Lecture Notes in Computer Science 502

Edited by G. Goos and J. Hartmanis

J. Bārzdiņš D. Bjørner (Eds.)

Baltic Computer Science

Selected Papers

Springer-Verlag
Berlin Heidelberg New York
London Paris Tokyo
Hong Kong Barcelona
Budapest

Series Editors

Gerhard Goos
GMD Forschungsstelle
Universität Karlsruhe
Vincenz-Priessnitz-Straße 1
W-7500 Karlsruhe, FRG

Juris Hartmanis
Department of Computer Science
Cornell University
Upson Hall
Ithaca, NY 14853, USA

Volume Editors

Jānis Bārzdiņš
Institute of Mathematics and Computer Science
University of Latvia
Boulevard Rainis 29, Riga 226250, Latvia

Dines Bjørner
Department of Computer Science, Building 344
Technical University of Denmark
DK-2800 Lyngby, Denmark

CR Subject Classification (1991): D.1-3, F.1-3

ISBN 3-540-54131-4 Springer-Verlag Berlin Heidelberg New York
ISBN 0-387-54131-4 Springer-Verlag New York Berlin Heidelberg

Printing and binding: Druckhaus Beltz, Hemsbach/Bergstr.
2145/3140-543210 - Printed on acid-free paper

Preface

There is no 'Soviet Computer Science'.

There are Estonian, Latvian, and Lithuanian cultures, as there are Armenian, Russian, Ukrainian, and many other cultures within the USSR. The cultures of the Baltics have bound together by centuries of history, some of it not so enlightening.

The Baltics computer science culture is amply demonstrated in this volmune. It has for too long not been widely accessible in the English literature. It is a refreshing reminder of man's ability to contribute despite troublesome times.

The usual benefits of free, international scientific co-operation, as most readers of this volume experiences it, of unhindered access to literature, of speedy exchange of results in the form, for example, of broad, international conference participation, was not a basic instrument of our colleagues in the east.

Science is international, and the more local science fits in with international developments, the more it obviously demonstrates its internationality. The present volume reflects work that is both internationally as well as locally inspired.

It should surprise me if the present volume could not - now - inspire research on a broader, international scale, as it has inspired other researchers in the USSR.

Attempts to formulate computer science results in the USSR in the classical framework of mathematics, but cast in the dialectical constructs of so-called cybernetics seems to have failed. Luckily the Baltics scientists did not fall into that trap. With a strong background - also in Russian mathematical logic - we see in this volume refreshing contributions, which, in addition, seem to fit better into the computer science tradition generally propagated.

Things are changing, however. We have seen, in the span of a few years, several productive, international conferences in the USSR[1]. This volume did not grow

[1]See for example: *COLOG'88*, Springer Lecture Notes in Computer Science, Vol. 417, and *Logic at Botik'89*, Springer Lecture Notes in Computer Science, Vol. 363.

out of such a conference, however, although it seems to me that its publication could set a precedence for other groupings of scientists across the combine of Russia, Ukraine, etc., to demonstrate their insight and results.

I am sure that, in future, we shall see the Baltic Republics form a vital link between the science of Russia - et cetera - on one hand, and the rest of the world, on the other hand.

The foreword by the main editor, Jan Bārzdiņš, gives, as could be expected, a clear overview of this volume and its contributions. I shall therefore only here express the joy and pleasure I feel in having been able to bring this volume out.

Dines Bjørner

Technical University of Denmark

Foreword

This volume offers a significant insight into Baltic computer science within the scope of the last 10-15 years. The volume contains both the results published mainly in Russian and completely new results.

Four research directions can be distinguished in Baltic computer science. They are represented in four parts of the volume:

- Deductive synthesis of programs (Estonia),
- Inductive synthesis of programs (Latvia),
- Automatic test case generation (Latvia),
- Specification and verification of distributed systems (Lithuania).

Several other research activities are included in the fifth part:

- Miscellaneous.

Deductive synthesis of programs. In the 1980s at the Institute of Cybernetics, Tallinn, an advanced knowledge-based programming system PRIZ was developed by E. Tyugu and his research group. The system PRIZ combines conventional programming technique with automatic synthesis of programs from problem specifications. The paper by G. Mints and E. Tyugu contains a general description and logical basis of the system PRIZ. A new approach to the semantics of specification languages based on structural synthesis ideas is proposed in the paper by G. Mints, J. Smith and E. Tyugu. A knowledge-based approach to the semantics of problem-oriented languages is considered in the paper by M. Meriste, J. Penjam. T. Tammet's paper is devoted to automatic theorem proving.

Inductive synthesis of programs. In the 1970s and early 1980s the problem of inductive synthesis was investigated mainly on a recursive-theoretic level. Major results concerning this approach are presented in the papers by R. Freivalds and by R. Freivalds, J. Bārzdiņš and J. Podnieks.

In the 1980s new models of inductive synthesis based on detection of purely syntactical analogies were developed by a research group at the University of Latvia. The papers by A. Brāzma and E. Kinber are devoted to these models. A new approach to the problem of inductive synthesis based on TRS is presented in the paper by G. Bārzdiņš.

Automatic test case generation. The theoretical basis of automatic test generation is developed in the paper by A. Auziņš, J. Bārzdiņš, J. Bičevskis, K. Čerāns, and A. Kalniņš.

it is proved that for a wide class of programs the problem of automatic construction of complete test sets according to criterion $C1$ is algorithmically solvable. The paper by J. Borzovs, A. Kalniņš and I. Medvedis is devoted to practical methods of automatic test generation for distributed real time systems.

Specification and verification of distributed systems. In H. Pranevitchius' paper new methods and tools for specification and verification of computer network protocols are proposed. In K. Gečas' paper the axiomatic approach for formalization of distributed systems is discussed. The completeness problems of temporal logic are considered in R. Pliuškevičius'paper.

Miscellaneous. The paper by M. Auguston describes a powerful compiler writing system successfully used in many projects.

The paper by R. Freivalds contains several important results showing the advantages of probabilistic automata over deterministic ones.

In conclusion it should be pointed out that many activities in the field of computers in the Baltic states are not featured in the volume. First, those related to computer networks, digital exchange systems, artificial intelligence are not reported. Also, finite automata research carried out in the late 1960s and early 1970s is not reflected in this volume. Nonetheless we hope the volume to be of interest for the people working in computer science.

Riga
April 1991

Jānis Bārzdiņš

Dedication

This volume is dedicated to
Professor Boris Avramovich Trakhtenbrot
Father of Baltic Computer Science
on the occasion of his 70th birthday in June 1991

Contents

Deductive Synthesis of Programs

Inductive Synthesis of Programs

Automatic Test Case Generation

Specification and Verification of Distributed Systems

Miscellaneous

The Programming System PRIZ

G. MINTS AND E. TYUGU

Institute of Cybernetics, Estonian Academy of Sciences, Tallinn 200108, *USSR*

(*Received* 26 *May* 1986)

The programming system PRIZ combines conventional programming technique with automatic synthesis of programs from specifications. It enables one to build specifications from descriptions of application domains. They are automatically encoded into propositional calculus and used by the system for the program synthesis. PRIZ is not bound to any particular problem domain, but applicable for synthesis of programs solving problems of a wide class called computational problems. From the theoretical side it has the deductive power of the intuitionistic propositional calculus.

1. Introduction

The programming system PRIZ combines conventional programming technique with automatic synthesis of programs from specifications. Its input language UTOPIST (Universal Translator Of Problems Including Specifying Texts) enables one to write specifications. Such a specification is automatically encoded into propositional calculus as it will be shown in section 4 of this paper, and used by the system for the program synthesis.

However, PRIZ is not problem oriented, but rather method oriented. It is not bound to any particular problem domain, but applicable for synthesis of programs solving problems of a definite class which we call *computational problems.* Our method of automatic program construction is called *structural synthesis.* From the theoretical side the structural synthesis has the deductive power of the intuitionistic propositional calculus (Mints & Tyugu, 1982) or pure typed lambda calculus. (Programs can be built as lambda-terms which are realisations of propositional formulas, see (Kleene, 1952; Howard, 1980).)

We can also compare PRIZ with PROLOG. Both of them exploit the structural similarity of constructive proofs and programs and build a program by proving solvability of a problem. PROLOG system works in a first order calculus and uses resolution principle very efficiently. Pure PROLOG handles objects of types zero and one (individuals and predicates). The logic of PRIZ system is restricted to propositional level. However, it can handle objects of any finite type, because it uses objects which are realisations of formulas. (The full force of pure typed lambda calculus is used in PRIZ system!) This comparison is illustrated in Fig. 1 where complexity of objects is increasing along the horizontal axis and order of logic is shown on the vertical axis.

Today PRIZ is a program product installed on more than 1000 Ryad computer mainframes; it was originally developed as a practical programming system, and the Russian abbreviation is deciphered as "programs for solving engineering problems". Its

Reprinted with permission from J. Symbolic Computation (1988) 5, 359-375

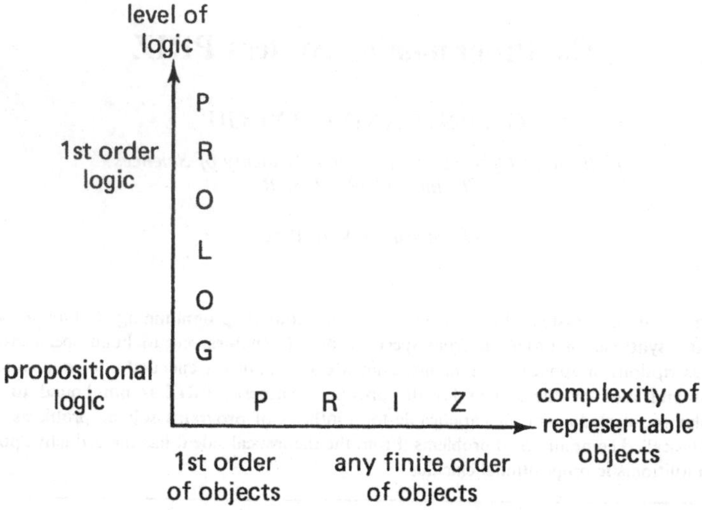

Fig. 1. Logic of PROLOG and PRIZ.

logical background is not at all visible for a practically minded user. From the user's point of view UTOPIST is essentially a nonprocedural language.

We completely agree with the characterisation of programming in nonprocedural languages given by N. S. Prywes and A. Pnueli in the introduction to (Prywes & Pneuli, 1983). Moreover, PRIZ system is a compiler, like the implementation of MODEL language specified in (Prywes & Pnueli, 1983), and both systems use data dependency for operations scheduling, i.e., for program synthesis. However, MODEL language is oriented on sequential data processing and has specific facilities for representing multidimensional arrays. We have no predefined means for array processing in PRIZ. In order to process sequentially an array or a file one must preprogram proper functional constants. We shall demonstrate this in an example of solving minimax problem for matrices in the end of section 3 and also in an example of data base language given in appendix 4.

We start our representation of the PRIZ system with a general description of its architecture in section 2. Thereafter we describe the nonprocedural part of its input language UTOPIST which is intended for writing specifications. In sections 4 and 5 we briefly discuss logical basis of the PRIZ system, giving propositional semantics of specifications and referring to more detailed papers on logics of structural synthesis of programs. Implementation of the synthesizer which is the principal part of PRIZ is discussed in section 6.

2. System Architecture

Since automatic program synthesis is the main distinctive feature of PRIZ, we present the system here mainly from that angle. The part of the PRIZ system shown in Fig. 2 is intended for processing *problem statements* of the form

$$M|-x_1, \ldots, x_k \rightarrow y \tag{1}$$

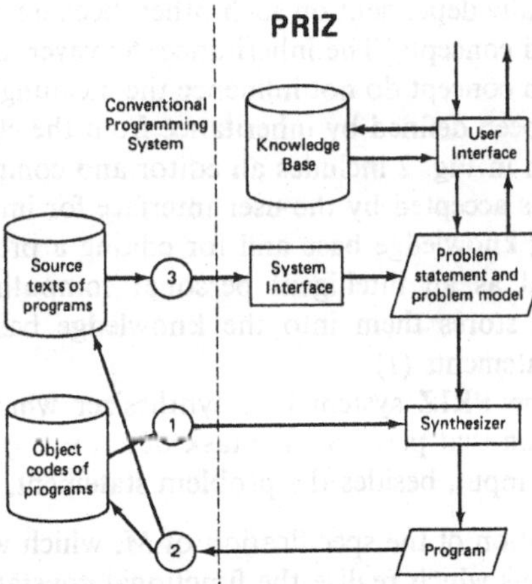

Fig. 2. Architecture of PRIZ system.

which means "Knowing M compute y from $x_1, \ldots, x_k$", i.e. it represents a computational problem. The following is an example of the problem statement:

$$\text{triangle} \mid - a, b, c \rightarrow \text{alpha}.$$

It is assumed that given a specification of M it is possible to obtain the value for y depending on the given value of $x_1, \ldots, x_k$. (Obviously, the variables $x_1, \ldots, x_k$ and y must be specified in the specification of M.)

Actually, PRIZ does more than calculating the value of y. It proves the solvability of the problem and from this proof derives a program, which calculates the value. If the solvability cannot be proved, then we say that the problem statement is semantically invalid.

An essential part of the system is knowledge base (*KB*). It contains specifications of concepts and it is easily accessible by a user who can manipulate knowledge by adding specifications of new concepts and by editing the existing specifications. From the user's point of view the knowledge base constitutes a hierarchy of concepts, for example, as it is shown in Fig. 3, where the knowledge base *KB* immediately contains concepts "geometry" and "physics" which in their turn contain "point", "triangle" etc. The

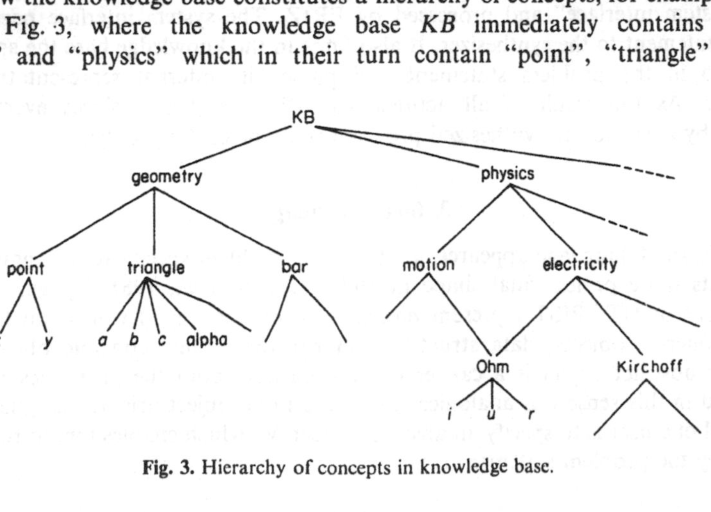

Fig. 3. Hierarchy of concepts in knowledge base.

specifications are conceptually dependent on each other, because new concepts can inherit properties of earlier defined concepts. The inheritance, however, is implemented in such a way that changes made in a concept do not influence the meaning of other concepts in the case when the latter have been defined by inheritance from the changed one.

The user interface shown in Fig. 2 includes an editor and compiler for concepts. There are a number of commands accepted by the user interface for immediate execution, such as commands for handling knowledge base and for editing a problem specification. The PRIZ system can be used as an intelligent personal computing system that accepts specifications of concepts, stores them into the knowledge base and solves problems represented by problem statements (1).

The principal part of the PRIZ system is a synthesizer which translates a problem statement (1) into a program that performs the task described by this statement.

The synthesizer takes as input, besides the problem statement,

—the internal representation of the specification of M, which we call *problem model*,
—programs and equations which realise the functional constants used in the problem model.

By proving solvability of the problem, the synthesizer builds the schema of a program for solving it. Thereafter, it assembles the program from solving functions of equations and program modules from the library. This program can be immediately applied for computations, or it can be used in a conventional programming system as any other program module.

The part of PRIZ shown in Fig. 2 is tightly coupled with a conventional programming system in the following three ways:

(1) Any program that satisfies standard calling conventions of the conventional programming system can be used as an implementation of some functional constant in a specification.

(2) A synthesized program can be used in the conventional programming system as any other program module. It can be represented either in assembler language or as an object module.

(3) Programs written in FORTRAN or assembler language can contain problem statements as comments in these languages. These comments are detected by a program called "system interface" and processed by PRIZ. The system interface passes such a problem statement to the synthesizer. It also finds in the knowledge base the specification referred to in the problem statement and passes its internal representation to the synthesizer. As the result of all actions, the PRIZ system replaces every problem statement by a call to the synthesized program that solves the problem.

3. Input Language

The UTOPIST language appeared in 1974 as a problem specification language and it obtained its more or less final shape in 1977 (Kahro *et al.*, 1981; Tyugu, 1987). The specifications in UTOPIST represent *abstract objects* (concepts) which can be used for creating concrete objects (data structures) in run-time. Only concrete objects possess values. An abstract object is a carrier of information about the properties of concrete objects and in this sense it is analogical to a class in an object oriented language.

The goal of a user is to specify an abstract object M, which enables him to represent his program by the problem statement (1).

This cannot be always done, and a problem must often be broken into subproblems where every subproblem can be represented by its own problem statement. Therefore, a program may contain a considerable imperative part written in a procedural language. We are going to consider here only the declarative nonprocedural part of UTOPIST, that is the part which is used for specifying abstract objects.

A specification has the following form

$$\langle\text{identifier}\rangle : \langle\text{specifier}\rangle$$

and it represents an abstract object with the name ⟨identifier⟩ and with the properties represented by the ⟨specifier⟩.

$$\langle\text{specifier}\rangle ::= \left\{\begin{matrix}\langle\text{inheritance}\rangle\\ \langle\text{compound}\rangle\end{matrix}\right\}$$

The inheritance is a powerful means of the UTOPIST language. The complete syntax of inheritance is

$$\langle\text{inheritance}\rangle ::= \langle\text{name}\rangle[\langle\text{amendment}\rangle, \ldots]$$

In its simplest case the inheritance specifier is just a name of an abstract object. Then the new object inherits all the properties of the object that is used as the specifier. There are predefined abstract objects *numeric*, *text*, *boolean* and *undefined*, so we can write

x: numeric
b: boolean etc.

Any object *y* specified as

y: undefined

has no special properties, but it can be redefined later, as we shall see below.

The compound specifier is a sequence of specifications and relations which, in particular, can be expressed by equations. Examples of specifications with compound specifiers are, for instance,

```
point: (x: numeric;
        y: numeric)
```

and

```
bar: (P1: point;
      P2: point;
  length: numeric;
   angle: numeric;
    length^2 = (P1.x-P2.x)^2+(P1.y-P2.y)^2;
        length* sin (angle) = P2.y-P1.y)
```

The two equations specify the properties of a bar operationally, so that they can be used for computing the values of coordinates, the length or an angle, depending on the problem statement.

A compound specifier represents an object that can contain other objects which are called then its components. Compound names can be used for naming components of an object. A component *a* of an object *b* is called *b.a* outside of *b*. If *b*, in its turn, is the component of an object *c*, then outside of *c*, the name of the inner object is *c.b.a*, etc.

In general a compound specifier has the following form

$$(x_1 : t_1; \ldots; x_k : t_k; R_1; \ldots; R_m)$$

where $x_1, \ldots, x_k$ are identifiers of components, $t_1, \ldots, t_k$ are their specifiers and $R_1, \ldots, R_m$ are relations. Any component is an abstract object which in its turn is specified by a specification. Recursive specifications are prohibited. The value of a compound object consists of the values of its components.

Relations are the means for specifying the properties of objects. A relation included into the specification of an object Z represents the constraints on Z. It can also be regarded as an implicit or explicit representation of computation of the values of some components from the values of other components. A relation can be labelled and this label can be used as the name of a procedure or a function.

Relation can be either an equation or an axiom with realisation. In the case of equation the system takes for granted that every variable occurring there can be computed from the remaining ones. There are various implementations for solving equations: numeric, symbolic and also user-supplied.

In another case the relation is specified by an axiom of the form

$$\langle \text{axiom} \rangle ::= \left\{ \begin{matrix} \langle \text{name} \rangle \\ (\langle \text{name} \rangle, \ldots \rightarrow \langle \text{name} \rangle) \end{matrix} \right\}, \ldots \rightarrow \langle \text{name} \rangle, \ldots$$

that represent applicability of a program which is realisation of the relation.

We do not specify the syntax of the realisation. In the simplest case it is a name of a program from the program library written in parentheses after the axiom. For example

$$X \rightarrow Y(f).$$

As an example of a compound specification we present here the following abstract object:

matrix : (m : *text;*
    e : *numeric;*
    i : *numeric;*
    j : *numeric;*
    create: $\rightarrow m(A)$;
    put : $m, i, j, e \rightarrow m(B)$
    get : $m, i, j \rightarrow e(C)$);

This abstract object represents a matrix and it can be used as an abstract data type. Here A, B and C are names of the programs which are respectively realisations of the relations create, put and get.

Let us return now to the inheritance. The name of the abstract object used in an inheritance specifier can be followed by amendments which bind components of the object. For instance, having specifications of a point and a bar we can write

P : point $x = 0$;
AB : bar length $= 15$, $P1 = P$;

The meaning of amendments $x = 0$ and length $= 15$, is obvious. The amendment $P1 = P$ in the specification of the bar AB means that the point $P1$ of the bar AB is the same as point P specified above.

Let us consider an example of a problem shown in Fig. 4. The distance v must be computed depending on the value of the angle u.

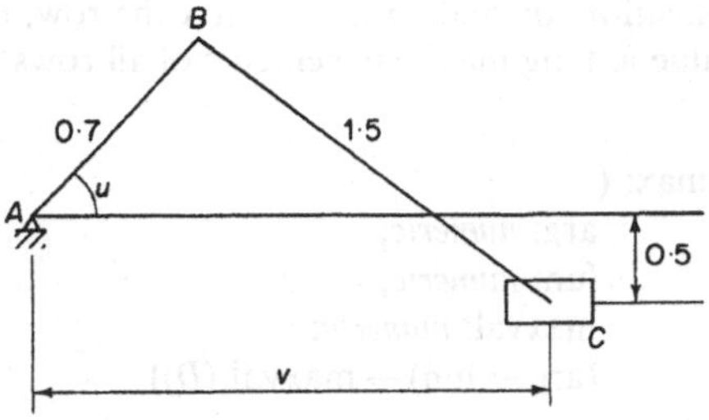

Fig. 4. Example problem.

If we have specified the point and the bar as shown above, then we can specify this problem as follows:

mech : (u : *numeric;*
v : *numeric;*
AB : bar length = 0·7, $P1$ = (0, 0), angle = u;
BC : bar length = 1·5, $P1 = AB.P2$, $P2.y = -0{\cdot}5$, $P2.x = v$)

The problem

$$\text{mech}|-u \rightarrow v$$

is solvable and the algorithm built by the PRIZ system where justification of each step is also shown is given in appendix 3.

This example demonstrates how specifications are used in the PRIZ system, but it does not show the logic behind the specifications. This will be considered in sections 4 and 5. Let us return to the language itself.

We can use the amendment

⟨name⟩ : ⟨name⟩

if the left name belongs to the object which has been specified as *undefined*. In this case this object obtains the type of the object with the name from the right-hand side. This gives us generic types.

Indeed, we can specify

y : (. . . x : *undefined*; . . .)

and then use any abstract object z for concretisation of x:

$a : y \quad x : z.$

For instance, after specifying

set: (elem : *undefined*; . . .)

we can create sets

points: set elem: point

and

people: set elem: person

etc.

Let us consider a specification for finding in a matrix the row, the maximal element of which has the minimal value among maximal elements of all rows. First of all we define a concept of maximum:

max: (
arg: *numeric*;
fun: *numeric*;
maxval: *numeric*;
(arg → fun) → maxval (*D*))

We use here a program *D* for representing a relation specified by the axiom

$$(\text{arg} \to \text{fun}) \to \text{maxval}.$$

This relation binds the maximal value of a function with the function itself represented by the subformula

$$\text{arg} \to \text{fun}.$$

The concept of minimum can be specified by using the same program *D*:

min: (
arg: *numeric*;
fun: *numeric*;
negfun: *numeric*;
minval: *numeric*;
maxval: *numeric*;
negfun = −fun;
minval = −maxval;
(arg−→ negfun)−→ maxval (*D*)).

And the specification of the desired concept minimax is as follows:

minimax: (
value: *numeric*;
m: *matrix*;
*r*1: max arg = *m.j*, fun = *m.e*;
*r*2: min arg = *m.i*, fun = *r*1 . maxval,
maxval = value).

The specifications we presented in this example are written in a "weak" specification language without using any powerful means for representing the properties of functions. Actually, our axioms can represent only the types of functions (possibly of higher order). However, we needed here only one predefined functional constant *D* for a program which would find the maximum of a function.

4. Axiomatic Semantics of Specifications

A precise representation of the semantics of UTOPIST can be given by means of a simple language (to be called the semantic language) which is a restricted (but still universal) form of the intuitionistic propositional calculus. The propositional variables X, Y etc. express the computability (existence) of values of objects presented by a specification. Let us denote the objects by small letters: a, b, x, y, a_1, a_2, ... For any object x we introduce a propositional variable X which denotes the computability of x.

(X is true if x is computable or x already has a value). The language includes only propositonal formulas of the following forms:

$$X_1 \& \ldots \& X_k \rightarrow Y, \qquad (2)$$

or in a shorter way:

$$\mathbf{X} \rightarrow Y;$$

as well as

$$(\mathbf{U}^1 \rightarrow V^1) \ \& \ldots \& \ (\mathbf{U}^m \rightarrow V^m) \rightarrow (\mathbf{X} \rightarrow Y), \qquad (3)$$

or in a shorter way:

$$(\underline{\mathbf{U} \rightarrow \mathbf{V}}) \rightarrow (\mathbf{X} \rightarrow Y).$$

From the logical point of view these formulas are implications. But from the computational point of view they can be considered as functional dependencies. The formulas (3) express functional dependencies of higher order (with functions as arguments).

To analyse the solvability of the computational problem given by a problem statement (1) and to find the applicative structure of the resulting program, only the purely propositional structure shown explicitly in (2), (3) is essential. However, to write the resulting program in all details, formulas (2), (3) have to be expanded as follows

$$\mathbf{X} \underset{f}{\rightarrow} Y \qquad (4)$$

and

$$(\mathbf{U} \underset{g}{\rightarrow} V) \rightarrow (\mathbf{X} \underset{F(g)}{\rightarrow} Y), \qquad (5)$$

where $g = g_1, \ldots, g_m$.

Functions f, F in (4), (5) are realisations of (2), (3) respectively. The formula (4), for example, means that the realisation of Y can be computed from the realisations of $\mathbf{X}$ by means of f, or that f is a procedure for computing y from $\mathbf{x}$. The formula (5) means that the procedure F produces from any functions g computing v from u some new function $F(g)$ computing y from x.

Since any computational model consists of specifications, it is sufficient to define a function sem which, for any specification S, computes a set sem(S) of formulas of the form (4), (5) which are axioms describing the possible computations according to the specification S. (A computation with input variables $x_1, \ldots, x_k$, and an output variable y is possible according to the specification S if and only if the formula $X_1 \& \ldots \& X_k \rightarrow Y$ is constructively derivable from sem (S)). The function sem is defined as follows.

(1) Let t be a predefined type *numeric*, *text*, *undefined* or *boolean*. Then

sem $(x : t) = \phi$ (the empty set)

Let Π be the set of axioms for the type t and Π^t_x is obtained from Π by substituting x instead of t for every occurrence of t, then

(2) sem $(x : t) = \Pi^t_x$

(3) sem $(x : (x_1 : t_1; \ldots; x_k : t_k)) =$
$= \{X_1 \& \ldots \& X_k \rightarrow X; X \rightarrow X_1; \ldots; X \rightarrow X_k\} \cup$
X.sem $(x_1 : t_1) \cup \ldots \cup X$.sem $(x_k : t_k)$

where X.sem (S) is the set of axioms obtained from sem (S) by adding prefix X. to every propositional variable.

(4) sem $(E_1(x_1, \ldots, x_k) = E_2(x_1, \ldots, x_k)) =$
$= \{X_1 \& \ldots \& X_{i-1} \& X_{i+1} \& \ldots \& X_k \rightarrow X_i |$ the equation $E_1(x_1, \ldots, x_k) = E_2(x_1, \ldots, x_k)$ is solvable for $x_i\}$

(5) sem $((u \rightarrow v), x \rightarrow y(G)) = \{(U \rightarrow V) \rightarrow (X \rightarrow Y)\}$, where G is any realisation

(6) sem $(x : (x_1 : t_1; \ldots; x_k : t_k; R_1; \ldots; R_m)) =$
sem $(x : (x_1 : t_1; \ldots; x_k : t_k)) \cup$ sem $(R_1) \cup \ldots \cup$ sem (R_m),
where $R_1, \ldots, R_m$ are relations.

(7) Simple amendment. If the component u of the object y has a type different from *undefined*, then

$$\text{sem}\,(x : y\ u = v) = \text{sem}\,(x : y) \cup \text{sem}\,(x.u = v)$$

(8) Defining amendment. If u is of the type *undefined* in y, then

$$\text{sem}\,(x : y\ u : v) = \text{sem}\,(x : y) \cup \text{sem}\,(x.u : v)$$
$$\text{sem}\,(x : y\ u = v) = \text{sem}\,(x : y\ u : v) \cup \text{sem}\,(x.u = v).$$

5. Program Synthesis

The synthesizer of PRIZ employs the schema

$$\text{SPECIFICATION} \xrightarrow{\text{I}} \text{PROOF} \xrightarrow{\text{II}} \text{PROGRAM}. \tag{6}$$

Input data for the step I are produced by the function sem described above in the form of a sequent $\Gamma \vdash P \rightarrow Q$ with Γ (the axioms) being the list of propositional formulas (2), (3). The proof is a formal derivation of $P \rightarrow Q$ from Γ according to the so called Structural Synthesis Rules (SSR) listed in appendix 1. Its structure and the search strategy is best of all illustrated for the case when all axioms in Γ are of the form (2). Then one proceeds stepwise by gradually enlarging the set C of computed variables. Initially this set C for the goal sequent $\Gamma \vdash P \rightarrow Q$ consists of P (since its computability is assumed) and the variables given as separate members of Γ. Each search step simply adds to C all conclusions Y of a formula (2) if all premises $X_1, \ldots, X_k$ of this formula are already in C. Then the formula (2) used in this way is simply discarded. The goal $\Gamma \vdash P \rightarrow Q$ is proved if Q is eventually included in C. This proof search can be organised so that it is completed in linear time.

In the case when axioms of the form (3) are present in Γ, the proof search is more complicated and the resulting system turns out to be equivalent to the intuitionistic propositional calculus (Vološ *et al.*, 1982).

The step II of the schema (6), that is, the extraction of the program from a constructed proof uses the same basic ideas as the standard intuitive interpretation for the intuitionistic system. Expanded versions (4), (5) of the formulas (2), (3) are used here to assign typed lambda-terms (realisations) to the axioms from Γ, which are beginning formulas (leaves) of the proof (tree). Then we can proceed along the applications of the rules assigning realisations to further formulas. This assignment (see appendix 2) uses a known device traceable to the Heyting–Kolmogorov interpretation of intuitionistic connectives, or more precisely, the Kleene (1952) realisability. The lambda-term assigned to final formula $P \rightarrow Q$ is the schema of required program.

The minimax problem described in section 3 can be represented in logical language by the following three axioms, where the propositional variables M, I, J, E and MAXINROW denote computability of a matrix, of its number of row, number of column, element and maximal element in a row. The variable MINIMAX denotes computability of the desired result of the problem.

$$M \& I \& J \underset{get}{\rightarrow} E$$

$$(J \rightarrow E) \underset{max}{\rightarrow} \text{MAXINROW}$$

$$(I \rightarrow \text{MAXINROW}) \underset{min}{\rightarrow} \text{MINIMAX}$$

These three axioms are a complete specification for synthesizing a program which finds the minimal value of maximal elements of rows in a matrix.

The proof of solvability of this problem is

$$\cfrac{\cfrac{M \& I \& J \rightarrow E \qquad (J \rightarrow E) \rightarrow \text{MAXINROW}}{M \& I \rightarrow \text{MAXINROW}} \qquad (I \rightarrow \text{MAXINROW}) \rightarrow \text{MINIMAX}}{M \rightarrow \text{MINIMAX}}$$

The complete program of this problem is

$$\lambda m \text{ min } (\lambda i \text{ max } (\lambda j \text{ get } (m, i, j))).$$

6. Implementation of the Synthesizer

The synthesizer shown in Fig. 2 transforms a problem statement into a program for solving the problem, using knowledge from a given problem model. It operates exactly in accordance with the logic described above. (In this sense the PRIZ system differs from PROLOG which, besides the exact logic, allows tricks with cut operator and predicates of higher order.) The fact that logics of the PRIZ system is equivalent to the intuitionistic propositional calculus (Volož *et al.*, 1982) implies that structural synthesis of programs is *P*-SPACE complete. Nevertheless, the synthesizer handles practical problems rather efficiently. This is achieved by careful design of internal representation of problem model so that its data structures match data flow model of the program to be synthesized. Besides that, a restricted but faster strategy based on modal logic *S*4 can be used for program synthesis in many cases (Mints, 1984).

Let us consider a set Γ of computability statements representing a problem model, and a sequent which must be proved for solving the problem: $\Gamma \vdash X \rightarrow Y$. A proper data structure for representing Γ is a network. Every propositional variable and every computability statement is represented as a node in the network. The node of any computability statement is connected with the nodes of the propositional variables which occur in this formula. The computability statements are connected with each other in the network through the common propositional variables. A position of the propositional variable in a formula is represented by a labelling (*in*, *out*, *arg*1, *res*1, *arg*2, *res*2, . . .) on the edges. Fig. 5(a) shows the network for the minimax problem.

Having the network representation of the problem conditions, it is possible to transform this network into a data-flow schema for any program which can be synthesized from these conditions. For this purpose we determine a direction for every edge in the network by the following rule: the arrows lead from negative occurrences of

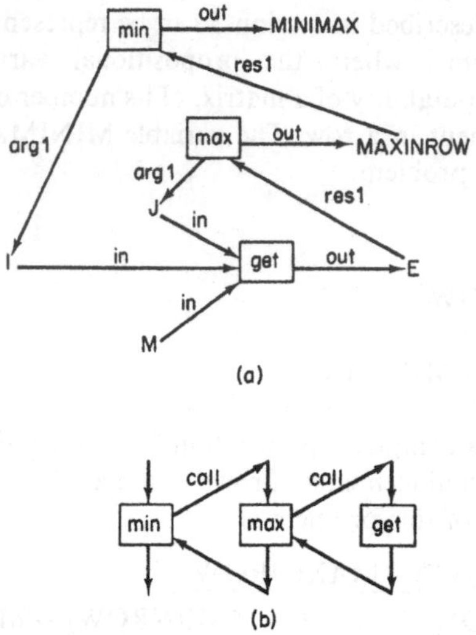

Fig. 5. Internal representation of problem model (a) and program schema (b) for minimax problem.

propositional variables to positive occurrences of propositional variables. As usually in logic, we say that an occurrence of a subformula is negative when it is on the left side of an odd number of implications in the formula. Otherwise the occurrence is positive. The rule for data flow directions is suggested by SSR rules. A negative occurrence of a subformula $A \to B$ in an axiom determines a description of a function, and its positive occurrence introduces a call of the function in the final program. "A" corresponds to the input and "B" to the output of the function of the implication $A \to B$. This gives the directions for the edges connecting A and B.

The directions have already been determined in Fig. 5(a) and the network can be considered as a data-flow schema for the minimax problem. Two cycles are visible on the data flow schema. The larger (external) cycle

min arg1 I in get out E res1 max out MAXINROW res1 min

and the internal cycle

max arg1 J in get out E res1 max

These cycles correspond to the two subproblems $I \to$ MAXINROW and $J \to E$ appearing in the problem specification.

The data-flow schema is very useful for building a proof of the solvability theorem. In the case where there are only axioms of the form (2) in Γ, the search becomes a simple flow analysis on a graph. (It has been shown by Dikovski (1985) that this search can be done in linear time.) If Γ contains conditional computability statements (3), the search is done on an and-or-tree of subproblems. Subproblems are generated for negative occurrences of subformulas $A \to B$ in the computability statements. No pattern matching is needed, because the data-flow schema explicitly represents all possible connections between the formulas. An algorithm built by the synthesizer contains initially 2 parts:

(1) data flow schema which is part of the internal representation of the problem model (the whole schema in Fig. 5(a) for our example);

(2) program schema which determines the order of execution of operators of the data flow schema (Fig. 5(b) for our example).

This representation is translated into the object code of the conventional programming system.

7. Concluding Remarks

We have presented here PRIZ as a system which automatically transforms problem statement (1) into programs, using specifications as a source of information for automatic program synthesis. However, the key issues to practical success of PRIZ have been, firstly, its ability to support various combinations of manual programming with automatic program construction and, secondly, its extensive usage of common program libraries.

There are various ways to combine manual and automatic programming. Quite often an engineer specifies in UTOPIST one single model of a device and uses this specification for solving various optimisation problems. Optimisation algorithms are presented as FORTRAN programs that contain problem statement for finding values of parameters of the device. Another approach is to write a collection of specifications that represent concepts for specifying problems from some restricted domain. This approach is demonstrated in appendix 4 for data base problems.

We hope that, as time passes, the users of PRIZ will develop their own specification libraries which are sufficiently rich to cover a number of interesting problem domains.

Appendix 1

The inference rules for structural synthesis of programs (SSR)

$$\frac{\vdash \underline{\mathbf{X}} \to V;\ \underline{\Gamma \vdash X}}{\underline{\Gamma} \vdash V},\ (\to -)$$

where $\underline{\Gamma \vdash X}$ is a set of sequents for all X in $\mathbf{X}$.

$$\frac{\vdash \underline{(\mathbf{U} \to V)} \to (\mathbf{X} \to Y);\ \underline{\Gamma \vdash X};\ \underline{\mathbf{Z}, \mathbf{U} \vdash V}}{\Gamma, \mathbf{Z} \vdash Y}\ (\to - -)$$

where $\underline{\Gamma \to \mathbf{X}}$ is a set of sequents for all X in $\mathbf{X}$, and $\underline{\mathbf{Z}, \mathbf{U} \vdash V}$ is a set of sequents for all $(\mathbf{U} \to V)$, in $\underline{(\mathbf{U} \to V)}$.

$$\frac{\Gamma, \mathbf{X} \vdash Y}{\Gamma \vdash \mathbf{X} \to Y}\ (\to +)$$

In fact, the planner of PRIZ uses some additional rules which can be derived from the basic ones listed above. For example in the rule $(\to - -)$ the rightmost **U** above the line can be replaced by **W&U**, and **W** added below the line.

The structural synthesis rules described above allow to synthesize applicative programs. An option used less frequently permits to synthesize recursive programs. This option has some interesting applications, in particular, to the semantics of algorithmic languages (Penyam, 1983).

Appendix 2

We present here program derivation rules. Taking into account that

$$X \underset{f}{\rightarrow} Y = (\forall s)(X(s) \rightarrow Y(f(s)))$$

and

$$(U \underset{g}{\rightarrow} V) \rightarrow (X \underset{F(g)}{\rightarrow} Y) = (\forall g)((\forall u)(U(u) \rightarrow V(g(u))) \rightarrow (\forall x)(X(x) \rightarrow (Y(F(g, x))),$$

we can extend the inference rules SSR so that they will contain the rules for building new terms:

$$\frac{\vdash X \underset{f}{\rightarrow} V; \quad \Gamma \vdash X(t)}{\Gamma \vdash V(f(t))} (\rightarrow -)$$

$$\frac{\vdash (U \underset{g}{\rightarrow} V) \rightarrow (X \underset{F(g)}{\rightarrow} Y); \quad \Gamma \vdash X(s); \quad Z, U \vdash V(t)}{\Gamma, Z \vdash Y(F(\lambda u . t, s))} (\rightarrow - -)$$

$$\frac{\Gamma, X \vdash Y(t)}{\Gamma \vdash X \underset{\lambda x . t}{\rightarrow} Y} (\rightarrow -)$$

These rules represent the method for constructing a program simultaneously with the proof.

Appendix 3

Computer printout of the algorithm for the problem mech.

$AB.1 = 0{\cdot}7 \rightarrow AB.1$
$AB.P1.x = 0 \rightarrow AB.P1.x$
$AB.P1.y = 0 \rightarrow AB.P1.y$
$BC.1 = 1{\cdot}5 \rightarrow BC.1$
$BC.P2.y = -(0{\cdot}5) \rightarrow BC.P2.y$
$\rightarrow u$
$AB.\mathrm{angle} = u \rightarrow AB.\mathrm{angle}$
$\sin(AB.\mathrm{angle}) * AB.1 = AB.P2.y - AB.P1.y \rightarrow AB.P2.y$
$BC.P1.y = AB.P2.y \rightarrow BC.P1.y$
$AB.1 * AB.1 = (AB.P2.x - AB.P1.x)\hat{}2 + (AB.P2.y - AB.P1.y)\hat{}2 \rightarrow AB.P2.x$
$BC.P1.x = AB.P2.x \rightarrow BC.P1.x$
$BC.1 * BC.1 = (BC.P2.x - BC.P1.x)\hat{}2 + (BC.P2.y - BC.P1.y)\hat{}2 \rightarrow BC.P2.x$
$BC.P2.x = v \rightarrow v$
*** end of algorithm ***

Appendix 4

This appendix contains systematic specification of concepts for data description and data handling that constitute a data base language.

SET

Let us specify a concept of a set with the following properties:

(1) A set is an object the value of which is represented by its single nonvirtual components "val".

(2) A set can contain elements of any type, its component "elem" has type *undefined*. All elements of one and the same set must have one and the same type.

(3) Knowing a property of elements of a set, which determines any element uniquely, it is possible to retrieve the element from the set. This property is represented by a component "key" of the set. We don't put any restrictions here on the representations of keys in the elements.

(4) It is always possible to select an arbitrary element from a set. If the set is empty, then the result of the selection will be the value *empty*.

(5) All the sets are finite, and we can arrange the selection of elements in such a way that repeating the selection we can get all elements of a set once at a time and after that get the value *empty*.

In order to express the last two properties we must introduce a component "selector" which controls the selection of elements. If it has the value *true* then one particular element of a set is selected. If the value of the selector is *false* then an element which is different from previously selected elements is selected.

The following specifications can be used for describing a concept with properties listed above:

set1: (val : *space*;
 elem : *undefined*;
 key : *undefined*;
 selector : *bool*;
 *r*1 : val, selector → elem(*A*);
 *r*2 : val, key → elem(*B*)).

This concept doesn't possess any facilities for changing a value of a set. These facilities are added in the following version of a set concept:

set : (*copy* set1;
 create: → val(*C*);
 addelem : elem, val → val(*D*);
 deletelem : elem, val → val(*E*))

Here we use a feature of superclasses, i.e. inheritance of all properties of an abstract object by a new defined abstract object which is supported by a very simple construction:

copy ⟨*name*⟩ set1;

which copies the whole specification of set1 into the place where it is written.

We don't discuss implementation of the functions *A*, *B*, *C*, *D*, *E* which represent the relations *r*1, *r*2, create, addelem and deletelem. But the properties of the set described above must be taken into consideration when the functions are being programmed. A special care must be taken for satisfying the restrictions (4) and (5).

SUBSET

We shall specify a concept of a subset also in the most general way—as a relation between two sets which is determined by a predicate *p*:

$$B = \{x | x \in A \& p(x)\}.$$

The value of a subset will be the single nonvirtual component of this concept.

subset: (*copy* : set;
of : set;
cond : *bool*;
R : (of . selector → cond), of → val(F))

In this specification we have used the names "val", "of" and "cond" for the sets B, A and for the predicate p respectively. The following are some examples of application of these concepts:

people : set elem = person;
children : subset of = people, elem = person,
cond = person . age < 16

It is easy to demonstrate that these specifications are sufficient for solving the problem

people → children

i.e. for finding all children from a given set of people.

Actually the concept of subset specified above can be used for generating new sets which are not contained in any other set. Therefore we shall call this concept also a filter:

filter : subset

The following example demonstrates how a set of unitvectors can be specified by using a filter which takes points one by one (see the specification of a set) and computes the values for vector . mod and vector . arg which constitute a vector. These computations are initiated when the subproblem

of . selector → cond

is solved for the relation R of the filter for unitvectors.

point : (x, y : *num*);
vector : (mod, arg : *num*);
vector . mod = *sqrt*(x^2+y^2);
vector . arg = *if* $x = 0$ & $y = 0$ *then* 90 *elif* $x = 0$ & $y = 0$ *then* −90
elif $x > 0$ *then atan* (y/x) *elif* $x < 0$ *then* 180+ *atan* (y/x) *fi*;
points : set of = point;
unitvectors : filter of = points, elem = vector, cond = vector . mod = 1

OPERATIONS WITH SETS

Having two finite sets A and B represented by their components A . val and B . val it is possible to build a value of a new set, using set-theoretical operations: union, intersection, difference and direct product. The first operation is a partial operation, because we have a restriction that all elements of a set must have one and the same type. The specifications of operations can be very simple:

union: (*copy* set;
A, B : set;
R : A . val, B . val → val(G));

intersection: (*copy* set;
A, B : set;
$R : A.\text{val}, B.\text{val} \rightarrow \text{val}(H)$);
difference: (*copy* set;
A, B : set;
$R : A.\text{val}, B.\text{val} \rightarrow \text{val}(K)$);
product: (*copy* set;
A, B : set;
$R : A.\text{val}, B.\text{val} \rightarrow (L)$)

It may seem that the programs G, H, K, L depend very much on the representation of sets. But it is not necessarily so, because it is possible to use operations create and addelem for constructing new sets and the relation $r1$ for selecting elements of sets which are given as operands.

QUANTIFIERS

In representing conditions like "there exists an element with the property p in the set S" or "all elements of the set S have the property p" we need quantifiers over sets. They can be specified analogically to the concept of subset, only the result will be a boolean value and not a set value. The specifications of quantitifers are as follows:

all: (S : set);
cond : *bool*;
result : *bool*;
(S.select → cond), S.val → result(M));
exist: (S : set;
cond : *bool*;
result : *bool*;
(S.select → cond), S.val → result(N))

References

Dikovski, A., Kanovich, M. (1985). Computational models with separable problems. *Cybernetics* (Technicheskaya Kibernetika) **N5**, 36–59 (In Russian).

Howard, P. (1980). The formulae-as-types notion of construction. In: *To H. B. Curry. Essays on logic, lambda calculus and formalism.* Pp. 479–490.

Kahro, M., Kalja, A., Tyugu, E. (1981). *Instrumental Programming System ES EVM (PRIZ).* Moscow: Finansy i Statistika (in Russian).

Kleene, S. (1952). *Introduction to Metamathematics.* Amsterdam: North-Holland.

Mints, G., Tyugu, E. (1982). Justification of the structural synthesis of programs. *Science Comput. Prog.* **N2**, 215–240.

Mints, G. (1984). Structural synthesis with independent subtasks and modal logic S4. Eesti NSV TA Toimetised (Proc. of the Estonian Academy of Sci). *Mathem.*, **33, N2**, 147–151.

Penyam, J. (1983). Synthesis of semantic processors from attribute grammars. *System Programming Comput. Software* **N1**, 50–60.

Prywes, N. S., Pnueli, A. (1983). Compilation of Nonprocedural Specifications into computer programs. *Software Engineering* **N3**, 267–279.

Tyugu, E. (1987). *Knowledge based programming.* New York: Addison-Wesley.

Volož, B., Matskin, M., Mints, G., Tyugu, E. (1982). Theorem proving with the aid of program synthesizer. *Cybernetics* **N6**, 63–70.

TYPE-THEORETICAL SEMANTICS OF SOME DECLARATIVE LANGUAGES

Grigory Mints[1)], Jan M. Smith[2)], Enn Tyugu[3)]

[1)3)]Institute of Cybernetics, Akademia tee 21, Tallinn 200108, Estonia
[2)]University of Göteborg/Chalmers, Göteborg, S-41296, Sweden

1. Introduction

We can usually agree easily about the meaning of a text written in a programming language. In general, it is not so with meaning of texts in specification languages for knowledge representation. However, there is a kind of declarative languages with precise semantics. These are languages for specifying automatic program synthesis problems [1,2]. In this case a specification S must contain the information needed, firstly, for comprehending the input x and output y of a program and, secondly, for synthesizing the program which computes y from x. Meaning of the specification S can be thought of as a set of all programs which can be synthesized on the basis of this specification. We can be more precise. Let us consider the collection of all objects specified by S which can occur as input or output of a program. Let x and y be tuples of such objects. Then a pair (x,y) represents a problem on S which can be formulated as follows: "compute y from x knowing S". We define the meaning of S as the set of all pairs ((x,y),f) where (x,y) is a solvable problem on S and f is the program for solwing the problem i.e. for computing y from x. In [3,4] a function <u>sem</u> has been defined for a particular declarative language, which produces a set of specific axioms U_S for any given specification S written in this language. There is a program synthesis method - structural synthesis of programs implemented in several programming systems [1,5] which enables us automatically to produce programs from axioms U_S for a number of problems (x,y) on S. This is a deductive program synthesis method which derives a program from a solvability proof of the given problem (x,y). The question of provability is solvable for the theories used in the structural synthesis of programs, consequently, the set of solvable problems on S is well defined, and so is the meaning of S.

Looking at specification languages used in the structural

synthesis of programs we can see the similarity of basic constructions of these languages with the constructions of Martin-Löf's type theory [6]. Bearing in mind the notion formulas-as-types this analogy must not be surprising. This provoked us to give another definition of semantics of declarative languages, based on the type theory, and this semantics seems very natural. We call it type-theoretical semantics, because the meaning of a specification is represented as cl type in this case. Types can also be used for synthesizing programs [7] and we can establish that, according to this semantics, the same problems are solvable which are solvable by means of the structural synthesis of programs.

2. The language

In this paper we consider the kernel of several languages which are input languages of programming systems of the PRIZ family [1,2,5]. Most of extensions needed to get UTOPIST language [5] which is the input language of the PRIZ system can be handled syntactically, i.e. the extensions can be reduced to the kernel language by rather simple textual transformations. This kernel is slightly different also from the language used in [3]. Only semantically essential constructions of the language are preserved in the kernel.

The language is intended for specifying abstract objects. A specification written in this language is a sequence of statements of the following form:

a:(x:s;...;y:t).

where a is a name given to the object specified, and x,...,y are names given to its components. Also the components are objects. They have types specified by the type-specifiers s,...,t. Names of the components x,...,y of the object a used outside the specification of a are a.x,...,a.y., i.e. the prefix 'a.' is added to the names. Iteration of this construction, i.e. a name like a.x.z.u is also allowed.

The objects which are not components of other objects are called sometimes also concepts.

Let us give precise definitions.

There are primitive objects with predefined types: text and numeric.

A specification of a component of an object has always the form

$$x:s$$

where s can be

1) name of a primitive object:

2) name of an object specified earlier (recursive specifications are not allowed):

3) an expression of the following forms:

$$u_1,...,u_m \text{->} u_{m+1}$$

$$\text{or } u_1,...,u_m \text{->} u_{m+1}(f)$$

where $u_1,...,u_{m+1}$ are names of objects, m>0, f is a name of a predefined function.

Specifications of components of objects have the following meaning.

If s is a name of an object then the component x has the same type as the object s.

If s is of the form

$$u_1,...,u_m \text{->} u_{m+1}(f)$$

then the component x is a function f which computes the object u_{m+1} from the objects $u_1,...,u_m$. If s is of the form

$$u_1,...,u_m \text{->} u_{m+1}$$

then the difference with the previous case is only that the function for computing u_{m+1} from $u_1,...,u_m$, i.e. the value of the object x specified by s, is not given explicitly, but must be synthesized automatically.

This is the whole kernel language.

We make the following definitional extensions to this language immediately.

1) Equality:

We can use equalities like

$$b=c,$$

where b and c are names of objects, which will be expanded to objects of a primitive type as follows:

$$r_1 : b \text{ -> } c(Id);\ r_2 : c \text{ -> } b(Id),$$

where Id is an identity function, and r_1, r_2 are new names.

For objects of nonprimitive type the equality a = b is expanded firstly for all their components, i.e. the equalities

$$a.u = b.v$$

are added for every pair a.u, b.v of corresponding components of the objects. Thereafter, the equalities for primitive objects are expanded as described above.

2) Amendments:

A component x can be specified as follows:

$$x : b \quad u_1 = v_1, \ldots, u_k = v_k$$

and this means

$$x : b; \quad x.u_1 = v_1; \ldots; x.u_k = v_k$$

3) Polymorphism:

A new primitive object <u>any</u> is introduced. If this is used in a specification of an object

b : (...u:<u>any</u>;...)

then

(1) the specification of b can contain any names of objects which start with the prefix 'u.' and these objects are considered as being completely specified as components of u;

(2) this object b can be used as a specifier only in the following way:

$$x : b \quad u = v$$

where v is an object which does not contain components of type <u>any</u>, and contains all components of u referred to according to (1).

4) Equations:

Analogically to equality we can use equations as sources of functions. Given an equation

$$E(u_1, \ldots, u_m, v_1, \ldots, v_n) = 0$$

with stipulation that it is uniquely solvable for the variables $u_1, \ldots, u_m$, we use this equation as an abbreviation for

$$r_1 : u_2, \ldots, u_m, v_1, \ldots, v_n \rightarrow u_1 \ (f_1):$$

$$\vdots$$

$$r_m : u_1, \ldots, u_{m-1}, v_1, \ldots, v_n \rightarrow u_m \ (f_m):$$

where $r_1, \ldots, r_m$ are new names, $f_1, \ldots, f_m$ are function solwing equation for the variables $u_1, \ldots, u_m$ respectively.

5) Subproblems:

An expression of the form

$$(u_{11}, \ldots, u_{1m} \rightarrow u_{1(m+1)}, \ldots, (u_{k1}, \ldots, u_{kl} \rightarrow u_{k(l+1)}).u_1, \ldots, u_n \rightarrow u_{n+1} (f)$$

can be used as an abbreviation for thhe following:

$$r_1 : u_{11}, \ldots, u_{1m} \rightarrow u_{1(m+1)}$$

$$r_k : u_{k1}, \ldots, u_{kl} \rightarrow u_{k(l+1)}$$

$$r_1, \ldots, r_k, u_1, \ldots, u_n \rightarrow u_{n+1} (f).$$

where $r_1, \ldots, r_k$ are new names.

The objects $r_1, \ldots, r_k$ are called subproblems, because their programs which are their values must be synthesized on the basis of the specification in the same way as a program for any other solvable problem.

Examples:

As the first example, we specify an object that represents a matrix. The component val of this object is the value of matrix (so to say the matrix itself), i and j are number of a row and number of a column. The only function we use is for selecting an element of the matrix. This function is represented by the component r1.

```
matrix: (val:text;
         i:numeric;
         j:numeric;
         e:numeric;
         r1:val,i,j ->e (get);
* comment: r1 selects element of m from the row i and column j).
```

The following two objects represent concepts of minimum and maximum of a function. Pay attention to the fact the function itself is not a component of these objects. The components arg and funval are argument and corresponding value of the function to be minimized or maximized.

```
min: (arg:numeric;
      funval:numeric;
      minval:numeric;
      r1: (arg -> funval) -> minval (fmin);
* comment: r1 computes minimal value of a function).

max: (arg:numeric;
      funval:numeric;
      maxval:numeric;
      r1: (arg -> funval) -> minval (fmax);
* comment: r1 computes maximal value of a function).
```

The name for the function to be optimized in min or max is to be introduced when these specifications are translated into the kernel language. Both of them are extended by introducing the new specification

fun: arg -> funval

and specification for r1 is transformed by replacing (arg->funval) by fun.

Having the specifications of objects matrix, min and max, we can specify the following problem 'find the minimal element among the maximal elements of rows of a matrix m'. The specification is as follows:

minimax:

(m:matrix;
result: numeric;
r1:max arg = m.j, funval = m.e;
r2:min arg = m.i, funval = r1.maxval, minval = result).

Recall that equalities are transformed into pairs of implications when this text is reduced to kernel language.

3. Axiomatic semantics of the language

Let us agree that we use only small letters in the names of objects. With any object x we associate a propositional variable to be denoted by X with the intended meaning 'x can be computed'. The same is done for objects with compound names, i.e. the propositional variable corresponding to an object x.a....b is written in capital letters X.A....B.

Firstly, we introduce the rules for transforming a specification S into a set of propositional formulas U_S = sem(S): which contain only propositional variables introduced as above. To each formula F in the set U_S we assign also a function constant to be called the realization of F. These realizations will be either names of predefined functions or standard lambda terms connected with cartesian product. These are: $comp_m$ forming a compound object from its m components, projections $p_{m,i}$ producing these components from the given object, application Ap_m of m-ary functions to its arguments and identity Id.

The realization will be written in brackets alongside the formula.

1) if s is a primitive object, then

sem(x:s) = 0:

2) sem (a:(x:s;...;y:t) = A.sem(x:s) U...U a.sem(y:t)U
{A.X&...&A.Z -> A($comp_m$),
A -> A.X($p_{m,1}$),...,A->A.Z($p_{m,m}$)},
where A.sem(x:s),...,A.sem(y:t) are obtained from sem(x:s),...,sem(y:t) by adding the prefix 'A.' to every

propositional variable; x,...,z are those of the components for which corresponding specification s is not an implication.

3) if s is specified as s:u, i.e. it is not a primitive object,

then sem(x:s) is obtained from sem(s:u) by changing the prefix 'S.' at all propositional variables to the prefix 'X.';

4) $\underline{sem}(x: u_1,\ldots,u_m \rightarrow u_{m+1}) =$
$= \{X\&U_1\&\ldots\&U_m \rightarrow U_{m+1}(Ap_m).$

$(U_1\&\ldots\&U_m \rightarrow U_{m+1}) \rightarrow X(Id\}$

5) $\underline{sem}\ (x: u_1,\ldots,u_m \rightarrow u_{m+1}(f)) =$
$= \{U_1\&\ldots\&U_m \rightarrow U_{m+1}(f)\}.$

Using these rules, any specification S of the kernel language can be translated into a set of implication υ_S.

An implication

$$X \rightarrow Y$$

can be associated with any problem 'compute y from knowing S'. Constructive proof of this implication which uses axioms υ_S obtained from S contains an algorithm for solving the problem (see [8]), which uses the realizations of formulas in υ_S.

The following are the inference rules needed for deriving the formula X -> Y representing a goal from a set of axioms υ_S and logical axioms $X_1\&\ldots\&X_m \rightarrow X_i$:

$$\frac{\underline{X} \rightarrow Y \quad \underline{U \rightarrow X}}{\underline{U} \rightarrow Y} \quad (*)$$

$$\frac{(\underline{U} \rightarrow V) \rightarrow Y \quad \underline{W}\ \&\ \underline{U} \rightarrow V}{\underline{W} \rightarrow Y} \quad (**)$$

where $\underline{A}$ stands for a conjunction $A_1\&\ldots\&A_k$ if A is a subformula, and for a list of formulas $A_1\ldots A_k$, if A is an antecedent in an inference rule.

These inference rules are obtained in an obvious way as simplifications of the SSR rules given in [8].

4. Type - theoretic semantics

Type theory can be seen as a tool both for writing specifications and constructing programs. A program derivation method has been described in [7] which is analogical to theorem prowing. This is a good reason for transforming specifications from a useroriented language into a precise language of types. This can be done using the transformation rules described below for our kernel language. In this description familiar type - theoretic abbreviations are used:

$$A \to B \equiv (\Pi x{:}A)B$$

$$A \,\&\, B \equiv (Ex{:}A)B$$

where B does not depend on x.

Assume that a distinct type symbol is fixed for any object or component in a given specification. Let us agree that we shall denote the type symbol corresponding to an object x by X, as we did it for propositions in the previous section.

So for example the type symbol X.A.Z corresponds to the object x.a.z. The translation Θ(a:u) [or shorter Θ(a)] of a specification

a : u

of an object a into type theory is defined as follows.

1. If u is primitive object then Θ(a:u)=0.

2. If u is a non-primitive object then Θ(a:u) is obtained from Θ(u) by changing the prefix 'U.' at all types to the prefix 'A.'.

3. If u is of the from

$$u_1,\dots,u_m \to u_{m+1}$$

then

$\Theta(a) = A \equiv U_1 x \dots x U_m \to U_{m+1}$

4. If a is specified as

$a{:}(x{:}s;\dots{:}y{:}t;\ u_1,\dots,u_m \to u_{m+1}(f);\dots;v_1,\dots,v_n \to v_{n+1}(g))$

where s,...,t are objects, then

$\Theta(a) \equiv$

$A \equiv A.X\ x \dots x\ A.Y$;

$f{:}\ U_1 x \dots x\ U_m \to U_{m+1}$;

$g{:}\ V_1\ x \dots x\ V_n \to V_{n+1}$

and it is understand that the global names of components are used, i.e. for those of u_i, v_j that are components of the object a, corresponding U_i, V_j have prefix 'A.'.

For the computational problem

P: S |- x -> y

its translation into type theory is defined as

"find a term such that Θ(s) |- f:X -> Y".

where Θ(S) consists of all Θ(a:s) for a:s in S.

Example.

Let S be the specification of minimax presented in section 2. Then θ(S) is as follows:

```
MATRIX ≡ MATRIX.VAL x MATRIX.I x MATRIX.J x MATRIX.E;
      get:(MATRIX.VAL x MATRIX.I x MATRIX.J x MATRIX.E)
MIN ≡ MIN.ARG x MIN.FUNVAL x MIN.MINVAL
MIN.FUN ≡ MIN.ARG -> MIN.FUNVAL
     min: MIN.FUN -> MIN.MINVAL

     MAX ≡ MAX.ARG x MAX.FUNVAL x MAX.MAXVAL
     MAX.FUN ≡ MAX.ARG -> MAX.FUNVAL
     max: MAX.FUN -> MAX.MAXVAL

MINIMAX ≡ MINIMAX.MATRIX x MINIMAX.RESULT x MINIMAX.R1 x MINIMAX.R2

Id: MINIMAX.R1.ARG -> MINIMAX.M.J;
Id: MINIMAX.R2.ARG -> MINIMAX.M.I;
Id: MINIMAX.R1.FUNVAL -> MINIMAX.M.E;
Id: MINIMAX.R2.FUNVAL -> MINIMAX.R1.MAXVAL;
Id: MINIMAX.R2.MINVAL -> MINIMAX.RESULT;
Id: MINIMAX.M.J -> MINIMAX.R1.ARG;
Id: MINIMAX.M.I -> MINIMAX.R2.ARG;
Id: MINIMAX.M.E -> MINIMAX.R1.FUNVAL;
Id: MINIMAX.R1.MAXVAL -> MINIMAX.R2.FUNVAL;
Id: MINIMAX.RESULT -> MINIMAX.R2.MINVAL;
```

It can be used together with the types MIN and MAX of the objects min and max for deriving a program for computing a value of minimax (i.e. minimax.result) from a given value of m.val. Corresponding natural deduction which can easily be read as a derivation according to the rules in section 3 has the following form, where some of the qualifying names are not shown explictitly:

```
1:MIN.ARG MIN.ARG -> M.I 2:MAX.ARG MAX.ARG ->M.J
        M.I                        M.J     3:M.VAL M.VAL, M.I, M.J ->M.E
M.E -> MAX.FUNVAL                 M.E
            (2) ______MAX.FUNVAL________
            MAX.ARG -> MAX.FUNVAL (MAX.ARG ->MAX.FUNVAL) -> MAX.FUN
MAX.FUN -> MAXVAL                 MAX.FUN
                 MAXVAL                    MAXVAL -> MIN.FUNVAL
            (1)______MIN.FUNVAL_________
                 MIN.ARG -> MIN.FUNVAL (MIN.ARG ->MIN.FUNVAL) -> MIN.FUN
MIN.FUN -> MINVAL                -> MIN.FUN
                 ->MINVAL                      MINVAL -> RESULT
                 (3)_______________-> RESULT
                              M.VAL -> RESULT
```

Corresponding program in the form of lambda term has the following form (modulo some lambda conversions taking into account Id(x) = x):

$$\lambda m\ \min(\lambda_j \max(\lambda_i \mathrm{get}(m,i,j)))$$

5. Equivalence of type-theoretical and axiomatic semantics

Theorem. Let a specification S in the kernel language and a problem x -> y on this specification be given. If the problem x -> yis solvable on S according to the axiomatic semantics then a program which computes y from x is derivable in the type theory from θ(S).
Moreover under suitable identification of lambda constructions

$$\mathrm{Sem}(S) \mid\!- X \to Y\ (t)$$

implies.

$$\theta(S) \mid\!- t : X \to Y$$

in type theory.

Proof. The definition of θ(S) is quite parallel to the definition of Sem(S). In particular the realization of implication in Sem is the same as in type theory. So one can apply the (obvious modification of) translation θ to any propositional intuitionistic natural deduction d of Sem(S)|- X -> and obtain a type theory derivation θ(d). Here we use the fact that the structural synthesis rules are essentially intuitionistic natural deduction rules for & and ->. Since program extraction rules for the

intuitionistic propositional logic are essentially the same as in the intuitionistic type theory, the term for the final E-introduction in $\theta(d)$ is the same as the program extracted from d, which was to be proved.

Remark. Consider the converse implication: derivability of the term f such that $\theta(S) \vdash (f:X \to Y)$ implies solvability of $S \vdash x \to y$ with the same program. We expect that this can be proved by careful analysis of normal derivations in type theory.

6. Interpretation using the notion of subset

The translation outlined in the section 4 stresses structural character of the kernel language dealing only with types but not with the values of these types. We outline here an alternative semantics where values i.e. elements of the types considered enter explicitly. One can recall that the translation of the kernel language into a weak second order language [9] also used values.

Instead of Σ which is implicit in type-theoretic definition of product we will use subsets. The sets used are of the form

$$\{z \in A_1 x \ldots x_n \mid P(z)\}$$

where every A_j is either one of the basic sets, like text and numeric, or again of the form $\{z \in B_1 x \ldots x B_m | Q(z)\}$. $P(z)$ is a propositional function on $A_i x \ldots x A_n$. A PRIZ specification

$$(i_1:A_1; \ldots; i_n:A_n; R_1: \ldots :R_m)$$

is interpreted as

$$\{z \in A_1 x \ldots x A_n \mid R(z)\} \qquad (0)$$

where $R(z)$ is the conjunction of $R_1 \ldots R_m$. One difference, though, is that all declarations $i \in B$ in the relations $R_1, \ldots, R_m$ should instead be among $A_1, \ldots, A_n$.

The difference of (0) from

$$(\Sigma\, x_1 \in A_1) \ldots (\Sigma\, x_n \in A_n)\; R(x_1, \ldots, x_n)$$

is that then $R(x_1, \ldots, x_n)$ is a proposition understood as a set, using the Curry-Howard interpretation. In the interpretation of PRIZ we propose now, $R(z)$ is a "real" proposition in the sense of the chapter on subsets in [7].

Using $A_1 x \ldots x A_n$ means that we must use notation like fst., snd, ... for the components of objects which is rather cumbersome compared with dot notation like x.a.b... But we could replace $A_1 x \ldots x A_n$ by

$$(\Pi x \in \{i_1,\ldots,i_n\})A(x)$$

where $i_1,\ldots,i_n$ are identifiers and A a family of sets on the enumeration set $\{i_1,\ldots,i_n\}$ such that

$$A(i_k) = A_k \qquad 1 \le k \le n$$

Such a family can easily be defined, using a universe and enumeration-elimination. Now we can introduce previous notation of projection by

$$c.i_k = \text{apply}\ (c,\ i_k)$$

where $c \in (\Pi x \in \{i_1,\ldots,i_n\})A(x)$. In the sequel, we abbreviate $(\Pi x \in \{i_1,\ldots,i_n\})\ A(x)$ by $(i_1 \in A_1;\ldots;i_n \in A_n)$.

Example. Using this notation, we make the following definitions of matrix, max, min and minimax.

```
matrix =
   { z ∈ {val ∈ text;
          e  ∈ numeric;
          i  ∈ numeric;
          j  ∈ numeric;
          get ∈ (text x numeric x numeric -> numeric)
     | apply (z.get, <z.val, z.i, z.j>) = z.c &
       z.get = C}
```

where C ∈ text x numeric x numeric -> numeric is the function (program) realizing get. An alternative would be do view C as a parameter so that matrix is introduced in the context

C ∈ text x numeric x numeric -> numeric

where C then is a variable. The equalities should actually be decorated with the set (for instance, $=_A$) but since the set is always clear from the context we omit it.

```
max =
   { z ∈ {arg ∈ numeric;
          funval ∈ numeric;
          maxval ∈ numeric;
          maxfun ∈ (numeric -> numeric) ->numeric)
     | (∀f ∈ numeric -> numeric) (apply(f,z.arg) = z.funval ⊃
       apply (z.maxfun, f ) = z.maxval) &
       z.maxfun  = fmax }
```

where fmax ∈ (numeric -> numeric) -> numeric

```
min =
   { z ∈ (arg ∈ numeric;
          funval ∈ numeric;
          minval ∈ numeric;
          minfun ∈ (numeric -> numeric) ->numeric)
       | (∀f ∈ numeric -> numeric) (apply(f,z.arg) = z.funval ⊃
          apply (z.minfun, f ) = z.minval) &
          z.minfun  = fmin }
where fmin ∈ (numeric -> numeric)  ->  numeric.
```

```
minimax =
{ z ∈ ( m ∈ matrix;
        result ∈ numeric;
           r1 ∈ max;
           r2 ∈ min)
|z.r1.arg        = z.m.j         &
 z.r1.funval     = z.m.e         &
 z.r2.arg        = z.m.i         &
 z.r2.funval     = z.r1.maxval   &
 z.r2.minval     = z.result    }
```

Now the derivation, which we do "bottom up", although "top down" would be more natural.

Problem

Find an element S in the set

matrix -> numeric

such that the proposition

apply (S, x.m) = x.value

holds in the context x ∈ minimax.

Solution

We place ourselves in the context

x ∈ minimax

We have C ∈ text x numeric x numeric -> numeric such that

```
apply (C, <x.m.val, x.m.i, x.m.j>) = x.m.e          (1)
```

Formally, the derivation of (1) is made by first using the subset-elimination rule

$$\frac{a \in \{x \in A \mid P(x)\}}{a \in A}$$

twice and then using the subset-elimination rule

$$\frac{a \in \{x \in A \mid P(x)\}}{P(a)}$$

followed by some elementary steps involving & and =.

Define F by

$$F(z) = \lambda y.apply\ (C, \langle x.m.val,\ z,\ y\rangle) \qquad (2)$$

We than have

$$F(x.m.i) = \lambda y.apply(C, \langle x.m.val,\ x.m.i,\ y\ \rangle) \in numeric \rightarrow numeric \qquad (3)$$

We have

$$fmax \in (numeric \rightarrow numeric) \rightarrow numeric$$

such that

$$(\forall\ f \in numeric \rightarrow numeric)\ (apply(f,\ x.r1.arg) = x.r1.funval \supset apply\ (fmax,\ f) = x.r1.maxval) \qquad (4)$$

We also obtain

$$x.r1.funval \quad = \quad x.m.e \qquad (5)$$

From (1) - (5) we get

$$apply\ (fmax,\ F(x.m.i)) = x.r1.maxval \qquad (6)$$

We can also derive

$$x.r2.arg \quad = x.m.i \qquad (7)$$

$$x.r2.funval \quad = x.r1.maxval \qquad (8)$$

(6) - (8) give

$$apply\ (fmax,\ F(x.r2.arg)) = x.r2.funval \qquad (9)$$

Analogically we get

$$apply\ (fmin,\ H) = x.r2.minval \qquad (10)$$

where

$$H = \lambda z.apply(fmax,\ F(z)) \qquad (11)$$

We also have

$$x.r2.minval \quad = x.value \qquad (12)$$

(11) and (12) give

$$apply\ (fmin,\ H) = x.value$$

Since

$$apply\ (fmin,\ H) = apply\ (fmin,\ \lambda z.apply(fmax,\ \lambda y.apply(C,\ \langle x.m.val,\ z,\ y)))$$

we finally obtain the solution

$$S = \lambda u.apply(fmin.\lambda z.apply(fmax,\ \lambda y.apply(C,\ \langle u.val,\ z,\ y)))$$

Except for notation, this is the same program that was derived at the section 4. If we had used Σinstead of subsets, and sets instead of propositions, the program would contain a lot of proof-elements coming from all the manipulations with equalities.

References

1. G. Mints, E. Tyugu. The programming System PRIZ. J. of Symbolic Computation, 1988, N5, pp. 359-375.

2. M. Koov et al. (Eds). MicroPRIZ - intelligent software system. Acad. of Sciences of the Estonian SSR. Tallinn, 1986.

3. G. Mints, E. Tyugu. Semantics of a declarative language. Information Processing Letters 23, 1986, pp. 147-151.

4.E. Tyugu. Language and Example of Knowledge-based Programming. Proceedings of the International Spring School, Akademie-Verlag Berlin, 1986, pp. 59-72.

5. E. Tyugu. Knowledge Based Programming. Addison-Wesley Publ. Co, 1988.

6. Per Martin-Löf. Intuitionistic Type Theory. Bibliopolis, Napoli, 1984.

7. B. Nordström, K. Petersson, J. M. Smith. Programming in Martin-Löf's Type Theory, Programming Methodology group. Dep. of. Comp. Sc., University of Göteborg/Chalmers, 1989.

8. G. Mints, E. Tyugu. Justification of the structural synthesis of programs. Science of Computer Programming. 1983, vol. 2, N 3, pp. 215-240.

9. G. Mints, E. Tyugu. The completeness of structural synthesis rules. Soviet Math. Doklady 1982, v. 25, pp. 343-346.

USING RESOLUTION FOR DECIDING SOLVABLE CLASSES AND BUILDING FINITE MODELS

Tanel Tammet

Institute of Cybernetics
Akadeemia tee 21, 200108, Tallinn, Estonia
e-mail: tanel@ioc.ew.su

Abstract

The paper consists of two parts. In the first part we briefly describe the resolution strategy devised by N.Zamov which decides a number of solvable classes, including Maslov's Class K (this class contains most well-known decidable classes like Gödel's Class, Skolem's Class, Monadic Class). We give a strategy close to Zamov's, deciding a a wide class with functional symbols. A short description of our theorem-prover implementing the decision strategies is given.

The second part presents the main result of the paper: a new, resolution-based method for showing the existence of finite models and an algorithm for building such models for several solvable classes. For small formulas our method often generates considerably smaller models than known methods of B.Dreben and W.D.Goldfarb, although it doesn't improve the known upper bounds on the size of the models.

The work described here has been guided by G.Mints. We would also like to thank N.Zamov for helpful discussions.

1. Deciding formulas in solvable classes using resolution

Since the first-order predicate calculus is undecidable, the complete proof methods (Gentzen's method and the resolution method, for example) are guaranteed to terminate only in case the answer is positive, e.g. in case of resolution method, the examined formula is refutable. If it is not, they will in general loop, since (except the positive result) there can't be any effective criteria for stopping the search.

Algorithms which are guaranteed to stop and provide correctly not only the positive but also the negative answers (decision algorithms), exist for the solvable subclasses of first order predicate calculus only. Well-known solvable classes are, for example, Gödel's Class, Skolem's Class, Maslov's Class (see [3]). Familiar decision algorithms for these sub-classes are specialized and in general based on testing a formula on a model of (super)exponential size.

It seems quite desirable to modify a general method like resolution in such a way that it became, besides being a complete proof procedure, also a decision procedure for some solvable classes. N.Zamov [15], [16] has shown that using a special ordering of literals, close to but stronger than J.Maslov's pi-orderings (see [10]), it is possible to guarantee termination of the resolution method for all formulas (including invalid ones) of a wide decidable class, the so-called Maslov's Class K (see [9], [16]).

This class contains most well-known decidable classes, like Gödel's Class (prefix $(\forall y_1)(\forall y_2)(\exists z_1)\ldots(\exists z_n)$, Skolem's Class (prefix $(\forall y_1)\ldots(\forall y_m)(\exists z_1)\ldots(\exists z_n)$ and every literal contains either one variable z_i or all variables $y_1,\ldots,y_m$), Monadic Class, etc. Strategies of the same kind were also investigated by V.Šaronov [20] and W.Joyner[4]. Using somewhat different methods, A.Leitsch (see [6]) has been investigating the decidability of horn clause implication problem ($\forall A \Rightarrow \forall B$ where A and B are horn clauses) by ordinary hyperresolution and has found several decidable suclasses of this class of formulas.

The strategy proposed by Zamov is complete in the general case, requires a small modification of the resolution method and proves in experiments to be much more efficient than building the countermodel of a formula. Since for decidable formulas it reduces the search space to a finite set of disjuncts, in addition of being a decision procedure it often discovers the validity of a formula in a decidable class much faster than the familiar modifications of the resolution method.

In the following we will give a short presentation of Zamov's strategy and give definitions of Maslov's Class K and a Class E+, the last one being decidable by a certain ordering strategy close to Zamov's strategy.

1.1 Zamov's strategy

At first we bring the outline of the strategy given in [16]. We will call it Z1-strategy.

Definition: The term t covers the term s if at least one of the following conditions is satisfied:

1) t=s
2) $t=f(t_1,...,t_n)$, s is a variable and $s=t_i$ for some i, $i=1,...,n$
3) $t=f(t_1,...,t_n)$, $s=g(t_1,...,t_m)$, $n \geq m \geq 0$.

Definition: The relation $>_1$ between literals is defined as follows: A $>_1$ B if for every argument t_2 of the literal B there exists an argument t_1 of the literal A such that t_1 covers t_2 or t_2 is a subterm of the term t_1.

Notice that the relation $>_1$ between literals is not a strict linear ordering relation, since it leaves some pairs of literals uncomparable and for other pairs A, B it might be case that $A>_1B$ and $B>_1A$. Nevertheless the $>_1$ relation is transitive and is preserved under substitution: if $A>_1B$, then As $>_1$ Bs for any substitution s.

Z1-strategy is defined by a restriction on a resolution rule (we prefer a formulation of resolution method where resolution rule and factorization rule are separated. See [5] for differences between definitions of resolution method). It is impotant to notice that Zamov's strategy does not allow eliminating tautologous disjuncts, and eliminating subsumed disjuncts is allowed only in case the ordering of the subsuming disjunct corresponds exactly to that of the subsumed one.

Restriction on resolution rule: only maximal literals (that is, those for which there are no strictly bigger ones in the sense of ordering $>_1$) in the disjunct are allowed to be resolved upon.

Example: In the disjunct {A(f(x,g(x)),y), B(g(x),g(x)), C(x,0), D(y,x), E(g(x),z)} only the literals A(f(x,g(x)),y), E(g(x),z) and C(x,0) are allowed to be resolved upon.

N.Zamov has shown (see [15], [16]) that Z1-strategy is complete and for the formulas of Maslov's Class K, only terms of the certain kind will be generated. These terms cannot contain proper subterms with the same or bigger arity, therefore the set of generated terms is finite. As the length of generated disjuncts is shown to be bounded by a certain function from the size of generated terms, the search space is finite and the Z1-strategy solves Maslov's Class K. We give the definiton of Class K in the section 1.3.

1.2 Z3-strategy

Throughout the section 2 of our paper and also in sections 1.4 and 1.5 we are going to use a certain ordering strategy, the completeness of which is proven analogically to the completeness of Zamov's strategy. We will not describe the completeness proof in the current paper. However, we notice that this strategy is not generally complete, but complete only for the specific classes (eg E+ and AMS intoduced later).

We will call it **Z3-strategy.**

By **maxdepth(x,L)** we denote the maximal depth of occurrence of the variable x in literal L.

Splitting is a following well-known rule: if a disjunct D in a set of disjuncts S can be split into two parts A and B such that A and B do not share variables, then S is contradictory iff both (S-D)+A and (S-D)+B are.

Definition: Let $\overline{x}$ be a set of variables in a literal A, $\overline{y}$ be a set of variables in a literal B. We say that $A >_3 B$ iff the following single condition holds:

$$\overline{y} \leq \overline{x} \text{ and } \forall y_i \in \overline{y}\ (\text{maxdepth}(y_i,B) < \text{maxdepth}(y_i,A))$$

The new ordering $>_3$ is transitive and is preserved under substitution in the weak sense: if $A >_3 B$ then it is guaranteed that $Bs >_3 As$ cannot be the case, but it is not guaranteed that $As >_3 Bs$).

Z3-strategy is defined by a restriction on a resolution rule analogous to the restriction used for Z1-strategy, and an additional restriction on the factorization rule.

Restriction on the resolution rule: only the maximal (in the sense of new ordering $>_3$) literals in a disjunct are allowed to be resolved upon.

Example. In the disjunct {A(f(f(x,y),y),1), B(2,g(y,x)), C(y,z), C(x,x), D(1,f(2,1))} the literals B(2,g(y,x)) and C(x,x) are not allowed to be resolved upon.

Restriction on the factorization rule:

Let $D=\{L_1,\ldots,L_n\}$ be some disjunct. If some pair of literals L_i, L_j in D does not share variables, then it is not allowed to generate such a factorization $(Ds)-(L_is)$ (where $s=MGU(L_i, L_j)$ is obtained by unifying L_i and L_j, not some other pair of literals in D) that D is not subsumed by $(Ds)-(L_is)$.

Example: It is not allowed to generate a factorization {P(f(x,g(x))), P(g(x))} from the disjunct {P(f(x,y)), P(y), P(g(x))}. On the other hand, generating {P(g(x))} from {P(g(x)), P(y)} is allowed.

The completeness of Z3-strategy is preserved for AMS class introduced later even if the elimination of tautologies and subsumed disjuncts is used. These elimination strategies will be used in the proof of the correctness of the algorithm for building finite models.

In a paper [13] we show that Z3-strategy, when complemented with the splitting rule, decides the Class E+ introduced in section 1.3.

1.3 Maslov's Class K

The prefix of the literal L in a prenex predicate formula F is obtained from the prefix of F by discarding quantifiers for those variables, which do not occur in L.

The definition we are going to present is given in terms of refutability, not provability as in [9].

F is said to belong to the Class K if it does not contain function symbols and there are variables $x_1,\ldots,x_n$ in a set of variables of F such that every $x_i (1 \le i \le n)$ is situated in the prefix of F to the left of all existential quantifiers and for every prefix $\underline{P}$ of a literal in F at least one of the following is true:

1) $\underline{P}$ consists of the single general quantifier $\forall$.
2) $\underline{P}$ ends with the existential quantifier $\exists$.
3) $\underline{P}$ is of the form $(\forall x_1)(\forall x_2)\ldots(\forall x_n)$.

Maslov's Class K is introduced and shown to be solvable in [9]. See [15], [16] for an overview of Class K and the proof of its decidability by Z1-strategy.

1.4 Class E+

We have shown that Z3-strategy with splitting decides the following class of formulas with functional symbols (proof can be found in [13]).

The definition is presented in terms of refutability:
We say that the first-order predicate calculus formula F in the prenex form belongs to the Class E+ iff the prefix of F consists only of the general quantifiers and the matrix of F has the following properties:

A) if a term t in some literal L contains variables, then it contains all the variables present in L.

B) if two literals L and L' in some disjunct D share a variable, all the variables in L and L' are shared.

The class just presented contains the Class E of formulas with function symbols where every atom contains only one variable (in terms of derivability, formulas in Class E can be said to be of the form (∃x)M). Solvability of Class E, also called N_1, has been shown in various ways, see [17], [18]. We consider the class E+ to be a "natural" superclass of E.

1.5. Overview of our theorem-prover

Our theorem prover [13] is designed for an interactive use and includes a large set of different resolution strategies. In addition to well-known strategies it also features Maslov's inverse method (see [8], [16]) and Z1- and Z3-strategies. The prover is implemented on IBM-PC-AT in LISP and assembler. It has decided all the first-order formulas from Church [2] (some of them are valid, some are not), the longest runtimes for these problems were less than 3 minutes. Without Zamov's strategy the prover was unable to refute the most complicated valid formula in [2]. We also experimented with W.McCune's OTTER theorem-prover: version 0.9 of OTTER running on IBM-PC-AT couldn't refute this formula either: after a long search OTTER ran out of memory.

Our prover has solved most first-order predicate calculus problems found in automated deduction literature (Schubert's steamroller, for example, was solved in about 4 minutes). Several experiments and applications of the prover are described in [11] and [13].

Resolution theorem provers with the capability to decide nontrivial solvable classes have in seventies been written by W.Joyner

[4] and A.Sochilina [19]. Joyner's prover used a weaker strategy than Zamov's method. We do not know exactly which modifications of Zamov's strategy were implemented by Sochilina's prover.

2. The resolution-based method for building finite models

In the following we will present an algorithm for building finite models for formulas in the class we call AM, which is the union of Initially-extended Ackermann and Initially-extended Essentially Monadic Classes. Initially extended Ackermann's Class is the class of formulas with prefix $(\exists x_1),\ldots,(\exists x_n),(\forall y),(\exists z_1),\ldots,(\exists z_m)$ (when given in terms of refutability). Initially-extended Essentially Monadic Class is a class of formulas with such atoms which after Skolemization will contain no more than one non-ground term among arguments of the atom. For example, the atom (in a Skolemized form) P(1,f(x,y),2,f(x,y)) will be considered to be Monadic.

Our method is practically in no way related to the methods of building finite models described in [14]; the last methods rely totally on the human user and except the theorem-prover (which does not use decision strategies) offer only a helpful housekeeping environment to keep track of the investigated search space.

The proof of the termination of our algorithm uses only the theorems about the completeness of pi-strategies of resolution method [10] and the theorem about narrowing [12], thus being the proof of the finite controllability of AM.

We have not set ourselves the task to improve the known upper bounds on the size of the model of Ackermann and Monadic classes (see [3]). Neither can we show that our method has a better upper bound on a computational complexity of building the model than is given in [7].

Nevertheless, our algorithm is capable of computing for "small formulas" considerably smaller models than classical methods given, for example, in [3] (such optimisations obviously were not the aim of the authors of [3]); it uses more of the structure of the investigated formula, being more flexible, so to say. Since it relies on a certain decision strategy (Z3-strategy) of resolution method, we have an opinion that it shares some of the good properties of resolution. For example, our method performs the satisfiability checking incrementally (satisfiability checking must be performed many times for generating even the smallest models) and uses an efficient resolution strategy.

It would be interesting to compare the implementation of our method with the implementation of classical methods; unfortunately no implementations of the classical methods are known to us.

Last not least, we hope that the general outline of the soundness and termination proof of the algorithm might be useful for showing finite controllability and devising analogous algorithms for other solvable classes for which we have the decision strategies of resolution (Classes K and E+, for example) and giving some additional insight to related problems.

2.1. Terminology

In order to avoid misinterpretation of several notions used in our text we will define some of them.

Definition: Constant is a functional symbol with arity 0.

Definition: Term, its arguments and leading functional symbol are defined as follows:

1. A variable is a term and a constant is a term.
2. If f_i is a functional symbol with arity af>0, and $t_1,...,t_{af}$ are terms, then $f_i(t_1,...,t_{af})$ is a term, $t_1,...,t_{af}$ are the arguments of the term $f_i(t_1,...,t_{af})$, f_i is a leading functional symbol of the term $f_i(t_1,...,t_{af})$.

Definition: of a subterm and proper subterm:

1. If t is a term, t is a subterm of t.
2. If $t=f_i(t_1,...,t_{af})$ is a term, then subterms of $t_1,...,t_{af}$ are subterms and proper subterms of t.

Definition: Term t is called functional term if it is neither a variable nor a constant.

Definition: An expression L is called ground if L does not contain variables. Expression L is called non-ground if it contains variables (or is a variable itself).

Definition: Atom is an expression of the form $P(t_1,...,t_n)$, where P is a predicate symbol and $t_1,...,t_n$ are terms, called arguments of the atom.

Definition: Literal is either an atom or the negation of an atom. If L is an expression, then ¬L denotes the negation (complement) of L, so ¬(¬L)=L for any L. Arguments of the literal are arguments of the atom in literal.

Definition: Disjunct denotes either a set of literals (written $\{L_1,\ldots,L_n\}$) or a disjunction of literals (written $L_1|\ldots|L_m$), depending upon context.

Definition: Formula denotes either a set of disjuncts or the first order predicate calculus formula in the ordinary sense, depending upon context.

Definition: A substitution is a finite set of the form $\{t_1/v_1,\ldots,t_n/v_n\}$, where $v_1,\ldots,v_n$ are different variables, $t_1,\ldots,t_n$ are terms, t_i do not contain any v_j ($1\le j\le n$) as subterms.

Definition: Let $s=\{t_1/v_1,\ldots,t_n/v_n\}$ be some substitution and L some expression. We denote by $s*L$ the expression obtained from L by replacing all occurrences of variables $v_1,\ldots,v_n$ by terms $t_1,\ldots,t_n$, respectively. $s*L$ is called a **substitution instance** of L.

Definition: Let $s_1=\{t_1/v_1,\ldots,t_n/v_n\}$ and $s_2=\{d_1/w_1,\ldots,d_m/w_m\}$ be substitutions.

The **composition** s_1*s_2 of s_1 and s_2 is a substitution which is obtained from $\{t_1*s_2/v_1,\ldots,t_n*s_2/v_n,d_1/w_1,\ldots,d_m/w_m\}$ by omitting all elements of the form t_j*s_2/v_j where $t_j*s_2=v_j$ and all elements d_j/w_j, where w_j belongs to $\{v_1,\ldots,v_n\}$.

Definition: A substitution s is called a **unifier** of two expressions L_1 and L_2 if $s*L_1=s*L_2$. L_1 and L_2 are called **unifiable** if there exists a unifier for them.

Definition: A unifier s is called the most general unifier of $L_1$1, L_2 if for every unifier s' of L_1, L_2 there exists a substitution s_1 such that $s'=s_1*s$. $MGU(L_1, L_2)$ denotes the most general unifier of expressions L_1, L_2.

Definition: Disjunct is called a **tautology** if it contains some literal L and its negation ¬L.

Definition: Disjunct D_1 **subsumes** the disjunct D_2 if there exists such a substitution s that $s*D_1$ is a subset of D_2.

Definition: The set of disjuncts S **subsumes** the disjunct D if either D is a tautology or some disjunct D' in S subsumes D.

Definition: The set of disjuncts S_1 **subsumes** the set of disjuncts S_2 if S_1 subsumes every disjunct in S_2.

2.2 The Class AM

We present the description of the classes AM and AMS. AM is the union of the Initially-extended Ackermann Class and the Initially-extended

Essentially Monadic Class. AMS is the class used while building a model for a formula in AM: it is essentially the Class AM with arbitrary ground substitutions allowed.

Definition: Let F be a formula of the first order predicate calculus (without functional symbols and without the equality predicate). Let SF be the skolem form of F. Let $A=P(t_1,...,t_n)$ be an atom in SF. By Args(A) we denote the set $\{t_1,...,t_n\}$. One element of Args(A) may then correspond to many syntactically equal terms among $t_1,...,t_n$. Then formula F belongs to the Class AM iff for every atom A in SF at least one of the following possibilities holds:

1. Args(A) contains at most one non-ground term.
2. Every functional term in Args(A) has an arity at most 1 and A contains only one variable (this variable may have several occurences in A).

We give the definition of the Class AMS as a class of sets of disjuncts.

Definition: A set S of disjuncts belongs to the Class AMS iff the following properties Pa, Pb and Pc hold for all literals in S and the property Pd holds for all disjuncts in S.

Property Pa(L) Every functional argument term t of literal L contains all the variables in L.

Property Pb(L) No term in L may contain variables deeper than at depth 1.

Example: term f(1,x,g(y)) contains x at depth 1, y at depth 2, thus Pb does not hold for any literal containing this term.

Property Pc(L) Either all nonconstant argument terms of L are syntactically equal or L is a substitution instance of some literal L′ such that each argument of L′ is either a constant, a variable x, or a functional term with arity 1 and a single argument x.

Examples: Pc(A(1,f(x,y,g(2)),2,f(x,y,g(2)))), Pc(B(4,g(x),d(x),x)), Pc(B(4,g(g(g(1))),d(g(g(1))),g(g(1)))), ¬Pc(C(f(x,y),f(y,x))), ¬Pc(D(x,y)), ¬Pc(E(g(x),d(1))), ¬Pc(F(g(1),x)).

Property Pd(D) Let a variable (say x) occur in D as a k-th argument of some term t in D. If x occurs in D as an argument of some other term d, then x is a k-th argument of d. Let a variable (say y) occur in D as argument of some atom. If y occurs in D as an argument of some term g, then y is a first argument of g.

It is easy to see that AM is the subclass of AMS.

In the following we will say that atom A is of the **Ackermann type** if and only if A has at least two such different arguments t_1 and t_2 that t_1 and t_2 are not constants; if A is not of the Ackermann type, we will say it is of the **Monadic type**. Notice that our usage of the names "Ackermann" and "Monadic" does not exactly correspond to the "normal" usage of these names (in our usage, for example, Monadic atoms can't be Ackermann). For literals the same classification is defined analogously.

2.3. Deciding formulas in AMS with Z3-strategy

We say that a disjunct D is an **abcd-disjunct** iff every literal in D has properties Pa, Pb and Pc and D has a property Pd.

We say that a disjunct D is a **Z3-resolvent** of disjuncts D_1 and D_2 iff D is obtained from D_1 and D_2 using resolution with Z3-strategy. We say that a disjunct D is a Z3-factorization of disjunct D' iff D is obtained from D' using factorization with Z3-strategy.

Lemma 1: Let disjuncts $D=\{L_1,\ldots,L_n\}$ and $D'=\{L'_1,\ldots,L'_m\}$ both be abcd-disjuncts. Let $R=s*L_2|\ldots|s*L_n|s*L'_2|\ldots|s*L'_m$ (where $s=MGU(L_1,\neg L'_1)=\{t_1/x_1,\ldots,t_r/x_r\}$) be a Z3-resolvent of D and D'. If some variable x_i ($1\le i\le r$) is a proper subterm of some term of some literal in the set $\{L_2,\ldots,L_n\}$, then the term t_i must be a proper subterm of some term f in L'_1 or L_1.

Proof: Suppose that x_i is a proper subterm of term t in some literal L_j in D. At first we show that in this case x_i must be a proper subterm of some term f in L_1.

Suppose that x_i is not a proper subterm of any term in L_1. Then, since we use the Z3-strategy and therefore $L_j \le_3 L_1$, one of the following three cases must hold:

1. L_1 does not contain x_i, contrary to the assumption.

2. L_1 contains x_i and also a variable (let it be x_u) not in L_j. Then L_1 contains more than one variable, but in this case (since $Pc(L_1)$) all the variables (including x_i) in L_1 are proper subterms of some term in L_1, contrary to the assumption.

3. Some variable (let it be x_u) occurs in L_1 deeper than in L_j. Then either $x_u=x_i$ (and, contrary to the assumption, x_i is a proper subterm of some term in L_1) or $x_u\ne x_i$ and again L_1 contains more than one variable, thus x_i must be a proper subterm of some term in L_1, contrary to the assumption.

Now we have shown that x_i is a proper subterm of some term f in L_1. Let f be a k-th argument of L_1, x_i be a l-th argument of f (such k and l exist due to $Pb(L_1)$). Assume that a functional term t_i is not a proper subterm of any term in L'_1 or L_1. Then s could contain t_i/x_i only in two cases:

1. a k-th argument of L'_1 were some term g such that f and g were unifiable, l-th argument of g were some variable x_j (then $t_i=t_j$), and x_j occured also in some other place in L'_1.

Suppose x_j occurred in L'_1 as the p-th argument. Due to $Pc(L_1)$, the p-th argument of L_1 could be either some constant (but t_i is supposedly not a constant), a variable x_i (this binding we have already), or some functional term (due to $Pc(L_1)$, it has the same list of arguments as f. Then, due to $Pa(L_1)$, f contains x_i, thus L_1 and L'_1 are not unifiable).

Suppose x_j occurred in L'_1 as a proper subterm of some term d. Due to $Pa(L'_1)$, d is the v-th argument of L'_1. Then, since Pa and Pc hold for L_1 and L'_1, either the v-th argument of L_1 is f (due to $Pc(L'_1)$ this does not introduce any new bindings to x_j) or L_1 and L'_1 are not unifiable.

2. a k-th argument of L'_1 were some variable x_j, which also occurred in other places in L'_1. Due to $Pa(L_1)$ and $Pc(L_1)$, x_j could then be bound only to f, but this binding we had already.

END OF PROOF

Lemma 2: Let disjunct $D=\{L_1,\ldots,L_n\}$ be an abcd-disjunct. Let $R=(s*D)-(s*L_i)$ (where $s=MGU(L_i,L_j)=\{t_1/x_1,\ldots,t_r/x_r\}$ for some i,j: $1\le i,j\le n$) be a Z3-factorization of D. If R is not a subset of D, then each term t_i ($1\le i\le r$) is either a variable, a constant, or a functional term which is a proper subterm of some term in L_i or L_j.

Proof: Suppose R is not a subset of D, some t_l ($1\le l\le r$) is a functional term and not a proper subterm of any term in L_i or in L_j. Then t_l must be a substitution instance of some functional term g which is a k-th (for some k) argument of L_i or L_j (in the following we assume that g is a k-th argument of L_i) and the k-th argument of L_j must be x_l. Consider following cases:

1. g does not contain x_l. Then, due to $Pa(L_i)$, L_i does not contain x_l. Since $Pc(L_j)$, L_j does not contain variables except x_l. Then L_i and L_j do not share variables. Then (since we use Z3-strategy)

either R subsumes D (in this case R is a subset of D, contrary to the assumption) or the factorization is not allowed, contrary to the assumption.

2. g contains x_1. Then, contrary to the assumption, L_i and L_j are not unifiable.

END OF PROOF

Lemma 3: Let disjuncts $D=\{L_1,\ldots,L_n\}$ and $D'=\{L'_1,\ldots,L'_m\}$ both be abcd-disjuncts. If the disjunct R is either a Z3-resolvent of D and D' or a Z3-factorization of D, then R is an abcd-disjunct.

Proof: 1. Properties Pa, Pc. The preservation of these properties is obvious, since they are preserved by any substitution.

2. Property Pb.

A) Resolution rule. $R=s*L_2|\ldots|s*L_n|s*L'_2|\ldots|s*L'_m$ (where $s=MGU(L_1,L'_1)=\{t_1/x_1,\ldots,t_r/x_r\}$). Suppose that for some literal $L=s*L_j$ $(2\le j\le n)$ in R Pb(L) does not hold. Then some term in L_j must contain some variable x_k as a proper subterm and the corresponding t_k must contain variables as proper subterms. Since $Pb(L_1)$ and $Pb(L'_1)$, t_k cannot be a proper subterm of any term in L_1 or L'_1. Then, due to lemma 1, t_k/x_k cannot be an element of s.

B) Factorization rule. Let R be a result of the application of factorization rule to D. If R is a subset of D, the preservation of property Pb is obvious. Assume that R is not a subset of D. Suppose that for some literal $L=s*L_j$ in R Pb(L) does not hold. Then some term in L_j must contain some variable x_k as a proper subterm and the corresponding t_k must contain variables as proper subterms, which is impossible due to $Pb(L_j)$ and lemma 2.

3. Property Pd. Let D be an abcd-disjunct. Let $s=\{t_1/x_1,\ldots,t_n/x_n\}$ be some substitution such that no t_i $(1\le i\le n)$ is a non-ground functional term. Then Pd(s*D). Let $s'=\{d_1/x_1,\ldots,d_m/x_m\}$ be some substitution such that no x_j occurs in D as a proper subterm of some term and no pair d_i,d_j $(1\le i,j\le m)$ shares variables. Then no literal in D contains more than one variable, therefore Pd(s*D). It is easy to see that every substitution applied by factorizing or resolution step to some disjunct D has one of the beforementioned forms, either s or s'.

Thus factorization step preserves Pd. Consider resolution step. Let D and D' be abcd-disjuncts and literals L and L' in D and D' be resolved upon. Since D and D' are assumed not to share variables, Pd(D

| D'). Since we already know that properties Pa, Pb and Pc are preserved, D | D' is an abcd-disjunct. Since MGU(L,L') has one of the beforementioned forms (s or s'), Pd(MGU(L,L')*(D | D')) holds.
END OF PROOF

Theorem 1: Let S be a set of disjuncts in Class AMS. Then Z3-strategy derives only a finite number of disjuncts from S.

Proof: Due to the definition of Class AMS, all disjuncts in S are abcd-disjuncts. Lemma 3 guarantees that every disjunct derived from S with Z3-strategy is also an abcd-disjunct. Therefore Lemma 1 and Lemma 2 guarantee that the depth of functional nesting in any derived disjunct is not greater than the maximal depth of functional nesting in S. Lemma 3 also guarantees that the length of derived disjuncts is restricted (since properties Pc and Pd are preserved, disjuncts longer than some known length bound will be subsumed by their own factorizations).
END OF PROOF.

2.4. The algorithm for building finite models for formulas in AM

We start with a definition of a function *stable* we will need later.
Definition: Function *stable*, when given some set of disjuncts A as an argument, computes the set of disjuncts A' by applying resolution with Z3-strategy to A until no more new disjuncts can be derived, thus A'=*stable*(A') (remember that we assume resolution to incorporate the strategy of eliminating subsumed and tautologous disjuncts).

Since the termination of Z3-strategy on formulas from Class AMS is guaranteed, *stable* is a total function on Class AMS. Since Z3-strategy is complete for Class AMS, ø ∈ *stable*(A) (then *stable*(A)={ø} due to subsumption) if and only if A is unsatisfiable. In the following we will say that some set of disjuncts G is in the **stable** form iff G=*stable*(G).

Let F be a satisfiable formula from Class AM and SF={$D_1,\dots,D_n$} be the conjunctive normal form of the skolemized F (set of disjuncts obtained from F, for short).

We will use the Herbrand universe H: {$h_1,h_2,\dots$} built from the constant and function symbols of SF as a domain of the model M for F (Herbrand's theorem implies that if a first order predicate calculus formula has a model, it has a model with the domain of elements of Herbrand universe). In order to build the finite model, we must build the finite domain. We will select a set of equations $E=\{e_1,...,e_m\}$ (where each e_i is of the form $h_k=h_l$ for some k,l), that would decompose H into a finite number of different equivalence classes $\{c_1,...,c_r\}$ such that the formula SFE: $\{D_1,...,D_n,e_1,...,e_m\}$ would be satisfiable. In this case SFE would have a finite model MF with the domain D constructed by choosing one arbitrary element from each c_i. Obviously MF would be a model for F.

Let H be a Herbrand universe of a satisfiable F from AM. We will use the same main idea for building the finite model for F as is used for building finite models in [3], for example: we will traverse the Herbrand universe (considering it as a certain directed non-cyclical graph with infinite levels (the depth of terms at each level is by one less than the number of level) and with m starting points at the first level (m is either 1 or a number of constant symbols in F)), moving from level 1 to deeper levels and trying to add equations between terms on the current level and some earlier level. We also try to add equations between terms on the same level. Each equation cuts short some branches, until the branches in H are pruned.

The **minimal consistent criteria** for accepting some equation a=b between herbrand terms is the satisfiability of a conjunction (F & a=b & E) where E is the set of equations found so far. Such a criteria gurantees that F will have a model with the constructed interpretation of function symbols (but it generally does not guarantee finding a finite model, since we do not backtrack to try all possible combinations of equations). We will bring a simple example of the process.

Example: Formula F=(P(x,f(x)) & ¬P(f(y),y)) has a Herbrand universe with a single branch: {0, f(0), f(f(0)), f(f(f(0))), f(f(f(f(0)))), ... }. At first try to add equation f(0)=0. But F & f(0)=0 is unsatisfiable, therefore this equation cannot be added. At the next step try to add f(f(0))=0, but again F & f(f(0))=0 is unsatisfiable. Then try f(f(0))=f(0) and fail again. The first equation which can be added consistently is f(f(f(0)))=0, which prunes our single branch, thus giving the finite domain with four elements.

In the general case we have more than one branch and therefore need more than one equation. One of the most important properties of our model-building algorithm is an absence of backtracing. Notice that using total backtracing (checking all possible interpretations for function symbols) for searching a finite model would prevent finding any but the smallest models: for example, a single functional symbol with arity 2 on a ten-element domain yields 10^{10} different interpretations.

Unfortunately, as we do not use backtracing, for testing the acceptability of an equation it is not possible to rely just on testing the satisfiability of the conjunction of our original formula, so far obtained equations and the tested equation: we have no means for a proof that such a process of finding the equations will terminate. In order to guarantee termination of the search for a finite domain we will use stronger criteria. The criteria we have chosen differ from those given in [3] for the Ackermann Class, for example, in such a way that as one of the consequences we can almost always build much smaller models for the small formulas, although for "very saturated" formulas the worst case bounds in [3] are probably better.

2.5 The criteria for accepting a set of equations

In the general case we have more than one branch in the Herbrand universe and therefore need many equations to prune all the branches. We will describe the algorithm *ok_equations* which determines whether a certain set of equations is acceptable. The main idea is that two terms d and t are allowed to be set equal in case they are "similar enough": they must have the same leading functional symbols, the equation must not allow any additional unifications between substitution instances of the atoms in the original formula (the exact definitions are given later) and they must "behave similarly in respect to possible models of F", so to say.

The main problem is selecting such a criteria *ok_equations* that we could prove the following three propositions:

1. termination of a single step, *ok_equations*.
2. termination of the search: our algorithm of constructing the finite domain is guaranteed to stop.
3. soundness: if *ok_equations*(E′), then the set of disjuncts E′ ∪ F is satisfiable.

In the following we will use the notion **narrowing** of Slagle (see [12]): if E is a confluent term rewriting system, **narrowing** of any expression e is obtained by unifying a left side term h of some rewrite rule in E with some non-variable subterm t of e, applying the obtained substitution s:=MGU(h_k,t) to e, and rewriting the expression s*e to its normal form. The narrowing of the narrowing of e is also considered to be a narrowing of e.

Remark 2 in forthcoming section 2.6 demonstrates that the set of equations generated by our algorithm can be always oriented to a confluent term rewriting system. In the following it is always assumed that when equations in E are oriented into reductions, the left side term of the reduction is deeper than the right side term.

We will say that an expression e is **narrowable** iff there is a narrowing of e (in respect to some known E).

We will say that an expression e is **narrowable** to some expression e' iff there is a narrowing e' of e (in respect to some known E).

Example: Let E={f(f(0))->0, g(1)->0}. The single narrowing of an atom P(f(x),x) is P(0,f(0)).

We select the following criteria *ok_equations* (we assume the set of disjuncts F to be in the stable form).

1. Empty set satisfies *ok_equations*.
2. Assume that the set E satisfies *ok_equations*. In order to test whether E & {fa->fb} (fa and fb must have the same leading functional symbol f) satisfies ok_equations, at first construct two sets of literals, FA_LIT and FB_LIT, in the following way:

A. Let FA_ATOMS be the set of all such substitution instances I of atoms in F that I contains the term fa among its deepest arguments.

Let FB_ATOMS be the set of all such substitution instances I of atoms in F that I contains the term fb among its deepest arguments.

Let A' be an element of FA_ATOMS and A' be such a substitution instance of an atom A in F that A' contains fa among its deepest arguments. We say that atom B' in FB_LIT **corresponds to** A' iff B' is such a substitution instance of A that B' contains fb among its deepest arguments.

Since every atom in F has properties Pa, Pb and Pc, there is a one-to-one correspondence between FA_ATOMS and FB_ATOMS.

Since every atom in F has properties Pa, Pb and Pc, the number of elements in FA_ATOMS (and of FB_ATOMS) is not bigger than the number of atoms (up to renaming the variables) in F. Also notice that the elements of FB_LIT generally aren't the normal forms of corresponding elements of FA_LIT.

B. Construct the set of literals FA_LIT by assigning signs to atoms in FA_ATOMS so that F ∪ E ∪ FA_LIT were satisfiable. Since we assumed that F ∪ E were satisfiable, it is always possible (FA_LIT is a subset of the model for F ∪ E).

In the following algorithm the sets FA_ATOMS and FA_LIT will be constructed by the procedure *findsign*, which is described in section 2.7.

C. Construct the set FB_LIT from the sets FB_ATOMS and FA_LIT by assigning every atom in FB_ATOMS the same sign as was assigned to the corresponding atom in FA_ATOMS for constructing FA_LIT. In the following algorithm FB_ATOMS and FB_LIT will be built from fb, F and FA_LIT by the procedure *samesign*.

We say that some set of reductions R **preserves disunification in F iff** the following holds: if two atoms A and B in the formula F are not unifiable, then no narrowing A' of A (in respect to E) unifies neither with B nor with any narrowing B' of B. Disunification preserving is in the following algorithm tested by the procedure *ok_disunific* (see section 2.7).

Now let E ∪ {fa->fb} satisfy *ok_equations* iff the set F ∪ E ∪ FA_LIT ∪ FB_LIT is satisfiable and E ∪ {fa->fb} preserves disunification in F.

Example: Let us take the formula S={{P(x,f(x))}, {¬P(f(y),y)}, {Q(z), Q(f(z))}, {¬Q(u), ¬Q(f(u))}} as an example. Recall that the Herbrand universe of S consists of the single branch 0,f(0),f(f(0)),... . We'll see how the *ok_equations*, given S, will treat several reductions.

1. f(0)->0 is rejected, since f and 0 are different functional symbols. f(f(0))->0 is rejected for the same reasons.

2. f(f(0))->f(0) is rejected, since disunification is not preserved (the narrowing of P(x,f(x)) as well as of P(f(y),y) is P(f(0),f(0))). f(f(f(0)))->f(0) and f(f(f(0)))->f(f(0)) do not preserve disunification either.

3. f(f(f(f(0)))->f(0) preserves disunifications in S. Form FA_ATOMS and FB_ATOMS:

FA_ATOMS={P(f^3(0),f^4(0)), P(f^4(0),f^3(0)), Q(f^4(0))}.

FB_ATOMS={P(0,f(0)), P(f(0),0), Q(f(0))}.

Form FA_LIT by selecting signs for elements of FA_ATOMS. Following set FA_LIT will be ok:

FA_LIT={P(f^3(0),f^4(0)), ¬P(f^4(0),f^3(0)), Q(f^4(0))}.

Then FB_LIT={P(0,f(0)), ¬P(f(0),0), Q(f(0))}.

Since S U FA_LIT U FB_LIT is not satisfiable, f(f(f(f(0)))->f(0) will be rejected.

4. The reduction f^5(0)->f(0) will preserve disunification and the set S ∪ FA_LIT ∪ FB_LIT (with FA_LIT and FB_LIT corresponding to the new reduction rule) is satisfiable, thus the reduction will be accepted.

2.6 The algorithm for building finite models: details

We present an algorithm for building a finite domain for a Skolemized formula SF, the original unskolemized version of which belonged to the Class AM. The following algorithm constructs a finite domain for a formula F=*stable*(SF), interpretation of functional symbols on this domain and a subset of the model for F by adding new ground literals to the original set of disjuncts F. The full model for F can then be built from the domain in different simple ways (for example, applying resolution with no strategies (except elimination of subsumed disjuncts) to the set obtained from F by substituting elements of a domain to variables in F in all possible ways and normalizing all atoms) which are not investigated in our paper.

Notice that since F is a set of disjuncts derived from SF, F might subsume several disjuncts in SF and several function and predicate symbols in SF might not appear in F. In the model of F these symbols can be interpreted in an arbitrary way.

In addition to the procedures *groundatoms*, *stable findsign*, *samesign* and *ok_disunific* we use also the procedure *satisfiable* for testing the satisfiability of the argument. It uses the procedure *stable* in the obvious way: *satisfiable*(F) computes *true* iff *stable*(F)≠{ø} (remember the use of subsumption).

The algorithm is written rather with clarity than efficiency in mind: it could be rewritten into a more efficent algorithm.

```
F:=stable(SF);
D:= {x | x is a constant symbol in F};
IF D={} THEN D:={1};
FNEW:=F; DNEW:=D; DLAST:=D; E={};
WHILE  DNEW≠{ø}
  |BEGIN
  |  DNEW:={};
  |  FOR EACH f IN {x| x is a functional symbol in F, arity(f)>0}
  |    |BEGIN
  |    |  af:=arity(f);
  |    |  FOR EACH fa IN {f(t_1,...,t_af)| ∀i.t_i∈D & ∃i.t_i∈DLAST}
  |    |     |BEGIN
  |    |     |  FA_LIT:=findsign(fa, F, FNEW);
  |    |     |  foundflag:=FALSE;
  |    |     |  FOR EACH fb IN D
  |    |     |  WHILE foundflag=FALSE & ok_disunific(E ∪ {fa->fb})
  |    |     |     |BEGIN
  |    |     |     |  FB_LIT:=samesign(fb, F, FA_LIT);
  |    |     |     |  IF  satisfiable(FNEW ∪ FA_LIT ∪ FB_LIT) THEN
  |    |     |     |    |BEGIN
  |    |     |     |    |   E:=E ∪ {fa->fb};
  |    |     |     |    |   FNEW:=stable(FNEW ∪ FA_LIT ∪ FB_LIT);
  |    |     |     |    |   foundflag:=TRUE
  |    |     |     |    |END
  |    |     |     |END
  |    |     |  IF foundflag=FALSE then DNEW:=DNEW ∪ {fa}
  |    |     |END
  |    |END
  |  DLAST:=DNEW;  D:=D ∪ DNEW
  |END.
```

The well-known theorem of Slagle [12] states that if E is a complete term rewriting system (set of simplifiers in his terminology) and F is a set of disjuncts without equality, then E ∪ F is refutable if and only if the full narrowing of F (in respect to E) is refutable. The full narrowing of F is a sum of F and all narrowings of all disjuncts in F.

Remark 1: The left side term of any equation in E has only a single occurrence in E.

Remark 2: The set E of all equations generated at each step of our algorithm is always such that orienting all equations $h_k=h_l$ in E into rewrite rules $h_k \to h_l$ produces a complete term rewriting system.

Proof: We have to show termination and confluency of the rewriting relation (see [1]). Most important, notice that all terms in E are ground.

1. Termination of the rewriting relation. The left side of each rewrite rule in E is deeper than its right side.

2. Confluency. Guaranteed by a remark 1 and the fact that terms in E are ground.

END OF PROOF.

Remark 3: Left side terms of rewrite rules in E cannot be constants and cannot contain only constants as proper subterms.

Remark 4: If a literal L in F is narrowable with some rule l->r in E, then FNEW subsumes either the disjunct s*L or ¬(s*L), where s=MGU(l,t), where t is some term in L and t is neither a variable nor a constant.

Proof: By definition of FA_ATOMS, since every element of FA_ATOMS (with a positive or a negative sign) is included in FNEW.
END OF PROOF.

Remark 5: If a literal L in F does not contain functional terms and contains a variable (say x), then FNEW subsumes either the disjunct {s*L} or {s*¬L} for every such s={l/x} where l is the left side of some rewrite rule in E.
Proof is analogous to the proof of remark 4.

In view of remark 2, in the following we will treat E as a set of rewrite rules or as a set of equality units, depending on context.

2.7 Termination of ok_equations

Given that our original formula SF belongs to Class AM, termination of every subprocedure in our program is easy to prove.

We have to show that *stable* always terminates. We use the fact that Z3-strategy decides the Class AMS: *stable's* argument set of disjuncts S in the given algorithm always belongs to Class AMS by the fact that elements of FA_ATOMS and FB_ATOMS are ground substitution instances of atoms in AMS and by lemmas 1, 2 and 3 in section 2.3.

If *stable* terminates on a set S, then *satisfiable* terminates on S also.

findsign(fa, F, FNEW) could be computed as follows: At first make the set FA_ATOMS=$\{A_1,\ldots,A_n\}$. For each atom A_i in FA_ATOMS do the following: Let $\{L_1,\ldots,L_{i-1}\}$ be a set of already computed elements in FA_LIT. If *satisfiable*($\{A_i\} \cup \{L_1,\ldots,L_{i-1}\} \cup$ FNEW), then let L_i=A_i, else let L_i= $\neg A_i$.

ok_disunific(E ∪ {fa->fb}) could be computed in the following way: for all pairs of nonunifiable atoms in F generate all narrowings of both elements of the pair with $E \cup \{fa\to fb\}$ and test whether any narrowing of the first element (or the first element itself) doesn't unify with any narrowing of the second element (or with the second element itself).

Computing *samesign* is trivial.

2.8. Termination of the model construction algorithm

We prove the termination by giving an upper bound on the number of elements in the computed domain. Recall that the finite domain D is constructed by finding a set of rewrite rules E such that terms containing elements of D are reduced by rewrite rules in E to terms in D.

Let $B_m=\{d_1,\ldots,d_m\}$ be a tuple of m first elements of the constructed domain D. As our algorithm has added all elements of B_m to D, it can't have added any equation of the form $d_i=t$ (where t is any term and $1\le i\le m$) to E, since adding any such equation to E would have meant pruning the sequence B_m. Nevertheless, during the generation of D the algorithm has for every equation of the form $d_i=d_j$ (where all pairs of i,j are such that $1<i<m$ and $1<j<i$) examined the possibility to add this equation to E. There are 3 possible causes for rejecting the examined equation $d_i=d_j$:

A) the leading functional symbol of d_i is not the same as the leading functional symbol of d_j.

B) equation $d_i=d_j$ does not preserve disunification in F.

C) There is no model for $F \cup E$ which would contain both the literals in FA_LIT and FB_LIT (FA_LIT and FB_LIT are the sets of such signed atoms in the Herbrand expansion of F which have either the term d_i or d_j, correspondingly, among their deepest argument terms. Theorem 2 in section 2.9 demonstrates that if such a model existed, a model for $F \cup E \cup \{d_i=d_j\}$ would exist also).

In the following we show that each of abovementioned conditions A, B, C decomposes the Herbrand domain of F into a finite number (n_A, n_B, n_C, accordingly) of classes so that if an element d_i belongs to the same class (for each of the conditions A, B, C) as an element d_j, then the equation $d_i=d_j$ would be accepted by our algorithm. From this it immediately follows that if the number m (which represents the number of domain elements constructed) $> n_A*n_B*n_C$, the set E will contain one equation of the form $d_i=t$ ($1<i\le m$, t is some term), thus pruning the sequence D. The upper bound we will give is by no means

the best: we give it only in order to prove the termination of the search and have not tried to improve it.

We say that a term contains itself at depth 0, arguments of its leading functional symbol at depth 1, etc.

By the inequality of structures up to some depth n we mean that when we replace the subterms deeper than n both in d_i and d_j by a new common constant c, the resultant terms are not syntactically equal. For example, the structures of terms f(0,g(h(1,2),2)) and f(0,g(g(3,2),2)) are equal up to depth 1, but inequal up to depth 2.

A) Obviously n_A is equal to the number of functional symbols in F.

B) Equation $d_i = d_j$ may not preserve disunification for atoms in F only if one of the following holds:

1) d_i contains d_j as a subterm at depth less than 3: We can say that "the cause" for this condition is the occur check: let us take atoms P(f(x),x), P(y,f(y)) and equation f(f(f(f(0))))=f(f(f(0))), for example. The chosen atoms are not unifiable, but their narrowings with the chosen equation are both P(f(f(f(0))),f(f(f(0)))). The depth boundary 3 is sufficient since Ackermann-type atoms in F do not contain more than one variable and depth of terms in these atoms is 0 or 1. Notice that the current restriction has to consider only the unification of Ackermann-type atoms.

2) the structure of d_i is up to depth 1 not equal to the structure of d_j: the current condition covers the condition A, which is the same as the equality of structures up to depth 0.

We can take $n_B = 3 * (n_{fn} * (n_{cn} + n_{fn})^m)$ where n_{fn} is the number of the functional symbols in F, n_{cn} is the number of constant symbols in F, and m is the maximal arity of function symbols in F.

C) $n_C = 2^w$, where w is the number of atoms in F (up to renaming variables). Notice that it is the case only because we do not generally use the normal forms of Ackermann-type atoms in FA_LIT for the atoms in FB_LIT.

2.9 Soundness of ok_equations

Now we will prove that our algorithm is sound in the sense that if it accepts some set of equations E, the formula F ∪ E is satisfiable.

Proof: We show that the full narrowing of the final formula FNEW (computed by our algorithm) with respect to the set E is satisfiable.

Since F is subsumed by FNEW, by theorem of Slagle [12] F ∪ E will then also be satisfiable. In order to show the satisfiability of the full narrowing of FNEW, we prove the following (forthcoming theorem 2): any disjunct derivable with Z3-strategy from the full narrowing of FNEW is subsumed by the full narrowing of FNEW.

END OF PROOF

Let FNEW' be the full narrowing of FNEW. Let FNEW_NARROWED be the set obtained from FNEW' by removing all tautologies and subsumed disjuncts.

By norm(t) where t is any expression we denote the normal form of t with respect to E.

In the following we will use the notion of **narrowing substitution**: let expression e be narrowable to expression e' and some rule $f_i a \to f_i b$ be used for normalizing during narrowing. Then e contains some term t such that $f_i a = MGU(f_i a,t)*t$. Then we say that $MGU(f_i a, t)$ is a **narrowing substitution** for e,e'. Generally e,e' might have many narrowing substitutions, but since in our case all atoms have the properties Pa, Pb and Pc, each pair e,e' cannot have more than a single nonempty narrowing susbtitution.

Lemma 4: No term t in any FNEW can contain narrowable proper subterms.

Proof: Lemmas 1, 2 and 3 in section 2.3 demonstrate that no term in FNEW can contain non-ground functional terms as proper subterms and neither the resolution nor factorization rule of Z3-strategy can generate (that is, by substitution) literals where the terms occur deeper than they occured in the argument literals of these rules. Since terms in E do not contain narrowable proper subterms (due to remark 1), no term in any FA_ATOMS or FB_ATOMS does. Then no term in FNEW contains narrowable proper subterms.

END OF PROOF

Lemma 5: If L' is the narrowing of some literal L in FNEW, then L = ∓ s*OL (we write ∓L for "either L or ¬L") for some substitution s and some non-ground literal OL in F.

Proof: All atoms in FNEW are substitution instances of atoms in F. Since atoms in F cannot contain terms deeper than 1, due to remark 3 ground atoms in F are not narrowable.

END OF PROOF.

Lemma 6: If a literal $s*L$ is narrowable with some rewriting rule $l\text{->}r$, then at least one of the following must hold:

1) L is narrowable with $l\text{->}r$.

2) s contains terms which are narrowable with $l\text{->}r$.

Proof: Suppose neither L nor any term in s is narrowable with $l\text{->}r$. Then neither L nor s contain terms which are not variables and which are unifiable with l. Then $s*L$ cannot contain such terms either.
END OF PROOF.

Lemma 7: If the literal L in FNEW is narrowable with some narrowing substitution s, then FNEW subsumes either the disjunct $\{s*L\}$ or the disjunct $\{s*\neg L\}$.

Proof: Due to the lemma 5 $L = \mp(s_1*OL)$ for some substitution s_1 and some non-ground literal OL in F. We consider two possible cases:

1. OL contains non-ground functional terms. Then, due to lemma 4, s_1 does not contain narrowable terms. Then, due to lemma 6, OL is narrowable with the narrowing substitution s. By remark 4, FNEW subsumes $\{\mp s*OL\}$. Then FNEW subsumes also $\{\mp s*(s_1*OL)\}$. But $s_1*OL=\mp L$.

2. OL does not contain non-ground functional terms. Then either OL is ground, in which case OL=L and the assertion of the lemma holds by remark 4, or OL contains a single variable (let it be x). In the last case OL is not narrowable (by property Pc and remark 3), therefore $s_1=\{t/x\}$, where, by lemmas 6 and 4, t is some narrowable term which does not contain any narrowable proper subterms. By remark 5 FNEW subsumes $\{\mp\{l/x\}*OL\}$, where l is the left side of the rule used for narrowing L with a narrowing substitution s. Obviously $\{l/x\}*OL=s*(\{t/x\}*OL)$. But $\{t/x\}*OL = \mp L$.
END OF PROOF.

Lemma 8: If the disjunct D' in FNEW_NARROWED is a narrowing of some disjunct D in FNEW, then D' is a unit disjunct.

Proof: Let $D=L_1|\ldots|L_n$ and $D'=L_1'|\ldots|L_n'$ and some literal in D' (let it be L_1') be a narrowing of the corresponding literal L_1 in D using the narrowing substitution s. Lemma 7 says that in this case we have two possibilities:

1. FNEW subsumes $\{s*L_1\}$. Then FNEW_NARROWED subsumes $\{L_1'\}$, thus D' must be a unit disjunct.

2. FNEW subsumes $\{s^* \neg L_1\}$. We consider two possible cases:

A) L_1 contains non-ground functional terms. Then L_1 is among the biggest (in the sense of ordering $>_3$) literals in D, and since FNEW is in the stable form, FNEW subsumes the resolution of $\{s^* \neg L_1\}$ and D, that is $s^*(L_2|\ldots|L_n)$. In this case FNEW_NARROWED subsumes $L_2'|\ldots|L_n'$. But this is contrary to the assumption that D' is in FNEW_NARROWED.

B) L_1 does not contain non-ground functional terms. Then either L_1 is ground, in which case, contrary to the assumption that D is in FNEW, FNEW subsumes $L_2|\ldots|L_n$ (like the case A), or L_1 contains a variable and no narrowable terms. Then L_1 is not narrowable, contrary to the assumption.

END OF PROOF.

Lemma 9: Let L' be the narrowing of some literal L in FNEW and $L=s_1{*}OL$ for some literal OL in F (due to lemma 5 such OL, s_1 exist). If OL is of the Monadic type, then FNEW subsumes {∓_L'}.

Proof: Let s be the narrowing substitution of L, L'. Since OL is of the Monadic type, one of the following holds:

1. OL contains a variable (let it be x) and no functional terms. Then, due to lemma 4, L'={t/x}*OL, where t is the right side of some rule in E. Then ∓L' is the member of some FB_LIT, thus FNEW subsumes {∓L'}.

2. OL contains a single narrowable term (let it be g) and no variables outside g. Then, due to lemma 4, L'=norm(MGU(g, l)*OL), where l is a left side of some rule in E. As in case 1, FNEW subsumes {∓L'}.

END OF PROOF.

Lemma 10: Let A' be the narrowing of some atom A in FNEW. If A' is unifiable with some atom K in FNEW, FNEW subsumes {∓A'}

Proof: By lemma 5 $A=s_1{*}OA$, where s_1 is some substitution and OA is some atom in F. If OA is of the Monadic type, lemma 9 says that FNEW subsumes (∓A'}. In the following we therefore assume that OA is of the Ackermann type. Then A' is a narrowing of OA, since by lemma 4 s_1 cannot contain narrowable terms, therefore by lemma 6 OA contains them.

Let K be a atom in FNEW. By lemma 5 $K=s_k{*}OK$ for some atom OK in F.

Assume that A′ is unifiable with K. Here we can use disunification preserving: as E preserves disunification in F, OA is unifiable with OK. If OK is of the Monadic type, OK and OA cannot be unifiable (since the narrowing A′ of Ackermann-type OA is assumed to unify with Monadic-type OK, considering remark 3 OA does not have a variable as an argument, thus OA must contain at least two non-ground terms with different leading function symbols). In the following we therefore assume OK to be of the Ackermann type.

Since A′ is ground, A′=MGU(A′,K)*K=MGU(A′,OK)*OK. As A′ is a result of narrowing OA, OA contains some functional term $f_i(l)$, which is in A′ replaced by the right side $f_i(b)$ of some rule $f_i(a)$->$f_i(b)$ in E. As OK and OA are both of the Ackermann type, OK must then contain some term $f_i(k)$ on the place where OA has the term $f_i(l)$. Then (as A′ is ground and $f_i(k)$ contains all variables in OK) MGU(A′,OK)=MGU($f_i(b)$,$f_i(k)$). Therefore A′=MGU($f_i(b)$,$f_i(k)$)*OK. Consider cases A and B:

A. OK is ground. Then OA≠OK, since OK=A′ but A′ is not narrowable. Therefore OA is not ground, thus l in $f_i(l)$ is a variable. Then OK={b/l}*OA, and since OK=A′, A′={b/l}*OA. Then A′ is contained in some FB_LIT, thus FNEW subsumes {∓A′}.

B. OK is not ground. Then k in $f_i(k)$ is a variable, thus $f_i(k)$ is unifiable with $f_i(b)$, then ∓{b/k}*OK is a member of some FB_LIT. Then FNEW subsumes {∓{b/k}*OK}. Since A′ is unifiable with OK, A′={∓_{b/k}*OK}.

END OF PROOF.

Lemma 11: Let {L} be a disjunct in FNEW and L′ be a narrowing of L with some rule in E. Then FNEW does not subsume {¬L′}.

Proof: Due to lemma 5 L=s_1*OL for some substitution s_1 and some non-ground literal OL in F.

L′ is a narrowing of L with a narrowing substitution s_n. Then either L′ is a narrowing of OL (with the narrowing substitution s_{on}) or OL does not contain functional terms.

Suppose FNEW subsumes {¬L′}. We consider three possible cases:

1. OL does not contain functional terms. Then it has a variable (let it be x) among its arguments. Then some FB_LIT (therefore also FNEW) subsumes the disjunct {{l/x}* ¬OL} or {{l/x}*OL}, where l is

the left side of the rule used for narrowing L to L'. Since {l/x}*OL is unifiable with L, FNEW cannot subsume {{l/x}* ¬OL} (otherwise FNEW were contradictory). If FNEW subsumed {{l/x}* OL}, it also had to subsume {{r/x}*OL} (by the construction of FB_LIT from FA_LIT), where r is the right side of the rule used for narrowing L to L'. Since L'={r/x}*OL, FNEW must in this case be contradictory.

2. OL contains functional terms and is of the Monadic type. Since OL is narrowable to L' with the narrowing substitution s_{on}, FNEW subsumes either {s_{on}* ¬OL} or {s_{on}* OL}. Since s_{on}*OL is unifiable with L, FNEW cannot subsume {s_{on}* ¬OL}. If FNEW subsumed {s_{on}* OL}, it also had to subsume {L'} and were contradictory.

3. OL is of the Ackermann type. Since OL is narrowable to L' with the narrowing substitution s_{on}, FNEW subsumes either {s_{on}* -OL} or {s_{on}* OL}. Since s_{on}*OL is unifiable with L, FNEW cannot subsume {s_{on}* ¬OL}. In the following we assume that FNEW subsumes {s_{on}*OL}. We consider two possible cases (having in mind that FNEW subsumes {¬L'}):

A. L' = $\mp s_k$*OK for some literal OK in F and some substitution s_k. Then, as L' is a narrowing of OL, L'=s*OL for some substitution s. Since FNEW subsumes {s_{on}*OL}={{la/x}*OL}, where x is a single variable in OL and la is a single argument of the functional term which is the left side of some rule used for narrowing OL to L', FNEW also subsumes (due to construction of FB_LIT from FA_LIT) a disjunct {{ra/x}*OL} where ra is a single argument of the functional term which is the right side of some rule used for narrowing OL to L'. Obviously L'={ra/x}*OL, therefore FNEW must be contradictory.

B. L' is a narrowing of some Monadic literal OK in FNEW. Then, contrary to our assumption, L' cannot be a narrowing of OL.

END OF PROOF.

Theorem 2: Any disjunct derivable from FNEW_NARROWED with Z3-strategy is subsumed by FNEW_NARROWED.

Proof: At first we examine inference by factorization. Let D' be a disjunct in FNEW_NARROWED. If D' is also in FNEW, every factorization of D' is subsumed by FNEW. If D' is not in FNEW, lemma 8 says that D' is a unit disjunct. Then D' is not factorizable.

In the following we examine inference by resolution.

Let D_1' and D_2' be two such disjuncts in FNEW_NARROWED that a disjunct D_3 is inferred from D_1' and D_2' by a step of resolution of

Z3-strategy. If both D_1' and D_2' are subsumed by FNEW, then D_3 is subsumed by FNEW (as FNEW is in a stable form). Therefore we assume that at least one of D_1', D_2' is not subsumed by FNEW. We consider two possible cases.

1. Both D_1' and D_2' are the results of narrowing some disjuncts D_1 and D_2 in FNEW.

Due to lemma 8 D_1 and D_2 are both unit disjuncts. Then D_1:={L} and D_2:={¬R} for some literals L and R. Then D_1'={L'} and D_2={¬R'}, where L' is a narrowing of L and R' is a narrowing of R. As narrowings of any literal in FNEW with rules from E are ground, L'=R'.

Let OL be the literal in F such that L = ∓ s_1*OL and OR be the
literal in F such that R = ∓ s_r*OR (lemma 5 says that it is possible to
find such literals and substitutions).

If the literal OL is of the Monadic type, then due to lemmas 9 and 11 FNEW subsumes {L'}. Analogically, if OR is of the Monadic type, FNEW subsumes {R'}. The possibility that {L'} or {R'} is subsumed by FNEW is covered by a forthcoming case 2. During the analysis of the case 1 we therefore assume that OL and OR are of the Ackermann type.

Because E preserves disunification in F, OL and OR must be unifiable. Since OL and OR are of the Ackermann type, all functional symbols in OL and OR have the arity 1, OL contains a variable (let it be x) and OR contains a variable (let it be y). Let a rule f_i(c)->f_i(d) be used for narrowing L to L' and a rulef_j(e)->f_j(g) be used for narrowing R to R'.

Let the functional term t be the n-th argument of the atom in OL. Then the n-th argument of the atom in OR must be such functional term g that t and g are unifiable. Then f_i(d)=f_j(g) due to lemma 4.

By remark 3 neither c nor e may be constants. Since L'=R', L and R have the same sign. Then, since atoms in OL and OR are unifiable and L'=R', we have OR = ∓ {y/x}*OL. As L= o OL or L= o {c/x}*OL (o is either a positive or a negative sign), FNEW must also subsume {o {d/x}*OL} (because of the construction of FB_LIT from FA_LIT). As OL = ∓{x/y}*OR, OL is also narrowable with the rule f_j(e)->f_j(g), which, as we showed, is the same as f_i(e)->f_i(d). Thus FNEW must subsume {o {e/x}*OL}. Since L and R have the same sign, R= o {y/x}*OL or R= o {e/x}*OL. As FNEW contained {¬R}, FNEW must be contradictory. Since this is not true, case 1 is not possible.

2. FNEW contains D_1:={L} ∪ D for some disjunct D and literal L which is allowed to be resolved upon in D_1 (using Z3-strategy). Disjunct D_2' in FNEW_NARROWED is the result of narrowing some disjunct D_2 in FNEW, and FNEW does not subsume D_2'. As D_2' is a narrowing of some disjunct in FNEW, then due to lemma 8 D_2 is a unit disjunct. Then D_2={R} for some literal R in FNEW and D_2'={R'}. Since ¬R' must be unifiable with L, lemmas 10 and 11 say that FNEW subsumes {R'}. We got contradiction with the assumption that FNEW does not subsume {R'}.
END OF PROOF.

2.10. Experiments with the implementation

As noted before, we have an implementation of the resolution method of decision strategies. In order to experiment with finite-model building we also implemented the model construction algorithm with the minimal criteria, described in section 2.4. Notice that this is not the complete method decribed elsewhere in the paper. Nevertheless, the minimal-criteria method performed quite well in the experiments.

The following table presents the number of the formula (in exercises to section 46 of A.Church's book [2]), its prefix, time of deciding a formula, result found (negation of the formula satisfiable-/unsatisfiable), time of constructing a finite domain, size of the domain found. All times are given in seconds (shorter times are somewhat inaccurate). Star means that the model was not found (due to memory limitations or inherent incompleteness of the used method).

Formula	Prefix	Dec. time	Dec. result	Model time	Domain size
Ex2 No1	∃∀∃	0.11	unsat.	-	-
Ex2 No2	∀∃	0.06	sat.	0.05	2
Ex2 No3	∀∃∃∀	0.02	sat.	0.06	1
Ex2 No4	∃∃∀	0.11	unsat.	-	-
Ex2 No5	∀∀∃∃	0.38	unsat.	-	-
Ex3 No1	∃∀∃∃	0.05	sat.	0.17	2
Ex3 No2	∃∃∃∀∀	0.11	unsat.	-	-
Ex4 No1	∃∀	0.05	sat.	0.04	1
Ex4 No2	∃∀	0.17	unsat.	-	-
Ex9 No1	∀∃	0.17	sat.	0.55	2
Ex9 No2	∀∃	0.22	unsat.	-	-
Ex12 No1	∀∃∃	0.33	unsat.	-	-
Ex12 No2	∃∀∃	0.33	unsat.	-	-
Ex12 No3	∀∃∃	1.93	unsat.	-	-
Ex14 No1	∀∀∃	0.06	sat.	4.5	7
Ex14 No2	∀∀∃	2.69	sat.	***	***
Ex14 No3	∀∀∃	0.22	unsat.	-	-
Ex14 No4	∀∀∃	2.75	unsat.	-	-
Ex14 No5	∀∀∃	0.28	unsat.	-	-
Ex14 No6	∀∀∃	1.43	unsat.	-	-
Ex14 No7	∀∀∃	0.55	sat.	***	***
Ex15 No1	∃∀∀∃	0.11	unsat.	-	-
Ex15 No2	∃∃∀∃	0.11	sat.	0.05	2
Ex15 No3	∀∃∀	0.06	unsat.	-	-
Ex15 No4	∀∃∀	0.06	unsat.	-	-
Ex15 No5	∀∃∀∀	0.05	unsat.	-	-
Ex15 No6	∀∃∀∀	0.05	unsat.	-	-
Ex15 No7	∃∀∃∀	0.06	sat.	0.06	2
Ex16 No2	∃∀∀∃	0.06	unsat.	-	-
Ex16 No3	∃∀∀∃	0.11	sat.	0.17	2
Ex16 No4	∃∃∀∀∃	0.72	unsat.	-	-
Ex17 No2	∃∃∀∀∃∃	0.11	unsat.	-	-
Ex17 No3	∃∃∀∀∃	1.32	unsat.	-	-
Ex17 No4	∀∃∀∃	30.5	sat.	***	***
Ex17 No5	∀∃∀∃	7.58	unsat.	-	-
Ex18 No2	∃∀∀∃	1.43	unsat.	-	-
Ex18 No3	∃∃∀∀∃	2.04	sat.	8.79	4
Ex18 No4	∃∃∀∀∃	0.66	unsat.	-	-
Ex18 No5	∃∀∀∀∃	15.16	unsat.	-	-
Ex20 No1	∃∃∀∀∃	0.66	unsat.	-	-

References

1. Barendregt, H.P. The Lambda Calculus. (North Holland, Amsterdam, 1981).
2. Church, A. Introduction to mathematical logic I. (Princeton University Press, New Jersey, 1956).
3. Dreben, B., Goldfarb, W.D. The decision problem: solvable classes of quantificational formulas. (Addison-Wesley, Reading, 1979).
4. Joyner, W.H. Resolution strategies as decision procedures. J. ACM 23 (3)(1976), 396-417.
5. Leitsch, A. On different concepts of resolution. Zeitschr. f. math. Logik und Grundlagen d. Math. 35 (1989) 71-77.
6. Leitsch, A. Implication algorithms for classes of horn clauses. Statistik, Informatik und Ökonomie, hrsg. v. W.Janko. 172-189, Springer 1988.
7. Lewis, H.R. Complexity results for classes of quantificational formulas. J. Computer and System Sciences 21 (3) (1980) 317-353
8. Maslov, S.Ju. An inverse method of establishing deducibility in the classical predicate calculus. Dokl. Akad. Nauk. SSSR 159 (1964) 17-20=Soviet Math. Dokl. 5 (1964) 1420, MR 30 #3005.
9. Maslov, S.Ju. The inverse method for establishing deducibility for logical calculi. Trudy Mat. Inst. Steklov 98 (1968) 26-87= Proc. Steklov. Inst. Math. 98 (1968) 25-96, MR 40 #5416; 43 #4620.
10. Maslov, S.Ju. Proof-search strategies for methods of the resolution type. Machine Intelligence 6 (American Elsevier, 1971) 77-90.
11. Mints, G.E, Tammet, T. Experiments in proving formulas of non-classical logics with a resolution theorem-prover. To appear in the Journal of Automated Reasoning.
12. Slagle, J.R. Automated theorem-proving for theories with simplifiers, commutativity and associativity. J. ACM 21 (4) (1974), 622-642.
13. Tammet, T. A resolution program, able to decide some solvable classes. Proceedings of Colog-88, LNCS 417, 300-312, Springer Verlag 1990.
14. Wos, L., Overbeek, R., Lusk, E. Boyle, J. Automated reasoning: introduction and applications. (Prentice-Hall, New Jersey, 1984).
15. Zamov, N.K., On a bound for the complexity of terms in the resolution method. Trudy Mat. Inst. Steklov 128 (1972), 5-13.
16. Zamov, N.K., Maslov's inverse method and decidable classes. Annals of Pure and Applied Logic 42 (1989), 165-194.
17. Маслов С.Ю. Минц Г.Е. Теория поиска вывода и обратный метод. Доп. к русскому переводу: Чень,Ч., Ли, Р. Математическая лоогика и автоматическое доказательство теорем. (Наука, М., 1983) 291-314.
18. Оревков В.П. Один разрешимый класс формул классического исчисления предикатов с функциональными знаками. Сб: II симпозиум по кибернетике (тезисы), Тбилиси 1965, 176.
19. Сочилина А.В. О програме, реализующей алгоритм установления выводимости формул классического исчисления предикатов. Семиотика и информатика 12 (1979).
20. Шаронов В.И. Анализ полноты стратегий в методе резолюций. Диссертация. Ленинград 1973.

Toward knowledge-based specifications of languages

Merik Meriste
Department of Computer Science
University of Tartu
Liivi 2, 202400 Tartu, Estonia

Jaan Penjam
Institute of Cybernetics
Estonian Academy of Sciences
Akadeemia tee 21, 200108 Tallinn, Estonia
e-mail: jaan@ioc.ew.su

Abstract

In this paper the problem of embedding language design and implementation tools in knowledge-based systems is considered. On the one hand, this is the question of using object-oriented paradigm for the specification of a language treated as a collection of classes of concepts. On the other hand, this is the question of employing syntax-directed methods for software construction in knowledge-based systems.

1. Introduction

An attempt is made to unify a method for constructing a conceptual style language on the one hand, and the implementing language by the means of an attribute evaluating technique on the other hand. The problem is handled from the perspective of rising the intellectual level of language implementation systems. Attribute methods of language specification used on many compiler writing systems [1] are first of all implementation-oriented, i.e. the language must be specified in terms of attributed translations (for example in the MUG2 [2] or TOOLS/HLP [3] systems). The structure and meaning of language concepts are given through detailed specification of parts of language compiler (see also [4]). Thus, compiler writing systems are usually designed under the following presumption: user of a system must be an expert of translation methods and program compiler parts in specific terms.

New trends in computer applications which require more intelligent software for unexperienced users, are still not really accepted in the field of language implementation systems. New users are primarily interested in an easily understandable method for language specification.

When specifying a language, the main attention must be focused on language concepts described, their meaning and conceptual structure. This is exactly the way the problem-oriented language designer thinks. Our opinion is that a suitable basis for this approach is the method of knowledge-based programming [5]., successfully used for problem solving in various areas. The main aspects of knowledge-based programming are [5]:

- programming in terms of a problem domain;
- the use of the computer when the problem is being posed;
- automatic synthesis of programs;
- the use of the knowledge base to accumulate useful concepts.

We distinguish **language concepts** (classes of objects of a problem domain) and **language constructions** to present these concepts in the language. For each part of specification a special formalism is used. For example language concepts are specified by their **semantic models** and by **interpretation** of these models. Syntactic properties (including context-dependent properties) of language constructions are specified via abstract attribute grammars.

In the second section we show how to implement language specifications. In our opinion, the designed language specification must be implementable by a language implementation system.To implement semantic specifications, the structural synthesis of programs [5] is used. For implementing the semantics of real languages, it takes polynomial time to synthesize a semantic processor. The semantic processor has linear time complexity.

In the last section we compare our technique of implementation of semantics with evaluation of attributes, and present a classification of attribute grammars.

2. Specification of concepts (semantics)

Problem oriented languages are often designed by specialists of some problem area, who rather describe concepts they intend to represent in the language. In other words, they want to specify knowledge about their own subject. Keeping in mind further implementation of language specification, we suggest computational models [5] and metalanguage based on this formalism as a technique for representing knowledge about language concepts. Computational models will be considered in detail in the following chapter. Here we mention only that they are related to attribute grammars so that the implementation for conventional language schemes can be employed.

We describe a programming language in a semantics-oriented manner. At first we construct semantic models of classes of actual objects which we consider as concepts of the language. Every model of such kind characterizes the structure (possibly trivial) of an object and computational relations between its structural components. Context-sensitive relations between components are determined when a higher-order-class of objects is being described. Consequently, specifying language concepts, the constructor of the language determines the structure of these concepts, although he need not explicitly visualize the dependencies between the concepts being used. This is the usual situation in cognition. Conflicts in an implicitly generated system of concepts may be detected by the language implementation systems. Usually the completeness of the system of concepts is not requisite. This system may be improved by changes in our ideas about the actual world.

Through the rest of the paper we demonstrate our methods by the example of specification and implementation of a language of ordinary differential equations. Differential equation may be presented in usual mathematical notation. Although, in our approach the detailed syntax of the equation can considerably vary.

In the paper semantic models are written in source language NUT of a object-oriented system with program synthesis [6]. Briefly, the rules of the fragment of the used NUT-language are as follows.

The basic concept of the NUT language are object and class. Values, programs, data types etc. are objects. Objects of same kind are joined together into some abstract object called class. A class is a carrier of the knowledge about common properties of its objects, such as the structure of objects, relations applicable to them and so on.

In this paper semantic models are handled as NUT-classes. So, every declaration of semantic model begins with the name of the corresponding class followed by the class description in parenthesis. The structure of an object, i.e. components of the object, their names and types are defined at the beginning (after the keyword var). The type of component can be the name of some class (name of semantic model). There are also some predefined classes of objects in the NUT, these are numeric, bool, text, program, array and any.

The structure of semantic model is usually followed by relations (after the keyword **rel**). Relations in NUT-language have the following form:

name_of_relation: **rel** axiom {implementation}

The axiom is an implication of the form $X_1,\ldots,X_n$ --> Y (it means that Y is computable from $X_1,\ldots,X_n$). The interpretation (operational semantics) of that implication is presented by the program in braces.

For example, the following model represents the concept of ordinary first degree differential equation y' = f(x,y). That model contains numerical variables STEP, X0, X1, Y0, logical variable RESULT and relation PROCESS between these variables. Any text between /* and */ is an explaining commentary.

```
EQN:( var
    STEP:  numeric ;                    /* step of integration */
    X0, X1:  numeric ;                  /* interval of integration */
    Y0:  numeric ;                      /* initial value for solution */
    RESULT:  bool ;                     /* stop condition */

  /* loop over all basic nodes of integration */
      PROCESS:  rel (EXP ⊢ X,Y ---> VAL),X0,X1,Y0,STEP ---> RESULT
                               φ
             {RESULT :=  false ;
               for  X=X0  step  STEP  to  X1
                    do
                          printf ("y(%d)=%d\n",X,Y);
                          METHOD(φ, STEP, X, Y, NEWY);
                          Y := NEWY
                    od ;
             RESULT :=  true });
```

Model EQN determines the semantics of a differential equation (more precisely the semantics of an initial-value problem) as the process of its solution. Relation PROCESS expresses evaluation of the solution in all basic points of integration: output variable RESULT in computed (value true will be assigned to that variable) as soon as the unknown function is evaluated in all points to be computed. Program METHOD called by the relation computes the next value of the unknown function using any familiar standard computational technique. That program depends on a procedural parameter for computing of arithmetic expression which usually stands at the right side of the differential equation. Statement (EXP ⊢ X,Y $\xrightarrow[\varphi]{}$ VAL) shows that subroutine φ solving subproblem X,Y ---> VAL must be synthesized on computational model EXP.

Computational model EXP describes the semantics of an arithmetic expression. The value of the expression is defined to depend on the structure (type) of the expression. The type of expression represents here a property of the following kind: the expression consists of a single constant (type 'const') or one variable x or y (type of expression is accordingly 'varX' or 'varY'), or the expression consists of two subexpressions to be added (type 'add') etc. Let variable T denote the type of expression under the consideration.

```
EXP: (X,Y,VAL:  numeric ;
      T:  type of expr ;
      CASE:  rel  (CONST ⊢ T ------> VAL), varX ⊢ X ----> VAL),
                              φconst                φx
                (varY ⊢ Y ----> VAL),(ADD ⊢ T,X,Y ------> VAL),
                          φy                        φadd
                ...
                ...
                T,X,Y --> VAL
                      { case of    T = 'const' ==>   φconst(T,VAL) ||
                                   T = 'varX'  ==>   φx(X,VAL) ||
                                   T = 'varY'  ==>   φy(Y,VAL) ||
                                   T  = 'add'  ==>   φadd(T,X,Y,VAL) ||
                                   ...
                                   ...
                      });
```

Computational models of different component-expressions use functions left and right to obtain the value of left or right sub-expressions of an expression of type T. Variable VAL stands for the value of a subexpression.

```
     CONST:(T:  type of expr ;
            VAL:  numeric ;);
     varX: (X,VAL:  numeric ;
             rel  X --> VAL {VAL := X});
     varY: (Y,VAL:  numeric ;
             rel  Y --> VAL {VAL := Y});
     ADD: (T:  type of expr ;
           X,Y,VAL:  numeric ;
            rel (EXP ⊢ T,X,Y ---> VAL),T,X,Y --> VAL
                              φ
                 {T1 :=  left  (T);
                  T2 :=  right  (T);
                  VAL := φ(T1,X,Y) + φ(T2,X,Y)});
     ...
     ...
```

Binding semantics and syntax specifications: Specified semantic models generate some constraints to the syntactic structure of language constructions (but do not explicitly define this structure). For example, differential equation must include an arithmetic expression, an expression of the type "add" includes two sub-expressions, etc. To be exact, given semantic models describe for our language the following abstract syntax.

P_{EQN} : EQN --> EXP
P_{CONST}: EXP --> numeric
P_{varX} : EXP -->
P_{varY} : EXP -->
P_{ADD} : EXP --> EXP EXP

It is important to note, that the syntactic structure generated by semantic models may not coincide with the abstract syntactic structure of the corresponding language constructions. So, the problem of accordance of these structures arises. The analogous problem arises when detailed and abstract syntax of constructions are matched.

A simple solution is to fix the order of syntactic structures of a specification: from the detailed syntax to the structure of semantic models or vice versa. In this case the most detailed description must be an adjustment to a more abstract one. Exhaustive solution of these problems requires extending of the theory of covering CF-grammars [7] into the class of regular right part CF-grammars. From the practical point of view, it is sufficient to have some transformation method of the more detailed structure to a more abstract one and, accordingly to this transformation, to organize the correspondence of elements of these structures. As a basis for such transformation we use the concept of the sparse syntactic structure [7].

Thus, putting together syntactic structures leads us to the stepwise adjustment of independently designed specifications of semantics, context-dependent properties and syntax of the language. Let us note that the order of adjustment is free! This compromise solution allows, firstly, to choose more convenient syntactic structures, and secondly, to achieve acceptable efficiency of the implementation.

3. Implementation of a semantic specification

Semantic models provide the possibilities to implement language semantics using automatic structural synthesis of programs [8].

Structural synthesis of programs is based on specification of programs in the form easily translatable into propositional formulae. Structural synthesis of a program consists of two steps: planning (deriving a certain formula in intuitionictic propositional calculus) and generation of a program (extraction of the program from the proof obtained as a result of the first step).

The complete specification of a program to be synthesized consists of two parts: computational model and description of a problem. Both parts may be written in any problem-oriented specification language, but in order to use algorithms of structural synthesis, these are translated into formal description of the problem in a logical language. Following [8], a computation model is a set of axioms of two different forms (we shall use abbreviation A_k instead of conjunction A_1 & ... & A_k):

1. Unconditional computability statement:

$$(1) \qquad \vdash A_k \xrightarrow{f} C;$$

2. Conditional computability statement:

$$(2) \qquad \vdash \&_{(1 \le i \le l)} (A^i_{ki} \xrightarrow{\varphi_i} B_i) \; \& \; C_k \xrightarrow{F(\varphi_1, \ldots, \varphi_l)} D$$

In this section propositional variables that indicate computability of some objects denoted by corresponding lower case letters are denoted by capital letters.

The first form means that computability of some objects $a_1, \ldots, a_k$ implies computability of object c. That implication is implemented by function (program) f. More precisely, for any given values of objects

$a_1, \ldots, a_k$ the value of object c can be computed using function f, so that $f(a_1, \ldots, a_k) = c$.

Conditional computability statement expresses a situation where the computability of object d depends on the computability of $c_1, \ldots, c_k$ under the condition that there exist functions φ_i (i = 1,....,l) for computing object b_i from $a_1, \ldots, a_{ki}$. Similarly to the first case, conditional computability statement indicates the tool for

implementing the implication - functional F that operates on arguments (free function symbols) 1,...,n.

Let us denote by M any computational model which represents relations between objects of any application domain. The description of the problem over that domain for computing y from $x_1,\dots,x_n$ can be written in the logical language of synthesis as sequent

(3) $\exists f\,(M \vdash X_n \xrightarrow[f]{\quad\quad} Y)$.

We consider the set of formulae (1), (2) and (3) as the specification of a problem. The program is synthesized from such a specification in two steps. At first, the proof of existence of a solution of the problem is found, i.e. the system derives sequent (3) form the axioms of model M and from the so called logical axioms (axiom of form $A \vdash A$) by means of inference rules of structural synthesis [8]. After being successful in that step, the required program is derived from the proof obtained at the first step.

Our language specification method presumes separating the abstract level of syntax. To every abstract syntax rule corresponds a semantic model (class) described during language construction process. These semantic models are efficiently transformable into corresponding computational models [9]. The computational model M_p of production p consists of relations of the semantic model written in the form of propositional formulae. For example, the computational model of the production P_{EQN} includes exactly one axiom:

$$\vdash (X_{EXP} \,\&\, Y_{EXP} \xrightarrow[\varphi]{} VAL_{EXP}) \,\&\, X_0 \,\&\, X_1 \,\&\, Y \,\&\, STEP \xrightarrow[PROCESS(\varphi)]{\quad\quad} RESULT.$$

The obtained formal language description may be implemented by the use of the algorithms of structural synthesis of programs. It requires the corresponding formal specification to be composed. Some computational relations represent informational dependencies between semantic models that must be added to models M_p accordingly to abstract syntactic structure of the language [10]. If M (M is called a language model) is the result of such an addition, an appropriate semantic processor may be automatically generated by building derivation of the following sequent:

$$\exists f\,(M \vdash A \xrightarrow[f]{} B),$$

where A and B denote "contextual" and "semantic" properties the initial symbol of and abstract syntax correspondingly.

For example, if the language model for differential equations is denoted by EQN', then for

(4) $\exists$ f (EQN' $\vdash$ T,X0,Y0,X1,STEP $\xrightarrow[f]{}$ RESULT)

the synthesis algorithm generates the semantic processor.

This program computes semantics of any tree T of the abstract syntax of differential equation. In other words, system synthesizes function f for

T, X0, Y0, X1, STEP $\xrightarrow[f]{}$ RESULT.

Function f is compiled from relations of the classes EQN, EXP, CONST, VarX etc. and "elementary tree-walking" functions left and right.

Scheme of language translation: The translation follows three-pass scheme 1) syntax analysis; 2) context analysis; 3) interpretation or semantic synthesis. The first pass also includes construction of abstract syntax tree, the second pass includes construction of syntactic structure for determining of semantics. An advantage of this scheme is that the abstract program tree is constructed immediately (without previous complete parse tree).

4. Attribute grammars and computational models.

Computational models M_p that correspond to different productions may be considered as attribute models attaching the semantics to abstract syntactic structures of the language. The components described in the first part of the computational symbols of the corresponding productions. The dependencies among the attribute instances of a parse tree are defined by computational statements. In our example symbol EQN has inherited attributes X0, Y0, X1, STEP which are interpreted as limits of integration,initial condition and integration step. The non-terminal symbol EQN has a synthesized attribute RESULT for expressing the termination of integration process.

Inherited attributes X and Y and the synthesized attribute VAL of symbol EXP denote the arguments and the value of the righthand side expression of the equation.

Terminal symbol numeric has one synthesized attribute *value* (value of constant) given before evaluation of semantics.

The following attribute grammar corresponds to our example.

```
modEQN  :   EQN --> EXP
                    {RESULT := LOOP( EQN.XO, EQN.Y0, EQN.X1, EQN.STEP,
                                    (EXP: X,Y ---> VAL)) }

modCONST : EXP --> numeric
                    {EXP.VAL := numeric.value}.

modvalX  :  EXP -->
                    {EXP.VAL := EXP.X}

modvalY  : EXP -->
                    {EXP.VAL := EXP.Y}

modADD  :   EXP --> EXP EXP
                    {EXP.0.VAL := EXP.1.VAL + EXP.2.VAL;
                     EXP.1.X := EXP.0.X;
                     EXP.1.Y := EXP.0.Y;
                     EXP.2.X := EXP.0.X;
                     EXP.2.Y := EXP.0.Y}
...
...
```

Function **LOOP** in the first attribute model produces the termination condition of integration process from inherited attributes of EQN and functional attribute (EXP: X,Y --> VAL). The value of that attribute must be given by an arithmetic expression.

The obtained attribute grammar may be implemented by means of structural program synthesis. The proof of existence of a solution (for our example - derivation of formula (4)) coincides with deciding whether an attribute grammar is well defined. That derivation is constructive, i.e. the proof can be transformed into a program (semantic processor) with little effort [5,8,9].

It must be noted that the attribute evaluation method used by the synthesized semantic processor depends on the set of additional computational models (i.e. on the set $(M - (\cup M_p))$. In [10] two separate ways are developed to construct the set of additional relations corresponding to the dynamic and the static implementation of semantics.

In practice attribute grammars are used for context analysis and/or to determine the semantics of a parse tree. Context analysis results in some attributed structure of a program which are the initial data for computation of program semantics. In an exceptionally favorable case only synthesized attributes of the root of the parse tree are to be computed. Then many evaluated attributes may appear to be useless for finding the semantics of the program. So, the requirement to compute all the attributes of the parse tree (this is a conventional requirement for well-defined attribute grammars) appears to be excessively strong. We have introduced a new concept of well-definedness that does not require the evaluation of useless attributes of the semantics structure of a parse tree. A similar less restrictive concept of well-definedness was introduced in [11] by Filè. On the basis of a new concept of well-definedness new (large) classes of attribute grammars corresponding to any conventional grammar may be introduced. For example, for conventional classes of well-defined attribute grammars c-WAG and absolutely noncircular attribute grammars c-ANCAG [10] we obtain the corresponding larger classes WAG and ANCAG. The comparison of conventional and new classes gives the topology of well-defined attribute grammars presented in Fig.1.

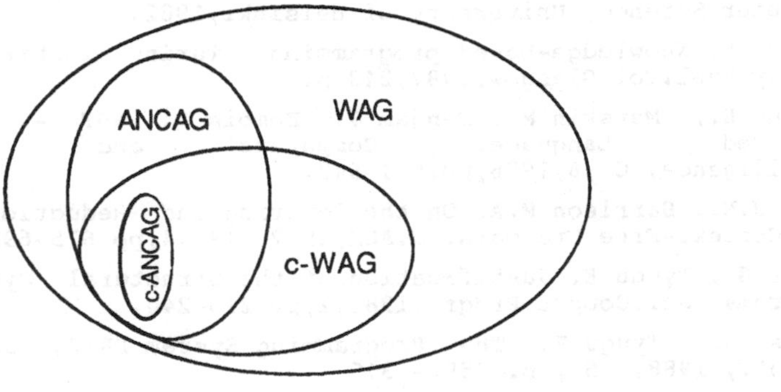

Fig.1. Classification of attribute grammars

In [12] a principal scheme to check whether an attribute grammar belongs to any enlarged class by means of an algorithm for reducing grammar is proposed. We demonstrated how computational models can be used for determining the semantics of programming languages and for computer-aided generation of translators as well. It appears to be another way to check whether an attribute grammar belongs to class ANCAG.

This classification allows us to indirectly estimate our semantics specification and implementation methods. The experience with attribute grammars shows that class c-ANCAG has quite an expressive power to specify actually used languages [1,11]. The technique for implementation of attribute grammars that uses computational models appears to be in practice quite effective for class ANCAG. In [10] the theorems are proved that show: the synthesis of a semantic processor for programming languages from their absolutely noncircular attribute grammar (class ANCAG) takes polynomial time.

References

[1] Deransart P., Jourdan M., Lorho B. Attribute Grammars. LNCS, 1988, 323, - 232 pp.

[2] Ganziger H., et al. A Truly Generative Semantics-Directed Compiler Generator. SIGPLAN Notices,1982, 17,6,pp.172-184.

[3] Koskimies K.,Elomaa T.,Lehtonen T., Paakki J.: TOOLS/HLP84 Report and User Manual. Report A-1988-2, Department of Computer Science, University of Helsinki,1988.

[4] Koskimies K. An Experience on Language Implementation Using Attribute Grammars. Report A-1982-2,Department of Computer Science, University of Helsinki,1982.

[5] Tyugu E. Knowledge-based programming. Turing Institute Press, Wesley Publ.Co.,Glasgow,1987,243 p.

[6] Tyugu E., Matskin M., Penjam J., Eomois P. NUT - an Object-Oriented Language. Computers and Artificial Intelligence, C ,6,1986,pp.521-542.

[7] Gray J.N., Harrison M.A. On the Covering and Reduction Problems for Context-Free Grammars. J.ACM,1972, 19 ,4,pp.675-698.

[8] Mints G., Tyugu E. Justification of the Structural Synthesis of Programs. Sci.Comput.Progr.,1982,2,pp.215-240.

[9] Mints G., Tyugu E. The Programming Sysrem PRIZ, J. Symbolic Comput., 1988, 5 , p. 359 - 375

[10] Penjam J. Computational and Attribute Models of Formal Languages. Theoret. Comput. Sci.,1990, 71 ,pp.241+264.

[11] Engelfriet J., Filè G. Simple Multi-visit Attribute Grammars. J. Comput. Syst. Sci.,1982,24,pp.283-314.

[12] Filè G. Interpretation and Reduction of Attribute Grammars. Acta Informatica,1983, 19 ,pp.115-150.

INDUCTIVE INFERENCE OF RECURSIVE FUNCTIONS: QUALITATIVE THEORY

Rūsiņš Freivalds
Institute of Mathematics and Computer Science
The University of Latvia
Raiņa bulvāris 29
226250, Riga, Latvia

Abstract

This survey contains both old and very recent results in non-quantitative aspects of inductive inference of total recursive functions. The survey is not complete. The paper was written to stress some of the main results in selected directions of research performed at the University of Latvia rather than to exhaust all of the obtained results. We concentrated on the more explored areas such as the inference of indices in non-Goedel computable numberings, the inference of minimal Goedel numbers, and the specifics of inference of minimal indices in Kolmogorov numberings.

Goedel numberings have many specific properties which influence the inference process very much. On the other hand, when discussing the desirability inductive inference we usually do not mention these properties. Hence the motivation is valid for inference of indices in non-Goedel computable numberings as well. Section 2 contains several results showing that the inference of indices in computable numberings can differ very much. For instance, there are computable numberings which are difficult for the inference, and only finite classes of total recursive functions can be identified. This shows that computable numberings can be very much removed from Goedel numberings.

We get rather similar results and even very similar methods of proofs when we consider the identification of minimal indices in Goedel numberings. It is difficult to express this similarity explicitly but many proofs can be expressed in parallel. Criteria for the identifiability of the minimal numbers, lattice - theoretical properties of the partial ordering of Goedel numberings with respect to identifiability of the minimal numbers, and identifiable classes with extremal characteristics are considered. Kolmogorov numberings which have special status in defining Kolmogorov complexity turn out to have special properties in inference of minimal numbers as well.

Section 9 presents results in abstract theory of identification types. It turns out that there are "typical" or "complete" classes of functions in many identification types $\mathfrak{M}, \mathfrak{L}$ such that to deside whether or not $EX_{\mathfrak{M}} \subseteq EX_{\mathfrak{L}}$ it suffices to check whether or not the "$\mathfrak{M}$-complete" class $V_{\mathfrak{M}}$ is in $EX_{\mathfrak{L}}$. Unfortunately, the proposed technique for constructing these classes does not work for those types with "identification of minimal indices in specific Goedel numberings".

1. INTRODUCTION

Recursion-theoretical concepts not explained below are treated in [Rog 67].

In textbooks motivating theory of numberings for programmers Goedel numberings usually are explained as follows [Ersh 77].

Compiling of computer programs may be quite a job. Sometimes the reason of this is not just technical but rather essential. By "a universal programming language" or "a universal computer" we will understand a 2-argument partial recursive function ψ universal for the class of all 1-argument partial recursive functions. By "program to compute a 1-argument partial recursive function" we will understand its index, i.e. a number $n \in N$ such that $\varphi(x)=\pi x \cdot \psi(n,x)$.

Hence if we have two universal programming languages (i.e. two universal functions ψ_0, ψ_1) then the translation problem is the problem how to obtain any ψ_1-index for the function whose ψ_0-index is the given n.

Unfortunately, not always the translation can be performed by an algorithm, i.e. by a total recursive function. Moreover, there are "universal programming languages" ψ_0 and ψ_1 such that the translation is impossible whichever direction.

On the other hand, there is a "distinguished" universal programming language which is "more universal" than the others. It allows translations from all universal programming languages to it. Clearly, only it deserves to be called "universal". It is the Goedel numbering. (Formally, there are many Goedel numberings but H.Rogers [Rog 58] proved that they all are recursively isomorphic.)

We are to feel the difference between the two subsequent definitions 1.1 and 1.3.

DEFINITION 1.1. A numbering ψ of partial recursive functions is called computable if:

1) for arbitrary n, $\psi_n(x)$ is a partial recursive function of the variable x,

2) for arbitrary partial recursive function χ of the variable x, there is an n such that $\psi_n(x)=\chi(x)$,

3) there is a uniform algorithm which computes the values $\psi_n(x)$ for all pairs (n,x).

DEFINITION 1.2. We say that the numbering ψ is reducible to the numbering φ ($\psi \leq \varphi$) if there is an algorithm g such that for arbitrary n, $\psi_n(x)=\varphi_{g(n)}(x)$ for all x.

DEFINITION 1.3. A computable numbering φ is a Goedel numbering if every computable numbering ψ of partial recursive functions is reducible to φ.

There exist Goedel numberings. More than that. All "natural" (i.e. not specially designed) computable numberings usually turn out to be Goedel ones. It is rather difficult to construct a non-Goedel computable numbering.

Section 2 shows that non-Goedel computable numberings may be very difficult for inductive inference. There is a computable numbering ψ such that ψ-indices can be identified in the limit only for finite classes of total recursive functions.

Section 3 contains a series of results showing that computable numberings can differ very much with respect to inferrability. We investigate the partial ordering of computable numberings with respect to the possibility of inductive inference. The structure turns out to be very regular.

Goedel numberings are very much different for identification of minimal indices. (We remind these results in much detail in Section 4.) There are Goedel numberings where only finite sets of functions are identifiable and there are Goedel numberings where rather rich classes can be identified. In [Fre 75] a criterion of identifiability in at least one Goedel numbering was proved (it is repeated as our Theorem 4.2). The lattice of equivalence classes of Goedel numberings was studied in a paper [FK77] apparently unknown in the West. These results are presented in Section 6 of this paper. E.Kinber [Kin77] proved a series of theorems (with very complicated ideas of proofs, by the way) on mindchange complexity for identification of minimal Goedel numbers. Another paper by Kinber [Kin 83] considers a modification of our notion of nearly minimal Goedel numbers. He considers what does it mean "the second minimal" (as opposite to "not much larger than the minimal" in [Fre 75]). The main result in [Kin 83] shows that c-minimal Goedel numbers can be identified in at least one Goedel numbering if and only if strictly minimal Goedel numbers can be identified in another Goedel numbering.

Unfortunately, it is still an open problem (since 1977!) whether or not for any two Goedel numberings φ_1 and φ_2 there is a third one where minimal numbers can be identified for every class such that for it the minimal numbers are identifiable in at least one numbering φ_1 or φ_2. We do not know even whether or not there are two classes U_1 and U_2 for which the minimal Goedel numbers are identifiable but never in the same numbering.

Our Section 8 shows that progress is made recently for Kolmogorov numberings. Kolmogorov numberings are "the most informative" ones. By the definition, every Goedel numbering can be reduced to the Kolmogorov numbering via a recursive function with no more rapid than linear growth.

Section 8 contains Theorem 8.3 solving a long standing open problem. (Unfortunately, the proof turned out to be not very much complicated). It was proved, in contrast to Theorem 1.1 , that for arbitrary Kolmogorov numbering there always is an infinite identifiable class of total recursive functions.

Let $\mathfrak{G}$ denote the family of all Goedel numberings. Let $\varphi \in \mathfrak{G}$. By $\mathfrak{R}$ we denote the class of all total recursive functions of one argument.

We fix a Cantor (i.e. computable one-one) numbering $<x_1,x_2,\ldots,x_n>$ of all n-tuples $\{x_1,x_2,\ldots,x_n\}$ of nonnegative integers as n varies. We fix also a Cantor numbering c(x,y) of all pairs of nonnegative integers (c(x,y)=z, l(z)=x, r(z)=y).

By $f^{[x]}$ we denote the (x+1)-tuple $\{f(0),f(1),\ldots,f(x)\}$.

Strategy is an arbitrary partial recursive function.

DEFINITION 1.4 A strategy F identifies in the limit a φ-number for a total recursive function F ($f \in EX_\varphi(F)$) if:

1) for every n the value $F(<f^{[n]}>)$ is defined,

and

2) the limit $\lim_{n\to\infty} F(<f^{[n]}>)=a$ exists and equals to a φ-index of the function f (i.e. $\varphi_a=f$).

There is a "folk lemma" used by nearly all authors in papers on inductive inference.

LEMMA 1.1. For arbitrary Goedel numbering $\{F_i\}$ of all partial recursive strategies there is a family $\{F'_i\}$ of total recursive strategies such that for arbitrary i and total recursive f, if $\lim_{n\to\infty} F_i(<f^{[n]}>)$ exists then $\lim_{n\to\infty} F'_i(<f^{[n]}>)$ exists as well and the limits are equal.

DEFINITION 1.5. A class U of total recursive functions is φ-identifiable in the limit ($U \in EX_\varphi$) if there is a strategy F which identifies in the limit a φ-index for every function in the class U.

It is easy to see that if φ and ψ are two Goedel numberings then $EX_\varphi=EX_\psi$. Hence it is natural to write just $U \in EX$ instead of $U \in EX_\varphi$.

To strengthen some of our results we use a modification of our Definitions 1.4 and 1.5.

DEFINITION 1.6. A strategy F identifies the class U of total recursive functions in the sense BC_φ if for every $f \in U$:

1) for every n the value $F(<f^{[n]}>)$ is defined,

2) there is an n_0 such that for every $n>n_0$ the value $F(<f^{[n]}>)$ equals a φ-index of the function f.

Like EX-identification, $BC_\varphi=BC_\psi$ for all Goedel numberings φ and ψ. Hence we use the notation BC.

J.M.Barzdin [Bar 74] proved that $EX \subset BC$ and $EX \neq BC$.

The minimal φ-index of a function f is denoted by $\min_\varphi(f)$.

DEFINITION 1.7. Let h(x) be a total recursive function. We say that h-minimal φ-indices are identifiable in the limit for a class U ($U \in EX_\varphi^{h\text{-}min}$) if there is a strategy F such that:

1) $U \subseteq EX_\varphi(F)$,

2) for arbitrary $f \in U$, $\lim_{n\to\infty} F(<f^{[n]}>) \leq h(\min_\varphi(f))$.

We pay somewhat more attention to the particular case h(x)=x. We use EX_φ^{min} instead $EX_\varphi^{h\text{-}min}$ for this function.

Now we introduce some more pieces of notation. Let α be an arbitrary string of integers. By $\alpha 0^k$ we denote a string the first elements of which are taken from α and the last k elements are zeros. Similarly, by $\alpha 0^\infty$ we denote a total function the first values of which correspond to the string α, and all the other values equal 0.

DEFINITION 1.8. A Goedel numbering æ is called Kolmogorov numbering if every computable numbering ψ is reducible to æ via total recursive function which never exceeds a linear function.

2.INFERENCE IN COMPUTABLE NUMBERINGS

It is natural to question which classes of total recursive functions are identifiable in the limit in all computable numberings. Theorem 2.1 in this Section shows that finite classes and only they are identifiable in all computable numberings. Afterwards we try to understand what properties of the numberings make them difficult for the inference.

LEMMA 2.1. There is a total function f, graph of which is in Π_1, such that:

1) for arbitrary partial recursive function ψ the equality $\psi(x)=f(x)$ can hold for no more than finite number of different x,

2) $(\forall x)\ (\exists p)\ (f(x)=c(x,p))$.

PROOF. To prove that the graph of a function f is in the class Π_1 of Kleene-Mostowski [Rog 67], we need to prove that there is an algorithm $\mathfrak{M}$ uniform in x and y such that it stops for all pairs (x,y) such that $f(x)\neq y$ and it does not stop for the pairs (x,y) such that $f(x)=y$.

We consider an auxiliary algorithm $\mathfrak{M}$ which has only one argument x and outputs an infinite sequence of all possible true inequalities $f(x)\neq y$. Since for arbitrary x inequalities $f(x)\neq y$ are produced for all nonnegative integers y but one, the function f will be defined unambiguously.

The algorithm $\mathfrak{M}$ works as follows. It computes in parallel $\varphi_0(x),\varphi_1(x),\dots,\varphi_x(x)$ (where φ is a fixed Goedel numbering) during 1,2,3,... steps. In parallel with these computations the following inequalities are output: $f(x)\neq 0$, $f(x)\neq 1$, $f(x)\neq 2,\dots$, $f(x)\neq c(x,0)-1$, $f(x)\neq c(x,0)+1$, $f(x)\neq c(x,0)+2,\dots$

If one of the computations $\varphi_0(x),\varphi_1(x),\dots,\varphi_x(x)$ stops then M compares whether the result equals c(x,0). If <u>not</u> then $\mathfrak{M}$ goes on to output the same sequence. If <u>yes</u> then $\mathfrak{M}$ outputs $f(x)\neq c(x,0)$, searches for the least p_1 such that $f(x)\neq c(x,p_1)$ has not yet been output and $c(x,p_1)$ does not equal the values $\varphi_0(x),\varphi_1(x),\dots,\varphi_x(x)$ computed up to this moment, and $\mathfrak{M}$ outputs inequalities ..., $f(x)\neq c(x,p_1)-2$, $f(x)\neq c(x,p_1)-1$, $f(x)\neq c(x,p_1)+1$, $f(x)\neq c(x,p_1)+2,\dots$

In parallel, the computation of $\varphi_0(x),\varphi_1(x),\dots,\varphi_x(x)$ is continued, and in the case of new results again it is checked whether the new result equals $c(x,p_1)$, etc.

There is a bounded number of computations $\varphi_0(x),\varphi_1(x),\dots,\varphi_x(x)$ that can change the current $c(x,p_i)$. Inevitably, there will be the last $c(x,p_i)$ and this value will become f(x). □

Relativizing this proof to a creative oracle, we get a proof for

LEMMA 2.2. There is a total function f, graph of which is in Π_2, such that:

1) for arbitrary partial function ψ, graph of which is in Σ_2, the equality $\psi(x)=f(x)$ can hold for no more than finite number of different x,

2) $(\forall x)\ (\exists p)\ (f(x)=c(x,p))$.

The graph of f being in Π_2 can be represented by an algorithm $\mathfrak{M}$ uniform in x and y such that for all pairs (x,y) it produces a sequence of zeros and ones, and if $f(x)\neq y$ then the sequence containes no more than a finite number of ones.

R.M.Friedberg [Fri 58] proved that there is a computable one-to-one numbering ν' of all 1-argument partial recursive functions. We use ν' and the algorithm $\mathfrak{M}$ to construct a computable numbering ν. The function $\nu_n(t)$ is defined as follows. It equals $\nu'_{l(n)}(t)$ if $\mathfrak{M}$ for $x=l(n)$ and $y=r(n)$ outputs a sequence containing no less than t ones, and it is undefined, otherwise.

LEMMA 2.3. ν is a computable numbering of all 1-argument partial recursive functions, and every total recursive function has only one index in ν.

PROOF. If a function ψ has a ν'-index n then its ν-index is $c(n,f(n))$, and all the numbers of type $c(n,p)$ where $p\neq f(n)$ are ν-indices of finite functions. Hence, if ψ has an infinite domain then it has no ν-indices differing from $c(n,f(n))$. ❑

THEOREM 2.1. There is a computable numbering ν of all 1-argument partial recursive functions such that no infinite class of total recursive functions is in EX_ν.

PROOF. Assume from the contrary that an infinite class of total recursive functions is ν-identifiable in the limit by a strategy F. We define an auxiliary function $\eta(x,t)$:

$$\eta(x,t)=\begin{cases}0, & \text{if } t=0,\\ F(\langle\nu'_x{}^{[t-1]}\rangle), & \text{if } t>0.\end{cases}$$

Unfortunately, the function $\eta(x,t)$ is only partial recursive. We define another auxilary function, a total one. To compute $g(x,t)$, compute sequentially $\eta(x,0),\eta(x,1),\eta(x,2),\ldots$ using t steps of computation in total. Then $g(x,t)$ equals the last computed value in the abovementioned sequence (and it equals 0 if t steps do not suffice to compute $\eta(x,0)$). We define $\psi(x)$ as $\lim_{t\to\infty} r(g(x,t))$. Since ψ is a limit of a total recursive function, its graph is in Σ_2.

Recall that every total recursive function has only one index in ν' and one index in ν. If the ν'-index of a total function is n then its ν-index is $c(n,f(n))$. If F identifies the ν-index of ν'_n then $\lim_{t\to\infty}\eta(n,t)=c(n,f(n))$. Hence $\lim_{t\to\infty} g(n,t)=c(n,f(n))$ and $\psi(n)=$ $=\lim_{t\to\infty} r(g(n,t))=f(n)$.

Lemma 2.2 implies that the values of ψ and f can equal only for finite number of values of the argument. Contradiction. □

3. PARTIAL ORDERING OF COMPUTABLE NUMBERINGS

The reducibility of computable numberings $\psi \leq \varphi$ means the existence of an algorithm which, for arbitrary function ψ_i finds its φ-index j ($\varphi_j = \psi_i$). There are equivalent numberings which are reducible two ways. For instance, all Goedel numberings are equivalent. The partial ordering P_1 of the equivalence classes of the computable numerings of all 1-argument partial recursive functions is studied intensively (see [Ersh 77]). It is known that P_1 is upper semilattice but it is not lower semilattice.

We could consider "limiting reducibility" and the corresponding partial order of equivalence classes of computable numberings. It would produce rather similar results. Instead, we considered another reducibility of the same computable numberings. We use $\psi \leq_{EX} \varphi$ to denote that for arbitrary class U of total recursive functions $U \in EX_\psi$ implies $U \in EX_\varphi$. It is easy to see that if $\psi \leq \varphi$ (and even if $\psi \leq \varphi$ in the limit) then $y \leq_{EX} \varphi$.

Let P_2 be the partial ordering of the equivalence classes with respect to $\leq_{EX}$. We will see that P_1 and P_2 are very much different.

The numbering considered in Theorem 2.1 is in the minimum element of P_2. On the other hand, there is no minimum element in P_1.

The ordering P_1 and P_2 have maximum elements, namely, the classes of computable numberings equivalent to Goedel numberings.

It is known (see [Ersh 77]) that P_1 is not a lower semilattice.

THEOREM 3.1. P_2 is a distributive lattice.

PROOF. The greatest lower bound for the equivalence classes containing the numberings ν' and ν'', respectively, is the equivalence class containing the numbering.

$$(\nu' \otimes \nu'')_{c(i,j)}(x) = \begin{cases} \nu'_i(x), & \text{if } \nu'_i(x) = \nu'_j, \\ \text{undefined}, & \text{if otherwise.} \end{cases}$$

To prove that $(\nu' \otimes \nu'')$ is contained in the greatest lower bound, we are to prove that if a computable numbering ψ is such that $\psi \leq_{EX} \nu'$ and $\psi \leq_{EX} \nu''$ then $\psi \leq_{EX} (\nu' \otimes \nu'')$. Indeed, let $\psi \leq_{EX} \nu'$, and $U \in EX_\varphi$. Then $U \in EX_{\nu'}$. We denote the strategy identifying in the limit ν'-indices for U by F. Let $\psi \leq_{EX} \nu''$. Then $U \in EX_{\nu''}$ as well. We denote the strategy identifying in the limit ν''-indices for U by G. We consider the strategy $H(<f^{[x]}>) = c(F(<f^{[x]}>), G(<f^{[x]}>))$. It is easy to see that H identifies in the limit the $(\nu' \otimes \nu'')$-indices for U.

The least upper bound for the equivalence classes containing the numberings ν' and ν'', respectively, is the equivalence class containing the numbering

$$(\nu' \oplus \nu'')_n(x)= \begin{cases} \nu'_i(x), \text{ if } n=2i, \\ \nu''_i(x), \text{ if } n=2i+1. \end{cases}$$

To prove that $(\nu' \oplus \nu'')$ is contained in the least upper bound, we are to prove that if a computable numbering ψ is such that $\nu' \leq_{EX} \psi$ and $\nu'' \leq_{EX} \psi$ then $(\nu' \oplus \nu'') \leq_{EX} \psi$. Indeed, let a strategy F identify in the limit $(\nu' \oplus \nu'')$-indices for functions in U. We divide U into two subclasses U_1 and U_2. If the strategy F assigns in the limit to the function $f \in U$ an even value 2i then $f \in U_1$ and strategy F_1 assigns in the limit to this function the ν'-index i. If the strategy F assigns in the limit to the function $f \in U$ an odd value 2i+1 then $f \in U_2$ and strategy F_2 assigns in the limit to this function the ν''-index i. Since $U_1 \in EX_{\nu'}$ and $\nu' \leq_{EX} \psi$, there exists a strategy G_1 identifying in the limit correct ψ-indices for $f \in U_1$. Since $U_2 \in EX_{\nu''}$ and $\nu'' \leq_{EX} \psi$, there exists a strategy G_2 identifying in the limit correct ψ-indices for $f \in U_2$. Hence U can be EX_ψ-identified by a strategy.

$$G(<f^{[x]}>)= \begin{cases} G_1(<f^{[x]}>), \text{ if } F(<f^{[x]}>) \text{ is even,} \\ G_2(<f^{[x]}>), \text{ if } F(<f^{[x]}>) \text{ is odd.} \end{cases}$$

To prove the distributivity of the lattice, we are to prove EX-equivalence of the numberings:

$\nu' \oplus (\nu'' \otimes \nu''')$ and $(\nu' \oplus \nu'') \otimes (\nu' \oplus \nu''')$,

$\nu' \otimes (\nu'' \oplus \nu''')$ and $(\nu' \otimes \nu'') \oplus (\nu' \otimes \nu''')$.

By our definitions above,

$$(\nu' \oplus (\nu'' \otimes \nu'''))_n(x)= \begin{cases} \nu'_i(x), \text{if } n=2i, \\ \nu''_k(x)=\nu'''_l(x), \text{ if } n=2c(k,l)+1 \text{ and } \nu''_k(x)=\nu'''_l(x), \\ \text{undefined, if otherwise.} \end{cases}$$

$$((\nu' \oplus \nu'') \otimes (\nu' \oplus \nu'''))_{c(i,j)}(x)= \begin{cases} \nu'_k(x)=\nu'_l(x), \text{ if } i=2k, j=2l \text{ and } \nu'_k(x)=\nu'_l(x), \\ \nu''_k(x)=\nu'_l(x), \text{ if } i=2k+1, j=2l \text{ and } \nu''_k(x)=\nu'_l(x), \\ \nu'_k(x)=\nu'''_l(x), \text{ if } i=2k, j=2l+1 \text{ and } \nu'_k(x)=\nu'''_l(x), \\ \nu''_k(x)=\nu'''_l(x), \text{if } i=2k+1, j=2l+1 \text{ and} \\ \qquad \nu''_k(x)=\nu'''_l(x), \\ \text{undefined, if otherwise.} \end{cases}$$

The numberings are EX-equivalent if for arbitrary class U of total recursive functions identifiability in the limit in the other numbering. The equivalence of these two numberings can be proved by simple modification of the outputs of the strategies. this modification relies heavily on our interest in total functions only. Indeed, for every index in one of these two numberings it is possible to find effectively an index in the other numbering such that if the given number is an index of a total function then the corresponding index in the other numbering is an index for the same function. (If the index is defined using a ν'_i in the first numbering then the corresponding index in the other numbering is defined either by ν'_i or by $\nu'_i = \nu'_i$. If ν'-indices are not involved in definition of the given index in the first numbering then it is defined by $\nu''_k = \nu'''_l$ and the other numbering contains the same function.)

The other two numberings are:

$$(\nu' \otimes (\nu'' \oplus \nu'''))_n(x) = \begin{cases} \nu'_i(x) = \nu''_k(x), \text{ if } n = c(i,2k), \text{ and } \nu'_i(x) = \nu''_k(x), \\ \nu'_i(x) = \nu'''_l(x), \text{ if } n = c(i,2l+1), \text{ and } \nu'_i(x) = \nu'''_l(x), \\ \text{undefined, if otherwise,} \end{cases}$$

$$((\nu' \otimes \nu'') \oplus (\nu' \otimes \nu'''))_n(x) = \begin{cases} \nu'_i(x) = \nu''_k(x), \text{ if } n = 2c(i,k), \text{ and } \nu'_i(x) = \nu''_k(x), \\ \nu'_i(x) = \nu'''_l(x), \text{ if } n = 2c(i,k)+1, \text{ and } \nu'_i(x) = \nu'''_l(x), \\ \text{undefined, if otherwise.} \end{cases}$$

For these numberings the proof is even simpler. □

Theorem 3.1 shows that P_2 is much more regular ordering than P_1 and hence it deserves some attention.

4. IDENTIFICATION OF MINIMAL INDICES

We try to describe

$$\bigcap_{\varphi \in \mathfrak{G}} \bigcap_{h \in \mathfrak{R}} EX_\varphi^{h\text{-min}} \text{ and } \bigcup_{\varphi \in \mathfrak{G}} \bigcup_{h \in \mathfrak{R}} EX_\varphi^{h\text{-min}}$$

in this Section. The results and the methods of proof remind very much the identification of arbitrary indices in computable (non-Goedel) numberings. However we have no formal linkage between these two areas.

THEOREM 4.1. For arbitrary total recursive function h(x) there is a Goedel numbering φ such that arbitrary class U of total recursive function is in $EX_\varphi^{h\text{-min}}$ iff card (U) is finite.

LEMMA. There exists a function $\chi(x,j)$ such that:

1) the graph of χ is in the class Π_2 of Kleene-Mostowski hierarchy,

2) $(\forall i)\ (\forall j)\ (\chi(i,j) \text{ defined} \Rightarrow \chi(i,j)=1)$,

3) $(\forall i)\ (\exists j<i+1)\ (\chi(i,j)=1)$,

4) $(\forall \psi \in PLR)(\exists i_0)(\forall i>i_0)(\psi(i) \text{ defined} \Rightarrow \chi(i,\psi(i)) \text{ not defined})$.

REMARK. It is convenient to regard $\chi(i,j)$ as a many-valued (many-many) mapping $N \rightarrow N$. The statement 3) asserts that χ maps every i to at least one integer not exceeding i+1. The statement 4) asserts that the mapping χ differs almost everywhere from any mapping definable by a function in Σ_2.

PROOF OF LEMMA. Let K be a creative set [Rog 67]. Let $\mathfrak{M}_m^K$ be a Turing oracle-machine with number m using the oracle K.

We define the function χ as follows. If j>i+1, then $\chi(i,j)$ is not defined. If j<i+1 and

there exists m<i such that $\mathfrak{M}_m^K(i)=j$, then $\chi(i,j)$ is not defined. Otherwise $\chi(i,j)=1$.

The checking of statements 1), 2), 3), 4) is not complicated.

PROOF OF THEOREM. Let $\chi(i,j)$ be the function defined in Lemma. The statements 1) and 2) imply the existence of a g.r. function h(i,j,t) such that for every i,j the following two assertions are equivalent:

a) $\chi(i,j)$ is defined, b) h(i,j,t)=1 for infinitely many t.

We shall regard the case EX_φ^{min} first. Let φ be an arbitrary Goedel numbering. Let Z(y,n) be a total recursive function such that

$$\varphi_{z(y,n)}(x)=\begin{cases}\varphi_y(x), \text{ if there are at least x such t that } h(y,n,t)=1\\ \text{not defined, otherwise}\end{cases}$$

We define a numbering ϖ as follows.

$\varpi_0\equiv\varphi_{z(0,0)}$, $\varpi_1\equiv\varphi_{z(0,1)}$, $\varpi_2\equiv\varphi_0$,

$\varpi_3\equiv\varphi_{z(1,0)}$, $\varpi_4\equiv\varphi_{z(1,1)}$, $\varpi_5\equiv\varphi_{z(1,2)}$, $\varpi_6\equiv\varphi_1$,

$\varpi_7\equiv\varphi_{z(2,0)}$, $\varpi_8\equiv\varphi_{z(2,1)}$, $\varpi_9\equiv\varphi_{z(2,2)}$, $\varpi_{10}\equiv\varphi_{z(2,3)}$, $\varpi_{11}\equiv\varphi_2$,

- -

The numbering ϖ is evidently computable. It is a Goedel numbering because φ is reducible to ϖ via

$$w(i)=\frac{i+7i+4}{2}$$

If f is a total recursive function and $i=min_\varphi(f)$, then by the statement 3)

$$\frac{(i-1)^2+7(i-1)+4}{2} < min_\varpi(f) < \frac{i^2+7i+4}{2}$$

Let an arbitrary strategy F identify in the limit the minimal ϖ-numbers for a class U of total recursive functions. We will prove thet the cardinality of U is finite.

We define auxiliary functions.

$$\eta(i,t)=\begin{cases}0, \text{ if } t=0\\ F(<\varphi_i(0),\varphi_i(1),\ldots,\varphi_i(t-1)>), \text{ if } t>0\end{cases}$$

Let a Turing machine $\mathfrak{M}$ computing η be fixed. Let g(i,t) be the maximal S not exceeding t, such that all the values $\eta(i,0),\eta(i,1),\ldots,\eta(i,s)$ are computable by $\mathfrak{M}$ in no more than t steps. If t steps do not suffice for computing $\eta(i,0)$, then g(i,t)=0.

Let

$$a \dot{-} b=\begin{cases}a-b, \text{ if } a>b\\ 0, \text{ if } a<b\end{cases}$$

$$\psi^1(i)=\lim_t g(i,t),\ \psi(i)=\lim_t (g(i,t) \dot{-} \frac{(i-1)2+7(i-1)+4}{2} \dot{-} 1)$$

If i is the minimal φ-number of a total recursive function and $\varphi_i \in U$, then $\psi^1(i)$ and $\psi(i)$ are defined, $\psi^1(i)$ is the minimal ϖ-number of φ_i and $\chi(i,\psi(i))=1$. The statement 4) implies there can be at most a finite number of such i. This concludes the proof for the case $h(x)\equiv x$.

For other functions h the definition of ϖ is to be slightly modified. We put functions into the following sequence to define the numbering ϖ:

$\varphi_{z(0,0)}, \varphi_{z(0,1)}, 0, 0, \ldots, 0, \varphi_0,$

$\varphi_{z(1,0)}, \varphi_{z(1,1)}, \varphi_{z(1,2)}, 0, 0, \ldots, 0, \varphi_1,$

$\varphi_{z(2,0)}, \varphi_{z(2,1)}, \varphi_{z(2,2)}, \varphi_{z(2,3)}, 0, 0, \ldots, 0, \varphi_2,$

where 0 is the empty function and if the "block" $\varphi_{z(1,0)}, \varphi_{z(i,1)}, \ldots, \varphi_{z(i,i+1)}$, has got numbers n,n+1,...,n+i+1 in the numbering ϖ, then 0 is repeated

$\max \{h(n), h(n+1), \ldots, h(n+i+1)\}$

times before the function φ_i. It is easy to see that every h-minimal ϖ-number of a g.r. function is absolutely minimal.

COROLLARY.
$\bigcap_{\varphi \in \mathfrak{G}} EX_\varphi^{min} = \bigcap_{h \in \mathcal{R}} EX_\varphi^{h\text{-}min}$ = the class of all finite sets.

DEFINITION 4.1. A class U of total recursive functions is φ-standardizable in the limit with a recursive bound ($U \in LSR\varphi$) if there are total recursive functions G(i,n) and v(i) such that if i is a φ-index of a function $f \in U$ then:

1) the limit $\lim_{n\to\infty} G(i,n)$ exists and equals to a φ-index of f;
2) if i and j are φ-indices of the same $f \in U$ then $\lim_{n\to\infty} G(i,n) = \lim_{n\to\infty} G(j,n)$;
3) card $\{G(i,0), G(i,1), \ldots\} \le v(i)$.

It is easy to see that if φ and ψ are two Goedel numberings then $LSR_\varphi = LSR_\psi$. Hence it is natural to write just LSR.

THEOREM 4.2. For arbitrary class U of total recursive functions
$(U \in \bigcup_{\varphi \in \mathfrak{G}} EX\varphi^{min}) \Leftrightarrow (U \in EX \;\&\; U \in LSR)$.

PROOF. $\Rightarrow$ Let $U \in EX_\varphi^{min}$. Then evidently $U \in EX$. To prove $U \in LSR$ it suffices to consider the functions v(i) and G(i,n), where v(i)=i+1

$$G'(i,n)=\begin{cases} F(<\varphi_i(0),\varphi_i(1),\ldots,\varphi_i(n)>), & \text{if } F(<\varphi_i(0),\varphi_i(1),\ldots,\varphi_i(n)>)<i, \\ i, & \text{if } F(<\varphi_i(0),\varphi_i(1),\ldots,\varphi_i(n)>)>i. \end{cases}$$

$$G(i,n)=\begin{cases} G'(i,t), & \text{where t is the maximal integer not exceeding n, such that all values } G'(i,0),G'(i,1),\ldots,G'(i,t), \text{ are computable in n steps of Turing machine,} \\ i, & \text{if n steps do not suffice to compute } G'(i,0). \end{cases}$$

$\Leftarrow$ Let $\varphi \in \mathfrak{G}$, $U \in EX$, $U \in LSR$. Let the φ-identification in the limit of the class U be carried out by a strategy F and the φ-standardization be carried out by G(i,n) with a recursive estimate v(i).

We define three auxiliary functions. P.r. function $\xi(i,j)$ is equal to G(i,k), where k is the minimal integer such that the set {G(i,0),G(i,1),...,G(i,k)} contains more than j different elements.

$$\varphi_{d(m)}(x)=\begin{cases}\varphi_m(x), \text{ if } (\exists y>x)\ (G(m,y)=m), \\ \text{not defined, otherwise}\end{cases}$$

$z(i,j)=d(\xi(i,j))$.

We define a numbering ϖ as follows:

$\varpi_0\equiv\varphi_{z(0,0)}, \varpi_1\equiv\varphi_{z(0,1)}, \ldots, \varpi_{v(0)-1}\equiv\varphi_{z(0,v(0)-1)}, \varpi_{v(0)}\equiv\varphi_0,$

$\varpi_{v(0)+1}\equiv\varphi_{z(1,0)}, \varpi_{v(0)+2}\equiv\varphi_{z(1,1)}, \ldots, \varpi_{v(0)+v(1)}\equiv\varphi_{z(0,v(1)-1)}, \varpi_{v(0)+v(1)+1}\equiv\varphi_1$

- -

$\varpi_{v(0)+...+v(i-1)+i}\equiv\varphi_{z(i,0)}, \varpi_{v(0)+...+v(i-1)+i+1}\equiv\varphi_{z(i,1)}, \ldots, \varpi_{v(0)+...+v(i)+i-1}\equiv\varphi_{z(i,v(i)-1)},$
$\varpi_{v(0)+...+v(i)+i}\equiv\varphi_i,$

- -

The numbering ϖ is a Goedel numbering because φ is reducible to ϖ via w(i)=v(0)+v(1)+...+v(i)+i.

We shall prove a following characteristics of the function d(m): if $\varphi_i\in U$, then for every natural m:

$(\varphi_{d(m)}\equiv\varphi_i)\Leftrightarrow(m=\lim_n G(i,n))$

Indeed, the implication $\Leftarrow$ follows from $\lim_t G(\lim_n G(i,n),t)=\lim_n G(i,n)$. The implication $\Rightarrow$ follows from the definition of the function d(m) (if G(m,y)=m for infinitely many y, then $\varphi_{d(m)}\equiv\varphi_m$ and hence $\varphi_m\equiv\varphi_i$ and $\lim_n G(m,n)=\lim_n G(i,n)$.

Thus no integer of type v(0)+...+v(i)+i can be the minimal ϖ-number of a function from the class U.

A strategy F' which identifies the minimal ϖ-numbers for the class U can be defined as follows. Let m(f,n) denote the value G(F(<f(0),f(1),...,f(n)>),n). To define F'(<f(0),f(1),...,f(n)>) we compute m(f,n) and use a fixed Turing machine, computing ξ, to calculate the following values

$\xi(0,0),\xi(0,1),...,\xi(0,v(0)-1),$

$\xi(1,0),\xi(1,1),...,\xi(1,v(1)-1),$ (*)

- - - - - - - - - - - - - - -

$\xi(m(f,n),0),\xi(m(f,n),1),...,\xi(m(f,n),v(m(f,n))-1).$

Let (i,j) be the first pair (according to the sequence (*)), such that the computation of $\xi(i,j)$ stops in no more than n steps and $\xi(i,j)$=m))f,n). Then F' gets a value equal to the number, which the function $\varphi_{z(i,j)}$ has in the numbering ϖ, i.e.

F,(<f(0),f(1),...,f(n)>)=v(0)+v(1)+...+v(i-1)+i-1+j.

Otherwise, F'(<f(0),f(1),...,f(n)>)=0.

COROLLARY 1. There exist Goedel numberings φ' and φ'', such that $EX_{\varphi'}^{min} \neq EX_{\varphi''}^{min}$.

COROLLARY 2. For every class U of g.r. functions and for every total recursive function h, such that h(x)≥x for all x, it is true that

$(U \in \bigcup_{\varphi \in \mathfrak{G}} EX^{h}_{\varphi}\text{-min}) \Leftrightarrow (U \in EX \ \& \ U \in LSR)$.

COROLLARY 3. $\bigcup_{h \in \mathfrak{R}} \bigcup_{\varphi \in \mathfrak{G}} EX^{h}_{\varphi}\text{-min} = \bigcup_{\varphi \in \mathfrak{G}} EX_{\varphi}^{min}$

REMARK. The class U_0 consisting of all {0,1}-valued total functions which equal 1 for at most finite number of values of the argument, is in EX but not in EX_{φ}^{min} for any $\varphi \in \mathfrak{G}$. Thus we have proved $U_0 \notin LSR$ and $EX \not\subseteq LSR$. Using a construction developed by E.B.Kinber it can be proved that $LSR \not\subseteq EX$ as well.

THEOREM 4.3. There are classes U_1 and U_2 of total recursive functions such that

$U_1 \in EX \setminus LSR$,

$U_2 \in LSR \setminus EX$.

Theorem 4.2 shows that there are Goedel numberings φ and ψ such that $EX_{\varphi}^{min} \neq EX_{\psi}^{min}$.This opens a rich area of investigation, e.g. to characterize the non - equivalent Goedel numberings.

We denote $\bigcup_{\varphi \in \mathfrak{G}} EX_{\varphi}^{min}$ by EX^{min}. Another corollary of Theorem 4.2 shows that

$\bigcup_{\varphi \in \mathfrak{G}} EX_{\varphi}^{h\text{-min}} = EX^{h\text{-min}}$

equals the same EX^{min} for arbitrary h(x)≥x.

E.B.Kinber [FK 77] proved very difficult theorem on the number of mindchanges in EX^{min} - identification. Mindchanges are characterised by a function whose argument is $\min_{\varphi}(f)$.

THEOREM 4.4. There is a class $U_1 \in EX^{min}$ which cannot be EX_{φ}^{min} - identified with a recursive bound on mindchanges for arbitrary Goedel numbering φ.

THEOREM 4.5. There is a Goedel numbering φ such that:

1) there is an infinite class U of total recursive functions such that $U \in EX_{\varphi}^{min}$,

2) there is no effectively enumerable class U of total recursive functions such that $U \in EX_{\varphi}^{min}$.

We consider two lemmas before the proof. It is known that Post's theorem on the existence of simple sets can be strengthened [Tra 65].

LEMMA 4.1. There is a set A such that:

1) A is recursively enumerable,

2) for arbitrary m there are at most $\log_2 m$ elements in $A \cap \{0,1,2,\dots,m\}$,

3) $\bar{A}$ has no infinite recursively enumerable subsets.

PROOF. By W_x we denote the domain of φ_x. Let $B=\{\langle x,y\rangle \mid y \in W_x \,\&\, \& y \geq 2^{x+1}\}$. We fix an effective enumeration of the set B, and construct a set $B'=\{\langle x,y\rangle \mid \langle x,y\rangle \in B \,\&\, (\forall z)\, [[z \neq y \,\&\, \langle x,z\rangle \in B] \Rightarrow \langle x,y\rangle$ succeeds $\langle x,y\rangle$ in the enumeration of B]]}. We define $A=\{y \mid (\exists x)(\langle x,y\rangle \in B')\}$. The properties 1),3) are proved in the same way as in Post's theorem (see [Rog 67]). The property 2) is implied by $y \geq 2^{x+1}$ in the definition of the set B. □

By relativization of this proof to a creative oracle we get the proof of

LEMMA 4.2. There is a set A such that:

1) $A \in \Sigma_2$ (A is enumerable with a creative oracle),

2) for arbitrary m there are at most $\log_2 m$ elements in $A \cap \{0,1,2,\dots,m\}$,

3) $\bar{A}$ has no infinite subsets from Σ_2.

We use these lemmas to prove the Theorem.

PROOF OF THEOREM. Let ψ be a Goedel numbering. We consider two auxiliary numberings of all partial recursive functions of 1 argument.

$$\beta_i(x)=\begin{cases}\psi_j(x), & \text{if } i=2j,\\ j, & \text{if } i=2j+1,\end{cases}$$

$$\gamma_i(x)=\beta_{l(i)}(x)$$

We use a specific c(x,y), namely, $c(0,0)=0$, $c(0,1)=1$, $c(1,0)=2$, $c(0,2)=3$, $c(1,1)=4$, $c(2,0)=5$, $c(0,3)=6$, $c(1,2)=7$,... Then for arbitrary n,k among the functions γ_0, $\gamma_1,\dots,\gamma_{k^2}$ the function ψ_n occurs no less than k-n times.

We define a numbering ν using the numbering γ and the set A from Lemma 4.2. $A \in \Sigma_2$. Hence, the partial characteristic function

$$\chi_A(y)=\begin{cases}1, & \text{if } y \in A,\\ \text{undefined}, & \text{if } y \in \bar{A}\end{cases}$$

can be represented as a limit of a total recursive function $\chi_A(y)=\lim_{s\to\infty} h(y,s)$. For arbitrary i,x the value $\nu_i(x)$ is defined as follows: if in the sequence h(i,0), h(i,1), h(i,2),... there are no less than x values differing from 1 then $\nu_i(x)=\gamma_i(x)$; otherwise ν_i is undefined. It is obvious that if i is a γ-index of a function with infinite domain then $(\nu_i=\gamma_i) \Leftrightarrow (i \in \bar{A})$.

Now we prove that for every function ψ_i (total or not) $\min_\nu(\psi_i)\le 2i^2$. Indeed, for arbitrary n,k among the functions $\gamma_0,\gamma_1,\ldots,\gamma_{k^2}$ there are no less than k-n occurences of β_n. For arbitrary n there is k such that $k-n>1+\log_2 k^2$. Hence for this k there is an $i\in\{0,1,2,\ldots,k^2\}$ such that $i\in\bar{A}$ and $\gamma_i=\beta_n=\nu_i$.

Now we prove that no infinite effectively enumerable class can be EX_ν^{min}-identifiable.

Assume that a strategy F EX_ν^{min}-identifies an effectively enumerable class $U=\{\alpha_i(x)\}$. Let $g(i,n)=F(<\alpha_i[n]>)$ and $\eta(i)=\lim_{n\to\infty} g(i,n)$. Since $\eta(i)$ is the limit of a total recursive function, its range is in Σ_2. Since F identifies U and all the functions in U are total, we conclude that $\{\eta(0),\eta(1),\eta(2),\ldots\}\subseteq\bar{A}$ and $\alpha_i\ne\alpha_j$ imply $\eta(i)\ne\eta(j)$. Then, by the assertion 3) of Lemma 4.2, the range of η is finite, and hence $card(U)<\infty$.

Now we prove that there is an infinite class of total recursive functions in EX_ν^{min}.

We consider the class U_0 of all constants. We define a strategy $G(<y_0,y_1,\ldots,y_n>)=$ $=s(2y_0+1,0)$. It identifies correct γ-indices for all functions in U_0. We will use the property of γ mentioned above, namely, if i is a γ-index of a total function then $(\nu_i=\gamma_i)\Leftrightarrow(i\in\bar{A})$.

We introduce a set $c=\{c(2\cdot 0+1,0),c(2\cdot 1+1,0),c(2\cdot 2+1,0),\ldots\}$. For arbitrary k the cardinality of $C\cap\{0,1,2,\ldots,2k^2\}$ is no less than k. On the other hand, in $\{0,1,2,\ldots,2k^2+k\}$ there are no more than $\log_2(2k^2+k)$ elements of A. Hence $C\cap\bar{A}$ is infinite. Hence G correctly identifies ν-indices for an infinite class of constant functions.

We will use this strategy G to define new Goedel numberings.

The numberings $\mu=\{\mu_j\}$ is defined by a shuffle of $\{\nu_i\}$ and $\{\psi_i\}$ which puts $2i^2$ equal functions ψ_i immediately after ν_{2i^2}. Note that all the minimal μ-indices come from $\{\nu_i\}$.

We denote by G' the strategy which produces as the results the corresponding μ-indices instead of ν-indices produced by G.

Now we describe the construction of the numbering φ. First we fix some procedures of parallel computation of functions μ_j, j=0,1,... . Let $\mu_i(x_1),\mu_i(x_2),\ldots,\mu_i(x_m),\ldots$ be values of μ_i in the order of their appearance during the parallel computation. Assume that $\mu_i(x_1),\ldots,\mu_i(x_r)$ are already computed and $(x_1,\mu_i(x_1)),\ldots,(x_r,\mu_i(x_r))$ are included in the graph of φ_i. Carry out the two following procedures simultaneously.

PROCEDURE 1. Compute $\mu_i(x_{r+1})$, $\mu_i(x_{r+2}),\ldots$. After every step k of computation find the maximal m_k such that the result $\mu_i^k(x)$ of computing k step for $\mu_i(x)$ is defined for every $x\le m_k$, and compute $a_k:=G'(<\mu_i^{[m_k]}>)$. If a_k appears with the property $a_k\le i$ then, for every $\mu_i(x_t)$ computed up to the moment k, include $(x_t,\mu_i(x_t))$ in the graph of φ_i.

PROCEDURE 2. Compute $\mu_i(x_{r+1})$. If $\mu_i(x_{r+1})$ halts in some step k, find $m \geq k$ and pairwise distinct numbers $j_1, j_2, \ldots, j_c \leq i$ such that $c > 2(j_1)^2$, and for every $j \in \{j_1, j_2, \ldots, j_c\}$ there holds $\mu_i^k[k] \subseteq \mu_i^m[m]$. If such m and $j_1, j_2, \ldots, j_c$ have been found, include $(x_{r+1}, \mu_i(x_{r+1}))$ in the graph of φ_i.

After any halting of PROCEDURE 1 or PROCEDURE 2 and after including a new pair in the graph of ji renew PROCEDURE 1 and PROCEDURE 2 for new $\mu_i(x_{r+1})$, $\mu_i(x_{r+2}), \ldots$.

The definition of φ_i is completed.

Clearly, φ is a computable numbering of partial recursive functions. To prove that $\varphi \in \mathfrak{G}$ it suffices to prove that μ is reducible to φ. We will use the following property of our construction. If i is not one of first $2(\min_\mu f)^2$ μ-indices of f then $\varphi_i = \mu_i$. (Indeed, for such an i PROCEDURE 2 halts for every $\mu_i(x_{r+1})$.)

Now we prove that φ is a Goedel numbering. Let μ_i be an arbitrary partial recursive function. Given j, one can effectively find a μ-index $i > j$ for μ_i such that at least $c > 2j^2$ μ-indices of μ_i are between j and i. (The well-known padding technique can be used, see [Rog 67]. Define $g(j) = i$. Obviously, g reduces μ to φ.

Now we prove that G' identifies minimal φ-indices for infinitely many total functions. Indeed, let $U \in EX_\mu(G')$, $f \in U$ and $\lim_{k \to \infty} G'(\langle f^{[k]} \rangle) = i$. Then $\mu_i = f$. We have to prove that $\varphi_i = f$ and $\varphi_j \neq f$ for all $j < i$. The functions φ_i and f equal since PROCEDURE 1 halts infinitely often. Further, i is one of the first $2(\min_\mu f)^2$ μ-indices of μ_i. Hence if $j < i$ and $\mu_i = f$ then there is no set $\{j_1, j_2, \ldots, j_c\}$ of m-indices for f such that $j_m < j$, $1 \leq m \leq c$.

Hence we get that there is a step k_0 such that for arbitrary $j_1, j_2, \ldots, j_c < j$, $c > 2(j_1)^2$, $m \geq k_0$ there is at least one $j \in \{j_1, j_2, \ldots, j_c\}$ with the property $\mu_i^{k_0}[k_0] \not\subseteq \mu_i^m[m]$.

Obviously, PROCEDURE 2 never halts after step k_0. On the other hand, $f \in EX_\mu(G')$. Hence there is a k_1 such that $a_k = G'(\langle \mu_i^{[m_k]} \rangle) = i$ and $i > j$ for all $k \geq k_1$ and m_k defined in PROCEDURE 1. Hence PROCEDURE 1 also never halts after the moment k_1. We see that no pair $(x, \mu_j(x))$ is included in the graph of φ_j at the steps $k \geq \max(k_0, k_1)$. Hence $\varphi_j \neq f$. ❑

THEOREM 4.6. There is a Goedel numbering φ such that:

1) there is an infinite class U of total recursive functions such that $U \in EX_\varphi^{min}$,

2) every class $U \in EX_\varphi^{min}$ is contained in an effectively enumerable cass V of total recursive functions such that $V \in EX_\varphi^{min}$.

PROOF. Let ψ be the Goedel numbering for which EX_ψ^{min} consists of finite classes only (see Theorem 4.1). Now we consider the numbering φ:

$$\varphi_i(x)=\begin{cases}\psi_j(0), & \text{if } i=2j,\\ \psi_j(x), & \text{if } i=2j+1.\end{cases}$$

The minimal φ-indices for the class of all constants can be identified in the limit by finding the minimal even i such that $\varphi_i(0)$ (which equals $\psi_j(0)$ such that i=2j) equals f(0) (where f is the function to be identified).

Now we prove the assertion 2). Let $U\in EX_\varphi^{min}$. We consider the class U \ CONSTANTS and denote it by U_1. Assume that U_1 is infinite. It is easy to see that all φ-indices for functions in U_1 are odd. Moreover, for arbitrary $f\in U_1$, $min_\varphi(f)=2min_\varphi(f)+1$. Hence, a strategy exists which identifies in the limit the minimal ψ-indices for an infinite class U_1. Contradiction. ❑

5. UNIONS OF IDENTIFIABLE CLASSES

J.M.Barzdin [Bar 74] constructed a pair of classes of total recursive functions U_1, U_2 such that $U_1\in EX$, $U_2\in EX$, and $U_1\cup U_2\notin BC$. Since then many similar results have been proved for another types of inductive inference. A similar theorem is valid for EX^{min}-identification as well.

THEOREM 5.1. There are classes U_1 and U_2 of total recursive functions and a Kolmogorov numbering ψ such that $U_1\in EX_\psi^{min}$, $U_2\in EX_\psi^{min}$ and $U_1\cup U_2\notin BC$.

PROOF. We fix a Kolmogorov numbering φ or all 1-argument partial recursive functions and a Goedel numbering $\{F_i\}$ of partial recursive strategies. Let $\{F'_i\}$ denote the corresponding numbering of total recursive strategies (see Lemma 1.1.).

The class $U=U_1\cup U_2$ is constructed such that it cannot be BC-identified by any F'_i. The total recursive function being the counterexample for F'_i will be connected (but maybe not quite identical) to the following function g_i constructed as follows.

STEP 0. Define $g_i(0)=i$. Go on to Step 1.

STEP m (m>0). Assume g_i is defined for $x\in[0,r-1]$. We denote the sequence $(q_i(0),q_i(1),\dots,q_i(r-1))$ by α. Include the value $F'_i(<\alpha>)$ in the list A.

SUBSTEP(m,t) (t=1,2,...) Define $g_i(r+t)=0$. (Note that $g_i(r)$ is not defined yet). Compute $F'_i(<\alpha 0^t>)$ and if it is not included in the list A, include it. Then for every $k\in A$ compute t steps of $\varphi_k(r)$. If $\varphi_k(r)=0$ for at least one $k\in A$ then define $g_i(r)=1$ and go to the Step 1. If for every $k\in A$ either $\varphi_k(r)\neq 0$ or t steps do not suffice for the convergence then go to the Substep (m,t+1).

It is easy to see that either g_i is total (if infinitely many steps are performed) or g_i is defined but for one value x=r.

We define

$$f_i(x)=\begin{cases} g_i(x), \text{ if } g_i(x) \text{ defined,} \\ 0, \text{ otherwise,} \end{cases}$$

and $U=\{f_i \mid i=0,1,...\}$. Every f_i is a total recursive function. From the construction, $U \notin BC$.

We define

$U_1=\{f_i \mid g_i \text{ is total}\}$,

$U_2=\{f_i \mid g_i \text{ is not total}\}$.

Now we will prove that $U_1, U_2 \in EX_\psi^{min}$. We construct the following Goedel numbering ψ. For every i, $\psi_{3i+2}=\varphi_i$ and hence ψ is a Kolmogorov numbering along with the given φ. For every i, the function $\psi_{3i}(x)=g_i(x)$, and $\psi_{3i}(x)$ is defined sequentially for x=0,1,2,... . For every x it is defined by a parallel computation of $\varphi_i(x)$ and $g_i(x)$. The value $\psi_{2i}(x)$ equals that of the two values which is computed first.

Note that ψ_{3i} is either empty function (if $\varphi_i(x)$ is not defined) or total one. There is an algorithm $\mathfrak{M}$ uniform in i and enumerating these i for which $\psi_{3i}(0)=\varphi_i(0)$ but ψ_{2i} is not equal f_i. This algorithm tries to find an x for which $\psi_{3i}(x)$ and $g_i(x)$ are defined but not equal.

To identify ψ-minimal indices for U_1, the strategy uses f(0) to find a corresponding ψ_{3i+1} with $\psi_{3i+1}(0)=f(0)$ (3i+1 is a correct ψ-index but may be not the minimal one) and then searches among all 3j and 3j+1 and where j<i for the minimal number z such that $\psi_z(0)=f(0)$, and either z=3j and the algorithm $\mathfrak{M}$ has not yet rejected z or z=3j+1, and $\mathfrak{M}$ has rejected z because of $\psi_{3j+1}(a)=\varphi_j(a)\neq g_j(a)$ but $g_j(a)=f(a)$.

To identify ψ-minimal indices for U_2, the strategy uses the initial fragment (f(0),f(1),...,f(y)) up to the latest value y for which f(y)=1. It searches among all 3j for the minimal one with $\psi_{3j}(0)=f(0),...,\psi_{3j}(0)=f(y)$. Since $f \in U_2$, the initial fragment is changed only finite number of times. ❑

On the other hand, we will see from the subsequent Theorem 2.2 that there are some classes U and some Goedel numberings such that union with such U does not decrease the identifiability of any class. Such a class U can be considered as the easiest for the identification of the minimal indices.

We do not know what can be said about existence of such easiest classes for EX_φ^{min}-identification in arbitrary Goedel numberings.

Theorem 1.1 shows that for some Goedel numberings there is no infinite easiest class but every finite class, of course, has the needed property.

Theorem 2.2 serves two purposes in this paper. One purpose is to show that there is no best (for the EX^{min}-identification) Goedel numbering. We shall reconsider this in Section 3. The other purpose is to show that Goedel numberings which allow the easiest classes are arbitrabily high in the partial ordering of Goedel numbering with respect to EX^{min}-identification.

THEOREM 5.2. For arbitrary $\varphi \in \mathfrak{G}$ there is a $\psi \in \mathfrak{G}$ and an effectively enumerable class U such that $U \notin EX_\varphi^{min}$ and for arbitrary class V either in EX_φ^{min} or in EX_ψ^{min} it holds $U \cup V \in EX_\psi^{min}$.

PROOF. Let w(i,k) be a total recursive function such that

$$\varphi_{w(i,k)}(x) = \begin{cases} \varphi_i(x), & \text{if } x \neq 2, \\ k, & \text{if } x = 2. \end{cases}$$

Let be $v(i) = \max(\max_{k \leq 2} w(i,k), i)$. Hence $v(i) \geq i$.

For arbitrary pair (i,j) we shall show how one can effectively enumerate a class U_{ij}. Then U equals $\bigcup_{i} \bigcup_{j} U_{ij}$. Since the enumeration of U_{ij} is uniform in i and j, the class U is enumerable as well.

Let i and j be given. We construct simultaneously the class U_{ij} and a partial recursive function $\varphi_{g_j(i)}$. At every stage m of our enumerating procedure we add no more than one new function to the class U_{ij} and the functions already in the class are additionaly defined either only for x=m or for all $x \geq m$. The function $\varphi_{g_j(i)}$ is additionally defined no more than for a finite number of values of the argument. Every integer $r \leq v(i)$ may be at some stage be marked. After being marked such an r never becomes unmarked again.

We fix a numbering of all possible strategies $\{F_j\}$.

We define $\varphi_{g_j(i)}(0)=i$, $\varphi_{g_j(i)}(1)=j$. Further on, every new function added to the class U_{ij} at an arbitrary stage will equal i at zero and equal j at one.

<u>Stage 1.</u> Go to the Stage 2.

<u>Stage 2.</u> The first function u(x) is added to the (empty up to now) class U_{ij} and u(2)=1 is defined. Go to the Stage 3.

<u>Stage m.</u> Let $\varphi_{g_j(i)}$ be defined for all $x \leq s$ (maybe but x=2). Let u(x) be the latest function added to U_{ij} up to this step. We assume that u(x) is defined for all x<m and all the other functions already in U_{ij} are total.

(1) We compute m steps for each of $\varphi_0(2), \varphi_1(2), \ldots, \varphi_i(2)$. We look for an n such that $\varphi_n(2)$ is defined and $\varphi_n(2)=u(2)$. If no such n is found, we go to the substage (2). If such an n is found, we mark it, define u(x)=0 for all $x \geq m$ and add the following function $u^{(1)}$ to U_{ij}:

$$u^{(1)}(x) = \begin{cases} u(x), & \text{if } x<m \text{ and } x \neq 2, \\ u(x)+1, & \text{if } x=2. \end{cases}$$

Go to the Substage (2).

(2) Let u' be the latest function in U_{ij}. For all $x<m$ let

$$\alpha_x=\begin{cases}\varphi_{g_j(i)}(x), & \text{if } \varphi_{g_j(i)}(x) \text{ already defined,}\\ u'(x), & \text{otherwise.}\end{cases}$$

We compute m steps for each of

$F_j(<\alpha_0\alpha_1\ldots\alpha_s>),F_j(<\alpha_0\alpha_1\ldots\alpha_{s+1}>),\ldots,F_j(<\alpha_0\alpha_1\ldots\alpha_{m-1}>)$. (*)

If no of these values is computed then we define $u'(m)=1$ and go to the stage $m+1$.

Assume that one abovementioned value is found. Let $r=F_j(<\alpha_0\ldots\alpha_k>)$ be the rightmost of them and r' be the rightmost of the same values (*) computed in m-1 steps.

If $r\neq r'$ or $r>v(i)$ or r marked then for all $x\in\{s+1,s+2,\ldots,k\}$ we define $\varphi_{g_j(i)}(x)=u'(x)$, $u'(m)=1$ and go the Stage $m+1$. Otherwise we go to the Substage (3).

(3) We have an unmarked $r\leq v(i)$. We compute m steps of $\varphi_r(k_1)$ where $k_1=\max(3,k)$. If $\varphi_r(k_1)$ does not converge in m steps or $\varphi_r(k_1)\neq u'(k_1)$ then we define $u'(m)=1$ and go to the stage $m+1$.

If $\varphi_r(k_1)$ converges and $\varphi_r(k_1)=u'(k_1)$ then we mark r and define $u'(x)=0$ for all $x\geq m$ and add a new function $u^{(2)}$ to the class U_{ij}:

$$u^{(2)}(x)=\begin{cases}u'(x), & \text{if } x\leq m \text{ and } x\neq k_1\\ u'(x)+1, & \text{if } x=k_1.\end{cases}$$

Subsequently, for all x such that $s\leq x\leq k_1$ we define $\varphi_{g_j(i)}(x)=u^{(2)}(x)$ and go to the Stage $m+1$.

We have concluded the description of the procedure. It is easy to see that U is effectively enumerable class of total recursive functions. For arbitrary j the function gj is total recursive. For arbitrary i,j all the functions $u^{(1)},u^{(2)},\ldots$ are different.

Note the following properties of $f\in U_{ij}$. If $f(x)=0$ for an $x\geq 3$ then $f(y)=0$ for all $y>x$. If f is the last function added to U_{ij} then $f(x)\neq 0$ for all $x\geq 3$.

Now we prove that $U\notin EX_\varphi^{min}$.

Assume from the contrary that F_j identifies in the limit the minimal φ-indices of the functions in U (and hence in $\bigcup_i U_{ij}$). Let a be a fixed point for g_j, i.e. $\varphi_{g_j(a)}=\varphi_a$.

Note that the class U_{aj} is finite. Indeed, at substages (1) no more than a+2 functions can be added to U_{aj}. At substages (2) no functions are added, and at substages (3) at most v(a)+2 are added to U_{aj}.

Let $\bar{u}$ be the last function added to U_{aj}. We shall prove that

$$\lim_{n\to\infty} F_j(<\bar{u}^{[n]}>)\neq \min\nolimits_\varphi(\bar{u}).$$

First we note that $p=\lim_{n\to\infty} Fj(<\bar{u}^{[n]}>)>v(a)$

since otherwise p would be marked at some stage and $\bar{u}$ would differ from φ_p. But we see that beginning from a stage m the integer p is the rightmost value in (*). It follows from the definition of the substage (2) that because of p>v(a) the function $\varphi_{g(a)}(x)$ is defined for all x≠2. Easy to see that $\varphi_{g(a)}$ equals $\bar{u}$ for all x≠2 since at every stage m the value $\varphi_{g(a)}$ is defined using the corresponding value of the latest function in U_{ij}. It follows from the definition of the substage (1) that $\bar{u}(2)\leq a+2$. Now from the definitions of w(a,k), v and

the equality $\varphi_a=\varphi_{g(a)}$ we get $p=\lim_{n\to\infty} F_j(<\bar{u}^{[n]}>)\leq v(a)$

Contradiction. Hence $U\notin EX_\varphi^{min}$.

Now we construct the needed numbering ψ. Between every two neighbouring functions φ_{l-1} and φ_l we insert v(l)+3 auxiliary functions. Hence it is easy to reduce φ to ψ. On the other hand, all the functions inserted between φ_{l-1} and φ_l are chosen to make difficult identification of the minimal ψ-indices.

If φ_l is not defined either on 0, or on 1, or on 2 then all the auxiliary functions between φ_{l-1} and φ_l are nowhere defined.

Let $\varphi_l(0)=i$, $\varphi_l(1)=j$ and $\varphi_l(2)$ be defined. By n_k we denote the ψ-index of the k-th function preceding φ_l in the numbering ψ:

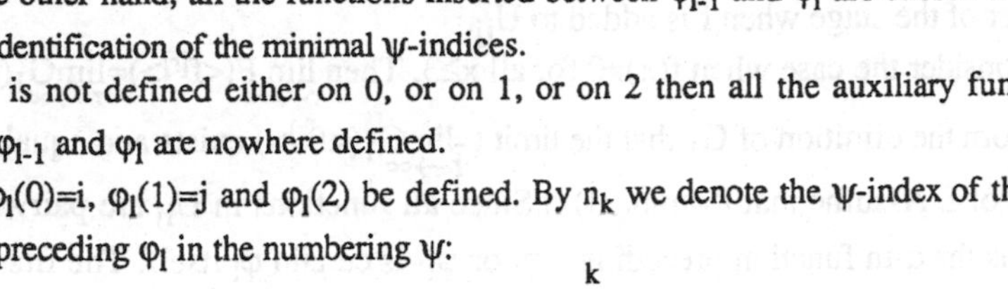

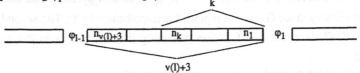

Fig.1.

At first we consider the case k<v(l)+3. To define ψ_{n_k} we enumerate the class U_{ij}. If this class contains less than k functions then ψ_{n_k} is nowhere defined. Let U_{ij} contain at least k functions, the k-th function in the enumeration of U_{ij} be u_k, and m be the number of the stage at which U_k is added to U_{ij}. We compute $\varphi_l^{[m]}$. If $\varphi_l^{[m]}=u_k^{[m]}$ then we define $\psi_{n_k}=u_k$, otherwise ψ_{n_k} is nowhere defined.

Now we define ψ_{n_k} for k=v(l)+3. We compute $\varphi_l(3),\varphi_l(4),...$ (in that order). If for an r we have got $\varphi_l(r)=0$ then $\psi_{n_k}=\varphi_l^{[r]}0^\infty$, otherwise ψ_{n_k} is nowhere defined.

This concludes the definition of the Goedel numbering ψ (which is computable and φ is reducible to ψ).

We are going to prove that $V\in EX_\varphi^{min}$ or $V\in EX_\psi^{min}$ imply $U\cup V\in EX_\psi^{min}$. First, we prove the case $U\in EX_\psi^{min}$.

To this goal, we consider two auxiliary strategies G_1 and G_2.

Let f be arbitrary function in U. For r≤2 we define $G_1(<f^{[r]}>)=0$. Let now be r>2. From i=f(0) and j=f(1) we find the index q in the enumeration of U_{ij} for the first function with the initial fragment $f^{[r]}$ which is in U_{ij}. Let m denote the stage at which this function is added to U_{ij}. We compute r steps of $\varphi_0^{[m]},\varphi_1^{[m]},\ldots\varphi_r^{[m]}$ and find the least l such that $\varphi_l^{[m]}$ is defined, $\varphi_l^{[m]}=f^{[m]}$ and q<v(l)+3. (If there is no such l then $G_1(<f^{[r]}>)=0$).

For $G_1(<f^{[r]}>)$ we take the ψ-index of the k-th function preceding φ_l in the numbering ψ (see Fig. 1). Thus G_1 is a partial recursive strategy defined for all $f\in U$.

Now we define the strategy G_2. If all $f(3),f(4),\dots,f(r)$ differ from 0 then $G_2(<f^{[r]}>)=G_1(<f^{[r]}>)$. Otherwise we find the least $k\geq 3$ such that $f(k)=0$ and compute r steps of $\varphi_0^{[k]},\varphi_1^{[k]},\dots,\varphi_r^{[k]}$. We search for the least $p\leq r$ such that $\varphi_p^{[k]}=f^{[k]}$ (if there is no such p then $G_2(<f^{[r]}>=G_1(<f^{[r]}>)$ and we take for $G_2(<f^{[r]}>)$ the ψ-index of the $(v(p)+3)$-th function preceding φ_p in the numbering ψ (see Fig.1). Again, G_2 is a partial recursive strategy defined for all $f\in U$. Now we consider the strategy $F(<f^{[r]}>)=\min(G_1(<f^{[r]}>),G_2(<f^{[r]}>))$. We are going to prove that $\lim_{r\to\infty} F(<f^{[r]}>)=\min_\psi(f)$ for all $f\in U$.

Let $f\in U,f(0)=i,f(1)=j$. Let f be the q-th function in the enumeration of U_{ij} and m be the number of the stage when f is added to U_{ij}.

We consider the case when $f(x)\neq 0$ for all $x\geq 3$. Then $\lim_{r\to\infty} F(<f^{[r]}>)=\lim_{r\to\infty} G_1(<f^{[r]}>)$. It follows from the efinition of G_1 that the limit $t=\lim_{r\to\infty} G_1(<f^{[r]}>)$ exists and equals a ψ-index of f. Assume that $t'=\min_\psi(f)<t$.Since all functions in U_{ij} are pairwise distinct, either $\psi_{t'}$ is the q-th function preceding a φ_l or $\psi_{t'}$ is certain φ_l itself. The first possibility is self-contradictory since G_1 would replace the hypothesis t by t'. The second possibility implies $q>v(l)+2$ since the q-th function preceding the function φ_l in the numbering ψ would be f.

We shall get the contradiction by proving $q\leq v(l)+2$.

It follows from the procedure enumerating U_{ij} that the class contains no more than $v(i)+2$ distinct functions. Since v is monotone, it suffices to prove that $i\leq l$. We have $\varphi_l(x)\neq 0$ for $x\geq 3$. It follows from the definition of U_{ij} that φ_l is the last function in U_{ij}. Such a function differs from all $\varphi_0,\varphi_1,\dots,\varphi_i$. Hence $\min_\varphi(\varphi_l)>i$. When φ is reduced to ψ, the index l becomes $t'=\min_\psi(\varphi_l)$. Hence $\min_\varphi(\varphi_l)=l$ and $l>i$. This concludes the consideration of the case $f(x)\neq 0$ for all $x\geq 3$.

Now we consider the case when there is a $p\geq 3$ such that $f(p)=0$. Let p be the minimal one. Then the limits $\lim_{r\to\infty} G_1(<f^{[r]}>)$ and $\lim_{r\to\infty} G_2(<f^{[r]}>)$ exist. Hence the limit $t=\lim_{r\to\infty} F(<f^{[r]}>)$ exists as well. First we consider the subcase $t=\lim_{r\to\infty} G_2(<f^{[r]}>)$. Since $f\in U$ the subcase $t=\lim_{r\to\infty} G_2(<f^{[r]}>)$. Since $f\in U$ then $f(p)=0$ implies $f(x)=0$ for all $x\geq p$. But then from the definition of G_2 we conclude that $t=\min_\psi(f)$.

Now we consider the subcase $t=\lim_{r\to\infty} G_1(<f^{[r]}>)$. Then $t=\lim_{r\to\infty} G_2(<f^{[r]}>)$ as well. Assume $t'=\min_\psi(f)<t$. The index t' cannot be in the interval between φ_{l-1} and φ_l since otherwise G_1 would change the hypothesis t into t'. Hence t' is an index for a φ_l. But then $\varphi_l=f$ and a function preceding φ_l in ψ would equal f. It follows from the definition of G_2that $\lim_{r\to\infty} G_2\ (<f^{[r]}>)<t'<t$. Contradiction.

Hence F identifies in the limit the minimal ψ-indices for U. We have either $V\in EX_\varphi^{min}$ or $V\in EX_\psi^{min}$. If $V\in EX_\varphi^{min}$ then we denote by G a strategy identifying in the limit the minimal φ-indices for the functions in V and by $\check{C}$ we denote a strategy which produces hypotheses being the results of reduction $\varphi\to\psi$ from hypotheses by G. If $V\in EX_\psi^{min}$ then we denote by $\check{C}$ a strategy identifying in the limit the minimal ψ-indices for the functions in V.

Let τ be a computable one-one numbering of U. The minimal ψ-indices for $V\cup U$ can be identified by the following strategy H. It tries to find an n such that $\tau_n(0)=f(0)$ and $\tau_n(1)=f(1)$. While no such n is found the strategy H outputs the same hypotheses as $\check{C}$. When H finds the first n with this property, H starts to output the same hypotheses as F and does this while $f^{[r]}=\tau_n^{[r]}$. When an r is found such that $f^{[r]}\neq\tau_n^{[r]}$ the strategy H again starts to output the same hypotheses as $\check{C}$ and, in parallel, tries to find new n such that $\tau_n(0)=f(0)$, $\tau_n(1)=f(1)$. After finding such an n the strategy H copies hypotheses of F while $f^{[r]}=\tau_n^{[r]}$, etc. Only a finite number of functions in τ have the property $\tau_n(0)=f(0)$ and $\tau_n(1)=f(1)$.

Hence either $\lim_{r\to\infty} H(<f^{[r]}>)=\lim_{r\to\infty} F(<f^{[r]}>)$ or $\lim_{r\to\infty} H(<f^{[r]}>)=\lim_{r\to\infty} \check{C}(<f^{[r]}>)$. The first case implies $f\notin U$ and $f\in V$. The intervals between any two φ_{l-1} and φ_l in the numbering ψ contain only functions from U (or empty functions). Hence $min_\varphi(f)$ is the result of the standard reduction of $min_\varphi(f)$. Hence

$\lim_{r\to\infty} H(<f[r]>)=min_\psi(f)$. Q.E.D. ❑

6. STRUCTURE OF THE PARTIAL ORDERING

The usual reducibility of computable numberings $\psi\leq\varphi$ means the existence of an algorithm which, for arbitrary function ψ_i finds its φ-index j ($\varphi_j=\psi_i$). There are equivalent numberings (e.g. all Goedel numberings are equivalent). The partial ordering P_1 of the equivalence classes of the computable numberings of partial recursive functions is studied intensively (see [Ersh 77]). It is known that P_1 is upper semilattice but it is not lower semilattice.

We considered another reducibility of the same computable numberings in [Fre 74]. We use $\psi\leq_{EX}\varphi$ to denote that for arbitrary class U of total recursive functions $U\in EX_\psi$ implies $U\in EX_\varphi$. It is easy to see that if $\psi\leq\varphi$ then $y\leq_{EX}\varphi$.

Let P_2 be the partial ordering of the equivalence classes with respect to $\leq_{EX}$. It was proved in {Fre 74] that P_1 and P_2 are very much different.

Now we introduce another reducibility $\psi\leq_{min}\varphi$. We use $\psi\leq_{min}\varphi$ to denote that if for arbitrary class U of total recursive functions $U\in EX\psi^{min}$ implies $U\in EX_\varphi^{min}$. Note that $\psi\leq\varphi$ does not imply $\psi\leq_{min}\varphi$. Theorems in Section 1 show that even Goedel numberings which are recursively isomorphic [Rog 58] are far from being min-equivalent.

The numbering constructed in Theorem 1.1.is in the minimum element of P_3 (the partial ordering of computable numberings with respect to $\leq_{min}$) but it is known that there is no minimum element in P_1.

Our Theorem 2.2. shows that there is no maximum element (and even no maximal elements) in P_3. On the contrary, there is the maximum element in P_1. This maximum element consist of Goedel numberings.

Now we will prove that P_3 is lower semilatice. To this, we will prove that for arbitrary $\varphi, \chi \in \mathfrak{G}$ there is the "best" numbering among the Goedel numberings ψ such that $EX_{\psi}^{min} \subseteq EX_{\varphi}^{min}$ and $EX_{\psi}^{min} \subseteq EX_{\chi}^{min}$.

THEOREM 6.1 Let $\varphi, \chi \in \mathfrak{G}$. There is a Goedel numbering ψ such that:
(a) $\psi \leq \varphi$, $\psi \leq \chi$,
(b) $(\forall æ \in \mathfrak{G})((æ \leq \varphi) \ \& \ (æ \leq \chi) \Rightarrow (æ \leq \psi))$.

PROOF. Let c(i,j) be a Cantor numbering of pairs:
c(0,0)=0,c(0,1)=1,,c(1,0)=2,c(0,2)=3,c(2,0)=5,c(0,3)=6,...
For all i,j,x we define

$$\psi_{c(i,j)}(x)= \begin{cases} \varphi_i(x), \text{ if } \varphi_i(x)=\chi_j(x), \\ \\ \text{undefined, if otherwise.} \end{cases}$$

$\psi_{c(i,j)}$ can be total only if φ_i is total, χ_j is total and $\varphi_i=\chi_j$. For our c(i,j) and for arbitrary total recursive function f, $\min_{\psi}(f)=c(\min_{\varphi}(f),\min_{\chi}(f))$.

This makes the properties (a) and (b) obvious. ❑

Unfortunately, we do not know whether P_3 is upper semilattice. This problem has resisted all attempts since 1977 when it was posed in [FK 77].

Another open problem in [FK 77] questions whether or not for two arbitrary classes $U_1 \in EX^{min}$ and $U_2 \in EX^{min}$ there is a Goedel numbering φ such that $U_1 \in EX_{\varphi}^{min}$ and $U_1 \in EX_{\varphi}^{min}$

I would not be much surprised to find out that the answers to these two problems may be opposite.

THEOREM 6.2 There are Goedel numberings $æ, \psi \in \mathfrak{G}$ and classes U_1, U_2 of total recursive functions such that $U_1 \in EX_{æ}^{min} \setminus EX_{\psi}^{min}$ and $U_2 \in EX_{\psi}^{min} \setminus EX_{æ}^{min}$.

PROOF. Let φ be arbitrary Goedel numbering. We define $æ_{3i+2}(x)=\psi_{3i+2}(x)=\varphi_i(x)$,

$$æ_{3i}(x)= \begin{cases} 2a, \text{ if } (\varphi_i(0)=2a) \ \& \ (\exists n)(F'_a(<(2a)^{x+n}>)\neq 3i), \\ 2a+1, \text{ if } \varphi_i(0)=2a+1, \\ \text{undefined, otherwise,} \end{cases}$$

$$æ_{3i+1}(x)=\begin{cases} 2a, \text{ if } (\varphi_i(0)=2a) \ \& \ (\exists n)(F'_a(<(2a)^{x+n}>)\neq 3i+1), \\ 2a+1, \text{ if } \varphi_i(0)=2a+1, \\ \text{undefined, otherwise,} \end{cases}$$

$$\psi_{3i}(x)=\begin{cases} 2a+1, \text{ if } (\varphi_i(0)=2a+1) \ \& \ (\exists n)(F'_a(<(2a)^{x+n}>)\neq 3i).. \\ 2a \ , \text{ if } \varphi_i(0)=2a, \\ \text{undefined, otherwise,} \end{cases}$$

$$\psi_{3i+1}(x)=\begin{cases} 2a+1, \text{ if } (\varphi_i(0)=2a+1) \ \& \ (\exists n)(F'_a(<(2a+1)^{x+n}>)\neq 3i+1),. \\ 2a, \text{ if } \varphi_i(0)=2a, \\ \text{undefined, otherwise,} \end{cases}$$

$U_1=\{2a+1 \mid a\in N\}$.
$U_2=\{2a \mid a\in N\}$.

$U_1\in EX_{æ}^{min}$ via strategy searching for the minimal 3i such that $\varphi_i(0)=f(0)$. The same strategy serves to prove that $U_2\in EX_{\psi}^{min}$.

Assume $U_1\in EX_{\psi}^{min}(F'_a)$ and consider the constant function $(2a+1)^{\infty}\in U_1$. Either $(\exists^{\infty}n)(F'_a(<(2a+1)^n>)\neq 3i)$ or $(\exists^{\infty}n)(F'_a(<(2a+1)^n>)\neq 3i+1)$, or both. Any case, the minimal ψ-index is either 3i or 3i+1 but F'_a does not identify it in the limit.

Similary, $U_2\notin EX_{æ}^{min}$. ❑

7. NEARLY MINIMAL INDICES

We allow only "special" (e.g. minimal) indices to be produced as the results of the identification in this paper. The restrictions are softened in this section and we prove that at least some properties that differ EX^{min} from EX are caused not by the minimality of the required results but merely by the fact that they are taken from a set of small cardinality.

Let ψ be an arbitrary computable numbering of 1-argument partial recursive functions and c be an arbitrary positive integer. We consider a set S of the "special" ψ-indices and demand that every total recursive function has at least one index in S. We call the set S c-bounded if for arbitrary total recursive function the set of the ψ-indices for f intersects with S in a set of cardinality not exceeding c. We say that a strategy F identifies in the limit the
S-ψ-indices for a class U($U\in EX_{\psi}^{S}$) if for arbitrary $f\in U$ the limit $\lim_{x\to\infty} F(<f^{[x]}>)$ exists and equals to a such that $a\in S$ and $\psi_a=f$.

THEOREM 7.1. Given an arbitrary computable numbering ψ, $c\geq 1$ and c-bounded set S of ψ-indices, there exists an effectively enumerable class U such that $U\notin EX_{\psi}^{S}$.

PROOF. Assume that there is ψ, $c\geq 1$ and a c-bounded S such that all effectively enumerable classes are in $EX_\psi{}^S$. Since the strategy F'_i (see Section 1) produces the same result as the corresponding strategy F_i, we can assume that the abovementioned effectively enumerable classes can be identified by strategies in $\{F'_i\}$.

We will construct classes $U_1, U_2, U_3, \ldots$ in this proof such that simultaneous $EX_\psi{}^S$-identifiability of $U_1, U_2, U_3, \ldots, U_{i+1}$ contradicts the c-boundedness of S since the strategies produce pairwise distinct results.

Induction basis. U_1 is defined as the class of all total functions f such that $\lim_{x\to\infty} f(x)=0$. The class U_1 is effectively enumerable. From the assumption, There is a strategy G_1 which identifies in the limit S-ψ-indices for U_1.

Induction step. Let $j\in\{1,2,3,\ldots\}$. Assume by induction that effectively enumerable classes $U_1,\ldots,U_j$ have already been constructed and they are $EX_\psi{}^S$-identifiable in the limit by strategies $G_1,\ldots,G_j$, respectively, and $G_1,\ldots,G_{j-1}$ are the strategies used to define the classes $U_2,\ldots,U_j$. Assume that there is an algorithm $\mathfrak{M}_j$ uniform in n and p where $U_j\in EX_\psi{}^S(F_n)$ and p is the Cantor index of an arbitrary string of integers $\{y_0,y_1,\ldots,y_m\}$ (m is arbitrary as well) and $\mathfrak{M}_j$ produces a φ-index of a total function f such that:

1) $f(0)=y_0$, $f(1)=y_1$,..., $f(m)=y_m$,

2) $f\in U_1\cap U_2\cap\ldots\cap U_j$,

3) the strategies $G_1,\ldots G_j$ produce pairwise distinct ψ-indices of f.

Returning to the induction basis, note that $\mathfrak{M}_1$ produces the program for the function $f(0)=y_0,\ldots f(m)=y_m$, $f(m+1)=f(m+2)=\ldots=0$.

We construct $U_{j+1}=\{h_z(x)\}$ by describing an algorithm uniform in z and x to compute $h_z(x)$. For every z the construction will be performed in stages. The function h_z is defined following a certain example f. We call it the current master-function.

Stage 0. Let $z=c(i,p)$ and $p=\langle y_0,y_1,\ldots,y_r\rangle$. We define $h_z(0)=y_0$, $h_z(1)=y_1$, ..., $h_z(r)=y_r$. If $p=0$, i.e. p is the index of the empty string then $h_z(0)=0$. We take for the master - function the function which is produced by $\mathfrak{M}_j$ from G_j and p.

Stage s+1. Let $z=c(i,p)$, $p=\langle y_0,y_1,\ldots,y_r\rangle$. Assume that $h_z(0),h_z(1),\ldots,h_z(k)$ have been already defined and $k\geq r$, $h_z(0)=y_0,h_z(1)=y_1,\ldots,h_z(r)=y_r$. Assume that the master-function f is such that:

1) $f\in U_1\cup U_2\cup\ldots\cup U_j$,

2) $h_z(0)=f(0),h_z(1)=f(1),\ldots,h_z(k)=f(k)$

3) no two strategies among $G_1,\ldots G_j$ identify in the limit the same ψ-index of f.

To define $h_z(k+1)$ we compute in parallel: 1) the sequences

$G_1(<f^{[k]}>), G_1(<f^{[k+1]}>), G_1(<f^{[k+2]}>), \ldots$

- -

$G_j(<f^{[k]}>), G_j(<f^{[k+1]}>), G_j(<f^{[k+2]}>), \ldots$

$F_i'(<f^{[k]}>), F_i'(<f^{[k+1]}>), F_i'(<f^{[k+2]}>), \ldots$

and the value

$\psi_{F_i'(<f^{[k]}>)}(k+1)$.

Now we describe a chain of tests connected with these computations. This chain may be cut because of several obstaes described below.

The chain of tests starts with testing whether or not $F_i'(<f^{[k]}>)=F'(<f^{[k+1]}>)$. If yes then we use $F_i'(<f^{[k]}>)=a(k)$ to compute 1 step of $\psi_{a(k)}(k+1)$ and to test whether $\psi_{a(k)}(k+1)=f(k+1)$. If it does not converge or the result differs then we test whether there are $r\in\{1,2,\ldots,j\}$ such that $G_r(<f^{[k]}>)=G_r(<f^{[k+1]}>)$. If there are then we test whether $F_i'(<f^{[k+1]}>)$ differs from all such $G_r(<f^{[k+1]}>)$. If it differs not from all such $G_r(<f^{[k+1]}>)$ then we test whether $F_i'(<f^{[k+1]}>)=F_i'(<f^{[k+2]}>)$. If yes then we use $F_i'(<f^{[k]}>)=a(k)$ to compute 2 steps of $\psi_{a(k)}(k+1)$ and to test whether $\psi_{a(k)}(k+1)=f(k+1)$. If it does not converge or the result differs then we test whether there are $r\in\{1,2,\ldots,j\}$ such that $G_r(<f^{[k]}>)=G_r(<f^{[k+1]}>)=G_r(<f^{[k+2]}>)$. If there are then we test whether $F_r'(<f^{[k+2]}>)$ differs from all such $G_r(<f^{[k+2]}>)$. If it differs not from all such $G_r(<f^{[k+2]}>)$ then we test whether $F_i'(<f^{[k+2]}>)=F_i'(<f^{[k+3]}>)$, etc.

This chain of tests can be cut because of several obstacles:

a) $\psi_{a(k)}(k+1)$ may converge and equal $f(k+1)$;

b) an m can be found such that $F_i'(<f^{[m-1]}>)\neq F_i'(<f^{[m]}>)$;

c) an $m>k$ can be found such that there are no $r\in\{1,2,\ldots,j\}$ such that $G_r(<f^{[k]}>)=G_r(<f^{[k+1]}>)= =\ldots=G_r(<f^{[m]}>)$;

d) an $m>k$ can be found such that $F_i'(<f^{[m]}>)$ differs from all $G_r(<f^{[m]}>)$ ($r\in\{1,2,\ldots,j\}$) such that $G_r(<f^{[k]}>)=G_r(<f^{[k+1]}>)=\ldots=G_r(<f^{[m]}>)$.

In the case a) we define $h_z(k+1)=f(k+1)+1$ and take another master - function being the result of $\mathfrak{M}_j$ from G_j and $<h_z(0),h_z(1),\ldots,h_z(k+1)>$.

In the cases b), c) and d) we define $h_z(k+1)=f(k+1)$, $h_z(k+2)=f(k+2),\ldots,h_z(m)=f(m)$ and the master - function is not changed.

This concudes the description of Stage s+1. Go to the Stage s+2.

We prove now that every stage definetely ends. To this, we prove that every chain of tests end. Ineed, the master - function f is in $U_1, U_2, \ldots, U_j$. The strategies EX - identify these classes. Hence the limits $\lim_{n\to\infty} G_r(<f^{[n]}>)$ exist and equal correct ψ - indices of f. Assume, the chain never ends. Then $F_i'(<f^{[k]}>)=\lim_{n\to\infty} F_i'(<f^{[n]}>)$ and there is an $r\in\{1,2,\ldots,j\}$ such that $\lim_{n\to\infty} G_r(<f^{[n]}>) =\lim_{n\to\infty} F_i'(<f^{[n]}>)$. But then $F_i'(<f^{[k]}>)=a(k)$ is a correct ψ-index of f and $\psi_{a(k)}(k+1)=f(k+1)$. Assumption on the infiniteness of the chain fails.

Now we prove that for arbitrary i and p the function $h_{c(i,p)}$ has the following properties:

A) Let $p=<y_0,y_1,...y_r>$. Then $h_{c(i,p)}(0)=y_0, h_{c(i,p)}(1)=y_1,...,h_{c(i,p)}(r)=y_r$.

B) If the strategy F'_i identifies in the limit a ψ-index for $h_{c(i,p)}$ then $h_{c(i,p)}$ is in all classes $U_1,U_2,...,U_j,U_{j+1}$.

C) If the strategy F'_i identifies in the limit a ψ-index for $h_{c(i,p)}$ then the strategies $G_1,G_2,...,G_j,F'_i$. identify pairwise distinct ψ-indices for this function.

The property A) is obvious. We prove B), C).

Every stage in the contruction of $h_{c(i,p)}$ ends in a), b), c), d). At least one of them occurs infinitely often. In our proof we distinguish between:

1) the case a) occurs infinitely often. Then $h_{c(i,p)} \notin EX_\psi(F_i')$ since F_i' makes infinitely many errors;

2) case b) occurs infinitely often. Then F_i' has infinitely many mindchanges;

3) the cases a) and b) occur no more than finite number of times. Then the master - function is changed only finite number of times. Hence $h_{c(i,p)}$ is in $U_1 \cap ... \cap U_j$. It is in U_{j+1} by the definition of U_{j+1}. We have proved B).

The strategies $G_1,G_2,...,G_j$ have only finite number of mindchanges on the master - function, and their limits are pairwise distinct. If F_i and F'_i as well have only finite number of mindchanges on $h_{c(i,p)}$ then almost all stages end in d). We have proved C).

To complete the induction step it remains to note that the algorithm $\mathfrak{M}_j$ for the number i of the strategy F_i and the Cantor index p of $\{y_0,y_1,...,y_n\}$ produces a φ-index of the function $h_{c(i,p)}$.

We conclude the proof of the Theorem by pointing at the contradiction between the assumed EX_φ^S - identifiability of U_{c+1} for the c-bounded S and the property c) for U_{c+1} which says that (c+1) strategies produce c+1 pairwise distinct results when EX_φ^S - identifying a function. ❑

8. KOLMOGOROV NUMBERINGS

Proofs of the most of theorems above are based on the following construction: an arbitrary Goedel numbering φ is taken and a new computable numbering ψ is constructed such that for a total recursive function g(i) it holds $\psi_{g(i)}=\varphi_i$. We conclude that computability of the numbering y implies its being Goedel, and we are free to use the intervals between $\psi_{g(i-1)}$ and $\psi_{g(i)}$ to construct sets of fuctions either helping to identify the ψ-minimal indices or vice versa: to fail attempts to identify them.

Only in Theorem 2.1 we have been able to keep these intervals of constant length. In most cases the method of the proof demand these intervals being of growing length.

Hence the function g(i) reducing φ to ψ cannot be linearly bounded and ψ cannot be a Kolmogorov numbering.

Theorems in this Section show that rather many of the above proved theorems fail to have counterparts for Kolmogorov numberings.

CONSTANTS= $\{f \mid (\exists c)(\forall x)(f(x)=c)\}$.

THEOREM.8.1. There is a Kolmogorov numbering ψ such that CONSTANTS$\in EX_\psi^{min}$.

PROOF. Let φ be an arbitrary Kolmogorov numbering. Let $\psi_{2i+1}=\varphi_i$ and

$$\psi_{2i}(x)=\begin{cases}\varphi_i(0), & \text{if } \varphi_i(0) \text{ defined,}\\ \text{undefined}, & \text{if } \varphi_i(0) \text{ not defined.}\end{cases}$$

The strategy always output the minimal 2i such that $\varphi_i(0)=f(0)$ for the given f. ❑

THEOREM.8.2. There is a Kolmogorov numbering ψ such that CONSTANTS$\notin EX_\psi^{min}$.

PROOF. Let ψ be an arbitrary Kolmogorov numbering and $\{F_i'\}$ be the family of total recursive strategies described in Section 1. Let $\psi_{3i+2}=\varphi_i$,

$$\psi_{3i}(x)=\begin{cases}\varphi_i(0), \text{ if } F'_{f(0)}(<f^{[y]}>)\neq 3i \text{ for no less than x distinct values of y,}\\ \text{undefined, otherwise,}\end{cases}$$

$$\psi_{3i}(x)=\begin{cases}\varphi_i(0), \text{ if } F'_{f(0)}(<f^{[y]}>)\neq 3i+1 \text{ for no less than x distinct values of y,}\\ \text{undefined, otherwise,}\end{cases}$$

Note that if $\varphi_i(0)$ is defined then at least one of the functions ψ_{3i}, ψ_{3i+1} is the constant $\varphi_i(0)$. Hence the minimal ψ-index for every constant function always equals 0 or 1 (modulo 3).

On the other hand, assume that F'_j EX_ψ^{min}-identifies CONSTANTS. Denote by i the minimal φ-index for functions such that $\varphi_i(0)=j$. Then the minimal ψ-index of the constant j equals either 3i or 3i+1. However it follows from the definitions of ψ_{3i} and ψ_{3i+1} that $\lim_{y\to\infty} F'_j(<f^{[y]}>)\neq 3i$ and $\lim_{y\to\infty} F'_j(<f^{[y]}>)\neq 3i-1$

Contradiction. ❑

THEOREM.8.3. For arbitrary Kolmogorov numbering ψ there is an infinite class U of total recursive functions such that U$\in EX_\psi^{min}$.

PROOF. Let $\{\alpha_i\}$ be arbitrary Kolmogorov numbering of 1-argument partial recursive functions. Consider auxiliary Kolmogorov numbering $\varphi=\{\varphi_i\}$:

$$\varphi_i(x)= \begin{cases} \alpha_j(x), \text{ if } i=2j+1, \\ j, \text{ if } i=2j. \end{cases}$$

Since ψ is Kolmogorov numbering, φ is reducible to ψ by linearly bounded total recursive function. Hence for ψ, there is a positive c such that for arbitrary n the minimal ψ-indices of all the constants $0,1,2,\ldots,n$ do not exceed $c\cdot n$.

Consider the set A_n of all $d\in\{0,1,2,\ldots,n\}$ such that the interval $[0,c\cdot n]$ contain no more than 2c ψ-indices of functions ψ_j such that $\psi_j(0)=d$. It is easy to see that the cardinality of A_n is less than n/2. Note that for these n/2 values d the interval $[0,c\cdot n]$ contains at least one ψ-index of the constant function d.

Now consider 2c strategies $G_1,G_2,\ldots,G_{2c}$. The strategy G_k having learned f(0) identify in the limit k-th minimal ψ-index of a function ψ_j such that $\psi_j(0)=f(0)$. At least one of these strategies identify the minimal ψ-index for infinitely many constants. ❑

9.ABSTRACT THEORY OF IDENTIFICATION TYPES

In this Section we prove a theorem saying that for "natural" identification types there is a "typical" class of total recursive function such that it is the most difficult for the identification.

When we say "identification types" we have in mind specific types stundied many times by many researchers, such types as EX, EX_n^m, EX^{cons} BC, FIN ([Gold 67], [Bar 72], [Pod 74], [Pod 75], [Wie 77], [Smi 82]).

DEFINITION 9.1. We define identification type $\mathfrak{M}$ as a predicate $\mathfrak{M}(f,\{n_i\})$ over functions and admissible recursive sequences of integers.

The predicate is understood as: "the sequence $\{n_i\}$ might be the sequence of hypotheses in $\mathfrak{M}$-identification of f".

We denote the set of all $\mathfrak{M}$-admissible sequences for f by $D_{\mathfrak{M}}(f)$. We denote the class of all identification types by Δ ($M\in\Delta$).

For instance, EX_φ is characterized by a predicate which is true for every pair $(f,\{n_i\})$ where f is a total recursive function and $\{n_i\}$ is a sequence such that $(\exists i_0)(\exists n)(\forall i>i_0)((n_i=n)\&(\forall x)(\varphi_n(x)=f(x)))$.

BC is characterised by a predicate which is true for every pair $(f,\{n_i\})$ where f is a total recursive function and $\{n_i\}$ is a sequence such that $(\exists i_0)(\forall i>i_0)\ (\forall x)\ (\varphi_{n_i}(x)=f(x))$.

EX^{cons} is characterized by a predicate which is true for every pair $(f,\{n_i\})$ where f is a total recursive function and $\{n_i\}$ is a sequence such that $(\forall i)(\forall x\leq i)(\varphi_{n_i}(x)=f(x))$ and $(\exists i_0)(\exists n)(\forall i>i_0)((n_i=n)$.

The family of all $\mathfrak{M}$-identifiable classes of total recursive functions is denoted by $EX_{\mathfrak{M}}$.

We prove going to prove that, provided certain "naturality" properties of the types, every identification type M has complete class U of total recursive functions such that:

1) $U \in \mathfrak{M}$,

2) for arbitrary "natural" type $\mathfrak{L}$ such that $\mathfrak{L} \subsetneq \mathfrak{M}$ the class $U \notin \mathfrak{L}$.

DEFINITION 9.2. We say that the identification type $\mathfrak{M}$ is reducible to the identification type $\mathfrak{L}$ ($\mathfrak{M} \leq \mathfrak{L}$) if there is an algorithm which transforms pairs (graph of a function f, $\mathfrak{M}$-admissible sequence for f) into a $\mathfrak{L}$-admissible sequence for the same f.

DEFINITION 9.3. We say that identification type $\mathfrak{M}$ is closed ($\mathfrak{M} \in \Delta_0$) if there are functions u(x,y) and v(z) such that:

1) for arbitrary $f \in \mathfrak{R}$ and $\{n_i\} \in D_{\mathfrak{M}}(f)$, the sequence $\{k_i\} = \{u(f(i), n_i)\}$ is in $D_{\mathfrak{M}}(g)$ for $g(x) = c(f(x), n_x)$;

2) for arbitrary $g \in \mathfrak{R}$, the sequence $\{n_i\} = \{v(g(i))\}$ is in $D_{\mathfrak{M}}(f)$ for $f(x) = l(g(x))$.

Informally, an identification type is closed when identifiability of a function implies identifiability of similar functions as well. The types EX, $EX_n{}^m$, EX^{cons}, BC are closed but identification of the minimal numbers in a Goedel numbering is not.

THEOREM 9.1. For arbitrary identification type $\mathfrak{M} \in \Delta_0$ there is a class $V_{\mathfrak{M}}$ of total recursive functions such that:

1) $V_{\mathfrak{M}} \in EX_{\mathfrak{M}}$,

2) if $\mathfrak{L} \in \Delta_0$ and $V_{\mathfrak{M}} \in EX_{\mathfrak{L}}$ then $EX_{\mathfrak{M}} \subseteq EX_{\mathfrak{L}}$,

3) if $V_{\mathfrak{M}} \notin EX_{\mathfrak{L}}$ then $EX_{\mathfrak{M}} \not\subseteq EX_{\mathfrak{L}}$.

PROOF. We define $V_{\mathfrak{M}}$ to consist of all the functions $g(x) = c(f(x), n_x)$ where f is arbitrary total recursive function and $\{n_x\}$ is arbitrary recursive sequence which is $\mathfrak{M}$-admissible for f. Now we use the function u(x,y) from the property 1) in the definition of closedness for $\mathfrak{M}$ and define a strategy $F(<g^{[k]}>) = u(l(g(k)), r(g(k)))$. We see that the strategy F $\mathfrak{M}$-identifies the class $V_{\mathfrak{M}}$. Hence $V_{\mathfrak{M}} \in EX_{\mathfrak{M}}$.

If $V_{\mathfrak{M}} \notin EX_{\mathfrak{L}}$ then, of course, $EX_{\mathfrak{M}} \not\subseteq EX_{\mathfrak{L}}$. If $V_{\mathfrak{M}} \in EX_{\mathfrak{L}}$ then we denote the strategy $\mathfrak{L}$-identifying $V_{\mathfrak{M}}$ by G. Let U be an arbitrary class in $EX_{\mathfrak{M}}$. We will prove that $U \in EX_{\mathfrak{L}}$ as well. There is a strategy H $\mathfrak{M}$-identifying U. If a total recursive function f is in U then the function $g(x) = c(f(x), H(<f^{[x]}>))$ is in $V_{\mathfrak{M}}$, and the sequence $\{G(<g^{[x]}>)\}$ is a $\mathfrak{L}$-admissing one for the function g. It follows from the property 2) in the definition of closedness for $\mathfrak{L}$ that the sequence $\{V(G(<g^{[x]}>))\}$ is a $\mathfrak{L}$-admissing sequence for f. Hence $U \in EX_{\mathfrak{L}}$. □

THEOREM 9.2. For arbitrary identification types $\mathfrak{M},\mathfrak{L}\in\Delta_0$,

$\mathfrak{M}\leq\mathfrak{L} \Leftrightarrow EX_{\mathfrak{M}}\subseteq EX_{\mathfrak{L}}$.

PROOF. $\Rightarrow$ Let U be a class of total recursive functions and F be a strategy $\mathfrak{M}$-identifying U. Then for arbitrary $f\in U$ the sequence $\{F(f^{[x]}>)\}$ is an $\mathfrak{M}$-admissible sequence for $\mathfrak{M}$. It follows from $\mathfrak{M}\leq\mathfrak{L}$ that there is an algorithm which transforms pairs (graph of a function f, $\mathfrak{M}$-admissible sequence for f) into a $\mathfrak{L}$-admissible sequence for the same f. It is easy to combine this algorithm and the strategy F to get the $\mathfrak{L}$-identifying strategy for U. Hence $EX_{\mathfrak{M}}\subseteq EX_{\mathfrak{L}}$.

$\Leftarrow$ Assume $EX_{\mathfrak{M}}\subseteq EX_{\mathfrak{L}}$. It follows from Theorem 9.1 that $V_{\mathfrak{M}}\in EX_{\mathfrak{L}}$. Let $V_{\mathfrak{M}}$ be $\mathfrak{L}$-identified by a strategy G.

It is possible to reduce $\mathfrak{M}\leq\mathfrak{L}$ in the following way. We take the graph of arbitrary function f, an $\mathfrak{M}$-admissible sequence for f, and apply the function U(x,y) from the property 1) in the definition of closedness for $\mathfrak{M}$. Since the $\mathfrak{M}$-admissible sequence for f is recursive, we get a total recursive function $g\in V_{\mathfrak{M}}$. Then the sequence $\{G(<g^{[x]}>)\}$ is a $\mathfrak{L}$-admissing sequence for g. It follows from the property 2) in the definition of closedness for $\mathfrak{L}$ that the sequence $\{v(G(<g^{[x]}>))\}$ is a $\mathfrak{L}$-admissing sequence for f. Hence $\mathfrak{M}\leq\mathfrak{L}$. □

Note that Theorem 9.2. establishes equivalence between a uniform and a non-uniform notion. $\mathfrak{M}\leq\mathfrak{L}$ postulates existence of a uniform reduction algorithm valid for all total recursive function and all recursive $\mathfrak{M}$-admissible sequences for them. On the other hand, $EX_{\mathfrak{M}}\subseteq EX_{\mathfrak{L}}$ means only that for arbitrary class U of total recursive functions, if U can be $\mathfrak{M}$-identifiable then it can be $\mathfrak{L}$-identifiable as well. There is no uniformity allowing to find a $\mathfrak{L}$-identifying strategy, given the $\mathfrak{M}$-identifying strategy.

It follows from Theorem 9.2 that if $EX_{\mathfrak{M}}\subseteq EX_{\mathfrak{L}}$ then $\mathfrak{M}\leq\mathfrak{L}$ and hence there is a uniform operator transforming $\mathfrak{M}$-identifying strategies into $\mathfrak{L}$-identifying strategies for the same classes of total recursive functions.

Theorems 9.1 and 9.2 have a certain defect. They are proved only for identification types in Δ_0 (rather than Δ). Unfortunately, the Theorems do not hold for Δ.

THEOREM 9.3. There are identification types $\mathfrak{M},\mathfrak{L}\in\Delta$ such that $EX_{\mathfrak{M}}\subseteq EX_{\mathfrak{L}}$ but $\mathfrak{M}\not\leq\mathfrak{L}$.

PROOF. The identification type $\mathfrak{M}$ is chosen such that only finite classes of total recursive functions are $\mathfrak{M}$-identifiable (see e.g. Theorem 4.1). The type $\mathfrak{L}$ is chosen among the continuum of the types such that for every total recursive function f the set $D_{\mathfrak{L}}(f)$ contains only one recursive sequence. Note that for every such $\mathfrak{L}$ all finite classes of total recursive functions are $\mathfrak{L}$-identifiable. On the other hand, if $\mathfrak{M}$ is fixed and $\mathfrak{L}_1$ and $\mathfrak{L}_2$ are two different identification types with the abovementioned property then $\mathfrak{M}\leq\mathfrak{L}_1$ and $\mathfrak{M}\leq\mathfrak{L}_2$ cannot be reduced by the same reduction algorithm. There is an enumerable set of reduction algorithms. We remove from the continuum of abovementioned types $\mathfrak{L}$ an enumerable family of types $\mathfrak{L}_i$ such that the type $\mathfrak{M}$ is reducible to $\mathfrak{L}_i$ via the corresponding reduction algorithm. Every $\mathfrak{L}$ from the remaining family of types can be used to complete the proof of our Theorem. ❑

ACKNOWLEDGMENT

Section 9 consists of results co-authored by Efim B.Kinber (Riga). Section 4-6 contain results from[FK 77]. Additionally I should say that it was my colleague's idea to return to these problems after 13 years. Our many discussions on them stimulated me to write this paper.

REFERENCES

[Bar 72] J.M.Barzdin. Prognostication of automata and functions,81-84, Elsevier-North Holland, 1972.

[Bar 74] J.M.Barzdin. Two theorems on limiting synthesis of functions. Theory of algorithms and programs, No. 1, 82-88, Riga, University of Latvia, 1974 (Russian).

[Ersh 77] Yu.L.E. Ershov. Theory of Numberings. Nauka, 1977 (Russian).

[Fre 74] R.Freivalds. On limiting synthesis of indices of total recursive functions in various computable numberings. Doklady AN SSSR, 219: 812, 1974 (Russian).

[Fre 75] R.Freivalds. Possibility to identify in the limit the indices of total recursive functions in various computable numberings. Theory of algorithms and programs, No.2, 3-25 (Russian).

[Fri 58] R.M.Friedberg. Three theorems on recursive functions: I Decomposition. II Maximal sets. III Enumeration without dublication. Symbolic Logic, 23:309-316, 1958.

[FK 77] R.Freivalds, E.B.Kinber. Limiting identification of the minimal Goedel numbers, Theory of algorithms and programms, No.3, 3-34 (Russian).

[Gold 67] E.M.Gold. Language identification in the limit. Information and Control, 10:447-474, 1967.

[Kin 77] E,B.Kinber. On limiting identification of minimal numbers for functions from effectively enumerable classes. Theory of algorithms and programs, No.3, 35-56 (Russian).

[Kin 83] E.B.Kinber. A note on limit identification of c–minimal indices. Elektronische Informationsverarbeiterung und Kybernetik, 19: 459–463, 1983.

[Pod 74] K.M.Podnieks. Comparing varions concepts of function prediction, part 1. Theory of algorithms and programs, 1:68-81, 1974 (Russian).

[Pod 75] K.M.Podnieks. Comparing varions concepts of function prediction, part 2.

Theory of algorithms and programs, 2:33-44, 1975 (Russian).

[Rog 58] H.Rogers. Goedel numberings of the partial recursive functions. J.Symbolic Logic, 23: 331–341, 1958.

[Rog 67] H.Rogers. Theory of Recursive Functions and Effective Computability. Mc Graw-Hill, 1967. Reprinted. MIT Press. 1987.

[Smi 83] C.H.Smith. The power of pluralism for automatic program synthesis. Journal of the ACM, 29:1144-1165, 1982.

[Tra 65] B.A.Trakhtenbrot. Optimal computations and the frequential phenomenon by Yablonski. Algebra i Logika. 4:5, 1965 (Russian).

[Wie 77] R.Wiehagen. Identification of formal languages. Lecture Notes in Computer Science, 53:571-579, 1977.

INDUCTIVE INFERENCE OF RECURSIVE FUNCTIONS: COMPLEXITY BOUNDS

Rūsiņš Freivalds, Jānis Bārzdiņš and Kārlis Podnieks

Institute of Mathematics and Computer Science
The University of Latvia
Raiņa bulv. 29, Rīga, 226250, Latvia

Abstract. This survey includes principal results on complexity of inductive inference for recursively enumerable classes of total recursive functions. Inductive inference is a process to find an algorithm from sample computations. In the case when the given class of functions is recursively enumerable it is easy to define a natural complexity measure for the inductive inference, namely, the worst-case mindchange number for the first n functions in the given class. Surely, the complexity depends not only on the class, but also on the numbering, i.e. which function is the first, which one is the second, etc. It turns out that, if the result of inference is Goedel number, then complexity of inference may vary between $\log_2 n+o(\log_2 n)$ and an arbitrarily slow recursive function. If the result of the inference is an index in the numbering of the recursively enumerable class, then the complexity may go up to const·n. Additionally, effects previously found in the Kolmogorov complexity theory are discovered in the complexity of inductive inference as well.

The time complexity of prediction strategies (the value f(m+1) is predicted from f(0),...,f(m)) is investigated. It turns out that, if a prediction strategy F is "error-optimal" (i.e. it makes at most $\log_2 n+O(\log_2\log_2 n)$ errors on the n-th function of the class), then the time complexity of computation of F(<f(0),...,f(m)>) (i.e. a candidate for f(m+1)) may go up, in some sense, to $2^{2^{cm}}$.

Special attention is paid to inductive inference by probabilistic algorithms. It turns out that arbitrary recursively enumerable class of total recursive functions can be identified with ln n + o(log n) mind- changes in an arbitrary numbering of the class.

1. Introduction

"Inductive inference" is the term coined for finding out the algorithm from sample computations. We restrict ourselves to the case when a total recursive function is to be identified. The first paper in this area was [Go 67], yet (sometimes indirectly) the research was influenced by the theory of experiments with finite automata [Moo 56].

There are several ways how to make this problem precise but all of them are based on the same paradigm. There is a "black box" with a given total recursive function f in it. We cannot see the program of the device computing f but we can get the values of the function. Since the function is total, with no restriction of generality we can assume that the black box outputs the values in the natural order: f(0),f(1),f(2),f(3),...

The inductive inference machine (or the *strategy*) tries to use the initial fragments of the function to figure out the algorithm computing it. Hence, from the recursion theory point of view, the strategy is a functional mapping the class of total recursive functions $\mathcal{R}$ into the set of nonnegative integers N. This functional is to be computable in some sense. Theory of recursive functions [Rog 67] has developed a precise notion for such a functional - the notion of a recursive functional. Informally, recursive functional is computed by a Turing machine with an input tape containing the graph of the function f and a work tape. The machine works for some time and then stops after finite number of steps (the machine decides itself when to stop) and produces the result needed.

Unfortunately, only very simple classes of functions are identifiable in this sense. Indeed, in finite number of steps only finite number of values of the function can be observed. If two functions differ only on a later value, then the machine nevertheless produces the same output.

A more interesting type of identification was "identification in the limit" considered in [Go 67]. Instead of being printed once forever, the output ("hypothesis") is shown on a "screenboard" and, if there is a need, it may be changed later. We say that the machine has resulted in y if at some moment it has produced the output y and after that moment this output is never changed.

Formally, the *identifying strategy* F is an arbitrary partial recursive function. $<x_1,x_2,...,x_n>$ is an effective numbering of all tuples of nonnegative integers, using as the numbers all nonnegative integers. $\{\varphi_i\}$ is a Goedel numbering of all partial recursive functions of one argument.

$F(<f(0),...,f(n)>)$ is referred to as the n-th *hypothesis* by F on the function f. The hypothesis p is called correct for f if $\varphi_p=f$.

We say that f is *identified in the limit* by F (denoted $f\in EX(F)$) if there is an n_0 such that for arbitrary $n>n_0$:

1) $F(<f(0),\ldots,f(n)>)=F(<f(0),\ldots,f(n_0)>)$,

2) the hypothesis $F(<f(0),\ldots,f(n_0)>)$ is correct for f.

We say that the class U of total recursive functions is identified in the limit by F (denoted $U\subseteq EX(F)$) if every function $f\in U$ is identified in the limit by F.

We say that the class U of total recursive functions is identifiable in the limit ($U\in EX$) if there is a strategy F identifying U in the limit.

The class U of total recursive function is called *recursively enumerable* if there is a total recursive function $g(i,x)$ such that:

1) for arbitrary i the function $\lambda x\cdot g(i,x)$ of one argument x is in the class U,

2) for arbitrary $f\in U$ there is an i such that $\lambda x\cdot g(i,x)=f(x)$.

The function g introduces a numbering $\tau=\{\tau_i\}$ of functions in U, namely, the number i is called the index of the function f if $\tau_i(x)=\lambda x.g(i,x)=f(x)$.

THEOREM 1.1. (E.M.GOLD [Go 67]) If a class U is a subclass of a recursively enumerable class of functions, then U is identifiable in the limit.

PROOF. The strategy produces as its n-th hypothesis

$$\begin{cases} i, \text{ if } i\le n \text{ and } i \text{ is the least} \\ \text{nonnegative integer } j \text{ such that} \\ <f(0),\ldots,f(n)>=<\tau_j(0),\ldots,\tau_j(n)>; \\ n, \text{ if there is no such } i \text{ for the given } n. \end{cases}$$

It is easy to see that the strategy is total recursive and it identifies U in the limit. Moreover, our strategy never allows more than n mindchanges on the functions with indices 0,1,2,...,n.

□

The worst-case number of mindchanges for the first n functions in the class U (more precisely: in the numbering τ of the class U) can be considered as a complexity measure for the pair (U,τ). Our paper is written to find out how the numbering influences this complexity for the given recursively enumerable class U. We make a terminological distinction: recursively enumerable class U of total recursive func- tions but *enumerated class* (U,τ), i.e. U with its fixed numbering τ.

This way, we try to understand in this paper how different complexities of distinct enumerated classes (U,τ) based on the same recursively enumerable class U can be.

We will show that the linear complexity in the proof of Theorem 1.1 can be improved if we are interested only in getting a correct Goedel number for the given function. On the other hand, the proof of Theorem 1.1 yields us more than it is said in the formulation of Theorem 1.1. The strategy with the linear complexity of mindchanges produces the τ-index, one can effectively find a Goedel number for the same function but in the general case it is a recursively unsolvable problem to find a τ-index, given arbitrary Goedel number. Hence we can expect higher complexity for identification of τ-indices when compared with the identification of Goedel numbers. In Section 3 we will see that this really is the case.

We will consider also a notion which appears to be closely connected with the identification in the limit, called prediction of functions.

In the *prediction of functions* the result $F(<f(0),\ldots,f(n)>)$ is expected to be $f(n+1)$. Nevertheless arbitrary finite number of errors is allowed (but it is not allowed for the value $F(<f(0),\ldots,f(n)>)$ to be undefined).

Prediction turns to be closely connected with identification in the limit. Given arbitrary recursively enumerable class U of total recursive functions and its numbering τ, if (U,τ) can be predicted with $\le g(n)$ errors, then (U,τ) can be identified in the limit with $\le g(n)$ mindchanges (see Theorem 1.2 below).

To be able to prove this (very simple) theorem and other results like it we introduce a useful notation.

The string of integers $f(0), f(1),\ldots,f(n)$ is denoted by $f^{[n]}$. This allows us to write $F(<f^{[n]}>)$ instead of $F(<f(0),\ldots,f(n)>)$.

We denote by $F^{NV}(f)$ the *number of errors* while predicting f by the predicting strategy F.

We fix a Goedel numbering $\varphi=\{\varphi_i\}$ of all partial recursive functions of one argument x. We denote by $F^{EX}(f)$ the *number of mindchanges* by F on f, provided F correctly identifies in the limit a φ-index of the function f.(Please notice that for the sake of brevity we have omitted φ in the notation $F^{EX}(f)$. Of course, it should be written).

We denote by $F^{NV}_{U,\tau}(n)$ the maximum among $\{F^{NV}(\tau_0), F^{NV}(\tau_1),\ldots,F^{NV}(\tau_n)\}$. Similarly, by $F^{EX}_{U,\tau}(n)$ we denote the max among $\{F^{EX}(\tau_0), F^{EX}(\tau_1),\ldots,F^{EX}(\tau_n)\}$.

We denote by $F^{\tau}(f)$ the *number of mindchanges* by F on f, provided F correctly identifies in the limit a τ-index of the function f. We denote by $F^{\tau}_{U,\tau}(n)$ the maximum among $\{F^{\tau}(\tau_0), F^{\tau}(\tau_1), \ldots, F^{\tau}(\tau_n)\}$.

THEOREM 1.2. For arbitrary enumerated class (U,τ) and arbitrary total recursive strategy F predicting U, there is a total recursive strategy G identifying U in the limit such that $G^{EX}_{U,\tau}(n) \le F^{NV}_{U,\tau}(n)$.

PROOF. Let $y_0, y_1, \ldots y_n$ be a tuple of nonnegative integers and F be the total recursive strategy predicting U. We consider a partial recursive function η defined as follows

$$\eta(x) = \begin{cases} y_x, & \text{if } x \le n, \\ F(<y_0, y_1, \ldots, y_n>), & \text{if } x = n+1, \\ F(<\eta(0), \eta(1), \ldots, \eta(x-1)>), & \text{if } x > n+1. \end{cases}$$

The algorithm for computing values of η is uniform in $n, y_0, y_1, \ldots, y_n$. Hence there is a total recursive function j such that $j(<y_0, y_1, \ldots, y_n>)$ is a φ-index of the function η, corresponding the tuple $(y_0, y_1, \ldots, y_n)$.

If f is a total recursive function and the predicting strategy F makes no more errors on initial fragments $(f(0), f(1), \ldots, f(x))$ containing $(f(0), f(1), \ldots, f(n))$, then η is total and $\eta = f$.

We consider a strategy G such that

$$G(<y_0, y_1, \ldots, y_n>) = j(<y_0, y_1, \ldots, y_n>)$$

for all values of the argument. For every total recursive function f, the number of mindchanges by G equals the number of errors by F.

□

A strategy F identifying τ-indices for a class U is called consistent if for arbitrary n and arbitrary $f \in U$ the value $F(<f(0), f(1), \ldots, f(n)>)$ is a τ-index i such that $\tau_i(0) = f(0)$, $\tau_i(1) = f(1)$, ... $, \tau_i(n) = f(n)$.

THEOREM 1.3. For arbitrary enumerated class (U,τ) and arbitrary consistent total recursive strategy H identifying for U τ-indices in the limit, there is a total recursive strategy F predicting U such that $F^{NV}_{U,\tau}(n) \le H^{\tau}_{U,\tau}(n)$.

PROOF. If $H(<f(0), f(1), \ldots, f(n)>) = i$, then set

$$F(<f(0), f(1), \ldots, f(n)>) = \tau_i(n+1).$$

Since H is consistent, every error by F implies a mindchange by H.

□

We need a useful "folk lemma" used by nearly all authors in papers on inductive inference. We have added the complexity bounds to the argument used in this lemma.

LEMMA 1.1. For arbitrary Goedel numbering $\{F_i\}$ of all partial recursive strategies there is a family $\{F'\}$ of total recursive strategies such that for arbitrary i and total recursive f if $\lim_{n\to\infty} F_i(<f^{[n]}>)$ exists, then $\lim_{n\to\infty} F'_i(<f^{[n]}>)$ exists as well, the limits are equal, and for all n

$$(F'_i)^{\tau}_{U,\tau}(n) \le (F_i)^{\tau}_{U,\tau}(n)+1, \; (F'_i)^{EX}_{U,\tau}(n) \le (F_i)^{EX}_{U,\tau}(n)+1.$$

PROOF. The strategy F'_i on $<f^{[n]}>$ simulates in total n steps of Turing machine computation for $F_i(<f^{[0]}>)$, $F_i(<f^{[1]}>)$, $F_i(<f^{[2]}>)$,... (in that order). The result $F'_i(<f^{[n]}>)$ equals the last completely computed value in this sequence. If time n does not suffice to compute $F_i(<f^{[0]}>)$, then $F'_i(<f^{[n]}>)=0$. □

2. Prediction and EX-identification

The proof of Theorem 1.1. provides strategies for prediction, identification in the limit and identification of τ-indices with the following complexity bounds:

$$F^{NV}_{U,\tau}(n) \le n,$$

$$G^{EX}_{U,\tau}(n) \le n,$$

$$H^{\tau}_{U,\tau}(n) \le n$$

for arbitrary enumerated classes (U,τ). We prove in this section that the first two bounds can be lowered.

THEOREM 2.1. ([BF 72], [BF 74]) For arbitrary enumerated class (U,τ) and arbitrary positive integer k, there is a total recursive strategy F such that for all n

$$F^{NV}_{U,\tau}(n) \le \log_2 n+\log_2\log_2 n+\ldots+\underbrace{\log_2\log_2\ldots\log_2}_{k\ times} n + o(\underbrace{\log_2\log_2\ldots\log_2}_{k\ times} n)$$

PROOF. The main idea is as follows. We associate a certain weight p_i $(\Sigma p_i=1)$ to every τ-index i, and, then, to predict the next value $y'_{n+1}=F(<y_0,y_1,y_2,\ldots,y_m>)$, we consider a parameter s, and for arbitrary fixed value of s we total the weights for all integers j such that

$$\tau_j(0)=y_0\&\tau_j(1)=y_1\&\tau_j(2)=y_2\&\ldots\&\tau_j(m)=y_m\&\tau_j(m+1)=s.$$

Our prediction of y'_{m+1} is the value of s for which the abovedescribed total is maximal.

We assert that if our strategy of prediction makes k errors on the function τ_n, then

$$2^k p_n \le 1. \qquad (2.1.)$$

Indeed, consider a graphical representation of the class U by an infinite tree.

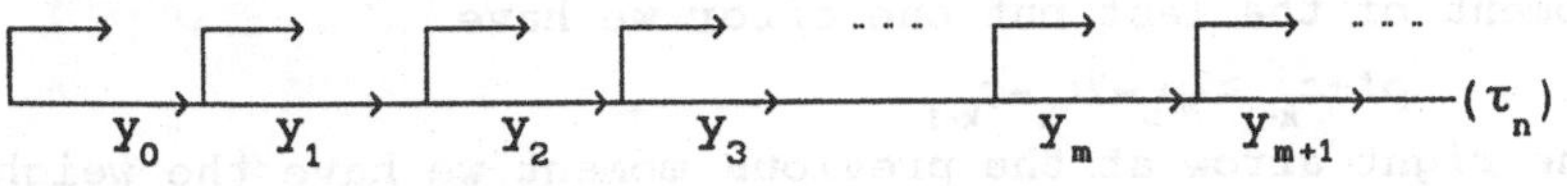

The infinite path drawn here corresponds to the function τ_n (which may have more than one τ-index, by the way). The outgoing arrows correspond to functions declining from τ_n.

The function τ_n has the total weights no less than p_n. Consider the last error, the error number k. If our strategy has chosen to predict a value differing from that of τ_n, it is only because the weight of the declining arrow has had a weight no less than p_n. Hence the weight of the correct prediction at the moment of the (k-1)-th error has been at least $2 \cdot p_n$. Since the (k-1)-th error has been commited, another declining arrow has had a weight $\ge 2 \cdot p_n$. Hence the weight of the correct prediction at the moment of the (k-2)-th error has been at least $4 \cdot p_n$. Continuing this consideration we get (2.1.).

We conclude that our strategy makes no more than $\log_2 \frac{1}{p_n}$ errors on the function τ_n. If we use the distribution of weights

$$p_n = \frac{c}{n \cdot (\log_2 n)(\log_2 \log_2 n) \ldots \underbrace{(\log_2 \ldots \log_2 n)}_{k-1 \text{ times}} \underbrace{(\log_2 \ldots \log_2 n)}_{k \text{ times}}^2}$$

(where c is a constant such that $\sum p_n = 1$), we get the upper bound

$$F^{NV}_{U,\tau}(n) \le \log_2 n + \log_2 \log_2 n + \ldots + \underbrace{\log_2 \log_2 \ldots \log_2 n}_{k \text{ times}} + o(\underbrace{\log_2 \log_2 \ldots \log_2 n}_{k \text{ times}}) \qquad (2.2.)$$

We have been slightly incorrect so far. We cannot guarantee the recursiveness of the strategy since absolutely precise computation of an infinite series of weights is expected. Now we redefine the strategy expecting the totals of weights being computed only approximately, namely, the totals needed for the current prediction being computed only up to a certain ε_t where ε_t depends only on the number of errors already commited.

We have that the total of weights p for the prediction at the moment of the k-th (the last) error always satisfies

$$p+\varepsilon_k \geq p_n-\varepsilon_k$$

i.e. the weight of the right arrow at the previous moment is no less than

$$2p_n-2\varepsilon_k.$$

For the moment of the last but one error we have

$$p'+\varepsilon_{k-1} \geq 2p_n-2\varepsilon_k-\varepsilon_{k-1}$$

and for the right arrow at the previous moment we have the weight

$$\geq 2^2 \cdot p_n-2^2 \cdot \varepsilon_k-2\varepsilon_{k-1}.$$

Continuing this argument we finally get a weight

$$\geq 2^k \cdot p_n-2^k \cdot \varepsilon_k-\ldots-2^2\varepsilon_2-2\varepsilon_1$$

which cannot exceed 1. If we take $\varepsilon_j=2^{-2j}$, we have $2^k \cdot p_n \leq 2$ and the same inequality (2.2.).

□

THEOREM 2.2. ([BF 74]) For arbitrary enumerated class (U,τ) and arbitrary positive integer k, there is a total recursive strategy G such that for all n

$$G^{EX}_{U,\tau}(n) \leq \log_2 n+\log_2\log_2 n+\ldots+\underbrace{\log_2\log_2\ldots\log_2}_{k\ \text{times}} n + o(\underbrace{\log_2\log_2\ldots\log_2}_{k\ \text{times}} n) .$$

PROOF. Immediately from Theorems 2.1 and 1.2.

□

In order to prove the lower bounds of the complexity of prediction we introduce some auxiliary notions and prove an important lemma.

We consider prediction of the values of nonrecursive functions. It is easy to see that the number of errors should equal infinity. However, we can consider the initial fragments $f^{[n]}=\langle f(0),f(1),\ldots,f(n)\rangle$. By $F_{NV}(f^{[n]})$ we denote the number of errors made by the strategy F when predicting the first n values f(1),f(2),...,f(n).

A.N.Kolmogorov [Kol 65] introduced a fundamental notion of complexity of finite objects. According to this idea the complexity of a function in a fixed numbering of functions is the binary logarithm of its minimum index. In the class of all partial recursive functions of one argument x, as shown by Kolmogorov [Kol 65], there is an optimal numbering x such that, if φ is an arbitrary computable numbering of partial recursive functions, then there is a constant c_φ such that for arbitrary partial recursive function f its complexity in κ does not exceed the complexity of f in φ plus c_φ.

We consider a counterpart of this complexity for numberings of total recursive functions. Note that there may exist no optimal (in this sense) numbering.

Let $\tau=\{\tau_i\}$ be an arbitrary computable numbering of total recursive functions. We consider the complexity of initial fragments of functions. By $k_\tau(f^{[n]})$ we denote the minimum τ-index of a function h such that $h^{[n]}=f^{[n]}$. By $K_\tau(f^{[n]})$ we denote $[\log_2 k_\tau(f^{[n]})]$. If f is nonrecursive, then $K_\tau(f^{[n]})\longrightarrow\infty$ with $n\longrightarrow\infty$. We try to find out a relation between $F_{NV}(f^{[n]})$ and $K_\tau(f^{[n]})$.

LEMMA 2.1. Let (U,τ) be an arbitrary enumerated class and $\eta(p)$ be a function such that $F^{NV}_{U,\tau}(p)\le\eta(p)$. Then for arbitrary (nonrecursive) function f and arbitrary n, $F_{NV}(f^{[n]})\le\eta(k_\tau(f^{[n]}))$.

PROOF. We have $F^{NV}_{U,\tau}(p)\le\eta(p)$. Hence for arbitrary p it is true that $F_{NV}(\tau_p^{[y]})\le\eta(p)$ for all y. Let $p_n=k_\tau(f^{(n)})$. Then for $x\le n$ we have $\tau_{p_n}(x)=f(x)$. Hence $F_{NV}(f^{[n]})=F_{NV}(\tau_{p_n}^{[n]})\le\eta(p_n)=\eta(k_\tau(f^{[n]}))$.

□

THEOREM 2.3. ([BF 74]) For arbitrary enumerated class (U,τ) and arbitrary positive integer k, there is a total recursive strategy F such that for arbitrary (nonrecursive) total function f and for all n,

$$F_{NV}(f^{[n]})\le K_\tau(f^{[n]})+\log_2 K_\tau(f^{[n]})+\ldots+\underbrace{\log_2\ldots\log_2}_{k\text{ times}} K_\tau(f^{[n]})+ o(\underbrace{\log_2\ldots\log_2}_{k\text{ times}} K_\tau(f^{[n]})).$$

PROOF. Immediately from Lemma 2.1 and Theorem 2.1.

□

THEOREM 2.4. ([BF 74]) There is an enumerated class (U,τ) such that for arbitrary strategy F and arbitrary positive integer k:

1) $(\forall n)\,(F^{NV}_{U,\tau}(n)>\log_2 n-3)$,

2) $(\exists^\infty n)\,(F^{NV}_{U,\tau}(n)>\log_2 n+\log_2\log_2 n+\ldots+\underbrace{\log_2\log_2\ldots\log_2}_{k\text{ times}} n)$

PROOF. We define two enumerated classes (V,τ') and (W,τ'') and then join them making the class $U=V\cup W$ and the numbering

$$\tau_n=\begin{cases}\tau'_k, & \text{if } n=2k-1,\\ \tau''_k, & \text{if } n=2k.\end{cases}$$

The enumerated class (V,τ') is constructed to have the property 1.

Let binary 0-1 strings be enumerated lexicographically. The infinite string of values $\tau'_i(0)\tau'_i(1)\tau'_i(2)\ldots$ is obtained from the i-th string in the lexicographical numbering by adding infinitely many zeros after the string. It is easy to see that $(\forall n)(F^{NV}_{V,\tau'}(n)\geq\log_2 n-2)$.

To construct the class (W,τ'') and to prove 2) we make use of the following theorem by P.Martin-Löf [ML 66] (see also [ZL 70]). Let h(n) be an arbitrary total recursive function such that the series $\sum 2^{-h(n)}$ diverges. Then for every 0-1 valued function f it is true that

$$(\exists^\infty n)(K_B(f^{[n]})\leq n-h(n).$$

In the abovecited theorem one can take, for instance, the function $h(n)=\log_2 n+\log_2 n+\ldots+\log_2\log_2\ldots\log_2 n+a(n)$, where a(n) is a function growing to infinity sufficiently slowly.

The Martin-Löf theorem uses an optimal numbering B of partial recursive functions. Hence we cannot use this result directly. On the other hand, the proof of the theorem is based on the construction of an effective coding of initial fragments of sequences. The effectiveness of the coding allows us to construct a numbering $\sigma=\{\sigma_i\}$ of total recursive functions as well, such that

$$(\exists^\infty n)(K_\sigma(f^{[n]})\leq n-h(n)).$$

For (W,τ'') we take the numbering $\tau''=\sigma$ and the class W numbered by σ.

Assume from the contrary that

$$(\forall^\infty n)(F^{NV}_{W,\sigma}(n)\leq\log_2 n+\log_2\log_2 n+\ldots+\underbrace{\log_2\log_2\ldots\log_2}_{k\ \text{times}} n)$$

Hence there is a constant c such that

$$(\forall n)(F^{NV}_{W,\sigma}(n)\leq\log_2 n+\log_2\log_2 n+\ldots+\underbrace{\log_2\log_2\ldots\log_2}_{k\ \text{times}} n+C).$$

We denote $\log_2 n+\log_2\log_2 n+\ldots+\log_2\log_2\ldots\log_2 n+C$ by $\eta(n)$ and use Lemma 2.1. We get

$$(\forall n)(F_{NV}(f^{[n]})\leq\log_2 k_\sigma(f^{[n]})+\log_2\log_2 k_\sigma(f^{[n]})+\ldots+$$
$$+\underbrace{\log_2\log_2\ldots\log_2}_{k\ \text{times}} k_\sigma(f^{[n]})+C)\leq K_\sigma(f^{[n]})+\log_2 K_\sigma(f^{[n]})+\ldots+$$
$$+\underbrace{\log_2\log_2\ldots\log_2}_{k-1\ \text{times}} K_\sigma(f^{[n]})+C'.$$

Up to now our function f was arbitrary. Now we take a specific one, and, namely, we take the 0-1 valued function which is predicted incorrectly at every step. Thus $(\forall n)(F_{NV}(f^{[n]})=n)$. We have

$$(\forall n)(n\le K_\sigma(f^{[n]})+\log_2 K_\sigma(f^{[n]})+\ldots+\underbrace{\log_2\log_2\ldots\log_2}_{k-1\text{ times}} K_\sigma(f^{[n]})+C'.$$

On the other hand, from the modified Martin-Löf theorem we have

$$(\exists^\infty n)(K_\sigma(f^{[n]})\le n-\log_2 n-\log_2\log_2 n-\ldots-\log_2\log_2\ldots\log_2 n-a(n)).$$

Hence

$$(\exists^\infty n)(n\le(n-\log_2 n-\log_2\log_2 n-\ldots-\log_2\log_2\ldots\log_2 n-a(n))+$$
$$+\log_2(n-\log_2 n-\log_2\log_2 n-\ldots-\log_2\log_2\ldots\log_2 n-a(n))+$$
$$+\log_2\log_2(n-\log_2 n-\log_2\log_2 n-\ldots-\log_2\log_2\ldots\log_2 n-a(n))+$$
$$+\ldots+$$
$$\log_2\log_2\ldots\log_2(n-\log_2 n-\log_2\log_2 n-\ldots-\log_2\log_2\ldots\log_2 n-$$
$$-a(n))+C').$$

Contradiction.

□

We are going to prove the counterpart of Theorem 2.4 for identification in the limit. For this, we need a counterpart of Lemma 2.1.

By $G_{EX}(f^{[n]})$ we denote the minimum (over all functions g such that $g^{[n]}=f^{[n]}$) of $G^{EX}(g)$.

LEMMA 2.2. Let (U,τ) be an arbitrary enumerated class and $\eta(p)$ be a function such that $G^{EX}_{U,\tau}(p)\le\eta(p)$. Then for arbitrary (nonrecursive) function f and arbitrary n, $G_{EX}(f^{[n]})\le\eta(k_\tau(f^{[n]}))$.

PROOF. We have $G^{EX}_{U,\tau}(p)\le\eta(p)$. Hence for arbitrary p it is true that $G_{EX}(\tau_p^{[y]})\le\eta(p)$ for all y. Let $p_n=k_\tau(f^{[n]})$. Then for $x\le n$ we have $\tau_{p_n}(x)=f(x)$. Hence $G_{EX}(f^{[n]})=G_{EX}(\tau_{p_n}^{[n]})\le\eta(p_n)=\eta(k_\tau(f^{[n]}))$.

□

THEOREM 2.5. ([BF 74]) There is an enumerated class (U,τ) such that for arbitrary strategy G and arbitrary positive integer k:

1) $(\forall n)(G^{EX}_{U,\tau}(n)>\log_2 n-\text{const})$,

2) $(\exists^\infty n)(G^{EX}_{U,\tau}(n)>\underbrace{\log_2 n+\log_2\log_2 n+\ldots+\log_2\log_2\ldots\log_2 n}_{k\text{ times}})$.

PROOF. As in proof of Theorem 2.4. we define two enumerated classes (V,τ') and (W,τ'') and then join them making the class $V\cup W$ and the numbering

$$\tau_n=\begin{cases}\tau'_k, & \text{if } n=2k-1,\\ \tau''_k, & \text{if } n=2k.\end{cases}$$

The enumerated class (W,τ'') is defined precisely as in the proof of Theorem 2.4, only instead of Lemma 2.1 we use Lemma 2.2.

The class V is a subclass of the one as in the proof of Theorem 2.4. Now we define the numbering τ'. With pairs (i,j) we associate 2^j τ'-indices. The corresponding functions are defined in such a way that the strategy F'_i (from Lemma 1.1) either makes on one of these functions no less than $\log_2 2^j=j$ mindchanges or does not identify at least one of these functions.

We divide the sequence of all nonnegative integers (the potential τ'-indices) into segments. The integers $2^k\le m<2^{k+1}$ make the segment S_{k+1}. Every segment is associated with a strategy from $\{F'_i\}$. Namely, the segments $S_0,S_2,S_4,S_6,S_8,\ldots$ are associated with F'_0. The segments $S_1,S_5,S_9,S_{13},\ldots$ are associated with F'_1. The segments $S_3,S_{11},S_{19},S_{27},\ldots$ are associated with F'_2, etc.

Thus we have the following property. If S_r and $S_{r+2^{i+1}}$ are two adjacent segments associated with the same strategy F'_i, and $d\in S_r, l\in S_{r+2^{i+1}}$, then l exceeds d no more than constant number of times. Every τ'-index in the segment $S_{r+2^{i+1}}$ does not exceed $2^{r+2^{i+1}+2}$. Our construction allows us to assert that at least one function f in S_r is such that $(F'_i)^{EX}(f)\ge r$. Hence, for every n from the segment $S_{r+2^{i+1}}$ or from the preceding segments, it is true that $(F'_i)^{EX}(\tau'_n)\ge\log_2 n-\text{const}$.

It remains to describe the functions in the segment S_{k+1} associated with F'_i. We define them in steps, first all the functions in the segment for $x=0$, then for $x=1$, $x=2$, $x=3$,.... For $0\le x\le i+k+1$ the functions are defined to encode i and k (the string of the first $i+k+1$ values equals 0^i10^k1). After that one half of the functions gets the current value 0 and the other half gets 1. The strategy F'_i is to change the hypothesis at least on one of these two functions. When it has changed the hypothesis for the corresponding indices we define again one half of the functions to be equal 0, and the other half to be equal 1, etc. Either there is a function in the segment which is not identified by F'_i or F'_i has at least k mindchanges.

□

3. Identification of τ-indices

The trivial strategies for prediction and identification in the limit provided by the proof of Theorem 1.1 were improved in Section 2. However, the counterpart of these improvements for identification of τ-indices was not proved there. We will show that such a counterpart is impossible.

THEOREM 3.1. ([Ba 74-1]) There is an enumerated class (U,τ) of total recursive functions such that for arbitrary total recursive strategy H there is a constant c>0 such that for all n (but a finite number of them)

$$H^{\tau}_{U,\tau}(n)>\frac{n}{c}.$$

PROOF. The construction of the class $U=\{\tau_0,\tau_1,\tau_2,...\}$ is based on a diagonalization. At first we divide the sequence of all nonnegative integers (the potential τ-indices) into segments. The integers $2^k \le m<2^{k+1}$ form the segment S_{k+1}. Every segment is associated with a strategy from $\{F'_i\}$ (see Lemma 1.1). Namely, the segments S_0, S_2, S_4, S_6, S_8,... are associated with F'_0. The segments $S_1,S_5,S_9,S_{13},...$ are associated with F'_1. The segments $S_3,S_{11},S_{19},S_{27},...$ are associated with F'_2, etc.

Thus we have the following property. If S_j and $S_{j+2^{i+1}}$ are two adjacent segments associated with the same strategy F'_i, and $d\in S_j$, $l\in S_{j+2^{i+1}}$, then l exceeds d and the length of S_j no more than constant number of times.

Now we define the functions τ_m where $2^k\le m<2^{k+1}$, i.e. in the segment S_{k+1}. Let this segment correspond to F'_i. Then

$$\tau_m(x)=\begin{cases} 1, \text{ if } x<i, \\ 0, \text{ if } x=i, \\ 1, \text{ if } i+1\le x\le i+k, \\ 0, \text{ if } x=i+k+1, \\ \text{to be defined below, if } x>i+k+1. \end{cases}$$

Thus we have coded i and k into an initial fragment of the function.

Let z>0, and we define $\tau_m(i+k+1+z)$. We consider $F'_i(<\tau_m^{[i+k+z]}>)$ supposed to be the τ-index of τ_m. If $\tau_m^{[i+k+z]}=(1^i01^k0^z)$ and $F'_i(<\tau_m^{[i+k+z]}>)=m$, then we define $\tau_m(i+k+1+z)=1$ and $\tau_m(x)=1$ for all $x>i+k+1+z$.

Let τ_m $(2^k\le m<2^{k+1})$ be either a function with i+k values 1 only or the function of this segment which has no less zeros than any other function τ_m in this segment. Then either F'_i does not identify its τ-index correctly or F'_i makes no less than 2^k-1 mindchanges. Thus we have proved that the worst-case mindchange complexity $(F'_i)^\tau(\tau_m)$ in the segment S_{k+1} is no less than $2^k-1\geq\frac{n}{2}$. Hence the worst-case mindchange complexity for the first segments $S_0,S_1,\ldots,S_r$ (where $k+1<r\leq k+1+2^{i+1}$) is no less than $2^k-1\geq n/2^{2^{i+2}}$.

□

THEOREM 3.2. There is an enumerated class (U,τ) of total recursive functions such that, for arbitrary total recursive strategy H and for infinitely many n,

$$H^\tau_{U,\tau}(n)>n-o(\sqrt{n}).$$

PROOF differs from the proof of Theorem 3.1 only in the length of the segments. Now the length of the segment S_k is 2^{2^k}. Hence the length and the worst-case mindchange complexity of every segment is no less than the square of the total length of all of the preceding segments.

Infinitely many segments are associated with every strategy F'_i. The functions in these segments which are the most complicated for identification of τ-indices by F'_i provide the needed complexity bound.

□

THEOREM 3.3. For arbitrary enumerated class (U,τ) of total recursive functions and for arbitrary constant $c>0$ there is a total recursive strategy H such that for infinitely many n,

$$H^\tau_{U,\tau}(n)<\frac{n}{c}.$$

PROOF. We denote by ρ the real number $\rho=\lim\sup\frac{d_n}{n+1}$, where d_n is the number of pairwise distinct functions among $\tau_0,\tau_1,\tau_2,\ldots,\tau_n$. The number ρ needs not to be a constructive real number but it can be approximated by rationals.

It is possible to find effectively infinitely many n such that $\rho-\varepsilon\leq\frac{d_n}{n+1}\leq\rho+\varepsilon$. Let $n_1,n_2,n_3,\ldots$ be effective increasing sequence of such n's. Such that for arbitrary k, $n_k>2^{n_{k-1}}$.

The strategy H searches the τ-index for the given function f, first, among $\tau_0,\tau_1,\ldots,\tau_{n_1}$. It begins with computing the initial segments of $\tau_0,\tau_1,\ldots,\tau_n$ until $\geq(\rho-\varepsilon)(n_1+1)$ distinct functions are found. Then with no more than $2\varepsilon\cdot(n_1+1)$ mindchanges the strategy either stabilizes to the correct output or finds out that f is not in this initial segment. In the latter case the strategy H goes on to search the τ-index among $\tau_0,\tau_1,\ldots,\tau_{n_2}$, and so on.

Any case, the total number of mindchanges does not exceed $n_k\cdot 2\varepsilon$ for every function among $\tau_0,\tau_1,\ldots,\tau_n$. For $n \in \{n_k-[n_k/2], n_k-[n_k/2]+1, \ldots ,n_k\}$ this makes no more than $n\cdot\varepsilon$ mindchanges.

□

4. Influence of the numbering

We have proved several lower bounds in Sections 2 and 3. We prove in this section that most of these lower bounds express the complexity of the numbering rather than the complexity of the class of functions.

THEOREM 4.1. ([BKP 74]) If the class U of total recursive functions has a numbering τ such that the property $(\tau_i\equiv\tau_j)$ is decidable, then, for arbitrary total recursive function g(n) which nondecreasingly grows to the infinity, there is a strategy H identifying in the limit τ-indices of U such that $H^{\tau}_{U,\tau}(n)\le g(n)$ for all n.

PROOF. Let $n_1,n_2,n_3,\ldots$ be the sequence of the least numbers such that $g(n_i)\ge i$. The strategy computes initial fragments of $\tau_0,\tau_1,\ldots,\tau_{n_1}$ sufficiently long until all functions which are different (as shown by the decidable property) really turn out to be different. Then solely one of these functions can be equal to the function under identification. The first hypothesis (with insufficient information about the function) is 0, and the second hypothesis is the abovementioned sole function in the segment.

If the function turns out to be this function, then the only suitable function is found among $\tau_0,\tau_1,\ldots,\tau_{n_2}$ (at cost of one additional mindchange), and so on.

□

COROLLARY. If the class U of total recursive functions has a numbering τ such that the property $(\tau_i\equiv\tau_j)$ is decidable, then for arbitrary total recursive function g(n) which nondecreasingly grows to the infinity there is a strategy G identifying U in the limit such that $G^{EX}_{U,\tau}(n)\le g(n)$ for all n.

PROOF. Immediately from Theorems 4.1, 1.2 and 1.3.

□

For the contrast, we note that the counterpart of Theorem 4.1 for the prediction fails.

THEOREM 4.2. ([BKP 74]) If for an enumerated class (U,τ) it is true that for arbitrary total recursive function $g(n)$ which nondecreasingly grows to the infinity there is a strategy F predicting U such that $F^{NV}_{U,\tau}(n) \le g(n)$ for all n, then there is a nonrecursive strategy K such that $K^{NV}_{U,\tau}(n)=o(1)$.

PROOF. We use the term "pxq table of (U,τ)" for the table of values $\tau_i(x)$ with $i \le p$, $x \le q$. All possible strategies H provide us only a finite number of variants which function isto prefered when predicting values for $\tau_0, \tau_1, \dots, \tau_p$ and for $x \le q$. All these variants can be enumerated and a number $S(p,q)$ be found such that:

a) arbitrary strategy H makes no less than $S(p,q)$ errors at a line of the (pxq)-table of (U,τ),

b) there is a strategy H_0 which makes at an arbitrary line of the (pxq)-table of (U,τ) no more than $S(p,q)$ errors.

Evidently, $S(p,q)$ is a total recursive function which is monotonic both in p and q. It is easy to see that

$$(\forall p)(\forall q) H^{NV}_{U,\tau}(p) \ge S(p,q) \qquad (4.1)$$

Since there is a total recursive strategy F with the property $F^{NV}_{U,\tau}(p) \le p$, we conclude that for a fixed p the function $S(p,q)$ is bounded. Indeed, if $S(p,q)$ were unbounded, then it would be possible to find a total recursive function $t(p)$ such that $S(p,t(p)) \longrightarrow \infty$ monotonically. By (4.1), this contradicts the provisions of the theorem.

We have proved $(\forall p)(\forall q)(S(p,q) \le C)$. Now we can prove the existence of the needed strategy K.

The inequality $S(q,q) \le C$ implies that, for every q the set $\tilde{H}_q$ of those strategies which make no more than C errors within the (qxq)-table of (U,τ), is nonempty. The set $\tilde{H}_q$ is divided into a finite system of equivalence classes where one class consists of strategies which function equally within the (qxq)-table of (u,τ). We denote this system by $\{\tilde{H}^1_q, \dots, \tilde{H}^{kq}_q\}$. It is easy to see that

$$(\forall k \le k_{q+1})(\exists l \le k_q)(\tilde{H}^k_{q+1} \subseteq \tilde{H}'_q).$$

Hence from the compactness theorem for trees with the finite branching property, there is a strategy H such that

$$(\forall q)(\exists k \le k_q)(H \in \tilde{H}^k_q)$$

or just $H \in \tilde{H}_q$ for all q . Thus H makes no more than C errors on every (qxq)-table of (U,τ), and $H^{NV}_{U,\tau}(q)=o(1)$.

□

5. Prediction and identification of finite automata

We saw in Section 2 that prediction and identification in the limit can be performed with a small number of errors (resp.,mindchanges). Section 3 contained disappointing results (Theorems 3.1 and 3.3) showing that for identification of τ-indices many mindchanges may be inevitable. On the other hand, we saw in Section 4 that the negative results just indicate that these are numberings which are complicate, not the classes of functions. Now we are about to ask whether "natural" numberings make identification easy or complicate.

For arbitrary classes of functions it is not possible to answer such a question since we do not know the criteria according to which numberings could be called "natural". Nevertheless, there is a happy exception. There are classes of objects that can be considered as recursively enumerable classes of total recursive functions, and simultaneously they have nontrivial natural numberings, the naturalness of which is widely accepted. We are talking about finite automata.

Finite automata were intensively studied in the fifties, and the pioneering paper [Moo 56] was a starting point in several directions of research, inductive inference including. Hence it is natural to consider such an example.

Initial finite automata with input and output are considered. The input alphabet is fixed X={1,2,...,a}. The output alphabet may vary. We restrict it only to be a subset of {1,2,...,n}. The class of all such automata is denoted by U_a. The subclass of U_a obtained by fixing the output alphabet to be Y={1,2,...,b} is denoted by $U_{a,b}$.

Automata are considered as "black boxes". We know only that they are in U_a. Let the sequence of the inputs of such an automaton A be

$$\omega=\{x(1), x(2), \ldots, x(t), \ldots\},$$

and

$$\{y(1), y(2), \ldots, y(t), \ldots\}$$

be the corresponding output sequence. The problem is, for an arbitrary t, given {x(1), ..., x(t)}, {y(1), ..., y(t)}, x(t+1), to predict y(t+1). Arbitrary effective rules (called strategies) are allowed.

We see that the problem cannot be solved without errors. We study the minimal number of errors needed for such a prediction. The main result of this section shows that the worst-case number of errors can be very small, namely, $o((a-1)\cdot k\cdot \log_2 k)$ for automata with k states and this estimate cannot be asymptotically improved. Note that any exhaustive search gives the upper bound of k^k type.

Let Σ be a strategy, i.e. a total recursive function of one argument. We say that Σ commits an error at moment t working on the sequence ω and the automaton A, if

$$\Sigma(<x(1),\ldots,x(t),y(1),\ldots,y(t),x(t+1)>)\neq y(t+1).$$

$\Sigma^*(\omega,A)$ is the cardinality of the set of those t when Σ commits an error at work on ω and A. For arbitrary class U of automata

$$\Sigma^*(\omega,U,k)=\max \Sigma^*(\omega,A),$$

where the maximum is taken over all automata $A\in U$ with no more than k states.

THEOREM 5.1. ([Ba 74-2]) Let $a\geq 2$. There is a strategy Σ such that for arbitrary input sequence ω,

$$\Sigma^*(\omega,U_a,k)\leq(a-1)k\cdot\log_2 k+o((a-1)\cdot k\cdot\log_2 k).$$

PROOF. Instead of automata from U_a we consider the corresponding automata graphs (see [TB 72]) with input alphabet $X=\{1,\ldots,a\}$. We take one representative per class of isomorphic graphs (isomorphism for graphs with a fixed initial vertice is considered). We order these representatives by the number of vertices. We remove the graphs for which the part reachable from the initial vertice coincides with a graph considered earlier (such graphs do not generate new automata operators). The graphs with the same number of vertices are ordered arbitrarily. We get a sequence of graphs $\mathcal{G}=(G_1,G_2,\ldots,G_i,\ldots\}$. Evidently, if the number of vertices $|G_i|$ in the graph G_i does not exceed k, then

$$i\leq I(a,k), \tag{5.1}$$

where I(a,k) is the number of all pairwise nonisomorphic initial automata graphs with k vertices and a-letter input alphabet. It follows from [Kor 67] that

$$I(a,k) \sim \begin{cases} \frac{k^{ak}}{k!}\cdot k, & \text{if } a\geq 3, \\ \frac{1}{e^{2\cdot e^4}} \cdot \frac{k^{ak}}{k!} \cdot k, & \text{if } a=2. \end{cases} \tag{5.2}$$

(Since we consider initial automata graphs, we have the multiplier k in (5.2), in contrast to the original version of the formula in [Kor 67]).

Following the idea of the proof of Theorem 2.1 we associate weights

$$p(G_i)=\frac{C_0}{i(\log_2(i+1))^2} \tag{5.3}$$

to graphs G_i. (Here the constant C_0 is chosen to have $\sum p(G_i)=s_0<1$. It is easy to see that the series converge effectively.)

First, we construct a nonrecursive "strategy" Σ which provides the needed complexity bound. This strategy in the computation process observes all the infinite sequence $\mathscr{G}$. Next, we use the effective convergence of $\sum p(G_i)$ and modify this "strategy" making it recursive.

The "strategy" Σ is described as a sequential process of predicting which ascribes output letters to the edges of the graph (thus converting the graph into an automaton). The "strategy" crosses out the graphs which have turned out to be inconsistent with the input x(1),...,x(t) and output y(1),...,y(t). Let the path x(1)...x(t) in the graph G be the path starting in the initial vertice and following the input word x(1)...x(t).

We start the prediction at t=1 when we are to predict y(2) by x(1), y(1), x(2). For the starting sequence of automata graphs we take the sequence $\mathscr{G}^0=\{G_1^0,\ldots,G_i^0,\ldots\}$ which is essentially the same $\mathscr{G}$, only on the edges outgoing from the initial vertice and labelled by input letter x(1) the output symbol y(1) is written. The weights of the automata graphs remain the same as before. This way, we get a sequence $\mathscr{G}^1=\{G_1^1,\ldots,G_i^1,\ldots\}$ with ascribed weights.

At the stage t we have the information x(1),...,x(t), y(1),...,y(t),x(t+1). We take the sequence $\mathscr{G}^{t-1}=\{G_1^{t-1},\ldots,G_i^{t-1},\ldots\}$ produced at the previous stage. All graphs in this sequence have output letters y(1), y(2),...,y(t) written on the edges of the path x(1) x(2) ... x(t), and no edges have been ascribed contradicting letters. In the general case $\mathscr{G}^{t-1}$ may have not all automata graphs, since some of the graphs may contradict the existing information on the input-output relation. In other terms, if G_i^{t-1} is considered as a partially defined automaton, then it produces $y(1)\ldots y(t)$ as its response to $x(1)\ldots x(t)$ and goes to the state $g_t=g_1x(1)\ldots x(t)$.

We say that G_i^{t-1} at input $x(t+1)$ outputs y if the edge outgoing g_t and corresponding $x(t+1)$ is on the path $x(1)\ldots x(t)$ and has the output symbol y. If G_i^{t-1} produces an output symbol in response to $x(t+1)$, i.e., if the edge $x(t+1)$ from g_t is on the path $x(1)\ldots x(t)$, then we say that G_i^{t-1} participates the prediction.

Additionally, the elements of $\mathcal{G}^{t-1}$ have got weights $p(G_i^{t-1})$ and the total $\sum p(G_i^{t-1})=S_0<1$. The "strategy" $\bar{\Sigma}$ predicts the output symbol with the maximal total weight.

To complete the description of the current stage t we have to say that the new information is used to transform $\mathcal{G}^{t-1}$ into $\mathcal{G}^t$. The output symbol $y(t)$ is ascribed to the edge of the graph corresponding to $x(t)$ on the path $x(1)\ldots x(t-1)x(t)$. If this output symbol contradicts to the earlier information for this graph, then the graph is removed from the sequence.

The new weight is defined as follows. If the graph has not participated in the prediction, then its weight is not changed. If the graph has participated and has not been removed, then its weight is multiplied to s_t/r_t, where s_t is the total of weights of the automata having participated in the prediction and r_t is the total of weights of the automata having produced the right outcome. Evidently, the total of weights over all the sequence $\mathcal{G}^t$ has not changed, i.e. $\sum p(G_i^t)=S_0$.

Note that, if $\bar{\Sigma}$ has made an error, then

$$\frac{S_t}{r_t}\geq 2. \tag{5.4}$$

Hence, every graph having produced a right prediction at least doubles its weight.

Let G_α be the first graph in the sequence which is consistent with the input-output information. At every moment of error, either G_α gets a new output symbol or doubles its weight. Hence the maximal number of errors does not exceed a number z such that $2^{z-ak}\cdot p(G_\alpha)=1$. From this equality, using (5.1), (5.2), (5.3), we can get

$$\bar{\Sigma}^*(\omega,U_a,k) < z \leq (a-1)k\cdot\log_2 k. \tag{5.5}$$

It remains to modify $\bar{\Sigma}$ and to get a recursive strategy Σ which computes the infinite series only approximately and does about the same as $\bar{\Sigma}$. We use the constructive convergence of the series of weights. This allows us to consider only finite initial fragments of this series. The strategy Σ predicts y only when it has checked that any other output symbol y′ may have the total of weights

$$p(y')\le p(y)+\frac{2}{j_t+1}\cdot p(y), \tag{5.6}$$

where j_t is the number of errors already made up to this moment (instead of $p(y')\le p(y)$ for $\bar{\Sigma}$). This modification does not influence (5.5).

□

THEOREM 5.2. ([Ba 72-2]) Let $a\ge 2$. There exists an input sequence ω_0 such that for every strategy Σ and for every $b\ge 2$

$$\Sigma^*(\omega_0,U_{a,b},k)\ge(a-1)\cdot k\cdot\log_2 k+o((a-1)\cdot k\cdot\log_2 k)$$

(consequently, $\Sigma^*(\omega_0,U_a,k)\ge(a-1)\cdot k\cdot\log_2 k+o((a-1)\cdot k\cdot\log_2 k))$.

PROOF. Let $X=\{x_1,\dots,x_a\}$ be an input alphabet and $Y=\{0,1\}$ be an output alphabet. Given any natural number $k\ge 64$, we define the automata class R_k as follows. A typical automaton in R_k is drawn in Fig.5.1 (containing only those arrows essential for further considerations). As it is shown in Fig.5.1, automata in R_k have

$$s+\mu\alpha=2[\log_2 k]+6+2^{[\log_2 k-\log_2\log_2 k]}\cdot[\log_2 k-\log_2\log_2 k]=k-o(k)$$

states. First s-1 states specify a subautomaton called k-*encipherator* (the same for all automata in R_k), the next k states form a different subautomaton called the *main*.

First we give the formal description of k-encipherator. Given the binary representation of the number k, we replace every occurrence of the symbol 1 by the word x_2x_1, replace every symbol 0 by the word x_1x_2 and add $x_1x_1x_1$ to the end of the word obtained so far. Let $\bar{k}$ denote the word we have obtained. Apparently, $s=2[\log_2 k]+6$ is the length of $\bar{k}$; let $\bar{k}=\nu_1,\nu_2,\dots,\nu_s$. The word $\bar{k}$ contains no subword $x_1x_1x_1$. $\bar{k}$-encipherator is supposed to "let through" (to the main subautomaton) only the words containing a subword $\bar{k}$, provided it starts updating in the initial state q_1. The definitions of k-encipherator (see Fig.5.1) and the word $\bar{k}$ imply that, provided x_1 repeated tree times preceeds $\bar{k}$, k-encipherator will reach the state q_1 and will stay in this state while x_1 is on input.

Now we describe the main subautomaton. It consists of many distinct blocks. The i-th block begins with the state $q_{s+i\alpha}$ (initial states in Fig.5.1 are marked by *), the length of each block (i.e.,

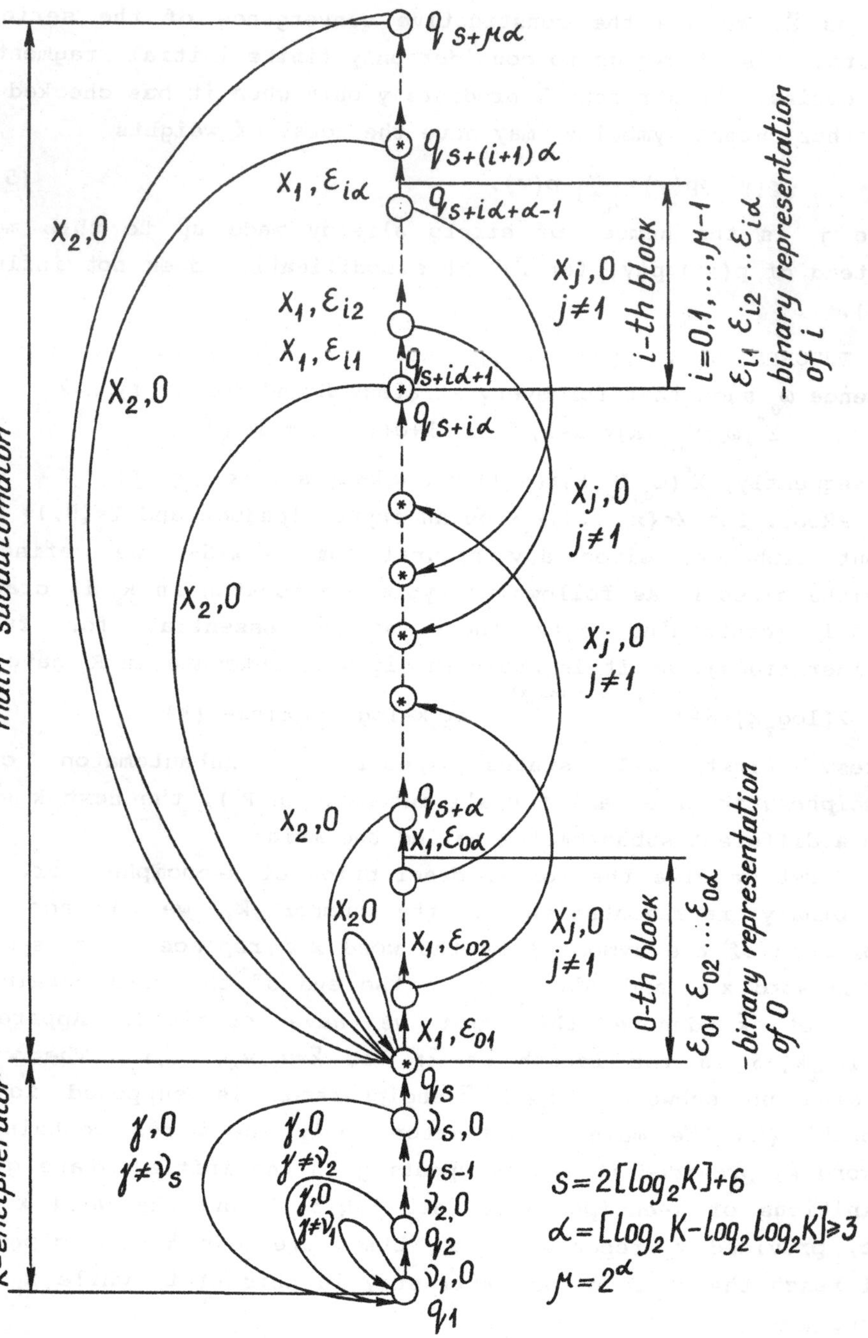

q s+μα
q s+(i+1)α
x1, εiα
q s+iα+α-1
x2,0
xj,0
j≠1
i-th block
i=0,1,...,μ-1
εi1 εi2 ... εiα
-binary representation of i
x1, εi2
x1, εi1
q s+iα+1
x2,0
q s+iα
main subautomaton
xj,0
j≠1
x2,0
xj,0
j≠1
q s+α
x2,0
x1,ε0α
x2 0
xj,0
j≠1
0-th block
ε01 ε02 ... ε0α
-binary representation of 0
x1,ε02
x1,ε01
qs
k-encipherator
γ,0
γ≠νs
γ,0
γ≠ν2
γ,0
γ≠ν1
νs,0
qs-1
ν2,0
q2
ν1,0
q1
s=2[log2K]+6
α=[log2K-log2log2K]≥3
μ=2^α

Fig.5.1

the number of states) is equal to $\alpha=[\log_2 k-\log_2\log_2 k]\geq 3$, the total number of blocks is $\mu=2^{\alpha}\leq\frac{k}{\log_2 k}$. The output labels on the arrows from the states in the i-th block labelled by x_1 form the binary word $\varepsilon_{i1}\varepsilon_{i2}\ldots\varepsilon_{i\alpha}$ that is the binary representation of the number i (containing so many zeros in the beginning that the total length is α).

The word $\varepsilon_{i1}\varepsilon_{i2}\ldots\varepsilon_{i\alpha}$ is said to be the characteristic sequence of the block i. Hence, every block specifies its own characteristic sequence. Note, that the number of distinct binary words of the length α is just equal to the number of blocks; therefore, every binary word of the length α is the characteristic sequence for some block. Arrows outgoing from the initial states of the blocks (i.e., from the states $q_{s+i\alpha}$, $i=0,1,\ldots,\mu$) and labelled by the input symbol x_2 link initial states with the state q_s. Arrows outgoing from inner states of blocks and labelled by input symbols differing from x_1 (call these arrows *variable* ones) link these states with arbitrary initial states of blocks (there are 2^{α} states of this kind). Just the latter property differs any automaton in R_k from any other.

Now we consider variable arrows. The total number of these arrows is equal to $u=(a-1)\mu(\alpha-1)$. Let us fix a linear ordering of these arrows: $d_1,d_2,\ldots,d_u$. Given any main subautomaton, associate with it the binary sequence

$$\delta_{11},\ldots,\delta_{1\alpha},\ldots,\delta_{j1},\ldots,\delta_{j\alpha},\ldots,\delta_{u1},\ldots,\delta_{u\alpha}$$

of the length αu defined as follows: $\delta_{j1},\ldots,\delta_{j\alpha}$ is the characteristic sequence of the block having the initial state the arrow d_j goes to. This sequence is called the characteristic sequence of the given main subautomaton. It is easy to see (taking into account values of α and μ) that every binary sequence of the length αu is the characteristic sequence for some main subautomaton.

Now we define one specific input sequence. Let d_j' stand for the input symbol labelling d_j, and V_j be the sequence "transferring" q_s to the state the arrow d_j is outgoing from. We set

$$D_k=\{V_1,d_1',\underbrace{x_1,\ldots,x_1}_{\alpha\ \text{times}},x_2,\ldots,V_j,d_j',\underbrace{x_1,\ldots,x_1}_{\alpha\ \text{times}},x_2,\ldots,$$
$$V_n,d_u',\underbrace{x_1,\ldots,x_1}_{\alpha\ \text{times}}\}.$$

Consider, for a while, the main subautomaton as an independent automaton with the initial state q_s. For input string D_k the automaton outputs the sequence

$$E=\{W_1,0,\delta_{11},\ldots,\delta_{1\alpha},0,\ldots,W_j,0,\delta_{j1},\ldots,\delta_{j\alpha},0,\ldots$$
$$\ldots,W_u\delta_{u1},\ldots,\delta_{u\alpha}\},$$

where W_j is the output sequence corresponding to the fragment V_j and $\delta_{j1},\ldots,\delta_{j\alpha}$ corresponds to the piece $\underbrace{x_1,\ldots,x_1}_{\alpha \text{ times}}$ directly following V_j. The subsequence

$$\delta_{11},\ldots,\delta_{1\alpha},\ldots,\delta_{j1},\ldots,\delta_{j\alpha},\ldots,\delta_{u1},\ldots,\delta_{u\alpha}$$

of the sequence E is, obviously, the characteristic sequence of the given main subautomaton.

Let Σ be any strategy. Now it is not difficult to show that there is a main subautomaton A_Σ that, provided A_Σ is treated as an independent subautomaton with the initial state q_s, the strategy Σ, being applied to the automaton A_Σ and the input sequence D_k, will make mistakes just in those places corresponding to the fragments $\underbrace{x_1,\ldots,x_1}_{\alpha \text{ times}}$ of D_k, i.e., for every j and $1\le l\le\alpha$, $1\le j\le u$, the inequality

$$\Sigma\{V_1,d'_1,\underbrace{x_1,\ldots,x_1}_{\alpha \text{ times}},x_2,\ldots,V_j,d'_j,\underbrace{x_1,\ldots,x_1}_{l-1 \text{ times}};$$
$$_1,0,\ \delta_{11},\ldots,\delta_{1\alpha},0,\ldots,W_j,0,\delta_{j1},\ldots,\delta_{j(l-1)},x_1)\ne\delta_{j\alpha}$$

will hold.

This inequality shows how the characteristic sequence of the required automaton A_Σ should be defined. Furthermore, given the characteristic sequence, one can easily restore unambiguously the automaton A_Σ. Hence,

$$\Sigma^*(D_k,A_\Sigma)\ \ge\ u\alpha\ =\ (a-1)\mu(\alpha-1)\alpha.$$

Finally, we are able to define the required input sequence:

$$\omega_0=\{\bar{k}_0,D_{k_0},(\overline{k_0+1}),D_{k_0+1},\ldots,\bar{k},D_k,\ldots\},\quad k_0=64.$$

Let A be an arbitrary automaton in R_k. As it follows from the definition of k-encipherator the automaton A reaches for the first time the state q_s on the input string ω_0 just after the initial fragment

$$\omega_0=\{\bar{k}_0,D_{k_0},\ldots,D_{k-1},\bar{k}\}.$$

Before A has reached q_s, k-encipherator runs on $\omega_0(k)$ (let $\Omega_0(k)$ denote the sequence k-encipherator outputs on $\omega_0(k)$). The sequence ω_0 is constructed so that D_k follows $\omega_0(k)$. Therefore, after the string $\omega_0(k)$ is updated, the main subautomaton can be considered as an independent automaton with the initial state q_s, input string D_k and prediction strategy according to

$$\Sigma'(\varphi,\xi;x_1)=\Sigma(\omega_0(k),\xi;\Omega_0(k),\xi;x_1).$$

Let us choose $A_{\Sigma'}$ as the main subautomaton for A. Then, clearly,

$$\Sigma^*(\omega_0,A)\geq\Sigma'^*(D_k,A_{\Sigma'})\geq(a-1)\mu(\alpha-1)\alpha.$$

Therefore, $\Sigma^*(\omega_0,U_{a,2},s+\mu\alpha)\geq(a-1)\mu(\alpha-1)\alpha$. Using values of s,α,μ, we obtain

$$\Sigma^*(\omega_0,U_{a,2},k)\leq(a-1)k\cdot\log_2k+o((a-1)k\cdot\log_2k).$$

□

One can consider identification in the limit of automata instead of prediction of their behaviour. In this case, given a pair $\{x(1),\dots,x(t)\}$, $\{y(1),\dots,y(t)\}$, one has to construct an automaton A′ non-distinguishable from the "black box" A on the string $\omega=\{x(1),\dots,x(t),\dots\}$. Let $\{A_\omega\}$ stand for the class of all such A′. Strategy Σ in this case is a general recursive function which, given any string $\{x(1),\dots,x(t)\}$, $\{y(1),\dots,y(t)\}$, finds an automaton in U_a(more precisely, given the number of the string, it finds the number of an automaton in U_a).

$$A_t=\Sigma(x(1),\dots,x(t);y(1),\dots,y(t))$$

is said to be the hypothesis generated at the moment t. Let us suppose that

a) for every t, the automaton A_t transforms the input word $x(1)\dots x(t)$ into $y(1)\dots y(t)$, i.e. A_t is not an "explicitly" incorrect guess;

b) there exists t such that $A_t=A_{t+1}=\dots=A'$ and $A'\in\{A_w\}$.

Then we say that the strategy Σ identifies in the limit the automaton A on the sequence ω.

By $\Sigma^\#(\omega,A)$ we denote the number of mindchanges, i.e. the number of moments when the automaton produced at this moment differs from the automaton produced at the previous moment. Additionally, $\Sigma^\#(\omega,A)=\infty$ if the strategy Σ does not identify in the limit the automaton A on ω. By analogy, we define $\Sigma^\#(\omega,U_a,k)=\max\Sigma^\#(\omega,A)$, where the maximum is taken over all automata $A\in U_a$ with no more than k states.

THEOREM 5.3. ([Ba 74-2]) Let a≥2. There exists a strategy Σ such that for every input sequence ω

$$\Sigma^*(\omega,U_a,k)\leq(a-1)k\cdot\log_2k+o((a-1)k\cdot\log_2k).$$

PROOF. Instead of the "strategy" $\bar\Sigma$ from the proof of Theorem 5.1 we use a "strategy" $\bar\Sigma'$ which differs only in one aspect. The "strategy" $\bar\Sigma'$ changes the sequence $\mathcal{G}$ only at the moments when an error is made. It is easy to see that the estimate (5.5) remains valid since it was proved actually using only those moments t when the strategy fails (i.e. the inequality (5.4) holds). Let $t_1, t_2, \ldots t_n$ denote moments when errors were made, $n=\bar{\Sigma}'^{*}(\omega,A)$. Therefore, our strategy $\bar{\Sigma}'$ will use only subsequences $\mathcal{G}, \mathcal{G}^{t_1}, \mathcal{G}^{t_2}, \ldots, \mathcal{G}^{t_n}$.

Now we are about, given the strategy $\bar{\Sigma}'$, to define an effective strategy Σ'. The symbol y, Σ' outputs at the moment t, has to satisfy the inequality 5.6. Let $t\in(t_i,t_{i+1}]$. Then inequality is transformed to

$$p(y')\le p(y)+\frac{2}{i}\,p(y). \qquad (5.7)$$

For any given $t\in(t_i,t_{i+1}]$, the symbol y can be defined using at most an initial fragment of the sequence $\mathcal{G}^{t_i}$. This fragment is said to be essential for the given moment t. Taking into account constructive convergence of the series $\sum_j p(\mathcal{G}_j)$ one can show easily that it can be effectively computed, given the pair $\{x(1),\ldots,x(t)\}$, $\{y(1),\ldots,y(t)\}$. Note, that, if an initial fragment, essential for the moment t, is long enough, then it can be equally essential for the next moment, and so on. Now, let $t_{i_1}, t_{i_2}, \ldots, t_{i_n}$ be the moments in $(t_i,t_{i+1}]$ when one has to change (i.e. to make longer) the essential initial fragment chosen earlier (in order to make it possible to check the inequality (5.7)). Note, furthermore, that, if an essential initial fragment containing the required graph G_α is found and this fragment contains a sufficiently long "tail" after G_α, then at least the inequality (5.7) protects it from replacement (it will be changed when an error is made, and $\mathcal{G}$ is to be changed itself). This consideration implies that, if we choose every next essential initial fragment sufficiently longer than the preceding one (for instance, of the length 2^n, where n is the length of the preceding fragment), then the total number of changes of essential initial fragments implied by inequality (5.7) will not exceed $o(|G_\alpha|\log_2|G_\alpha|)$. On the other hand, the number of changes of essential initial fragments implied by changes of the sequence $\mathcal{G}$ is equal to the number of $\mathcal{G}$ changes, i.e. the number of errors Σ' makes on the input string. The latter number, as it follows from the proof of Theorem 5.1, does not exceed $(a-1)k\cdot\log_2 k+o(k\cdot\log_2 k)$. We obtain now that our strategy Σ' changes essential initial fragments at most

$$(a-1)k\cdot\log_2 k+o(k\cdot\log_2 k)+o(|G_\alpha|\log_2|G_\alpha|)=$$
$$=(a-1)k\cdot\log_2 k+o(k\cdot\log_2 k)$$

times. While essential initial fragment is not changed the strategy Σ' predicts the next value using only this fragment and the current vertex of each graph from the fragment. Namely, it means the following. The current vertex of G_j at the moment t is just the vertex the automaton reaches reading x(1)...x(t) from the initial state. Therefore, if we know the current vertex of the graph G_j, then we can find the symbol y G_j (as an automaton) outputs reading x(t+1); there is no need to store information reflecting the word x(1)...x(t).

It means that a finite automaton is able to perform prediction which Σ' is making while essential initial fragment is not changed. The states of the required automaton are all possible orders of current vertices in the chosen initial fragments (i.e., each state is a chosen initial fragment, where just a single vertex, called current, is marked in every graph; the choice of current vertices distinguishes one state from the other). Transition from one state to another is performed according to the transition of current vertices in every graph while reading x. The automaton outputs the symbol the strategy Σ' is supposed to output in the given case.

The above automaton is just the hypothesis the required strategy Σ is suppoosed to guess during the timefragment under consideration. Evidently, the number of hypothesis changes is equal to the number of changes of essential initial fragments. Therefore,

$$\Sigma^{\#}(\omega,A)\le(a-1)k\cdot\log_2 k+o((a-1)\cdot k\cdot\log_2 k).$$

□

The lower bound proved in Theorem 5.2, clearly, holds in the given case too.

The cases considered above resemble in a way simple experiment. Now we consider the case which resembles multiple experiment. Let the sequence

$$\Omega=\{\varphi_1,\varphi_2,\ldots,\varphi_t,\ldots\}$$

be used as an input for a "black box" A and $\{\eta_1,\eta_2,\ldots,\eta_t,\ldots\}$ is the corresponding sequence of output words (A reads every new word starting from the initial state).

Prediction by the 3-tuple $\{\varphi_1,\ldots,\varphi_t\}$, $\{\eta_1,\eta_2,\ldots,\eta_t\}$, φ_{t+1} means prediction of η_{t+1}. In our case $\Sigma^{*}(\Omega,A)$ is the number of distinct t such that

$\Sigma(\varphi_1,\ldots,\varphi_t;\eta_1,\eta_2,\ldots,\eta_t;\varphi_{t+1})\neq\eta_{t+1}$.

Given any pair $\{\varphi_1,\ldots,\varphi_t\}$, $\{\eta_1,\eta_2,\ldots,\eta_t\}$, the goal of the identification in the limit is to define an automaton A' non-distinguishable from A on the input words Ω. $\Sigma^{\#}(\Omega,A)$ is defined like $\Sigma^{\#}(\omega,A)$, but the words φ_t,η_t are used instead of x(t) and y(t) respectively, and the hypothesis A_t is defined as $\Sigma(\varphi_1,\ldots,\varphi_t;\eta_1,\eta_2,\ldots,\eta_t)$.

Extending slightly proofs of Theorem 5.1 and Theorem 5.3, we obtain the following, slightly more general results.

THEOREM 5.1'. ([Ba 74-2]) Let $a\geq 2$. There exists a strategy Σ such that for every sequence Ω of input words

$$\Sigma^{*}(\Omega,U_a,k)\leq(a-1)k\cdot\log_2 k+o((a-1)k\cdot\log_2 k).$$

THEOREM 5.3'. ([Ba 74-2]) Let $a\geq 2$. There exists a strategy Σ such that, for every sequence Ω of input words,

$$\Sigma^{\#}(\Omega,U_a,k)\leq(a-1)k\cdot\log_2 k+o((a-1)k\cdot\log_2 k).$$

Theorem 5.3' is a very important tool for investigation of the synthesis of programs by hystories of their behaviour (see Section 6).

6. Notes on program synthesis from computational hystories

One of the most important problems in the theory of learning evidently is program synthesis from computational histories. Note, that even learning of such algorithms as addition and multiplication usually proceeds as follows: the teacher demonstrates how the algorithm is working on particular samples, i.e., gives the histories of computation and then the learners are synthesizing general algorithm (program) on the basis of this information themselves. In 1972 Bierman [Bie 72] proposed heuristic algorithms of synthesis from computational histories and implemented them on computer. Still the mathematical basis of the process of such synthesis have not been studied much at the time. Below we give the first results in this field we obtained in 1974 (first published in [Ba 74-3]).

As a model we consider the Post machine. All the results can be easily transformed for more general programming languages (to within multiplying constants in evaluations).

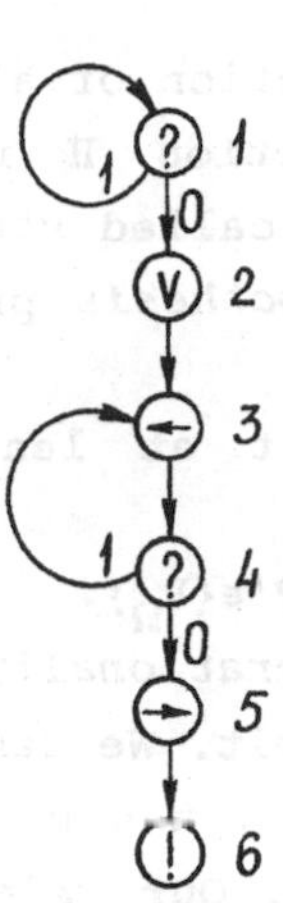

Fig.6.1

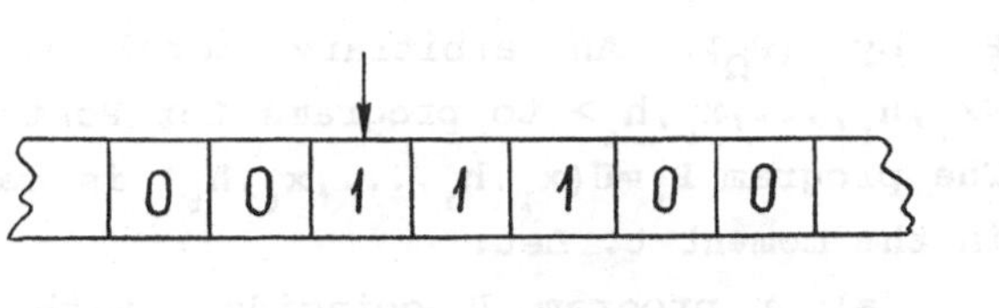

Fig.6.2

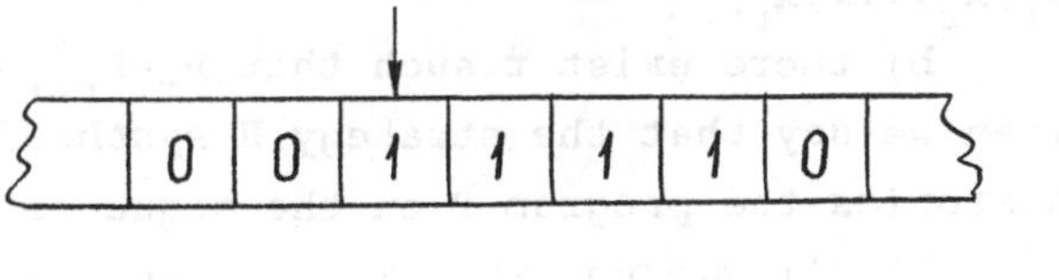

Fig.6.3

Let us consider one-tape Post machine with outer alphabet {0,1}. It is given by the instructions of the type:

← - shift the head one cell leftwards,

→ - shift the head one cell rightwards,

V - print '1' in the current cell,

0 - print '0' in the current cell,

? - conditional instruction: transfer by 1 if 1, transfer by 0 if 0,

! - instruction 'HALT'.

An example of a program is given in Fig.6.1.

Given the input x=111 (Fig.6.2), the program produces y=1111 (Fig.6.3) executing the following sequence of instructions:

$$? \rightarrow ? \rightarrow ? \rightarrow ?\ V \leftarrow ? \leftarrow ? \leftarrow ? \leftarrow ? \leftarrow ? \rightarrow !$$

The sequence is formed from all the instructions which are run by the program working on the given x. Such a sequence will be called *operationally-logic history* of the given program for the given x (the notion is introduced in [Er 71]).

Now let us state the problem. Let P be an arbitrary program of the Post machine and

$$\Omega=\{x_1,x_2,\ldots,x_t,\ldots\}$$

be an infinite sequence of natural numbers. We assume that the program P halts for any x_t from Ω and gives the result $P(x_t)$ (we call such Ω permissible for P). Let h_t - operationally-logic history of program P for x_t. Let there be given

$$\{(x_1,h_1),\ldots,(x_t,h_t)\}.$$

It is required to determine a program P' such that P' coincides with

P on Ω, i.e., $P'(x)=P(x)$ for $x\in\Omega$. We denote a collection of all such P' by $\{P_\Omega\}$. An arbitrary total recursive function Π mapping $<x_1,h_1,...,x_t,h_t>$ to programs for Post machines is called *strategy*. The program $P_t=\Pi(x_1,h_1,...,x_t,h_t)$ is called the *hypothesis* produced in the moment t. Let:

a) a program P coincide with P for any t at least for $x_1,x_2,...,x_t$,

b) there exist τ such that $P_\tau=P_{\tau+1}=...=P'$ and $P'\in\{P_\Omega\}$.

Then we say that the strategy Π *synthesizes from operationally-logic histories* the program P on the sequence Ω in the limit. We denote by $\Pi^{\#}(\Omega,P)$ the number of changing the hypothesis, i.e., the number of different t, such that $P_t\neq P_{t+1}$. Otherwise, $\Pi^{\#}(\Omega,P)=\infty$. Our aim is to evaluate $\Pi^{\#}(\Omega,P)$. Let us denote by $\|P\|$ the number of conditional instructions in P.

THEOREM 6.1. ([Ba 74-3]) There exists a strategy Π such that for any program P and any sequence Ω

$$\Pi^{\#}(\Omega,P)\le\|P\|\log_2\|P\|+o(\|P\|\log_2\|P\|).$$

Using advanced enough algorithmic languages $\|P\|$ usually is not too large. For instance, for the program of multiplication of matrices $\|P\|=3$. Therefore Theorem 6.1 shows that there exists a strategy which makes quite a few mistakes in the process of synthesis (almost comparable with the number of mistakes the programmers usually do when writing similar programs).

To prove Theorem 6.1 we associate with any program P the following automaton P_{aut} with input alphabet {0,1}. Let program P begin with a conditional instruction (this does not restrict the generality), and let us represent it as a graph. Let us keep in the graph only those vertexes corresponding to instructions "?" and "!", the paths consisting of other vertexes we replace by arrows. More precisely, if the path is of the type given in Fig.6.4a, we replace it by the arrow with *entry* label ε and *exit* label $(\gamma_1,\gamma_2,...,\gamma_s,\delta)$ (Fig.6.4b). As the result we obtain a diagram of a certain automaton, which we denote by P_{aut}. For the program given in Fig.6.1 the corresponding automaton is shown in Fig.6.5, the input alphabet is $\{(\rightarrow,?),(V,\leftarrow,?),(\leftarrow,?),(\rightarrow,!)\}$.

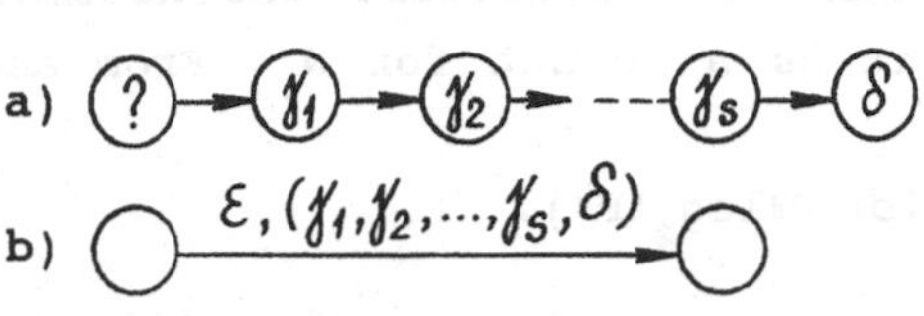

Fig.6.4

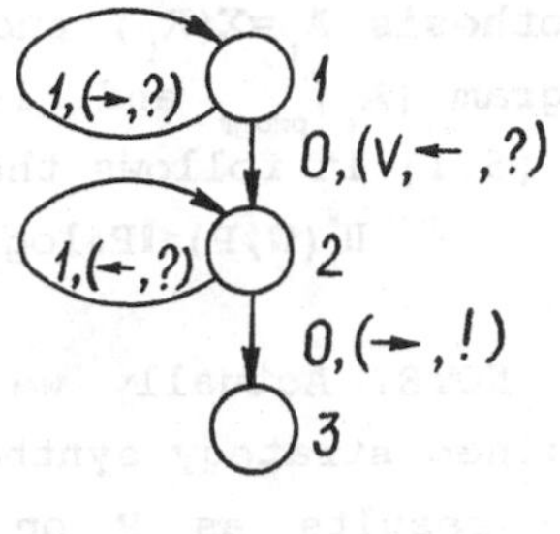

Fig.6.5

Evidently it is possible to restore the program P by P_{aut} q(we denote it by $(P_{aut})_{progr}$).

We associate the input word $\varphi_t=\varepsilon_{t_1}\varepsilon_{t_2}\ldots\varepsilon_{t l_t}$ $(\varepsilon_{t j}\in\{0,1\})$ with x_t and $h_t={?u_1}{?u_2}?\ldots{?u_{l_t}}$, where u_j is the sequence of instructions (unconditional) between conditional constructions, in the following way: $\varepsilon_{t_1}\varepsilon_{t_2}\ldots\varepsilon_{t l_t}$ are the sequences of values which take the conditional instructions working on x_t in correspondence to history h_t (we assume that conditional instruction "?" takes 1, if the cell in question contains 1, and 0 otherwise). To put it differently, the word φ_t in the diagram of automaton P_{aut} determines the same path as the word x_t with history h_t in the program P. Now, substituting φ_t for x_t in $\Omega=\{x_1,\ldots,x_t,\ldots\}$ we obtain the sequence of words

$$\Omega'=\{\varphi_1,\ldots,\varphi_t,\ldots\}.$$

The following assertion stating the relationship between synthesis of automata and programs is evident now:

A. If A is an arbitrary automaton undistinguishable from P_{aut} on the sequence of input words Ω' (input of all words starts on state 1), then the program $(A)_{progr}$ obtained from automaton A is undistinguishable from program P on the sequence Ω (i.e., they have the same histories and give the same results).

Let us apply the strategy Σ from Theorem 5.3′. We obtain

$$\Sigma^*(\Omega',P_{aut})<|P_{aut}|\log_2|P_{aut}| = (\|P\|+1)\log_2(\|P\|+1) \qquad (6.1)$$

The strategy Σ uses 2t-tuple

$$K_t=\langle\varphi_1,\ldots,\varphi_t,P_{aut}(\varphi_1),\ldots,P_{aut}(\varphi_t)\rangle$$

to produce (t+1)-hypothesis. On the other hand, the intended strategy Π can use only 2t-tuple $N_t=\langle x_1,h_1,\ldots,x_t,h_t\rangle$. Nevertheless, evidently it is possible to construct K_t effectively from N_t. Therefore the strategy Π works as follows. First, it finds the 2t-tuple K_t from N_t, then it applies the strategy Σ to K_t and finds hypothesis $A_t = \Sigma(K_t)$ and finally it transforms the automaton A_t to program $(A_t)_{progr}$ and gives it as a result for N_t. From assertion A and (6.1) it follows that

$$\Pi^*(\Omega,P) \le \|P\| \log_2 \|P\| + o(\|P\| \log_2 \|P\|).$$

□

NOTE. Actually we have proved a bit stronger assertion: the obtained strategy synthesizes a program which produces not only the same results as P on Ω, but also the same operationally-logic histories.

Let us consider the so-called *operational histories* [Er 71] instead of operationally-logic histories. Usually they are the minimal necessary information given to the learner in the process of learning some algorithm. They can be obtained from operationally-logic histories by omitting all conditional instructions. For instance, operational history corresponding to the example given above equals → → → V ← ← ← ← → !. Let us denote the number of changing the hypothesis in this case by $\Pi^*(\Omega,P)$. Let $|P|$ be the number of instructions in P. Then the following theorem holds.

THEOREM 6.2. ([Ba 74-3]) There exists a strategy Π such that for any program P and any sequence Ω

$$\Pi^*(\Omega,P) \le |P| \log_2 |P| + o(|P| \log_2 |P|).$$

Theorem 6.2 follows easily from Theorem 6.1. Note, that any program P can be transformed to an equivalent program P′ putting the conditional instruction "?" $O \longrightarrow O \rightrightarrows O$ between any two instructions $O \longrightarrow O$. Obviously, $\|P'\| \le |P|$ and operational histories of P and P′ coincide. On the other hand, it is possible to restore operationally-logic history $?K_1?K_2?\ldots?K_s!$ by operational history $K_1K_2\ldots K_s!$. Consequently, it is possible to use Theorem 6.1 for program P′. Therefore $\Pi^*(\Omega,P') \lesssim \|P'\| \log_2 \|P'\| \le |P| \log_2 |P|$.

□

The question whether a complete analogy with Theorem 6.1 holds in the case of operational histories is open. It is also interesting to study the synthesis of programs with small $\|P\|$: the given evaluations cannot be used reasonably for the case.

7. Errors versus complexity

Following the proof of Theorem 2.1 for an arbitrary enumerated class (U,τ) a total recursive prediction strategy F can be constructed such that for all n:

$$F^{NV}_{U,\tau}(n)\le\log_2 n+\log_2\log_2 n+o(\text{logloglog } n).$$

In this chapter a general result will be proved from which it follows that for such "error-optimal" strategies the time complexity of computation of the prediction $F(<f(0),\ldots,f(m)>)$ (i.e. a candidate for $f(m+1)$) may go up, in some sense, to $2^{2^{cm}}$.

To put it precisely, we investigate general algorithms of strategy construction instead of particular strategies. Such algorithms are called *uniform prediction strategies*. The precise definition is as follows.

Any numbering τ of total functions (not necessarily computable) can be treated as an oracle which answers to queries like "$\tau_i(j)=?$". Uniform prediction strategy F is a Turing machine with oracle τ which computes a candidate for $f(m+1)$ from the given values $f(0),\ldots,f(m)$ (it is assumed that the function f is in the numbering τ). We denote this candidate value, as usual, by $F_\tau(<f(0),\ldots,f(m)>)$. If the function f is not in the numbering τ, then the computation, maybe, does not halt. Thus, given any τ, F_τ is a partial recursive prediction strategy in the sense of Section 1.

The number of errors committed by the strategy F during the prediction of a function f from a numbering τ we denote, as usual, by

$$F^{NV}_\tau(f)=\text{card }\{m \mid F_\tau(<f(0),\ldots,f(m)>)\ne f(m+1)\}.$$

Let $h(x)$ be any function of a real variable x defined for all $x\ge0$. We say that a uniform strategy F *uses* $h(m)$ *queries*, if for any numbering τ, any function f from τ, and all $m\ge0$ the computation process of $F_\tau(<f(0),\ldots,f(m)>)$ issues $\le h(m)$ queries "$\tau_i(j)=?$" to oracle τ. The number of queries can be viewed as a rough lower bound for time complexity of the prediction.

Our main interest is to investigate the power of uniform prediction strategies which use $h(m)$ queries for $h(m)=2^m$, 2^{cm}, x^x, 2^{2^m}, $2^{2^{cm}}$. However, the obtained upper and lower bounds hold for any "reasonable" function h such that $\exp\le h\le 2^{\exp}$ (i.e. $h(x)$ grows at least as fast as 2^{cx}, but not faster than $2^{2^{cx}}$). To put it precisely, we introduce the following conditions for h:

C1) h is a computable function of real variable, h(x) is defined, positive and twice differentiable for all sufficiently large x. For any integers m,n≥0 it can be decided effectively whether h(m)=n or not.

C2) There is a real constant a>0 such that for all sufficiently large x:

$$(\log_2 h(x))' > a, \quad (\log_2 h(x))'' \geq 0.$$

These conditions are satisfied by any "reasonable" function growing at least as fast as 2^{cx}.

C3) There are two real constants b,d≥0 such that for all sufficiently large x:

$$(\log_2 h(x))' \leq 2^{bx+d}.$$

This condition is satisfied by any "reasonable" function growing not faster than $2^{2^{cx}}$.

One can verify easily that if the function h satisfies C1,C2,C3, then:

C4) so does the function $\frac{h(x)}{x+2}$,

C5) h(x) is strongly increasing and continuous for all sufficiently large x. This assures the existence of the inverse function $h^{-1}(x)$.

C6) For all sufficiently large integers m:

$$\frac{h(m+1)}{h(m)} \geq 1+a, \quad \sum_{i=0}^{m} h(i) < \frac{1}{a} h(m+1).$$

THEOREM 7.1.([Po 77-1]) Let function h satisfy the conditions C1,C2, and let F be a uniform prediction strategy using h(m) queries. Then there is a computable numbering τ such that for infinitely many n:

$$F_\tau^{NV}(\tau_n) > \log_2 n + h^{-1}(n) - O(1).$$

All functions of τ are of the type N⟶{0,1} with a finite number of 1's.

PROOF. For the given strategy F we define a numbering τ and some function f.

First, since C6 holds for h, let m_0 be an integer such that for all $m \geq m_0$: h(m+1)>h(m)+1.} Then, for $i \leq h(m_0)$ let all functions τ_i equal to zero. For all $i > h(m_0)$ and $j \leq m_0$ set f(j)=0 and $\tau_i(j)=0$. When during the computation of some $F_\tau(\langle f(0),\ldots,f(s)\rangle)$, $s\le m_0$, F issues a query "$\tau_1(j)=?$", set $\tau_1(j)=0$.

Suppose now that for some $m\ge m_0$ we have defined:

a) the functions τ_n for all $n\le h(m)$,

b) the values $f(0),\ldots,f(m)$, such that f coincides up to m with all τ_n for a sufficiently large n, and F_τ makes $m-m_0$ false predictions on f up to m,

c) the values $\tau_i(0),\ldots,\tau_i(m)$ for all $i>h(m)$.

Maybe, we have also defined a finite number of some other values $\tau_i(j)$.

Now we define all functions τ_n for $h(m)<n\le h(m+1)$, the value $f(m+1)$ and the values $\tau_i(m+1)$ for $i>h(m+1)$. Let us simulate the computation process of $F_\tau(\langle f(0),\ldots,f(m)\rangle)$. When F issues a query "$\tau_i(j)=?$" and the value $\tau_i(j)$ is not defined yet, set $\tau_i(j)=0$. The process will end up and yield the prediction $F_\tau(\langle f(0),\ldots,f(m)\rangle)$. (Suppose, this is not the case. Then we can set all the values $\tau_i(j)$ and $f(j)$ (not defined yet) equal to zero. Since f is now in τ, the prediction $F_\tau(\langle f(0),\ldots,f(m)\rangle)$ must be defined.)

Then we define $f(m+1)=s$ such that $s\in\{0,1\}$ and $s\ne F_\tau(\langle f(0),\ldots,f(m)\rangle)$. Thus, this prediction of F_τ is false, and the total of errors is now $m+1-m_0$. Next we define $\tau_i(m+1)$ for all i (if this value is not defined yet):

$$\tau_i(m+1)=\begin{cases} s, & \text{if } \tau_i \text{ coincides with f up to m,} \\ 0, & \text{otherwise.}\end{cases} \qquad (*)$$

Since only a finite number of $\tau_i(m+1)$ has been defined before, the function f will coincide up to m+1 with all functions τ_i for a sufficiently large i.

It remains to define other values of τ_n, $h(m)<n\le h(m+1)$, which have not been defined. Set $\tau_n(j)=0$ for all j, $m+1<j\le k$, where k is such that no value $\tau_i(j)$ has been defined up to now for $i>h(m)$ and $j>k$. The functions τ_n, $h(m)<n\le h(m+1)$, fall into natural equivalence classes:

$$n_1 \simeq n_2 \longleftrightarrow (\forall j\le m+1)\tau_{n_1}(j)=\tau_{n_2}(j)$$

(the values $\tau_n(j)$, $m+1<j\le k$, are equal to zero, i.e. they do not influence the equivalence). Let A be any of these classes, set $t=[\log_2\text{card}(A)]$. If $t>0$, we define for $n\in A$ the values $\tau_n(k+1),\ldots,\tau_n(k+t)$ using all 2^t binary words of length t. For $j>k+t$ and $n\in A$ set $\tau_n(j)=0$. Thus, predicting the values $\tau_n(k+1),\ldots,\tau_n(k+t)$

any strategy will fail t times on some τ_n, $n\in A$.

Iteration of such steps gives full definition of the numbering τ. Let us show that τ is the required numbering of the theorem.

One can easy verify the following

LEMMA 7.1. If $\tau_1(j)=f(j)$ for all $j<j_0$, and $\tau_1(j_0)\neq f(j_0)$, then $\tau_1(j)=0$ for all j, $j_0<j<k$.

The *rank* $r(A)$ of an equivalence class A (see above) is defined as the maximum number $r\le m+1$ such that

$$(\forall\tau_n\in A)(\forall j\le r)\tau_n(j)=f(j).$$

Clearly, $r(A)\ge m_0$, and by the Lemma 7.1, different classes A have different ranks. So we can denote all these classes by A_{m_0}, ..., A_r, ..., A_{m+1}. Predicting the values $\tau_n(0)$, $\tau_n(1)$, ..., $\tau_n(r)$ $(n\in A_r)$ the strategy F_τ will fail at least $r-m_0$ times. After that, predicting the values $\tau_n(k+1)$, ..., $\tau_n(k+t)$ for some $n\in A_r$, the strategy F_τ will fail another t times, $t=[\log_2 card(A_r)]$. Hence, F_τ fails on some τ_n, $n\in A_r$, at least $r+\log_2 card(A_r)-m_0-1$ times.

Some of the classes A_r are sufficiently large:

LEMMA 7.2. There exist three constants c,d,e (depending on function h) such that for all sufficiently large m there is r, $m+1-c\le r\le m+1$, such that

$$card(A_r)>dh(m+1)-e.$$

Having this lemma we can easily prove the assertion of Theorem 7.1. Indeed, take any sufficiently large m and the class A_r of the lemma. The strategy F_τ fails on some τ_n, $n\in A_r$, at least

$$r+\log_2 card(A_r)-m_0-1$$

times. Now recall that $h(m)<n\le h(m+1)$:

1) $h(m+1)\ge n$, hence $m+1\ge h^{-1}(n)$ and $r\ge m+1-c\ge h^{-1}(n)-c$.

2) $h(m+1)\ge n$, hence

$$\log_2 card(A_r)\ge\log_2(dh(m+1)-e)\ \ge\ \log_2(dn-e)\ge\log_2 n-e'$$

(e' - a constant depending on d,e). Hence,

$$F_\tau^{NV}(\tau_n)>\log_2 n+h^{-1}(n)-c-e'-m_0-1.$$

□

PROOF OF LEMMA 7.2. First, let us note that the classes A_r $(m_0\le r\le m+1)$ cover all the numbers n, $h(m)<n\le h(m+1)$. Hence, using C6,

$$\sum_{r=m_0}^{m+1} card(A_r)\ >\ h(m+1)-h(m)-1\ >\ (1-\frac{1}{1+a})h(m+1)-1.$$

Let us prove now that, if c is fixed but sufficiently large, then

$$\sum_{r=m_0}^{m-c} card(A_r) \le \frac{1}{a}(1+a)^{-c}h(m+1),$$

i.e. most of classes A_r are relatively small. Indeed, if $r<m+1$ and $n\in A_r$, then during the computation of some $F_\tau(<f(0),\ldots,f(j)>)$, $1\le j\le r$, the query "$\tau_n(r+1)=?$" must have been issued (otherwise, according to (*), $\tau_n(r+1)$ would have been defined equal to $f(r+1)$, and the rank of A_r were not r). Hence, the total of queries issued is at least

$$\sum_{r=m_0}^{m-c} card(A_r).$$

On the other hand, for the prediction $F_\tau(<f(0),\ldots,f(j)>)$ at most $h(j)$ queries could have been used, hence, using C6,

$$\sum_{r=m_0}^{m-c} card(A_r) \le \sum_{j=0}^{m-c} h(j) \le \frac{1}{a}h(m+1-c) \le \frac{1}{a}(1+a)^{-c}h(m+1).$$

Now we have:

$$\sum_{m+1-c}^{m+1} card(A_r) > (1-\frac{1}{1+a})h(m+1)-1-\frac{1}{a}(1+a)^{-c}h(m+1)=$$

$$=(1-\frac{1}{1+a} - \frac{1}{a}(1+a)^{-c})h(m+1)-1,$$

and for some r, $m+1-c\le r\le m+1$:

$$card(A_r) > \frac{1}{c+1}(1-\frac{1}{1+a} - \frac{1}{a}(1+a)^{-c})h(m+1)-\frac{1}{c+1}.$$

It remains to make c large enough to satisfy

$$1-\frac{1}{1+a} - \frac{1}{a}(1+a)^{-c}>0.$$

□

EXAMPLES. E1) For any uniform strategy F using 2^m queries:

$\exists\tau\exists^\infty n\ F_\tau^{NV}(\tau_n)>2\log_2 n-O(1)$.

E2) For any uniform strategy F using 2^{cm} queries:

$\exists\tau\exists^\infty n\ F_\tau^{NV}(\tau_n)>(1+\frac{1}{c})\log_2 n-O(1)$.

E3) For any uniform strategy F using m^m queries:

$$\exists\tau\exists^\infty n\ F_\tau^{NV}(\tau_n)>\log_2 n +\frac{\log_2 n}{\log_2\log_2 n} - O(1).$$

E4) For any uniform strategy F using 2^{2^m} queries:

$\exists\tau\exists^\infty n\ F_\tau^{NV}(\tau_n)>\log_2 n+\log_2\log_2 n-O(1)$.

E5) For any uniform strategy F using $2^{2^{cm}}$ queries:

$\exists\tau\exists^\infty n\ F_\tau^{NV}(\tau_n)>\log_2 n+\frac{1}{c}\log_2\log_2 n-O(1)$.

COROLLARIES. a) If $h(x)$ is growing slower than any exponent 2^{cx}, then no uniform strategy F using $h(m)$ queries can provide an upper bound $F_\tau^{NV}(\tau_n)\le const\cdot\log n$.

b) If $h(x)$ is growing as an exponent 2^{cx}, then no uniform strategy F using $h(m)$ queries can provide an upper bound $F_\tau^{NV}(\tau_n)\le\log_2 n+o(\log n)$.

c) If $h(x)$ is growing slower than any super-exponent $2^{2^{cx}}$, then no uniform strategy F using $h(m)$ queries can provide an upper bound $F_\tau^{NV}(\tau_n)\le\log_2 n+const\cdot\log\log n$.

d) The uniform strategy F defined in the proof of The- orem 2.1 uses (for some numbering τ and for infinitely many n) at least $2^{2^{cm}}$ queries to compute $F_\tau(\langle\tau_n(0),\dots,\tau_n(m)\rangle)$.

Now let us turn to upper bounds. Let $h(x)$ be a function satisfying the condition C1 and $\overline{\pi}=\{\pi_n\}$ be a recursive series of real numbers. By $\{h\overline{\pi}\}$ we denote the following modification of the uniform prediction strategy from the proof of Theorem 2.1.

The prediction $\{h\overline{\pi}\}_\tau(\langle f(0),\dots,f(m)\rangle)$ is computed as follows. We consider the functions τ_i only for $i\le h(m)$ and the weights π_i assigned to them. Find all numbers t such that

$$E_t=\{i \mid i\le h(m)\ \&\ (\forall j\le m)(\tau_i(j)=f(j)\ \&\ \tau_i(m+1)=t)\}\ne 0.$$

If there are no such t's, set the prediction equal to zero. For each t found compute its weight

$$w_t=\sum\{\pi_i \mid i\in E_t\}$$

with the precision 2^{-2m}, i.e. find rational number r_t such that $|r_t-w_t|\le 2^{-2m}$. Now find t with maximum r_t, and set

$$\{h\overline{\pi}\}_\tau(\langle f(0),\dots,f(m)\rangle)=t.$$

$\{h\overline{\pi}\}$ is a total recursive prediction strategy using $(m+2)h(m)$ queries. There are two different types of errors committed by the strategy $\{h\overline{\pi}\}_\tau$ during the prediction of values of the function τ_n:

- type 1:

$$\{h\overline{\pi}\}_\tau(\langle\tau_n(0),\dots,\tau_n(m)\rangle)\ne\tau_n(m+1)\ \&\ h(m)<n$$

(i.e. when computing the prediction, the function τ_n is ignored),

- type 2:

$$\{h\overline{\pi}\}_\tau(\langle\tau_n(0),\dots,\tau_n(m)\rangle)\ne\tau_n(m+1)\ \&\ h(m)\ge n.$$

Slightly modifying the proof of Theorem 2.1 we obtain the following

LEMMA 7.3. Let the function h satisfy conditions C1,C2 and the predictions $\{h\overline{\pi}\}_\tau(\langle\tau_n(0),\dots,\tau_n(m)\rangle)$ be false for $m=m_1,m_2,\dots,m_s$. Let us denote: s_1 - the number of type 1 errors, s_2 - the number of type 2 errors ($s=s_1+s_2$). Then:

a) $s_1<h^{-1}(n)$,

b) $2^{s_2}\pi_n < \sum_{i=1}^{s_2-1} 2^i\sigma_{s_1+i}+2+\sum_{j=0}^{\infty}\pi_j$,

where $\sigma_i=\sum \{\pi_j \mid h(m_i)<j\le h(m_{i+1})\}$.

Now we define a special sequence $\bar{\pi}^0$:

$$\pi_n^0 = \frac{1}{h'h^{-1}(n)2^{h^{-1}(n)}}.$$

LEMMA 7.4. Let the function h satisfy conditions C1,C2 and C3. Let the strategy $\{h\bar{\pi}^0\}_\tau$ predict the function τ_n. Let us denote: s_1 - the number of type 1 errors, s_2 - the number of type 2 errors. Then:

a) $s_1<h^{-1}(n)$,

b) $s_1+s_2-\log_2 s_2 < h^{-1}(n)+\log_2 h'h^{-1}(n)+O(1)$.

PROOF. One can verify easily that π_x^0 is a decreasing function, hence for all n:

$$\pi_n^0 < \int_{n-1}^{n} \frac{dx}{h'h^{-1}(x)2^{h^{-1}(x)}}.$$

Summing up we have

$$\sigma_i < \int_{h(m_i)}^{h(m_{i+1})+1} \frac{dx}{h'h^{-1}(x)2^{h^{-1}(x)}}.$$

Substitute h(t) for x:

$$\int_{h(m_i)}^{\infty} \frac{dx}{h'h^{-1}(x)2^{h^{-1}(x)}} = \int_{m_i}^{\infty} \frac{h'(t)dt}{h'(t)2^t} = \int_{m_i}^{\infty} \frac{dt}{2^t} = \frac{1}{\ln 2}2^{-m_i}.$$

Thus we have:

$$\sigma_i<\frac{1}{\ln 2}2^{-m_i} \le \frac{2}{\ln 2}2^{-i}$$

(since $m_i\ge i-1$). Hence, by Lemma 7.3:

$$2^{s_2}\pi_n^0 < \sum_{i=1}^{s_2-1} 2^i\sigma_{s_1+i}+2+\sum_{j=0}^{\infty}\pi_j^0 < \text{const}\cdot s_2 2^{-s_1},$$

$$s_2+\log_2\pi_n^0 < \log_2 s_2 - s_1+\text{const},$$

$$s_2-\log_2 h'h^{-1}(n)-h^{-1}(n) < \log_2 s_2 - s_1+\text{const}.$$

□

Now we can prove the upper bound:

THEOREM 7.2. ([Po 77-1]) Let the function h satisfy conditions C1,C2,C3. There is a total recursive uniform strategy F using h(m) queries such that for any numbering τ and all n:

$$F_{\tau}^{NV}(\tau_n) \le \log_2 n + (b+1)h^{-1}(n) + O(\log\log n)$$

(the constant b is from condition C3).

PROOF. Take $h_1(x) = \frac{h(x)}{x+2}$ and the strategy $\{h_1 \bar{\pi}^0\}$. Since h_1 also satisfies C1,C2,C3 (with the same constants b,d), we have:

$$h_1'(x) \le h_1(x) 2^{bx+d},$$

$$h_1' h_1^{-1}(n) \le h_1 h_1^{-1}(n) 2^{bh_1^{-1}(n)+d},$$

$$\log_2 h_1' h_1^{-1}(n) \le \log_2 n + bh_1^{-1}(n) + d.$$

Hence, by Lemma 7.4:

$$s_1 + s_2 - \log_2 s_2 \le \log_2 n + (b+1)h_1^{-1}(n) + O(1).$$

Since $x - \log_2 x \le y$ implies $x \le y + \log_2 y + O(1)$, and by C6, $h_1^{-1}(n) = O(\log n)$:

$$s_1 + s_2 \le \log_2 n + (b+1)h_1^{-1}(n) + O(\log\log n).$$

Since $F_{\tau}^{NV}(\tau_n) = s_1 + s_2$ and $h_1(n) = h^{-1}(n) + O(\log\log n)$, the proof is completed.

□

EXAMPLES. EE1) Let $h(x) = 2^x$, then b=0 in C3. There is a uniform strategy F using 2^m queries such that

$$F_{\tau}^{NV}(\tau_n) \le 2\log_2 n + O(\log\log n).$$

Compare example E1.

EE2) Let $h(x) = 2^{cx}$. There is a uniform strategy F using 2^{cm} queries such that

$$F_{\tau}^{NV}(\tau_n) \le \left(1 + \frac{1}{c}\right)\log_2 n + O(\log\log n).$$

Compare example E2.

EE3) Let $h(x) = x^x$. There is a uniform strategy F using m^m queries such that

$$F_{\tau}^{NV}(\tau_n) \le \log_2 n + O\left(\frac{\log n}{\log\log n}\right).$$

Compare example E3.

EE4) Let $h(x) = 2^{2^x}$. There is a uniform strategy F using 2^{2^m} queries such that

$$F_{\tau}^{NV}(\tau_n) \le \log_2 n + O(\log\log n).$$

Compare example E4.

8. Probabilictic strategies

In Sections 3,4 the complexity of *deterministic* identification of τ-indices was investigated, and the corresponding exact estimates were obtained. In this section we obtain the exact estimate ln n for the number of mindchanges for the *probabilistic* identification of τ-indices.

The hypotheses F(<f(0),...,f(m)>) of a *probabilistic strategy* F are random natural numbers which take their values over some fixed probability space P. Formally, probabilistic strategy F is a mapping which associates with each elementary event e∈P some deterministic strategy F_e. Thus the hypothesis F(<f(0),...,f(m)>) takes its values n with fixed probabilities

$$p_F(<f(0),...,f(m)>,n)=P\{F(<f(0),...,f(m)>)=n\}.$$

Recursive probabilistic strategies can be defined by means of probabilistic Turing machines introduced first in [LMS 56]. Let a random Bernoulli generator of some distribution (p,1-p) be fixed, 0<p<1. The generator is switched into deterministic "apparatus" of a Turing machine. As a result, the operation of the machine becomes probabilistic, and we can speak of the probability that the operation satisfies certain conditions.

Consider the following Turing machine M operating with a fixed Bernoulli generator. With input sequence

$$f(0),f(1),...,f(m),...$$

this machine prints as output an empty, finite or infinite sequence of natural numbers (hypotheses):

$$h_0,h_1,...,h_m,...,$$

where h_m depends only on the values f(0),...,f(m). To each infinite realization of Bernoulli generator's output (i.e. an infinite sequence of 0's and 1's) corresponds a completely determined operation of the machine M as a deterministic strategy in the sense of Section 1.

By P{M,τ,f} we denote the probability that a probabilistic strategy M identifies in the limit a τ-index of the function f.

By P{M,f,≤k} we denote the probability that probabilistic strategy M makes no more than k mindchanges by the function f.

THEOREM 8.1. ([Po 75]) For any enumerated class (U,τ) there exists a probabilistic strategy M such that $P\{M,\tau,f\}=1$ for all $f\in U$, and as $n\rightarrow\infty$

$$P\{M,\tau_n,\le\ln n+O(\sqrt{\log n}\cdot\log\log n)\}\rightarrow 1.$$

For a computable numbering τ, a recursive probabilistic strategy M can be constructed..

THEOREM 8.2. ([Po 75]) For any countable set Φ of probabilistic strategies there exists an enumerated class (U,τ) such that for any strategy $M\in\Phi$, if $P\{M,\tau,f\}=1$ for all $f\in U$, there is an increasing sequence $\{n_k\}$ such that as $k\rightarrow\infty$

$$P\{M,\tau_{n_k},\le\ln n_k-O(\sqrt{\log n_k}\cdot\log\log n_k)\}\rightarrow 0.$$

For the class of all recursive probabilistic strategies a computable numbering τ can be constructed.

Let M,τ,f be given. We consider some sufficient condition for $P\{M,\tau,f\}=1$. Let us denote by $f^{[m]}$ the code $<f(0),\dots,f(m)>$, then the random variable $M(<f(0),\dots,f(m)>)$ can be denoted by $M(f^{[m]})$. By $P_m(M,f)$ we denote the probability that M changes its hypothesis at step m, i.e. $P\{M(f^{[m]})\ne M(f^{[m+1]})\}$.

We say that strategy M is *τ-consistent* on the function f if, for all m,

a) $M(f^{[m]})$ is defined with probability 1,

b) if $P\{M(f^{[m]})=n\}>0$, then $\tau_n(j)=f(j)$ for all $j\le m$.

By Borel-Cantelli lemma, M is τ-consistent on the function f, then $\sum_m P_m(M,f)<\infty$ implies $P\{M,\tau,f\}=1$. Thus in the case of consistent strategies the fact of τ-identification can be established in terms of summing up the probabilities of mindchanges.

The upper bound $\ln n$ is proved by means of probabilistic counterpart of the strategy from the proof of Theorem 2.1. Essential difficulties arise, however, not in the construction of the strategy, but in its analysis.

Let (U,τ) be an enumerated class of total functions. Take some probability distribution $\{\pi_n\}$, where $\pi_n>0$ for all n and $\sum_n\pi_n=1$. Let $M_{\tau\pi}$ be the following τ-consistent probabilistic strategy.

If the set $E_0=\{n\mid\ \tau_n(0)=f(0)\}$ is empty, then we set $M_{\tau\pi}(f^{[0]})$ undefined with probability 1. If E_0 is nonempty, we put $M_{\tau\pi}(f^{[0]})=n$ with probability π_n/σ for every $n\in E_0$, where $\sigma=\Sigma\{\pi_n\mid n\in E_0\}$.

Let us assume now that the hypotheses $M_{\tau\pi}(f^{[j]})$ have already been determined for $j<m$, and $M_{\tau\pi}(f^{[m-1]})=p$. If p is "undefined",

then we set $M_{\tau\pi}(f^{[m]})$ undefined with probability 1. Else, if $\tau_p(m)=f(m)$ (i.e. the hypothesis p is correct also for the next argument m), we set $M_{\tau\pi}(f^{[m]})=p$ with probability 1. Now suppose $\tau_p(m)\neq f(m)$.

Let us take the set of all (for the time being) appropriate hypotheses, i.e.

$$E_m=\{n|\ (\forall j\le m)\tau_n(j)=f(j)\}.$$

If E_m is empty, we put $M_{\tau\pi}(f^{[m]})$ undefined with probability 1. If E_m is nonempty, we put $M_{\tau\pi}(f^{[m]})=n$ with probability π_n/σ for every $n\in E_m$, where $\sigma=\Sigma\{\pi_n|n\in E_m\}$.

LEMMA 0.1. For all n,

$$\sum_m P_m(M,\tau_n)\le\ln\frac{1}{\pi_n}.$$

From this it follows that for an arbitrary choice of distribution π, if $\pi_n>0$ for all n, the strategy $M_{\tau\pi}$ identifies in the limit τ-index of an arbitrary function in the class U with probability 1.

LEMMA 8.2. Let the function $f\in U$ be fixed. Then the following events are independent:

$$A_m=\{M_{\tau\pi}(f^{[m]})\neq M_{\tau\pi}(f^{[m+1]}\},\qquad m=0,1,2,\ldots.$$

It is curious that the events A_m(i.e. "at the m-th step strategy $M_{\tau\pi}$ changes its mind") do not display any striking indications of independence; nevertheless, they do satisfy the formal independence criterion.

If we take

$$\pi'_n=\frac{c}{n(\ln n)^2},$$

with the convention that 1/0=1 and ln 0=1, then by Lemma 8.1 the sum of the probabilities of hypothesis correcting of strategy $M_{\tau\pi'}$ with the function τ_n will not be greater than $\ln n+O(\log\log n)$. Lemma 8.2 and Chebyshev inequality allow to deduce from this that, as $n\to\infty$,

$$P\{M_{\tau\pi'},\tau_n,\le\ln n+O(\sqrt{\log n}\cdot\log\log n)\}\to 1.$$

It is easy to see that if the numbering τ is computable, the strategy $M_{\tau\pi'}$ can be made recursive.

The lower bound ln n is based upon Lemma 8.3, below. Let $\{X_j\}$ be a sequence of independent random variables such that

$$P\{X_j=1\}=\frac{1}{j},\quad P\{X_j=0\}=1-\frac{1}{j}.$$

It can be shown that, as $n\to\infty$,

$$P\{\sum_1^n X_j\ge\ln n-O(\sqrt{\log n}\cdot\log\log n)\}\to 1.$$

LEMMA 8.3. Let M be a probabilistic strategy, k and n natural numbers with k<n, and $\varepsilon>0$ a rational number. Then there is a set of n functions $\sigma_1,\dots,\sigma_n$ such that if M identifies with probability 1 the σ-number of an arbitrary function of the set, then with one of these functions M changes its mind $\geq k$ times with probability

$$\geq(1-\varepsilon)P\{\sum_{j=1}^{n} X_j \geq k\}.$$

If M is recursive strategy, the set $\sigma_1,\dots,\sigma_n$ can be constructed effectively.

Let $\{M_i\}$ be an enumeration of all probabilistic strategies from countable class Φ. With every pair (i,s) we associate the set of functions of Lemma 8.3 for $M=M_i$, $n=2^s$, $k=s \ln 2 - \sqrt{s} \log s$, $\varepsilon=2^{-s}$. Following the method of Section 4, a numbering τ can be constructed from these sets, thus proving Theorem 8.2.

For detailed proofs of lemmas see [Po 77-2].

References

[Ba 74-1] J.Barzdin. Limiting synthesis of τ-indices. Theory of Algorithms and Programs, vol.1, Latvia State University, 1974, pp.112-116 (in Russian)

[Ba 74-2] J.Barzdin. Prediction and limiting synthesis of finite automata. Theory of Algorithms and Programs, vol.1, Latvia State University, 1974, pp.129-144 (in Russian)

[Ba 74-3] J.Barzdin. A note on program synthesis from computational histories. Theory of Algorithms and Programs, vol.1, Latvia State University, 1974, pp.145-151 (in Russian)

[BF 72] J.Barzdin, R.Freivald. On the prediction of general recursive functions. Soviet Math. Dokl. 13, 1972, pp.1224-1228

[BF 74] J.Barzdin, R.Freivald. Prediction and limiting synthesis of effectively enumerable classes of functions. Theory of Algorithms and Programs, vol.1, Latvia State University, 1974, pp.101-111 (in Russian)

[BKP 74] J.Barzdin, E.Kinber, K.Podnieks. Speeding up prediction and limiting synthesis of functions. Theory of Algorithms and Programs, vol.1, Latvia State University, 1974, pp.117-128 (in Russian)

[Bie 72] A.W.Biermann. On the inference of Turing machines from sample computations. Artificial Intelligence, 1972

[Er 71] A.P.Ershov. Theory of program schemata. IFIP Congress 71, Ljubljana, 1971, 1, pp.144-163

[Go 67] E.M.Gold. Language identification in the limit. Information and Control, 10:5, 1967, pp.447-474

[Kol 65] A.N.Kolmogorov. Three approaches to the definition of the notion "quantity of information". Problemy peredachi informacii, 1:1, 1965 (in Russian)

[Kor 67] A.D.Korshunov. On asymptotic estimates of the number of finite automata. Kibernetika, 2, 1967 (in Russian)

[LMS 56] K. de Leeuw, E.F.Moore et al, Computability by probabilistic machines. Automata Studies (Ann. of Math. Studies, No.34), Princeton Univ. Press, Princeton, N.J., 1956, pp.183-212

[ML 66] P.Martin-Löf. On the notion of random sequence. Teoriya veroyatnosti i ee primeneniya, 2:1, 1966 (in Russian)

[Moo 56] E.F.Moore. Gedanken-experiments on sequential machines. Automata Studies (Ann. of Math. Studies, No.34), Princeton Univ. Press, Princeton, N.J., 1956, pp.129-153

[Po 75] K.M.Podnieks. Probabilistic synthesis of enumerated classes of functions. Soviet Math. Dokl. 16, 1975, pp.1042-1045

[Po 77-1] K.M.Podnieks. Computational complexity of prediction strategies. Theory of Algorithms and Programs, vol.3, Latvia State University, 1977, pp.89-102 (in Russian)

[Po 77-2] K.M.Podnieks. Probabilistic program synthesis. Theory of Algorithms and Programs, vol.3, Latvia State University, 1977, pp.57-88 (in Russian)

[Rog 67] H.Rogers, Jr. Theory of recursive functions and effective computability. McGraw-Hill, New York, 1967

[TB 73] B.A.Trakhtenbrot, J.M.Barzdin. Finite Automata (Behaviour and Synthesis). North-Holland, Amsterdam, 1972

[ZL 70] A.K.Zvonkin, L.A.Levin. Complexity of finite objects and foundations of the information and randomness notions by the theory of algorithms. Uspekhi matematicheskikh nauk, 25:6, 1970 (in Russian)

INDUCTIVE SYNTHESIS OF DOT EXPRESSIONS

Alvis Brāzma

Institute of Mathematics and Computer Science
The University of Latvia
Raiņa bulv.29, Rīga 226250, Latvia

Abstract. We consider the problem of the synthesis of algorithms by sample computations. We introduce a formal language, namely, the so-called dot expressions, which is based on a formalization of the intuitive notion of ellipsis ('...'). Whilst formally the dot expressions are simply a language describing sets of words, on the other hand, it can be considered as a programming language supporting quite a wide class of programs. Equivalence and asymptotical equivalence of dot expressions are defined and proved to be decidable. A formal example of a dot expression is defined in the way that, actually, it represents a sample computation of the program presented by the given dot expression. A system of simple inductive inference rules synthesizing dot expressions (programs) by their formal examples (sample computations) is developed and proved to synthesize a correct (i.e., asymptotically equivalent to the given) expression by one sufficiently long example. Some instances of the application of the model for program inductive synthesis are also given. Particularly, there are given examples of the euclidean and bubblesort algorithm synthesis within acceptable time from completely natural sample descriptions.

Introduction

When explaining different algorithms humans often use examples. Thus, if we denote the remainder from the whole division *a/b* by mod(*a*,*b*), one of the possible ways to describe the euclidean algorithm computing the greatest common divisor of natural numbers a1 and a2 is the following description by example in fig.1.

```
input a1, a2;
      let a3:=mod(a1,a2);
      is a3=0? suppose it is not;
      let a4:=mod(a2,a3);
      is a4=0? suppose it is not;
      let a5:=mod(a3,a4);
      is a5=0? suppose it is not;
      let a6:=mod(a4,a5);
      is a6=0? suppose it is not;
```

```
      let a7:=mod(a5,a6);
      is a7=0? suppose it is;
   return a6;
```

fig.1

Similarly, if by *a*:=:*b* we denote the operation of exchange of the values of *a* and *b*, bubblesort algorithm can be described as in fig.2.

```
   input a:array(1..4);
        if a(1)≤a(2) then; else a(1):=:a(2);
        if a(2)≤a(3) then; else a(2):=:a(3);
        if a(3)≤a(4) then; else a(3):=:a(4);
        if a(1)≤a(2) then; else a(1):=:a(2);
        if a(2)≤a(3) then; else a(2):=:a(3);
        if a(1)≤a(2) then; else a(1):=:a(2);
   return a;
```

fig.2

From descriptions (i.e., sample computations) like the given above a human evidently can restore the respective general algorithms. Therefore such descriptions by sample computations can be regarded as programs in a certain nontraditional programming language (the sample language) [2,3]. In this paper we formalize one of such languages, define the semantics and study the mathematical background. We will try to construct the semantics of the language as simple as possible and reflecting our intuition.

First we introduce the language of the so-called dot expressions [3]. This language is based on a formalization of the simplest cases of the intuitive notion *ellipsis* ('...') (which we call here *dots*). Formally the dot expressions is a language describing a class of sets of words (any dot expression describes a definite set), whilst, on the other hand, it can also be regarded as a programming language where a program is presented by a set of all the possible sample computations (i.e., by a description of such set).

An arbitrary element of the set presented by a certain dot expression is called a formal example of the given expression. In our context a formal example is in fact a sample computation of a program. The goal of inductive synthesis is to restore a dot expression (program) by a formal example (sample computation).

An algorithm of inductive synthesis constructing a dot expression from a formal example actually defines the semantics of the sample language, since it transforms examples into dot expressions, whose semantics is defined independently. Such an algorithm should be simple and natural (in the intuitive sense), otherwise, the semantics of the sample language would be complex and unnatural contrary to our goal. One of the most lucid means to present such an algorithm is to determine certain natural principles or rules of inference (i.e., a set of transformations) following which we obtain the intended expressions from their examples. In the given paper we propose such a system of inductive inference consisting of three simple rules and prove that the system constructs the correct expression by a single, sufficiently long example. This property we call the completeness of the inductive inference system. Particularly, the proposed system synthesizes a correct program for the general euclidean and bubblesort algorithm by the examples given in fig.1 and fig.2. Thus, the given paper can be regarded as a study of theoretical foundations of a certain inductive synthesis model, within which it is possible to synthesize a restricted, but quite a rich class of programs without using the exhaustive search. Note, that in recent years such models are widely developing [1,4,11,12].

The given paper can be regarded also as a study of the mathematical concept of *ellipsis* or *'and so on'*. Ellipsis (dots) in fact are a tool for description of certain general objects. For example, the expression $1,2,...,k$ is a general object for which $1,2,3,4,5,6,7$ is a particular example. It is natural to regard two dot expressions equivalent, if their corresponding sets of all the examples coincide. Here, a popular mathematical problem arises: is it possible to decide whether two dot expressions are equivalent? In the simplest cases considered here the answer is proved to be positive. Another natural question: is it possible to reconstruct the general object (i.e., the dot expression) by a sufficiently long particular example? Here again it turns out that within a certain degree of accuracy it is possible.

Finally, let us note, that an experimental system of program synthesis from sample computations based on the ideas of dot expressions is developed in Latvia University [10]. The system can synthesize quite a wide class of programs.

Let us sketch the framework of the given paper. In section 1 we introduce basic notions and concepts of the paper, formulate all principal results and give examples of their application for program synthesis. The rest of the paper is, in fact, a proof of one single theorem - the theorem of completeness of the given system of inductive inference rules. The proof of all the other assertions is either simple or simple corollary. In the end of the paper we list a number of open problems concerning dot expressions.

To conclude, let us note that the idea of the program synthesis by sample computations belong to A.Bierman and R.Chrishnaswamy [5]. The notion of the dot expressions was first introduced by J.Barzdin in [3], where also a certain system of inductive inference rules was proposed. Later in [9] the problem of the equivalence and inductive synthesis was solved for a particular, rather restricted subclass of dot expressions (the so called dot expressions of depth one). In [6] the proof of decidability of equivalence was first given for the general case. In [7] there was given another more simple system of rules of inductive inference, together with some idea of the completeness proof. Full proof turned out to be rather complex and is presented for the first time here.

The given proof to a large extent is a collective work of a group of researchers of the Institute of Mathematics and Computer Science, the University of Latvia and a lot of important ideas do not belong to the author of the paper but to J.Barzdin and also I.Etmane. The author has also received a valuable advice from A.V.Uspensky how to present the results. The author is deeply grateful to all of them and also to L.Zeltkalne for editing the paper.

1. Basic Notions and Main Results

Let $\mathbb{A}=\mathbb{A}'\cup \mathbb{Z}$ be an alphabet, where $\mathbb{A}'$ is a finite set ($<,>,\circ \notin \mathbb{A}'$) and $\mathbb{Z}$ is the set of integers. We represent integers in the decimal notation underlining the substrings representing them (except for one digit numbers) and we assume an underlined substring as one character.

The basic construction in the concept of dot expressions is a dot term. Dot terms are either constant or variable. A *constant dot term* is a word of the type:

$$<a_1a_2...a_n \circ\circ\circ b_1b_2...b_n>,$$

where $a_i, b_i \in \mathbb{A} \cup \{<,>,\circ\}$ $(i=1,...,n)$. We call a constant dot term *valid*, if for the strings $a_1a_2...a_n$ and $b_1b_2...b_n$ the following condition is held: there exists a constant $\phi\in\mathbb{Z}$, such that for each $i=1,...,n$, either $a_i=b_i$ or a_i, $b_i \in\mathbb{Z}$ and $b_i-a_i=\phi$. For example, T_1=<a(1)∘∘∘a(4)> and T_2=<a4b6∘∘∘a1b3> are valid dot terms. If a term is not valid, we call it *invalid*. By the *factor* and the *period* of a dot term we mean the integer ϕ and n respectively.

For a valid dot term T=<$a_1...a_n$ ∘∘∘ $b_1...b_n$> we can define the *unfoldment* unf(T) as follows:

$$\text{unf}(T)=d_1^0...d_n^0d_1^1...d_n^1...\ ...d_1^m...d_n^m,$$

where $m=|\phi|$, $d_i^0=a_i$, $d_i^m=b_i$ $(i=1,...,n)$ and d_i^j $(j=1,...,m-1)$ are defined as follows: if $a_i=b_i$, then $d_i^j=a_i$; if $a_i\neq b_i$ (consequently, a_i, $b_i \in\mathbb{Z}$) then

$$d_i^{j+1}-d_i^j = \begin{cases} +1, & \text{if } b_i>a_i; \\ -1, & \text{if } b_i<a_i. \end{cases}$$

If $\phi=0$, then we set

$$\text{unf}(T)=a_1...a_n.$$

For T_1 and T_2 given above

unf(T_1)=a(1)a(2)a(3)a(4),
unf(T_2)=a4b6a3b5a2b4a1b3.

A *constant dot expression* (or a *dot string*) is defined inductively:

1. Any word over the alphabet $\mathbb{A}$ is a dot string.
2. If A and B are dot strings, then the word AB is a dot string.
3. If A and B are dot strings and $|A|=|B|$, then the term <A∘∘∘B> is also a dot string.
4. There are no other dot string.

We call a dot string *valid* if all the composing dot terms are valid, otherwise we call it *invalid*. For example,

A_1=<<a4∘∘∘a0>∘∘∘<a0∘∘∘a0>><a1∘∘∘a5>,
A_2=<b<a11∘∘∘a14>∘∘∘b<a41∘∘∘a44>>c,
A_3=<<a11∘∘∘a41>∘∘∘<a11∘∘∘a44>>

are valid dot strings.

A dot term T is called *outermost* in a dot string A, if in A there does not exist a dot term S which contains T. The *depth* of a dot term is defined as the depth of the nesting of parenthesis '<','>'. The *depth* of a dot string is the maximal depth of terms, belonging to the string.

We define the *complete unfoldment* Unf(A) of a dot string A, as the result of the following procedure. If A is valid, then we substitute for unf(T) all the outermost terms T in A. If the obtained dot string A' is valid, then again we substitute for the unfoldments all the outermost terms. We repeat this operation till we obtain a dot string B, which either does not contain any dot term or is invalid. We set Unf(A)=B in the firs case and assume Unf(A) to be undefined in the second case (the complete unfoldment of an invalid dot string is also regarded to be undefined).

Let us consider, for example, the above given dot string A_1. Replacing the outermost terms of A_1 by their unfoldments we get

<a4∘∘∘a0><a3∘∘∘a0><a2∘∘∘a0><a1∘∘∘a0><a0∘∘∘a0>a1a2a3a4a5.

Next, unfolding the obtained terms we get

Unf(A_1)=a4a3a2a1a0a3a2a1a0a2a1a0a1a0a0a1a2a3a4a5.

In the same way we can obtain the complete unfoldment of the string A_2. In the case of A_3, on the contrary, after unfolding the outermost term we get dot string

<a11∘∘∘a41><a11∘∘∘a42><a11∘∘∘a43><a11∘∘∘a44>

which is invalid, since terms <a11∘∘∘a42> and <a11∘∘∘a43> are invalid.

If the complete unfoldment of a dot string A is defined, we call A *correct*, otherwise we call it *incorrect*. The last example shows, that also valid dot strings can be incorrect (this was first noted by *I.Etmane*). Further on we will consider mainly valid dot strings and, if the contrary is not said, by dot string we will understand exactly valid dot string.

Now, let us go back to the definition of a dot term. We will define a variable dot term which contrary to constant depends on a parameter, denoted by n. Let $\bar{\mathbb{X}}=\{\underline{n+c}\,|\,c\in\mathbb{Z}\}$. (Expressions $\underline{n+(-c)}$ and $\underline{n+0}$ will be denoted by $\underline{n-c}$ and $\underline{n}$, respectively.) Let $\mathfrak{y}$, $\mathfrak{z}$ $\in\mathbb{Z}\cup\bar{\mathbb{X}}$. By $\mathfrak{y}-\mathfrak{z}$ we understand the algebraic difference of $\mathfrak{y}$ and $\mathfrak{z}$. For example, $\underline{n+3}-4=\underline{n-1}$ and $\underline{n+3}-\underline{n+1}=2$.

We define a *dot term* as a word

$$<\mathfrak{a}_1\mathfrak{a}_2\ldots\mathfrak{a}_n \circ\circ\circ\ \mathfrak{b}_1\mathfrak{b}_2\ldots\mathfrak{b}_n>$$

where $\mathfrak{a}_i$, $\mathfrak{b}_i\in \mathbb{A}\cup\bar{\mathbb{X}}\cup\{<,>,\circ\}$ $(i=1,\ldots,n)$. A dot term is said to be *valid*, if for the words $\mathfrak{a}_1\mathfrak{a}_2\ldots\mathfrak{a}_n$ and $\mathfrak{b}_1\mathfrak{b}_2\ldots\mathfrak{b}_n$ the following condition holds: there exists $\phi\in\mathbb{Z}\cup\{n+c\,|\,c\in\mathbb{Z}\}\cup\{-n+c\,|\,c\in\mathbb{Z}\}$ (which we call the *factor*), such that either $a_i=b_i$ or $a_i, b_i \in \mathbb{Z} \cup \bar{\mathbb{X}}$ and $b_i-a_i=\phi$ ($i=1,\ldots n$). For example, $T_1'=<a(1)\circ\circ\circ a(\underline{n+1})>$ and $T_2'=<a\underline{n}\underline{n+2}\circ\circ\circ a13>$ are valid dot terms. Their factors are n and -n+1, respectively.

A *dot expression* can by defined exactly the same way as a constant dot expression (dot string), only in the first item of the definition, we take alphabet $\mathbb{A} \cup \bar{\mathbb{X}}$ instead of alphabet $\mathbb{A}$ and in the third item we take arbitrary term instead of constant term. A dot expression is *valid* if all the terms are valid. For example, the following dot expressions are valid:

$E_1=<<a\underline{n}\circ\circ\circ a0>\circ\circ\circ<a0\circ\circ\circ a0>><a1\circ\circ\circ a\underline{n+1}>$,

$E_2=<b<a11\circ\circ\circ a1\underline{n}>\circ\circ\circ b<a\underline{n}1\circ\circ\circ a\underline{n}\underline{n}>>c$,

$E_3=<<a11\circ\circ\circ a\underline{n}1>\circ\circ\circ<a11\circ\circ\circ a\underline{n}\underline{n}>>$.

The dot expressions given in fig.3 and fig.4 are also valid.

input a1, a2;
<let a3:=mod(a1, a2);
is a3=0? suppose it is not;
∘∘∘
let $a\underline{n-1}$:=mod($a\underline{n-3}$, $a\underline{n-2}$);
is $a\underline{n-1}$=0? suppose it is not;>
let $a\underline{n}$:=mod($a\underline{n-2}$, $a\underline{n-1}$);
is $a\underline{n}$=0? suppose it is;
return $a\underline{n-1}$;

Fig. 3

input a:array(1..n);
<<if a(1)≤a(2) then; else a(1):=:a(2); ∘∘∘
if a($\underline{n-1}$)≤a($\underline{n}$) then; else a($\underline{n-1}$):=:a($\underline{n}$);>
∘∘∘
<if a(1)≤a(2) then; else a(1):=:a(2); ∘∘∘
if a(1)≤a(2) then; else a(1):=:a(2);>>
return a;

Fig. 4

Let **E** be a dot expression. By **E**(α) ($\alpha \in \mathbb{Z}$) we denote the constant dot expression we obtain from **E** by substituting the integer α for the variable n in all the substrings $\underline{n+c}$ and computing the corresponding $\alpha+c$. For example, $E_1(4)=W_1$, $E_2(4)=W_2$ and $E_3(4)=W_3$.

An expression **E** is said to be *correct*, if **E**(n) is correct for all $n \in \mathbb{N}$. For example, E_1 and E_2 are correct, but E_3 is not. Later we prove

Assertion 1. The problem of correctness for dot expressions is decidable.

We define the *value* **VAL(E)** of a correct dot expression **E** as the set $\{\mathrm{Unf}(E(n)) \mid n \in \mathbb{N}\}$. The value of an incorrect dot expression is the empty set.

Dot expressions **E** and **F** are said to be *equivalent* (*asymptotically equivalent*) if the sets **VAL(E)** and **VAL(F)** coincide (coincide, except on possibly a finite number of elements). We denote the fact that **E** and **F** are equivalent (asymptotically equivalent) by **E≡F (E≅F)**.

For example, if

$$E_4 = \langle\langle a\underline{n-1}\circ\circ\circ a0\rangle\circ\circ\circ\langle a1\circ\circ\circ a0\rangle\rangle\langle a0\circ\circ\circ a\underline{n}\rangle,$$

$$E_5 = \langle\langle a\underline{n-1}\circ\circ\circ a0\rangle\circ\circ\circ\langle a0\circ\circ\circ a0\rangle\rangle\langle a1\circ\circ\circ a\underline{n}\rangle,$$

$$E_6 = a\langle\langle \underline{n-1}a\circ\circ\circ 0a\rangle\circ\circ\circ\langle 0a\circ\circ\circ 0a\rangle\rangle 1\langle a2\circ\circ\circ a\underline{n}\rangle,$$

then E_1, E_4, E_5 and E_6 are asymptotically equivalent.

Now, let us note that the dot expression given in fig.3 is, in fact, a program of the euclidean algorithm, since it describes all the possible sample computations of the algorithm (in the case a1>a2). Similarly, the dot expression given in fig.4 is a program of the bubblesort algorithm.

Along with dot expressions we will consider the so-called unary *for*-expressions (i.e. *for*-expressions depending on one variable that is called *external*), which, in fact, are simply another presentation of dot expressions. For example, the dot expression

$$\langle a(1)\circ\circ\circ a(\underline{n})\rangle$$

can be presented as the following unary *for*-expression:

$$\langle a(\underline{i}) \mid i{:=}1..\underline{n}\rangle. \quad (1.1)$$

Similarly, the dot expression

$$\langle\langle a1\circ\circ\circ a1\rangle\circ\circ\circ\langle a1\circ\circ\circ a\underline{n}\rangle\rangle$$

equals

$$\langle\langle a\underline{j} \mid j{:=}1..\underline{i}\rangle \mid i{:=}1..\underline{n}\rangle. \quad (1.2)$$

The bubblesort algorithm can be presented as in fig.5

```
input a:array(1..n);
     <<if a(j)≤a(j+1) then; else a(j):=:a(j+1);
                  |j:=1..i>
            |i:=n-1..1>
return a;
```

Fig. 5

The main construction in the language of *for*-expressions is *for-term*, namely, any word of the type:

$$<\bar{T}|i:=u..v>.$$

Substring $i:=u..v$ is called the *head* of the term, i the *proper variable*, u, v the *boundaries* and $\bar{T}$ the *body* of the term. Boundaries u and v are strings of the type c, $\underline{n+c}$, $\underline{i+c}$, ..., where $c\in\mathbb{Z}$ and n, i, ... is either an external variable or any of the proper variables of the terms outer to the considered one. The body of the term is a word $\bar{T}=a_1a_2...a_m$, where a_i is either a character of a certain alphabet $\mathbb{A}$ (which includes integers), or a string of the type $\underline{n+c}$, $\underline{i+c}$, ..., where n, i, ... is either the external variable, or the proper variable of the given term or the one outer to the given. If the body $\bar{T}$ of the term T contains a string $\underline{i+c}$ (where i is the proper variable of T) at least in one place, we call T *legitimate term*, otherwise, T is *illegitimate*. For example, the terms in (1.1) and (1.2) are legitimate, but the term <a$\underline{n}$|i:=1..$\underline{n}$> is illegitimate.

In case the term $<\bar{T}|i:=u..v>$ is such that $v-u\in\mathbb{Z}$, we can define the unfoldment unf(T) as the string

$$\bar{T}(u)\bar{T}(u+\sigma)\bar{T}(u+2\sigma)...\bar{T}(v),$$

where

$$\sigma = \begin{cases} +1, & \text{if } v-u\geq 0, \\ -1, & \text{if } v-u<0, \end{cases}$$

and we obtain $\bar{T}(w)$ from $\bar{T}$ substituting w for i in all the substrings $\underline{i+c}$ and computing the corresponding $w+c$.

A unary *for*-expression is obtained by concatenation of the characters of the alphabet $\mathbb{A} \cup \bar{\mathbb{X}}$ and *for*-terms (the body of which in turn, may contain other *for*-terms). Later we will give a recursive definition of a *for*-expression, but for the time being this descriptive one will be sufficient.

We call a unary *for*-expression *legitimate*, if all the terms with $v-u\notin\mathbb{Z}$ are legitimate (where u,v are the boundaries). Otherwise, we call the expression *illegitimate*.

The *value* **VAL(E)** of a unary *for*-expression can be defined the same way as for a dot expression: we replace the external variable **n** by all the integers $n \in \mathbb{N}$ and unfold all the terms of the expression **E**(n), beginning with the outermost. We call a unary *for*-expression **E** equivalent to the dot expression **F**, if their values coincide.

Assertion 2. There exists an algorithm which, given a correct dot expression, constructs an equivalent legitimate unary *for*-expression and, given a legitimate unary *for*-expression, constructs an equivalent correct dot expression.

Since *for*-expressions are, in fact, simply another presentation of dot expressions, we will not distinguish between them and speak simply of expressions.

We call an expression **E** *singular*, if there exists an illegitimate unary *for*-expression asymptotically equivalent to **E**, or **E** does not contain the external variable (i.e., **E** is constant). For instance, expression $<<1\circ\circ\circ 1><2\circ\circ\circ\underline{n}>\circ\circ\circ<1\circ\circ\circ\underline{n-1}><\underline{n}\circ\circ\circ\underline{n}>>$ is singular, since it is asymptotically equivalent to graphical expression $<<\underline{i}|i:=1..\underline{n}>|j:=1..\underline{n}>$, which is illegitimate (the body of the outermost term does not contain the proper variable). Underneath we prove

Theorem 1. Equivalence and asymptotical equivalence for nonsingular expressions are decidable.

Let us note that the singular expressions is a rather special class, therefore the restriction of nonsingularity is not particularly strong.

Now, let us pass to the problem of synthesis. A *formal example of expression* **E** is defined as an arbitrary element of the set **VAL(E)** (in case **E** is incorrect, a formal example is defined as special emptiness character Λ). For instance, the sample computations of the euclidean and bubblsort algorithm given above (fig.1 and fig.2) are formal examples of the expressions given in fig.3 and fig.4 (or fig.5), respectively.

The *problem of inductive synthesis* can be defined as follows: given a formal example X=**Unf(E(**n**))** of a certain expression **E**, it is required to find an expression asymptotically equivalent to **E**.

Let us note at the beginning that for any expression **E**, however large a number $n \in \mathbb{N}$ we take, there always exists an expression **F**, such that **F≢E**, but still, **Unf(E(**n**))=Unf(F(**m**))**, for a certain $m \in \mathbb{N}$. Nevertheless, it turns out, that it is possible to restore the correct expression by single sufficiently long example. We will prove

Theorem 2. There exists an algorithm, such that for any nonsingular expression E, there is a constant $n_E \in \mathbb{N}$, such that for any $n \geq n_E$, given an example Unf(E(n)), the algorithm constructs an expression F asymptotically equivalent to E. Additionally, n_E can be effectively found from E.

It may appear that it is possible to prove the theorem trivially using the exhaustive search algorithm, namely, for the given example we check all expressions one after another (we assume that all expressions are enumerated in a way that "simpler" expressions are before more "complex" ones) and choose the first that fits for the given example. Although, the given algorithm is indeed correct, it is not so easy to prove it. We have to prove that for any expression E there exists $n_E \in \mathbb{N}$, such that the first expression which fits for the example Unf(E(n_E)) (for the given enumeration) is asymptotically equivalent for all $n \geq n_E$. For this, actually, we have to prove that for any pair of expressions E and F, there exists $n_{E,F} \in \mathbb{N}$, such that for $n \geq n_{E,F}$ and $m \geq n_{E,F}$, Unf(E(n))=Unf(F(m)), yields E≅F. The proof of this assertion, in turn, is nearly as complicated as the proof of correctness of nonexhaustive search algorithm given here (a bit simpler proof of the former assertion is given in [6]).

An important question arises: is it possible to decide solely by example X=Unf(E(n)) (i.e., without knowing E), whether $n \in \mathbb{N}$ is large enough for the algorithm to construct the correct expression. From the above mentioned we get:

Assertion 3. Let there be given an algorithm constructing expressions by single example X. It is impossible to decide solely by X=Unf(E(n)) (i.e., without knowing E) whether the constructed expression is asymptotically equivalent to E or not.

Therefore, if we have an example X=Unf(E(n)) and do not know E itself, the algorithm will give us the "correct" expression, if n happens to be sufficiently large, still we never know whether n is large enough or not. At the same time in most cases it is possible to evaluate approximately the necessary minimal length of the example.

As it was already noted in the introduction, we deal with the problem of synthesis by means of inductive inference rules. We call a system S of inductive inference rules *complete* for a class $\mathfrak{C}$ of expressions, if for any E∈$\mathfrak{C}$ there is a constant $n_E \in \mathbb{N}$, such that for any $n \geq n_E$ the result of the application of the system S to the example Unf(E(n)) is an expression asymptotically equivalent to E.

The system we propose consists of three rules. The first rule - the rule of folding-up is based upon the notion of regular substrings. A dot string $A=\bar{T}_0\bar{T}_1\ldots\bar{T}_n$ is called *(π,ϕ)-regular* ($\pi\in\mathbb{N}$, $\phi\in\mathbb{Z}$), if it is the unfoldment of a dot term $T_A=<\bar{T}_0\circ\circ\circ\bar{T}_n>$ with the factor ϕ ($|\phi|=n$) and the period π. The term T_A is called the *producing term* of the given string, π and ϕ are called the *period* and the *factor* of the regular string. By the *attraction* of the given regular string we will mean $|\phi/\pi|$. Note, that for any (π,ϕ)-regular string there is only one producing term. The substrings $\bar{T}_1,\bar{T}_2,\ldots,\bar{T}_n$ we call the *atoms* of the given regular string.

Given a dot string X, the rule of *folding-up* looks for (π,ϕ)-regular substring Y with the largest attraction and factor $|\phi|\geq1$ and which are not inside any dot term and replaces it by the producing term. In case there are more than one such substring, the rule replaces the leftmost.

Let us denote by $f^i(X)$ the result of i applications of the folding-up to the string X. Then if, for example,

X=Unf($E_1(4)$)=a4a3a2a1a0a3a2a1a0a2a1a0a1a0a0a1a2a3a4a5,

then

$f^1(X)$=a4a3a2a1a0a3a2a1a0a2a1a0a1a0<a0∘∘∘a5>, (1.3)

$f^2(X)$=<a4∘∘∘a0>a3a2a1a0a2a1a0a1a0<a0∘∘∘a5>, (1.4)

....

$f^5(X)$=<a4∘∘∘a0><a3∘∘∘a0><a2∘∘∘a0><a1∘∘∘a0><a0∘∘∘a5>,

$f^6(X)$=<<a4∘∘∘a0>∘∘∘<a1∘∘∘a0>><a0∘∘∘a5>.

The next we define the rule of *generalization*. Let X be an arbitrary dot string and $\alpha_1,\ldots,\alpha_n$ be all the letters of X, such that $\alpha_i\in\mathbb{Z}$. The rule of *generalization* replaces every α_i in X, for which $\alpha_i>max\{\alpha_1,\ldots,\alpha_n\}/2$, by expression $\underline{n-\gamma_i}$, where $\gamma_i=max\{\alpha_1,\ldots,\alpha_n\}-\alpha_i$.

Let us denote the result of the application of the generalization to the string X by $g(X)$. Then, for X above

$g(f^6(X))$=<<a$\underline{n-1}$∘∘∘a0>∘∘∘<a1∘∘∘a0>><a0∘∘∘a$\underline{n}$>.

Note, that $g(f^6(X))=E_4\cong E_1$. This equivalence may lead to hypothesis that the system of the rules, where the rule of folding-up is applied repeatedly while possible and then the rule of generalization, is complete. For dot expressions of the depth less then three, apparently, it is so, nevertheless this system does not work, for instance, for expression <<<0∘∘∘0>∘∘∘<0∘∘∘0>>∘∘∘<<0∘∘∘0>∘∘∘<0∘∘∘$\underline{n}$>>>. To save the situation, we have to add one more, purely technical rule, namely, the rule of standardization.

This rule is based on the operations of expansion and shift of dot terms. For instance, if we expand maximally the term in expression

a1a2<a3∘∘∘a8>a9a

we get

<a1∘∘∘a9>a,

and after shifting it rightwards we get

a<1a∘∘∘9a>.

Similarly, after maximal expansion of the underlined term in the expression

a1a1a2<<a1∘∘∘a3>∘∘∘<a1∘∘∘a8>>a1<a2∘∘∘a9>

we get

<<a1∘∘∘a1>∘∘∘<a1∘∘∘a9>>.

In case it is possible to expand or shift the term *T* "at the expense" of another term *S* of the expression, we replace *S* by the complete unfoldment. For instance, expanding the underlined term in expression

<a1∘∘∘a5><a6∘∘∘a2><b1∘∘∘b5>

we get

<a1∘∘∘a6>a5a4a3a2<b1∘∘∘b5>.

We allow to expand or shift a term *T* at "the expense" of another term *S* in case the depth of *T* is greater than that of *S*, or *T* and *S* have equal depths and *T* is on the left to *S*.

Now, let us describe the procedure of the expansion and shift more formally.

We say that a *dot string A fits for a dot string B from left (right)*, if there exists $C \in A^*$, such that

$$\mathrm{Unf}(B)=\mathrm{Unf}(A)C \qquad (\mathrm{Unf}(B)=C\,\mathrm{Unf}(A)).$$

For instance, <a1 ∘∘∘ a3> fits for <a1 ∘∘∘ a5> from left. We call the string *C the left (right) difference of dot strings B and A* and denote by $D^*_L(B,A)$ ($D^*_R(B,A)$).

Let $T=\langle a_1 \ldots a_m \circ\circ\circ\ b_1 \ldots b_m \rangle$ and let

$$a_i^+ = \begin{cases} a_i\ , & \text{if } a_i=b_i; \\ a_i+1, & \text{if } a_i<b_i; \\ a_i-1, & \text{if } a_i>b_i; \end{cases} \qquad a_i^- = \begin{cases} a_i\ , & \text{if } a_i=b_i; \\ a_i-1, & \text{if } a_i<b_i; \\ a_i+1, & \text{if } a_i>b_i; \end{cases}$$

$(i=1,\ldots,m)$. Similarly we can define b_i^+, b_i^-. Let us consider a dot string *AT*, where *A* is an arbitrary dot string and *T* a term. We say that the *term T can be expanded leftwards in the dot string AT* if the dot string $a_1^-\ldots a_m^-$ fits for *A* from right. Let $A=A_1A_2$, for dot strings A_1 and A_2 such that $a_1^-\ldots a_m^-$ fits for A_2 from right and A_2 is the minimal one among such substrings of *A* (i.e., there does not exist nonempty dot strings A_1' and A_2', such that $A_2=A_1'A_2'$ and $a_1^-\ldots a_m^-$ fits for A_2' from right). Then by *expansion of the term T leftwards in the string AT* we mean the substitution of the string

$$B=A_1D_R^*(A_2,a_1^-\ldots a_m^-)<a_1^-\ldots a_m^- \circ\circ\circ\ b_1\ldots b_m>$$

for *AT*. Note, that Unf(B)=Unf(AT).

Similarly, it is possible to define the *expansion rightwards.*

Now let us pass to the definition of the shift. We call a dot string *D elementary,* if *D* is either a character or a dot term. Let *k* ($k\le m$) be such that the string $a_1\ldots a_k$ is elementary. We say that the term *T can be shifted rightwards in the dot string TC,* if the string $b_1^+\ldots b_k^+$ fits for the string *C* from the left. Let $C=C_1C_2$, for dot strings C_1 and C_2 such that $b_1^+\ldots b_k^+$ fits for C_1 from left and C_1 is the minimal one among such substrings of *C*. Then by *shift of the term T rightwards in the dot string TC* we understand the substitution of the string

$$B'= a_1\ldots a_k<a_{k+1}\ldots a_m a_1^+\ldots a_k^+ \circ\circ\circ$$
$$b_{k+1}\ldots b_m b_1^+\ldots b_k^+>D_L^*(C_1,b_1^+\ldots b_k^+)C_2$$

for the string *TC*. Let us note that Unf(B')=*TC*.

In general it is possible to expand or shift a term in the given string not only once, but also several times. Let us assume the following restriction: we allow expand a term *T* leftwards only up to the first term of the depth more or equal to the depth of *T* (i.e., within the substring having the depth less than that of *T*) and expand and shift rightwards up to the first term of the depth more than that of *T* (i.e., within the substring having the depth less or equal to that of *T*). If it is impossible to expand or shift the term *T* rightwards in the string *BTC* within these limits, we say that *T is maximally expanded and shifted rightwards.*

Now we can define the rule of standardization. Let us consider a dot string

$$A=B_1T_1B_2\ldots B_lT_lB_{l+1}\ldots B_mT_mB_{m+1},$$

where $T_1,\ldots,T_m$ are the outermost dot terms and $B_1,\ldots,B_{m+1}$ are words over the alphabet $\mathbb{A}$. The rule of *standardization* first maximally expands leftwards and rightwards and shifts rightwards all the terms $T_{11},\dots,T_{1n}$ having the maximal depth. Then, it maximally expands and shifts rightwards the terms $T_{1'1},\dots,T_{1'n'}$ with the depth by unity less than the maximal, and so on, till all the outermost terms are maximally expanded and shifted rightwards (each within the permitted limits).

Application order of the inference rules is as follows: first we apply the rule of folding-up, then the rule of standardization, then again the rule of folding-up, next the rule of standardization and so on, until it is not possible to apply the rule of folding-up (i.e., until the dot string does not contain a regular substring with the factor $|\phi|\geq 1$). Then we apply once and only once the rule of generalization. We denote the described *system of inductive inference* by S.

Let us denote the result of the application of standardization to the string X by $s(X)$. Then, for example, the process of the application of the system S to $X=\mathrm{Unf}(E_1(4))$ can be described as follows. After the first application of the rule of folding-up we get (1.3) and since standardization changes nothing, $s(f(X))=f(X)$. The next application of folding-up gives us (1.4) and after standardization we get

$$(sf)^2(X)=a<4a\circ\circ\circ 0a>3a2a1a0a2a1a0a1a0<a0\circ\circ\circ a5>.$$

Further

$$(sf)^4(X)=a<4a\circ\circ\circ 0a><3a\circ\circ\circ 0a><2a\circ\circ\circ 0a>1a0<a0\circ\circ\circ a5>,$$

$$f(sf)^4(X)=a<<4a\circ\circ\circ 0a>\circ\circ\circ<2a\circ\circ\circ 0a>>1a0<a0\circ\circ\circ a5>, \quad (1.5)$$

and after standardization:

$$(sf)^5(X)=a<<4a\circ\circ\circ 0a>\circ\circ\circ<0a\circ\circ\circ 0a>>1a2a3a4a5. \quad (1.6)$$

Note, that the rightmost term is unfolded. Next, we fold it back and after standardization we get:

$$(sf)^6(X)=a<<4a\circ\circ\circ 0a>\circ\circ\circ<0a\circ\circ\circ 0a>>1<a2\circ\circ\circ a5>. \quad (1.7)$$

The application of folding-up is not possible any more, therefore, we apply the rule of generalization and obtain:

$$g(sf)^6(X)=a<\underline{n-1}a\circ\circ\circ 0a>\circ\circ\circ<0a\circ\circ\circ 0a>>1<a2\circ\circ\circ a\underline{n}>, \quad (1.8)$$

which is asymptotically equivalent to E_1.

Let us denote by $(sf)^*(X)$ the string $(sf)^m(X)$, where $m\in\mathbb{N}$ is such that it is impossible to apply the folding-up to $(sf)^m(X)$. Then the result of the application of the rules of inference system S to X can be denoted by $g(sf)^*(X)$. The completeness of inductive inference system S for class $\mathfrak{G}$ of expressions can be put as follows: for each $E \in \mathfrak{G}$ there exists a constant $n_E \in \mathbb{N}$, such that for any $n \geq n_E$: $g(sf)^*(\mathbf{Unf}(E(n))) \cong E$.

Theorem 3. The system S of inductive inference consisting of the rules of *folding-up, standardization* and *generalization* is complete for the class of nonsingular dot expressions.

Particularly, the given system synthesizes a program for the euclidean algorithm asymptotically equivalent to the one given in fig.3 by the example given in fig.1 and the bubblesort algorithm given in fig.4 by the example given in fig.2. Let us note that translation of a dot expression into a program in some traditional programming language is purely technical problem (*for*-terms match *for*-loop structures in PASCAL-like programming languages).

The completeness theorem evidently yields the synthesis theorem (theorem 2). Let us touch the problem of time complexity of the synthesis algorithm based on the described inductive inference rule system S. Experience shows that for most expressions the algorithm works in polynomial time (by the length of examples). Nevertheless, there exist expressions for which this is not true. For instance, the algorithm works exponentially for expression $E=\langle\langle 2\circ\circ\circ 3\rangle\langle 4\circ\circ\circ 1\rangle\circ\circ\circ\langle 2\circ\circ\circ \underline{n}\rangle\langle \underline{n+1}\circ\circ\circ 1\rangle\rangle$. Still, it is easy to see, that this is a rather special class of expressions. It can be proved formally that, if we exclude this class of expressions, the algorithm works polynomially. On the other hand, apparently the system S can be slightly modified to make the algorithm polynomial time for all expressions (look open problem 6).

Let us prove the assertions. Before we pass to a strict proof, in the next section we will give the basic ideas.

2. The Basic Ideas of the Proof

Let us denote by /E\ the maximal absolute value of the integers $\gamma \in \mathbb{Z}$ belonging to the expression **E**. For instance, $/a2(\underline{n-3})\backslash = \max(2,3) = 3$. Let $|E|$ be the length of **E** and $\|E\| = \max(/E\backslash, |E|)$.

Along with the complete unfoldment **Unf(*W*)** of a dot string *W* (where all the terms of *W* are unfolded) we can also define partial unfoldments, where some of the terms may remain folded up (the dot string *W* itself and the complete unfoldment **Unf(*W*)** can also be regarded as partial unfoldments of *W*). Let E be an expression and let us consider a string E(*n*). For each term of E(*n*) we can define in a natural way the *corresponding term* in E. We call a partial unfoldment *X* of E(*n*) *substantial*, if there exists a term in E(*n*) whose corresponding term in E has a variable factor and which is unfolded in *X* . For instance, if E=<1∘∘∘$\underline{n}$><1∘∘∘2>, then the strings 123456<1∘∘∘2> and <1∘∘∘6>12 are partial unfoldments of E(6), the first of which is substantial and the second is not.

Further in this section the formulations are not quite formal and judgments are not mathematically strict. We will frequently give references to the corresponding formal assertions of the following sections in parenthesis. The reader, who dislike such mathematical inaccuracies, can pass directly to the next section.

In the most general terms essence of the proof of the completeness theorem can be characterized as follows. We construct a certain algorithm S transforming an arbitrary expression E into asymptotically equivalent expression S(E) for which the following properties are held:

a) if *X* is a substantial partial unfoldment of an expression E(*n*) (for sufficiently large *n*), then, there exists another partial unfoldment *X'* of the expression E(*n*), such that

$$sf(S(X))=S(X')$$

(lemma 8);

b) if *X* is a substantial unfoldment of E(*n*) and $n \gg \|E\|$, then S(*X*) contains a regular substring with attraction $\alpha=n/const$, where const=const(‖E‖) (i.e., const does not depend on *n*), and consequently, $\alpha \gg \|E\|$ (lemma 7);

c) if $n \gg \|E\|$, then

$$S(E(n))=(S(E))(n)$$

i.e., E(*n*) transforms, in a sense, the same way as the expression E itself (lemma 2, property of uniformness).

Now let us sketch how *a*), *b*) and *c*) yield the completeness of inductive inference system *S*. Let us show first that *a*), *b*) and *c*) yield the following: if $n \in \mathbb{N}$ is large enough ($n \gg \|E\|$), then for any $k \in \mathbb{N}$, the expression E can be transformed into an asymptotically equivalent expression E_k, such that there exists a partial unfoldment X_k of the expression $E_k(n)$, for which

$$S(X_k)=(sf)^k(\mathrm{Unf}(E(n))). \qquad (2.1)$$

Let us assume (2.1) by induction and show that the same is true for $k+1$. Let $Y=\mathrm{Unf}(\mathrm{E}(n))$ and $\mathrm{S}(X_k)=(sf)^k(Y)$. There are two possibilities: either the unfoldment X_k is substantial or not. In the first case we get directly from *a*), that there exists an unfoldment X_{k+1} of the expression $\mathrm{E}_k(n)$, such that

$$(sf)^{k+1}(Y)=sf(\mathrm{S}(X_k))=\mathrm{S}(X_{k+1}),$$

i.e., $\mathrm{E}_{k+1}=\mathrm{E}_k$.

In the second case, only the terms of $\mathrm{E}_k(n)$ whith the corresponding terms in E_k having constant factor can be unfolded in the unfoldment X_k. Let we obtain E_k' from E_k by unfolding these terms (note, that $\mathrm{E}_k'\cong\mathrm{E}_k$). Then $\mathrm{E}_k'(n)=X_k$ and

$$(sf)^k(Y)=\mathrm{S}(X_k)=\mathrm{S}(\mathrm{E}_k'(n))=(\mathrm{S}(\mathrm{E}_k'))(n),$$

and therefore

$$(sf)^{k+1}(Y)=sf(\mathrm{S}(\mathrm{E}_k')(n))=s((f\mathrm{S}(\mathrm{E}_k'))(n))$$

(the last equality holds because $n\gg\|\mathrm{E}\|$). Since $\mathrm{S}(\mathrm{E})\cong\mathrm{E}$, we get $\mathrm{S}(\mathrm{E}_k')\cong\mathrm{E}$, and evidently $f\mathrm{S}(\mathrm{E}_k')\cong\mathrm{E}$. Let $\mathrm{E}_{k+1}=f\mathrm{S}(\mathrm{E}_k')$ and let X_{k+1} be a partial unfoldment of the expression $\mathrm{E}_{k+1}(n)$ obtained by unfolding these terms of $\mathrm{E}_{k+1}(n)$ which would be unfolded, if the rule of standardization were applied to $\mathrm{E}_{k+1}(n)$. It can be proved that

$$s(\mathrm{E}_{k+1}(n))=\mathrm{S}(X_{k+1}).$$

Therefore,

$$(sf)^{k+1}(Y)=\mathrm{S}(X_{k+1}),$$

where X_{k+1} is a partial unfoldment of the expression $\mathrm{E}_{k+1}\cong\mathrm{E}$, i.e., what we needed, hence (2.1).

From (2.1) and *b*) we get that there exists an expression E^+ asymptotically equivalent to E, such that

$$\mathrm{S}(\mathrm{E}^+(n))=(sf)^*(\mathrm{Unf}(\mathrm{E}(n))). \tag{2.2}$$

Indeed, according to (2.1) there exist an expression $\mathrm{E}'\cong\mathrm{E}$ and an unfoldment X of $\mathrm{E}'(n)$, such that

$$\mathrm{S}(X)=(sf)^*(\mathrm{Unf}(\mathrm{E}(n))).$$

X is not substantial, since in the opposite case, according to *b*) $\mathrm{S}(X)$ would contain the regular substring with "large" attraction in contradiction to the definition of $(sf)^*(Y)$. Therefore only the terms of $\mathrm{E}'(n)$ with corresponding terms in E' having constant factors can be unfolded in X. We get (2.2) assuming that E^+ is obtained from E'

by unfolding these terms.

In section 6 we will show that for an arbitrary expression **F**, in case $n \gg \|F\|$, the generalization $g(\mathbf{F}(n))$ is asymptotically equivalent to **F** itself (i.e., $g(\mathbf{F}(n))\cong\mathbf{F}$). Consequently

$$\begin{aligned}&(sf)^{*}(\mathbf{Unf}(\mathbf{E}(n)))=g(\mathsf{S}(\mathbf{E}^{+}(n)))=\\&=g((\mathsf{S}(\mathbf{E}^{+}))(n))\cong\mathsf{S}(\mathbf{E}^{+})\cong\mathbf{E}^{+}\cong\mathbf{E},\end{aligned}\tag{2.3}$$

i.e., we get the theorem of completeness.

Now let us return to properties *a*), *b*) and *c*). To give some idea of their proof, first we will describe the idea of transformation S. The algorithm is based on the so-called procedure of equivalent expansion and shift of terms. This procedure, in fact is a generalization of the procedure of expansion and shift used in rule of standardization *s*. We denote this procedure by L. The application of procedure L in algorithm S is more complex than the expansion and shift in rule *s*: in algorithm S procedure L is applied not only to the outermost terms as in rule *s*, but also to inner ones. This leads us to the need to handle the expressions depending on an arbitrary number of variables. Let us show the work of algorithm S by the example. It is more convenient to describe the work of the algorithm not for dot expressions but for *for*-expressions. Let us consider the following expression:

$$\underbrace{\langle\underbrace{\langle \underline{i}\underline{j}\,|\,j:=1..\underline{i}\rangle}_{T_1}\underbrace{\langle \underline{i}\underline{j}\,|\,j:=\underline{i+1}..\underline{n}\rangle}_{T_2}\,|\,i:=1..\underline{n-1}\rangle}_{T_3}\underline{n}1\underbrace{\langle \underline{n}\underline{j}\,|\,j:=2..\underline{n}\rangle}_{T_4}$$

Algorithm S first maximally expands the term T_1 (in fact, it unites T_1 and T_2, step by step expansion would be infinite). We get

$$\underbrace{\langle\langle \underline{i}\underline{j}\,|\,j:=1..\underline{n}\rangle\,|\,i:=1..\underline{n-1}\rangle}_{T_3{}'}\underline{n}1\underbrace{\langle \underline{n}\underline{j}\,|\,j:=2..\underline{n}\rangle}_{T_4}$$

Next we expand the term $T_3{}'$ and obtain the result of transformation S:

$$\langle\langle \underline{i}\underline{j}\,|\,j:=1..\underline{n}\rangle\,|\,i:=1..\underline{n}\rangle.$$

Note that, in order to implement the procedure of equivalent expansion and shift for a term **T** of the depth *n*, actually we have to decide asymptotical equivalence for the expressions of the depth *n*-1. For instance, expanding the term $T_3{}'$, we should decide, whether expression $\mathbf{E}(n)=\langle\underline{n}\underline{j}\,|\,j:=1..\underline{n}\rangle$ is asymptotically equivalent to expression $\mathbf{F}(n)=\underline{n}1\langle\underline{n}\underline{j}\,|\,j:=2..\underline{n}\rangle$.

Algorithm S is constructed by recursion using the property, that

$E \cong F$ implies $\mathcal{S}(E)=\mathcal{S}(F)$ (lemma 2, item 1) what allows us to decide the asymptotical equivalence of E and F. Directly from the construction we will get property *c*). It follows that, if integers i_1, i_2 are such that $i_2-i_1 \gg \|E\|$, then

$$\mathcal{S}(E(i_1)E(i_1+1)\ldots E(i_2))=XE^*(i_1+g)E^*(i_1+g+1)\ldots E^*(i_2-g)Y, \qquad (2.4)$$

E^* being defined by $E^*(i)=\mathcal{S}(E_2(i)E_1(i+1))$, where E_1 and E_2 are such that $E_1(i)E_2(i)=E(i)$ and $g=\text{const}(\|E\|)\approx\|E\|$ (i.e., g does not depend on i_1 and i_2, and is comparatively small), X and Y are dot strings of the length of the same order as $|E|$. Actually (2.4) means that the string $\mathcal{S}(E(i_1)E(i_1+1)\ldots E(i_2))$ contains a regular substring with the factor $\phi=i_2-i_1-\text{const}$ $(\text{const}=\text{const}(\|E\|))$, the atoms $E^*(i)$ $(i=i_1+g,\ldots,i_2-g)$, the period $\pi=|E^*|\approx|E(i)|$ and, consequently the attraction $\alpha=(i_2-i_1)/\text{const}$ (proposition 7).

Let X be a certain substantial unfoldment of $E(n)$. Then it can be proved that

$$X=X_1\bar{T}(m)\bar{T}(m+1)\ldots\bar{T}(m+h)X_2,$$

where $\bar{T}$ is the body (possibly slightly changed) of a certain term of E and $h=n/\text{const}$. From here and (2.4) we get property *b*).

The proof of property *a*) is comparatively the most complex (most of section 5 is devoted to it). Very important in this proof is lemma about regular strings (lemma 1). If two regular strings W_1 and W_2 with periods π_1 and π_2 intersect on a common substring Z, as it is shown in fig.6, and Z is long enough, then either $\pi_1=\pi_2$ or one of the periods is almost as large as $|Z|$, i.e, one of the possibilities shown in fig.7 or fig.8 holds.

Now, let X be a partial unfoldment of $E(n)$ and $\mathcal{S}(X)$ be such that it can be presented in the form

$$\mathcal{S}(X)=X_1YX_2,$$

where Y is a regular substring with "large" attraction. It will be proved in section 5 that there exists a partial unfoldment X' of $E(n)$ and a term T of X', such that Y, in a sense, is the "image" of T in $\mathcal{S}(X)$, as it is shown in fig. 9 (lemma 10).

From there taking into account *b*) we will get property *a*).

Finally, let us describe briefly the content of the following sections. First, in section 3 we give a number of definitions and prove several lemmas which, are independent of algorithm $\mathcal{S}$. Section 4 is devoted to the construction of algorithm $\mathcal{S}$ and to the proof of its basic properties (excluding *a*)). In section 5 we prove property *a*).

Finally, in section 6, we show how the theorems of equivalence and completeness follow from the properties of algorithm S.

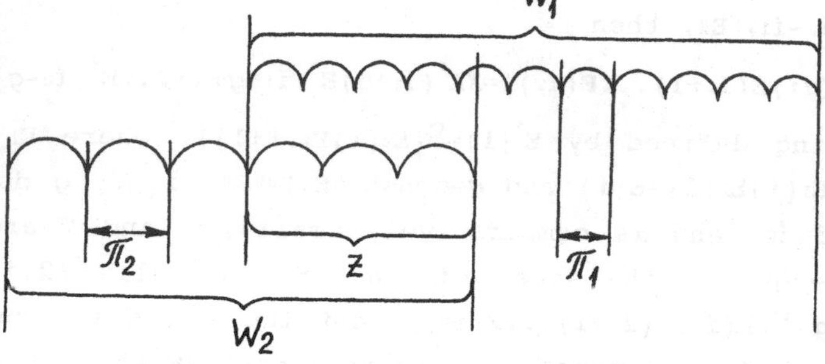

Fig.6

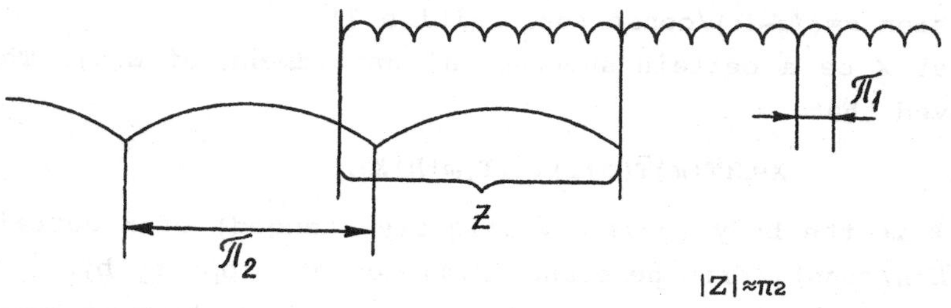

Fig.7

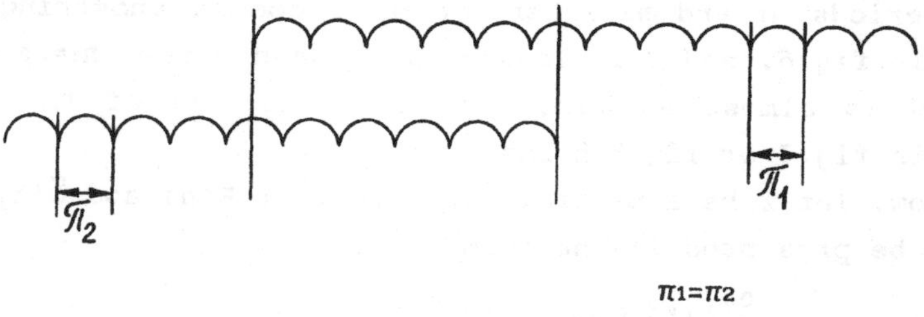

Fig.8

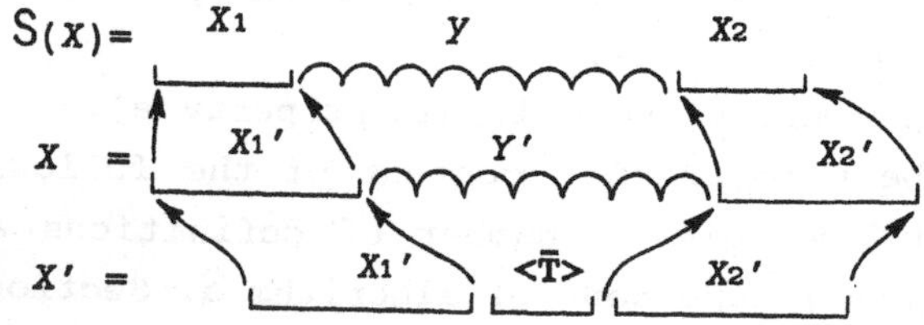

Fig.9

3. Auxiliary Notions and Assertions

In the beginning of the section we will give a number of definitions, which may be boring, but which are necessary for further proofs.

As it was mentioned above, we will need a kind of *for*-expressions depending on arbitrary number of variables. Let $\mathbb{A}$ be a finite alphabet, $\mathbb{X}=\{i,j,n,\ldots,n_1,n_2,\ldots\}$ be a set of the so-called variables and $\mathbb{P}=\{<,>,|,..,:=\}$ (we assume that $\mathbb{A}$, $\mathbb{P}$ and $\mathbb{X}$ do not intersect in pairs). Let $\bar{\mathbb{X}}=\{\underline{i+\gamma}\,|\,i\in\mathbb{X},\gamma\in\mathbb{Z}\}$. As before, an underlined substring we regard as one character. We also assume that $\mathbb{X}$ contains one special variable n^0, whose value always equals 0. Instead of $\underline{n^0+\gamma}$ we will write simply γ. Let $\mathbb{X}'=\mathbb{X}-\{n^0\}$.

Let A be a word over the alphabet $\mathbb{A} \cup \bar{\mathbb{X}} \cup \mathbb{P}$. Then any word of the type

$$<A|i:=\mathfrak{z}..\eta>,$$

where $i\in\mathbb{X}'$, $\mathfrak{z},\eta\in\bar{\mathbb{X}}$, is called *for-term*. As befor, A, $\mathfrak{z}$, η and i are called *body*, *borders* and *proper parameter*, respectively. The algebraic difference $\eta-\mathfrak{z}$ is called *factor* and the length $|X|$ *period* of the term. We say that the factor of a term T is *constant*, if $\eta-\mathfrak{z}\in\mathbb{Z}$, otherwise we say that T has *variable factor*. If the factor is constant, we can define the *step*: *step(T)*=1, if $\eta-\mathfrak{z}\geq 0$ and *step(T)*=-1, otherwise.

We define a *substitution* as an arbitrary word of the type $'\mathfrak{z}_{i1}/n_1,\ldots,\mathfrak{z}_{ik}/n_k'$, where $n_1,\ldots,n_k \in\mathbb{X}'$ and $\mathfrak{z}_{i1},\ldots,\mathfrak{z}_{ik} \in\bar{\mathbb{X}}$. Let Φ be a substitution and A be an arbitrary word over the alphabet $\mathbb{A} \cup \mathbb{P} \cup \bar{\mathbb{X}}$. By A[$\Phi$] we denote the word we obtain from A, by substituting expression $\mathfrak{z}_{ij}$ for the variable n_j ($j=1,\ldots,k$) in all the substrings $\underline{n_j+\gamma}$, and computing the corresponding algebraic sums $\underline{\mathfrak{z}_{ij}+\gamma}$. For instance, if $A=a\underline{n}b\underline{m+2}$, then $A[\underline{m+1}/n,1/m]=a\underline{m+1}b3$ and $A[\underline{m+1}/n,\underline{m}/m]=a\underline{m+1}b\underline{m+2}$.

Let a term $T=<\bar{T}|i:=\mathfrak{z}..\eta>$ have a constant factor. We define the unfoldment unf(T) as:

$$\mathrm{unf}(T)=\bar{T}[\mathfrak{z}/i]\bar{T}[\mathfrak{z}+\sigma/i]\ldots\bar{T}[\eta/i],$$

where σ=*step*(T). For instance, for T_1 above, unf(T_1)=$a\underline{n+5}a\underline{n+4}\ldots a\underline{n-1}$.

Let us set $\bar{\mathbb{Y}}=\{\underline{i+\gamma}\,|\,i\in\mathbb{Y}\}$, where $\mathbb{Y}\subseteq\mathbb{X}$. We define a *for-expression with the given set of free variables* inductively:

a) an arbitrary word over the alphabet $\mathbb{A} \cup \bar{\mathbb{Y}}$ is a *for*-expression with the set $\mathbb{Y}$ of free variables;

b) if **E** and **F** are *for*-expressions with the set $\mathcal{Y}$ of free variables, then **EF** is also a *for*-expression with the set of free variables $\mathcal{Y}$;

c) if **E** is a *for*-expression, $\mathcal{Y}$ is the set of free variables, $i \in \mathcal{Y} - \{n_0\}$ and $\xi, \eta \in \bar{\mathcal{Y}}$, then the term $\langle E | i := \xi .. \eta \rangle$ is a *for*-expression with the set of free variables $\mathcal{Y} - \{i\}$.

For instance, $E = \langle\langle a\underline{i}\underline{j} | i := \underline{k} .. \underline{j}\rangle \underline{n} | j := 0 .. \underline{n}\rangle b \langle c\underline{l} | l := \underline{m} .. 0\rangle \underline{m}$ is *for*-expression with the set of free variables $\{k, n, m\}$.

We will usually call *for*-expressions simply *expressions*.

An expression is called *legitimatc*, if the bodies of all the terms contain their respective proper parameters at least in one place, otherwise we call it illegitimate. Bellow, by the expression we will mean exactly legitimate expression if the contrary is not claimed. By *subexpression* we will mean any substring of the given expression, which is also expression. For instance, $F = \langle a\underline{i}\underline{j} | i := \underline{k} .. \underline{j}\rangle \underline{n}$ is a subexpression of the above given expression **E**. Note that some of the variables, which are not free in the expression, may be free in a subexpression. We call expression *constant*, if it does not contain any free variable. Usually, by the *variables* of the expression we will understand the free variables.

We define the *set* $V(E)$ *of unfoldments* of an expression **E** inductively:

a) $E \in V(E)$;

b) if $E' \in V(E)$, **T** is an arbitrary term of **E′** (not necessary the outermost) with a constant factor and **E′′** is obtained from **E** by substitution of **unf(T)** for **T**, then $E'' \in V(E)$.

For instance, if $E = \langle a\underline{i} \langle b\underline{j} | j := 1..2\rangle | i := 1..\underline{n}\rangle$, then $V(E)$ consists of two unfoldments, one of which is **E** itself and the other is $E' = \langle a\underline{i} b1b2 | i := 1..\underline{n}\rangle$.

Note, that for any **E** there exists $E' \in V(E)$, such that **E′** does not contain any terms with constant factor. It is evident that such **E′** is unique and we denote it by **Unf(E)** or in some cases by E^0. Note also that, if **E** is constant, then **Unf(E)** does not contain any terms at all. We say that an unfoldment **E′** is *finer* than **E′′**, if $E' \in V(E'')$. Note, that **Unf(E)** is finer than any other $E' \in V(E)$. We denote by $V^m(E)$ ($m \in \mathbb{N}$) the subset of $V(E)$ consisting of unfoldments obtained by unfolding only the terms with the factor $|\phi| \le m$.

In the same way as for dot expression we can define *depth(E)* of a *for*-expression **E**. Let us define $depth_m(E)$ ($m \in \mathbb{N}$) as the depth of the expression we obtain from **E** unfolding all the terms of **E** with the factor $|\phi| \le m$. We set *depth*$_\infty$*(*E*)=depth(*Unf(E)*)*. Note that, if **E** is constant, then *depth*$_\infty$*(*E*)=*0.

We define a *simple ordering* $\Sigma(n_1,\dots n_m)$ of the variables $n_1,\dots,n_m \in X$ as a word $n_{i_1} \le n_{i_2} \le \dots \le n_{i_m}$, where $i_1, i_2, \dots, i_m$ is a permutation of $1,2,\dots,m$. We say that an m-tuple $\alpha_1,\dots\alpha_m$ ($\alpha_i \in \mathbb{Z}$) is *permissible* for the ordering $\Sigma(n_1,\dots n_m)$, if $n_1=\alpha_1,\dots,n_m=\alpha_m$ is a solution of the inequality system $\Sigma(n_1,\dots,n_m)$ taking into account that, if for some j: $n_j=n^0$, then $\alpha_j=0$. We say that an m-tuple $\alpha_1,\dots,\alpha_m$ is π*-permissible* for Σ ($\pi \in \mathbb{N}$), if it is permissible for Σ and for each $i \ne j$: $|\alpha_i - \alpha_j| \ge \pi$.

By $E(n_1,\dots,n_m)$ we denote the fact that $n_1,\dots,n_m$ are free variables of expression **E**. Then, instead of $E[\xi_{i_1}/n_1,\dots,\xi_{i_m}/n_m]$, we simply write $E(\xi_{i_1},\dots,\xi_{i_m})$.

Let $n_1,\dots,n_m$ be the set of all the free variables of $E(n_1,\dots,n_m)$ and $F(n_1,\dots,n_m)$. We say that the expressions **E** and **F** are π*-equivalent* ($\pi \in \mathbb{N}$) *for given simple ordering* $\Sigma(n_1,\dots,n_m)$ if for any m-tuple $(\alpha_1,\dots\alpha_m)$ π-permissible for Σ:

$$\mathrm{Unf}(E(\alpha_1,\dots,\alpha_m))=\mathrm{Unf}(F(\alpha_1,\dots,\alpha_m)). \qquad (3.1)$$

We denote the fact by $E^{\Sigma \angle \pi}F$ or simply $E \overset{\pi}{\sim} F$ (assuming that Σ is fixed). We say that expessions **E** and **F** are *almost equivalent* for the given ordering Σ, if there exists $\pi \in \mathbb{N}$, such that $E^{\Sigma \angle \pi}F$. We denote the fact by $E \overset{\Sigma}{\sim} F$ (or simply $E \sim F$).

We call an expression *singular*, if there exists an illegitimate expression almost equivalent to the given, otherwise we call it *nonsingular*. Further on, if the opposite is not claimed, by *expression* we will understand exactly nonsingular expression.

Let us note that unary *for*-expressions defined in section 1 actually coincide with *for*-expressions with two variables n^0 and n, provided that $n^0 \le n$. Asymptotical equivalence $E \cong F$ equals the assertion that there exists $\lambda \in \mathbb{Z}$, such that $E(n) \overset{0 \le n}{\sim} F(n+\lambda)$. $E \equiv F$ equals $E^{0 \le n \angle\, 0}\, F$.

Now we can prove assertion 1, i.e., the decidability of correctness for dot expressions. We will present an algorithm, which constructs an equivalent *for*-expression for an arbitrary dot expression, if the given dot expression is correct and give the answer *'incorrect'*, otherwise.

It is easy to imagine expressions, where dot terms are used along with *for*-terms. The intended algorithm gradually replaces dot terms by appropriate *for*-terms, beginning with the outermost and checks in each step, whether inner dot terms (which are also changed) remain valid.

The algorithm works as follows. Let $T=\langle a_1\ldots a_n\circ\circ\circ b_1\ldots b_n\rangle$, where $a_i, b_i\in \mathbb{A}\cup\bar{\mathbb{X}}\cup\{<,>,\circ,|,..,:=\}$, is a valid dot-term. For any $i=1,\ldots,n$ there are two possibilities: either $a_i=b_i$ or $a_i=\underline{i_p+\alpha_i}$ and $b_i=\underline{i_q+\beta i}$, where $i_p, i_q\in\mathbb{X}$. Note, that for all i for which $\alpha_i\neq\beta_i$, the difference $\beta_i-\alpha_i$ is the same, say γ. The algorithm replaces T by $S=\langle c_1\ldots c_n|i:=\underline{i_p}..\underline{i_q+\gamma}\rangle$, where

$$c_i=\begin{cases} a_i, & \text{if} \quad a_i=b_i;\\ \underline{i+\alpha_i}, & \text{otherwise.}\end{cases}$$

It can be proved that the body $\bar{S}=c_1\ldots c_n$ is a valid dot expression if and only if T is correct (to prove this we use a comparatively simple fact that a term $\langle\bar{S}_1(i)\circ\circ\circ\bar{S}_2(i)\rangle$ is valid if and only if the term $\langle S_1(\alpha)\circ\circ\circ S_2(\alpha)\rangle$ is valid for three different $\alpha\in\mathbb{Z}$), hence assertion 1, by induction.

Similarly we can define an algorithm constructing correct dot expressions by given *for*-expressions and, consequently, obtain assertion 2.

We will need the following propositions.

Proposition 1. If $E\overset{\Sigma}{\simeq}F$, then $depth_\infty(E)=depth_\infty(F)$.

To prove the proposition note that for any expression $E(n_1,\ldots,n_k)$ (where $n_1,\ldots,n_k$ are all the free variables of E) we can find a polynomial $P_m(x)$ of the order $m=depth_\infty(E)$, such that for any k-tuple $\alpha_1,\ldots,\alpha_k$ for which $\alpha\le|\alpha_i-\alpha_j|\le\alpha\beta$ ($i\neq j$, $\alpha\in\mathbb{N}$, $\beta>1$) (we will call such k-tuples *(α,β)-expressive*): $P_m(\alpha)\le|\mathbf{Unf}(E(\alpha_1,\ldots,\alpha_k))|\le P_m(\alpha\beta)$. From there the proposition.

We say that an expression F *fits equivalently for expression* E *from left (right) for given ordering* Σ, if there is an expression G, such that $FG\overset{\Sigma}{\simeq}E$ ($GF\overset{\Sigma}{\simeq}E$). We denote it by $F\underset{\rightarrow}{\overset{\Sigma}{\varsigma}}E$ ($F\underset{\leftarrow}{\overset{\Sigma}{\varsigma}}E$). If $FG^{\Sigma\angle\alpha}E$ ($GF^{\Sigma\angle\alpha}E$), then we will also write $F^{\Sigma}\underset{\rightarrow}{\varsigma}^{\alpha}E$ ($F^{\Sigma}\underset{\leftarrow}{\varsigma}^{\alpha}E$). Sometimes, assuming that Σ is fixed, we will simply write $F\underset{\rightarrow}{\varsigma}E$ ($F\underset{\leftarrow}{\varsigma}E$) or $F\underset{\rightarrow}{\overset{\alpha}{\varsigma}}E$ ($F\underset{\leftarrow}{\overset{\alpha}{\varsigma}}E$). We call the expression G the *left (right) equivalent difference* of E and F.

Proposition 2. Let $E=E(n_1,\ldots,n_k)$ and $F(i)=F(i,n_1,\ldots,n_k)$ be expressions, and let $depth_\infty(E)\le depth_\infty(F)$. Then there exists a constant μ, such that

$$F(n_i)F(n_i+\sigma)\ldots F(n_i+\mu\sigma)\underset{\rightarrow}{\varsigma}E$$
$$(\ F(n_i)F(n_i+\sigma)\ldots F(n_i+\mu\sigma)\underset{\leftarrow}{\varsigma}E\ )$$

does not hold ($\sigma\in\{+1,-1\}$, $i=1,\ldots,k$).

We say that an *ordering* Σ *yields inequality* $i+\beta\le j+\gamma$, if there exists an $\alpha\in\mathbb{N}$, such that any α-separated solution of the inequality system Σ is also a solution of $i+\beta\le j+\gamma$. For instance, $0\le i\le j\le k$ yields $i\le j-5$.

We can generalize the step of a term also for terms with a variable factor. Let there be given an ordering $\Sigma(n_1,\dots,n_k)$ and let $T=\langle\bar{T}|i:=\underline{n_i+\alpha}..\underline{n_j+\beta}\rangle$. We define $step_\Sigma(T)$ for given Σ as follows:

$$step_\Sigma(T) = \begin{cases} +1, \text{ if } \Sigma \text{ yields } n_i+\alpha\le n_j+\beta; \\ -1, \text{ if } \Sigma \text{ yields } n_i+\alpha> n_j+\beta. \end{cases}$$

Note, that for any $T(n_1,\dots,n_k)$ there exists $\alpha\in\mathbb{N}$, such that for any α-separated $\alpha_1,\dots,\alpha_k$: $step(T(\alpha_1,\dots,\alpha_k))=step_\Sigma(T)$.

Let $\underline{n_h+\chi}$ $(h\in\{1,\dots,k\})$ be such that Σ yields either $n_i+\alpha\le n_h+\chi\le n_j+\beta$ (in case $step_\Sigma(T)=1$) or $n_j+\beta\le n_h+\chi\le n_i+\alpha$ (in case $step_\Sigma(T)=-1$). Then the expression

$$E=\langle\bar{T}(i)|i:=\underline{n_i+\alpha}..\underline{n_h+\chi}\rangle\langle\bar{T}(i)|i:=\underline{n_h+\chi+\sigma}..\underline{n_j+\beta}\rangle,$$

where $\sigma=step_\Sigma(T)$, is called a *partition* of the term $T=\langle\bar{T}(i)|i:=\underline{n_i+\alpha}..\underline{n_j+\beta}\rangle$.

We define the set $R_\Sigma(E)$ of *dischargements* of an expression E for given ordering Σ inductively:

a) $E\in R_\Sigma(E)$;

b) let $E'\in R_\Sigma(E)$, T be an outermost term of E' and let E'' be an expression we obtain from E' by replacing T, either by an arbitrary partition or (if T has constant factor) by the unfoldment $unf(T)$; then $E''\in R_\Sigma(E)$.

It is evident that for $E'\in R_\Sigma(E)$, $E'\overset{\Sigma}{\underset{\alpha}{\simeq}}E$.

Let $\alpha\in\mathbb{N}$ and let us define $R^\alpha_\Sigma(E)=\{E'\in R_\Sigma(E)\,|\,/E'\backslash\le\alpha\}$.

The notion of the set of dischargements of the expression will have an important role. We will show that, if $F\overset{\Sigma}{\underset{\rightarrow}{\subsetneq}}E$ $(F\overset{\Sigma}{\underset{\leftarrow}{\subsetneq}}E)$, then there exists $E'\in R_\Sigma(E)$, such that $E'=E_1E_2$ and $F\sim E_1$ $(F\sim E_2)$. Another property is related to algorithm S. We will show that for any E there exists $E'\in R_\Sigma(E)$, such that, if $S(E)=E_1E_2$, then $E'=E_1'E_2'$, $S(E')=S(E_1')S(E_2')$ and $S(E_1')=E_1$, $S(E_2')=E_2$.

We will need a notion of the so-called insolation of the term in the given expression. We say that the *insolation* of the outermost term $T=\langle\bar{T}(i)|i:=\jmath..\eta\rangle$ in an expression $E=E_1TE_2$ equals ρ $(\rho\in\mathbb{N})$ (for the given ordering Σ), if

$$\bar{T}(\jmath-\sigma\rho)\bar{T}(\jmath-\sigma(\rho-1))\dots\bar{T}(\jmath-\sigma)\underset{\leftarrow}{\subsetneq}E_1$$

and

$$\bar{T}(\jmath+\sigma)\bar{T}(\jmath+2\sigma)\ldots\bar{T}(\jmath+\sigma\rho)\underset{\rightarrow}{\subseteq}E_2,$$

where $\sigma=step_{\Sigma}(T)$.

Evidently, for any E and any ρ there is $E'\in R_{\Sigma}(E)$, such that for all outermost terms of E′ the insolation is more or equal to ρ.

Let Σ be a simple ordering. We call a term $T=\langle\bar{T}|i:=\underline{n_i+\alpha}..\underline{n_j+\beta}\rangle$ *elementary* for the given ordering, if there does not exist h: $h\neq i, h\neq j$ such that Σ yields $n_i\leq n_h\leq n_j$ or $n_j\leq n_h\leq n_i$. We define the *accessibility* of the given elementary term T as the integer $\nu=min(\alpha\sigma,-\beta\sigma)$. It is easy to prove

Proposition 3. Let Σ' be equal to $n_p\leq\ldots\leq n_l\leq i\leq n_m\leq\ldots\leq n_q$ ($n_p\leq\ldots\leq n_m\leq i\leq n_l\leq\ldots\leq n_q$) and let $\Sigma(n_1,\ldots,n_k)$ be obtained from Σ' by omission of i. Let $T=\langle F(i,n_1,\ldots,n_k)|i:=\underline{n_l+\alpha}..\underline{n_m+\beta}\rangle$ be an elementary term, let the accessibility of T be more or equal to ω ($\omega\in\mathbb{N}$) and let E be an expression, such that $E \overset{\Sigma'}{\angle}{}^{\omega} F$. Then $T\overset{\Sigma}{=}\langle E|i:=\underline{n_l+\alpha}..\underline{n_m+\beta}\rangle$.

Note that for any expression E and any $\nu\in\mathbb{N}$ there is $E'\in R_{\Sigma}(E)$, such that for all the outermost terms of E′ the accessibility is more or equal to ν.

Above we have defined only simple orderings, i.e., orderings of the type $n_{i1}\leq\ldots\leq n_{il}$. We will also need *ordering* of more general type:

$$n_{i1}+\chi_1\leq\ldots\leq n_{im}+\chi_m,$$

where $i_1,\ldots,i_m$ is not necessarily a permutation of $1,\ldots,l$, but the same index may occur several times. For instance, $0\leq n_1\leq n_2\leq 15\leq n_3$ is ordering. (The need for the orderings of this type comes from the following. Let us consider expression $E(n)=\langle F(i,n)|i:=0..\underline{n}\rangle$ and ordering $0\leq n$. Then $0\leq i\leq n$ holds for the variables of the subexpression $F(i,n)$. As we have mentioned in section 2, we also consider the expression $E(\alpha)$ ($\alpha\in\mathbb{N}$). For the corresponding subexpression $F(i,\alpha)$, $0\leq i\leq\alpha$ holds).

We say that an ordering is *noncontradicting,* if the inequality system defined by it has a solution. We define *scope*(Σ) of the noncontradicting ordering as follows: *scope*$(\Sigma)=\alpha$ ($\alpha\in\mathbb{N}$), if there is α, such that there exists α-separated k-tuple permissible for Σ and there does not exist β-separated k-tuple permissible for Σ, for $\beta>\alpha$; otherwise, *scope*$(\Sigma)=\infty$ (formally ∞ is a character for which for any $\alpha\in\mathbb{N}$, $\alpha<\infty$). If *scope*$(\Sigma)=\infty$, we call Σ *open ordering.*

It is possible to generalize α-equivalence and almost equivalence of expressions for arbitrary orderings. The additional requirement to (3.1) is that in order to consider two expressions *α-equivalent* for the given ordering Σ, $scope(\Sigma)\geq\alpha$ should hold.

Let $n_1,\ldots,n_k$ be all the free variables of an expression E and let $\{\mathfrak{z}_{i1},\ldots,\mathfrak{z}_{il}\}$ ($\mathfrak{z}_{ij}\in\bar{\mathbb{X}}$) be a set containing all substrings of E of the type $\underline{n_i+\gamma}$ ($i=1,\ldots,k$; $\gamma\in\mathbb{Z}$). We say the ordering $\Sigma(n_1,\ldots,n_k)$ to be *in concord* with E, if Σ is of the type $\mathfrak{z}_{j1}\leq\ldots\leq\mathfrak{z}_{jl}$, where $j_1,\ldots,j_l$ is a permutation of $i_1,\ldots,i_l$. Note, that for any ordering $\Sigma(n_1,\ldots,n_k)$ and any expression $E(n_1,\ldots,n_k)$ we can find an ordering Σ', such that: Σ' is in concord with E, and for any F, $E\overset{\Sigma'}{\simeq}F$ if and only if $E\overset{\Sigma}{\simeq}F$. We say that Σ' is *equivalent* to Σ.

Let us define the set $\tilde{R}^{\lambda}_{\Sigma}(E)$, where $\lambda\in\mathbb{N}$, as follows. $E'\in\tilde{R}^{\lambda}_{\Sigma}(E)$ if and only if there exist expressions $\tilde{E}$, $\tilde{E}'$, an ordering $\tilde{\Sigma}$ and a substitution Φ^*, such that $/\tilde{E}\backslash\leq\lambda$, $E=\tilde{E}[\Phi^*]$, $\Sigma=\tilde{\Sigma}[\Phi^*]$, $\tilde{E}'\in R^{\lambda}_{\tilde{\Sigma}}(\tilde{E})$ and $\tilde{E}'[\Phi^*]\in R_{\Sigma}(E)$.

For instance, if

$$E=\langle a\underline{i}\,|\,i:=0..\underline{100}\rangle\langle a\underline{i}\,|\,i:=\underline{100}..\underline{101}\rangle,$$
$$E'=a0\langle a\underline{i}\,|\,i:=1..\underline{99}\rangle a\underline{100}a\underline{100}a\underline{101}\ ,$$

then, $E'\in\tilde{R}^{1}_{\Sigma}(E)$ (where Σ is the empty ordering), since for $\tilde{\Sigma}$ equal to $0\leq n$ and

$$\tilde{E}=\langle a\underline{i}\,|\,i:=0..n\rangle\langle a\underline{i}\,|\,i:=n..\underline{n+1}\rangle,$$
$$\tilde{E}'=a0\langle a\underline{i}\,|\,i:=1..\underline{n-1}\rangle a\underline{n}a\underline{n}a\underline{n+1},$$

$\tilde{E}'\in R^{1}_{\tilde{\Sigma}}(\tilde{E})$, $E'=\tilde{E}'[n/\underline{100}]$ and $E'\in R_{\Sigma}(E)$.

Note that for given E and λ, $\tilde{R}^{\lambda}_{\Sigma}(E)$ is finite and can be effectively enumerated.

By $\alpha=\alpha(|E_1|,\ldots,|E_m|)$ ($\alpha=\alpha(\|E_1\|,\ldots,\|E_m\|)$) we will mean that α depends only on $|E_1|,\ldots,|E_m|$ ($\|E_1\|,\ldots,\|E_m\|$).

As it was noted in section 2, to prove theorems of equivalence and synthesis we use certain algorithms transforming expressions. Let W be an algorithm transforming expressions $E_1(n_1,\ldots,n_k),\ldots,E_l(n_1,\ldots,n_k)$ into expression $F=W_{\Sigma}(E_1,\ldots,E_l)$ for the given ordering $\Sigma(n_1,\ldots,n_k)$. The algorithm W is called *bounded*, if $depth(F)\leq max(depth(E_1),\ldots,depth(E_l))$. W is said to *conserve the equivalence*, if $l=1$ and there exists a constant $\omega=\omega(|E_1|)$, such that for any Σ: $W_{\Sigma}(E_1)\overset{\Sigma}{\sim}{}^{\omega}E_1$. Finally, W is called *uniform*, if for any Σ:

a) for any $\beta\in\mathbb{N}$, for which $\Sigma[\underline{n_i+\beta}/n_i]$ ($i=1,\ldots,k$) is noncontradicting

$$W_{\Sigma[\underline{n_i+\beta}/n_i]}(E_1[\underline{n_i+\beta}/n_i],\ldots,E_l[\underline{n_i+\beta}/n_i])=$$
$$=W_{\Sigma}(E_1,\ldots,E_l)[\underline{n_i+\beta}/n_i];$$

b) let $\mathbb{Y}$ be the set of subexpressions $\underline{n_i+\gamma}\in\bar{\mathbb{X}}$ contained in some of the expressions $E_1,\dots,E_l$; there exists $\bar{\alpha}=\bar{\alpha}(|E_1|,\dots,|E_l|)$, such that for any $\alpha\in\mathbb{Z}$, for which $\min_{u\in\mathbb{Y}}|(n_i+\alpha)-u|\geq\bar{\alpha}$ $(i=1,\dots,k)$, and $\Sigma[\underline{n_i+\alpha}/n_j]$ is noncontradicting, the following holds:

$$W_{\Sigma[\underline{n_i+\alpha}/n_j]}(E_1[\underline{n_i+\alpha}/n_j],\dots,E_l[\underline{n_i+\alpha}/n_j])=$$
$$=W_{\Sigma}(E_1,\dots,E_l)[\underline{n_i+\alpha}/n_j]$$

$(j=1,\dots,k)$.

It can be easily proved that, if algorithm W is uniform, then there exists a constant $\alpha_0=\alpha_0(|E_1|,\dots,|E_l|)$, such that for α_0-separated k-tuple $\alpha_1,\dots,\alpha_k$ permissible for Σ:

$$W_{\Sigma}(E_1,\dots,E_l)[\alpha_1/n_1,\dots,\alpha_l/n_l]=$$
$$=W_{\Sigma(\alpha_1,\dots,\alpha_k)}(E_1(\alpha_1,\dots\alpha_k),\dots,E_l(\alpha_1,\dots,\alpha_k)) \qquad (3.2)$$

Let $E_1,\dots,E_l$ and $\tilde{E}_1,\dots,\tilde{E}_l$ be expressions, Σ be an ordering, $\tilde{\Sigma}$ be an open ordering and Φ^* a substitution such that $E_1=\tilde{E}_1[\Phi^*],\dots,E_l=\tilde{E}_l[\Phi^*]$ and $\Sigma=\tilde{\Sigma}[\Phi^*]$. We call expressions $\tilde{E}_1,\dots,\tilde{E}_l$ and ordering $\tilde{\Sigma}$ *canonical* for the given W, $E_1,\dots,E_l$ and Σ if

$$W_{\tilde{\Sigma}}(\tilde{E}_1,\dots,\tilde{E}_l)[\Phi^*]\doteq W_{\Sigma}(E_1,\dots,E_l) \qquad (3.3)$$

Actually (3.3) means that $\tilde{E}_1,\dots,\tilde{E}_l$ transforms in a sense the same way as $E_1,\dots,E_l$.

Let $n_1,\dots,n_m$ be variables. We say that a certain assertion P *holds for reasonable orderings* $\Sigma(n_1,\dots,n_m)$, if there exists $\gamma\in\mathbb{N}$, such that assertion P holds for any ordering $\Sigma(n_1,\dots,n_m)$, for which $scope(\Sigma)\geq\gamma$.

It can be proved

Proposition 4. Let $E_1,\dots,E_k$ be expressions. If W is uniform and Σ is reasonable, then there exist a constant $\rho=\rho(|E_1|,\dots,|E_k|)$, expressions $\tilde{E}_1,\dots,\tilde{E}_k$ and ordering $\tilde{\Sigma}$ canonical for W, $E_1,\dots,E_k$, and Σ, such that $|\tilde{E}_i|\leq\rho$ $(i=1,\dots,k)$.

Now, let us formulate the lemma about regular strings mentioned in the previous section. Evidently, the notion of regular string can be generalized for the alphabet which includes $\bar{\mathbb{X}}$. In this case we will talk about regular words.

Lemma 1. Let a word **A** be (π_1,ϕ_1)-regular and **B** (π_2,ϕ_2)-regular. Let **A** and **B** intersect on a common substring **C**. If $|\mathbf{C}|\geq max(\pi_1,\pi_2)+4min(\pi_1,\pi_2)$ then $\pi_1=\pi_2$.

The proof of the lemma, which is mostly technical, is given in [6].

We say that E *can be obtained from* F *by inner substitution* $i \leftarrow j+\chi$ ($i,j \in \mathbb{X}'$, $\chi \in \mathbb{Z}$), if we can obtain E from F substituting term $S=\langle \bar{S}(j+\chi) \mid j:=\zeta-\chi..\eta-\chi \rangle$ for term $T=\langle \bar{T}(i) \mid i:=\zeta..\eta \rangle$ (T may not be outermost). By $E \doteq F$ we will mean, that there exists a sequence of inner substitutions by which E can be obtained from F.

It is evident that the assertion of lemma 1 is also true for the case, then the words A and B do not actually intersect, but only contain substrings C_1 and C_2, such that $C_1 \doteq C_2 \doteq C$.

Finally, let us introduce one more notion. Let us consider a sequence of expressions $X^i=(sf)^i(Y)$. Let $\xi=\xi(\nu)$ ($\xi \in \mathbb{N}$, $\nu>0$) be such that for all $i=0,\ldots,\xi(\nu)-1$ the expression X^i contains a regular substring with attraction ν or more, but the string X^ξ does not. We call such $\xi(\nu)$ the *ν-level step* for the expression *Y*, and denote by *level(ν)*.

4. Algorithm of Complete Standardization

As it was noted in section 2, the proof of the completeness theorem will be obtained as corollary of properties of a certain algorithm transforming expressions, namely, the algorithm of complete standardization. In this section we will construct the algorithm and prove a number of its properties.

The algorithm, which we denote by S, will be constructed recursively. Operating on expressions of depth *N*+1 ($N \in \mathbb{N}$), algorithm S will apply auxiliary algorithm D to expressions of depth *N*, auxiliary algorithms L and T to expressions of depth *N*+1 and algorithm S itself to expressions of depth *N* and less. Auxiliary algorithms in turn use algorithm S for expressions of depth *N* and less as it is shown in fig. 10.

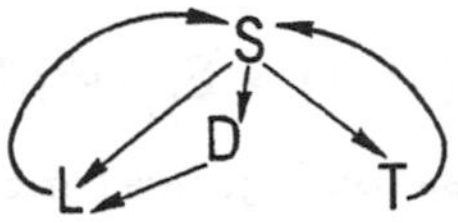

Fig. 10.

By $S_\Sigma(E)$ we denote the expression we obtain applying algorithm S to the expression E given the ordering Σ. We can assume without loss of generality that Σ is in concord with E.

Lemma 2. Let $E(n_1,\ldots,n_k)$ be an expression, $n_1,\ldots,n_k$ be all the free variables of E and $\Sigma(n_1,\ldots,n_k)$ an arbitrary ordering. There exists bounded, uniform and conserving equivalence algorithm $\mathcal{S}$, such that, if Σ is reasonable, then $\mathcal{S}_\Sigma(E)$ is defined and the following properties are held:

1. Let F be an expression and let the ordering Σ be open. If $E \overset{\Sigma}{=} F$, then

$$\mathcal{S}_\Sigma(E^0) \doteq \mathcal{S}_\Sigma(F^0).$$

2. There can be found effectively a constant $\mu=\mu(|E|)$ and an expression $E' \in \tilde{R}^{\mu}_{\Sigma}(E)$, such that, if $\mathcal{S}_\Sigma(E)=E_1E_2$ for certain E_1 and E_2, then $E'=E_1'E_2'$, $\mathcal{S}_\Sigma(E')=\mathcal{S}_\Sigma(E_1')\mathcal{S}_\Sigma(E_2')$, $\mathcal{S}_\Sigma(E_1')=E_1$ and $\mathcal{S}_\Sigma(E_2')=E_2$. If $E=E'$ for all possible E_1 and E_2, we call E *separable*.

3.*a*) Let expressions E_1, E_2 and E_3 be such that $\mathcal{S}_\Sigma(E_1E_2)=\mathcal{S}_\Sigma(E_1)\mathcal{S}_\Sigma(E_2)$ and $\mathcal{S}_\Sigma(E_2E_3)=\mathcal{S}_\Sigma(E_2)\mathcal{S}_\Sigma(E_3)$. Then $\mathcal{S}_\Sigma(E_1E_2E_3)= =\mathcal{S}_\Sigma(E_1)\mathcal{S}_\Sigma(E_2)\mathcal{S}_\Sigma(E_3)$.

3.*b*) Let $dpth(E)=depth(\mathcal{S}_\Sigma(E))$. Let $\mathcal{S}_\Sigma(E_1E_2)=\mathcal{S}_\Sigma(E_1)\mathcal{S}_\Sigma(E_2)$ and let E' be such that $dpth(E')\le dpth(E_1)$ $(dpth(E')\le dpth(E_2))$. Then $\mathcal{S}_\Sigma(E'E_1E_2)=\mathcal{S}_\Sigma(E'E_1)\mathcal{S}_\Sigma(E_2)$ $(\mathcal{S}_\Sigma(E_1E_2E')=\mathcal{S}_\Sigma(E_1)\mathcal{S}_\Sigma(E_2E'))$.

3.*c*) Let $\mathcal{S}_\Sigma(E'E_1E_2)=\mathcal{S}_\Sigma(E'E_1)\mathcal{S}_\Sigma(E_2)$ $(\mathcal{S}_\Sigma(E_1E_2E')= =\mathcal{S}_\Sigma(E_1)\mathcal{S}_\Sigma(E_2E'))$ and let $dpth(E')\le dpth(E_1)$ $(dpth(E')\le dpth(E_2))$. Then $\mathcal{S}_\Sigma(E_1E_2)=\mathcal{S}_\Sigma(E_1)\mathcal{S}_\Sigma(E_2)$.

4. Let expression $E(n_i)=E(n_1,\ldots,n_k)$, $(i=1,\ldots,k)$ be such, that the expression $E(n_i)E(n_i+\sigma)$, where $\sigma\in\{+1,-1\}$, is separable. Then, there exist expressions E_1 and E_2, such that $E=E_1E_2$ and

$$\mathcal{S}_\Sigma(E(n_i)E(n_i+\sigma))=\mathcal{S}_\Sigma(E_1(n_i))\mathcal{S}_\Sigma(E_2(n_i)E_1(n_i+\sigma))\mathcal{S}_\Sigma(E_2(n_i+\sigma)).$$

5. Let an ordering Σ be open and $\vec{\alpha}=(\alpha_1,\ldots\alpha_k)$ be (α,β)-expressive k-tuple (i.e., $\alpha\le|\alpha_i-\alpha_j|\le\alpha\beta$) permissible for Σ, $\alpha\in\mathbb{N}$, $\beta>1$. Let us consider a sequence of strings $X^i=(sf)^i(\mathrm{Unf}(E(\vec{\alpha})))$ $(i\in\mathbb{N})$. There exist constants $\mu=\mu(\|E\|,\beta)$ and $\bar{\alpha}=\bar{\alpha}(\|E\|,\beta)$, such that for any $\alpha\ge\bar{\alpha}$

$$((sf)^{level(\alpha/\mu)}(\mathrm{Unf}(E(\vec{\alpha}))))_f \doteq \mathcal{S}_{\Sigma_0}(E^0(\vec{\alpha})), \qquad (4.1)$$

where by X_f we mean a *for*-expression equivalent to the dot expression X, $E^0=\mathrm{Unf}(E)$ and Σ_0 is an ordering containing the only variable n_0 (and being in concord with $E^0(\vec{\alpha})$).

A number of important facts follows directly from lemma 2. First of all, note that since $\mathcal{S}$ is uniform, we get from (3.2), that, if $E(n_1,\ldots,n_k)$ is an arbitrary expression and Σ is an open ordering, then there exists $\alpha=\alpha(\|E\|)$, such that for all α-separated k-tuples $\alpha_1,\ldots,\alpha_k$ permissible for Σ:

$$S_{\Sigma}(E)[\alpha_1/n_1,\dots,\alpha_k/n_k]=S_{\Sigma_0}(E(\alpha_1,\dots,\alpha_k)). \qquad (4.2)$$

From the fact that S is uniform we also get that for S, for any expression E and reasonable ordering Σ there exists canonical expression $\tilde{E}$, such that $\|\tilde{E}\|\le\gamma$, where $\gamma=\gamma(|E|)$. Taking into account items 3 and 4 of lemma 2 we can get a stronger version of this assertion: in case E has the form $E(n)=G(n)G(n+\sigma)\dots G(n+\mu\sigma)$ ($\sigma\in\{+1,-1\}$, $\mu\in\mathbb{N}$ and n is a certain variable of E), then there exists expression $\tilde{G}$ canonical for G, such that $\|\tilde{G}\|\le\gamma(|G|)$ and $\tilde{E}(n)=\tilde{G}(n)\tilde{G}(n+\sigma)\dots\tilde{G}(n+\mu\sigma)$ is canonical for E (i.e., γ does not depend on μ).

The existence of canonical substitution and item 1 of lemma 2 yield

Corollary 1. For the given E, F and Σ, there exist a constant $\lambda=\lambda(|E|,|F|)$, expressions $\tilde{E}$, $\tilde{F}$, an open ordering $\tilde{\Sigma}$ and a substitution Φ^*, such that $\|\tilde{E}\|\le\gamma$, $\|\tilde{F}\|\le\gamma$, $\tilde{E}=\tilde{E}[\Phi^*]$, $\tilde{F}=\tilde{F}[\Phi^*]$, $\tilde{\Sigma}=\tilde{\Sigma}[\Phi^*]$ and $\tilde{E}\overset{\tilde{\Sigma}_L\alpha}{}\tilde{F}$ if and only if $E\overset{\Sigma_L\alpha}{}F$.

For the case $E=G(n)G(n+\sigma)\dots G(n+\nu\sigma)$ and $F=H(n)H(n+\sigma')\dots H(n+\mu\sigma')$ ($\sigma,\sigma'\in\{+1,-1\}$, $\nu,\mu\in\mathbb{N}$) a stronger version of the assertion holds: there exist $\lambda=\lambda(|G|,|H|)$, $\tilde{G}$, $\tilde{H}$, $\tilde{\Sigma}$ and Φ^*, such that $\|\tilde{G}\|\le\lambda$, $\|\tilde{H}\|\le\lambda$, $G=\tilde{G}[\Phi^*]$, $H=\tilde{H}[\Phi^*]$ and $\Sigma=\tilde{\Sigma}[\Phi^*]$ and $\tilde{E}\overset{\tilde{\Sigma}_L\alpha}{}\tilde{F}$ if and only if $E\overset{\Sigma_L\alpha}{}F$, where $\tilde{E}=\tilde{G}(n)\dots\tilde{G}(n+\nu\sigma)$, $\tilde{F}=\tilde{H}(n)\dots\tilde{H}(n+\mu\sigma')$.

Corollary 1 is very important, as it frequently allows us to consider an equivalence for an open ordering instead of an equivalence for the given arbitrary ordering. Furthermore, instead of arbitrary expression E, we can consider an expression $\tilde{E}$, such that $\|\tilde{E}\|\le\gamma(|E|)$.

From the corollary and item 1 of lemma 2 we also get: if $E\overset{\Sigma}{\sim}F$, where Σ is an arbitrary ordering, then there exist a constant $\lambda=\lambda(|E|,|F|)$, and expressions $E'\in V^{\lambda}(E)$ and $F'\in V^{\lambda}(F)$, such that

$$S_{\Sigma}(E')\doteq S_{\Sigma}(F') \qquad (4.3)$$

(we denote the fact by $S_{\Sigma}(E)\approx S_{\Sigma}(F)$). In case $E=S_{\Sigma}(E)$, we say that E is in *standard form.*

According to item 4 of lemma 2

$$S_{\Sigma}(E(n_1)E(n_1+\sigma))=S_{\Sigma}(E_1(n_1))S_{\Sigma}(E_2(n_1)E_1(n_1+\sigma))S_{\Sigma}(E_2(n_1+\sigma)).$$

We call the expression $E^*(n_1)=S_{\Sigma}(E_2(n_1)E_1(n_1+\sigma))$ the *complete standard form* of E *with respect to variable* n_1 *for given* σ *and* Σ. The expression $E_2(n_1)E_1(n_1+\sigma)$ is called the *basis* of E^*, $E_2(n_1)$ and

$E_1(n_1+\sigma)$ are its *left* and *right part*. We say that the expression E is in *complete standard form* (with respect to n_1 for given σ and Σ) if $E(n_1)E(n_1+\sigma)=S_\Sigma(E(n_1)E(n_1+\sigma))$.

Finally note that item 5 of lemma 2 and (4.2) yield

Corollary 2. For the given E, F, open ordering Σ and (α,β)-expressive k-tuple $\vec{\alpha}$, there exists $\bar{\alpha}=\bar{\alpha}(\|E\|,\beta)$, such that if $\alpha\geq\bar{\alpha}$, then $Unf(E(\vec{\alpha}))=Unf(F(\vec{\alpha}))$ yields $E\overset{\Sigma}{\simeq}F$.

Now, let us pass to the auxiliary algorithms. We begin with algorithm D. In fact we have two algorithms: D^L and D^R, called the algorithm of *left and right equivalent difference* respectively. Given expressions E and F and an ordering Σ, algorithm D^L (D^R) decides, whether $F\underset{\to}{\subseteq}E$ ($F\underset{\leftarrow}{\subseteq}E$) holds, and, if it does, then finds the left (right) equivalent difference denoted by $D^L_\Sigma(E,F)$ ($D^R_\Sigma(E,F)$). The algorithm is specified more precisely by

Lemma 3. Let E and F be expressions and Σ an arbitrary ordering. There exists a limited and uniform algorithm D^L (D^R), such that if the ordering Σ is reasonable, then D^L_Σ (D^R_Σ) is defined and

1) if $F\overset{\Sigma}{\underset{\to}{\subseteq}}E$ ($F\overset{\Sigma}{\underset{\leftarrow}{\subseteq}}E$), then $FD^L_\Sigma(E,F)\overset{\Sigma}{\simeq}E$ ($D^R_\Sigma(E,F)F\overset{\Sigma}{\simeq}E$), else $D^L_\Sigma=$*'no'* ((D^R_Σ)=*'no'*);

2) there exist $\mu=\mu(|E|,|F|)$ and $E'\in\tilde{R}^{\mu}_{\Sigma}(E)$, where $E'=E_1E_2$ for certain E_1 and E_2, such that $E_1\overset{\Sigma}{\simeq}F$ ($E_2\overset{\Sigma}{\simeq}F$) and $D^L_\Sigma(E,F)=E_2$ ($D^R_\Sigma(E,F)=E_1$).

Since D^L (D^L) is uniform, there exists canonical expressions $\tilde{E}$ and $\tilde{F}$ for D^L (D^R) (for any E, F and Σ) such that $\|\tilde{E}\|\leq\gamma$ and $\|\tilde{F}\|\leq\gamma$ (for certain constant $\gamma=\gamma(|E|,|F|)$. It follows

Corollary 3. For the given E, F and reasonable Σ there exist a constant $\lambda=\lambda(|E|,|F|)$, expressions $\tilde{E}$, $\tilde{F}$, an open ordering $\tilde{\Sigma}$ and a substitution Φ^*, such that $\|\tilde{E}\|\leq\gamma$, $\|\tilde{F}\|\leq\gamma$, $E=\tilde{E}[\Phi^*]$, $F=\tilde{F}[\Phi^*]$ and $\Sigma=\tilde{\Sigma}[\Phi^*]$, and $\tilde{F}\overset{\tilde{\Sigma}}{\underset{\to}{\subseteq}}{}^{\alpha}\tilde{E}$ ($\tilde{F}\overset{\tilde{\Sigma}}{\underset{\leftarrow}{\subseteq}}{}^{\alpha}\tilde{E}$) if and only if $F\overset{\Sigma}{\underset{\to}{\subseteq}}{}^{\alpha}E$ ($F\overset{\Sigma}{\underset{\leftarrow}{\subseteq}}{}^{\alpha}E$).

We will use algorithm D for the construction of algorithm L of equivalent expansion and shift of terms. In the simplest case then the expression has the form

$$E=E_1TE_2=E\langle\bar{T}(i)\,|\,i:=\jmath..\eta\rangle E_2$$

and $depth(E_2)<depth(T)$, T can be expanded rightwards equivalently, if $\bar{T}(\eta+\sigma)\overset{\Sigma}{\underset{\to}{\subseteq}}E_2$, where $\sigma=step_\Sigma(T)$, and the result of the expansion is

$$E'=E_1\langle\bar{T}(i)\,|\,i:=\jmath..\eta+\sigma\rangle D^L_\Sigma(E_2,\bar{T}(\eta+\sigma)).$$

Let us consider an example of a more complex case of the work of aalgorithm L. Let Σ be equal to $0\leq n_1\leq n_2\leq n_3$ and E be equal to

$a0\langle a\underline{i}\,|\,i:=1..\underline{n_1}\rangle a\underline{n_1+1}\langle a\underline{i}\,|\,i:=\underline{n_1+2}..\underline{n_2}\rangle\langle a\underline{i}a\underline{i+1}\,|\,i:=\underline{n_2+1}..\underline{n_3}\rangle.$

After the equivalent expansion of the leftmost term leftwards and rightwards the algorithm produces:

$\langle a\underline{i}\,|\,i:=0..\underline{n_1+1}\rangle\langle a\underline{i}\,|\,i:=\underline{n_1+2}..\underline{n_2}\rangle\langle a\underline{i}a\underline{i+1}\,|\,i:=\underline{n_2+1}..\underline{n_3}\rangle.$

Further, the algorithm unites the leftmost term with the term on the right:

$\langle a\underline{i}\,|\,i:=0..\underline{n_2}\rangle\langle a\underline{i}a\underline{i+1}\,|\,i:=\underline{n_2+1}..\underline{n_3}\rangle.$

Next, it expands the obtained term "at the expense" of the term on the right twice. We get

$\langle a\underline{i}\,|\,i:=0..\underline{n_2+2}\rangle\langle a\underline{i}a\underline{i+1}\,|\,i:=\underline{n_2+2}..n_3\rangle.$

It is not possible to expand the obtained term any more, but still it can be shifted rightwards "at the expense" of the term on the right. We obtain

$a\langle \underline{i}\underline{a}\,|\,i:=0..\underline{n_2+2}\rangle\underline{n_2+2}a\underline{n_2+3}\langle a\underline{i}a\underline{i+1}\,|\,i:=\underline{n_2+3}..\underline{n_3}\rangle.$

Formally algorithm L is specified by lemma 4.

Let $\bar{T}(i)$ and $\bar{S}(i)$ be expressions and let there exist $\bar{T}_1(i)$, $\bar{T}_2(i)$, $\alpha\in\mathbb{Z}$ and $\sigma\in\{+1,-1\}$, such that $\bar{T}(i)=\bar{T}_1(i)\bar{T}_2(i)$ and $\bar{S}(i)=\bar{T}_2(i+\alpha)\bar{T}_1(i+\alpha+\sigma)$. We say that $\bar{T}$ and $\bar{S}$ *coincides to within shift* and write $\bar{T}\overset{\sigma}{\simeq}\bar{S}$. If $\bar{S}(i)\underset{\cdot}{=}\bar{T}_2(i+\alpha)T_1(i+\alpha+\sigma)$, then we write $\bar{T}\underset{\cdot}{\overset{\sigma}{\simeq}}\bar{S}$.

Lemma 4. Let $E=F\underline{T}G$ be an expression, Σ be an ordering and let the term $T=\langle\bar{T}(i)\,|\,i:=\mathfrak{z}..\eta\rangle$ be marked in a certain way (say, underlined). Let *depth(F)<depth(T), depth(G)≤depth(T).* There exists a limited, uniform and conserving equivalence algorithm L, such that, if Σ is reasonable, then $\mathsf{L}_\Sigma(E)$ is defined, and the following properties are held:

1) $\mathsf{L}_\Sigma(E)=F'T'G'=F'\langle\bar{T}'(i)\,|\,i:=\mathfrak{z}'..\eta'\rangle G'$ and for $\sigma=step_\Sigma(T)$:

a) $\bar{T}'(i)\overset{\sigma}{\simeq}\bar{T}(i)$;

b) there does not hold $\bar{T}(\mathfrak{z}'-\sigma)\underset{\leftarrow}{\subsetneq}F'$;

c) there do not exist $\bar{T}_1(i)$ and $\bar{T}_2(i)$, such that $\bar{T}(i)=\bar{T}_1(i)\bar{T}_2(i)$ and $\bar{T}_1(\eta'+\sigma)\underset{\rightarrow}{\subsetneq}G'$;

d) $G'\underset{\leftarrow}{\subsetneq}G$ and $F'\underset{\rightarrow}{\subsetneq}F\bar{T}(\mathfrak{z})$.

2) If Σ is open there exists a constant $\mu=\mu(|E|)$, such that if the accessibility and the insolation of all the outermost terms of E are more or equal to μ, then

$F=F'F''$, $G=G''G'$ and $\mathsf{L}_\Sigma(E)=F'\mathsf{L}_\Sigma(F''TG'')G'=F'T'G'$.

3) If G (F) has the form $H(n_p)H(n_p+\sigma')$ $(\sigma'\in\{+1,-1\})$, then

depth(G′)=*depth*(G) (*depth*(F′)=*depth*(F)).

Directly from lemma 4 we get

Corollary 4. Let Σ be an open ordering, $E_1=F_1T_1G_1$, $E_2=F_2T_2G_2$, *depth*(F_i)<*depth*(T_i), *depth*(G_i)≤*depth*(T_i), *i*=1,2. Let

$$L_\Sigma(E_i)=F_i'T_i'G_i'.$$

If $E_1\overset{\Sigma}{\sim}E_2$ and $\bar{T}_1\overset{\sigma}{\doteq}\bar{T}_2$, where $\bar{T}_1$ and $\bar{T}_2$ are respective bodies of T_1 and T_2, and $\sigma=step_\Sigma(T_1)=step_\Sigma(T_2)$, then

$$T_1'\doteq T_2',\quad F_1'\sim F_2' \text{ and } G_1'\sim G_2'.$$

Now let us pass to the specification of algorithm T. Algorithm T can be applied only to the expressions of the type $E=\langle\bar{T}\,|\,i:=\xi..\eta\rangle$. The result of the transformation is specified by

Lemma 5. Let $T=\langle\bar{T}(i)\,|\,i:=\xi_1..\xi_k\rangle$ be an expression and Σ an ordering. There exists a limited, uniform and conserving equivalence algorithm T, such that if Σ is reasonable, then $T_\Sigma(T)$ is defined,

$$T_\Sigma(T)=E_0T_1...E_lT_{l+1}E_{l+1} \quad (\text{or } T_\Sigma(T)=E_0),$$

$l\geq0$, *depth*(E_j)<*depth*(T) and $T_j=\langle\bar{T}_j(i)\,|\,i:=\xi_j'..\xi_{j+1}'\rangle$, where $\bar{T}_j$ is the complete standard form of $\bar{T}$ for ordering $u\leq...\leq\xi_j'\leq i\leq\xi_{j+1}'...\leq v$, such that the ordering obtained from it by omission of i is equivalent to Σ.

The essence of algorithm T is to split the term T into terms $T_1,...,T_k$, such that the variables of the body $\bar{T}_i$ (*i*=1,...,*k*) are ordered and then, to transform each $\bar{T}_i$ into the complete standard form. For example, if the ordering Σ equals $0\leq n_1\leq n_2$ and $T=\langle a\underline{i}\,|\,i=0..\underline{n_2}\rangle$, then

$$T_\Sigma(T)=\langle a\underline{i}\,|\,i:=0..n_1\rangle\langle a\underline{i}\,|\,i:=\underline{n_1+1}..\underline{n_2}\rangle$$

($a\underline{i}$ is in complete standard form, since any expression of the depth 0 is in complete standard form).

Now we can pass to the construction of algorithm S. Let E be an expression and Σ be an ordering. <u>Algorithm</u> S <u>operates as follows</u>.

If *depth*(E)=0, then it sets $S_\Sigma(E)=E$.

Let *depth*(E)=*N*, *N*>0. E can be presented in the form

$$E=E_1T_1...E_kT_kE_{k+1},$$

where *depth*(T_i)=*N* (*i*=1,...,*k*), *depth*(E_i)<*N* (*i*=1,...,*k*+1). The algorithm carries out three following steps.

1. It sets $E'=E_1T_\Sigma(T_1)...E_kT_\Sigma(T_k)E_{k+1}$.

2. It applies algorithm L to E′ marking (underlining) in turn all terms of the depth *N* of the expression E′ starting from the left.

Let the obtained expression be $E''=E_1'T_1'\ldots E_l'T_l'E_{l+1}'$, where $depth(T_l')=N$, $depth(E_l')<N$.

3. Finally the algorithm sets

$$S_\Sigma(E)=S_\Sigma(E_1')T_1'\ldots S_\Sigma(E_l')T_l'S_\Sigma(E_{l+1}').$$

To prove that algorithm S satisfies lemma 2, first we will construct the auxiliary algorithms and prove that they satisfy their respective specifications.

Let us assume by induction that lemma 2 is true for expressions of depth N and less (it is evident that in the case of expression of zero depth, the lemma holds).

Let us consider algorithm D and prove

Proposition 5. Let **E** and **F** be expressions (of depth N or less) and Σ be an ordering. Let $F\underset{\rightarrow}{\subset}E$ ($F\underset{\leftarrow}{\subset}E$). If Σ is reasonable, then there can be found effectively a constant $\mu=\mu(|E|,|F|)$ and an expression $E'\in\tilde{R}^{\mu}_{\Sigma}(E)$, such that $E'=E_1E_2$ and $E_1\sim F$ ($E_2\sim F$) for certain E_1 and E_2.

Proof. First of all let us introduce several notions. Let W be a constant expression and W' be a certain unfoldment. We can define *images* in W' for any subexpression W_1 of W. For instance, if

$$W=a\langle b\underline{i}\,|\,i:=1..3\rangle b4,$$
$$W'=ab1b2b3b4, \qquad (4.4)$$

then, b1b2b3 is the image of $\langle b\underline{i}\,|\,i:=1..3\rangle$, b1, b2 and b3 are the images of $b\underline{i}$, and b4 is the image of b4. Formally, image can be defined inductively.

Let $W'=W_1'w'W_2'$ be an unfoldment of W and $w'\in\mathbb{A}$. We say that w' is a *free image*, if there exists $w\in\mathbb{A}$, such that W has a form $W=W_1wW_2$ and w' is the image of w. For instance, character 4 in (4.4) is a free image, but 3 is not.

Let **E** be an expression, Σ be an open ordering and let the accessibility of all of the outermost terms of **E** be more or equal to ρ ($\rho\in\mathbb{N}$). Let $\vec{\alpha}$ be α-separable k-tuple ($\alpha\in\mathbb{N}$) permissible for Σ, and let us consider the unfoldment $\mathrm{Unf}(E(\vec{\alpha}))=w_1w_2\ldots w_l$ ($w_i\in\mathbb{A}$). It is evident that, if α is large enough, then all these $w_i\in\mathbb{Z}$, for which there exists $j=1,\ldots,k$, such that $|\alpha_j-w_i|<\rho$, are free images. Consequently, it follows from corollary 2 that, if Σ is open and $F\underset{\rightarrow}{\subset}E$ ($F\underset{\leftarrow}{\subset}E$), then there exists a constant $\rho=\rho(\|F\|)$, such that if the accessibility and insolation of all the outermost terms of **E** are more or equal to ρ, then $E=E_1E_2$ and $E_1\sim F$ ($E_2\sim F$). Proposition 5 follows by corollary 3.

Now we can construct algorithm D. We describe algorithm D^L (D^R

can be constructed by analogy).

From proposition 5 we get that there can be found a constant $\mu=\mu(|F|)$ and an expression $E'\in\tilde{R}^{\mu}_{\Sigma}(E)$, such that if $F\underset{\to}{\overset{\Sigma}{\lessapprox}}E$, then $E'=E_1E_2$ and $E_1\overset{\Sigma}{\sim}F$. According to (4.3) there can be found a constant $\lambda=\lambda(|E|,|F|)$, such that if $E_1\sim F$, then there exist $E_1'\in V^{\lambda}(E_1)$ and $F'\in V^{\lambda}(F)$ such that $S_{\Sigma}(E_1')\doteq S_{\Sigma}(F')$. We check for all possible E_1 and E_2, such that $E_1E_2=E'$, and all possible $E_1'\in V^{\lambda}(E_1)$ and $F'\in V^{\lambda}(F)$, whether $S_{\Sigma}(E_1')\doteq S_{\Sigma}(F')$ holds. If it does for a certain E_1', we set $D^{L}_{\Sigma}(E,F)=E_2$, else $D^{L}_{\Sigma}(E,F)=$'*no*'. It is evident that the algorithm satisfies lemma 3.

Let us pass to algorithm L. In the beginning we prove proposition 6 from where we will get: if two terms **T** and **S** cannot be united, it is possible to expand (or shift) the term **T** "at the expense" of the term **S** only a definite number of times.

Proposition 6. Let $E(i)=E(i,n_1,\ldots,n_k)$, $F(i)=F(i,n_1,\ldots,n_k)$ and $G=G(n_1,\ldots,n_k)$ be expressions (of depth less or equal to N), let ordering Σ' be equal to $\mathfrak{z}\le\ldots\le\mathfrak{w}\le i\le\mathfrak{v}\le\ldots\le\mathfrak{y}$ ($\mathfrak{z}\le\ldots\le\mathfrak{u}\le i\le\mathfrak{w}\le\ldots\le\mathfrak{y}$), where $\mathfrak{z},\mathfrak{u},\mathfrak{v},\mathfrak{y}\in\bar{Y}$, $Y=\{n_1,\ldots,n_k\}$ and let Σ be obtained from Σ' by omission of i. There exists and can be effectively found a constant $\gamma=\gamma(|E|,|F|,|G|)$, such that if Σ is reasonable, $\sigma=+1$ ($\sigma=-1$) and for certain $\eta\in\mathbb{N}$, $\sigma'\in\{+1,-1\}$

$$E(\mathfrak{w})E(\mathfrak{w}+\sigma)\ldots E(\mathfrak{w}+\eta\sigma)\ \underset{\to}{\overset{\Sigma}{\lessapprox}}\ GF(\mathfrak{w})F(\mathfrak{w}+\sigma')\ldots F(\mathfrak{w}+\gamma\sigma')$$

(where, $E(\mathfrak{w})=E(i)[\mathfrak{w}/i]$) holds and

$$E(\mathfrak{w})E(\mathfrak{w}+\sigma)\ldots E(\mathfrak{w}+\eta\sigma)\ \underset{\to}{\overset{\Sigma}{\lessapprox}}\ GF(\mathfrak{w})F(\mathfrak{w}+\sigma')\ldots F(\mathfrak{w}+(\gamma-1)\sigma')$$

does not hold, then $\sigma=\sigma'$ and there exist a constant $\omega=\omega(|E|,|F|,|G|)$ and an expression $F'\in\tilde{R}^{\omega}_{\Sigma}(F)$, such that $F'=F_1F_2$ and

a) $E(i+(\rho+1)\sigma)\overset{\Sigma'}{\sim}F_2(i)F_1(i+\sigma')$,

b) $E(\mathfrak{w})\ldots E(\mathfrak{w}+\rho\sigma)\overset{\Sigma}{\sim}G(\mathfrak{w})F_1(\mathfrak{w})$,

for certain $\rho\in\mathbb{N}$. Analogous assertion is true for relation $\underset{\leftarrow}{\lessapprox}$.

To prove preposition 6 let us first prove simpler propositions 7 and 8.

Proposition 7. Let $E(i)=E(i,n_1,\ldots,n_k)$, $F(n_1,\ldots,n_k)$ and $G=G(n_1,\ldots,n_k)$ be expressions (of depth less or equal to N), Σ' be an ordering equal to $\mathfrak{z}\le\ldots\le\mathfrak{w}\le i\le\mathfrak{v}\le\ldots\le\mathfrak{y}$ ($\mathfrak{z}\le\ldots\le\mathfrak{u}\le i\le\mathfrak{w}\le\ldots\le\mathfrak{y}$) and Σ be obtained from Σ' by omission of i. Let E^* be the complete standard form of E with the respect to i for $\sigma=1$ ($\sigma=-1$) and Σ', and let E_2, E_1 be the left and the right part of the basis of E^*. Finally, let us consider the expression

$$FE(\varpi)E(\varpi+\sigma)\ldots E(\varpi+\nu\sigma)G$$

($\nu\in N$). There exists a constant $\mu=\mu(|E|,|F|,|G|)$, such that if $\nu>2\mu$ and *scope*(Σ')$\ge\nu$, then

$$S_\Sigma(H)=F^+E^*(\varpi+\mu\sigma)E^*(\varpi+(\mu+1)\sigma)\ldots E^*(\varpi+(\nu-\mu)\sigma)G^+,$$

where $F^+=S_\Sigma(FE(\varpi)\ldots E(\varpi+(\mu-1)\sigma)E_1(\varpi+\mu\sigma))$, $G^+=S_\Sigma(E_2(\varpi+(\nu-\mu+1)\sigma)E(\varpi+(\nu-\mu+2)\sigma)\ldots E(\varpi+\nu\sigma)G)$.

Proposition 7 follows from the uniformity of S and items 3 and 4 of lemma 2.

Proposition 8. Let $E(i)=E(i,n_1,\ldots,n_k)$ and $F(i)=F(i,n_1,\ldots,n_k)$ be expressions (of depth less or equal to N), Σ' be equal to $\jmath\le\ldots\le\varpi\le i\le\upsilon\le\ldots\le\eta$ ($\jmath\le\ldots\le u\le i\le\varpi\le\ldots\le\eta$), and let Σ be obtained from Σ' by the omission of i. Let there exist F_1, F_2, F_1' and F_2', such that $F_1F_2\in R_\Sigma(F)$, $F_1'F_2'\in R_\Sigma(F)$ and

$$E(\varpi)E(\varpi+\sigma)\ldots E(\varpi+\nu\sigma)\overset{\Sigma}{\simeq}F_1(\varpi)F(\varpi+\sigma')\ldots F(\varpi+\mu\sigma')F_2'(\varpi+\mu\sigma)\qquad(4.5)$$

for certain $\nu,\mu\in N$ and $\sigma=+1$ ($\sigma=-1$). Let $E^*(i)$ and $F^*(i)$ be the complete standard forms of E and F (with respect to i for Σ' and σ and σ', respectively). Then, there exist constants $\bar\nu=\bar\nu(|E|,|F|)$ and $\bar\mu=\bar\mu(|E|,|F|)$, such that if Σ' is reasonable, then $\sigma=\sigma'$ and

1) there exist $F^{*\prime}$ and $E^{*\prime}$, such that $E^{*\prime}\overset{\cdot}{\simeq}F^{*\prime}$, $E^{*\prime}\approx E^*$ and $F^{*\prime}\approx F^*$,

2) there exist constants $\varepsilon=\varepsilon(|E|,|F|)$, $\omega=\omega(|E|,|F|)$ and expressions E_1' and E_2', such that $E_1'E_2'\in\tilde R^{\varepsilon}_\Sigma(E)$ and

$$F(i)\sim E_2'(i+\omega)E_1'(i+\omega-\sigma).$$

Proof. 1) Let us first consider the case when Σ' is open. Let

$$L=E(\varpi)E(\varpi+\sigma)\ldots E(\varpi+\nu\sigma)$$

and

$$M=F_1(\varpi)F(\varpi+\sigma')\ldots F(\varpi+\mu\sigma')F_1'(\varpi+\mu\sigma').$$

We can assume that the expressions are separable without any loss of generality. From proposition 7 we get

$$S_\Sigma(L)=E_1^+E^*(\varpi+\rho\sigma)\ldots E^*(\varpi+(\nu-\rho)\sigma)E_2^+$$

and

$$S_\Sigma(L)=F_1^+F^*(\varpi+\rho'\sigma')\ldots F^*(\varpi+(\mu-\rho')\sigma')F_2^+,$$

for certain expressions E_i^+, F_i^+, $i=1,2$, $\rho=\rho(|E|)$ and $\rho'=\rho'(|F|)$. Since L~M according to item 1 of lemma 2:

$$E_1^{+0}E^{*0}(\varpi+\rho\sigma)\ldots E^{*0}(\varpi+(\nu-\rho)\sigma)E_2^{+0}\overset{\cdot}{=}$$
$$\overset{\cdot}{=}F_1^{+0}F^{*0}(\varpi+\rho\sigma)\ldots F^{*0}(\varpi+(\nu-\rho)\sigma)F_2^{+0}.$$

Further, it follows from propositions 1 and 2 that the regular subexpressions $E^{*0}(\varpi+\rho\delta)\dots E^{*0}(\varpi+(\nu-\rho)\sigma)$ and $F^{*0}(\varpi+\rho\delta)\dots F^{*0}(\varpi+(\nu-\rho)\sigma)$ intersect on an arbitrary long common subexpression, if ν and μ are sufficiently large. Therefore, we can use lemma 1, from there we get $E^{*0} \overset{\sigma}{\underset{\bullet}{\simeq}} F^{*0}$. Evidently $\sigma=\sigma'$, and consequently 1).

For the case of arbitrary Σ', let us first note that from the stronger version of corollary 1 we get that there exist a constant $\lambda=\lambda(|E|,|F|)$, expressions $\tilde{E}$, $\tilde{F}$, $\tilde{F}_1$, $\tilde{F}_2$, an open ordering $\tilde{\Sigma}$ and a substitution Φ^*, such that $\|\tilde{E}\|\le\lambda$, $\|\tilde{F}\|\le\lambda$, $\|\tilde{F}_1\|\le\lambda$, $E=\tilde{E}[\Phi^*]$, $F=\tilde{F}[\phi^*]$, $F_i=\tilde{F}_i[\Phi^*]$ $(i=1,2)$ and $\Sigma=\tilde{\Sigma}[\Phi^*]$, and (4.5) yields

$$\tilde{E}(\varpi)\dots\tilde{E}(\varpi+\sigma\nu) \overset{\tilde{\Sigma}}{=} \tilde{F}_1(\varpi)\tilde{F}(\varpi+\sigma')\dots\tilde{F}(\varpi+(\mu-1)\sigma')\tilde{F}_2'(\varpi+\mu\sigma').$$

Since $\tilde{\Sigma}$ is open we come to the case proved above.

2) The above proved means that there exist $\lambda=\lambda(|E|,|F|)$ and E_1, E_2, such that $E_1E_2\in\tilde{R}^{\lambda}_{\Sigma}(E)$ and

$$S_{\Sigma}(E(\varpi)E(\varpi+\sigma))=S_{\Sigma}(E_1(\varpi))S_{\Sigma}(E_2(\varpi)E_1(\varpi+\sigma))S_{\Sigma}(E_2(\varpi+\sigma)),$$

F_1, F_2, such that $F_1F_2\in\tilde{R}^{\lambda}_{\Sigma}(F)$ and

$$S_{\Sigma}(F(\varpi)F(\varpi+\sigma))=S_{\Sigma}(F_1(\varpi)S_{\Sigma}(F_2(\varpi)F_1(\varpi+\sigma))S_{\Sigma}(F_2(\varpi+\sigma)),$$

and E_1^* and E_2^*, such that

$$E^*(i)=E_1^*(i)E_2^*(i),$$
$$F^*(i)=E_2^*(i+\omega)E_1^*(i+\omega+\sigma),$$

where $E^*(i)=S(E_2(i)E_1(i+\sigma))$, $F^*(i)=S(F_2(i)F_1(i+\sigma))$ and $\omega\in\mathbb{Z}$.

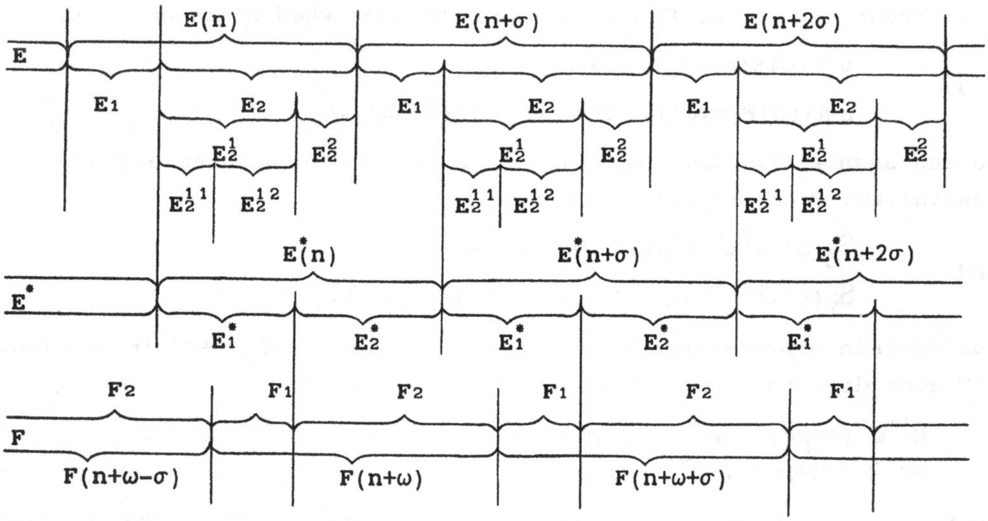

Fig. 11

Let us consider fig. 11, where one of the possible relations between E_1, F_1, E_i^*, E_i^* and F^* $(i=1,2)$ is shown (others can be considered similarly).

It is evident that there exist E_2^1 and E_2^2, such that $E_2^1E_2^2\in R_\Sigma^\lambda(E_2)$ and $E_2^1\sim E_1^*$ and $E_2^2E_1\sim E_2^*$. Furthermore, since $F_1 \underset{\leftarrow}{\subseteq} E_2^1$, there exist E_2^{11} and E_2^{12}, such that $E_2^{11}E_2^{12}\in R_\Sigma(E_2^1)$ and $E_2^{12}\sim F_1$. Therefore

$$F(i+\omega)\sim E_2^{12}(i)E_2^2(i)E_1(i)E_2^{11}(i+\sigma),$$

what we needed.

Propositions 8, 1 and 2 yield proposition 6.

From item 1 of proposition 8 we can also get

Proposition 9. Let $E(n,i)=E(n,i,n_1,\ldots,n_k)$ be an expression (of the depth less or equal to N), Σ be an arbitrary ordering and $\sigma\in\{+1,-1\}$. Let us consider the expressions $F(i)=E(n,i)$ and $G(i)=E(n+\sigma,i)$. There do not exist expressions $F_1(i)$ and $F_2(i)$ and a constant $\omega\in\mathbb{N}$, such that simultaneously $F_1(i)F_2(i)\sim F(i)$ and $F_2(i+\omega)F_1(i+\omega+\sigma')\sim G(i)$ $(\omega\in\mathbb{N},\ \sigma'\in\{+1,-1\})$.

It will follow from proposition 9 that in the process of equivalent expansion of terms, the term $T(n)=\langle\bar{T}(n,i)\,|\,i:=\mathfrak{z}..\mathfrak{y}\rangle$ cannot be united with the term $T(n+\sigma)=\langle\bar{T}(n+\sigma,i)\,|\,i:=\mathfrak{z}'..\mathfrak{y}'\rangle$. Item 3 of lemma 4 and, further, item 4 of lemma 2 will follow in turn.

Now let us pass to the construction of algorithm L of equivalent expansion and shift of the terms. The algorithm is based on the so-called procedures of elementary equivalent expansion and shift, elementary expansion and shift at the expense of another term and uniting of terms.

The simplest procedure is the first. Let $E=FTG$ be an expression such that $depth(T)=N+1$, $depth(F)\le N$ and $depth(G)\le N$. Let $T=\langle\bar{T}(i)\,|\,i:=\mathfrak{z}..\mathfrak{y}\rangle$, $step_\Sigma(T)=\sigma$ and Σ be an arbitrary ordering. We say that T can be *equivalently expanded rightwards (leftwards)* in the expression E, if

$$\bar{T}(\mathfrak{y}+\sigma) \underset{\rightarrow}{\subseteq} G \quad (\bar{T}(\mathfrak{z}-\sigma) \underset{\leftarrow}{\subseteq} F). \tag{4.6}$$

By *right (left) equivalent expansion* of the term T we will understand substitution of the expression

$$E'=F\langle\bar{T}(i)\,|\,i:=\mathfrak{z}..\mathfrak{y}+\sigma\rangle \mathsf{D}_\Sigma^{L}(G,\bar{T}(\mathfrak{y}+\sigma))$$
$$(E'=\mathsf{D}_\Sigma^{R}(F,\bar{T}(\mathfrak{z}-\sigma))\langle\bar{T}(i)\,|\,i:=\mathfrak{z}-\sigma..\mathfrak{y}\rangle G)$$

for the expression E.

We say, that the term T can be *equivalently shifted rightwards* in the expression E, if there exist expressions $\bar{T}_1(i)$ and $\bar{T}_2(i)$, such that $\bar{T}(i)=\bar{T}_1(i)\bar{T}_2(i)$ and

$$\bar{T}_1(\eta+\sigma) \underset{\rightarrow}{\subsetneq} G. \tag{4.7}$$

By *right equivalent shift* of the term T we understand substitution of the expression

$$E'=F\bar{T}_1(\xi)\langle\bar{T}_2(i)\bar{T}_1(i+\sigma)\,|\,i:=\xi..\eta\rangle D^L_\Sigma(G,\bar{T}_2(\eta+\sigma))$$

for the expression E.

Note that (4.6) and (4.7) can be decided and $E'\sim E$.

Now let us consider the expression

$$E=TFS=\langle\bar{T}(i)\,|\,i:=\xi..\eta\rangle F\langle\bar{S}(i)\,|\,i:=\xi'..\eta'\rangle,$$

where *depth(T)=depth(S)=N+1* and *depth(F)≤N.* We say that the *term* T *can be equivalently expanded at the expense of the term* S, if there exist $\mu\in\mathbb{N}$, such that $\mu<|\eta'-\xi'|$ and

$$\bar{T}(\eta+\sigma)\underset{\rightarrow}{\subsetneq}F\bar{S}(\xi')\bar{S}(\xi'+\sigma')\ldots\bar{S}(\xi'+\mu\sigma'), \tag{4.8}$$

where $\sigma=step_\Sigma(T)$, $\sigma'=step_\Sigma(S)$. By *equivalent expansion of the term* T *at the expense of the term* S, we understand the substitution of the expression

$$E'=\langle\bar{T}(i)\,|\,i:=\xi..\eta+\sigma\rangle D^L_\Sigma(F\bar{S}(\xi')\bar{S}(\xi'+\sigma')\ldots$$
$$\ldots\bar{S}(\xi'+\mu\sigma'),\bar{T}(\xi+\sigma))\langle\bar{S}(i)\,|\,i:=\xi'+(\mu+1)\sigma'..\eta'\rangle.$$

for the expression E. Let us note that (4.8) is decidable and $E\sim E'$.

Similarly we can define the procedure of the *shift of a term at the expense of another term.*

Let Σ be equal to $u\le\ldots\le\xi'\le\eta'\le\ldots\le v$ ($u\le\ldots\le\eta'\le\xi'\le\ldots\le v$) and the term S be elementary. We say that the *term* T *can be united with the term* S, if $step_\Sigma(T)=step_\Sigma(S)=\sigma$, $\xi'-\eta\in\mathbb{Z}$ and there exist expressions $\bar{S}_1$ and $\bar{S}_2$, such that $\bar{S}_1\bar{S}_2\in R_{\Sigma'}(S)$ and

1) $\bar{T}(\eta+\sigma) \overset{\Sigma}{\simeq} G\bar{S}_1(\xi')$,
2) $\bar{T}(i) \overset{\Sigma'}{\simeq} \bar{S}_2(i+\gamma)\bar{S}_1(i+\gamma+\sigma)$,

where $\gamma=\xi'-\eta$ and Σ' equals $u\le\ldots\le\xi'\le i\le\eta'\le\ldots\le v$ ($u\le\ldots\le\eta'\le i\le\xi'\le\ldots\le v$). Note that 1) and 2) can be decided. Note also that, if T can be united with S, then there exists $\kappa\in\mathbb{N}$, such that

$$E'=\langle\bar{T}(i)\,|\,i:=\xi..\eta'-\kappa\sigma\rangle\bar{S}_2(\eta'-\kappa\sigma+\gamma)\bar{S}(\eta'-\kappa\sigma+\kappa+\sigma)\ldots\bar{S}(\eta') \tag{4.9}$$

is asymptotically equivalent to E. By *uniting the terms* T and S we understand substitution of E' for E.

Using described procedures we can construct algorithm L. First, let us construct a simplified version of the algorithm (which we denote by L^∞) that will work only in the case of an open ordering Σ.

Let $E=FSG\underline{T}HUI$, where S, T and U are terms, F, G, H and I are subexpressions, $depth(E)=N+1$, $depth(S)=depth(T)=depth(U)=N+1$, $depth(G)\leq N$, $depth(H)\leq N$, and let the term T be marked in a certain way (say, underlined). Algorithm L^∞ works as follows.

1. It maximally equivalently expands rightwards and leftwards and shifts rightwards the term T in the subexpression GTH (i.e., it expands and shifts the term T repeatedly, till it is possible).

2. It checks whether it is possible to unite the terms T and U. If it is, it unites them, underlines the obtained term and returns to 1.

3. If $depth_\infty(T)<depth_\infty(U)$, then the algorithm checks whether it is possible to expand or shift the term T (i.e., the underlined term) at the expense of the term U. If it is, it expands (shifts) T and returns to 1.

4. If $depth_\infty(T)>depth_\infty(U)$, then the algorithm finds the minimal $\kappa\in N$, such that for the expression $U^{(\kappa)}$ which we obtain from U by unfolding all terms having the factor less or equal to κ, $depth(U^{(\kappa)})<N+1$ holds, substitutes $U^{(\kappa)}$ for U and checks, whether it is possible to expand (shift) T. If it is, it does it and returns to 1, else it stops (substituting back U for $U^{(\kappa)}$).

It follows from propositions 1, 2 and 6, that algorithm L^∞ stops after finite number of steps. It is evident also that $L^\infty_\Sigma(E)\sim E$. The uniformity of algorithm L^∞ follows from the uniformity of algorithm D. Item 1 of lemma 4 (for the case of open orderings) follows from the construction of algorithm L^∞. Finally, item 2 of lemma 3 and proposition 6 yield item 2 and proposition 9 yields item 3 of lemma 4 (in the case of open ordering).

To generalize algorithm L^∞ for arbitrary orderings, first let us prove stronger version of proposition 1.

Proposition 1A. Let E and F be expressions (of the depth less or equal to N) and Σ be an arbitrary ordering. There exists and can be found effectively a constant $\lambda=\lambda(|E|,|F|)$, such that

$$depth_\lambda(E)=depth_\lambda(F).$$

Proof. It follows from corollary 1 that there exists a constant $\mu=\mu(|E|,|F|)$, expressions $\tilde{E}$, $\tilde{F}$, open ordering $\tilde{\Sigma}$ and a substitution Φ^*, such that $\|\tilde{E}\|\leq\mu$, $\|\tilde{F}\|\leq\mu$, $\tilde{E}=E[\Phi^*]$, $\tilde{F}=F[\Phi^*]$ and $\tilde{\Sigma}=\Sigma[\Phi^*]$ and $\tilde{E}\overset{\tilde{\Sigma}}{\simeq}\tilde{F}$ if and only if $E\overset{\Sigma}{\simeq}F$. Let $\phi=max\{|\phi_1|,\dots,|\phi_l|\}$, where $\phi_1,\dots,\phi_l$ are all constant factors of the terms of $\tilde{E}$ and $\tilde{F}$. Then, $depth_{\phi+1}(\tilde{E})=depth_\infty(\tilde{E})$ and $depth_{\phi+1}(\tilde{F})=depth_\infty(\tilde{F})$. On the other hand, since $\tilde{E}\overset{\tilde{\Sigma}}{\simeq}\tilde{F}$, proposition 1 yields $depth_\infty(\tilde{\mathrm{E}})= depth_\infty(\tilde{\mathrm{F}})$. Therefore $depth_{\phi+1}(\mathrm{E})=depth_{\phi+1}(\mathrm{F})$. Taking into account $\|\tilde{\mathrm{E}}\|\le\mu$, $\|\tilde{\mathrm{F}}\|\le\mu$ we get proposition 1A.

Let L^μ be the algorithm obtained from L^∞ by substitution of $depth_\mu$ for $depth_\infty$. Taking into account proposition 1A, it can be proved that for any E, we can found a constant $\mu=\mu(|\mathrm{E}|)$, such that the algorithm L^μ satisfies lemma 4. (In fact we only have to prove that there is a constant $\theta=\theta(|\mathrm{E}|)$, such that after θ steps algorithm stops. This follows from proposition 6.) Therefore algorithm L is as follows: first we compute $\mu=\mu(|\mathrm{E}|)$ and then $\mathsf{L}^\mu_\Sigma(\mathrm{E})$.

Finally, let us pass to algorithm T. Let us apply the algorithm to the term $\mathrm{T}=\langle\bar{\mathrm{T}}(\mathrm{i})\,|\,\mathrm{i}:=\mathfrak{z}..\mathfrak{y}\rangle$.

First let us assume that the ordering Σ is obtained from ordering Σ' equal to $\mathfrak{u}\le\ldots\le\mathfrak{z}\le\mathrm{i}\le\mathfrak{y}\le\ldots\mathfrak{v}$ by omission of i. Let $\bar{\mathrm{T}}^*$ be the complete standard form of $\bar{\mathrm{T}}$ (with respect to i for the ordering Σ' and $\sigma=step_{\Sigma'}(\mathrm{T})$), $\bar{\mathrm{T}}^+$ be the basis of $\bar{\mathrm{T}}^*$, and $\bar{\mathrm{T}}_2$, $\bar{\mathrm{T}}_1$ be the left and the right part of $\bar{\mathrm{T}}^+$. Then we can find $\omega_1\in\mathbb{N}$ and $\omega_2\in\mathbb{N}$, such that $\bar{\mathrm{T}}\ {}^{\Sigma'}\!\lambda_{\,\omega_1}\ \bar{\mathrm{T}}_1\bar{\mathrm{T}}_2$ and $\bar{\mathrm{T}}^+\ {}^{\Sigma'}\!\lambda_{\,\omega_2}\ \bar{\mathrm{T}}^*$. Let $\omega=max(\omega_1,\omega_2)$ and $\gamma=\gamma(|\bar{\mathrm{T}}|)$ be such that, if $scope(\Sigma')\ge\gamma$ then $\mathsf{S}_{\Sigma'}(\bar{\mathrm{T}})$ is defined. Algorithm T operates as follows.

If $\mathfrak{y}-\mathfrak{z}\notin\mathbb{Z}$ or $|\mathfrak{y}-\mathfrak{z}|>2\omega+2\gamma$, then $\mathsf{T}_\Sigma(\mathrm{T})=\bar{\mathrm{T}}(\mathfrak{z})\ldots\ldots\bar{\mathrm{T}}(\mathfrak{z}+\omega)\bar{\mathrm{T}}_1(\mathfrak{z}+\omega+1)\langle\bar{\mathrm{T}}^*(\mathrm{i})\,|\,\mathrm{i}:=\mathfrak{z}+\omega+1..\mathfrak{y}-\omega-1\rangle\bar{\mathrm{T}}_2(\mathfrak{y}-\omega)\bar{\mathrm{T}}(\mathfrak{y}-\omega+1)\ldots\bar{\mathrm{T}}(\mathfrak{y})$, else $\mathsf{T}_\Sigma(\mathrm{T})=\mathrm{unf}(\mathrm{T})$.

By analogy we can define the algorithm for the case when Σ equals $\mathfrak{z}\le\ldots\le\mathfrak{y}\le\mathfrak{z}\le\ldots\le\mathfrak{v}$.

In the general case, when Σ equals $\mathfrak{u}\le\ldots\le\mathfrak{z}_0\le\mathfrak{z}_1\ldots\le\mathfrak{z}_k\le\ \ldots\le\mathfrak{v}$, and $\mathrm{T}=\langle\bar{\mathrm{T}}(\mathrm{i})\,|\,\mathrm{i}:=\mathfrak{z}_0..\mathfrak{z}_k\rangle$ $(\mathrm{T}=\langle\bar{\mathrm{T}}(\mathrm{i})\,|\,\mathrm{i}:=\mathfrak{z}_k..\mathfrak{z}_0\rangle)$, we define

$$\mathsf{T}_\Sigma(\mathrm{T})=\mathsf{T}_\Sigma(\mathrm{T}_0)\ldots\mathsf{T}_\Sigma(\mathrm{T}_{k-1}),$$

where $\mathrm{T}_0=\langle\bar{\mathrm{T}}_0(\mathrm{i})\,|\,\mathrm{i}:=\mathfrak{z}_0..\mathfrak{z}_1\rangle$, $\mathrm{T}_j=\langle\bar{\mathrm{T}}_j(\mathrm{i})\,|\,\mathrm{i}:=\mathfrak{z}_j+\sigma..\mathfrak{z}_{j+1}\rangle$, $j=1,\ldots,k-1$ $(\mathrm{T}_0=\langle\bar{\mathrm{T}}_0(\mathrm{i})\,|\,\mathrm{i}:=\mathfrak{z}_k..\mathfrak{z}_{k-1}\rangle$, $\mathrm{T}_j=\langle\bar{\mathrm{T}}_j(\mathrm{i})\,|\,\mathrm{i}:=\mathfrak{z}_j+\sigma..\mathfrak{z}_{j-1}\rangle$, $j=k-1,\ldots,1)$.

From the construction of the algorithm and the inductive assumption it is evident that T satisfies the specification given in lemma 5.

Thus we have completed the construction of algorithm S. Let us prove that it satisfies lemma 2. Boundedness, uniformness and equivalence conservation follow directly by induction from respective properties of algorithms D, L, T and S, for expressions of smaller depth. Items 2 and 3 also follow by induction from item 2 of lemma 4, the existence of canonical expression and items 2 and 3 of lemma 2 itself. Item 4 follows from item 3 of lemma 4, items 2 and 3 of lemma 2 and uniformness of algorithm S. Let us prove item 1.

Firs of all, let us note that item 1 of lemma 2 (for expressions of the depth less than *N*+1), corollary 4 and the construction of the algorithm S, yield

Corollary 5. Let $E_1=F_1T_1G_1$, $E_2=F_2T_2G_2$ be expressions, where $T_1=\langle\bar{T}(i)\,|\,i:=\jmath_1..\eta_1\rangle$, $T_2=\langle\bar{T}_2(i)\,|\,i:=\jmath_2..\eta_2\rangle$, *depth*$(T_i)=N+1$, *depth*$(F_i)\le N$, *depth*$(G_i)\le N$ $(i=1,2)$ and let Σ be an open ordering. If $E_1\overset{\Sigma}{\simeq}E_2$ and $\bar{T}_1\dot{\simeq}\bar{T}_2$, then

$$S_\Sigma(E_1^0)\dot{=}S_\Sigma(E_2^0).$$

It follows

Proposition 10. Let $E=FTG$ and H be expressions, such that *depth*$(T)=N+1$, *depth*$(F)\le N$, *depth*$(G)\le N$ and *depth*$(H)\le N+1$, and let Σ be an open ordering. If $E\overset{\Sigma}{\simeq}H$, then

$$S_\Sigma(E^0)\dot{=}S_\Sigma(H^0).$$

Proof. In case $depth_\infty(E)<N+1$, we get the proposition directly from the inductive assumption of lemma 2. Let us assume $depth_\infty(E)=N+1$. It follows from proposition 1 that $depth_\infty(H)=N+1$, therefore $H=H_1T_1\ldots H_kT_kT_{k+1}$, where $depth_\infty(H_i)\le N$, $depth_\infty(T_i)=N+1$. Let $T=\langle\bar{T}(i)\,|\,i:=\jmath..\eta\rangle$ and $T_1=\langle\bar{T}_1(i)\,|\,i:=\jmath_1..\jmath_2\rangle$. Since $E\overset{\Sigma}{\simeq}H$, it follows from proposition 2 that for any μ there exists ν, such that

$$F\bar{T}(\jmath)\bar{T}(\jmath+\sigma)\ldots\bar{T}(\jmath+\mu\sigma) \precsim H_1\bar{T}_1(\jmath_1)\bar{T}_1(\jmath_1)\bar{T}_1(\jmath_1+\sigma')\ldots\bar{T}_1(\jmath_1+\nu\sigma')$$

holds, but

$$F\bar{T}(\jmath)\bar{T}(\jmath+\sigma)\ldots\bar{T}(\jmath+\mu\sigma) \precsim H_1\bar{T}_1(\jmath_1)\bar{T}_1(\jmath_1)\bar{T}_1(\jmath_1+\sigma')\ldots\bar{T}_1(\jmath_1+(\nu-1)\sigma')$$

does not hold. Assuming the contrary from proposition 1 we get that $\jmath=\jmath_1+\eta$ $(\eta\in\mathbb{Z})$. Therefore, it follows from proposition 6 that for respective complete standard forms $\bar{T}^*$ and $\bar{T}_1^*$ of $\bar{T}$ and $\bar{T}_1$: $\bar{T}^*\dot{\simeq}\bar{T}_1^*$. Further, from corollary 5 by induction we get proposition 10.

Proposition 10 yields item 1 of lemma 2 by induction.

Thus, to complete the proof of lemma 2 only item 5 remains to be proved. We will do it in the next section.

5. Intermediate Results of the Synthesis

In the beginning, let us introduce a number of notions. Above, we have defined image of a subexpression of a given expression in an unfoldment. If the subexpression is a term, then we will distinguish *unfolded image* and *folded image*. For example, if

$$W=a\underbrace{<\underbrace{<b\underline{i}\,|\,i:=1..\underline{j}>}_{T_1}\,|\,j:=1..4>}_{T_2}c$$

is the expression and

$$W'=a\underbrace{<b\underline{i}\,|\,i:=1..1>}_{T_1'}\underbrace{<b\underline{i}\,|\,i:=1..2>}_{T_2'}\underbrace{<b\underline{i}\,|\,i:=1..3>}_{T_3'}\underbrace{b1b2b3b4c}_{H}$$

is the unfoldment, then T_1', T_2', and T_3' are folded images of T_1, H is an unfolded image of T_1 and $T_1'T_2'T_3'H$ is an unfolded image of T_2.

In section 3 there is defined the set of dischargements $R_\Sigma(E)$. Let us define by analogy the set $R^*_\Sigma(E)$ of *total dischargements* of the expression E, which we obtain by partition and unfolding of all the terms of the expression E, not exclusively the outermost. We define it inductively.

a) If *depth*$(E)=0$, then $R^*_\Sigma(E)=\{E\}$.

b) $R_\Sigma(E)\subset R^*_\Sigma(E)$.

c) Let $E'\in R^*_\Sigma(E)$ and $E'=E_1TE_2$, where $T=<\bar{T}\,|\,i:=\xi..\eta>$, let the accessibility of T equal ρ ($\rho\in\mathbb{N}$) and let Σ' be an ordering equal to $u\le\ldots\le\xi\le i\le\eta\le\ldots\le\upsilon$ (or $u\le\ldots\le\eta\le i\le\xi\le\ldots\le\upsilon$), where $u\le\ldots\le\xi\le\eta\le\ldots\le\upsilon$ ($u\le\ldots\le\eta\le\xi\le\ldots\le\upsilon$) is equivalent to Σ. If $\bar{T}'\in R^*_{\Sigma'}(\bar{T})$ is such that $\bar{T}\overset{\Sigma'}{\sim}{}^{\rho}\bar{T}'$, then $E_1<\bar{T}'\,|\,i:=\xi..\eta>E_2\in R^*_\Sigma(E)$.

For instance, if $E=<a\underline{i}<b\underline{j}\,|\,j:=1..\underline{i}>\,|\,i:=1..\underline{n}>$ and $E^*=a1b1a2b1b2<a\underline{i}b1<b\underline{j}\,|\,j:=2..\underline{i-1}>b\underline{i}\,|\,i=3..\underline{n-2}>a\underline{n-1}<b\underline{j}\,|\,j:=1..\underline{n-1}>an<b\underline{j}\,|\,j:=1..\underline{n}>$, then $E^*\in R^*_{0\le n}(E)$.

It follows from proposition 3 that, if $E'\in R^*_\Sigma(E)$, then $E'\overset{\Sigma}{\sim}E$.

Let us set define $R^{*\alpha}_\Sigma(E)=\{E'\in R^*_\Sigma(E)\,|\,/E'\backslash\le\alpha\}$.

We call, an unfoldment E' of an expression E *minimal* (for given Σ), if there does not exist an unfoldment E'', such that E' is finer than E'' and $S_\Sigma(E')=S_\Sigma(E'')$.

Let Σ_0 be an empty ordering (i.e., containing the only variable n^0), and let us denote $S_{\Sigma_0}(E)$ by $S\ (E)$.

Proposition 11. Let $E(n_1,\ldots,n_k)$ be an expression (of depth less or equal to N), Σ be an ordering and $\vec{\alpha}=(\alpha_1,\ldots,\alpha_k)$ be α-separated k-tuple permissible for Σ. There exist a constant $\gamma=\gamma(|E|)$ and an expression $E'\in R^{*\gamma}_\Sigma(E)$, such that if $A\in V(E'(\vec{\alpha}))$, then

a) if $S(A)=A_1'A_2'$ for certain A_1' and A_2', then $A=A_1A_2$ and $S(A)=S(A_1)S(a_2)$, $S(A_1)=A_1'$, $S(A_2)=A_2'$;

b) if the unfoldment A is minimal and has the type

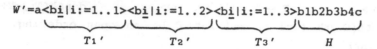

$A=A_1B_1\ldots B_nA_2$, where A_1, A_2 are certain subexpressions of A, $B_1\ldots B_m$ is an unfolded image of a certain term and $B_1,\ldots,B_n$ are the images of the body of the term, then there exist B_1^1, B_1^2, such that $B_1=B_1^1B_1^2$, B_n^1, B_n^2, such that $B_n=B_n^1B_n^2$ and

$$\mathrm{S}(A)=\mathrm{S}(A_1B_1^1)\mathrm{S}(B_1^2B_2B_3\ldots B_{n-1}B_n^1)\mathrm{S}(B_n^2A_2).$$

Note that in fact this proposition is a generalization of item 2 of lemma 2. The proof is mostly technical. If E=E′, then the expression E′ is called *completely separable*.

We call an expression E λ-*attracting*, if the attraction (i.e., |factor/period|) of the terms with constant factor is more or equal to λ. By $V_\lambda(E)$ we denote the subset of all unfoldments which are λ-attracting.

Item 5 of lemma 2 will follow from lemma 6 and lemma 7.

Lemma 6. Let $E(n_1,\ldots,n_k)$ be a completely separable expression (of depth less or equal to N), Σ be an open ordering and $\vec{\alpha}=(\alpha_1,\ldots,\alpha_k)$ be (α,β)-expressive k-tuple permissible for Σ ($\alpha\in\mathbb{N}$, $\beta>1$). Let $Y=\mathrm{Unf}(E(\vec{\alpha}))$, and let us consider the sequence $(sf)^1(Y),\ldots,(sf)^\zeta(Y)$. For any $\mu>1$ and $\beta>1$ there exist constants $\bar{\alpha}=\bar{\alpha}(\|E\|,\beta,\mu)$ and $\gamma=\gamma(\|E\|,\beta)$, such that if $\alpha\geq\bar{\alpha}$ then for any $i=0,\ldots,level(\alpha/\mu)$, there exists a minimal unfoldment $A_i\in V_{\alpha/\gamma}(E^0(\vec{\alpha}))$, such that

$$((sf)^i(\mathrm{Unf}(E(\vec{\alpha}))))_f \doteq \mathrm{S}_{\Sigma_0}(A_i).$$

In fact, this lemma means that if during the synthesis regular substrings with a "large" attraction only is folded up, then for each "step of the synthesis" - i there exists α/γ-attracting unfoldment A_i of the expression $E^0(\vec{\alpha})$, such that the complete standardization $\mathrm{S}(A_i)$ coincides with the result of the synthesis at this step.

Recall that an unfoldment $A\in V(E(\vec{\alpha}))$ is said to be *substantial*, if at least one of the terms of $E(\vec{\alpha})$, whose corresponding term in E has a variable factor, is unfolded in A.

Lemma 7. Let $E(n_1,\ldots,n_k)$ be a completely separable expression (of depth less or equal to N), Σ be an open ordering and $\vec{\alpha}$ be an α-separated k-tuple permissible for Σ ($\alpha\in\mathbb{N}$). There exist constants $\tau_0=\tau_0(\|E\|)$, $\bar{\alpha}'=\bar{\alpha}'(\|E\|)$ and $\mu_0=\mu_0(\|E\|)$, such that, if $\alpha\geq\bar{\alpha}'$, $\tau\geq\tau_0$ and $A\in V_\tau(E(\vec{\alpha}))$ is substantial, then $\mathrm{S}(A)$, contains outermost regular expression with the attraction $\chi\geq\alpha/\mu_0$ (i.e., $\mathrm{S}(A)=A_1BA_2$, where B is a regular subexpression and has the attraction $\chi\geq\alpha/\mu_0$).

The lemma actually means that, if an unfoldment A is substantial, then $\mathrm{S}(A)$ contains a regular substring with "large" attraction.

Before we pass to the proofs of lemmas 6 and 7, let us show, how they yield item 5 of lemma 2. Let E be an arbitrary expression, Σ an open ordering and $\vec{\alpha}$ be (α,β)-expressive k-tuple permissible for Σ. There exist $\rho=\rho(|E|)$ and $E'\in R_{\Sigma}^{*\rho}(E)$, such that E' is completely separable. Let $\mu_0=\mu_0(\|E'\|)=\mu_0'(\|E\|)$ be from lemma 7 and $\xi=level(\alpha/\mu_0)$ (for $Unf(E(\vec{\alpha}))$). According to lemma 6, there exist constants $\gamma=\gamma(\|E'\|,\beta)$ and $\bar{\alpha}=\bar{\alpha}(\|E'\|,\beta,\mu_0)$, such that if $\alpha\geq\bar{\alpha}$, then there exists an unfoldment $A_{\xi}\in V_{\alpha/\gamma}(E'(\vec{\alpha}))$, such that

$$(sf)^{\xi}(Unf(E(\vec{\alpha}))_{f} \doteq S(A_{\xi}).$$

If α is sufficiently large (i.e., $\alpha\geq max\{\bar{\alpha},\tau*\gamma\}$) then it follows from lemma 7 and the definition of $level(\alpha/\mu_0)$, that $A_{\xi}=E'^{0}(\vec{\alpha})$. Indeed, in the oposit case A_{ξ} is substantial and therefore, according to lemma 7, $S(A_{\xi})$ contains a regular substring with the attraction $\alpha_0\geq\alpha/\mu_0$ in contradiction to the assumption that $\xi=level(\alpha/\mu_0)$. Therefore,

$$((sf)^{\xi}(Unf(E(\vec{\alpha}))))_{f}\doteq S_{\Sigma}(E'^{0}(\vec{\alpha}))\doteq S_{\Sigma}(E^{0}(\vec{\alpha})),$$

i.e., item 5 of lemma 2.

Thus, to complete the proof of lemma 2, we have to prove lemmas 6 and 7. Let us begin with

Proof of lemma 7. In case τ is sufficiently large, all the terms of E with constant factor are unfolded in $A'\in V_{\tau}(E(\vec{\alpha}))$, therefore we can assume that E does not contain such terms. Since A is substantial and τ-attracting, evidently at least one of the outermost terms of the expression E is unfolded. Let $E=E_1TE_2$, $T=\langle\bar{T}(i,n_1,\ldots,n_k)\,|\,i:=\underline{n_p+\tau_p}..\underline{n_q-\tau_q}\rangle$ and

$$A=A_1\bar{T}_0(\alpha_p+\tau_p)\bar{T}_1(\alpha_p+\tau_p+\sigma)\ldots\bar{T}_l(\alpha_q+\tau_q)A_2,$$

where $A_i\in V(E_i(\vec{\alpha}))$ $(i=1,2)$, $\bar{\bar{T}}_j(\alpha_p+\tau_p+j\sigma)\in V(\bar{T}(\alpha_p+\tau_p+j\sigma,\alpha_1,\ldots,\alpha_k))$, $(j=0,\ldots,l)$, $\sigma=step_{\Sigma}(T)$.

From proposition 11 we get $S(A)=S(A_1\bar{T}_1(\alpha_p+\tau_p)\ldots$
$\ldots\bar{T}_{\nu-1}(\alpha_p+(\nu-1)\sigma)\bar{T}_{\nu}^{1}(\alpha_p+\nu\sigma))S(\bar{T}_{\nu}^{2}(\alpha_p+\nu\sigma)\bar{T}_{\nu+1}(\alpha_p+(\nu+1)\sigma)\ldots$
$\ldots\bar{T}_{\pi-1}(\alpha_p+(\pi-1)\sigma)\bar{T}_{\pi}^{1}(\alpha_p+\pi\sigma))S(\bar{T}_{\pi}^{2}(\alpha_p+\pi\sigma)\bar{T}_{\pi+1}(\alpha_p+(\pi+1)\sigma)\ldots\bar{T}_l(\alpha_l+\tau_q)A_2)$

Let $\nu=[|\alpha_q-\alpha_p|/3]$ and $\pi=[2*|\alpha_q-\alpha_p|/3]$, where notation $[x]$ is used to mean the largest integer smaller than x. Let us consider the expression:

$$S(\bar{T}_{\nu}^{2}(\alpha_p+\nu\sigma)\bar{T}_{\nu+1}(\alpha_p+(\nu+1)\sigma)\ldots\bar{T}_{\pi-1}(\alpha_p+(\pi-1)\sigma)\bar{T}_{\pi}^{1}(\alpha_p+\pi\sigma)).$$

In case $depth(E)=1$, the assertion of the lemma follows from proposition 7. Let us assume by induction that the lemma is true for expressions of the depth k, where $depth(E)=k+1$. There are two possibilities.

1.None of the subexpressions $\bar{T}\hat{\nu}(\alpha_p+\nu\sigma)$, $\bar{T}_{\nu+1}(\alpha_p+(\nu+1)\sigma),\ldots,$ $\bar{T}_{\pi-1}(\alpha_p+(\pi-1)\sigma)$, $\bar{T}\hat{\pi}(\alpha_p+\pi\sigma)$ contains an unfolded image of a term of the expression $E(\vec{\alpha})$.

2.At least one of the subexpressions $\bar{T}\hat{\nu}(\alpha_p+\nu\sigma)$, $\bar{T}_{\nu+1}(\alpha_p+(\nu+1)\sigma),\ldots,$ $\bar{T}_{\pi-1}(\alpha_p+(\pi-1)\sigma)$, $\bar{T}\hat{\pi}(\alpha_p+\pi\sigma)$ contains an unfolded image of a term of the expression $E(\vec{\alpha})$.

In the first case for all $i=\nu+1,\ldots,\pi-1$: $\bar{T}_i(\alpha_p+i)=\bar{T}(\alpha_p+i)$, therefore, the assertion of the lemma follows directly from proposition 7. In the second case let us consider one of the expressions which contains an unfolded image, say

$$\bar{T}\mu(\alpha_p+\mu\sigma)\in V(\bar{T}(\alpha_p+\mu\sigma,\alpha_1,\ldots,\alpha_k)).$$

$\bar{T}\mu(\alpha_p+\mu\sigma)$ satisfies the conditions of the lemma, if instead of α we take $\alpha/4$ (in fact $\alpha/(3+\varepsilon)$, for any $\varepsilon>0$). Since $depth(T)=k$, we get the assertion of the lemma from inductive assumption.

Let us pass to the proof of lemma 6. In the beginning let us note that instead of synthesizing dot expressions and transforming them into equivalent *for*-expressions, we can synthesize *for*-expressions directly. We will do it by using rule f' of *alternative folding-up*, which looks for the subexpression C, such that $C \doteq C'$, where C' is regular and satisfies the conditions of rule f and replaces C by an appropriate graphical term. The body of this term is called *body of regular string* C'. By analogy, let s' be the rule of standardization for *for*-expressions.

Lemma 6 will follow from lemma 8 by induction.

Lemma 8 (the basic lemma of synthesis). Let $E(n_1,\ldots,n_k)$ be a completely separable expression, Σ be an open ordering, and $\vec{\alpha}$ be (α,β)-expressive k-tuple permissible for Σ ($\alpha\in\mathbb{N}$, $\beta>1$). There exist $\bar{\alpha}=\bar{\alpha}(\|E\|,\beta)$ and $\gamma=\gamma(\|E\|,\beta)$, such that if $\alpha>\bar{\alpha}$ and unfoldment $A\in V_{\alpha/\gamma}(E(\vec{\alpha}))$ is substantial, then there exists an unfoldment $A'\in V_{\alpha/\gamma}(E(\vec{\alpha}))$, such that

$$s'f'(S(A)) \doteq S(A').$$

The proof of this lemma will follow from propositions 12 and 13. In the beginning, let us introduce one more notion.

Let us consider expressions $A=A_1''B'A_2''$ and $A'=A_1'TA_2'$, where $B'=\mathring{B}(0)\ldots\mathring{B}(\eta)$ is a regular subexpression, $\mathring{B}(i)$ are the atoms of B' and T is a term (see fig. 12). We say that the regular subexpression B' in A *corresponds to* the term T in A', if there exist expressions

C_1 and C_2, and unfoldments $C_1'\in V(C_1)$, $C_2'\in V(C_2)$, such that

1) $\mathrm{unf}(T)=C_1B'C_2$, $A_1'C_1'=A_1''$, $C_2'A_2'=A_2''$;

2) $\bar{T}(i)\doteq\mathring{B}(i)$ (where $\bar{T}$ is the body of the term T and $\mathring{B}(i)$ is the body of the regular expression B').

The following fact is the key in the proof of lemma 8. If A is a certain unfoldment of a completely separable expression $E(\vec{\alpha})$, such that $S(A)=A_1^+B^+A_2^+$, where B^+ is a regular subexpression with "large" attraction, then there exists another unfoldment A' of $E(\vec{\alpha})$, such that $A'=A_1TA_2'$ and the subexpression B of A, corresponding to B^+ (i.e. $S(B)=B^+$) contains a regular subexpression B' which corresponds to the term T in A' (see fig. 12).

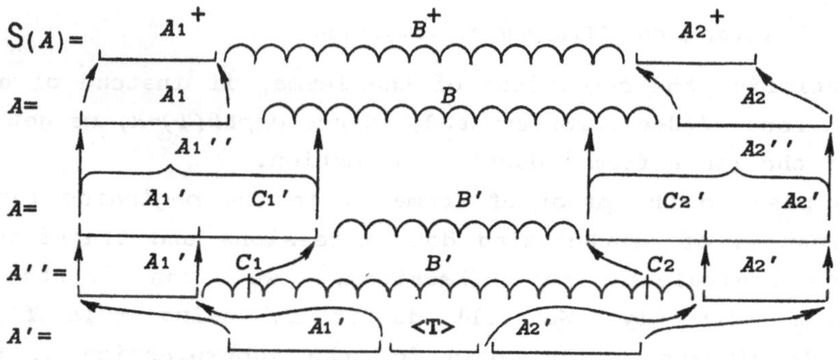

Fig. 12

More formally this assertion can be formulated as follows

Proposition 12. Let **E** be a completely separable expression (of the depth less or equal to N), Σ be an open ordering and $\vec{\alpha}$ be (α,β)-expressive k-tuple permissible for Σ ($\alpha\in\mathbb{N}$, $\beta>1$). Let $A\in V_{\alpha/\gamma}(E^0(\vec{\alpha}))$ ($\gamma>1$) be minimal and have the type $A=A_1BA_2$, and let

$$S(A)=A_1^+B^+A_2^+, \tag{5.1}$$

where $A_i^+=S(A_i)$ ($i=1,2$), $B^+=S(B)$ and $B^+=\mathring{B}^+(0)\ldots\mathring{B}^+(\eta)$ is a regular subexpression with the atoms $\mathring{B}^+(j)$ ($j=1,\ldots,\eta$). Let $\mu>1$ and the attraction of B^+ be $\chi\geq\alpha/\mu$. There exist constants $\bar{\alpha}=\bar{\alpha}(\|E\|,\beta,\mu)$ and $\gamma=\gamma(\|E\|,\beta)$, such that if $\alpha\geq\bar{\alpha}$ then there exists $A'\in V_{\alpha/\gamma}(E(\vec{\alpha}))$ of the form $A'=A_1'TA_2'$ and B contains a regular subexpression B' corresponding to the term T.

Proof. Let us call a subexpression of unfolded image of a certain term *n-bodied subexpression* ($n\in\mathbb{N}$), if it contains at least n images of the body of the given term. Let $\pi>1$ and A have the type

$A=D_1DD_2$, where D is an $[\alpha/\pi]$-bodied subexpression of a certain unfolded image of a certain term of $E(\vec{\alpha})$. Dividing the subexpression D repeatedly in three parts (similarly as in the proof of lemma 7), taking into account the definition of α/γ-attractive expression and the fact that the attraction of a regular expression is more or equal to modulus of the factor, we can prove inductively that there exists a constant $\rho=\rho(\|E\|,\gamma,\pi)$, such that D has the type $D=E_1EE_2$, where $E=\bar{T}(\omega)\bar{T}(\omega+\sigma)\ldots\bar{T}(\omega+[\alpha/\rho]\sigma)$ $(\omega\in\mathbb{N},\ \sigma\in\{+1,-1\})$, and $\bar{T}(\omega+i\sigma)$ $(i=0,\ldots,[\alpha/\rho])$ is an image of the body of a certain term of $E(\vec{\alpha})$. It follows from propositions 7 and 11 that there exists a constant $\rho'=\rho'(\|E\|,\gamma,\pi)$, such that

$$\mathrm{S}(A)=\mathrm{S}(D_1E_1')\bar{T}^*(\omega')\ldots\bar{T}^*(\omega'+[\alpha/\rho']\sigma)\mathrm{S}(E_2'D_2), \tag{5.2}$$

where $\bar{T}^*(i)$ is the complete standard form of $\bar{T}(i)$, E_1' and E_2' are certain subexpressions and $\omega'\in\mathbb{N}$.

Since E is completely separable, B can be presented in the form $B=\mathring{B}_0\ldots\mathring{B}_\eta$, where $\mathring{B}^+(i)=\mathrm{S}(\mathring{B}_i)$ $(i=0,\ldots,\eta)$. Taking into account uniformness of algorithm S it can be proved that there exist constants $\psi=\psi(\|E\|)$ and $\zeta\in\mathbb{Z}$, such that the expression $\mathring{B}_i$ contains an integer ζ_i, for which $|\zeta+i-\zeta_i|\le\psi$ $(i=0,\ldots,\eta)$. On the other hand, it is easy to prove from the contrary that for any $\psi\in\mathbb{N}$ there exist constants $\bar{\phi}=\bar{\phi}(\|E\|,\psi)$ and $\tau=\tau(\|E\|,\psi)$, such that if A has the type $A=A_1BA_2$, B contains characters $\xi_0,\ldots,\xi_\eta\in\mathbb{Z}$ for which $|\xi+i-\xi_i|\le\psi$ $(\xi\in\mathbb{Z},\ i=0,\ldots,\eta)$ and $\eta>\bar{\phi}$, then B contains $[\eta/\tau]$-bodied subexpression of a certain image of a certain term of $E(\vec{\alpha})$. Therefore, according to the mentioned above, from (5.2) we get that

$$\mathrm{S}(A)=\mathrm{S}(A_1B_2'')\bar{T}^*(\delta)\ldots\bar{T}^*(\delta+\phi\sigma)\mathrm{S}(B_2''A_2), \tag{5.3}$$

where $\delta\in\mathbb{Z}$, $\phi=[\alpha/\rho'']$, $\rho''=\rho''(\|E\|,\beta,\mu,\gamma)$, $\bar{T}^*(i)$ is the complete standard form of an unfoldment of a certain term of $E(\vec{\alpha})$ and B_1'', B_2'' are certain subexpressions.

To complete the proof of propositionn 12 we have to show that $\bar{T}(i)\underset{\bullet}{\approx}\mathring{B}(i)$. According to lemma 1 about regular strings, there are two possibilities:

a) $|\mathring{B}^+|=|T^*|$,

b) $|\mathring{B}^+|\ge|\bar{T}^*|(\phi-3)\ge|\bar{T}^*|\alpha/\nu$, where $\nu=\nu(\|E\|,\beta,\mu,\gamma)$ is a constant.

Let us assume the second case. Let χ be the attraction of the expression B^+. Since $\vec{\alpha}$ is (α,β)-expressive, there exists $\varepsilon=\varepsilon(\|E\|)$, such that

$$\chi \le \frac{\alpha\beta+\varepsilon}{|\mathring{B}^{+}|} \le \frac{(\alpha\beta+\varepsilon)\nu}{|\bar{T}^{*}|\alpha} \le \eta, \tag{5.4}$$

where η is a constant (i.e., it does not depend on α). Note that in this point we use the fact that $\vec{\alpha}$ is (α,β)-expressive. On the other hand, according to the conditions of the lemma

$$\chi \ge \alpha/\mu, \tag{5.5}$$

where μ also does not depend on α. Therefore, if α is sufficiently large, (5.4) contradicts (5.5). Hence *b*) is impossible and consequently $|\bar{T}^{*}|=|\mathring{B}^{+}|$. It follows that $\bar{T}(i) \overset{\sim}{\cdot}\!\!= \mathring{B}(i)$. Proposition 1 is proved.

Let us introduce the algorithm of the so-called *equivalent standardization* of expressions. The algorithm, which we denote by S^{0} operates the same way as rule of standardization *s'*, except that it uses algorithm L for expansion and shift of the terms (i.e., algorithm S^{0} first applies algorithm L to the outermost terms of maximal depth, then to the outermost terms of the depth by unity less than maximal and so on, till all outermost terms are maximally equivalently expanded and shifted rightwards). Let us note that the following properties of S^{0} holds:

a) a constant expression A is separable if and only if $s'(A)=\mathsf{S}^{0}(A)$;

b) for any constant expression A there exists an unfoldment $A'\in V(A)$, such that if a certain term T of A is unfolded in A then all subterms of T are also unfolded (we call such unfoldments *nonstopping*) and $s'(A)=\mathsf{S}^{0}(A')$;

c) if expressions $\mathbf{E}$ and $\mathbf{F}$ are such that the expression $\mathsf{S}(\mathbf{E})\mathsf{S}(\mathbf{F})$ is separable, then $\mathsf{S}(\mathbf{EF})=\mathsf{S}^{0}(\mathsf{S}(\mathbf{E})\mathsf{S}(\mathbf{F}))$ (we assume that the ordering Σ is fixed and instead of S_{Σ} (S^{0}_{Σ}) write S (S^{0});

d) if $\mathsf{S}^{0}(\mathbf{E})$ has standard form (i.e., $\mathsf{S}^{0}(\mathbf{E})=\mathsf{S}(\mathbf{E})$) and an unfoldment $\mathbf{E}'\in V(\mathbf{E})$ is nonstopping, then $\mathsf{S}^{0}(\mathbf{E}')=\mathsf{S}(\mathbf{E}')$;

e) if $A'\in V(\mathsf{S}(A))$ is a nonstopping unfoldment, then there exists an unfoldment $A''\in V(A)$, such that $\mathsf{S}(A'')=\mathsf{S}^{0}(A')$.

Let us consider a string $X=X_1YX_2$, where Y is regular (or there exists Y', such that $Y \overset{\cdot}{=} Y'$, and Y' is regular). Let us denote by $f'_{Y}(X)$ the string we obtain from X substituting the producing term for Y.

Proposition 13. Let $A=A_1BA_2$ be a separable constant expression and let

$$\mathsf{S}(A)=A^{+}B^{+}A_2^{+}=A_1^{+}\mathring{B}^{+}(0)\ldots\mathring{B}^{+}(\eta)A_2^{+}$$

where, $A_i^+=S(A_i)$ $(i=1,2)$, $B^+=S(B)$. Let $\mathring{B}(i)$ be an expression such that $S(\mathring{B}(i))=\mathring{B}^+(i)$ and $\mathring{B}^+(i)$ is the complete standard form of $\mathring{B}(i)$. There exists an unfoldment $\hat{A}\in V(A)$ such that $\hat{A}=\hat{A}_1B\hat{A}_2$ and

$$s'f'_{B^+}(S(A))=S(\hat{A}_1<\mathring{B}(i)\,|\,i:=0..\eta>\hat{A}_2) \tag{5.6}$$

Proof. Let us consider expression (5.6). According to property *b*) of algorithm S^0, there exist nonstopping unfoldments $\hat{A}_i^+\in V(A_i^+)$, such that

$$s'(A_1^+<\mathring{B}^+(i)\,|\,i:=0..\eta>A_2^+)=S^0(\hat{A}_1^+<\mathring{B}^+(i)\,|\,i:=0..\eta>\hat{A}_2^+).$$

Evidently the last equals

$$S^0(S^0(\hat{A}_1^+)<\mathring{B}^+(i)\,|\,i:=0..\eta>S^0(\hat{A}_2^+)). \tag{5.7}$$

According to property *e*) there are unfoldments $\hat{A}_i\in V(A_i)$, such that (5.7) equals

$$S^0(S(\hat{A}_1)<\mathring{B}^+(i)\,|\,i:=0..\eta>S(\hat{A}_2)). \tag{5.8}$$

Taking into account that $\mathring{B}^+(i)=S(\mathring{B}(i))$ and $\mathring{B}^+(i)$ is in the complete standard form where $\mathring{B}(i)$ is the base, (5.8) equals

$$S_0(S(\hat{A}_1)<S(\mathring{B}(i))\,|\,i:=0..\eta>S(\hat{A}_2)),$$

which, in turn, according to property *c*), equals

$$S(\hat{A}_1<\mathring{B}(i)\,|\,i:=0..\eta>\hat{A}_2).$$

Therefore the proposition is proved.

Now we can complete the **proof of lemma 8.**

Taking into account lemma 7 we get that $S(A)$ contains a regular substring with the attraction $\chi\geq\alpha/\mu$, for certain $\mu=\mu(\|E\|,\beta)$. Let B^+ be the substring with the maximal attraction. From proposition 12 we get that

$$s'f'_{B^+}(S(A))=s'f'_{B'}(S(A)),$$

where $B'=\bar{T}^*(\delta)...\bar{T}^*(\delta+\phi\sigma)$ is from (5.3). From proposition 13 we get that there exists an unfoldment $\hat{A}\in V(A)$, which can be presented in form $\hat{A}=\hat{A}_1'\hat{C}_1'B'\hat{C}_2'\hat{A}_2'$ (where $B=C_1'B'C_2'$), and

$$s'f_{B'}(S(A))=S(\hat{A}_1'\hat{C}_1'<\bar{T}(i)\,|\,i:=\delta..\delta+\phi\sigma>\hat{C}_2'\hat{A}_2').$$

The last evidently equals $S(A_1'TA_2')=S(A')$. Since B^+ has the maximal attraction,

$$s'f'(S(A))=s'f'_{B^+}(S(A))=S(A').$$

The lemma 8 is proved. From there taking into account lemma 7 we get lemma 6 by induction. Therefore, lemma 2.

6. Completion of the Proof

Let us finally show, how the properties of algorithm $\mathcal{S}$ yield decidability of equivalence (asymptotical equivalence) and completeness of inductive inference rules. Let us begin with equivalence.

Let there be given two unary expressions **E(n)** and **F(n)** and let the ordering of the parameters be $n_0 \le n$. From item 1 of lemma 2 we get that for a certain $\alpha \in \mathbb{N}$: $E \overset{\alpha}{\sim} F$ holds if and only if $\mathcal{S}(E^0) \doteq \mathcal{S}(F^0)$. Consequently, to decide, if there exists $\alpha \in \mathbb{N}$ such that $E \overset{\alpha}{\sim} F$, we check whether $\mathcal{S}(E^0) \doteq \mathcal{S}(F^0)$. Furthermore, if $\mathcal{S}(E^0) \doteq \mathcal{S}(F^0)$ holds, α can be found effectively and therefore, we can check whether $\mathrm{Unf}(E(\alpha'))=\mathrm{Unf}(F(\alpha'))$ for all $\alpha' < \alpha$, and consequently $E \equiv F$.

To decide asymptotical equivalence, let us remember that $E \cong F$ equals the assertion that there exists $\delta \in \mathbb{Z}$, such that $E(n) \sim F(n+\delta)$. Taking into account that $E(n) \sim F(n+\delta)$ yields $\mathrm{Unf}(E(\alpha))=\mathrm{Unf}(F(\alpha+\delta))$ (for sufficiently large α), we can prove that, if such δ exists, then $|\delta| \le \delta_E + \delta_F$, where δ_E, δ_F depends only on $\|E\|$ and $\|F\|$ respectively and can be effectively found. Therefore, we can decide if $E \cong F$ by checking for all δ: $|\delta| \le \delta_E + \delta_F$, whether $E(n) \sim F(n+\delta)$ (i.e., whether $\mathcal{S}(E^0(n)) \doteq \mathcal{S}(F^0(n+\sigma)))$.

Theorem of equivalence is proved.

Let us pass to synthesis theorem. We call an expression **E** *almost α-attractive* $(\alpha>0)$, if **E** does not contain a term which has the attraction less than α and at the same time is a subterm of a term with the attraction more or equal to α. It is evident that lemmas 7 and 8 remain true if we take the set $V'_{\alpha/\gamma}(E(\vec{\alpha}))$ $(V'_{\tau}(E(\vec{\alpha})))$ of all almost α-attractive unfoldments instead of the set $V_{\alpha/\gamma}(E(\vec{\alpha}))$ $(V_{\tau}(E(\vec{\alpha})))$ of all α/γ-attractive unfoldments. It follows

Lemma 9. Let $E(n_1,\ldots,n_k)$ be a completely separable expression, Σ an open ordering and $\vec{\alpha}$ be (α,β)-expressive k-tuple permissible for Σ $(\alpha \in \mathbb{N},\ \beta>1)$. Let ξ be the number of possible applications of folding-up and standardization to $\mathrm{Unf}(E(\vec{\alpha}))$. (i.e., $(sf)^{\xi}(\mathrm{Unf}(E(\vec{\alpha})))=(sf)^{*}(\mathrm{Unf}(E(\vec{\alpha})))$). For any β there exist constants $\bar{\alpha}=\bar{\alpha}(\|E\|,\beta)$ and $\gamma=\gamma(\|E\|,\beta)$, such that for any $\alpha \ge \bar{\alpha}$, and for any $i=1,\ldots,\xi$ there exist an expression $E_i \sim E$ and an unfoldment $A_i \in V'_{\alpha/\gamma}(E_i(\vec{\alpha}))$, such that

$$((sf)^{i}(\mathrm{Unf}(E(\vec{\alpha}))))_f \doteq \mathcal{S}(A_i).$$

Proof. We prove the lemma inductively by i. For $i=0$ the assertion is obvious. Let us assume that the assertion is true for

$i<\xi$. Let $\mu_0=\mu_0(\|E_i\|)$ be from lemma 7 and $\gamma=\gamma(\|E\|,\beta)$ from lemma 8. There are two possibilities: either A_i is substantial or not In the first case the lemma follows directly from lemma 8 (actually., from the case of almost α/γ-attractive unfoldments) taking $E_{i+1}=E_i$.

Let us consider the second case. Then there exists $E_i'\in V'_{\alpha/\gamma}(E_i)$, such that $E_i'(\vec{\alpha})=A_i$. Therefore

$$(s'f')^{i}(\mathrm{Unf}(E(\vec{\alpha})))\doteq\mathcal{S}(E_i'(\vec{\alpha}))=(\mathcal{S}(E_i'))(\vec{\alpha}).$$

Let $E_{i+1}=f'(\mathcal{S}(E_i'))$. Then

$$(s'f')^{i+1}(\mathrm{Unf}(E(\vec{\alpha})))=s'(E_{i+1}(\vec{\alpha})).$$

According to property *b*) of algorithm $\mathcal{S}^0$, there exists nonstopping $A_{i+1}\in V'_{\alpha/\gamma}(E_{i+1}(\vec{\alpha}))$, such that

$$s'(E_{i+1}(\vec{\alpha}))=\mathcal{S}^0(A_{i+1}),$$

and from property *d*)

$$\mathcal{S}^0(A_{i+1})=\mathcal{S}(A_{i+1}),$$

therefore

$$(s'f')^{i+1}(\mathrm{Unf}(E(\vec{\alpha})))\doteq\mathcal{S}(A_{i+1}),$$

i.e., the lemma is proved.

Further, in the same way as in the proof of item 5 of lemma 2, we obtain from lemma 7 and lemma 9

$$(s'f')^{*}(\mathrm{Unf}(E(\vec{\alpha})))\doteq\mathcal{S}(E_\xi(\vec{\alpha})).$$

For unary expressions it means that, if $\alpha\in\mathbb{N}$ is sufficiently large, then

$$((sf)^{*}(\mathrm{Unf}(E(\alpha))))_{f}\doteq\mathcal{S}(E_\xi(\alpha)).$$

To finish the proof, let us return to inductive inference rule of generalization. Let us prove that for any unary expression $F(n)$ for sufficiently large α: $g(F(\alpha))\cong F(\alpha)$. Indeed, if α is large enough, then all the characters b_i of $F(\alpha)=b_1\ldots b_m$, belonging to $\mathbb{Z}$ and exceeding $b=max\{b_i|b_i\in\mathbb{Z}\}/2$, corresponds to subexpressions $\underline{n+\gamma_i}$ in $F(n)$, where $\gamma_i=b_i-\alpha$. If we substitute $\underline{n+(b_i-b)}=\underline{n+\gamma_i-(b-\alpha)}$ for all these b_i, then we obtain the expression $F(n-(b-\alpha))$, which is almost equivalent to $F(n)$. Therefore

$$g(((sf)^{*}(\mathrm{Unf}(E(\alpha))))_{f}\doteq g((\mathcal{S}(E_\xi))(\alpha))\cong\mathcal{S}(E_\xi)\sim E,$$

i.e., theorem 3.

Finally let us note, that we have actually proved equivalence and synthesis theorems not only for unary, but also for arbitrary expressions. Directly from (4.3) we get

Theorem 4. There exists an algorithm which decides, whether $E\overset{\Sigma}{\sim}F$ ($E\overset{\Sigma}{\sim}{}_{L}^{\gamma}G$), for arbitrary nonsingular expressions E and F, and ordering Σ (and $\gamma\in\mathbb{N}$).

To generalize synthesis theorem, let us define the notion of *formal example of for-expression* $E(n_1,\ldots,n_k)$ as a k+1-tuple $(Unf(E(\alpha_1,\ldots,\alpha_k)),\alpha_1,\ldots,\alpha_k)$, where $\alpha_1,\ldots,\alpha_k\in\mathbb{Z}$. Furthermore, let us introduce the following rule of inductive inference, namely, the rule of *polyvalent generalization*. Let $(W,\alpha_1,\ldots\alpha_k)$ be a formal example and let $\psi_1,\ldots,\psi_l$ be the characters of W which belong to $\mathbb{Z}$. We substitute $\underline{n_j+\gamma_j^i}$ for ψ_i, where $j\in\{1,\ldots,l\}$ is such that $|\alpha_j-\psi_i|<|\alpha_h-\psi_i|$ $(h\neq j)$ and $\gamma_j^i=\alpha_j-\psi_i$.

We call the system of inductive inference rules *complete for the class* $\mathfrak{C}$ *of for-expressions,* if for an arbitrary $E(n_1,\ldots,n_k)\in\mathfrak{C}$ and arbitrary $\beta>1$, there exists a constant $\alpha_{E,\beta}\in\mathbb{N}$, such that for any $\alpha\geq\alpha_{E,\beta}$ and any (α,β)-expressive k-tuple $\alpha_1,\ldots,\alpha_k$ permissible for Σ, given the example $(Unf(E(\alpha_1,\ldots,\alpha_k)),\alpha_1,\ldots,\alpha_k)$, the system constructs an expression F, such that $F\overset{\Sigma}{\sim}E$.

It is evident that the following theorem is true.

Theorem 5. The system of inductive inference rules consisting of rules of graphical folding-up, graphical standardization and polyvalent generalization is complete for the class of all nonsingular *for*-expressions.

We get the corresponding synthesis theorem as a corollary.

7. Open Problems

1. According to theorem 3, there exists a constant α_E, such that for $\alpha\geq\alpha_E$, given the example $Unf(E(\alpha))$, system S synthesizes an expression F, such that $E\sim F$. How α_E depends on E?

The next two problems deal with the problem of singularity of expressions.

2. The problem of *singularity*: is it possible to decide for an arbitrary expression whether it is singular or not?

3. Are theorems 1, 2 and 3 true for the class of all expressions (including the singular ones)?

The next two problems deal with further simplification of inductive inference rules.

4. Let f'' be the rule of inductive inference similar to rule f'

(i.e., the rule of folding-up for *for*-expressions) with the only difference that instead of folding up the regular substring with maximal attraction, f'' folds up the regular substring with maximal modulus of factor. (In this case it is necessary to fold up also the strings which are inside terms.) Is system $S''=\{f'',s',g\}$ complete?

5. (J.Barzdin). Let us consider the system S''' consisting of two following rules. Rule of *simple folding-up*: any regular substring can be replaced by the producing term. The second rule is rule of *generalization g* from *S*. Order of application of the rules is the following. First we nondeterministically apply rule of simple folding-up a number of times. If, in a certain moment for the obtained string *X* the following *condition of generalizability* is held: for any character $\alpha_i \in \mathbb{Z}$ of the string *X*, either $\alpha_i \leq max\{\alpha_i\}/3$ or $\alpha_i \geq 2max\{\alpha_i\}/3$, then we can apply rule of generalization and complete the synthesis. Whether system S''' is complete?

The next problem concerns computational complexity of synthesis algorithm.

6. Synthesis algorithm based on inference system *S* apparently is not optimal. Let us introduce rule of *accelerated standardization* which differs from rule of standardization only with the following. Expanding and shifting a term *T* at the expense of another term *S*, instead of unfolding *S* as in the rule of standardization, rule of accelerated standardization only cuts off from *S* the "necessary" part (for example, in section 1 from (1.5) we would directly obtain (1.7)). One of the possible ways to enhance the efficiency of *S* is to substitute rule of accelerated standardization for rule of standardization. Is the system of inductive inference consisting of the rules of folding-up, accelerated standardization and generalization complete? Note, that the synthesis algorithm based on the system has polynomial time complexity.

7. A number of problems is related to possible generalizations of the model of dot (*for*-) expressions. Particularly we can consider the generalization of dot (*for*-) expressions for two or more dimensions (e.g., we can consider objects such as matrices) or graphs. There can also be considered dot expressions having an arbitrary step (instead of just +1 and -1).

A number of problems are mentioned also in [8].

REFERENCES

1.Angluin D. *Finding patterns common to a set of strings.* J.Compt. Syst. Sci., V21, 1980.,46-62.

2.Barzdin J. *On inductive synthesis of programs.* Springer-Verlag, Lecture notes in Computer Sci., V122, 1981. 235-254.

3.Barzdin J. *Some rules of inductive inference and their use for program synthesis.* IFIP - 83, North-Holland, 1983, 333-338.

4.Barzdin J., Brāzma A., Kinber J. *Models of inductive syntactical synthesis.* Machine Intellegece, 1990, N12, 139-148.

5.Bierman A.W., Krisnaswamy R. *Constructing programs from example computations.* IEEE Trans.Soft.Eng., SE-2-1976, 141-153.

6.Brāzma A. *The decidability of equivalence for graphical expressions.* Theory of algorithms and programming, Riga, 1986, 103-156 (in Russian).

7.Brāzma A., Etmane I. *Inductive synthesis of for-expressions.* Theory of algorithms and programming, Riga, 1986, 156-189 (in Russian).

8.Brāzma A., Kinber J. *Generalized regular expressions - a language for synthesis of programs with branching in loops.* Theoretical computer sc. V.46, North-Holland, 1986, 175-195.

9.Etmane I. *A certain formalization of the ellipsis notion.* Informatics and semantics. V.27, Moscow, 121-141 (in Russian).

10.Etmane I. *An approach to inductive synthesis of programms.* Programming, Moscow, 1988, N4, 5-16 (in Russian).

11.Shapiro E. *Algorithmic program debugging.* MIT Press, 1983.

12.Muggleton S.,Buntine W. *Towards constructive induction in first-order predicate calculus.* TIRM-88-031, 1988.

SOME MODELS OF INDUCTIVE SYNTACTICAL SYNTHESIS FROM SAMPLE COMPUTATIONS

EFIM KINBER

Institute of Mathematics and Computer Science
The University of Latvia
Raiņa bulv.29, Rīga 226250, Latvia

Abstract. The paper is a survey of several models of inductive program synthesis from sample computations. Synthesis tools are basically syntactical: the synthesis is based on the detection of "regular" fragments related with "shuffled" arithmetical progressions. Input sample computations are supposed to be "representative": they have to "reflect" all loops occurring in the target program. Programs are synthesized in nontraditional form of "generalized" regular expressions having Cleene stars and unions for loops and CASE-like operators. However, if input samples are somehow "annotated" (we consider two different approaches), then loops can be synthesized in more traditional WHILE-form, where loop conditions are separated from actions. The model in Section 3 is developed to handle the synthesis from incomplete sample computations (initial fragments). This model can be useful for the synthesis of some divide-and-conquer algorithms.

Introduction

Several models of inductive synthesis of programs from sample computations explaining their behaviour are presented in this paper. Synthesis methods are purely syntactical: input information is treated as a string of symbols, taking into account no semantics. The synthesis itself is based on the detection of purely syntactical regularities in sample computations.

The boundedness of purely syntactical tools for inductive program synthesis is quite evident; for example, syntactical tools clearly are not sufficient to separate predicates from actions in a sample computation text. For instance, an explanation of standard sort-merge behaviour can begin with

a(1)≤b(1)? yes; then a(1)→c(1);

a(2)≤b(1)? no; then b(1)→c(2);

or with

a(1)≤b(1)Y; c(1):=a(1);

a(2)≤b(2)N; c(2):=b(1);

(the choice of the language depends on the user); any syntactical synthesizer is hardly able to select the logical condition in this case. Moreover, syntactical methods possess an important advantage: they actually do not depend on the language chosen by the user to explain the target algorithm's behaviour. This advantage is particularly important for nonprofessional users.

The first general method for inductive synthesis from sample computation (full computation traces) was developed by A.Biermann and R.Krishnaswamy in [1]. This method does not put any significant restrictions on the class of synthesizable programs, however, it yields an exhaustive search. Furthermore, the presentation of full computation traces is inconvenient for the user. From this point of view an approach seems to be more natural when sample computations, being not full, are sufficient to explain essentially the target algorithm's behaviour in a natural way. Besides, effectiveness of a synthesis method is of importance; for instance, it is natural to require the running time to be a polynomial of the input sample's length.

The first model, more or less satisfying the above requirements, was developed by J.M.Barzdin in [2] (the so-called dots expressions). Dots expression is a form of program presentation particularly convenient for inductive generalization (or synthesis) of FOR-loops. J.M.Barzdin is the first who has noted that already purely syntactical regularities in sample computations allow to synthesize inductively quite complicated programs. J.Barzdin's ideas were developed in the works by A.Brazma and I.Etmane [3,4,5]. In particular, A.Brazma has constructed a convenient and quite natural collection of syntactical inductive inference rules allowing, given any sufficiently long sample computation, to synthesize a dots expression almost equivalent to the target one. In addition, the synthesis method is effective almost always (except very artificial cases).

However, the power of dots expressions is quite restricted. For example, programs allowing branching not only in loop termination conditions cannot be expressed by dots expressions.On the other hand, it is quite evident that the power of syntactical tools is not exhausted by dots expressions. Therefore two problems arise naturally: (1) to estimate the power and boundaries of purely syntactical methods; (2) to develop models for restricted (but still wide) classes of programs convenient from the practical point of view. A solution to the first problem is presented in [6], where syntactical tools are shown to be sufficient for an effective synthesis of a program class universal (in a sense) for the class of all partial recursive functions. The current paper is a survey of some researches concerning the second problem.

The paper consists of three sections. The first section is devoted to a quite general model of inductive syntactical synthesis, where sample computations are not annotated and no information concerning target program complexity is available to the synthesizer [9]. The model is oriented basically to data processing programs. For instance, standard sort-merge algorithm, algorithms decomposing tables are synthesizable within the model.

The corresponding language is a restricted version of the generalized regular expressions - the languge introduced in [7]. The union and iteration used in the language allow to synthesize a general structure of the target program usually not separating logical conditions from actions in loops and conditional operators.

The model defined in Section 2 [10] is convenient for effective synthesis of programs containing FOR-loops and special (however, very natural), interpreted functions. For instance, it is convenient to synthesize various algorithms within the model executing algebraic operations and various algorithms updating tables. The constraint for the loop conditions (only predicates $x \leq y$) is supposed to be known to the synthesizer; it allows, unlike the model in Section 1, to synthesize a loop in much more traditional WHILE...DO-form. However, in this case sample computations have to contain some additional information; we consider the case when they are annotated by (exact) loop boundaries. Of course, it is more natural (and more convenient from the user's point of view) to provide only approximate loop boundaries - in this case one has to transform the synthesis algorithm, using heuristical considerations. The running time of the synthesizer is a polynomial on the input sample length provided the loop depth in the target program is bounded.

Despite the polynomial running time, the synthesis methods in the above models have a disadvantage: the length of samples necessary for the correct synthesis can be very large in comparison to the length of the target program. At the same time in many cases a sample computation can be divided into fragments that actually do not differ in respect to the sequence and the entity of actions performed by the target algorithm (for example, parameters of these fragments can differ on an increment of arithmetical progression). If sample computations of the target program possess this property, then it is natural to use for the synthesis only an initial fragment of the sample fully describing the program's behaviour, and then to inform the synthesizer that "further the program behaves similarly". The model presented in Section 3 [1] is developed to express and synthesize programs having sample computations of the above kind. The corresponding language combines traditional programming tools (like WHILE-statements) with the tools convenient for the syntactical synthesis (iteration, union). Unlike previous models, some algorithms with recursion (for example, quick-sort) can be written within this model. Sample computations are annotated with the variables whose values occur in samples. Thus, an initial sample fragment of the quick-sort annotated this way is, in fact, a linear presentation of the quick-sort (informal) description given in [8]. The synthesis from the samples of this kind is quite natural and effective.

1. Iterative Programs

We begin with sample computations explaining the behaviour of two popular algorithms.

EXAMPLE 1. The ordered arrays $a=a(1), a(2),\dots,a(m)$ and $b=b(1),b(2),\dots,b(n)$ are to be merged into the array $c=c(1),c(2),\dots,c(m+n)$. The following sample computation explains the algorithm behaviour in a natural way:

Input: a,b;

$a(1)\le b(1)$? yes, then $a(1)\to c(1)$;
$a(2)\le b(1)$? yes, then $a(2)\to c(2)$;
$a(3)\le b(1)$? yes, then $a(3)\to c(3)$;
$a(4)\le b(1)$? no, then $b(1)\to c(4)$;
$a(4)\le b(2)$? no, then $b(2)\to c(5)$;
$a(4)\le b(3)$? yes, then $a(4)\to c(6)$;

$a(5)=\lambda$; then

$b(3)\to c(7)$;

$b(4)\to c(8)$;

$b(5)\to c(9)$;

$b(6)=\lambda$; then STOP

Output: c.

Note that the predicate $a(x)=\lambda$? is mentioned only at the point where $a(x)=\lambda$. It seems quite natural when we explain the algorithm's behaviour informally.

EXAMPLE 2. The negative and nonnegative numbers are to be selected in every row of the table $a(i,j)$, $1\le i\le m, 1\le j\le m$. The following sample explains the algorithm:

Input: a;

$a(1,1)<0$? yes, then $a(1,1)\to b(1,1)$;

$a(1,2)<0$? yes, then $a(1,2)\to b(1,2)$;

$a(1,3)<0$? yes, then $a(1,3)\to c(1,1)$;

$a(1,4)<0$? no, then $a(1,4)\to c(1,2)$;

$a(1,5)<0$? yes, then $a(1,5)\to b(1,3)$;

$a(1,6)=\lambda$, then

$a(2,1)<0$? yes, then $a(2,1)\to b(2,1)$;

$a(2,2)<0$? no, then $a(2,2)\to c(2,1)$;

$a(2,3)<0$? no, then $a(2,3)\to c(2,2)$;

$a(2,4)<0$? no, then $a(2,4)\to c(2,3)$;

$a(2,5)<0$? yes, then $a(2,5)\to b(2,2)$;

$a(2,6)<0$? yes, then $a(2,6)\to b(2,3)$;

$a(2,7)=\lambda$, then

$a(3,1)<0$? yes, then $a(3,1)\to b(3,1)$;

$a(3,2)<0$? yes, then $a(3,2)\to b(3,2)$;

$a(3,3)<0$? no, then $a(3,3)\to c(3,1)$;

$a(3,4)<0$? no, then $a(3,4)\to c(3,2)$;

$a(3,5)=\lambda$, then

$a(4,1)=\lambda$, then STOP

Output: b,c.

Now we shall define the language within which the above samples can be generalized (we omit some technical details).

Let **N** be the set of all natural numbers (including $\emptyset$), A' is a finite alphabet, $A=A'\cup$**N**, X is a set of variables, $X\cap A=\emptyset$. Let the set OP contain the following symbols of operations: :=(assignment), *(iteration), $^+$(adding 1), also brackets $($,$)$ and comma, ; $OP\cap(AUX)=\emptyset$. For the sake of brevity we write x^+ instead of $x:=x+1$.

Let $X(M)$ denote the set of variables occurring in the expression M.

The alphabet A plays a special role: it is used to represent sample computations.

Now we describe the structure of an iterative program.

The main part P of a program is a string

$$(1.1) \quad A_0B_1A_1B_2A_2...B_mA_m,$$

where $A_0, A_1, A_2, ..., A_m$ are words over the alphabet $A\cup X$, and $B_1, B_2, ..., B_m$ are loops.

A loop is an expression

$$(1.2) \quad R=(x_1:=\mu_1, ..., x_r:=)\ (P_1y_1^+...y_p^+ \cup P_2z_1^+...z_k^+),$$

where P_1 is a word

$$V_0W_1V_1...W_sV_s,\ s\leq 0,$$

where $V_0, ..., V_s$ are words over the alphabet $A\cup X$, $W_1, ..., W_s$ are loops, variables $y_1, ..., y_p$ occur in $V_0V_1...V_s$ (the same holds for P_2 and $z_1, ..., z_k$);

$x_1, x_2, ..., x_r \in X, \mu_1, ..., \mu_r \in \mathbf{N}\cup X$;

variables $z\in\{x_1, ..., x_r\}\cap(\{y_1, ..., y_p\}\cup\{z_1, ..., z_k\})$ are called l o c a l in the loop R.

The initial part of a program P is an expression

$$(x_1, :=c_1, ..., x_k:=c_k),$$

where $c_1, c_2, ..., c_k \in \mathbf{N}$ and $x_1, x_2, ..., x_k \in X$ are variables that are local in no loop in P.

Some simple natural constraints have to hold for programs (the detailed definition of iterative programs is given in [9]). However, one constraint is implied due to effective synthesis:

(*) for any expression

$$M=(T_1T_1' \cup T_2T_2')^*SR(U_1U_1' \cup U_2U_2')^*$$

in a program P, where T_1', T_2', U_1', U_2' are words containing all y^+, z^+ (see (1.2)) and R contains all assignments in front of the loop $(U_1U_1' \cup U_2U_2')^*$, no $W\in\{T_1, T_2, SU_1, SU_2\}$ is an initial fragment of any other $W'\in\{T_1, T_2, SU_1, SU_2\}$.

The constraint (*) means that elements of any two consequent loops have to differ in quite a strong sense. Versions of (*) can vary, however, at least one constraint of this kind is necessary.

Now we give some examples of iterative programs. Perhaps, the simplest ones are:

$P_1: (x:=0)(axx^+)^*$

$P_2: (x:=0, y:=0)(axx^+ \cup byy^+)^*$

$P_3: (x:=0)(ax(y:=x)(byy^+)^* x^+)^*$.

The following two iterative expressions are programs for the standard sort-merge and for separating negative and nonnegative numbers in a table.

$P_4: (x:=1, y:=1, z:=1)$ Input: a, b;
$(a(x) \le b(y)$? yes, then $a(x) \to c(z); x^+ z^+$
$\cup a(x) \le b(y)$? no, then $b(y) \to c; y^+, z^+)^*$
$((a(x)=\lambda$, then $(b(y) \to c(z); y^+ z^+)^*$
$b(y)=\lambda$, then STOP $)$
$\cup\ (b(y)=\lambda$, then $(a(x) \to c(z); x^+ z^+)^*$
$a(y)=\lambda$, then STOP.$))$ Output: c.

(Brackets (,) in $a(x)$, $b(y)$, $c(y)$ belonging to the alphabet A' are written in bold in order to separate them from the same symbols in OP).

$P_5: (i:=1)$ Input: $a; ((j:=1, m:=1, n:=1)$
$(a(i,j)<0$? yes, then $a(i,j) \to b(i,m) j^+ m^+$
$\cup a(i,j)<0$? no, then $a(i,j) \to c(i,n) j^+ n^+)^*$
$a(i,j)=\lambda$, then $i^+)^*$
$a(i,j)=\lambda$, then STOP.

The alphabet A plays an important role in our model: the set of words over A is the language of sample computations. The symbols in OP and variables are used only in programs and do not occur in samples.

Let $\mathscr{P}$ denote the set of all iterative programs.

Now we define the notion of a sample computation. To begin with, we define the notion of an unfoldment of a program $P \in \mathscr{P}$. Let us replace every loop $(R_1 \cup R_2)^*$ in P by an expression $R_{1_1} R_{1_2} \ldots R_{1_k}$, $R_{1_j} \in \{R_1, R_2\}, 1 \le i \le k$, and then replace every expression $S \cup T$ by either S, or T. The expression $\bar{P}$ we have obtained is said to be an unfoldment of the program $\bar{P}$. For example,

$$\bar{P}_2: \ (x:=o, y:=o) axx^+ axx^+ byy^+ byy^+ byy^+ axx^+ byy^+ byy^+$$

is an unfoldment of the above program P_2.

Now, for each variable x in $\bar{P}$, we enumerate all its occurrences in P (including x^+-s) from left to right. For our example $\bar{P}_2$ we obtain

$$(x(1):=o, y(1):=o) ax(2) x(3)^+ ax(4) x(5)^+ by(2) y(3)^+ by(4) y(5)^+$$

$by_{(6)}y_{(7)}^{\dagger}ax_{(6)}x_{(7)}^{\dagger}by_{(8)}y_{(9)}^{\dagger}by_{(10)}y_{(11)}^{\dagger}$.

Then we set $v(a)=a$ for every number a in $\bar{P}$. Now, for every $x \in X(P)$ for each $\nu_{(i)} \in \{x_{(i)}, x_{(i)}^{\dagger}\}, i=1,2,...,$ define the value $v(\nu_{(i)})$ as follows:

(a) if $\nu_{(i)}$ is $x_{(i)}$ in an assignment $x_{(i)}:=\mu$, then
$v(\nu_{(i)})=v(\mu)$

(b) otherwise, $v(x_{(i)})=v(\nu_{(i-1)})$,
$v(x_{(i)}^{\dagger})=v(\nu_{(i-1)})+1$.

Then delete all words $c:=c, c\in\mathbf{N}$, values of $x_{(i)}^{\dagger}, i=1,2,... x\in X$, and brackets $(,)\in OP$. The expression $v(\bar{P})$ we have obtained is called a v a l u e or a (formal) s a m p l e c o m p u t a t i o n of the iterative program P.

Thus, for our example $\bar{P}_2$ we get

$v(\bar{P})=a0a1b0b1b2a2b3b4$.

One can easily check that the expression in Example 1 is a value of the program P_4, and the expression in Example 2 is a value of P_5.

For an arbitrary $P\in\mathscr{P}$ let $V(P)$ denote the set of all sample computations of P. The set $V(P)$ can be treated as free semantics of the program P.

The equivalence relation can be naturally defined for iterative programs: $P_1 \equiv P_2$ iff $V(P_1)=V(P_2)$. Iterative programs constitute a subclass of the generalized regular expressions ([7]). Therefore the decidability of the equivalence problem follows from the decidability of this problem for g.r.e.-s ([7]).

It is quite apparent that some programs can be hardly synthesized from arbitrary sample computations. So we have to define a subclass of r e p r e s e n t a t i v e sample computations suitable for the inductive syntactical synthesis.

First we need some auxiliary notions.

For any loop $E=(P_1 \cup P_2)^*$ a 1-u n f o l d m e n t $\bar{E}$ is any expression $P_{i_1}P_{i_2}...P_{i_m}, P_{i_j}\in\{P_1,P_2\}, 1\le j\le m$. We obtain a 1-value of E replacing first occurrences of variables x_j in $\bar{E}$, such that assignments $x_j:=c, c\in\mathbf{N}$ stand just in front of $\bar{E}$, by numbers c and performing obvious calculations in $P_{i_1}, P_{i_2}..., P_{i_m}$.

For example, the word $(y:=u)a1a2byy^{+}a3a4byy^{+}byy^{+}$ is a 1-value of $(x:=1, y:=u)(axx^{+} \cup byy^{+})^{*}$.

Computing 1-values of all loops in a 1-value of E, we obtain a 2-value of E. Continuing this procedure, one can define a

k-value of E for an arbitrary k not larger than the loop depth of E (obviously defined).

Similarly, a k-value can be defined for an arbitary iterative program P.

Now let $R=(R_1 \cup R_2)^*$ be a loop in P and let $\bar{R}=R_{i_1}\ldots R_{i_k}$ be its 1-unfoldment such that

(1) for each $i\in\{1,2\}$ there is a subword R_iR_i in $\bar{R}$;

(2) there is either subword $R_1R_2R_1R_2$, or $R_2R_1R_2R_1$ in R.

$\bar{R}$ is called a r e g u l a r 1-unfoldment.

We can define the notion of regular unfoldment similarly; in this case $\bar{R}=R_{i_1}\ldots R_{i_k}$ must be replaced by $\bar{R}_{i_1}\bar{R}_{i_2}\ldots\bar{R}_{i_k}$, where each $\bar{R}_{i_j}$ is an unfoldment of R_{i_j}.

Let μ be an occurrence of x^+ in the unfoldment $\bar{P}$ such that x^+ does not occur between μ and the first assignment $x:=v$ to the right from μ. The value μ gets when $v(\bar{P})$ is computed is called an x-i n d e x for $v(\bar{P})$ ($v(x^+)$ is removed from $v(\bar{P})$; however $v(x)$ such that $v(x^+)-v(x)\leq 1$ is presented in $v(\bar{P})$).

Variables $x,y\in X(P)$ are called s e p a r a t e d in P iff, for some loop $T=(T_1\cup T_2)^*$, there is either x^+, or y^+ in some $T_i, i\in\{1,2\}$; the loop T is called (x,y)-s e p a r a t i n g.

Let c_1 be the maximal number occurring in the program $P, c_2=\mathrm{card}(X(P)$, and $c\geq\max(c_1,c_2)$.

We call an unfoldment $\bar{P}$ of the program P c-representative iff:

(I) for any separated variables x and y, if an initial fragment $\bar{P}'$ of $\bar{P}$ contains an unfoldment of some (x,y)-separating loop, then x- and y- indices for $v(P)$ to the right from $v\bar{(}P')$ are different;

(II) for any variable x all x-indices for $v(P)$ are different;

(III) for any loop $E=(E_1\cup E_2)$ any its unfoldment $\bar{E}_{i_1}\ldots\bar{E}_{i_k}$ without first c occurrences of $\bar{E}_1$ and without first c occurrences $\bar{E}_2$ is a regular unfoldment of E.

Finally, we call a sample computation $v(P)$ c-representative iff $v(P)=v(\bar{P})$ for a c-representative unfoldment $\bar{P}$ of P.

The conditions (I) and (II) are necessary to separate the values of different variables in the sample. The condition (III) "confirms" the presence of the loop E in the target program.

Unfortunately, sometimes the synthesis is impossible even from the representative samples. For example, let us consider the following expressions:

$\alpha=axx^{+}axx^{+}axx^{+}(axx^{+})^{*}$
$\beta=(axx^{+})^{*}axx^{+}axx^{+}axx^{+}axx^{+}$
$\gamma=(axx^{+})^{*}$.

These expressions have a (sufficiently long) common value, say,

(1.3) $v=a3a4a5a6a7a8$;

however, all three expressions are mutually inequivalent. Of course, given the sample v, a synthesizer can synthesize only one program; γ seems to be the most natural one, since α and β are in a sense "subprograms" of γ. The expression γ can be considered as a "canonical" program for samples like *(1.3)*. We will define the subclass of all "canonical" programs which are synthesizable from the representative samples.

First we define a collection of simple transformations over programs $P\in\mathscr{P}$. These transformations maximally "extend" and "shift" to the left all the loops in a program.

Let $P\in\mathscr{P}$,R is a fragment of P and R' is a fragment of any program $P'\in\mathscr{P}$.R is said to be similar to $R'(R\approx R')$ if, substituting R in P by R', one obtains the program P'' equivalent to P. Evidently, $\approx$ is an equivalence relation.

The first transformation "shifts" loops to the left (if it is possible).

Π_1. Let R be a loop in P and TR be an expression in P similar to $R'T'$ for some loop R' and some expression T'. Then, to obtain $\Pi_1(P)$, replace TR in P by $R'T'$.

For example, $a(xax^{+})^{*}$ is to be replaced by $(axx^{+})^{*}a$.

Π_2. Iff there is an expression $(R_1,R_2)^{*}S$ in P, R_2 contains only symbols x^{+} for $x\in X$, and $R_1\approx S$, then, to obtain $\Pi_2(P)$, replace $(R_1R_2)^{*}S$ in P by $(R_1R_2)^{*}$.

The next transformation (used 3 times) replaces, for example, $a2a3a4(x:=5)(axx^{+})^{*}$ by $(x:=2)(axx^{+})^{*}$.

G_3. Suppose there is an expression

(1.4) $S(y_1:=a_1,\ldots,y_m:=a_m,z_1:=u_1,\ldots,z_p:=u_p)(R_1T_1\cup R_2T_2)^{*},y_i,z_i,u_i\in X$

in P, all $a_i\geq 1$ (for the sake of simplicity all $y:=\mu$ with $\mu\in N$ are assumed to occur before $y:=\mu$ with $\mu\in X$), and S being similar to an expression $\tilde{R}_1$ obtained from R_1 by substituting the numbers $a_1-1,a_2-1,\ldots,a_m-1$ instead of all $y_1,y_2,\ldots,y_m$ occurrences. Let T_1 contain all symbols w^{+}in R_1T_1 (outside of loops), and T_1 be a word over $\{y_1^{+},\ldots,y_m^{+}\}$. Then, to obtain $\Pi_3(P)$, replace *(1.4)* in P

by

$$(y_1:=a_1-1,\dots,y_m:=a_m-1,z_1:=u_1,\dots,z_p:=u_p)(R_1T_1\cup R_2T_2)^*$$

(for R_2T_2 the definition is similar).

Inverse transformations $\Pi_i^{-1}, 1\le i\le 3$, can be defined naturally for $\Pi_i, 1\le i\le 3$.

The next transformation is similar to Π_3, but it is used for expressions of a higher loop-depth. For example, it transforms the expression

$$(x:=1)(axx^+)^*(y:=3)(a1(x:=y)(axx^+)\,y^+)^*$$

first to

$$a1(x:=2)(axx')^*(y:=3)(a1(x:=y)(axx^+)^*y^+)^*$$

(using Π_3^{-1}) and then to

$$(y:=2)(a1(x:=y)(axx^+)^*y^+)^*$$

(using Π_3).

Π_4. Suppose there is an expression *(1.4)* in *P* such that, if finite sequences of transformations Π_3^{-1} and, after that, possibly, Π_1^{-1} are applied to some loops in *S*, then Π_3 can be applied to the obtained expression

$$(1.5)\quad S'(y_1:=a1,\dots,z_p:=u_p)(R_1T_1\cup R_2T_2)^*$$

Then, to obtain $\Pi_4(P)$ apply Π_3 to *(1.5)*.

The inverse transformation Π_4^{-1} can be obviously defined also for Π_4, too.

Applying obvious transformations (for example, of the type $M(R_1\cup R_2)\to(MR_1\cup MR_2))$ to any $P\in\mathscr{P}$, we can transform *P* to an equivalent program $P_1\cup P_2\cup\dots\cup P_m$ where each P_i contains the symbol $\cup$ connecting expressions R_1,R_2 only in loops $(R_1\cup R_2)^*$. We call programs $P_1,P_2,\dots,P_m$ indecomposable.

An indecomposable program *P* is said to be c a n o n i c a l iff no transformation $\Pi_i, 1\le i\le 4$, is applicable to it.

An iterative program is called canonical iff it is equivalent to a finite union of indecomposable canonical programs.

Let $\mathscr{P}_0$ denote the set of all canonical iterative programs.

Multiple examples show that "real" programs are basically canonical. For instance, the above sort-merge program and the program separating negative and nonnegative numbers are canonical.

For any program $P,P'\in\mathscr{P}$, P' is called a p a r t i a l u n f o l d m e n t of *P* iff it is obtained from *P* by a finite sequence of transformations Π_1^{-1}–Π_4^{-1}.

PROPOSITION 1.1 ([7]). Every sequence of transformations Π_1–Π_4

applicable to *P* is finite.

PROPOSITION 1.2 ([7]). For every $P\in\mathcal{P}$ there exists $P'\in\mathcal{P}_0$ such that *P* is a partial unfoldment of *P*.

Now, given $P\in\mathcal{P}$ and $m\in\mathbf{N}$, let $V_{\geq m}(P)$ denote the set of values $v\in V(P)$ obtained from unfoldments $\bar{P}$ satisfying the following condition: for every loop $E=(E1\cup E2)^*$ in *P*, for every unfoldment $\bar{E}=\bar{E}1_1\bar{E}1_2\ldots\bar{E}1_k$ in $\bar{P}$ ($\bar{E}1_j$ is an unfoldment of $E1_j$, $1\leq j\leq k$), $\bar{E}1$ occurs in $\bar{E}$ at least *m* times, and $\bar{E}2$ occurs in $\bar{E}$ at least *m* times.

PROPOSITION 1.3 ([7]). If $P\in\mathcal{P}$ is a partial unfoldment of *R*, then $V_{\geq m}(P)\subseteq V_{\geq m}(R)$ for some $m\in\mathbf{N}$.

Propositions 1.2 and 1.3 actually mean that every iterative program can be asymptotically "embedded" into some canonical program.

Now we are about to describe the synthesis algorithm. First we do it informally considering the synthesis from the sample computation

$$v=a1a2a3a4a5a6a7a8a9a\underline{10}a\underline{11}$$
$$a1a3a4a5a6a7a8a9a\underline{10}a\underline{11}a\underline{12}a\underline{13}a\underline{14}a\underline{15}$$
$$a1a4a5a6a7a8a9a\underline{10}a\underline{11}a\underline{12}a\underline{13}a\underline{14}$$
$$a\underline{15}a\underline{16}a\underline{17}a\underline{18}a\underline{19}b\underline{19}\underline{19}cb\underline{20}\underline{20}c$$
$$b\underline{21}\underline{21}cd2\underline{23}cd3\underline{24}cd4\underline{25}cb\underline{26}\underline{26}c$$
$$b\underline{27}\underline{27}cd5\underline{26}cd6\underline{27}cb\underline{28}\underline{28}cd7\underline{29}c$$
$$b\underline{30}\underline{30}cd8\underline{31}cb\underline{32}\underline{32}cb\underline{33}\underline{33}cb\underline{34}\underline{34}c$$
$$d9\underline{35}cd\underline{10}\underline{36}cd\underline{11}\underline{37}cd\underline{12}\underline{38}cd\underline{13}\underline{39}c$$
$$d\underline{14}\underline{40}cd\underline{15}\underline{41}cd\underline{16}\underline{42}cd\underline{17}\underline{43}cd\underline{18}\underline{44}c$$
$$d\underline{19}\underline{45}cd\underline{20}\underline{46}cd\underline{21}\underline{47}cd\underline{22}\underline{48}c$$

(two digit numbers are underlined) of the indecomposable canonical program

$$(y:=2)(a1(x:=y)(axx^{+})^{*}y^{+})^{*}bx$$
$$(u:=2)(bxxcx^{+}\cup duxcu^{+}x^{+})^{*}. \qquad (1.6)$$

The basic idea of the synthesis algorithm is to detect the longest leftmost fragment related with one or two "shuffled" arithmetical progressions.

For example, this fragment may be

$$a1a2a3a4a5a6$$

or

$$a1a2a3b1b2a4a5b3b4$$

or

$$a2a3b4b4b6a7a8b9.$$

In our case first the algorithm finds the fragment

$\alpha=a1a2a3a4a5a6a7a8a9a\underline{10}a\underline{11}$.

Then it transforms α to the loop $(x:=1)(ax_1x_1^+)^*$ and marks by x_1 all numbers $\underline{11}$ to the right from α (possible places where the values of x_1 can occur). Similarly, the subwords $a3a4\ldots a\underline{15}$ and $a4a5\ldots a\underline{19}$ are transformed to $(x_2:=3)(ax_2x_2^+)^*$ and $(x_3:=4)(ax_3x_3^+)^*$, respectively. Accordingly, the numbers $\underline{15}$ occurring to the right from $a3\ldots a\underline{15}$ are marked by x_2, and numbers $\underline{19}$ to the right from $a4\ldots a\underline{19}$ are marked by x_3 (in the subword $\underline{19}b\underline{19}\underline{19}c$). Then the synthesis algorithm finds the leftmost longest fragment

$p=\underline{19}\underline{19}cb\underline{20}\underline{20}c\ldots d\underline{22}\underline{48}c$

related with two progressions $19,20,21,22$ and $19,20,21,22,\ldots,48$; here the values of the expressions bx_4x_4 and dx_5x4 are "shuffled".

β is transformed to

$(x_4:=\underline{19},x_5:=2)(bx_4x_4cx_4^+\cup dx_5x_4x_4^+x_5^+)^*$,

and the number $\underline{19}$ in $x_4:=\underline{19}$ is marked by x_3 (because $\underline{19}$ is the last value of x_3).

Now let us consider the second stage, where loops of higher depth are synthesized. First the synthesis algorithm, using Π_3^{-1}, transforms $(x:=1)(ax_1x1^+)^*$ to $a1(x:=2)(ax_1x_1^+)^*$ trying to construct a possibly longer expression related with an arithmetical progression. Thus, the expression

$a_1(x_1:=2)(ax_1x_1^+)^*a1(x_2:=3)(ax_2x_2^+)^*a1(x_3:=4)(ax_3x_3^+)^*$

is obtained. It is transformed to

$(y:=2)(a1(x:=y)(axx^+)^*y^+)^*$

and the markers x_3 associated with numbers $\underline{19}$ are replaced by x. Then the algorithm replaces all numbers with markers in the expression (in our case the numbers $\underline{19}$) by corresponding markers. Thus, the program

$(y:=2)(a1(x:=y)(axx^+)^*y^+)^*bx$
$(z:=x,u:=2)(bzzcz^+\cup duzcu^+z^+)^*$

is obtained. The program is evidently equivalent to that of *(1.6)*.

Now we describe the synthesis algorithm in the general form. First we define auxiliary operations over loops. Let $\alpha=\alpha_1\alpha_2\ldots\alpha_m$ be a 1-value of a loop

$E=(x1:=a_1,\ldots,x_{1_p}:=a_p,y_{j_1}:=b_1,\ldots,y_{j_t}:=b_t,z_1:=u_1,\ldots,z_s:=u_s)$
$(E_1x_1^+\ldots x_k^+\cup E_2y_1^+\ldots y_m^+)^*$

(for the sake of simplicity assignments $x_i:=a$ and $y_j:=b$ for $a,b\in N$

are put in front of $z:=u$ with $u\in X$). Let $\bar{\alpha}$ be the initial fragment of α containing at least n_1 1-values of $E_1x_1^+\dots x_k^+$ and n_2 1-values of $E_2y_1^+\dots y_m^+$ for any $n_1,n_2\le c$ (c is the parameter of representativeness). For each $i_r\in\{i_1,i_2,\dots,i_p\}$ we define

$$\delta(i_r)=\begin{cases} n_1+n_2, & \text{if } x_{i_r}\in\{y_1,y_2,\dots,y_m\}\\ n_1, & \text{otherwise,}\end{cases}$$

Let $\Delta_{n_1+n_2}(E,\alpha)$ denote the result of the application of Π_1 to the expression

$$\bar{\alpha}(x_{i_1}:=a_1+\delta(i_1),\dots,x_{i_p}:=a_p+\delta(i_p),y_{j_1}:=b_1+n_2,\dots,y_{j_t}:=b_t+n_2,$$
$$z_1:=u_1,\dots,z_s:=u_s)(E_1x_1^+\dots x_k^+\cup E_2y_1^+\dots y_m^+)^*.$$

Let P be an indecomposable canonical program, c_1 stands for the maximal number occurring in P, $c_2=card(X(P))$, $c_0\ge max(c_1,c_2)$, and v is a c_0-representative sample computation of P. The algorithm uses an auxiliary set of variables Z, the marker □ and the markers Z for all $z\in Z$.

Let k be the loop depth of P. The algorithm operates on v k stages. Assume that an expression $v^{(m-1)}$ is constructed up to some stage m and some symbols in $v^{(m-1)}$ are marked by the markers defined above.

Stage m. A finite number of steps is performed at the stage. Assume that $v^{(m-1)}$ has been transformed to $w'w$ up to a step r, where w' is the initial fragment of $w'w$ with the last symbol marked by □ (maybe $w'=\lambda$). For each loop E in $w'w$, let $\sigma(E)$ denote the subword transformed to E in the previous step.

Step r. If $w=\lambda$, then define $v^{(m)}=w'$, put □ just in front of $v^{(m)}$ and go to stage $m+1$. Otherwise, go to Substep 1.

Substep 1. Search for the leftmost subword α in $w'w$, which can be represented as concatenation of the subwords $\beta_i, 1\le i\le p$, and $\gamma_i, 1\le i\le s$, so that after

a) the application of $\Delta_{n_1+n_2}(E,\delta(E))$ for $n_1+n_2\le c_0$ to some loops E in α contained in no other loops,

b) the replacement of variables in $\beta_i, 2\le i\le p$, by variables occurring in β_1, and variables in $\gamma_i, 1\le i\le s$, by variables occurring in γ_1, α is transformed to a c_0-representative 1-value $\tilde{\alpha}$ of some loop

$$(y_1:=a_1,y_2:=a_2,\dots,y_n:=a_n,\dots,y_n:=a_n,$$

(1.7) $\qquad z_1:=b_1,\ldots,z_t:=b_t)(R_1y_1^+\ldots y_n^+\cup R_2z_1^+\ldots z_t^+)^*.$

Assume no $\tilde{\alpha}$ we need is found. Then, if $r=1$, go to Substep 3. If $r>1$, then define $v^{(m)}=w'w$, put □ just in front of $v^{(m)}$ and go to Stage $m+1$.

If $\tilde{\alpha}$ is found, then go to Substep 2.

Substep 2. A loop corresponding to $\tilde{\alpha}$ is to be defined on this substep. In fact, the loop (1.7) is to be synthesized.

First, for every α_1, we can choose maximal sets S_i of numbers that may be values of one and the same variable. Choose a new (not occurring in $w'w$) variable $y\in Z$ for every collection $\bar{S}=\{S_i\}, 1\le i\le m$. Every α_i is a value of either some R_1 (see (1.7)), or some R_2, therefore, the set of all new variables can be divided into the sets $\{y_1,y_2,\ldots,y_n\}$ and $\{z_1,\ldots,z_n\}$; values of R_1 contain values of $y\in\{y_1,\ldots,y_n\}$, and values of R_2 contain values of $\{z_1,\ldots,z_n\}$ (sets $\{y_1,\ldots,y_n\}$ and $\{z_1,\ldots,z_n\}$ can intersect). Replace the subword α in w by the loop (1.7) where $a_1,a_2,\ldots,a_n,b_1,b_2,\ldots,b_t,R_1$ and R_2 are defined as follows.

Assume that β_1 lies to the left from γ_1 (the second case can be handled similarly). Then, if y_1 is a variable corresponding to S_j, a_1 is a number in S_1 (note that all $a\in S_1$ are equal). If $z_1\in\{z_1,\ldots,z_t\}\setminus\{y_1,\ldots,y_n\}$, then b_1 is equal to a number in the corresponding S_j. Replacing all numbers $a\in S_i, i=1,2,\ldots,$ in β_1 by the variables corresponding to $S_i, i=1,2,\ldots,$ we obtain R_1. Similarly, we obtain R_2 from γ_1. If a_1 (or b_1) corresponds to a number marked by $z\in Z$, then a_1 (respectively, b_1) gets the same marker.

Now, for each variable $y\in\{y_1,\ldots,y_n,z_1,\ldots,z_p\}$, let $a(y)$ be the maximal number in α that occurs in some β_i or γ_j in a set $S\in\{S_i\}i=1,2,\ldots$ corresponding to y. If $a(y)$ is not a part of an expression $y:=a(y)$, then by y mark all numbers in w equal to $a(y)$ and occurring to the right from α. Then delete from w all marker-variables equal to variables occurring in $\beta_i, i<p$, and $\gamma_j, j<t$, and replace marker-variables occurring in β_p and γ_t by variables having the same positions in β_1 and γ_1, respectively.

Put the marker □ at the end of the synthesized expression and go to step $r+1$.

Substep 3. All loops are already "folded up". Replace each symbol in $v^{(m)}$ marked by $z\in Z$ to this marker (if the symbol is marked by many markers, then choose any of them). The obtained expression is the program P' we need.

The synthesis method is proved to be correct ([7]). The running time of the synthesis is $O(l^5)$, where l is the length of the input sample ([7]). Of course, the length l can be considerably larger than the length of the target program. However, if the loop depth is bounded, then the length of input samples can be comparable with the length of the target program. Note that translation of iterative programs into a natural programming language is a technical task; it can be done, if iterative programs are interpreted in a certain way.

2. Syntactical Inductive Synthesis of Programs Containing FOR-loops and Interpreted Functions

In this section we consider the case when complexity of loop conditions in target programs is bounded and it is known to a synthesizer. In particular, the case is of interest when loop conditions are elements of the boolean algebra over the set of inequalities $x \le y$ (x,y may be variables over the domain **N**). The syntactical synthesizer, provided the bound on the loop condition complexity, is able to synthesize loops in a traditional WHILE (or FOR)-form. However, syntactical synthesis of WHILE-loops in general case is hard: it needs a huge number of sample computations and is ineffective. So we have to impose constraints upon the class of target programs. These constraints can be of two types: (1) on complexity of loop conditions; (2) on the class of elementary actions occurring in the "bodies" of loops. Thereby, we consider the class of target programs satisfying a strong constraint of the type (1) (only FOR-loops, which are presented as WHILE-loops with conditions $x \le y$) and some weak constraints of the type (2) (see also [10]).

Syntactical inductive synthesis of programs containing only FOR-loops has been investigated ([2,3]) in the case when elementary operations are just addition and subtraction of 1 (or a constant $c \in \mathbf{N}$), and conditional statements are absent. In this section we consider the case when the amount of elementary operations (interpreted functions) in target programs is extended considerably, allowing also conditional statements.

Sample computations of these programs contain fragments much more complicated than arithmetical progressions; the languages developed in [2,3] do not suffice to handle their inductive generalization.

The constraints chosen to define our class seem to be quite natural. However, they do not suffice yet to synthesize target programs effectively. Thereby input sample computations are assumed to be annoted by "loop bounds". We consider the case when these annotations reflect exactly "loop bounds" in an input sample; then the synthesis algorithm can be proved to be correct. Of course, from the user's point of view, it is more natural to provide only approximate "loop bounds": in this case our synthesis method can be transformed using certain heuristics. The loops in programs of the class defined below are synthesized in a traditional WHILE-form, whereas conditional operators are synthesized in a general "neutral" form, usual for syntactical methods.

To begin with, we consider sample computations explaining some popular algorithms.

EXAMPLE 1. A program separating nonnegative and negative numbers in an array. Let *a=a(1),a(2),...,a(7)* be an array. The arrays *b* and *c* are used for nonnegative and negative numbers, respectively. A sample computation, explaining the algorithm's behavoiur, can look as follows:

Input *(7);*

a(1)≥0? yes, then *a(1)→b(1);*

a(2)≥0? yes, then *a(2)→b(2);*

a(3)≥0? *no,* then *a(3)→c(1);*

a(4)≥o? no, then *a(4)→c(2);*

a(5)≥o/ yes, then *a(5)→b(3);*

a(6)≥o? no, then *a(6)→c(3);*

a(7)≥o? yes, then *a(7)→b(4);*

Output *(b,c).*

EXAMPLE 2. An algorithm for computing the sum *S(x)* of the first *x* natural numbers. A sample computation explaining the algorithm's behaviour:

Input *(5);*

0+1⇒1;

1+2⇒3;

3+3⇒6;

6+4⇒10;

10+5⇒15;

Output *(15);*

The above samples are apparently sufficient to explain the behaviour of the corresponding algorithms. On the other hand, they are formal and get a real sense being interpreted in a certain way.

Now we define the class of programs. Let **N** be the set of all natural numbers (including o); A' is an alphabet of auxiliary symbols; X stands for the set of variables; F is the set of the constructions

$$f(x,y_1,y_2,\ldots,y_n)\Rightarrow x;\ x,y_1,y_2,\ldots,y_n\in X, n\geq o;$$

OP contains the following symbols *::=* (assignment), ∪ (union), *(,)* (brackets), ",", ≤, ≥, | (separator), WHILE, DO, Input, Output.

For any string of symbols $X(Q)$ denote the set of variables occurring in Q. The subalphabet

$$A=A'\cup N\cup\{f(m,n_1,\ldots,n_k)\Rightarrow r\,|\,m,n_1,\ldots,n_k,r\in \mathbf{N},\ f(x,y_1,\ldots,y_k)\Rightarrow x\in F, x,y_1,\ldots,y_k\in X,\ k\geq o\}$$

is the alphabet of sample computations. Passing to the target program during the synthesis, the words over A are not changed.

The domain of $x\in X$ is **N**; we assume that some variables $x\in X$ have indices in **N**.

There are two types of actions over variables: assignments and processings. An assignment is a construction $x:=\mu$, where $x\in X, \mu\in X\cup\{0,1\}$. A processing is $f(x,y_1,\ldots,y_n)\Rightarrow x\in F$; we say that the value x is c h a n g e d, and values $y_1,\ldots,y_n$ are u s e d. The subset F_0 of F contains special constructions $x+1\Rightarrow x$ and $x-1\Rightarrow x, x\in X$; for the sake of brevity x^+ and x^- will stand for $x+1\Rightarrow x$ and $x-1\Rightarrow x$, respectively. Let $\bar{F}_0$ denote the set of strings over F_0 containing either x^+ or x^- for $x\in X$.

Now we describe the structure of a program. A program is a string consisting of two nonempty parts. The first one is of the type

$$\text{Input}(z_1,z_2,\ldots,z_e), e\geq 1,$$

where $z_1,z_2,\ldots,z_e$ are variables occurring in the second part; $z_1,z_2,\ldots,z_e$ are called input variables.

The second part can be presented as a sequence

$V_1W_1V_2W_2...V_sW_sV_{s+1}, s\geq 0,$

where $V_1,V_2,...,V_{s+1}$ are strings over $A'\cup X$ (may be empty), and $W_1,W_2,...,W_s$ are loops.

Every loop is a concatenation of two fragments, say R_1 and R_2. R_1 is a sequence of assignments:

$(x_1:=\mu_1, x_2:=\mu_2, ..., x_e:=\mu_e), e\geq 0,$

where $x_1,...,x_e$ are mutually different variables in $X(R_2)$, and $\mu_1,\mu_2,...,\mu_e$ are either numbers $0,1$, or variables occurring in the program before the loop; variables $\mu_1,\mu_2,...,\mu_e$ can occur in R_2 only as right parts of assignments just in front of subloops of R_2.

The fragment R_2 is any of the expressions

$$\begin{aligned} &\text{WHILE}(x\leq y)\text{DO}(T|x^-),\\ (2.1)\quad &\text{WHILE}(x\geq 1)\text{DO}(T|x^-),\\ &\text{WHILE}(x\leq y)\text{DO}(T|x^+),\end{aligned}$$

where $x,y\in X, x\neq y$. T denote a string

$T_1\cup T_2\cup...\cup T_k, k\geq 1,$

where $T_1,T_2,...,T_k$ are substrings

$A_1B_1A_2B_2...A_mB_mA_{m+1}C, m\geq 0;$

here $B_1,B_2,...,B_m$ are loops, the fragments $A_1,...,A_{m+1}$ are (but one, may be) strings over $A'\cup X$, and just one A can be equal to (g) for some $g\in F$; finally, $C\in\bar{F}_0$ (C can be the empty word).

The variable x in (2.1) is called the loop counter. Variables in $A_1,...,A_{m+1}$ are called m a i n and subloops $B_1,...,B_m$ are called i n n e r for the loop in question.

Variables in loops are assumed to satisfy several natural restrictions:

a) the left part of each assignment in (2.1) is either the counter, or a main variable;

b) the value of a variable can be changed in a loop by at most one processing; it means, in particular, that the counter x cannot be changed in T;

c) the variable y in the loop condition $x\leq y$ is not changed in the loop;

d) inner subloops can use main variables of the outer loop only in the right parts of assignments;

e) C can contain only main variables of the loop.

The following explanation can be given to our loop construction. First, some values are assigned to some variables used in the loop. Then, one of the loop statements

for $x:=x0$ down to y do T,

for $x:=x0$ down to 1 do T,

for $x:=x0$ to y do T,

corresponding to *(2.1)* is executed; the counter is assumed to contain $x0$ in the beginning. Suboperator consists of branches $T_1, T_2, \ldots, T_k$; one and only one branch T_i is supposed to be executed on each loop turn.

Clearly, T is generalization of CASE and IF...THEN...ELSE-statements. Propositions and actions over items processed by the program are collected in strings $A_1, \ldots, A_{m+1}$ occurring in branches.

Several natural constraints have to be fulfilled for programs and loops. Some of them hold for all "real" programs containing FOR-loops, but some constraints are necessary for correct synthesis from representative samples.

CONSTRAINT 1. Every non-input variable x can occur in an expression A, provided an assignment $x:=\mu$ in front of A.

CONSTRAINT 2. For every variable x, at most one assignment $x:=\mu$ occurs in the program.

CONSTRAINT 3. (variables separation principle): for every two main variables x and y in an arbitrary loop

WHILE(...)DO($T_1 \cup T_2 \cup \ldots \cup T_k | z^{\times}$),

$(z^{\times} \in \{z^{+}, z^{-}\})$ there is T_i such that either

a) T_i contains $\Rightarrow x$ or $\Rightarrow y$, or

b) $x^{+} \in X(T) \Rightarrow y^{+} \notin X(T)$, and $x^{-} \in X(T) \Rightarrow y^{-} \notin X(T)$.

CONSTRAINT 4. If the loop B=WHILE(S)DO($T|x^{+}$), then x occurs in no loop following B, and it occurs in no expression $y=x, y \leq x$ in T.

CONSTRAINT 5. For every main variable x in a loop B=WHILE(...)DO($T_1 \cup T_2 \cup \ldots \cup T_k | z^{\times}$), if there is an expression $f(x, y_1, \ldots, y_m) \Rightarrow x$ in T_r, then every variable $y_i, 1 \leq i \leq m$, occurs in no $T_j, 1 \leq j \leq k$, in the form y_i^{-} or $\Rightarrow y_i$.

CONSTRAINT 6.For every loop WHILE(S)DO($T_1 \cup \ldots \cup T_k | x^{\times}$), for every replacement of variables, no T_i is an initial fragment of any T_j for $i \neq j$.

Constraint 4 is quite essential: it yields that every program has sample computations, where each loop is executed "sufficiently many" times; the last statement does not hold for many array processing algorithms. Constraints 4 and 5 are implied by the necessity to provide the existence of "representative" samples reflecting the structure of a program. Constraint 5 seems to be quite natural, since different T_i and T_j correspond to different values of the predicate S; on the other hand, this constraint provides a possibility to construct a polynomial-time synthesis algorithm.

Besides the above constraints, programs have to satisfy some simple technical restrictions (we omit them for the sake of brevity).

Let $\mathcal{P}$ denote the set of all programs.

Now we consider two examples of programs $P\in\mathcal{P}$ (brackets **(,)** and symbol **≤** that do not belong to A are bold).

EXAMPLE 3. The program separating nonnegative and negative numbers in an array:

P_1: Input $(u)(x:=1,y:=1,z:=1)$
WHILE$(x\le u)$DO$(a(x)\ge 0?$ yes; then $a(x)\to b(y)y^+$;
$\cup a(x)\ge o?$ no; then $a(x)\to c(z)z^+|x^+)$
Output (b,c).

EXAMPLE 4. The program computing $S(x)$:

P_2: Input $(x)(z:=1,y:=0)$WHILE$(z\le x)$DO$((y+z\Rightarrow y);|z^+)$ Output (y).

Now we define (formal) sample computations of programs $P\in\mathcal{P}$.

First, it is necessary to associate a computable function $I_f:\mathbf{N}^n\to\mathbf{N}$ with every symbol f of an n-ary function. The following *m o n o t o n i c i t y* condition is assumed to hold for the correspondence I_f: if for any $(a_1,a_2,\dots,a_n)$ and $(b_1,b_2,\dots,b_n)a_i\le b_i, 1\le i\le n$, then $I_f(a_1,a_2,\dots,a_n)\le I_f(b_1,b_2,\dots,b_n)$.

To define an *u n f o l d m e n t* of $P\in\mathcal{P}$, we apply the following procedure to P. Every loop B=WHILE(S)do$(T_1\cup\dots\cup T_k|x^\times)$ (for instance, let $x^\times$ be x^-) is to be replaced by any of expressions

$$\bar{B}=\{S\}T_{i_1}x^-\{S\}T_{i_2}x^-\dots\{S\}T_{i_m}x^-\{\underline{S}\}, m\ge 1,$$

where $m\in\mathbf{N}, T_{i_1},\dots,T_{i_m}\in\{T_1,T_2,\dots,T_k\}$ (the last $\{S\}$ is underlined), $\{,\}\notin A$, and all separators | are deleted; $\bar{B}$ is called an unfoldment of B. The whole expression we have obtained is said to be an unfoldment of P. For example, an unfoldment of the above example P_2 may be

$\bar{P}_2$: Input $(x),(z:=1,y:=0)\{z\le x\}(y+z\Rightarrow y);z^+$
$\{z\le x\}(y+z\Rightarrow y);z^+\{z\le x\}(y+z\Rightarrow y);z^+\{z\le x\}$

Output (y).

Now, for each $z \in X(\bar{P})$, enumerate all occurrences of z in P (from left to right): $z_{(1)}, z_{(2)}, \ldots$ (including z^+ and z^-).

Then, for every $z \in X(\bar{P})$, replace $z_{(1)}$ by some $V(z_{(1)}) \in \mathbf{N}$ and, for each $x \in X(\bar{P})$, define the value $V(\nu_i)$ of every $\nu_i \in \{x_{(i)}, x^+_{(i)}, x^-_{(i)}\}$ as follows:

(a) if $\nu_{(i)}$ is $x_{(i)}$ in an assignment $x_{(i)} := \mu$ then $V(\nu_{(i)}) = V(\mu)$;

(b) if $\nu_{(i)}$ is $x_{(i)}$ in an expression $f(x_{(i-1)}, y_1, \ldots, y_n) \Rightarrow x_{(i)}$ then $V(x_{(i)})$ is

$$f(V(x_{(i-1)}), V(y_1), \ldots, V(y_n));$$

(c) in other cases,

$$V(x_{(i)}) = V(\nu_{(i-1)}),$$
$$V(x^+_{(i)}) = V(\nu_{(i-1)}) + 1,$$
$$V(x^-_{(i)}) = V(\nu_{(i-1)}) - 1.$$

Now delete all assignments $c := c (c \in \mathbf{N})$. The obtained expression is said to be the s t r o n g v a l u e of the unfoldment $\bar{P}$; let $W(\bar{P})$ denote the strong value of $\bar{P}$.

Further the strong value $W(\bar{P})$ is called c o r r e c t iff:

(I) all inequalities in $W(P)$ that are not underlined are fulfilled;

(II) no underlined inequality holds;

(III) $W(\bar{P})$ contains no negative integer.

Now delete all strings in brackets $\{,\}$ (including brackets themselves), all brackets $(,) \in OP$ and values of $x^+, x^-, x \in X$, from $W(\bar{P})$. The expression we have obtained is called v a l u e or s a m p l e c o m p u t a t i o n of the program P. Let $V(P)$ denote the set of all values of P.

The reader can easily check that samples in Examples 1 and 2 are values of the above programs P_1 and P_2 respectively.

Programs P_1 and P_2 are called equivalent iff $V(P_1) = V(P_2)$.

If sample computations contain no additional information, then any effective synthesis algorithm is hardly possible. Hence, we consider the case when sample computations are "annotated" by "loop boundaries".

Formally one can obtain an annotated sample computation enclosing the unfoldment of each loop into some special brackets (for example, [,]). "Loop boundaries" of this kind facilitate the synthesis, however, some serious problems remain.

Besides, to make an effective synthesis possible, sample computations have to be quite "representative" reflecting the program's structure.

Informally, a sample computation $v=v(P)$ of $P\in\mathcal{P}$ is r e p r e s e n t a t i v e if
(1) the unfoldment of every loop WHILE(S)DO$(T_1\cup\ldots\cup T_k|x^{\times})$ contains the subword $\{S\}T_r x^{\times}\{S\}T_r$ for every $r\in\{1,\ldots,k\}$;
(2) for each variable $x,y\in X(P)$ and every initial fragment w of v, if, computing w, no loop WHILE$(S)(\ldots)$ with $S\in\{x\geq 1, y\geq 1\}$ together with loops having loop conditions $x\leq z_1, z_1\leq z_2,\ldots,z_p\leq y$ has been unfolded, then the last values of x and y in w are different (formal definition needs some technical details, omitted for the sake of brevity).

Representative samples actually correspond to any choice of sufficiently large and very different initial values of input variables. It facilitates the choice of representative samples for the user.

To construct the synthesis algorithm we need an auxiliary useful notion of a p a r t i a l value (or partial sample).

Let v denote any annotated sample of $P\in P$. Apply to loops in v the following "folding-up" procedure. Replace some fragments in annotating brackets, having no imbedded fragment of the same type, by corresponding loops.

If, for some of these loops, an assignment $x:=\mu$ (where y is the main variable in the loop) stands in front of it in the program, insert the assignment $y:=c$ at the corresponding place in v; here, if $\mu\in\mathbf{N}$, then $c=\mu$, if $\mu=x\in X(P)$, then c is the value of the rightmost $v\in\{x,x^{+},x^{-}\}$ in front of $y:=x$ in the unfoldment of P used to compute v. We let $v_{(1)}$ to denote the obtained expression. One can apply the same procedure to $v_{(1)}$ getting $v_{(2)}$, etc. All expressions obtained in this way are called partial values of P. If m is the loop depth of P and all loops in v are folded up to the loop depth m-k, then the corresponding partial value is said to be a k-value of the program. $1,2,\ldots$-values can be easily defined for k-values: they are $k+1,k+2,\ldots$-values of P.

The synthesis algorithm presented below copies, in fact, the process of partial value definition; just the difference is that in advance the synthesis algorithm has no information concerning the target program structure, except loop boundaries.

Our synthesis algorithm is based on the detection of some regularities in samples (and also in partial values as intermediate results of the synthesis). We can say that the notion of a r e g u l a r fragment is essential for our method. For the sake of simplicity we explain this notion informally. Let R be a 1-value of some program (or partial value) P. Then any regular fragment $\alpha=\alpha_1\alpha_2\ldots\alpha_m$ corresponds to an arbitrary loop

$$A=\text{WHILE}(S)\text{DO}(T_1\cup T_2\cup\ldots\cup T_s\,|\,x^{\times})$$

in P, and every α_j is, in fact, a 1-value of some T_j.

Our goal now is to present the main ideas of the synthesis algorithm 𝔄. From this point of view it is convenient to consider the synthesis process for the target program

P: Input $(u,z,y,t)(x:=0)$WHILE$(x\le u)$
DO$(x;y;(w:=y,s:=0)$
WHILE$(w\ge 1)$DO$((s+t\Rightarrow s);|w^-)y^+\cup x;$
$z;x;z^+|x^+)$
Output(s)

using the input sample

$v=[0;4;[0+11\Rightarrow 11;11+11\Rightarrow 22;22+11\Rightarrow 33;$
$33+11\Rightarrow 44;]$
$1;5;[0+11\Rightarrow 11;11+11\Rightarrow 22;22+11\Rightarrow 33;$
$33+11\Rightarrow 44;44+11\Rightarrow 55;]$
$2;17;2;3;18;3;$
$[4;6;[0+11\Rightarrow 11;11+11\Rightarrow 22;22+11\Rightarrow 33;$
$33+11\Rightarrow 44;44+11\Rightarrow 55;55+11\Rightarrow 66;]$
$5;19;5;6;20;6;7;21;8;22;8;]$.

The algorithm 𝔄 is supposed to use also initial values of the input variables $v(u)=8, v(z)=17, v(y)=4, v(t)=11$ and a sufficiently large collection Z of variables.

The leftmost expression in annotating brackets having no inner expression of this kind has to be treated and transformed on any stage of the synthesis in order to get a partial value of a program $P'\in\mathcal{P}$. For functions $I_f(y,x_1,\ldots,x_t)\to y$, the algorithm 𝔄 restores the variables $y,x_1,\ldots,x_t$ taking into account only identical positions of their values in the values of identical expressions. For variables x, changing in loops by operators x^+ and x^-, the synthesizer identifies corresponding fragments of arithmetical progressions in an input sample.

So let us consider our sample v. The word

$$\alpha=[0+11\Rightarrow 11;11+11\Rightarrow 22;22+11\Rightarrow 33;33+11\Rightarrow 44;]$$

is to be handled at the first stage. First, α has to be divided (or transformed) to subwords $\alpha_1,\alpha_2...,\alpha_m$ so that $\alpha_1\alpha_2...\alpha_m$ should become a regular fragment. The corresponding procedure searches for the shortest initial subword γ such that, for some subword $\gamma_1\gamma_2$ of α, words γ,γ_1,γ_2 are 1-values of the same expression T (γ has to contain the whole expression $f(a_1,a_2,...,a_p)\Rightarrow a$, if any; it is convenient to remind here that $a+b\Rightarrow c$ is a form of $+(a,b)\Rightarrow c$). In our case, $\gamma(=\alpha)$ is $0+11\Rightarrow 11$, and

$$\gamma_1\gamma_2=0+11\Rightarrow 11;11+11\Rightarrow 22;$$

the expression $s+11\Rightarrow s;$ can be chosen as T (the collection of necessary variables is to be chosen minimal). Further, $\mathfrak{A}$ searches for the shortest subword after $0+11\Rightarrow 11;$ that is a 1-value of the same T - it will be $\alpha_2=11+11\Rightarrow 22;$. Similarly $\mathfrak{A}$ comes across $\alpha_3=22+11\Rightarrow 33;$ and $\alpha_4=33+11\Rightarrow 44;$.

Then $\mathfrak{A}$ replaces $\alpha_1\alpha_2\alpha_3\alpha_4$ by a loop. For our $\alpha_1\alpha_2\alpha_3\alpha_4$, the corresponding loop

$$(w:=u,s:=0)\text{WHILE}(w\geq 1)\text{DO}(s+11\Rightarrow s;|w\bar{1})$$

is obtained as follows. As for $T=s+11\Rightarrow s;$, it is actually constructed. The initial value 0 is assigned to the variable s_1 introduced at this step. Values of the loop counter (a new variable $w\in Z$) do not occur in α - an assignment $w:=4$ (4 is the maximal value of a possible counter) is to be inserted in front of the loop in this case, and the loop condition has to be $w\geq 1$.

Similarly, the expressions

$$(w:=5,s:=0)\text{WHILE}(w\geq 1)\text{DO}(s+11\Rightarrow s;|w^-)$$
$$(w:=6,s:=0)\text{WHILE}(w\geq 1)\text{DO}(s+11\Rightarrow s;|w^-)$$

are synthesized. Now the algorithm $\mathfrak{A}$ handles the leftmost expression in annotating brackets on the next level (taking into account the expressions synthesized at the previous stages); denote it again by α. Again $\mathfrak{A}$ searches for the shortest initial subword γ such that, for some subword $\gamma_1\gamma_2$ of α, γ,γ_1,γ_2 are 1-value of the same expression, say, T_1. Given our α, $\mathfrak{A}$ comes across

$$\gamma(=\alpha_1):0;4;(w:=4,s:=0)\text{WHILE}(W\geq 1)\text{DO}(s+11\Rightarrow s;|w^-),$$

taking

$$x;y;(w:=4,s:=0)\text{WHILE}(w\geq 1)\text{DO}(s+11\Rightarrow s;|w^-)x^+y^+$$

for T_1 (searching for γ,γ_1 and γ_2 is facilitated by part *(5)* of the program definition). Then $\mathfrak{A}$ tries to find the next 1-value of

T_1 just after α_1; it comes across

$$\alpha_2=1;5;(w:=5,s:=0)\text{WHILE}(w\geq 1)\text{DO}(s+11\Rightarrow s;|w^-).$$

Now $\mathfrak{A}$ again tries to find a 1-value of T_1 just after α_2. However, it fails, and $\mathfrak{A}$ comes across (the shortest) subword $\alpha_3=2;17;2;$ that is a 1-value of the different expression $T_2=x;z;x;z^+x^+$ ($\mathfrak{A}$ is able to identify the variable in T_1 because their values are very close). Further, $\mathfrak{A}$ finds $\alpha_3=3;18;3;$,

$$\alpha_4=4;6;(w:=6,s:=0)\text{WHILE}(w\geq 1)\text{DO}(s+11\Rightarrow s;|w^-),$$

$\alpha_5=5;19;5;$ that are 1-values of the above expressions T_1,T_2. Then $\mathfrak{A}$ concludes that only x can be the counter in the loop to be synthesized; x is "removed" from T_1 and T_2. The inequality $x\leq 8$ is chosen for the loop condition, since 8 is the last value of the counter in α. The last step of the synthesis is to replace values of the input variables by these variables

Formal definition of the above synthesis algorithm can be given, and its correctness can be proved formally.

The algorithm is polynomial-time, if the loop depth of the target program is bounded. Of course, arbitrary sample computations can be very long, since every loop has to be unfolded quite many times to make the sample representative. However, numerous examples convince us that the synthesis from "natural" short sample computations is correct almost always.

3. Inductive Synthesis from Incomplete Sample Computations

To begin with, we consider some incomplete sample computations actually fully describing the behaviour of some well-known algorithms. Natural numbers in the samples that are variable values annotated by the corresponding variables (for example, $5[=x]$, $7[=y]$). Annotations of this kind are quite natural: for example, they play, in fact, the role of moving markers used to explain quick-sort and other popular algorithms in [8] (see [11, 12]).

EXAMPLE 1. Gauss matrix diagonalization algorithm (the main part of the corresponding algorithm solving systems of linear equations). The matrix consists of the elements $a(i,j),1\leq i\leq m,1\leq j\leq n$. The following sample seems to explain fully the target algorithm's behaviour:

Input: array $a(i,j), 1 \le i \le 4[=m],$

$1 \le j \le 5[=n];$

$i:=2, j:=1[=i-1];$

$$a(2[=i],1[=j]):=\frac{a(2[=i],1[=j])}{a(2[=i],1[=j-1])} * a(1=[=i-1],1[=i-1])-a(1[=i-1],1[=j]);$$

$$a(2,2):=\frac{a(2,2)}{a(2,1)} * a(1,1)-a(1,2);$$

$$a(2,3):=\frac{a(2,3)}{a(2,1)} * a(1,1)-a(1,3);$$

$$a(2,4):=\frac{a(2,4)}{a(2,1)} * a(1,1)-a(1,4);$$

$$a(2,5[=n]):=\frac{a(2,5[=n])}{a(2,1)} * a(1,1)-a(1,5[=n]);$$

$i:=3, j:=2[=i-1]; P$

If $i=4[=m]$; then STOP.

The symbol P stands here (and in the sample computations below) for "repeat the above actions for new values of the variables".

EXAMPLE 2. Sorting by search for the maximal element. The array $K(1),K(2),...,K(m)$ is to be sorted and located in the array $M(1),M(2),...,M(m)$. The following sample describes the target algorithm's behaviour:

Input: array $K(1),K(2),...,K(12[m])$;

$y:=12[=m]; x:=1;$

$K(1[=x]) \le K(2[=x+1])?$; suppose yes;

$K(2[=x]) \le K(3[=x+1])?$: suppose yes;

$K(3[=x]) \le K(4[=x+1])?$; suppose yes;

$K(4[=x]) \le K(5[=x+1])?$: suppose no;

then $K(4[=x]) \Leftrightarrow K(5[=x])$;

$K(5[=x]) \le K(6[=x+1])?$; suppose yes;

$K(6[=x]) \le K(7[=x+1])?$; suppose yes;

$K(7[=x]) \le K(8[=x+1])?$; suppose no;

then $K(7[=x]) \Leftrightarrow K(8[=x+1])$;

$K(8[=x]) \le K(9[=x+1])?$; suppose yes;

$K(9[=x]) \le K(10[x+1])?$; suppose yes;

K(10[=x])≤K(11[=x+1])?; suppose yes;
K(11[=x])≤K(12[=x+1=y])?; suppose no;
then *K(11[=x])⇔K(12[=x+1=y])*;
M(12[=y])⇐K(12[=y]);
y:=11;x:=1;P;
If *y=1*, then *M(1)⇐K(1)*; STOP.

EXAMPLE 3. Quick-sort. The reader can easily check that the following sample presents, in fact, a linear form of the quick-sort explanation given in [8] (using markers $\boxed{i}$ and $\boxed{j}$):

Input: array *K(1),K(2),...,K(16=[m])*;
x_0*:=1;*y_0*:=16[=m];x:=1[=*x_0*];y:=16[=*y_0*]*;
K(1[=x])≤K(16[=y])?; suppose yes;
K(1[=x])≤K(15[=y])?; suppose yes;
K(1[=x])≤K(14[=y])?; suppose yes;
K(1[=x])≤K(13[=y])?; suppose yes;
K(1[=x])≤K(12[=y])?; suppose no;
then *K(1[=x])⇔K(12[=y])*;
K(2[=x])≤K(12[=y])?; suppose yes;
K(3[=x])≤K(12[=y])?; suppose no;
then *K(3[=x])⇔K(12[=y])*;
K(3[=x])≤K(11[=y])?; suppose yes;
K(3[=x])≤K(10[=y])?; suppose yes;
K(3[=x])≤K(9[=y])?; suppose yes;
K(3[=x])≤K(8[=y])?; suppose no;
then *K(3[=x])⇔K(8[=y])*;
K(4[=x])≤K(8[=y])?; suppose yes;
K(5[=x])≤K(8[=y])?; suppose yes;
K(6[=x])≤K(8[=y])?; suppose yes;
K(7[=x])≤K(8[=y=x+1])?; suppose no;
K(7[=x])⇔K(8[=y=x+1]);
stack:=(*x+1,*y_0*);*y_0*:=x-1;x:=*x_0*);y:=*y_0*);*
P; If x_0=y_0 then
WHILE(¬Emp(stack))**DO**((x_0,y_0):=stack);

here stack is the special variable and Emp(stack) checks whether the stack is empty.

The quick-sort fully uses the divide-and-conquer mechanism. No inductive synthesis model developed up to now (including models in Sections 2 and 3) covers algorithms of this kind.

NOTE. We present quick-sort in a simplified form: the

boundaries of the "right" array are pushed into stack instead of the "smaller" ones. It enables us to stress the recursive nature of the algorithm, getting rid of the calculation of complex predicates connected with algebraic operations over variables.

In this section we develop a programming language oriented on inductive formalization of sample computations containing the above symbol P (together with the corresponding semantics). The synthesis method is mainly syntactical.

To define the language we use an alphabet $A', A=A' \cup \mathbf{N}$, a finite set of variables $X (A \cap X = \emptyset)$, the special variable stack$\notin X$ and the set OP containing symbols $+, -, (,), *$(Cleene star)$, \pm, =$, WHILE, DO, $\boxed{\neq}$ (predicate); $\cup$(union) P(special symbol); $OP \cap (A \cup X) = \emptyset$.

As usual, the alphabet A is of special importance: words over A are sample computations.

$\mathbf{N}$ is the domain of variables $x \in X$. Let $X(Q)$ denote for any word Q the set of variables occurring in Q. The atoms x^+ and x^- stand for assignments $x:=x+1$ and $x:=x\dot{-}1 (x \in X)$, respectively.

Every program is a string $A_1 B A_2$, where A_1 and A_2 are words over the alphabet A, and B is an expression

(3.1) C_1WHILE$(x \boxed{\neq} \mu)$DO$(C_2$WHILE$(y \boxed{\neq} \nu)$ DO$(Q) Q_1 D)$,

where

(1) $x, y \in X(QQ_1D), \mu, \nu \in \mathbf{N} \cup X$;

(2) if $\mu \in X$ then $\mu \in X(Q_1 D)$,
if $\nu \in X$ then $\nu \in X(Q)$,

(3) C_1 contains an assignment
$x:=a, a \in \mathbf{N} \cup X \cup \{$stack$\}$,
and if $\mu \in X$ then C_1 contains an assignment
$\mu:=b, b \in \mathbf{N} \cup X \cup \{$stack$\}$,

(4) C_2 contains an assignment
$y:=a, a \in \mathbf{N} \cup X \cup \{$stack$\}$,
and if $\nu \in X$ then C_2 contains an assignment $\nu:=b$,
$b \in \mathbf{N} \cup X \cup \{$stack$\}$,

(5) Q_1 is a word over $A \cup X$,
$D \in \{\lambda, x^+, x^-, \mu^+, \mu^-, x^+\mu^-, x^-\mu^+\}$,

(6) Q is defined as follows: let $\tilde{X}$ be the set of atoms $z, z+c, z-c$ for $z \in X, c \in \mathbf{N}$. then Q is either an expression

(3.2) $T_1 M_1 \cup T_2 M_2 \cup \ldots \cup T_m M_m$,

or

(3.3) $R_0(T_1M_1)^*R_1K_1(T_2M_2)^*R_2K_2...(T_mM_M)^*R_mK_m$,

where

(a) $T_i, 1\le i\le m$, and $R_i, 0\le i\le m$, are strings over the alphabet $A\cup\tilde{X};\exists i(R_i\ne\lambda)$;

(b) $M_i, 1\le i\le m, K_i, 1\le i\le m$, are strings $x_1^{a_1}\ x_2^{a_2}...x_p^{a_p}$, where all $x_i, 1\le i\le p$, are mutually different, and $a_1,...,a_m\in\{+,-\}; x\in\{x_1,...,x_p\}, y\in\{x_1,...,x_p\}$ for at least one M_i or K_i;

(c) if $z^+\in M_1M_2...M_mK_1K_2...K_m$ then $z^-\notin M_1M_2...M_mK_1K_2...K_m$ and vice versa; if $\nu\in\{x_1,x_2,...,x_p\}$ for some M_i or K_i then $y^+\in M_1...M_mK_1...K_m \Leftrightarrow \nu^-\in M_1...M_mK_1...K_m$ and vice versa.

(7) A_2 contains a subword $x=c$ for $c\in N\cup X\setminus\{x\}$.

Expressions WHILE($z\boxed{\ne}\mu$)DO(Q) occurring in programs are called s p e c i f i e d l o o p s ; consequently, expressions $(M)^*$ are called u n s p e c i f i e d l o o p s.

In this section we consider only programs of the loop depth 2 (see (3.1)). Moreover, the same ideas can be applied to algorithms of a higher loop depth.

Predicates $x\boxed{\ne}\mu$ occurring in our programs are interpreted; the symbol $\boxed{\ne}$ stands for $\ne$ to separate it from other predicate symbols that can occur in a program (for example, $\ne,\le$,EMP). Like in dots expressions ([2]), the last ones are not interpreted; they are treated by a synthesizer purely syntactically.

Predicates in unspecified loops are not isolated; it is stipulated by the impossibility to synthesize them directly,given purely syntactical information. The same reason implies the use of the union $\cup$ instead of the usual IF...THEN...ELSE (or case).

Let $\mathscr{P}$ denote the class of all programs.

To illustrate the definition of programs we construct programs for the Gauss algorithm, sorting by search for the maximal element and Quick-sort.

P_1: Input: array $a(i,j), 1\le i\le m, 1\le j\le n$;

$i:=2$

WHILE($i\boxed{\ne}m$)DO(($j:=i-1$)WHILE($j\boxed{\ne}n$)DO

$(a(i,j):=\dfrac{a(i,j)}{a(i,i-1)} * a(i-1,i-1)-a(i-1,j)j^+)i^+)$

```
        If i=m then STOP.
P2:     Input: array K(1),K(2),...,K(m),
              y:=m
        WHILE(y[≠]1)DO(x:=1)WHILE(x[≠]y)DO(
        (K(x)≤K(x+1)?; suppose no;
        K(x)⇔K(x+1)x⁺∪
        K(x)≤K(x+1)? suppose yes; x⁺)
        M(y)⇐K(y);y⁻)
        If y=1 then M(1)⇐K(1);STOP
P3:     Input: array K(1),K(2),...,K(m);
              x0:=1;y0:=m;
        stack:=(x0,y0)WHILE(¬Emp(stack))
        DO((x0,y0):=stack);
        WHILE(x0[≠]y0)DO((x:=x0,y:=y0)
        WHILE(x[≠]y)DO((K(x)≤K(y)?; suppose yes; y⁻)*
        K(x)≤K(y)?; suppose no; K(x)⇔K(y);x⁺
        (K(x)≤K(y)?; suppose yes; x⁺)*
        K(x)≤K(y)?; suppose no; K(x)⇔K(y);y⁻)
        stack:=(x+1,y0);y0:=x-1;))
```

Bold symbols (for example, **WHILE**, **DO**, **(**,**)**) belong to A and have nothing to do with the same symbols in OP. Moreover, whenever a program is interpreted, the same symbols in A and OP are supposed to be treated equally.

Divide-and-conquer algorithm's behaviour usually is explained (informally) up to the point where the main problem is divided into subproblems. Taking this into account, we define below the notion of program value - i n c o m p l e t e sample computation.

Let $P\in\mathscr{P}$. Unfold R as follows. First, replace the outer loop WHILE(α)DO(T) by the expression TP, where $P\notin A\cup X\cup OP$ is the special symbol. Further, let C_2 be defined according to (3.1). Replace $T=C_2$WHILE(β)DO(Q) by some $C_2(Q)^n, n\in\mathbf{N}$, and insert C_2 in front of P. Now replace each expression $(S)^*$ by some $(S)^m, m\in\mathbf{N}$, and then replace each expression $U_1\cup U_2\cup\ldots\cup U_r$ by any U_1.
Finally, insert the word $x\boxed{\neq}y$ between each two subsequent symbols $\}_1, \}_2\in\{x^+, x^-, y^+, y^-, \}$.

The obtained expression $\bar{P}$ is said to be a (f u l l) u n f o l d m e n t of P.

For example, given the above program P_3, one can get an

unfoldment

```
P̄3:     Input: array K(1),K(2),...,K(m);
                    x0:=1;y0:=m;
        stack:=(x0,y0)WHILE(¬Emp(stack))DO(
              (x0,y0):=stack;
              x:=x0;y:=y0;
        K(x)≤K(y)?; suppose yes; y^-  x[≠]y
        K(x)≤K(y)?; suppose yes; y^-  x[≠]y
        K(x)≤K(y)?; suppose yes; y^-  x[≠]y
        K(x)≤K(y)?; suppose yes; y^-  x[≠]y
        K(x)≤K(y)?; suppose no;
            K(x)⇔K(y); x^+  x[≠]y
        K(x)≤K(y)?; suppose yes; x^+  x[≠]y
        K(x)≤K(y)?; suppose no;
            K(x)⇔K(y); y^-  x[≠]y
        K(x)≤K(y)?; suppose yes; y^-  x[≠]y
        K(x)≤K(y)?; suppose yes; y^-  x[≠]y
        K(x)≤K(y)?; suppose yes; y^-  x[≠]y
        K(x)≤K(y)?; suppose no;
            K(x)⇔K(y); x^+  x[≠]y
        K(x)≤K(y)?; suppose yes; x^+  x[≠]y
        K(x)≤K(y)?; suppose yes; x^+  x[≠]y
        K(x)≤K(y)?; suppose yes; x^+  x[≠]y
        K(x)≤K(y)?; suppose no;
            K(x)⇔K(y) y^-  x[≠]y
        stack:=(x+1,y0);y0:=x-1;x:=x0;y:=y0;P)
```

Any expression, obtained from a full unfoldment deleting the fragment between any $x \boxed{\neq} y$ and the last $x \boxed{\neq} y$ (including the last $x \boxed{\neq} y$) is called an unfoldment of P, too. Thus,

```
P̄3:     Input: array K(1),K(2),...,K(m);
                    x0:=1;y0:=m;
        stack:=(x0,y0)WHILE(¬Emp(stack))DO(
              (x0,y0):=stack
              x:=x0;y:=y0;
        K(x)≤K(y)?; suppose yes; y^-  x[≠]y
        K(x)≤K(y)?; suppose yes; y^-  x[≠]y

        K(x)≤K(y)?; suppose yes; y^-  x[≠]y
        stack:=(x+1;y0);y0:=x-1;x:=x0;y:=y0;P)
```

is an unfoldment of P_3.

To define a value of the program, enumerate all occurrences of every variable in $\bar{P}$ from left to right, except stack and occurrences like $x:=$ and $y=\mu$. Thus, for $\bar{P}_3$, one obtains

Input: array $K(1),K(2),...,K(m^{(1)})$;

$x_0:=1;y_0:=m^{(2)}$;

stack$:=(x_0^{(1)},y_0^{(1)})$WHILE(¬Emp(stack)DO(

(x_0,y_0):=stack

$x:=x_0^{(2)};y:=y_0^{(2)}$;

$K(x^{(1)})\leq K(y^{(1)})$?; suppose yes; $y^{(2)-}$ $x^{(2)}\boxed{\neq}y^{(3)}$

$K(x^{(3)})\leq K(y^{(4)})$?; suppose yes; $y^{(5)-}$ $x^{(4)}\boxed{\neq}y^{(6)}$

$K(x^{(5)})\leq K(y^{(7)})$?; suppose yes; $y^{(8)-}$ $x^{(6)}\boxed{\neq}y^{(6)}$

$K(x^{(7)})\leq K(y^{(10)})$?; suppose yes; $y^{(11)-}$ $x^{(8)}\boxed{\neq}y^{(12)}$

$K(x^{(9)})\leq K(y^{(13)})$?; suppose no;

$K(x^{(10)})\leq K(y^{(14)});x^{(11)+}$ $x^{(12)}\boxed{\neq}y^{(15)}$,

etc.

Now we set $v(c)=c$ for all $c\in$**N** and define the value $v(t^{(i)})$ for the i-th occurrence of every variable $t\in X$ as follows:

1. $i=1$

If there is an assignment $t:=\mu$ to the left from $t^{(1)}$ in $\bar{P}$, then $v(t^{(1)})=v(\mu)$, otherwise $v(t^{(1)})=c$ for some $c\in$**N**.

2. $i>1$

$v(t^{(i)})=v(t^{(i-1)})$,

$v(t^{(i)+})=v(t^{(i-1)})+1$;

$v(t^{(i)-})=v(t^{(i-1)})-1$.

Execute all additions $a+b$ and subtractions $a-b$. For our example $\bar{P}_3$ one obtains

Input: array $K(1),K(2),...,K(16)$

$x_0:=1;y_0:=16$;

stack$:=(1,16)$WHILE(¬Emp(stack))DO(

(x_0,y_0):=stack;

$x:=1;y:=16$;

$K(1)\leq K(16)$?; suppose yes; 15 $1\boxed{\neq}15$

$K(1)\leq K(15)$?; suppose yes; 14 $1\boxed{\neq}14$

$K(1)\leq K(14)$?; suppose yes; 13 $1\boxed{\neq}13$

$K(1)\leq K(13)$?; suppose yes; 12 $1\boxed{\neq}12$

$K(1)\leq K(12)$?; suppose no;

$K(1)\Leftrightarrow K(12)$; 2 $2\boxed{\neq}12$,

etc.

Now let us interpret $\neq$ in $\boxed{\neq}$ as standard relation on N×N. If all unequalities $a \neq b$ hold, except just the last one, then delete all these unequalities and the values of z^+, z^- for $z \in X$ from the given expression. The expression we have obtained is called a value or an (incomplete) sample computation of the program P. Thus, for P_3, given the unfoldment $\bar{P}_3$, we obtain the incomplete sample

```
          Input: array K(1),...,K(16),
                        x0:=1;y0:=16;
                 stack:=(1,16)WHILE(¬Emp(stack))DO(
                        (x0,y0):=stack;
                        x:=1;y:=16;
         K(1)≤K(16)?; suppose yes;
         K(1)≤K(15)?; suppose yes;
         K(1)≤K(14)?; suppose yes;
         K(1)≤K(13)?; suppose yes;
         K(1)≤K(12)?; suppose no;
             K(1)⇔K(12);
         K(2)≤K(12)?; suppose yes;
         K(3)≤K(12)?; suppose no;
             K(3)⇔K(12);
         K(3)≤K(11)?; suppose yes;
         K(3)≤K(10)?; suppose yes;
         K(3)≤K(9)?; suppose yes;
         K(3)≤K(8)?; suppose no;
             K(3)⇔K(8);
         K(4)≤K(8)?; suppose yes;
         K(5)≤K(8)?; suppose yes;
         K(6)≤K(8)?; suppose yes;
         K(7)≤K(8)?; suppose no;
             K(7)⇔K(8)
         stack:=(8,16);y0:=6;x:=1;y:=6;P).
```

In turn, Examples 1 and 2 are sample computations of the programs P_1 and P_2 respectively. Example 3 is a sample computation of a slightly different version of P_3.

Note that not every unfoldment $\bar{P}$ specifies the value of P. The value $v(\bar{P})$ is defined iff all unequalities $a \boxed{\neq} b$, except the last one, are fulfilled.

Unfortunately, given an arbitrary incomplete sample, no

syntactic synthesizer is able to restore exactly all variables and necessary connections between them. Therefore, there is a reason to annotate input samples in some way. Annotations in our model are expressions $[=x-c]$, $[x+c]$, where $x\in X, c\in \mathbf{N}$, and $[,]\in A\cup OP\cup X$. Every annotation $[=x\pm c]$ is associated with a value of the expression $x\pm c$. Besides, if $x\boxed{\neq}y$ is a loop condition in the program and values of the variable x in the fragment, obtained from the l a s t expression Q in the unfoldment $C_2(Q)^n$ of $T=C_2\mathrm{WHILE}(\beta)\mathrm{DO}(Q)$, are equal to values of y (or $y\pm 1$), then these values of x are additionally annotated by $[=y]$ ($[=y\pm 1]$, respectively). If Q does not contain unspecified loops and symbols $\cup$, then only the initial fragment corresponding to the first Q in the unfoldment suffices to be annotated. On the contrary, if Q in T is of the type (3.3), then all values of the variables must be annotated. Finally, all values of the variables not occurring in $(Q)^n$ are to be annotated anyway.

The reader can easily ascertain that numbers in Examples 1-3 are annotated in accordance with the above requirements.

To yield successful synthesis, programs and sample computations have to satisfy some natural constraints.

To formulate necessary constraints we introduce some auxiliary notions.

Words $\alpha=a_1a_2\ldots a_k$ and $\beta=b_1b_2\ldots b_m$ are said to be e s s e n t i a l l y d i f f e r e n t iff $a_i\neq b_i$ for some $i\leq\min(k,m)$. Let the word Q in $P\in\mathscr{P}$ be of the type $R_0(T_1M_1)^*R_1K_1(T_2M_2)^*R_2K_2\ldots(T_mM_m)^*R_mK_m$.

We define three transformations over Q:

G1. Let $\alpha R_{i-1}=R'_{i-1}\alpha, T_i=T'_i\alpha$ for some words α, R'_{i-1}, T'_i and $i\in\{1,\ldots,m\}$. Then, to obtain $G_1(Q)$, replace $R_{i-1}K_{i-1}(T_iM_i)^*$ in Q by $R'_{i-1}K_{i-1}(\alpha T'_iM_i)^*\alpha$.

G2. Let $R_{i-1}=R'_{i-1}T_i$ for some R'_{i-1} and $i\in\{1,\ldots,m\}$. Then, to obtain $G_2(Q)$, replace R_{i-1} in Q by R'_{i-1}.

G3. If $Q=(R)^k$ for some subword R and $k>1$, then $G_3(Q)=R$.

A program P is called c a n o n i c a l iff no G_1, G_2, G_3 is applicable to it (more precisely, to Q in P). In fact, almost all "natural" algorithms are canonical or can be transformed easily to the equivalent canonical form. Below we deal with the synthesis of canonical programs satisfying the following condition:

(*) all words T_i and $R_j, 1 \le i,j \le m$, in Q are mutually essentially different.

The constraint (*) seems to be quite natural, since different T_i and R_i correspond to different values of predicates in loop conditions occurring in Q (see, for example, the above programs P_1, P_2, P_3).

Let $\mathscr{P}_0$ denote the class of canonical programs satisfying (*).

Now we define the class of representative sample computations enabling us to synthesize canonical programs.

Let $P \in \mathscr{P}_0$. An unfoldment $\bar{P}$ of P is called r e p r e s e n t a t i v e iff to construct $\bar{P}$

(1) T=C_2WHILE(β)DO(Q) (see the def. of unfoldment) is replaced by $C_2(Q)^n$ with $n \ge 2$;

(2) if Q is of the type (3.2), then, for each $i, 1 \le i \le m$, the subword $T_iM_iT_iM_i$ occurs in $\bar{P}$;

(3) if Q is of the type (3.3), then each $(T_iM_i)^*$ is replaced by $(T_iM_i)^r$ with $r \ge 2$.

An annotated sample computation v is called representative iff $v=v(\bar{P})$ for a representative unfoldment $\bar{P}$.

Now we are able to describe the synthesis method. The general idea is like in Sections 1 and 2: given input sample, detect the leftmost fragment that can be a value of some loop, and replace this fragment by an appropriate loop; then repeat the procedure.

In view of the loop structure the target program is supposed to have, the synthesis algorithm (say, $\mathfrak{A}$) can be divided into three stages: first, the expression Q (see(3.1)) is to be synthesized, then $\mathfrak{A}$ constructs the loop

(3.4) C_2WHILE($y \boxed{\ne} v$)DO(Q),

and, finally, $\mathfrak{A}$ constructs the target program (3.1).

Let w be an input sample.

We begin with the first stage. Here the case is possible when some values of the variables are not annotated (see Example 1). Then $\mathfrak{A}$ searches for a subword w_1w_2 in w such that, omitting annotations, the length of $w_1=a_1a_2...a_k$ is equal to the length of $w_2=b_1b_2...b_k$, and if symbols a_i, a_j in w_1 have been annotated by the same $[=x]$ then either $b_i=a_i=b_j=a_j$, or $b_i-a_i=b_j-a_j=\pm 1$.

To define T in $Q=TM$, $\mathfrak{A}$ takes w_1 and replaces a_i, having annotation $[=x+c], c \in Z$, by this annotation (in case $[=x]$ - simply by x). M is defined as follows: for each new variable x in w_1, it contains x^+, if the values of x increase in w_2, and x^-, if the values of x in w_2 are smaller than the values of x in w_1.

Now we consider the case when all values of the variables in w are annotated. Then the process defining Q can be divided to a finite number of steps. Let some expressions $T_1,T_2,\dots,T_l$ and $R_0,R_1,\dots,R_j$ be defined before some step p, and, maybe, a symbol a_0 in w is marked by □.

<u>Step p.</u> If no symbol in w is marked by □, then stop the procedure. Otherwise, search for the leftmost subword $a_0a_1\dots a_k$ equal to some T_s, provided all values of variables are replaced by the corresponding annotations. If the required $a_0a_1\dots a_k$ is found, then put □ on a_{k+1} and go to step $p+1$. Otherwise, search for the leftmost subword $\bar{a}=a_1a_2\dots a_k$ of maximal length to the right from □, satisfying the condition

(*) there is a subword w_1w_2 in w such that

(a) if all values of variables in $\bar{a}$ and in any $w_i, i\in\{1,2\}$ are replaced by corresponding annotations, the transformed words (say, $\bar{a}'$ and w_i') are equal;

(b) $w_1\neq w_2$.

If no $\bar{a}$ is found, replace values of variables in w to the right from □ by corresponding annotations and stop the procedure. Otherwise, let u denote the fragment of w between □ and $\bar{a}$. Replace the values of variables in u by their annotations; denote the obtained expression by R_{j+1}. Further, replace the values of variables in $\bar{a}$ by annotations and denote the new word by T_{l+1}. Finally, put □ on a_{k+1} and go to step $p+1$.

Thus, all T_i and R_i in Q are defined. The definition of M_i and K_i (see (3.2)) is quite obvious: if x increases, then x^+ is put to M_i; otherwise, x^- is put to M_i; K_i is defined similarly.

Now 𝔄 has to choose the form of Q ((3.2) or (3.3)). If at least one R_j is not the empty word, then Q is of the type (3.3) (to be constructed quite apparently), otherwise, Q is a union.

The loop (3.4) is constructed on the second stage. Variables for the loop condition $y \boxed{\neq} v$ are taken from the annotations $[=x=y\pm c]$ (see Examples 2 and 3).

The expression (3.1) is to be constructed on the third stage. Let u denote the fragment in w corresponding to Q. To define x in the condition $x \boxed{\neq} \mu$, find either x occurring in u and such that the increment of the values assigned to x before and after u is equal to *1* (like the variable *i* in Example 1 and *y* in Example 2), or the variable not occurring in annotations in *u* and such that different values are assigned to it before and after *u* (y_0 in Example 3). For μ, in the first case, take either the variable occurring in the annotation of the equality $x=c$ just after the symbol *P* (the required expression is in input sample, due to the program definition), or the symbol *c* itself if the equality $x=c$ is not annotated. In the second case define μ to be equal to *c* in $x=c$ just after *P*.

Now we are about to define assignments in C_2. If, for any $z \in X, z^+$ or z^- occurs in *Q*, then the assignment $z:=c$ stands in *w* before the fragment corresponding to *Q*. If *c* is annotated by $[=\delta]$, then put $z:=\delta$ into C_2, otherwise put $z:=c$.

Finally, replace numbers still annotated . The obtained expression is the target program.

The reader can easily check that, given Examples 1,2,3, the synthesis algorithm $\mathfrak{A}$ constructs the programs P_1, P_2 and P_3 respectively.

Correctness of the synthesis algorithm follows from the following

THEOREM. Given any annotated representative sample *w* of a program $P \in \mathscr{P}$, the algorithm $\mathfrak{A}$ constructs the program $P(w)$ equivalent to *P*.

PROOF. We only describe the essential steps of the proof, omitting technical details.

Let us consider an arbitrary step at the first construction stage. Nonapplicability of G_1 and G_2 (to the target program) implies the choice of the leftmost subword $\bar{a}$ possessing necessary properties. The condition *(a)* implies unambiguous choice of "patterns" T_i and R_j; the length of T_i is specified by the representativeness of the input sample *w*. Nonapplicability of G_3 implies the choice of "the shortest" *Q*. Stages 2 and 3 are quite apparent. *Q.E.D.*

It is very important that input samples are of the length comparable with the length of the target program. The synthesis algorithm apparently is polynomial-time (on the length of input sample). If iteration and union in subprograms are interpreted in a convenient way, the above synthesis method can be easily implemented.

The author is grateful to J.M.Barzdin for a valuable discussion.

REFERENCES

1. Biermann A.W., Krishnaswamy R. *Constructing programs from example computations.* - IEEE Trans. Software Eng., v.2, 1976, p.141-153
2. Barzdin J.M. *Some rules of inductive inference and their use for program synthesis.* - In: Inform. Proc. 83, Amsterdam, North-Holland, 1983, p.333-338
3. Brazma A.N. *Inductive synthesis of programs.* - In: Problems of Theor. Cybern., Proc. of 7th USSR Conf., Irkutsk, Irkutsk State Univ., 1985, p.32-33 (in Russian).
4. Brazma A.N. *The decidability of the equivalence for the graphical expressions.* - In: Theory of algorithms and programs, Latvia State Univ., Riga, 1986, p.156-189 (in Russian).
5. Brazma A.N., Etmane I.E. *Inductive synthesis of graphical expressions.* - In: Theory of algorithms and programs, Latvia State Univ., Riga, 1986, p.156-189 (in Russian).
6. Kinber E.B. *Inductive synthesis of programs for recursive functions from sample computations.* - Journ. Inf. Process. Cybern. EIK, v.25, No.8/9, 1989, p.435-456
7. Brazma A.N., Kinber E.B. *Generalized regular expressions - a language for synthesis of programs with branching in loops.* - Theor.Comp.Sci., v.46, 1986, p.175-195
8. Knuth D. *The art of computer programming.* v.3, Addison-Wesley, Reading, Mass., 1973
9. Kinber E.B. *Syntactical inductive synthesis of iterative programs.* - Computers and Art.Int., v.8, No.6, 1989, p.565-580
10. Kinber E.B. *On syntactical inductive synthesis of programs with FOR-loops and interpreted functions from sample computations.* - Programmirovanie, No.2, 1988, p.14-25 (in Russian).

11. Kinber E.B. *Inductive synthesis of programs from incomplete samples.* - In: Theoretical questions of programming, Latvia State Univ., Riga, 1988, p.4-23 (in Russian).

12. Kinber E.B. *Syntactical inductive synthesis from incomplete sample computations.* - In: COLOG-88, Proc. Intern. Conf. in Comp. Logic, v.1, Tallinn, 1988, p.177-180.

INDUCTIVE SYNTHESIS OF TERM REWRITING SYSTEMS

Guntis BARZDINS

Institute of Mathematics and Computer Science
The University of Latvia
Raina bulv. 29, Riga, Latvia, 226250

Abstract. Fast algorithm for inductive synthesis of term rewriting systems is described and proved to be correct. It is implemented and successfully applied for inductive synthesis of different algorithms, including the binary multiplication. The algorithm proposed supports automatic learning process and can be used for designing and implementation of ADT.

1 Introduction

The way how a person creates new algorithms seems to be based on the generalization of observed certain samples. The result of such observation is some hypothesis about algorithm producing these samples. For example, if we want to find a sorting algorithm, we can look at the certain sorting samples:

3,2 → 2,3
1,3,2 → 1,2,3
3,2,7,1 → 1,2,3,7
1,2,3,2 → 1,2,2,3
. . . .

and find some hypothetical algorithm (for example, bubble-sort algorithm) which works correct on these samples. After that we prove the correctness of the hypothetical algorithm in respect to the specification of the sorting problem. Thus most of the well known algorithms could be invented, such as decimal adding, multiplication, etc.

So, the process of creating a new algorithm is split into two parts: finding a hypothetical algorithm and proving its correctness. If the second part - proving correctness - is a well studied topic today, then the first part - generation of "sound", "reliable" hypothetical algorithms reasonably quickly (without exhaustive search), - remains to be a problem.

Construction of general algorithms from samples is the topic of computer science field called *inductive synthesis* (or *inductive inference*) including some hundred papers for the present moment. These papers could be divided into two groups. *The first group* are those that study inductive synthesis on recursive-theoretical level (see survey [AS83]). They describe which classes of recursive functions can be or cannot be synthesized in limit (i.e. from sufficiently large samples). But these results are of theoretic importance only because the synthesis method there usually is exhaustive search which is impossible for applications.

The second group of papers is related to more restricted computational models which are of pragmatic interest on the one hand and can be synthesized without exhaustive search on the other hand. Several of the studied models can be listed there:

- synthesis of programs from example computations [BK76],
- synthesis of regular LISP-programs [Sum77,Bie78],
- synthesis of dots expressions [Bar83] and some generalizations [BK86],
- synthesis of patterns in pattern languages [Ang80],
- synthesis of grammars [Cre72,Yok89],
- synthesis of PROLOG-programs [Sha83].

Each of these inductive synthesis models cover very different classes of algorithms which can be synthesized. These different models could be wished to be generalized into one, yet, the problem is that they are extremely different and synthesis methods are very closely related to certain models. It seems that a person uses some more general inductive synthesis method than a certain computational model listed above.

The inductive synthesis problem was treated excellently by D.Angluin in her paper "Easily inferred sequences" [Ang74]. Some hundred sequences of numbers were collected there having an obvious, or easy inferred, pattern, such that from a few successive terms of it a person very easily guesses the correct rule of generation. There are some of these sequences:

2,4,6,8,...

1,4,9,16,25,...

2,1,4,4,6,9,8,16,...

1,1,2,3,5,8,...

1,1,2,1,2,3,1,2,3,4,1,...

1,10,11,100,101,110,...

A question is: what formalism allows a person to generalize these quite different sequences very quickly in the right way? It should be noted that inductive synthesis models listed above don't cover all Angluin's sequences. Finding answer to the question is the topic of this paper.

Our approach is based on the idea of abstract data types. Functions in abstract data types are defined by sets of their independent properties, called algebraic axioms. Independence means that adding a new axiom other axioms remain unchanged. At the same time in the traditional programming languages commands are closely related and the meaning of one command depends on other commands in program. This is the point why exhaustive search appears quickly in the inductive synthesis models using traditional languages.

Yet the inductive synthesis method based on finding independent axioms faces another problem - not always we can compute the value of the function by its axiomatic description. A well known method how to convert an axiom system into the executable program is transforming it into the terminating and confluent rewrite system by Knuth-Bendix algorithm and some simplification ordering [BW89]. But the problem is that Knuth-Bendix algorithm can't be applied to incomplete axiom systems and it works only for very restricted classes of rewrite systems (actually, inductive synthesis was first applied to term rewriting systems in order to improve the power of Knuth-Bendix algorithm [TJ89,Lan89]).

The idea of this paper is to synthesize confluent and terminating rewrite systems directly. Although rewrite rules in a rewrite system are not so independent as axioms in an axiom system they remain much more independent than commands in the traditional programming languages. This allows us to synthesize a rewrite system by finding its rules independently, what *reduces search by exponent* with respect to the number of rules in the rewrite system to be synthesized. The termination of the synthesized rewrite system is guaranteed by means of quasi-simplification ordering.

Another source of economy is related with the search for a certain rewrite rule. It can be reduced sufficiently by "liquid-flow" method of graph analysis which allows to consider only "meaningful" rules - i.e. rules that work at least in one place in a sample and can't be derived from the other rules already found.

The mathematical foundations of such inductive synthesis approach are worked out in the paper. Efficient inductive synthesis algorithm QUITA is described and proved to be correct. QUITA algorithm is implemented and examples of its usage are described. Inductive synthesis of binary multiplication algorithm serves as an example characterizing QUITA's power - it takes only 10 minutes on IBM/PC.

The described approach has some other significant properties. First, it is possible to use partial specifications of the function to be synthesized if these specifications are in the form of algebraic axioms. In this case we can orient these axioms as rewrite rules and only insufficient rewrite rules are to be synthesized from the sample. The other property related with the first is that our approach supports learning process, i.e. it allows to collect rewrite rules of already synthesized functions into knowledge base and to reuse them afterwards during the synthesis of other functions.

We are sure that our approach offers a possibility to synthesize efficiently quite complicated algorithms from their input/output samples and partial specifications.

2 The Problem of Inductive Synthesis of Rewrite Systems

2.1 TERM REWRITING SYSTEMS

Let T_Σ be a set of *ground terms* (i.e. terms without variables) over finite *signature* Σ of functional symbols. Let $T_\Sigma(V)$ be a set of *open terms* (i.e. terms with variables) over signature Σ and set of variables V. By *v(t)* we denote the set of variables in term *t*.

A *substitution* σ of ground terms for variables appearing in the open term $t \in T_\Sigma(V)$ is a function of format $\sigma : v(t) \to T_\Sigma$. We denote by $t\sigma$ the ground term which is obtained from term *t* by substitution σ of its variables by ground terms.

We consider two types of *rewrite rules* which are oriented pairs of terms $l, r \in T_\Sigma \cup T_\Sigma(V)$:

- *well oriented* rules $l \to r$ such that $v(r) \subseteq v(l)$,
- *quasi oriented* rules $l \leftrightarrow r$ such that $v(l) = v(r)$.

A term *rewriting system* R is a finite set of rewrite rules. When a quasi oriented rule $l\leftrightarrow r$ is applied it should be interpreted as a pair of well oriented rules $l\to r$, $r\to l$. A rule $l\to r$ *applies* to a term t if a subterm s of t matches the left-hand side l by substitution σ of variables by ground terms (i.e. $s=l\sigma$). The rule is applied by replacing the subterm s in t with the corresponding right-hand side $r\sigma$ of the rule, within which the same substitution σ of variables by ground terms has been made. We write $t\Rightarrow u$ to indicate that the term t *rewrites* this way to the term u by a single application of some rule in the given rewrite system R. A *derivation* is a sequence of rewrites; if $t\Rightarrow\ldots\Rightarrow u$ in zero or more steps, then we say that u is *derivable* from t; by $R(T)$ we denote the set of terms which are derivable in the given rewrite system R from the set of terms T.

A rewrite system R is *quasi-terminating* (for ground terms) if every infinite derivation $t_1\Rightarrow t_2\Rightarrow t_3\Rightarrow\ldots$ for ground terms contains only finite number of different terms (i.e. $\forall t\in T_\Sigma$ the set $R(\{t\})$ is finite).

A rewrite system R is *ground-confluent* if the following property for the set of ground terms holds:

$$\forall t,u,v\in T_\Sigma\ [(u\in R(\{t\})\&v\in R(\{t\}))\Rightarrow \exists w\in T_\Sigma(w\in R(\{u\})\&w\in R(\{v\}))].$$

A rewrite system R is *ground-complete* if it is quasi-terminating and ground-confluent.

The *normal-form* of the ground term $t\in T_\Sigma$ in the quasi-terminating rewrite system R is the set of ground terms $t_R\in T_\Sigma$ such that

$$t_R\subseteq R(\{t\})\ \&\ R(t_R)=t_R.$$

If a rewrite system R is ground-complete, then each ground term $t\in T_\Sigma$ in R has a unique, finite and nonempty normal form set t_R which can be efficiently constructed from the given term t and rewrite system R.

Two ground terms are said to be *equivalent* in the ground-complete rewrite system R if and only if they have the same normal form.

2.2 ASSOCIATIONS, SAMPLES, INDUCTIVE SYNTHESIS

An equivalence relation on the set of ground terms T_Σ (for example, defined by the ground-complete rewrite system) splits all ground terms into equivalence classes.

The *association* $A=(a_1,a_2,\ldots)$ over the signature Σ is the splitting of the set of ground terms T_Σ into subsets called *equivalence classes*:

$$a_1, a_2, a_3, \ldots$$

$$(a_1 \cup a_2 \cup \ldots = T_\Sigma \text{ and } i \neq j \Rightarrow a_i \cap a_j = \emptyset)$$

such that the following property holds: if two ground terms $u, v \in T_\Sigma$ belong to the same equivalence class a_i, then any two ground terms $f(\ldots u \ldots), f(\ldots v \ldots) \in T_\Sigma$ differing only by subterms u and v also belong to the same equivalence class a_j.

A ground-complete rewrite system R over the signature Σ *realizes* the association A over the signature Σ if these and only these ground terms in R are equal which belong to the same equivalence class of the association A. The association A is called *constructive* if it can be realized by some ground-complete rewrite system. The same association can be realized by different rewrite systems; these rewrite systems are "equivalent" in some sense.

A *sample* $Ex=(e_1, e_2, \ldots, e_n)$ of the association $A=(a_1, a_2, \ldots)$ is a finite system of subsets of equivalence classes:

$$e_1 \subseteq a_{i1}, e_2 \subseteq a_{i2}, \ldots, e_n \subseteq a_{in} \qquad (k \neq m \Rightarrow i_k \neq i_m).$$

The sample $Ex=(e_1, e_2, \ldots, e_n)$ of the association $A=(a_1, a_2, \ldots)$ is *finite* if all sets e_i $(i \in [1,n])$ are finite.

The extra property of finite samples of associations is that they are constructive objects and can be given as input for some algorithm. The rewrite systems *inductive synthesis machine* M is the precisely described algorithm $M(\Sigma, Ex)$ which inputs finite signature Σ and finite sample Ex of some association over the signature Σ. M should terminate on any such input and produce some rewrite system $R=M(\Sigma, Ex)$ of signature Σ.

The sequence $Ex_1, Ex_2, Ex_3, \ldots$ of samples for the association A is called *complete* if the following properties hold:

- $\forall i \geq 1 \ \forall t \in Ex_i : t \in Ex_{i+1}$,
- $\forall t \in T_\Sigma \ \exists n \in \mathbb{N} \ t \in Ex_n$.

We say that an inductive synthesis machine M *synthesizes in limit* a constructive association A over the signature Σ if, for any complete sequence $Ex_1, Ex_2, \ldots$ of samples for the association A, the sequence of rewrite systems $R_1, R_2, \ldots$ $(R_i=M(\Sigma, Ex_i))$ has the property: $\exists n \in \mathbb{N}$ such that $\forall i \geq n$ R_i realizes the association A.

Hypothesis. There exists no inductive synthesis machine M which synthesizes in limit any constructive association.

The confidence in the hypothesis follows from the fact that constructive associations cover all total recursive functions, but Golds [Gol67] theorem claims the impossibility to synthesize in limit any total recursive function from input/output samples. The Golds theorem can't be applied directly in this case because a sample of association contains more than input/output samples of the goal function (it contains also samples of intermediate functions).

So, according to this hypothesis we have to restrict the class of constructive associations in order to gain some positive results.

2.3 S-ASSOCIATIONS, THEIR INDUCTIVE SYNTHESIS

In this section we introduce the class of S-associations which appears to be synthesizable in limit.

A *quasi-ordered set* $(S,\geq)$ consists of a set S and a transitive and reflexive binary relation $\geq$ defined on elements of S. Given a quasi-ordering $\geq$ on a set S, we define the associated *equivalence relation* $\approx$ as both $\geq$ and $\leq$ and *strict partial ordering* $>$ as $\geq$ but not $\leq$. A quasi-ordering on S is *total* if, for any two elements s and t in S, either $s\geq t$ or else $t\geq s$.

A total quasi-ordering $\geq_S$ on the set of ground terms T_Σ is a *quasi-simplification ordering*[1] if for all terms in T_Σ:

- $t>_S u \Rightarrow f(\ldots t\ldots)>_S f(\ldots u\ldots)$,
- $t\approx_S u \Rightarrow f(\ldots t\ldots)\approx_S f(\ldots u\ldots)$,
- $f(\ldots t\ldots)>_S t$.

Lemma 1. If $\geq_S$ is a quasi-simplification ordering on T_Σ, then any quasi-decreasing sequence of ground terms

$$t_1\geq_S t_2\geq_S t_3\geq_S\ldots \qquad (t_i\in T_\Sigma)$$

contains only a finite number of different elements.

---

[1] In [Der87] the quasi-simplification ordering is defined weaker: a quasi-ordering $\geq$ of the ground terms is a quasi-simplification ordering if for any ground terms u,v:
$f(\ldots u\ldots)\geq u$ and $u\geq v \Rightarrow f(\ldots u\ldots)\geq f(\ldots v\ldots)$.

This lemma follows from the results of [Der87] where orderings having this property are called *well founded* and *thin*.

A rewrite system R of signature Σ is *S-oriented* with respect to the quasi-simplification ordering $\geq_s$ on T_Σ if for any

- well oriented rule $l \rightarrow r \Rightarrow l\sigma >_s r\sigma$,
- quasi oriented rule $l \leftrightarrow r \Rightarrow l\sigma \approx_s r\sigma$,

for any substitution σ of variables by ground terms.

According to Lemma 1 any S-oriented rewrite system is quasi-terminating. A ground-confluent rewrite system R is called *S-complete* if it is S-oriented. A constructive association A is called *S-association* if it can be realized by some S-complete rewrite system.

A quasi-simplification ordering $\geq_s$ is *efficient* if there exists an algorithm for computing it, and we denote its Goedel number by s.

Theorem 1. For any efficient quasi-simplification ordering $\geq_s$ there exists inductive synthesis machine M^s which synthesizes in limit any S-association. M^s can be efficiently constructed from the Goedel number s of the ordering predicate $\geq_s$.

The proof of this theorem is based on exhaustive search. All rewrite systems of the given signature Σ can be efficiently enumerated. A rewrite system is called incorrect for S-association A if it isn't S-complete or it doesn't derive exactly the same ground term equalities as in A. There exists an algorithm Q^s that recognizes any incorrect rewrite system on sufficiently large sample of association A (it can be recognized in finite time because of Lemma 1). So, there exists an algorithm M^s which synthesizes a correct rewrite system from sufficiently large sample of the S-association A.

3.Inductive synthesis algorithm "QUITA"

Theorem 1 claims the possibility to synthesize in limit S-associations but nothing was said there about time complexity of such synthesis and how compact the synthesized rewrite systems are. Now we describe a certain inductive synthesis algorithm QUITA which is very efficient and produces compact rewrite systems (we say that a rewrite system is compact if it contains no rules derivable from other rules of the system).

We define QUITA algorithm for an unsubstantially restricted class of S-associations, for which S-orientation of rewrite rules is efficiently decidable. It seems impossible to avoid exhaustive search without this restriction . The point is that such efficient S-orientation predicate can be given for the majority of the known quasi-simplification orderings.

Let $\geq_s$ be a quasi-simplification ordering on the set of ground terms T_Σ. We denote by $C_s(\alpha)$ a predicate which determines whether a rewrite rule α is S-oriented. $H_s(\alpha)$ is called a *sufficient S-orientation predicate* if there holds:

- if rule α contains no variables, then $H_s(\alpha)=C_s(\alpha)$,
- if rule α contains variables, then $H_s(\alpha)\Rightarrow C_s(\alpha)$.

Let a quasi-simplification ordering $\geq_s$ and a predicate $H_s(\alpha)$ be given for signature Σ. A rewrite system *R* over signature Σ is called *(S,H)-oriented* if

$$\forall\alpha\in R : H_s(\alpha)=\mathit{true}.$$

Any (S,H)-oriented rewrite system is S-oriented and therefore quasi-terminating. A ground-complete rewrite system *R* is *(S,H)-complete* if it is (S,H)-oriented. A constructive association *A* is *(S,H)-association* if it can be realized by some (S,H)-complete rewrite system.

A predicate $H_s(\alpha)$ is efficient if there exists an algorithm for computing it, and we denote its Goedel number by *h*.

QUITA algorithm uses several independent natural ideas which are nested together. We begin by separate description of these ideas and then proceed by describing QUITA algorithm itself, and, finally, its correctness theorem will be given.

3.1 TESTING HYPOTHETICAL REWRITE SYSTEM

Let *A* be an S-association of signature Σ. A rewrite rule α is called *correct* for association *A* if, for any substitution σ of variables by ground terms in rule α, both sides of α are ground terms equivalent in association *A* (i.e. belonging to the same equivalence class). A rewrite system is called *correct* if all its rules are correct. A rewrite system *R* is called *sufficient* for the association *A* if from any two ground terms equivalent in

A a common ground term can be derived in *R*. The next lemma can be proved easily:

Lemma 2. Let *A* be an S-association and *R* be an S-oriented rewrite system. *R* is S-complete and realizes *A* if and only if *R* is correct and sufficient for *A*.

So, to guarantee that a hypothetical rewrite system *R* is S-complete and realizes the given S-association *A*, we have to ensure that:

- *R* is S-oriented,
- *R* is correct for *A*,
- *R* is sufficient for *A*.

For testing S-orientation of the hypothetical rewrite system we will use sufficient S-orientation predicate H_S. For fast testing of other two properties special methods will be described in the following sections.

3.2 EXPANSION OF SAMPLE, ITS GRAPHIC INTERPRETATION

Here we study more deeply the nature of association samples.

A sample *Ex* is called *correct* if it contains all subterms of its terms.

Let $Ex=(e_1,e_2,\dots,e_n)$ be a sample of the association *A* of signature Σ. We say that terms $t_1,t_2\in T_\Sigma$ are *equivalent according to the sample Ex* in the following cases:

- if $\exists i\in[1,n]$: $t_1,t_2\in e_i$,
- if $t_1=f(\dots u\dots)$ and $t_2=f(\dots s\dots)$ and u,s are equivalent according to the sample *Ex*,
- if $\exists t_3\in T_\Sigma$, such that t_1,t_3 and t_2,t_3, are equivalent according to the sample *Ex*.

It is clear that two terms $t_1,t_2\in T_\Sigma$ are equivalent according to the sample of an association *A* only when they are equal in *A*.

The *extension* of sample $Ex=(e_1,e_2,\dots,e_n)$ is a system of minimal sets $Ex'=(e_1',e_2',\dots,e_n')$ such that for any $i\in 1,\dots n$:

- $e_i\subseteq e_i'$,
- e_i' contains all terms that are equal to the terms of the set e_i according to the sample *Ex*.

The extension *Ex'* of the sample *Ex* of the association *A* is a sample of the association *A*, too. It should be noted that an extension of a finite sample may be an infinite sample.

The sequence $Ex_1, Ex_2, Ex_3, \dots$ of the samples of an association *A* is called *quasi-complete* if the corresponding sequence of extended samples $Ex_1', Ex_2', Ex_3', \dots$ is complete.

Further we will consider inductive synthesis from quasi-complete sequences of correct samples instead of considering complete sequences of samples. This is not a restriction of generality because from any complete sequence of samples it is possible to cut out efficiently a sequence of correct samples and this sequence is complete, too.

The point is that there exists a good graphic interpretation of correct samples and their extension.

Let us first consider an example of signature Σ containing only constants and unary operation names:

$$\Sigma=\{o(), a(\_), b(\_)\},$$

and the following correct sample:

$$Ex=\{\ e_1=\{o, b(o), b(b(o)), b(b(b(o)))\},$$
$$e_2=\{a(o), a(b(o)), a(b(b(o)))\},$$
$$e_3=\{a(a(o)), b(a(o)), a(a(b(o))), b(a(b(o)))\}\ \}.$$

Graphically such a sample can be realized by graph in the following way: each equivalence class is realized by a node; an arc *w* (*w* is the operation name) is drawn from a node e_i to a node e_j in case the sample *Ex* contains terms *t* and *w(t)*, where $t \in e_i$ and $w(t) \in e_j$. Hence the above sample *Ex* is realized by the following graph:

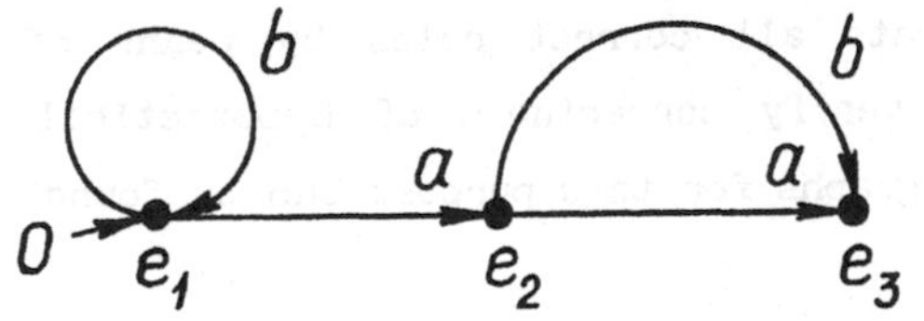

The extra property of such graph, called *graphic sample*, is:

- Any path, beginning from a constant and ending in a node e_i, interpreted as a ground term belongs to the class e_i' of the extended sample.
- Any term of class e_i' of the extended sample realizes a path beginning from the constant and ending in the node e_i.

There exists an analogous graphic interpretation for n-argument operations, too. In this case a graph will contain *n-arcs*, i.e. arcs with n enumerated inputs and one output:

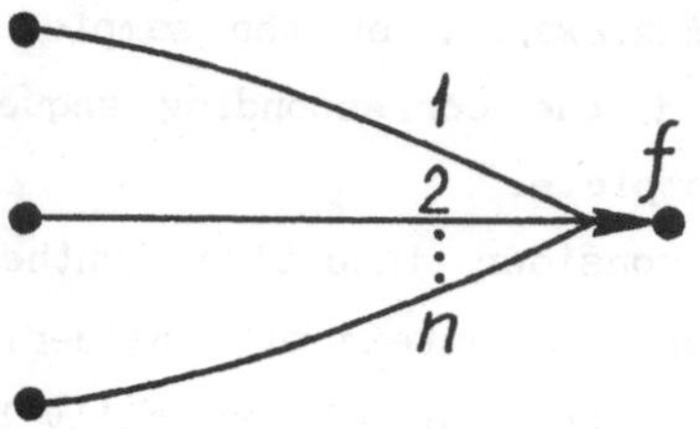

For rewrite rules there is also a good graphic interpretation. Rewrite rules stand for special kind of loops: for example, the rule

$$b(a(X))\to a(a(b(X)))$$

stands for the loop

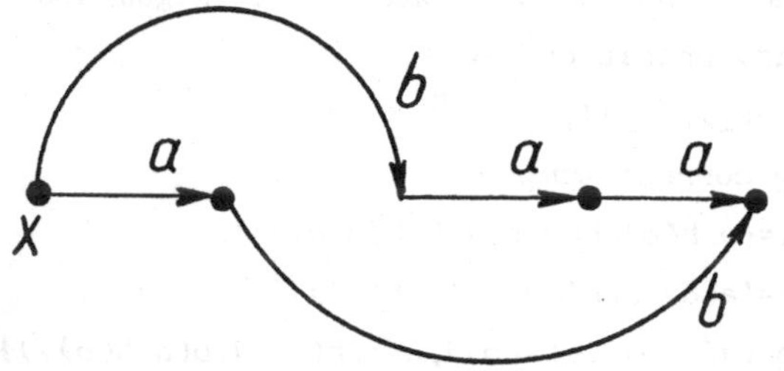

Similar more complicated loop stands for a rule with several variables.

The following observation is important: if some rewrite rule α is correct for the association A, then it appears as a loop in a sufficiently large graphic sample of A. This observation is used in two aspects: it allows to enumerate all correct rules by means of "liquid-flow" graph analysis and to verify correctness of hypothetical rules. More details about the use of graphs for this purpose can be found in [Bar90].

3.3 S-NORMALIZED SAMPLES

The next simple lemma is very important for QUITA algorithm and, what is important, it is valid only for the definition of quasi-simplification ordering given in this paper (see Section 2.3). The point is that well known quasi-simplification orderings, such as recursive path ordering, are quasi-simplification orderings also in our sense.

Lemma 3. Let $\geq_S$ be a quasi-simplification ordering and $A=(a_1,a_2,a_3,\ldots)$ be an S-association realized by the S-complete rewrite system R. Let us denote by l_i the set of the lightest terms of class a_i in ordering $\geq_S$. Then in the rewrite system R the normal form of the terms of class a_i is exactly the set l_i.

A correct sample $Ex=(e_1,e_2,\ldots,e_n)$ is *S-normalized* with respect to the quasi-simplification ordering $\geq_S$ if:

- In any class e_i there is chosen the *main* term m_i such that $\forall t\in e_i$: $t\geq_S m_i$.
- Sample Ex contains only those terms whose all proper subterms are main terms.

Because of Lemma 3 we may hope that in a sample most of the main terms will be the normal form terms.

If the Goedel number s of a quasi-simplification ordering $\geq_S$ is given, there exists an efficient algorithm which converts any correct sample Ex_1 into an S-normalized sample Ex_2 so that the extensions of Ex_1 and Ex_2 coincide. The idea of this conversion is to use the graphic presentation of correct sample and to mark the main path to any node to be the lightest among other paths in the ordering $\geq_S$.

The next lemma shows the main property of the S-normalized samples:

Lemma 4. Let $\geq_S$ be a quasi-simplification ordering, $Ex=(e_1,\ldots,e_n)$ be an S-normalized sample with main terms $m_1,\ldots,m_n$, $Ex'=(e_1',\ldots,e_n')$ be an extension of Ex, R be some S-oriented rewrite system and V be some ground term. In the rewrite system R the main term m_i is derivable from any term $u\leq_S V$ of the class e_i ($u\in e_i$: $m_i\in R(\{u\})$) if and only if the main term m_i is derivable from any term $t\leq_S V$ of class e_i' in extended sample Ex' ($t\in e_i'$: $m_i\in R(\{t\})$).

The proof of this lemma is based on the contrary assumption that there exists a term $t\in Ex'$: $t\notin Ex$ and $t\leq_S V$. It can be shown that in this case from term t the main term of the appropriate class can be derived in R, what contradicts with our assumption.

We will say that terms $m_1,m_2,\ldots$ are *main* terms of equivalence classes of some S-association $A=(a_1,a_2,a_3,\ldots)$ if

$\forall t \in a_i: m_i \in a_i \; \& \; t \geq_S m_i.$

A term $t=f(\ldots)$ which is not main term is called *quasi-main* if all its proper subterms are the main terms. Next Lemma 5 follows easily from Lemma 4. Quick sufficiency control of hypothetical rewrite system becomes possible due to it.

Lemma 5. Let $m_1, m_2, m_3, \ldots$ be the main terms of some S-association $A=(a_1, a_2, a_3, \ldots)$. An S-oriented and correct rewrite system R is sufficient for association A if and only if from any quasi-main term u the main term of the same equivalence class is derivable in R:

$$u \in a_i \; : \; m_i \in R(\{u\}).$$

So, to test the sufficiency of S-oriented and correct rewrite system we have to control only the possibility to derive the main terms from quasi-main terms.

3.4 HOW TO FIND AN INSUFFICIENT RULE?

Let A be an S-association and R be a rewrite system *insufficient for* A, i.e.:

- R is S-oriented,
- R is correct for association A,
- R is not sufficient for association A (i.e. not all term equalities of A can be derived in R).

We call a rewrite rule α *substantially new* with respect to the insufficient rewrite system R if it is S-oriented and correct and derives some ground term equalities which are not derivable in R:

$$\exists t \in T_\Sigma: \; R(\{t\}) \subset' R \cup \alpha'(\{t\}).$$

We want to consider only substantially new rules in order not to waste time on finding only syntactically new rules which don't carry any new information; this will guarantee the compactness of the synthesized rewrite systems, too.

So, the problem is to find some substantially new rule α for the given insufficient rewrite system R. The proposed idea will work for "sufficiently large" finite samples of A; therefore, first we define what "sufficiently large" sample is.

Let the *level* of a term be defined as follows: the level of the term which is constant symbol is 1; the level of the term which is variable is 0; the level of any other term $f(t_1,\dots,t_n)$ is the maximal level of the terms $t_1,\dots,t_n$ plus one. The level of rewrite rule is the maximal level of its right- and left- hand side terms.

Let A be an (S,H)-association. Among the (S,H)-complete rewrite systems realizing A there is a system R with the smallest maximal level *max* of its rules. Let W be the set of all (S,H)-oriented and correct for A rewrite rules of level no more than *max*. W is a finite set. W is sufficient for A because $R\subseteq W$. We denote by $r_1,r_2,\dots,r_k$ all subsets of W.

We define a set GR_{r_j} to consist of the lightest in the ordering $\geq_S$ ground terms t such that not all lightest terms of the same equivalence class can be derived in r_j, i.e:

$$t\in GR_{r_j} : (t\in a_i \Rightarrow \exists q\in l_i: q\notin r_j(\{t\})),$$

where l_i is a set of the lightest terms in the class a_i.

The set GR_{r_j} is a finite set according to Lemma 1 and because it consists of terms of the same weight in quasi-simplification ordering $\geq_S$. The significant property of the set GR_{r_j} is that $r_j(GR_{r_j})=GR_{r_j}$.

We denote by GR the union of all such sets GR_{r_j}, $j\in[1,k]$.

A rewrite rule α is *incorrect* for association A if it is not correct, i.e. there exists some substitution σ of variables by ground terms in rule α, such that two sides of the rule become ground terms unequal in A. This pair of unequal ground terms will be called a *counter-sample* for incorrect rule α.

Let Ex_A be a sample of association A containing all terms of:

- set W(GR) (i.e. all terms derivable in W from terms of set GR),
- counter-samples for all incorrect for A rewrite rules of level no more than *max*.

It is obvious that Ex_A is finite. A sample Ex is called *sufficiently large* if its extension contains sample Ex_A.

Let $Ex=(e_1,e_2,\dots,e_n)$ be a sufficiently large S-normalized sample of association A with main terms $m_1,m_2,\dots,m_n$ and let r_j be some subset of W.

We define a set G_{r_j} to consist of the lightest in the ordering $\geq_S$ terms $t\in Ex$ such that the main term of the same equivalence class can not be derived in r_j (and no lightest than m_i term can be derived from m_i in r_j), i.e:

$t \in G_{rj}$: $(t \in e_i \Rightarrow m_i \notin r_j(\{t\})$ & $\neg \exists q \in r(\{m_i\}): m_i >_S q)$.

The point is that the set G_{rj} can be found constructively from the sample *Ex* and the rewrite system r_j.

It follows from the definition of sufficiently large sample and Lemma 5 that $r_j \subseteq W$ is sufficient for association *A* if and only if the set G_{rj} is empty.

Let $r \in W$ be a rewrite system insufficient for association *A*. We denote by G^i_r a nonempty subset of set G_r containing only terms from class e_i. The next lemma is valid:

Lemma 6. Let *Ex* be a sufficiently large sample of S-association *A* and $r \subseteq W$ (set *W* for association *A* was defined above) be a rewrite system insufficient for *A*. Then for any nonempty set G^i_r there exists a substantially new with respect to *r* rule $\alpha \in W$ such that it applies to some term *t* of the set $r(G^i_r)$ at the root level and rewrites it into the equivalent according to the sample *Ex* term $t' \notin r(G^i_r)$.

The proof of this lemma consists of three parts. First of all it can be proved that the set G^i_r is a subset of GR_r and, therefore, the set $r(G^i_r)$ also is a subset of GR_r. Secondly from the definition of the sufficiently large sample follows that the main term m_i of class e_i is the lightest term in the whole class a_i of association *A*. Thirdly it is proved that there is a rule $\alpha \in W$ which having been applied to some term $t \in r(G^i_r)$ in the root level rewrites it into the term $t' \notin r(G^i_r)$. The rule α is substantially new because $t' \notin r(G^i_r)$ and $t' \in' r \cup \alpha'(G^i_r)$.

Lemma 6 gives the idea for quick finding of sufficiently new rules. In fact two sets of ground terms which are "patterns" for substantially new rules are defined by this lemma: the abovementioned set $r(G^i_r)$ and the set C^i_r of all terms such that:

- $C^i_r \cap r(G^i_r) = \emptyset$,
- $\forall t \in C^i_r$: $t \leq_S r(G^i_r)$,
- $C^i_r \subseteq e_i'$.

We have to consider only rules (both well oriented and quasi oriented) whose left-hand-side matches in the root level some term from the set $r(G^i_r)$ and right-hand-side matches in the root level some ground term from the set C^i_r. The graphic interpretation of the samples makes it possible to find all such matching rules of the fixed length in the time proportional to their length. More precisely the use of graphs for this purpose is described in [Bar90]; here we give only some ideas.

Any correct rule in the graphic sample appears as a loop consisting of two branches corresponding to left- and right- hand sides. The left-hand-side branch of the loop can be found easily because it has to match a term of the finite set $r(G^{i}_{r})$. So, the problem is to find right-hand-side branch of this loop. To do this we have to find in the graph all paths that connect the beginning and the ending of the left-hand-side branch and contain only arcs belonging to the terms of the set C^{i}_{r}. All such paths with fixed length can be found by the "liquid flow" method in the time proportional to their length. The "liquid flow" method can be extrapolated easily for the graphs with n-arcs, too.

We have to test all rules matching the patterns beginning with the rules of the smallest level. We test the S-orientation of the rule α by the given predicate h. We can test the correctness of the rule α for the extension of the given S-normalized sample quickly by graphic presentation of the sample. The idea is to test the rule α not for any substitution of variables in rule α by ground terms, but for any substitution of variables by equivalence classes. It means that we substitute a certain node in the graph for each variable of α. Using the graph we can immediately control whether the endings of both branches of the rule match the same node (i.e. the same equivalence class). According the definition of sufficiently large sample it contains counter-samples of all rules incorrect for A of the level no more than *max*. As we start from the rules of the smallest level we find a rule $\alpha \in W$ of the level no more than *max*.

Thus an algorithm which for any insufficient for A rewrite system $r \subseteq W$ quickly finds a substantially new rule $\alpha \in W$ from a sufficiently large sample of association A is described.

3.5 THE STRUCTURE OF THE "QUITA" ALGORITHM

Now we have to put together the above described ideas to obtain QUITA algorithm. QUITA inputs the sample *Ex*, Goedel number *s* of quasi-simplification ordering $\geq_{s}$ and Goedel number *h* of sufficient S-orientation predicate H_{s}.

```
algorithm QUITA(Ex,s,h);
      begin
            Ex:=Normalize(Ex,s);
            R:=∅;
NEXT:       (G,i):=FindPattern(Ex,R,s);
            if G=∅ then goto STOP;
            G':=DeriveAll(R,G);
            α:=NewRule(Ex,G',s,h);
            R:=R∪α;
            goto NEXT;
STOP:       return(R);
      end.
```

The function *Normalize(Ex,s)* cuts out from the sample *Ex* its correct part and rebuilds it into the S-normalized sample in which the main terms are tagged.

The function *FindPattern(Ex,R,s)* finds some set G^i_R and its index *i* (see Section 3.4) from the S-normalized sample *Ex* and the rewrite system *R*.

The function *DeriveAll(R,G)* for the set of terms G and rewrite system *R* builds the set of terms *R*(G).

The function *NewRule(Ex,G,s,h)* finds a substantially new S-oriented rule according to the methodology described in Section 3.4. It outputs such rule of the smallest level which is (S,H)-oriented and correct on the extension of *Ex*.

We denote by $QUITA_{s,h}(Ex)$ algorithm QUITA(*Ex,s,h*) with fixed parameters *s* and *h* for certain efficient quasi-simplification ordering $\geq_s$ and its efficient sufficient S-orientation predicate H_s.

<u>Theorem 2.</u> For any efficient quasi-simplification ordering $\geq_s$ of the signature Σ and efficient sufficient S-orientation predicate H_s algorithm $QUITA_{s,h}$ synthesizes in limit any (S,H)-association of the signature Σ from any quasi-complete sequence of its samples. The synthesized rewrite system always is (S,H)-oriented. The algorithm $QUITA_{s,h}$ terminates on any sample of the signature Σ.

The proof of this theorem follows from Lemmas 2-6.

The time complexity of the algorithm depends on many factors: the number of rules in the system and their length, the number of variables in the rule, the size of the sample and etc. We will not present precise theoretical estimation of the number of steps of this algorithm. Let us mention only that during synthesis of a certain rule search in algorithm QUITA appears only in the function *NewRule*, but it is reduced sufficiently according to the methodology proposed in Sect 2.4. In this paper the main criteria of the efficiency of QUITA is its real applicability to nontrivial examples, such as binary multiplication algorithm and others described in Part 3.

4 Methodology

In this part we present the ideas necessary for successful application of QUITA algorithm. It includes the definition of a certain quasi-simplification ordering, called recursive path ordering, the use of rewrite systems in the learning process and examples.

4.1 RECURSIVE PATH ORDERING

The algorithm $QUITA_{s,h}$ described in Section 2 is parameterized by the Goedel numbers of a certain quasi simplification ordering $\geq_s$ and sufficiency predicate H_s. When QUITA is applied they must be fixed. Further we will use only a certain quasi-simplification ordering of ground terms (called recursive path ordering [Der87]) which is parameterized by the quasi-ordering of signature Σ.

The definition of the recursive path ordering uses the notion of the multiset ordering. *Multisets* , or *bags*, are unordered sequences; they are like sets , but allow multiple occurrences of identical elements. For example, multiset {3,3,3,4,0,0} of natural numbers is identical to multiset {0,3,3,0,4,3}, but distinct from {3,4,0}. A quasi-ordering $\geq$ on any given set S induces a quasi-ordering $\underset{\sim}{\gg}$ on the set $M(S)$ of finite multisets over S in the following way.

For a set S, quasi-ordered by $\geq$, the *multiset ordering* $\underset{\sim}{\gg}$ on the set $M(S)$ of finite multisets over S is defined recursively as follows:

$X=\{x_1,\dots,x_m\} \underset{\sim}{\gg} (y_1,\dots,y_n\}=Y$

if $X=Y$ or if

$x_i \approx y_j$ and $X-\{x_i\} \underset{\sim}{\gg} Y-\{y_j\}$,

for some $i\in[1,m]$ and $j\in[1,n]$, or

$x_i > y_{j1}, y_{j2},\dots,y_{jk}$ and $X-\{x_i\} \underset{\sim}{\gg} Y-\{y_{j1},y_{j2},\dots,y_{jk}\}$,

for some $i\in[1,m]$ and $1\le j_1<j_2<\dots<j_k\le n$ $(k\ge 0)$.

Now we can define a recursive path ordering itself.

Let $\ge_\omega$ be a quasi-ordering on the functional symbols of signature Σ. The *recursive path ordering* $\ge_{S(\omega)}$ on the set T_Σ of ground terms over signature Σ is defined recursively as follows:

$s=f(s_1,\dots,s_m) \ge_{S(\omega)} g(t_1,\dots,t_n)=t$

if

$s_i \ge_{S(\omega)} t$ for *some* $i\in[1,m]$,

or

$f >_\omega g$ and $s >_{S(\omega)} t_j$ for *all* $j\in[1,n]$,

or

$f \approx_\omega g$ and $\{s_1,\dots,s_m\} \underset{\sim S(\omega)}{\gg} \{t_1,\dots,t_n\}$,

where $\underset{\sim S(\omega)}{\gg}$ is the multiset ordering induced by $\ge_{S(\omega)}$.

The main property of the recursive path ordering is the following [Der87]:

Theorem. For any complete quasi-ordering $\ge_\omega$ of functional symbols in signature Σ, the recursive path ordering $\ge_{S(\omega)}$ on the set T_Σ of ground terms is a quasi-simplification ordering.

It is easy to prove that this theorem is correct also for our a bit restricted definition of the quasi-simplification ordering.

There should be mentioned another simple property of recursive path ordering which will be of importance further.

Lemma 7. Let $\ge_\omega$ be a quasi-ordering on the set of functional symbols of signature Σ and let $\ge_{S(\omega)}$ be the induced recursive path ordering on the set of ground terms T_Σ. If the greatest in the ordering $\ge_\omega$ functional symbol of the term $t_1\in T_\Sigma$ is greater than the greatest functional symbol of the term $t_2\in T_\Sigma$, then $t_1 \ge_{S(\omega)} t_2$ in the induced recursive path ordering $\ge_{S(\omega)}$.

There exists a natural extension of the recursive path ordering $\ge_{S(\omega)}$ for terms with variables (open terms). The definition of the *extended* recursive path ordering differs by additional relation which should be added to the above definition:

$s \geq_{S(\omega)} t$, *if t is a variable appearing in s.*

If under extension of $\geq_{S(\omega)}$ term s is equal or greater than term t, then for any substitution σ of variables by ground terms $s\sigma \geq_{S(\omega)} t\sigma$. So, the extension of recursive path ordering yields a sufficient $S(\omega)$-orientation condition $H_{S(\omega)}$ for rewrite rules:

$H_{S(\omega)}(l \to r)$ if $l >_{S(\omega)} r$

and

$H_{S(\omega)}(l \leftrightarrow r)$ if $l \approx_{S(\omega)} r$.

It is easy to see that if a total quasi-ordering $\geq_{\omega}$ on the signature Σ is given, then the corresponding recursive path ordering $\geq_{S(\omega)}$ and the sufficient $S(\omega)$-orientation condition $H_{S(\omega)}$ are efficient; we denote by $s(\omega)$ and $h(\omega)$ their Goedel numbers.

Now we can define an inductive synthesis algorithm QUITA_{ω} having already included the recursive path ordering and its extension:

$$\text{QUITA}_{\omega} \stackrel{def}{=} \text{QUITA}_{s(\omega),h(\omega)}.$$

Further we will only consider the algorithm QUITA_{ω} which is parameterized by the total quasi-ordering $\geq_{\omega}$ of the functional symbols of signature Σ.

An association A of signature Σ is called *ω-association* if there exists a total quasi-ordering $\geq_{\omega}$ for the signature Σ such that A is an $(S(\omega),H_{S(\omega)})$-association, where $S(\omega)$ is the recursive path ordering of T_{Σ} induced by ordering $\geq_{\omega}$ of Σ.

4.2 A MORE PRAGMATIC APPROACH FOR QUITA_{ω} ALGORITHM

Let D be an enumerable set of finite objects (for example, natural numbers, finite sequences, finite sets). Let F_D be a set of all total functions defined over the domain set D: $f \in F_D \Rightarrow f: D^n \to D$.

Two ground terms of signature F_D are called *semantically equal* if their values in D are the same.

Let $f_1,\ldots,f_n$ be some functions from F_D. We denote by $A_{f_1,\ldots,f_n}$ an association containing all ground terms of signature $\{f_1,\ldots,f_n\}$ split into the equivalence classes according to semantic equality relation.

Let D_i be some finite subset of the domain set D. A *D_i-sample of function* $f \in F_D$ is a set of all equalities of form

$$f(x_1,\ldots,x_k)=y,$$

where $y,x_1,\ldots,x_k \in D_i$.

A *D_i-sample of association* $A_{f_1,\ldots,f_n}$ is a set of all equalities of form

$$f_i(x_1,\ldots,x_k)=y,$$

where $f_i \in \{f_1,\ldots,f_n\}$ and $y,x_1,\ldots,x_k \in D_i$.

If the sequence of finite subsets of the domain set D

$$D_1, D_2, D_3, \ldots$$

is such that:

- $\forall i \in \mathbb{N}: D_i \subseteq D_{i+1}$,
- $\forall d \in D\ \exists n \in \mathbb{N}: d \in D_n$,

then the corresponding sequence $D_1Ex, D_2Ex,\ldots$ of D_i-samples of association A is called *complete*.

It is easy to see that any D_i-sample is a finite object which describes some sample of association $A_{f_1,\ldots,f_n}$. A modification of QUITA_ω algorithm for inputting D_i-samples instead of the samples defined above will be called *QUITA'_ω*. It follows directly from Theorem 2 and definition of the quasi-complete sequence of samples that QUITA'_ω algorithm synthesizes in limit any ω-association from the complete sequence of its D_i-samples.

The QUITA'_ω algorithm is implemented by the author in Turbo-Pascal on IBM/PC (it contains ≈1500 lines) and the further examples are computed by this experimental implementation.

4.3 INDUCTIVE SYNTHESIS OF FUNCTIONS - THE SIMPLEST CASE

In this section basic notations are retained the same as they were introduced in the previous section.

A set of functions $h_1,h_2,\ldots,h_a \in F_D$ will be called *constructors* of the domain set D if for any $d \in D$ there exists a ground term t of signature $\{h_1,\ldots,h_a\}$ such that the value of t is d.

We say that a rewrite system R *implements* function $f \in F_D$ by constructor functions $h_1,\ldots,h_a$ of the domain set D if R rewrites any term of signature $\{f,h_1,\ldots,h_a\}$ into the semantically equal term of signature $\{h_1,\ldots,h_a\}$. (A rewrite system R may use some intermediate functions $g_1,\ldots,g_k$ differing from $f, h_1, \ldots, h_a$, what will be of importance in the next section.)

Such interpretation of function implementation seems to be quite natural. For example, natural numbers can be constructed by functions $o=0$ and $s(X)=X+1$. In this case a natural number n is represented (encoded) by term of the form $\underbrace{s(s(s\ldots s(0)))}_{n}$. To find an implementation of some function f defined over natural numbers means to find an algorithm (rewrite system R) which rewrites any term of form $f(s(s(s\ldots s(0))))$ into the semantically equal term of form $s(s(s\ldots s(0)))$. If we want to operate with binary encoding of natural numbers, we have to choose another set of constructor functions, for example, functions $o=0$, $d(X)=2*X$, $t(X)=2*X+1$.

Now we can define a problem we consider in the current section. Let D be a domain set and $h_1, \ldots, h_a$ - its constructors completed with some algorithm Val which yields a value $d \in D$ for any term of signature $h_1, \ldots, h_a$. Let there be given a finite set of input/output samples for some function $f \in F_D$:

$$f(\overrightarrow{x_1})=y_1$$
$$f(\overrightarrow{x_2})=y_2$$
$$\cdots\cdots$$
$$f(\overrightarrow{x_n})=y_n \qquad (\overrightarrow{x_i}, y_j \in D).$$

Our aim is to synthesize from such sufficiently large sample a rewrite system which implements function f by constructor functions $h_1, \ldots, h_a$.

To solve this problem we suppose that the given input/output sample of function f is a D_1-sample of function f. By the abovementioned algorithm Val the D_1-sample of function f can be extended to the D_1-sample of association $A_{f,h_1,\ldots,h_a}$.

We define an ordering $\geq_\omega$ of functions $f, h_1, \ldots, h_a$ in the following way:

$$f >_\omega h_1 =_\omega h_2 =_\omega \ldots =_\omega h_a.$$

It follows from Theorem 2 that if association $A_{f,h_1,\ldots,h_a}$ is ω-association, then it can be synthesized by QUITA'_ω algorithm from sufficiently large D_1-sample of $A_{f,h_1,\ldots,h_a}$. It follows from Lemma 7 and our choice of ordering $\geq_\omega$ that synthesized rewrite system R is ω-complete and therefore implements function f by constructor functions $h_1, \ldots, h_a$.

Now we can summarize our methodology of function implementation synthesis. Let there be given some D_1-sample of a new function f. First we have to extend this sample to the D_1-sample of the association $A_{f,h_1,\ldots,h_a}$, where $h_1, \ldots, h_a$ are constructors of domain set D. After that for this sample we use the QUITA$'_\omega$ algorithm with the abovementioned ordering $\geq_\omega$. The obtained rewrite system R is the hypothesis of the rewrite system implementing f by constructor functions $h_1,\dots,h_n$.

Let us consider a simple example. Let functions 0 and $s(X)=X+1$ be chosen as constructors of domain set, i.e. natural numbers:

$o=0$

$s(o)=1$

$s(s(o))=2$

$s(s(s(o)))=3$

. . . .

We consider a usual addition operation $+(X,Y)=X+Y$. Let the following D_3-sample of function $+(X,Y)$ be given:

$+(0,0)=0$	$+(2,0)=2$	$+(3,0)=3$
$+(1,0)=1$	$+(0,2)=2$	$+(0,3)=3$
$+(0,1)=1$	$+(2,1)=3$	
$+(1,1)=2$	$+(1,2)=3$	

It can be easily extended to the D_3-sample of association $A_{+,s,o}$ by the following equalities (obtained by the algorithm Val), which in our case relates terms of signature $s,0$ to the decimal realization of natural numbers:

$o=0$

$s(0)=1$

$s(1)=2$

$s(2)=3$

Frequently it is more easy to give graphical form of D_1-sample:

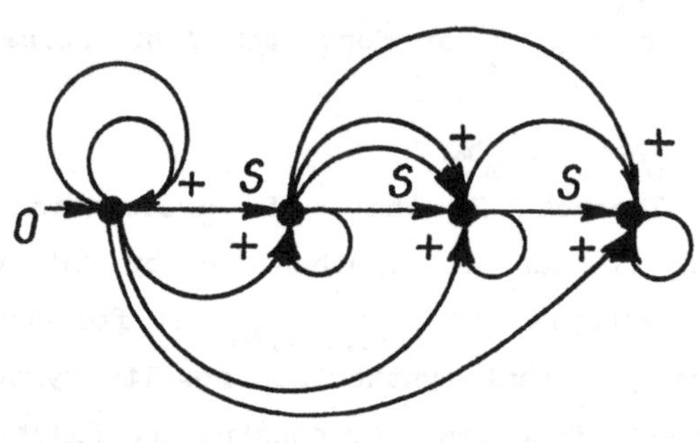

The ordering $\geq_\omega$ is fixed in the following way:

$$+ >_\omega s =_\omega 0.$$

Now we apply the algorithm QUITA$'_\omega$ and obtain the following rewrite system (within 5 seconds by QUITA$'_\omega$ implementation on IBM/PC):

$+(X,s(Y)) \to s(+(X,Y))$

$+(X,Y) \leftrightarrow +(Y,X)$

$+(X,0) \to X$

It is easy to see that this rewrite system is ground-complete and actually implements the function $+(X,Y)$ by constructor functions o and $s(X)$.

Unfortunately implementations of many functions can't be synthesized this way because they can't be implemented by the constructor functions without the use of intermediate functions. A square function $q(X)=X^2$ over natural numbers (with the same constructors 0 and $s(X)=X+1$) can serve as an example. According to our methodology from any D_1-sample of the function q we will obtain only some partial implementation rewrite system like this:

$q(0) \to 0$

$q(s(0)) \to s(o)$

$q(s(s(0))) \to s(s(s(q(s(0)))))$

$q(s(s(s(0)))) \to s(s(s(s(s(q(s(s(0))))))))$

$q(s(s(s(s(0))))) \to s(s(s(s(s(s(s(q(s(s(s(0)))))))))))$

Some regularity can be frequently detected when examining such a sequence of rewrite rules:

$$qs^{n+1}0 \to s^{2n+1}qs^{n}0.$$

Detected regularity can be used to replace a sequence by, in some sense equal, finite system of rewrite rules. Such approach is developed in [TJ89,Lan89] and seems to be useful in some situations. In the next section we will consider other, more pragmatic approach, for solving this problem by "learning" intermediate functions.

4.4 INDUCTIVE SYNTHESIS USING KNOWLEDGE BASE

Let $h_1,\dots,h_a$ be constructors of the domain set D. Let $f_1,\dots,f_n$ be an ordered set of functions from F_D such that association $A_{f_1,\dots,f_n,h_1,\dots,h_a}$ is an ω-association with respect to ordering $\geq_\omega$:

$$f_n >_\omega f_{n-1} >_\omega \dots >_\omega f_1 >_\omega h_1 =_\omega h_2 =_\omega \dots =_\omega h_a.$$

The sequence of functions $f_1,\dots,f_n$ ordered this way and the ω-complete rewrite system R realizing association $A_{f_1,\dots,f_n,h_1,\dots,h_a}$ will be called a *knowledge base* with respect to constructors $h_1,\dots,h_a$, and will be denoted:

$$B(f_1,\dots,f_n;R)/h_1,\dots,h_a.$$

It follows from Lemma 7 that for any knowledge base $B(f_1,\ldots,f_n;R)/h_1,\ldots,h_a$ a rewrite system R implements all functions $f_1,\ldots,f_n$ by constructors $h_1,\ldots,h_a$. The choice of constructor functions $h_1,\ldots,h_a$ is important because it fixes the encoding according to which functions are implemented. It is a well known fact that different algorithms are necessary to implement the same function with respect to different encodings (for example, multiplication by 10 is trivial for decimal encoding of natural numbers but much complicated for binary encoding; different algorithms are necessary for these different cases).

We say that knowledge base $B_1(f_1,\ldots,f_n;R_1)/h_1,\ldots,h_a$ is *bigger* than the other knowledge base $B_2(g_1,\ldots,g_m;R_2)/h_1,\ldots,h_a$ if there exists a subsequence $f_{i_1},f_{i_2},\ldots,f_{i_m}$ of sequence $f_1,\ldots,f_n$ such that:

- $1\le i_1<i_2<\ldots<i_m\le n$,
- $f_{i_1}=g_1,\ f_{i_2}=g_2,\ \ldots\ ,\ f_{i_m}=g_m$
- the rewrite systems R_1 and R_2 realize the same association over the signature $\{g_1,\ldots,g_m\}$ (which is the same as $\{f_{i_1},f_{i_2},\ldots,f_{i_m}\}$).

We say that function f can be *expressed* by rewrite system R' in knowledge base $B(f_1,\ldots,f_n;R)/h_1,\ldots,h_a$ if the association $A_{f,f_1,\ldots,f_n,h_1,\ldots,h_a}$ is an ω-association realized by ω-complete rewrite system R', where ordering $\ge_\omega$ is defined as follows:

$$f >_\omega f_n >_\omega f_{n-1} >_\omega \ldots >_\omega f_1 >_\omega h_1 =_\omega h_2 =_\omega \ldots =_\omega h_a.$$

The following properties of knowledge bases are important:

- If the function $f\in F_D$ is expressed by rewrite system R' in the knowledge base $B(f_1,\ldots,f_n;R)/h_1,\ldots,h_a$, then R' implements function f by constructors $h_1,\ldots,h_a$. The object $B'(f,f_1,\ldots,f_n;R')/h_1,\ldots,h_a$ is a knowledge base, too.

- If the function $f\in F_D$ can be expressed in the knowledge base $B(\ldots)/h_1,\ldots,h_a$, then f can be expressed in any knowledge base bigger than $B(\ldots)/h_1,\ldots,h_a$.

- Let $B_1(f_1,\ldots,f_n;R_1)/h_1,\ldots,h_a$ and $B_2(g_1,\ldots,g_m;R_2)/h_1,\ldots,h_a$ be knowledge bases. Then an object $B_3(f_1,\ldots,f_n,g_1,\ldots,g_m;R_1\cup R_2)/h_1,\ldots,h_a$ is a knowledge base, too, and all functions $f\in F_D$ which can be expressed in B_1 or B_2 can be expressed in B_3.

These three properties of knowledge bases form the key idea of learning process we are willing to use in inductive synthesis of nontrivial function implementations.

In this case we suppose that besides the domain set D and its constructors $h_1,\dots,h_a$ with algorithm Val some knowledge base $B(f_1,\dots,f_n;R)/h_1,\dots,h_a$ is also given. Let there be given a D_1-sample of some new function $f \in F_D$. Our aim is to synthesize a rewrite system R' which implements a function f by constructors $h_1,\dots,h_a$.

The methodology is very similar to that in Section 4.3. First we extend this D_1-sample of function f to the D_1-sample of the association $A_{f,f_1,\dots,f_n,h_1,\dots,h_a}$ by means of the algorithm Val and the rewrite system R of the knowledge base. After that we apply the QUITA$'_\omega$ algorithm for this D_1-sample of association with ordering $\geq_\omega$:

$$f >_\omega f_n >_\omega f_{n-1} >_\omega \dots >_\omega f_1 >_\omega h_1 =_\omega h_2 =_\omega \dots =_\omega h_a.$$

The obtained rewrite system R' is the hypothesis of rewrite system implementing f by constructor functions $h_1,\dots,h_a$.

Let us consider an example. The function we want to implement is the square function $q(X)=X^2$. The knowledge base contains previously synthesized rewrite system implementing addition function $+(X,Y)=X+Y$:

$B(+(X,Y),R)/s(X),0,$

where R is

$+(X,s(Y)) \to s(+(X,Y))$

$+(X,Y) \leftrightarrow +(Y,X)$

$+(X,0) \to X.$

Let there be given D_9-sample of function $q(X)$:

$q(0)=0$
$q(1)=1$
$q(2)=4$
$q(3)=9.$

First the D_9-sample of function $q(X)$ is extended to the D_9-sample of the association $A_{q,+,s,0}$ by means of rewrite system R and the algorithm H.

Ordering $\geq_\omega$ is defined in the following way:

$$q >_\omega + >_\omega s =_\omega 0$$

and the QUITA$'_\omega$ algorithm is applied for the D_9-sample of association $A_{q,+,s,0}$. In 25 seconds by experimental implementation on IBM/PC we obtain the rewrite system

$q(s(X)) \to s(+(+(X,X),q(X)))$

$q(0) \to 0$

$+(X,s(Y)) \to s(+(X,Y))$

$+(X,Y) \leftrightarrow +(Y,X)$

$+(X,0) \to X$

which implements the function q by the constructors $s,0$. The obtained rewrite system yields a new, bigger knowledge base containing functions q and +.

It is easy to see that this way all primitive recursive functions can be learned by $QUITA'_\omega$, if they are learned in the right order.

There is a possibility to improve the $QUITA'_\omega$ algorithm when it is used for learning by means of knowledge bases. As it can be seen in the example above a rewrite system implementing function q completely contains a rewrite system implementing function +, which was used as a knowledge base. According to our non-improved methodology every time when we use some knowledge base $B(f_1,\dots,f_n;R)/h_1,\dots,h_a$ we have to resynthesize all rules of R again. Such resynthesis can be excluded if we modify the $QUITA'_\omega$ algorithm so that it does not start from an empty set of rules (see variable R in the program of QUITA in Section 3.5) but inputs initial value of R containing the rewrite system of the knowledge base used. In this case we have to synthesize only additional rules.

In fact, this way we can also input some properties of the new function to be synthesized, what makes synthesis process faster and reduces the size of the necessary sample. So we can use partial specifications of the form of algebraic axioms - we have to orient them by means of predicate $H_{S(\omega)}$ and input as the initial set of rules R.

4.5 AN EXAMPLE

Here we show a typical learning session by the $QUITA'_\omega$ algorithm. We synthesize the implementations of several basic arithmetic functions for the binary encoding of natural numbers.

For that we have to choose specific constructor functions: 0, $d(X)=2*X$ and $t(X)=2*X+1$. In this case natural numbers are encoded in the following way: operation d stands for "0" and operation t for "1" in the inverted binary code of naturals:

o=0

$t(o)$=1

$d(t(o))$=10

$t(t(o))$=11

$d(d(t(o)))$=100

$t(d(t(o)))=101$

$d(t(t(o)))=110$

. . . .

These constructor functions do not encode natural numbers uniquely because a significant part of binary number can precede some nonsignificant zeros. So, some non-empty rewrite system realizes the association of constructors $A_{t,d,0}$. Let us consider a D_2-sample of association $A_{t,d,0}$:

$0=0$

$d(0)=0$

$t(0)=1$

$d(1)=10$

Applying QUITA$'_\omega$ algorithm to this sample we obtain immediately the rewrite system of one rule:

$d(0) \rightarrow 0$ (R1)

The meaning of this rule is a well known property that in the beginning of the number zero may be deleted.

So, we have a simple knowledge base already:

$B_1(\{\ \};\{\text{R1}\})/t,d,0.$

Now we are ready to learn some functions defined for natural numbers. We start with successor function $s(X)=X+1$. The next is D_4-sample of function s:

$s(0)=1$

$s(1)=10$

$s(10)=11$

$s(11)=100.$

Using the knowledge base B_1 from this sample the following additional rules to rule R1 are synthesized by QUITA$'_\omega$ algorithm (in 4 seconds on IBM/PC):

$s(0) \rightarrow t(0)$ (R2)

$s(d(X)) \rightarrow t(X)$ (R3)

$s(t(X)) \rightarrow d(s(X))$ (R4)

Each of the synthesized rule has a clear meaning describing how the binary code of the successive natural number can be obtained from the given number.

Rules R1,R2,R3,R4 form a new, bigger knowledge base:

$B_2(s;\{\text{R1,R2,R3,R4}\})/t,d,0.$

The next function we learn will be addition: $+(X,Y)=X+Y$. Let D_8-sample of adding function be given:

+(0,0)=0	. . . . .
+(0,1)=1	+(101,1)=110
+(1,0)=1	+(1,101)=110
+(0,10)=10	+(0,110)=110
. . . . .	+(110,0)=110

Using the knowledge base B_2 by QUITA'_{ω} algorithm from this sample the following additional rules to rules R1,...,R4 are synthesized (within 198 seconds on IBM/PC):

$$+(X,0) \rightarrow X \qquad \text{(R5)}$$

$$+(X,Y) \leftrightarrow +(Y,X) \qquad \text{(R6)}$$

$$+(t(X),d(Y)) \rightarrow t(+(X,Y)) \qquad \text{(R7)}$$

$$+(d(X),d(Y)) \rightarrow d(+(X,Y)) \qquad \text{(R8)}$$

$$+(t(X),t(Y)) \rightarrow d(s(+(X,Y))) \qquad \text{(R9)}$$

Rules R5,R6 are general adding function properties, but rules R7,R8,R9 describe how two binary codes have to be added . The size of the sample necessary for inductive synthesis of adding function could be reduced substantially if some properties of adding function were given a priori, for example, commutativity property R6.

Now we have a new, bigger knowledge base:

$B_3(+,s;\{\text{R1,R2,R3,R4,R5,R6,R7,R8,R9}\})/t,d,0$

The next function we learn will be multiplication: $*(X,Y)=X*Y$. Let D_8-sample of multiplication function be given:

*(0,0)=0	. . . . .
*(0,1)=0	*(100,10)=1000
*(1,1)=1	*(10,100)=1000
*(1,10)=10	*(1000,1)=1000
. . . . .	*(1,1000)=1000

Using the knowledge base B_3 by the QUITA'_{ω} algorithm from this sample the following additional rules to rules R1,...,R9 are synthesized (within 316 seconds on IBM/PC):

$$*(X,0) \rightarrow 0 \qquad \text{(R10)}$$

$$*(X,Y) \leftrightarrow *(Y,X) \qquad \text{(R11)}$$

$$*(X,d(Y)) \rightarrow d(*(X,Y)) \qquad \text{(R12)}$$

$$*(X,t(Y)) \rightarrow +(X,d(*(X,Y))) \qquad \text{(R13)}$$

This is a complete set of well-known binary multiplication properties. For example, let us compute the value of expression 11*100 by the synthesized rewrite system R1-R13. For that we have to find a normal form of term

$*(t(t(0)),d(d(t(0))))$. We obtain the normal form term $d(d(t(t(0))))$ that stands for binary number 1100.

Thus we have quite rich knowledge base

$B_4(*,+,s;\{R1,...,R13\})/t,d,0$

sufficient for inductive synthesis of many functions defined over natural numbers.

It is easy to see that rewrite system R1,...,R13 implements all functions $*,+,s$ by constructor functions $t,d,0$, i.e. in the binary encoding of natural numbers.

5 Conclusion

The described approach provides explicit mathematical background for efficient inductive synthesis of primitive recursive functions. The method is implemented and approved to be quite efficient. So, it can be used, for example, for inductive synthesis of implementations of abstract data types.

We are going to develop this approach in the following three directions:

- Inductive synthesis of implementations for partially defined functions. Rewrite systems implementing such functions usually are not completely terminating what causes specific problems during their inductive synthesis. At the same time there are wide partially defined function classes which can be synthesized efficiently by methods similar to those described in this paper.
- Automatic inductive "invention" of the necessary intermediate functions. This is the problem considered in Section 4.3 where square function couldn't be implemented because the intermediate adding function was necessary. For primitive recursive functions this problem theoretically can be solved by exhaustive search but more economical methods could be wished.
- Development of methodology for solving PROLOG-like problems in rewrite systems which, besides other benefits, leads to efficient inductive synthesis of inverse functions. Any set of PROLOG clauses can be interpreted as a rewrite system: for example, clauses

Is_elem(E,[E|A]).

Is_elem(E,[X|A]) :- Is_elem(E,A).

are interpreted as

$$Is\_elem(E,push(E,A)) \rightarrow true$$

$$Is\_elem(E,push(X,A)) \rightarrow Is\text{-}elem(E,A).$$

The point is that duality of PROLOG and rewrite systems lead to backtracking/unification strategy for solving term equations. For example, this way by the rewrite system which implements a square function $q(X)=X^2$ we can find a term X such that $q(X)=s(s(s(s(0))))$, i.e. compute a square root function.

REFERENCES

[Ang74] D.Angluin, Easily inferred sequences, *Memorandum No.ERL-M499, University of California*, 1974.

[AS83] D.Angluin and C.H.Smith, Inductive Inference: Theory and Methods, *Computing Surveys* 15, 237-264, 1983.

[Ang80] D.Angluin, Finding patterns common to a set of strings, *J.Comput. Syst. Sci.*, 21, 46-62, 1980.

[Bar90] J.M.Barzdin and G.J.Barzdin, Rapid construction of algebraic axioms from samples, (*Will appear in North-Holland)* 1990.

[Bar89] G.Barzdin, Inductive synthesis of encoding for algebraic data types, *Lect. Notes Artif. Intelligence* 397, 328-338, 1989.

[Bar83] J.M.Barzdin, Some rules of inductive inference and their use for program synthesis, *Information Processing 83*, 333-338, Amsterdam, North-Holland, 1983.

[BW89] L.G.Bouma and H.R.Walters, Implementing algebraic specifications, *Algebraic specification*, ACM Press frontier series,. 1989.

[BK76] A.W.Biermann and R.Krishnaswamy, Constructing programs from example computations, *IEEE Trans.Software Eng.* 2, 141-153, 1976.

[Bie78] A.W.Biermann, The inference of regular LISP programs from examples, *IEEE Trans. Systems Man Cybernet.* 8, 585-600, 1978.

[BK86] A.Brazma and E.B.Kinber, Generalized regular expressions - a language for synthesis of programs with branching in loops, *Theor. Comp. Sci.* 46, 175-195, 1986.

[Cre72] S.Crespi-Reghizzi, An effective model for grammar inference, *Information Processing 71*, New York, North-Holland, 524-529, 1972.

[Der87] N.Dershowitz, Termination of Rewriting, *Symbolic Computation* 3, 69-116, 1987.

[Gol67] E.M.Gold, Language identification in the limit, *Information and control* 10, 447-474, 1967.

[Lan89] S.Lange, Towards a set of inference rules for solving divergence in Knuth-Bendix completion, *Lect. Notes Artificial Intelligence* 397, 304-316, 1989.

[Sha83] E.Shapiro, Algorithmic program debugging, *Cambridge(Mas.) MIT Press*, 1983.

[Sum77] P.D.Summers, A Methodology for LISP program construction from examples, *J. ACM* 24-1, 161-175, 1977.

[TJ89] M.Thomas and K.P.Jantke, Inductive inference for solving divergence in Knuth-Bendix completion, *Lect. Notes Artificial Intelligence* 397, 288-303, 1989.

[Yok89] T.Yokomori, Learning context-free languages efficiently, *Lect. Notes Artificial Intelligence* 397, 104-123, 1989.

AUTOMATIC CONSTRUCTION OF TEST SETS: THEORETICAL APPROACH

Andrejs Auziņš, Jānis Bārzdiņš, Jānis Bičevskis, Kārlis Čerāns, Audris Kalniņš
The University of Latvia
Raiņa bulv. 19, Rīga 226250, Latvia

Abstract

We consider the problem of automatic construction of complete test set (CTS) from program text. The completeness criterion adopted is C_1, i.e., it is necessary to execute all feasible branches of program at least once on the tests of CTS. A simple programming language is introduced with the property that the values used in conditional statements are not arithmetically deformed. For this language the CTS problem is proved to be algorithmically solvable and CTS construction algorithm is obtained. Some generalizations of this language containing counters, stacks or arrays are considered where the CTS problem remains solvable. In conclusion the applications of the obtained results to CTS construction for real time systems are considered.

1 Introduction

Program testing remains the least automated and most resource–demanding step in the program development process. There are several testing methods: functional testing, structural testing, random testing, etc. In this paper we consider only structural testing. In the structural testing all activities, including test case selection, are based on program structure. The question about the completeness of the selected test set appears naturally. In the case of structural testing the most widely accepted completeness criterion is C_1 [11]: a test set is said to satisfy criterion C_1 if all feasible branches of program can be executed on this set. We shall not discuss how complete criterion C_1 is (see, e.g. [1,15]), we just note once more that this criterion is widely accepted in practice and there seems to be found no better criterion up to the moment.

For a fixed completeness criterion the problem of automatic construction of complete (with respect to the criterion) test set from program text arises. In this paper we consider the automatic construction of complete test sets according to criterion C_1. Such test sets will be simply called complete test sets (CTS), and the construction problem of such test sets will be called CTS problem.

We note just now that CTS problem is algorithmically unsolvable in general case, besides, as further results show, the algorithmic unsolvability appears swiftly. The aim of the paper is to find sufficiently large program classes with algorithmically solvable CTS problem and to develop the corresponding algorithms.

Yet, another remark. The variable value ranges are limited for real programming languages. For example, integer variable in Pascal can assume values from –2147483648 to 2147483647. These value limits formally yield the algorithmic solvability of CTS problem: the set of theoretically possible values of all internal variables of program can be used as the set of program states (this set will always be finite for the assumed restrictions), hence, CTS can be constructed by means of exhaustive search. However, it is clear that such a method is unusable in practice. A question arises how to exclude the trivial solution by means of exhaustive search. One of the ways is to drop the restrictions on variable value ranges. In this case the variable value range is infinite and thus the trivial solution to CTS problem by means of exhaustive search is excluded. If we, nevertheless, find an algorithm for CTS construction, it is probable that this algorithm will not use exhaustive search. Therefore we can hope that this algorithm will not use exhaustive search also for finite value ranges. Namely this way will be used in the paper. The obtained results confirm that the CTS construction algorithms obtained this way don't use exhaustive search indeed and are practically usable in many cases.

To conclude the introduction we give brief characteristics of program classes for which the solvability of CTS problem has been proved and corresponding algorithms obtained. Firstly these program classes have the property that variable values used in conditional statements are not arithmetically deformed, i.e., these values are read directly from program input data. The second characteristic property of these classes is connected with some restrictions on direct access to data. An important class of programs is formed by programs with counters. The CTS construction problem is obviously unsolvable for programs with free use of counters. Nevertheless, sufficiently general program classes with counters having solvable CTS problem can be found. One of the most important of such classes with solvable CTS problem is programs with real time counter.

In the conclusion some methods are presented for reducing real time programs to the models considered.

The paper contains results obtained by the authors at various times [2–10], as well as new results. New results are presented in Section 5 (J.Bārzdiņš) and Sections 9, 10 (K.Čerāns).

2 The First Solvable Case: Programs in Base Language L_0

2.1 Description of Language L_0

In order to expose the principal ideas we introduce a very simple programming language L_0 for the processing of sequential files. Nevertheless, a large part of business data processing in the sequential files area can be formalized in this language (adequately enough to investigate the construction of complete test set). This language can be characterized by the fact that values taking part in comparison statements are undeformed (i.e., such as read from input). This restriction is acceptable in practice because it is typical for data processing programs that program logic is controlled only by input data (e.g., record type) and that these data are used in comparison statements undeformed.

Now let us describe the language L_0. Programs in L_0 use external variables of special type, named tapes. We shall use tapes to represent finite sequences of integers. We shall say that tape X contains a sequence of integers $(x_1, x_2, \ldots, x_r)$, if the first cell of the tape contains x_1, the second - x_2, . . . , the r-th - x_r, but the other cells are empty (fig.1).

X: | x_1 | x_2 | . . . . | x_r |

Fig. 1

To put it otherwise it means that the value of the variable X is $(x_1, x_2, \ldots, x_r)$ in this case. We shall denote the i-th cell of X by X_i, this notation being used also as an integer - valued variable (the value of X_i is undefined if X_i is empty).

A program in L_0 has a finite number of input tapes and a finite number of output tapes associated with it. The program processes the values of its input tapes into values of its output tapes.

Initially the reading (writing) head is located on the first cell. The execution of an input (output) statement moves the head one position right. A program also has a finite number of integer-valued internal variables. We assume that all internal variables are initialized to 0 in the beginning. Now let us describe the statements of L_0. Let X be an input tape, Y - output tape, t, u - internal variables and c - constant (fixed integer). The following statements are available:

1. **X→ t** . The current cell of tape X is assigned to variable t. Thus, if $X = (x_1, x_2, \ldots, x_p)$, the first occurrence of statement **X→ t** assigns the value x_1 to t, the second - x_2 and so on. The statement has two exits: "+" if the current cell is nonempty and exit "-" if the cell is empty (tape is exhausted). In the last case the value of t is not changed. (Input statement).

2. **t→Y** . The value of variable t is assigned to the current cell of tape Y. (Output statement).

3. **u→t** (respectively **c→t**). The value of variable u (constant c) is assigned to variable t. (Assignment statement).
4. **u<t** (respectively **c<t, u<c**). The statement has two exits: if the value of u (respectively c) is less than the value of t (respectively c), then the exit "+" is used, otherwise, the exit "-". (Comparison statement).
5. **NOP**. Dummy statement (nothing is done). It is used instead of statements not essential for the construction of complete test set when more general programing languages are reduced to L_0. (Informally, these are unconditional statements not affecting the variable values used in comparisons).

6. **STOP**.

Statements 1 and 4 having two exits are called conditional statements, the other ones are called unconditional.

Informally a program in L_0 is a program constructed from the abovementioned statements in a normal way. Formally we define a *program in the language* L_0 as a quadruple

$$(\mathbf{X}, \mathbf{Y}, \mathbf{Z}, \mathbf{P}),$$

where $\mathbf{X}$ is a set of input tapes (e.g., $\mathbf{X}$={ A, B, . . . , C }), $\mathbf{Y}$ is a set of output tapes (e.g., $\mathbf{Y}$={ U, V, . . . , T }), $\mathbf{Z}$ is a set of internal variables (e.g., $\mathbf{Z}$={ a, b, . . . , v }), **P** is a flowchart constructed from statements of L_0. We require also all exits of statements in flowchart to be attached to some statements, i.e., no pending exits are allowed (c.f. the case in Section 4). We also assume the flowchart to be connected. The execution starts from the first statement (marked by the label "→"). Program stops when it reaches a STOP statement.

Fig. 2 gives an example of a program which creates a new sorted tape (file) by merging sorted tapes A and B. The program has a bug: control from statement 7 is passed to statement 8 (instead of 10).

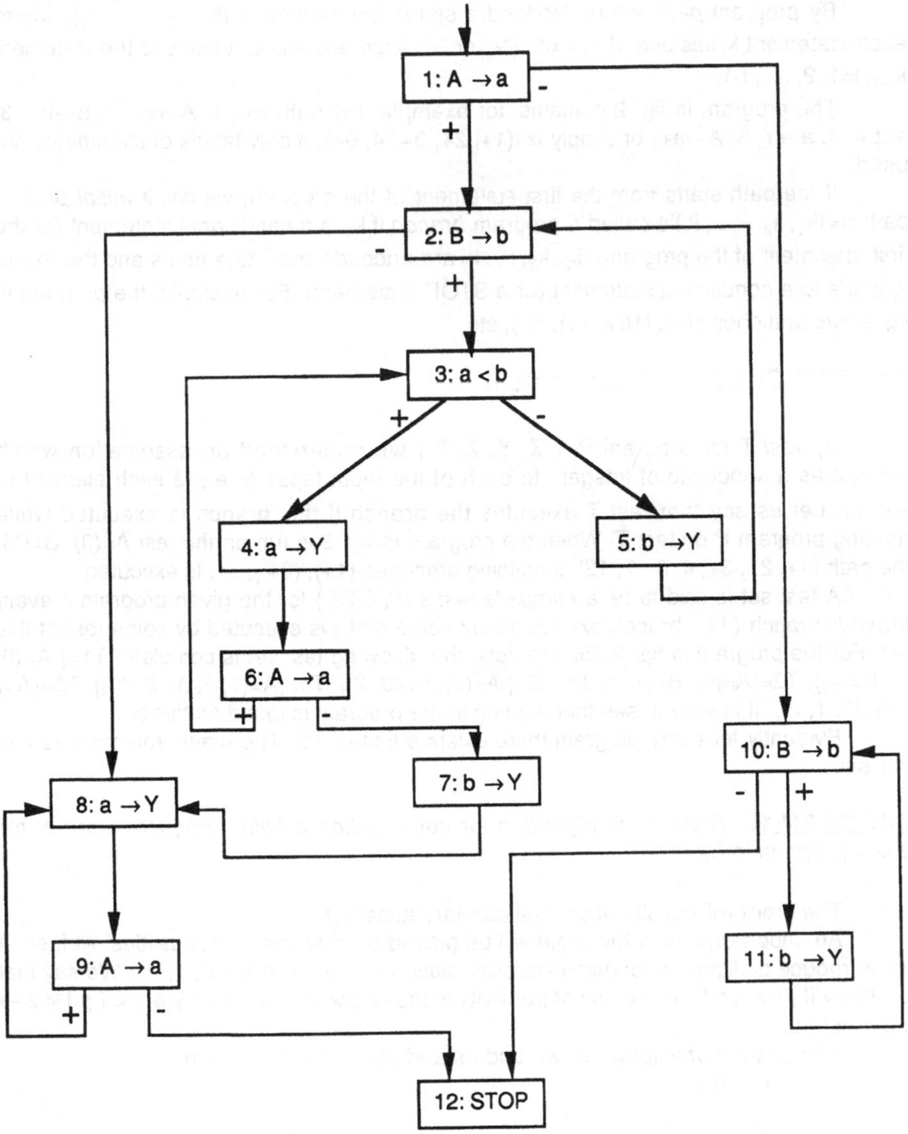

Fig. 2

By program *path* we understand a statement sequence $(k_1, k_2, \ldots, k_r)$, where each statement k_i has one of its exits ("+" or "-") fixed and this exit leads to the statement k_{i+1}, i=1, 2, . . ., r-1.

The program in fig. 2 contains, for example, the path α=(1: A→a+, 2: B→b+, 3: a<b+, 4: a→Y, 6: A→a+) or simply α=(1+, 2+, 3+, 4, 6+), if only labels of statements are used.

If the path starts from the first statement of the program, we call it *initial path.* A path $\alpha=(k_1, k_2, \ldots, k_r)$is called a program *branch* if k_1 is a conditional statement (or the first statement of the program), $k_2, k_3, \ldots k_r$ are unconditional statements and the exit of k_r leads to a conditional statement (or a STOP statement). For example, the program in fig. 2 has branches (1+), (10+, 11), (1-), etc.

2.2 CTS Construction Problem

By *test* T for program P=(**X**, **Y**, **Z**, **P**) we understand an association which associates a sequence of integers to each of the input tapes (i. e., to each element of set **X**). Let us say that test T executes the branch if this branch is executed while running program P on test T. When the program in fig. 2 is run on the test A=(0), B=(1), the path (1+, 2+, 3+, 4, 6-, 7, 12) containing branches (1+), (2+), . . . is executed.

A test set is said to be a *complete test set* (CTS) for the given program if every *feasible* branch (i.e., branch executable by some test) is executed by some test of this set. For the program in fig. 2, for example, the following test set is complete: T1={ A=(0, 1), B=(2)}, T2={A=(6), B=(1, 2, 3)}, T3={ A=(2), B=(0, 2)}, T4={A=(1, 2, 3), B=(0)}, T5={A=( ), B=(0, 1, 2)}. It is easy to see that the bug in the program is found on this set.

Evidently for every program there exists a finite CTS. The main problem is to find this set.

THEOREM 1. *There is an algorithm for constructing a finite complete test set for every program in* L_0.

The proof will consist of several auxiliary assertions.

An important role in the proof will be played by systems of inequalities. At first let us introduce a slightly extended inequality relation <(r)<, where r=0, 1, . . . We say that x < (r) <y if y - x ≥ r. Now the rule of transivity is the following: x < (r) < y & y < (p) < z → x < (r+p)< z.

By *a system of inequalities* we understand the following system

$$x_1 < (r_1) < y_1$$
$$\ldots\ldots$$
$$x_n < (r_n) < y_n,$$

where $x_1, \ldots, x_n, y_1, \ldots, y_n$ are variables or integer constants, for example,

a < (0) < 3
b < (2) < a
b < (5) < 3
b < (3) < c
c < (0) < d
d < (0) < c
-4 < (1) < b
-4 < (2) < 3.

We represent systems of inequalities also as *graphs*: vertices are labeled by variables and constants of the system and an edge of the weight r is drawn from vertex y to vertex x if the system contains inequality x < (r) < y. So the previous example of inequality system corresponds to the graph in fig. 3.

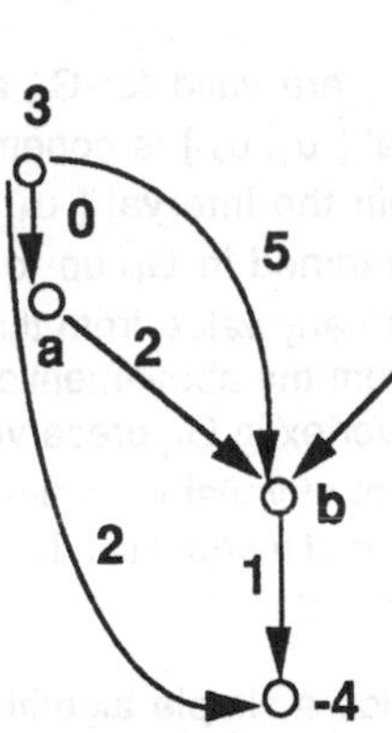

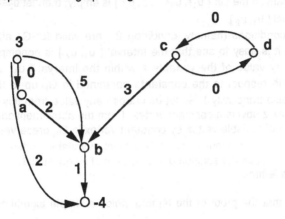

Fig. 3

Vertices labeled by variables are called *variable vertices* (vertices a, b, c, d in fig. 3), and vertices labeled by constants are called *constant vertices* (vertices 3 and -4).

Let us consider a directed path in the graph of inequality system. We define the weight of the path to be the sum of weights of the edges contained in the path.

Let us remark the following simple lemma.

LEMMA 1. *The inequality system N has a solution iff its graph G_N has the following properties:*

1. There is no cyclic path with the weight greater than 0.

2. The weight of every path leading from a constant vertex c_1 to a constant vertex c_2 is not greater than c_1-c_2.

The necessity is obvious. Let us prove the sufficiency. We build the solution by induction: at every induction step we assign constant value to some variable vertex of G_N in such a way that, first, the assigned constant satisfies all inequalities of the graph concerning the given vertex and, second, the replacement of the variable vertex by the constant vertex in the graph preserves validity of lemma conditions. To do this we need some additional notions. Let us say that vertex x is p units (p>0) greater (less) than vertex y if the maximum weight of paths leading from x to y (from y to x) is equal to p. Let us consider a variable vertex z in G_N with no constant value assigned in the previous steps. Let us find all constant vertices (including the ones created in the previous steps) with the paths leading to them from z.

Let $c_1^1, c_2^1, \ldots, c_k^1$ be the values of these vertices and $p_1^1, p_2^1, \ldots, p_k^1$ be numbers showing how many units the corresponding vertex is less than z. Similarly we find all constant vertices with the paths leading from them to z. Let $c_1^2, c_2^2, \ldots, c_l^2$ be their values and $p_1^2, p_2^2, \ldots p_l^2$ be numbers showing how much they are greater than z. Now let us consider numbers

$u_i^1=c_i^1+p_i^1$, i=1, 2, . . . , k, and

$u_i^2=c_i^2-p_i^2$, i=1, 2, . . . l.

Let $u_1=\max(u_1{}^1, u_2{}^1, \ldots, u_k{}^1)$ and $u_2=\min(u_1{}^2, u_2{}^2, \ldots, u_l{}^2)$. If the set $\{u_1{}^1, u_2{}^1, \ldots, u_k{}^1\}$ is empty (i.e., there are no paths from z to constant vertices), then let us assume $u_1=-\infty$. Similarly, if the set $\{u_1{}^2, u_2{}^2, \ldots, u_l{}^2\}$ is empty, then let $u_2=+\infty$. Now let us consider the interval $[u_1, u_2]$.

If the lemma conditions (namely, condition 2) are valid for G_N after previous induction steps, then it is easy to see that the interval $[u_1, u_2]$ is nonempty. It is also easy to see that every value of the variable z within the interval $[u_1, u_2]$ satisfies inequalities of G_N with respect to the constants contained in G_N up to that moment (taking into account also transitivity). So let us choose any value from this interval and assign it to z. So vertex z now is a constant vertex. From the abovementioned it is clear that such replacement of variable vertex by constant vertex in G_N preserves the validity of the lemma conditions. By continuing the replacement of variable vertices by constant ones the same way we obtain the solution of the system of inequalities N.

This proves the lemma.

Let us remark that the proof of the lemma yields a simple algorithm for solving inequality systems.

Let P be a program in $\mathbf{L_0}$ and $\alpha=(k_1, k_2, \ldots, k_r)$ an initial path in this program. Now let us define a system of inequalities $N(\alpha)$ corresponding to path α. $N(\alpha)$ will describe the feasibility conditions of path α. Let α_i denote the initial segment $(k_1, k_2, \ldots, k_i)$ of path α, $i=1, 2, \ldots, r$, and α_0 the empty initial segment. Let X be an input tape and t, u internal variables of program P. Let t_k, u_l be variables denoting the values of variables t, u after the execution of path $\alpha_{i-1}=(k_1, k_2, \ldots, k_{i-1})$ and X_s the last cell of tape X read during the execution (at the beginning the corresponding variables are t_0, u_0, X_0). Let c be a constant.

The system $N(\alpha)$ will be defined inductively: $N(\alpha_0), N(\alpha_1), \ldots, N(\alpha_r)= N(\alpha)$. Let us remember that internal variables are equal to 0 in the beginning. Therefore we define

$$N(\alpha_0)= \begin{cases} t_0=0 \\ u_0=0 \\ \ldots \end{cases}$$

Now let us assume that the system of inequalities $N(\alpha_{i-1})$ is already defined. Then we define $N(\alpha_i)$ as a system obtained from $N(\alpha_{i-1})$ by adding the following inequalities (in the sequel we use also standard inequality and equality relations $x\leq y$, $x<y$, $x=y$ understanding by them $x<(0)<y$, $x<(1)<y$, $x<(0)<y$ & $y<(0)<x$ respectively):

(1) If $k_i=(X\rightarrow u-)$, then inequality $X<0$ is added. By inequality $X<0$ we code the fact that integer sequence on tape X is exhausted.

(2) If $k_i=(X\rightarrow u+)$ and $N(\alpha_{i-1})$ does not contain inequality $X<0$ (i.e., no statement of type $X\rightarrow u-$ has been performed), then equality

$$u_{l+1}=X_{s+1}$$

is added. In this case new variables u_{l+1} and X_{s+1} are introduced which have the same sense for statement k_{i+1} as u_l and X_s have for k_i. If inequality $X< 0$ has already occured, then inequality $0< X$ is added in order to obtain a contradictory system.

(3) If $k_i=(t\rightarrow u)$ (or $k_i=(c\rightarrow u)$), then equality

$$u_{l+1}=t_k \text{ (or } u_{l+1}=c\text{)}$$

is added. A new variable u_{l+1} is again introduced in this case.

(4) If k_i=(t<u+) (or k_i=(c<u+) or k_i=(t<c+)), then inequality $t_k<(1)<u_l$ (or $c<(1)<u_l$) or $t_k<(1)<c$) is added.

(5) If k_i=(t<u-) (or k_i=(c<u-) or k_i=(t<c-)), then inequality $t_k>(0)>u_l$ (or $c>(0)>u_l$ or $t_k>(0)>c$) is added.

Let us give an example. For α^*=(1+, 2+, 3+) (see fig. 2) we have the inequality system

$$N(\alpha^*) = \begin{cases} a_0=0 \\ b_0=0 \\ a_1=A_1 \\ b_1=B_1 \\ a_1<(1)<b_1 \end{cases}$$

$N(\alpha^*)$ is represented as a graph in fig.4.

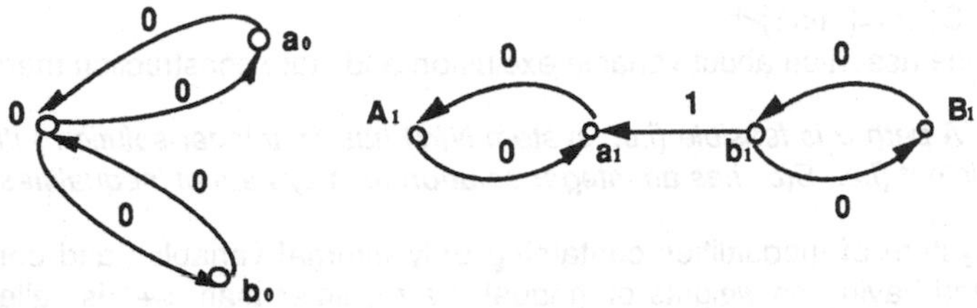

Fig.4

From the construction of $N(\alpha)$ there follows:

LEMMA 2. *The path α is feasible iff the system $N(\alpha)$ has an integer solution. Any solution of $N(\alpha)$ with respect to variables - cells of input tapes yields a test executing path α.*

Our aim is to reduce $N(\alpha)$ while preserving the existence (or the nonexistence) of the solution in such a way that there will be only a finite number of possible reduced systems for the given program P. This reduction relies on a variable exclusion method. Let us introduce some notations for this purpose.

Let us consider all the constants of program P (including 0). Let c_1 be the minimal and c_2 the maximal among these constants. Let $c_0 = c_2 - c_1$. Let us consider an arbitrary system of inequalities N (e.g. $N(\alpha)$) where all constants are within the segment $[c_1, c_2]$ and weights of edges within $[0, c_0+1]$. Let y be a variable in system N. Now let us define the exclusion of variable y. We consider all the pairs x, z of variables and / or constants distinct from y for which there exist inequalities $x < (p_1) < y$ and $y < (p_2) < z$ in the system N. For each of these pairs we add a new inequality $x < (r) < z$ to N where $r=p_1+p_2$ if $p_1+p_2 \le c_0+1$ and $r=c_0+1$ if $p_1+p_2 > c_0+1$. Then we delete all inequalities containing y from N. If N contains inequality of the type $y<(p)<y$ with $p > 0$, then this inequality is replaced by some standard contradicting inequality, e.g., $0 < (1) < 0$ (because the new system must have no solutions). So obtained inequality system is denoted by N'. From the construction of N' there follows an assertion:

The conditions for solution existence from Lemma 1 hold for inequality system N iff these conditions hold for inequality system N'. In other words, *inequality system N has a solution iff N' has a solution.*

Now let us return to inequality system $N(\alpha)$. Let program P have input tapes A, B,

. . . and internal variables t, u, ... Then the system $N(\alpha)$ contains, in general, variables A, B, . . . ; $A_1, A_2, \ldots, A_d$; $B_1, B_2, \ldots, B_e$; . . . ; $t_1, t_2, \ldots, t_f$; $u_1, u_2, \ldots, u_g$; . . . . Let us remember that internal variables with maximal subscripts t_f, u_g, . . . denote values of internal variables t, u, . . . after the execution of path α. These variables t_f, u_g, . . . , as well as variables A, B, . . . denoting input files are called active variables, the other ones - inactive. For example, the system $N(\alpha^*)$ from the previous example has active variables a_1, b_1. Now let us exclude, one after another, all inactive variables from $N(\alpha)$. It is easy to see that the order of variable exclusion does not affect the resulting system. Thus, we obtain a new system of inequalities containing only active variables. Then we drop all subscripts of the variables in it. The resulting system is denoted by $S(\alpha)$ and called a *program state after the execution of path* α.

Informally the state describes relations between current values of internal variables. The state corresponding to the path α^*=(1+, 2+, 3+) from the previous example, as it can be easily deduced from the inequality system $N(\alpha^*)$, is

$S(\alpha^*)$={ a<(1)<b.

From the assertion about variable exclusion and state construction there follows

LEMMA 3. *A path α is feasible (i.e., system $N(\alpha)$ has an integer solution) iff the state $S(\alpha)$ is consistent (i.e., $S(\alpha)$ has an integer solution as a system of inequalities).*

The system of inequalities containing only internal variables and constants of program P and having no weights of inequalities r greater than c_0+1 is called *state* of the program P. Like every system of inequalities a state can be represented by a graph. Two states will be called equal if the corresponding graphs are isomorphic (as graphs with labeled vertices and edges). It is easy to see that every program P has a finite number of distinct states. This fact together with the next lemma will play the main role in the proof of Theorem 1.

Now we need to generalize slightly the notion of the system of inequalities $N(\alpha)$ for path. At first there will be no longer the requirement for a path α=($k_1, k_2,.., k_r$) to be initial. Further, we allow to have arbitrary state σ of program P as an initial inequality system for construction. Under these conditions we define the system

$N(\sigma,\alpha)$

the following way. $N(\sigma,\alpha_0)$ is the same initial inequality system σ with only zero subscripts added to internal variables: t_0, u_0, ...

Further, $N(\sigma,\alpha_i)$ is defined from $N(\sigma,\alpha_{i-1})$ and statement k_i just as before. For example, if σ={a<(1)<b and α=(4, 6+, 3+), then

$N(\sigma,\alpha_0)$={a_0<(1)<b_0 ,

$N(\sigma,\alpha_1)$={a_0<(1)<b_0 (output statement adds nothing),

$N(\sigma,\alpha_2)$={a_0<(1)<b_0 , $a_1=A_1$,

$N(\sigma,\alpha)=N(\sigma,\alpha_3)$={$a_0$<(1)<$b_0$, $a_1=A_1$, a_0<(1)<b_0 .

Just as before we define state $S(\sigma,\alpha)$ corresponding to system $N(\sigma,\alpha)$, the state is obtained by excluding inactive variables from $N(\sigma,\alpha)$ the same way. For example, the state

$S(\sigma,\alpha)$={a<(1)<b

corresponds to the system $N(\sigma,\alpha)$ from the previous example. Let us note that this time state $S(\sigma,\alpha)$ occurs to be equal to σ. It has the following simple graph depicted in fig. 5.

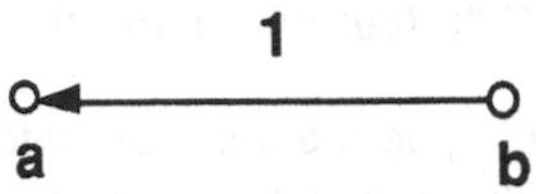

Fig. 5

A path β is said to be a continuation of a path α if the exit of the last statement of the path α leads to the first statement of the path β. The concatenation of paths α and β is denoted by $\alpha+\beta$.

LEMMA 4. *Let σ be a state of program P, α a path and β a continuation of path α. Then*

$$S(\sigma,\alpha+\beta)=S(S(\sigma,\alpha), \beta).$$

To prove the lemma we consider systems of inequalities $N(\sigma,\alpha+\beta)$, $N(\sigma,\alpha)$ and $N(S(\sigma,\alpha), \beta)$. By excluding inactive variables we obtain states $S(\sigma,\alpha+\beta)$, $S(\sigma,\alpha)$ and $S(S(\sigma,\alpha), \beta)$ from them. Let us remember that the order of exclusion of inactive variables does not affect the result. Therefore while constructing $S(\sigma,\alpha+\beta)$ from $N(\sigma,\alpha+\beta)$ we can exclude inactive variables in the starting period just in the same order as when constructing $S(\sigma,\alpha)$ from $N(\sigma,\alpha)$. It means that while constructing $S(\sigma,\alpha+\beta)$ we obtain $S(\sigma,\alpha)$ as an intermediate result and the construction of $S(S(\sigma,\alpha), \beta)$ from $N(S(\sigma,\alpha), \beta)$ follows just after that. In this consideration we have essentially used two facts; first, inactive variables in system $N(\sigma,\alpha)$ are also inactive in $N(\sigma,\alpha+\beta)$ and, second, inequalities in $N(\sigma,\alpha+\beta)$ generated by the path (i.e., the continuation of $N(\sigma,\alpha)$ up to $N(\sigma,\alpha+\beta)$) do not contain inactive variables of $N(\sigma,\alpha)$. It means that the exclusion of these inactive variables does not affect the continuation of $N(\sigma,\alpha)$ up to $N(\sigma,\alpha+\beta)$. All this becomes completely clear if we represent systems of inequalities and the exclusion process as graphs.

This completes the proof of Lemma 4.

Now let us construct the reachability graph for program P. Vertices of this graph are labeled by pairs (n,S), where n is a statement label and S a state of P. There will be as many edges issuing and with the same labels from the vertex (n,S) as from the statement n in P. Simultaneously with the vertex we also build the edges issuing from it (for the moment they are pending). The construction of the graph will be by induction. The initial vertex of the reachability graph will be the pair (n_0,S_0), where $n_0=1$ and S_0 is the initial state of program P: t=0, u=0, ... Edges issuing from this vertex will be pending for a while.

Let us assume that part of reachability graph has been constructed. Edges issuing from its vertices can be in three different states:

(1) an edge can be pending,

(2) an edge can be joined to a vertex,

(3) an edge can be forbidden (the emergence of forbidden edges will be explained further).

Only the pending ones will be of interest. So we choose a vertex (n_i,S_i) with a pending edge labeled by ε issuing from it (ε belongs to {+, -, e}). Let γ_i denote a path consisting of the sole statement n_i with exit ε : $n_i\varepsilon$. Let us build the state $S_j=S(S_i,\gamma_i)$. Two cases are possible:

(1) the state S_j is contradictory, i.e., it has no solution as a system of inequalities; in this case the exit ε from the vertex (n_i,S_i) is said to be forbidden (for example, the edge

is marked by special label "X"). (Let us remind that our notion of directed graph allows pending edges in it),

(2) the state S is consistent. Let n_j be the label of statement entered by exit ε of the statement n_i. Let us consider the pair (n_j,S_j). Again two cases are possible:

(a) the vertex (n_j,S_j) exists in the part of reachability graph already constructed; in this case we join the edge ε from vertex (n_i,S_i) to vertex (n_j,S_j),

(b) the vertex (n_j,S_j) does not exist in the part already constructed; in this case we build a new vertex (n_j,S_j) together with all the pending edges issuing from it and then join the edge labeled by ε from vertex (n_i,S_i) to the new vertex.

The described procedure is continued until we obtain a graph with no unmarked pending edges. Since the program P has a finite number of different states the before mentioned procedure will stop after a finite number of steps. The graph obtained as a result of this procedure we call *reachability graph* of the program P.

This graph has several important properties. Let us consider a path

$$v=((n_0,S_0)\varepsilon_0,\ (n_1,S_1)\varepsilon_1,\ldots,(n_r,S_r)\varepsilon_r)$$

in this graph starting from the initial vertex. Such a path will be called an *initial path.* Such a path may not contain forbidden edges. It means that edge ε_r leads to some vertex, say (n_{r+1},S_{r+1}).

We shall say that the path v is *feasible* if there is a test T such that the program P executes the path

$$\alpha=(n_0\varepsilon_0,\ n_1\varepsilon_1,\ldots,n_r\varepsilon_r)$$

and passes the state sequence

$$S_1,\ S_2,\ldots,S_{r+1} \text{ on this test.}$$

From the construction of reachability graph and Lemma 4 there follow equalities $S_i=S((n_0\varepsilon_0,\ n_1\varepsilon_1,\ldots,n_{i-1}\varepsilon_{i-1}))$ for $i=1,2,\ldots,r+1$. The state S_{r+1} is consistent by construction. Thus the state $S((n_0\varepsilon_0,\ n_1\varepsilon_1,\ldots,n_r\varepsilon_r))$ is also consistent and the path α in P is feasible by Lemma 3. This proves the following

LEMMA 5. *Every initial path in reachability graph is feasible.*

Let v be the beforementioned path in rechability graph. In this case the path

$$\alpha=(n_0\varepsilon_0,\ n_1\varepsilon_1,\ldots,n_r\varepsilon_r)$$

in program P will be said to be the *projection* of path v .

LEMMA 6. *An initial path α in program P is feasible iff there is an initial path v in rechability graph whose projection is α.*

The sufficiency of lemma condition follows directly from Lemma 5. Let us prove the necessity. Let

$$\alpha=(n_0\varepsilon_0,\ n_1\varepsilon_1,\ldots,n_r\varepsilon_r)$$

be an initial path in program P. Let us consider the sequence of current states $S_0=S(\alpha_0)$, $S_1=S(\alpha_1)$, $S_2=S(\alpha_2),\ldots,S_{r+1}=S(\alpha_{r+1})=S(\alpha)$, where $\alpha_i=(n_0\varepsilon_0,\ n_1\varepsilon_1,\ldots,n_{i-1}\varepsilon_{i-1})$. It follows from Lemma 3 that the path α is feasible iff the states $S_0, S_1,\ldots, S_{r+1}$ are consistent. Further it follows from Lemma 4 that the states $S_0, S_1,\ldots, S_{r+1}$ can be obtained also in a different manner:

$$S_1=S(S_0,n_0\varepsilon_0),\ S_2=S(S_0,\ n_1\varepsilon_1),\ldots,S_{r+1}=S(S_r,n_r\varepsilon_r),$$

i.e., by constructing the new state from the previous one and the current statement.

Hence, and from the construction of reachability graph, it follows that feasibility of path α implies the existence of path

$$((n_0,S_0)\varepsilon_0, (n_1,S_1)\varepsilon_1, \ldots, (n_r,S_r)\varepsilon_r)$$

in the reachability graph whose projection is path α.
This proves the lemma.

Let U be a set of initial paths in the reachability graph. U is said to be a *complete path set* if it contains all edges of the graph. Let us denote by pr_U a set of paths in the program P obtained by taking projections of paths in U.
From Lemma 6 there follows an obvious

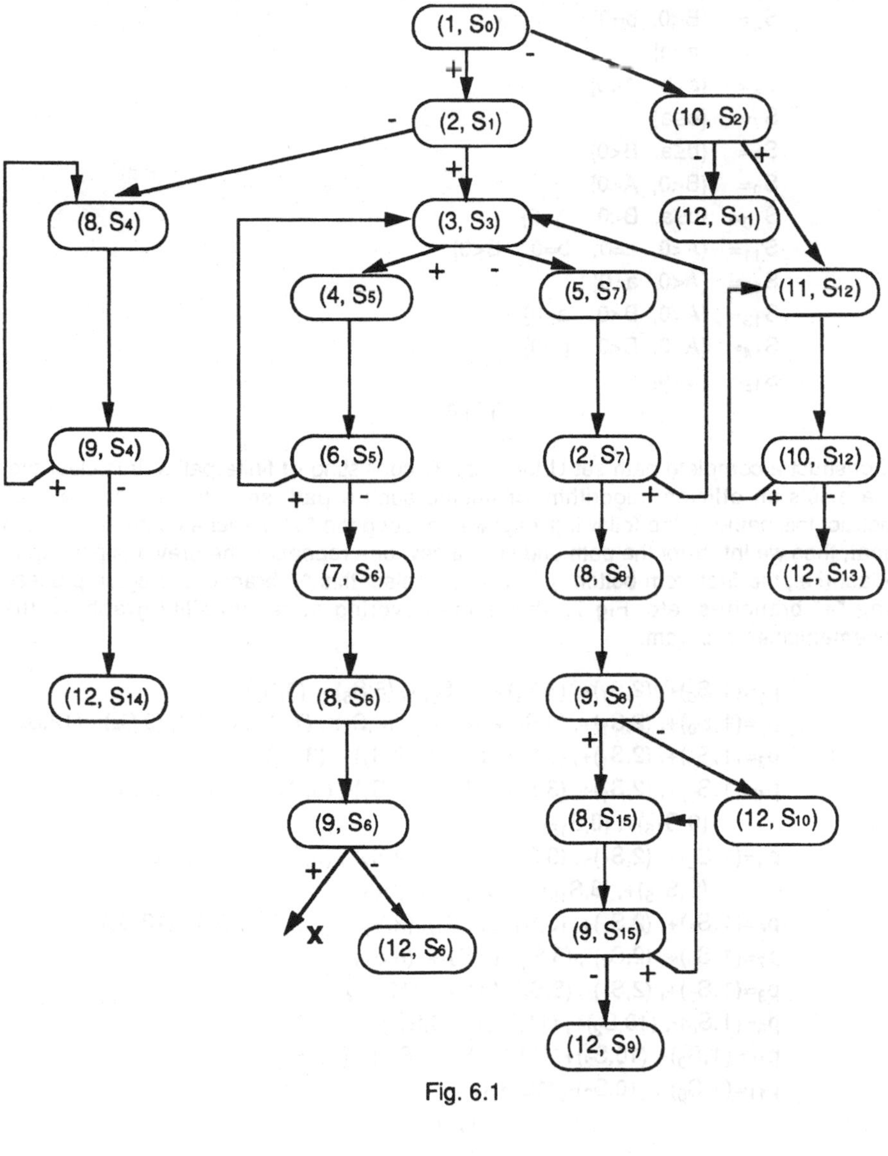

Fig. 6.1

COROLLARY. *Let U be a complete path set of the reachability graph of program P. Then the set of program P paths pr_U contains all feasible branches of program P.*

Hence follows the algorithm constructing CTS for a program P:

1. Construct reachability graph G for the program P. Fig. 6.1 and 6.2 show the reachability graph for the program in fig. 2.

S_0= {a=0, b=0}
S_1= {b=0}
S_2= {A<0, a=0, b=0}
S_3= {}
S_4= {B<0, b=0}
S_5= {a<b}
S_6= {a<b, A<0}
S_7= {b≤a}
S_8= {b≤a, B<0}
S_9= {B<0, A<0}
S_{10}= {b≤a, B<0, A<0}
S_{11}= {A<0, a=0, b=0, B<0}
S_{12}= {A<0, a=0}
S_{13}= {A<0, B<0, a=0}
S_{14}= {A<0, B<0, b=0}
S_{15}= {B<0}

Fig.6.2

2. Construct a complete path set U for graph G consisting of finite paths. It is clear that there exists an efficient algorithm for finding such a path set. Henceforth we shall construct this path set the following way: we go along the "+" branches until the vertices repeat, then we interrupt the path and start a new one repeating the previous path up to the last (i.e., the first from bottom) "-" branch, select this "-" branch and again proceed along "+" branches, etc. Fig 7. shows the covering of reachability graph for the abovementioned program.

p_1=(1,S_0)+, (2,S_1)+, (3,S_3)+, (4,S_5)+, (6,S_5)+, (3,S_3)
p_2=(1,S_0)+, (2,S_1)+, (3,S_3)+, (4,S_5)+, (6,S_5)-, (7,S_6), (8,S_6), (9,S_6)-, (12,S_6)
p_3=(1,S_0)+, (2,S_1)+, (3,S_3)-, (5,S_7), (2,S_7)+, (3,S_3)
p_4=(1,S_0)+, (2,S_1)+, (3,S_3)-, (5,S_7), (2,S_7)-, (8,S_8), (9,S_8)+, (8,S_{15}), (9,S_{15})+, (8,S_{15})
p_5=(1,S_0)+, (2,S_1)+, (3,S_3)-, (5,S_7), (2,S_7)-, (8,S_8), (9,S_8)+, (8,S_{15}), (9,S_{15})+, (8,S_{15}), (9,S_{15})-, (12,S_{12})
p_6=(1,S_0)+, (2,S_1)+, (3,S_3)-, (5,S_7), (2,S_7)-, (8,S_8), (9,S_8)-, (12,S_9),
p_7=(1,S_0)+, (2,S_1)-, (8,S_4), (9,S_4)+, (8,S_4)
p_8=(1,S_0)+, (2,S_1)-, (8,S_4), (9,S_4)-, (12,S_{14})
p_9=(1,S_0)-, (10,S_2)+, (11,S_{12}), (10,S_{12})+, (11,S_{12})
p_{10}=(1,S_0)-, (10,S_2)+, (11,S_{12}), (10,S_{12})-, (12,S_{13})
p_{11}=(1,S_0)-, (10,S_2)-, (12,S_{11})

Fig. 7

3. Take pr_U. For every $\alpha \in$ pr_U construct the inequality system $N(\alpha)$ and find its solution with respect to variables-cells of input tapes. This solution forms the test T_α.

The test set

$T = \{ T_\alpha \mid \alpha \in pr\_U \}$

is obtained as a result.

Test set corresponding to the covering in fig. 7 is depicted in fig. 8.

$T_1 = \{ A = (0,1), \quad B = (1)\}$
$T_2 = \{ A = (0), \quad B = (1)\}$
$T_3 = \{ A = (1), \quad B = (0,1)\}$
$T_4 = \{ A = (1,2,3), \quad B = (0)\}$
$T_5 = \{ A = (1,2), \quad B = (0)\}$
$T_6 = \{ A = (1), \quad B = (0)$
$T_7 = \{ A = (0,1), \quad B = ( )\}$
$T_8 = \{ A = (0), \quad B = ( )\}$
$T_9 = \{ A = ( ), \quad B = (0)\}$
$T_{10} = \{ A = ( ), \quad B = (0)\}$
$T_{11} = \{ A = ( ), \quad B = ( )\}$

Fig. 8

It is clear that test T_2 reveals the bug yielding wrong result Y=(0, 1, 0).

It follows from the beforementioned that T is a complete test set for program P.

This completes the proof of the Theorem.

2.3 Termination Problem

Some problems of program static analysis are closely related to the construction of CTS, reachability problem is one of them. The problem is to find out whether all program branches are feasible (reachable). It is easy to see that this problem is a special case of CTS problem and therefore no more attention is paid to it.

The second important problem is termination problem. The problem is to find out for a program whether it terminates on all input data selections. If there exist input data where the program does not stop, the program is said to be *nonterminating.* The decidability of reachability problem for a class of programs does not imply the decidability of termination at all. Therefore the following theorem arouses some interest.

<u>**THEOREM 2.**</u> *There is an algorithm which determines for every program in L_0 whether the program is nonterminating.*

To prove the theorem we use substantially the notion of reachability graph from the proof of the previous theorem.

Path $\beta=((n_1,S_1)\varepsilon_1, \ldots, (n_k,S_k)\varepsilon_k)$ in the reachability graph G is said to be *closed* if

(1) β is a cyclic path, i.e., the exit ε_k leads to the vertex (n_1, S_1),

(2) β contains no input statement with "+" exit, i.e., if n_i is statement $X \to t$, then ε_i is "-".

<u>**LEMMA 7**</u>. *Program P does not terminate on a test T iff a vertex of a closed path in the*

reachability graph can be reached on this test. Program P is nonterminating iff there is a closed path in its reachability graph.

At first let us assume that there is a test T on which the program P does not terminate. It means that the execution of P on T creates an infinite path

$$v=(n_1\varepsilon_1, n_2\varepsilon_2, \ldots).$$

Since the test T is finite, there is l such that l-tail of path v

$$\delta=(n_l\varepsilon_l, n_{l+1}\varepsilon_{l+1}, \ldots)$$

contains no more input statements with "+" exit. Since the set of program states is finite and the number of statements is finite, the path δ certainly will contain a segment

$$(n_j\varepsilon_j, \ldots, n_{j+u}\varepsilon_{j+u})$$

such that ε_{j+u} leads to the statement n_j and states S_j and S_{j+u+1} are equal. It means that there is a closed path, namely,

$$((n_j,S_j)\varepsilon_j, \ldots, (n_{j+u}, S_{j+u})\varepsilon_{j+u})$$

in the reachability graph reached on the test T. This proves the necessity of lemma condition.

Let us prove sufficiency. Let us assume that there is a closed path

$$\beta=((n_1,S_1)\varepsilon_1, \ldots, (n_k,S_k)\varepsilon_k)$$

in the reachability graph G. Let α be an initial path leading to the vertex (n_1,S_1). Let us consider path $\alpha\beta\beta\ldots\beta$ with the segment β repeated v times, v - "large enough". This path, like every path in a reachability graph, is feasible. Since the segment $\beta\beta\ldots\beta$ contains no input statements with "+" exit, the values of internal variables will begin to repeat. It means that, if the program executes path $\alpha\beta\beta\ldots\beta$ on some test T, then it will continue to repeat the segment β on the same test, i.e., it will loop forever. Hence, by the way, follows that a closed path β has the property that conditional statements contained in the path have only one of their exits executable, namely, the one contained in the path β. In other words, there can be no paths γ branching off the closed path in the reachability graph. Actually, were such a path γ, then, taking into consideration that all paths are feasible in reachability graph the test forcing the path $\alpha\beta\beta \ldots \beta\beta$ would also force the path $\alpha\beta\beta\ldots\beta\gamma$. This yields a contradiction. It means that the program loops forever on every test where some vertex of the closed path is reached. It proves the sufficiency of lemma conditions.

The condition of nontermination used in the lemma is algorithmically decidable. This proves the theorem.

3 Efficient Algorithms for CTS Construction

The proof of Theorem 1 gives us an algorithm for CTS construction which is not very efficient, especially because of the size of reachability graph. To reduce the size of this graph we introduce two notions: essentially located statements and essential variables.

A set of program statements is selected in such a way that every program loop contains at least one statement from this set.The first statement of the program and STOP statements are also included in this set. We call the statements from this set *essentially located statements* (ELS's). Our intent is to keep the set of ELS's as small as possible, therefore, if several loops have a common part, ELS is selected from this common part. In the program of fig. 2, for example, statements 1, 3, 9, 10, 12 form a set of ELS's.

Associated with every ELS there is a list of variables called *essential variables associated with the ELS.* An internal variable t is said to be an essential variable for a certain ELS if there exists a path beginning with the ELS such that the value possessed by the variable t immediately before the execution of the ELS is used unchanged in some comparison statement of the path.The use of unchanged value in comparison statement means that either the variable t is contained in some comparison statement (e.g., t<9) of the path before the new value is assigned to t or the unchanged value of t is assigned to some other variable u which, in turn, is used unchanged in a comparison statement.

There are several ways to find out whether the given variable is essential for the given ELS. We give an algorithm which is based on reverse analysis of program path from the end to the beginning. When traversing a path in a reverse order, a set of essential variables V is formed according to the following rules depending on the current statement K:

(1) if K is t<v (both "+" and "-" exit), then $V:= V\cup\{t, v\}$;
(2) if K is t<c (both exits), then $V:= V\cup\{t\}$;
(3) if K is $X\rightarrow t+$, then $V:= V\setminus\{t\}$;
(4) if K is $X\rightarrow t-$, then V is not changed;
(5) if K is $t\rightarrow v$, then $V:=$ if $v\in V$ then $V\cup\{t\}\setminus\{v\}$ else V;
(6) if K is $c\rightarrow v$, then $V:= V\setminus\{v\}$.

Further we form a graph for program P with ELS's as vertices and program paths e_i^j from one ELS to another as edges. Each vertex n has a set of essential variables V_n ascribed, initially all V_n are empty. Each vertex has also a status assuming one of the three values: not visited, active, inactive. Initially all vertices except those corresponding to STOP statements are not visited, STOP statements are marked active. On each step of the algorithm an active vertex n is selected, it is marked inactive and all edges e_i^j entering it are traversed as program paths in the reverse order as described before (V_n is taken as the initial value of V). When another ELS m is reached in the reverse analysis the resulting value of V is added to V_m. If V_m is actually increased, the status of m is set to active (also in the case when n=m). If the status of m was 'not visited', it is set to active anyway. Algorithm proceeds until all vertices are inactive. If the situation occurs where all vertices are either inactive or not visited, one of the not visited vertices is made active. The resulting values of V_n are the sets of essential variables for each of the ELS's. The termination of the algorithm is guaranteed by the monotonity of V_n for all n.

Of course, the feasibility of paths is not taken into account. In the program example considered, statement 1 has no essential variables because a and b are given new values from input tapes before using them. Statement 3 obviously has a and b as essential variables because the statement itself is a comparison statement using them. Statements 9, 10, 12 have no essential variables.

After these preparations a *reduced reachability graph* is constructed. Its construction is similar to that of the reachability graph. The main difference is that vertices correspond only to ELS's, other statements are not included. For each of the ELS's we build a set of all paths in the program starting with it and leading to some other ELS. These paths, let them be $e^i_1, e^i_2, \ldots, e^i_{r^i}$ for ELS i, will play the role of edges in reachability graph construction. The choice of ELS's guarantees us the boundedness of this set for every ELS. The other difference is that when constructing a state for the given ELS we exclude from the corresponding system of inequalities also those internal variables which are not essential for this ELS. Let us remark that formal variables A, B,... used to code the exhaustion of input tape (e.g., A<0) are retained in state.

Likewise for reachability graph, the construction starts from the first statement of the program (which is ELS by definition) and empty state. For the given ELS i and state S_j, we consider the paths e^i_k from this ELS one after another. The system of inequalities $N(S_j,e^i_k)$ and state $S(S_j,e^i_k)$ (in the new sense with respect to ELS reached by e^i_k) are constructed for each path. If the path is infeasible (i.e., $S(S_j,e^i_k)$ is contradictory), it is labeled by X. Otherwise we check whether ELS i' reached by e^i_k and state $S(S_j,e^i_k)$ form a vertex already in the reduced reachability graph and join edge e^i_k to the existing vertex or build a new vertex respectively.

We also have to change the definition of path projection in reduced reachability graph, replacing every edge e^i_k by the corresponding sequence of program statements.

It can be shown that Lemmas 5 and 6 from Theorem 1 hold also for reduced reachability graph (the proof will not be given here).

The construction of CTS using reduced reachability graph is similar to the previous case. A more economical covering principle can be used where a path traverses all loops at the given vertex once and then proceeds further. For nearly all real programs the reduced reachabilty graph is considerably less than full reachability graph and thus completely outweighs some additional efforts to build it.

Now let us return to our example. ELS's and their essential variables had

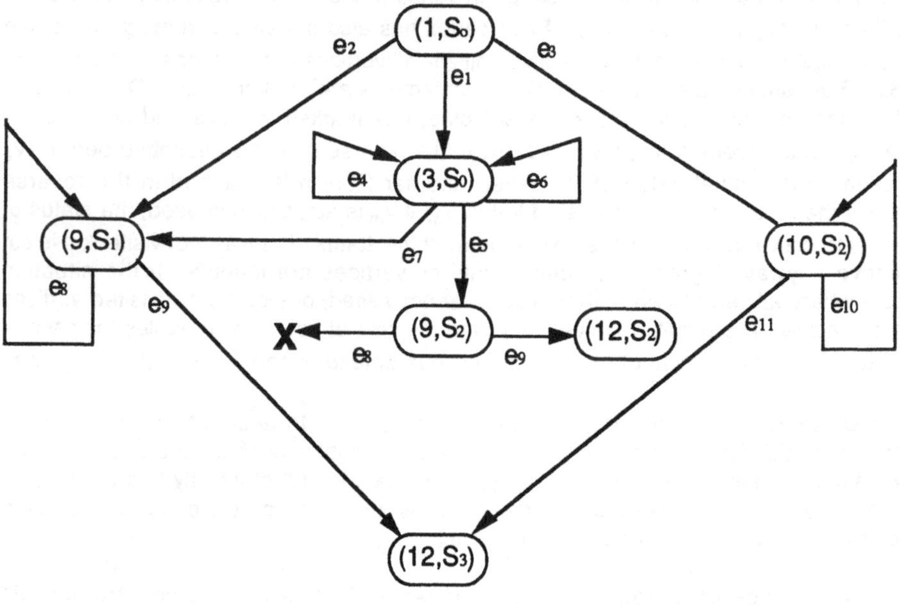

$S_0 = \{$ $S_1 = \{ B<0$ $S_2 = \{ A<0$ $S_3 = \{ A<0\ B<0$

Fig. 9.

already been mentioned. Paths leading from one ELS to another are the following:

from 1	e_1=(1+, 2+)	to 3 ,
	e_2=(1+, 2-, 8)	to 9 ,
	e_3=(1-)	to 10 ,
from 3	e_4=(3+, 4, 6+)	to 3 ,
	e_5=(3+, 4, 6-, 7, 8)	to 9 ,
	e_6=(3-, 5, 2+)	to 3 ,
	e_7=(3-, 5, 2-, 8)	to 9 ,
from 9	e_8=(9+, 8)	to 9 ,
	e_9=(9-)	to 12 ,
from10	e_{10}=(10+, 11)	to 10,
	e_{11}=(10 -)	to 12

The reduced reachability graph is shown in fig.9, its covering in fig.10 and the corresponding CTS in fig.11. The bug is detected by T_1. It can be seen that states in fact contain no internal variables, for they don't affect the feasibility of paths in this simple program (c.f., in fact, surplus states S_{10}, S_{11}, S_{12}, S_{13}, . . . in fig.6.). The test set is also reduced but it still detects the bug.

$p_1 = (1, S_0)\, e_1, (3, S_0)\, e_4, (3, S_0)\, e_6, (3, S_0)\, e_5, (9, S_2)\, e_9, (12, S_2)$
$p_2 = (1, S_0)\, e_2, (9, S_1)\, e_8, (9, S_1)\, e_9, (12, S_3)$
$p_3 = (1, S_0)\, e_3, (10, S_2)\, e_{10}, (10, S_2)\, e_{11}, (12, S_3)$
$p_4 = (1, S_0)\, e_1, (3, S_0)\, e_7, (9, S_1)\, e_9, (12, S_3)$

Fig. 10

$T_1 = \{ A = (0,1), B = (1,2)\}$
$T_2 = \{ A = (0,1), B = (\,)\}$
$T_3 = \{ A = (\,), B = (0)\}$
$T_4 = \{ A = (0), B = (0)\}$

Fig. 11

The reduced reachability graph can also be used for termination analysis of programs described in the previous section. We just note that every cyclic path will certainly contain some ELS and therefore will be present in the reduced reachability graph (in most cases as loop with one vertex in it).

There can be some further improvements of the algorithm for constructing CTS. At first let us remark the simple fact that for a program with all feasible paths we can simply construct its covering by paths and solve the corresponding inequality system by the method described. If it is not completely so, we start to construct the reduced reachability graph for the part of the program not traversable so simply and we look at every step of its construction (i.e., adding a path from one ELS to another) whether all branches have been covered. So with all statements reachable, usually only a small part of reachability graph is to be constructed. Both the original and improved algorithms are obviously exponential with respect to the size of the program in the worst case. Therefore no theoretical complexity analysis of the algorithms is given here. Nevertheless the performance of the algorithm described in this section is quite acceptable, for most real programs the numbers of steps required is nearly linear with respect to the size. The practical aspects of CTS construction will be covered more thoroughly in [17].

There is another aspect of optimality, namely, the optimality of CTS obtained. It is reasonable to minimize the number of tests or the total size. Here the main issue is to find the optimal (with respect to the criterion selected) covering of the reduced reachability graph. Obviously it is very difficult to find the absolute optimum, nevertheless, algorithms yielding nearly optimal covering can be devised. The covering proposed in this section (traversing all the loops at the given vertex once and then proceeding further) is clearly oriented towards minimizing the number of tests.

4 Conditional Programs and Programs with Preconditions

In previous sections we have discussed only programs without pending exits, i.e, there was a requirement that every exit of a statement should be attached to some other statement. In the sequel such programs will be called *closed programs.* In this section we drop the requirement and consider also programs with pending exits, i.e., exits not attached to other statements. We shall say such exits to be *forbidden* exits and programs with forbidden exits to be *conditional programs.* Conditional programs offer us some new possibilities. By means of forbidden exits we can specify conditions on input data. Fig. 12 shows us a program for merging two nondecreasing files which in addition check whether the input files are really nondecreasing. To describe formally the meaning of such checks we introduce the notion of a correct test. A test is said to be *correct* if the program running on this test never reaches a forbidden exit. It is easy to see that for the program in fig. 12 only nondecreasing input files serve as correct tests.

In the case of a conditional program a test set will be called a *correct complete test set* if

(1) the test set contains only correct tests,

(2) all program branches executable on correct tests are executed on tests of this set.

It is clear that the construction of a correct complete test set is more complicated than the construction of usual CTS. Nevertheless there holds

THEOREM 3. *There is an algorithm constructig a finite correct complete test set for every conditional program in* $\mathbf{L_0}$.

To prove the theorem we consider an arbitrary program in $\mathbf{L_0}$ and its reachability graph. The definition of reachability graph for a conditional program is similar to that for a closed program. Let us remember that we already had a kind of forbidden edges when constructing the reachability graph, namely, we said that an edge ε from a vertex (n_i, S_i) is forbidden if the state $S(S_i,n_i\varepsilon)$ is contradictory, i.e., the exit ε of the statement n_i is infeasible in the state S_i. We call these forbidden edges the forbidden edges of the first type. Reachability graph for a conditional program will also have forbidden edges of the second type: we say that an edge ε from a vertex (n_i, S_i) is also forbidden in the case when the exit ε from the statement n_i is forbidden. There are no other differences in the construction of reachability graph for a conditional program. Lemma 6 holds true also for this case.

The main problem in the construction of correct CTS is to prevent the constructed tests from generating paths in the reachability graph leading to the forbidden edges of

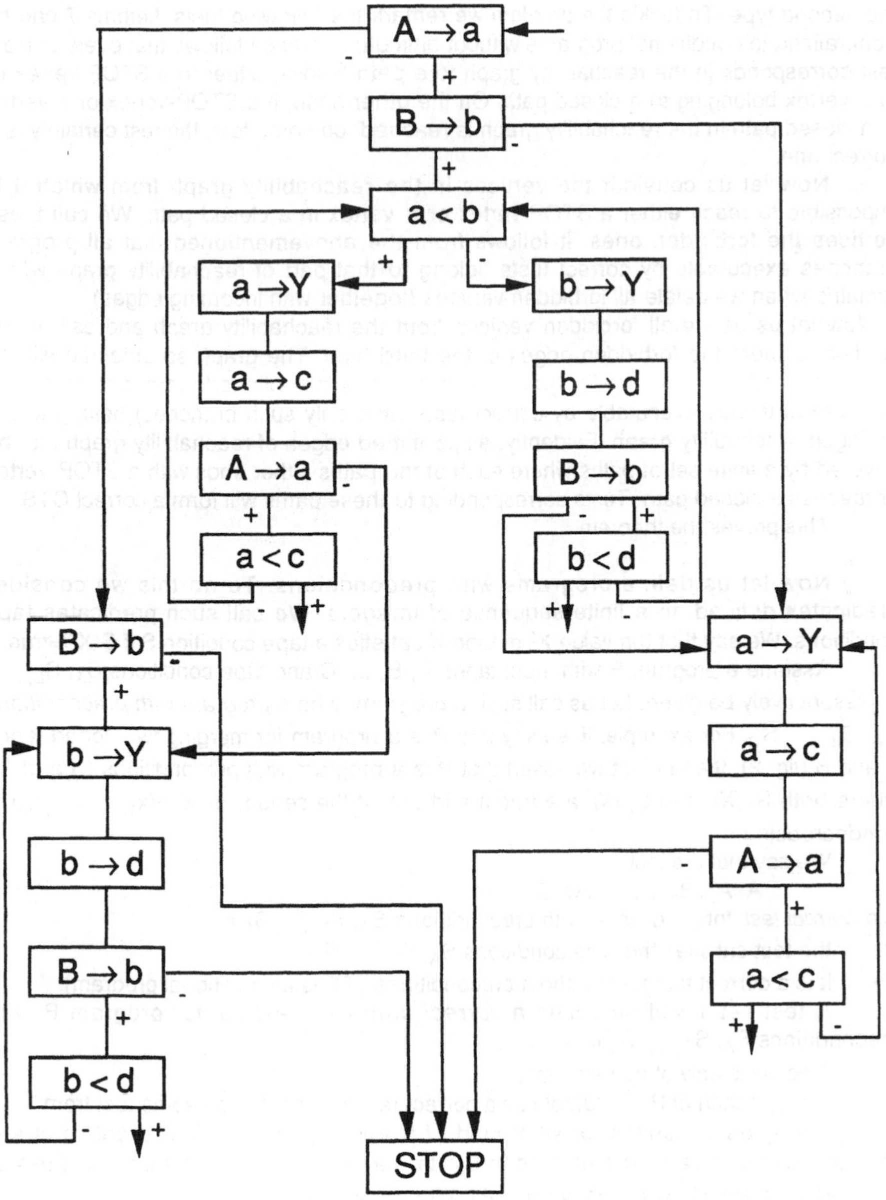

Fig. 12

the second type. To tackle the problem we remark the following facts. Lemma 7 can be generalized to conditional programs without difficulties. Hence follows that every correct test corresponds in the reachability graph to a path leading either to a STOP-vertex or to a vertex belonging to a closed path. On the other hand, if a STOP-vertex or a vertex in a closed path in the reachability graph is reached on some test, the test certainly is a correct one.

Now let us consider the vertices in the reachability graph from which it is impossible to reach either a STOP-vertex or a vertex in a closed path. We call these vertices the forbidden ones. It follows from the abovementioned that all program branches executable by correct tests belong to that part of reachability graph which remains when we delete all forbidden vertices (together with incoming edges).

Now let us delete all forbidden vertices from the reachability graph and call edges leading to them the forbidden edges of the third type. The graph so obtained will be called the abridged reachability graph. From the abovementioned there follows that all program branches executable by correct tests (and only such branches) belong to the abridged reachability graph. Evidently, all permitted edges of reachability graph can be covered by a finite set of paths where each of the paths either ends with a STOP-vertex or reaches a closed path. Tests corresponding to these paths will form a correct CTS.

This proves the theorem.

Now let us define programs with preconditions. To do this we consider predicates defined on a finite sequence of integers. We call such predicates tape conditions. We say that the value X^0 of tape X satisfies a tape condition S if $S(X^0)$=true.

Assume a program P with input tapes A, B, ... ,C and tape conditions S_A, $S_B, \ldots,$ S_C respectively be given. Let us call such a program to be a *program with preconditions* S_A, $S_B, \ldots, S_C$. For example, if we say that P is a program for merging two sorted tapes A and B (fig. 2), then in fact we assert that P is a program with preconditions S_A and S_B where both $S_A(X)$ and $S_B(X)$ are true if and only if the sequence $X = (x_1, x_2, \ldots, x_n)$ is nondecreasing.

We say that the test

$$A=A^0, B=B^0, \ldots, C=C^0$$

is a *correct test* for program P with preconditions S_A, $S_B, \ldots, S_C$ if

(1) the test satisfies the tape conditions S_A, $S_B, \ldots, S_C$,

(2) it is a correct test for P without preconditions (if P is a conditional program).

A test set T will be called a *correct complete test set* for program P with preconditions S_A, $S_B, \ldots, S_C$ if

(1) T consists only of correct tests,

(2) every branch of P executable by a correct test is executed on some test from T.

The question arises for what kind of preconditions the CTS problem is still solvable algorithmicaly for programs in $\mathbf{L_0}$. In the sequel we define a natural class of preconditions and show the solvability of CTS problem for it.

We consider tape conditions definable as programs in $\mathbf{L_0}$. One of the most natural ways to do this is as follows. Let S_X be a program in $\mathbf{L_0}$ with one input tape X. A predicate is associated with S_X which is true for those and only those values of tape X where the program S_X stops. Namely this predicate is called *tape condition specified by S_X*.

A tape condition specified by a program could be defined also otherwise. We could say that a tape value X^0 satisfies the condition if and only if X^0 is a correct test for the program S_X ,i.e., the program S_X when executed on X^0 does not reach a forbidden exit (we allow S_X to be a conditional program). It is not difficult to show by using previous results on program termination that both definitions are uniform, i.e., describe the same class of conditions.

THEOREM 4. *There is an algorithm constructing a finite correct CTS for every program in L_0 with preconditions also specified by programs in L_0.*

The proof of the theorem follows from Theorem 3 and Lemma 1.

LEMMA 1. *For every program P in L_0 with preconditions specified by programs in L_0 there is a conditional program P^* in L_0 without preconditions such that every correct CTS for P^* is a correct CTS for P with its preconditions. There is an algorithm constructing P^* from P and its preconditions.*

The idea of the proof of the lemma is simple. Let us assume for the simplicity that P has only one input tape A with a tape condition specified by a program S_A. It is not difficult to see that we can merge the reading of tape A for checking the precondition S_A and the reading of A during the execution of P into a single process. It means that we can build a program that will execute the job of both program P and program S_A between two consecutive reads from tape A. If a statement has a pending exit in program S_A, then the corresponding exit is left pending for "maps" of this statement in P^*. In such a way the program P^* will contain, on the one hand, the maps of all branches of program P and, on the other hand, all the restrictions in the form of forbidden exits imposed by the condition S_A. If P has more than one input tape with corresponding tape conditions, the method just described allows us, first, to insert the check of the first tape condition into P, then that of the second tape and so on. In such a way we can always build the desired program P^*. This completes the proof.

It is easy to see that for programs in L_0 with preconditions in L_0 there also holds an equivalent of Theorem 2 stating the decidability of nontermination.

5 Programs with Other Simple Data Types

So far we have considered only one simple type – integer in the language L_0. The aim of this section is to generalize the previous results to arbitrary simple types with comparison operators defined. There can be a great variety of such types and comparison operators can be defined in a highly different manner in respect to types. For example, let us consider charstring type. The comparison operator "<" can be defined for it according to the lexicographic ordering: $x_1...x_n < y_1...y_m$ if $\exists i_0$ such that $x_1=y_1, \ldots, x_{i0-1}=y_{i0-1}$ and $x_{i0}<y_{i0}$, or n<m and $x_1=y_1, \ldots, x_n=y_n$ (the ordering adopted in Turbo Pascal). New situations arises for this ordering as there are infinitely many words between some two words x and y and a finite number of words between some other words. The relation "<" can be defined for this type also otherwise: $x_1...x_n < y_1...y_m$ if n<m or n=m and $\exists i_0$ such that $x_1=y_1, \ldots, x_{i0-1}<y_{i0-1}$ and $x_{i0}=y_{i0}$, (ordering used by some other Pascal

implementations). In this case there will be only a finite number of words between any two words x, y. This example shows us the variety of possible situations here. To comprise all the cases we use an "axiomatic" approach in this section: the comparison operator will be requested only to satisfy some "axioms" of constructivity. All the types appearing in real programming languages will satisfy these "axioms". On the other hand we will show that these axioms are sufficient to make the CTS construction problem algorithmically solvable. Our aim is to investigate more deeply what is essential and what is not essential for the algorithmic solvability of the CTS construction problem. So,let

$$\mathbf{T}_1, \mathbf{T}_2, \ldots, \mathbf{T}_a$$

be arbitrary simple types with comparison operators $=, \neq, \leq, <$ defined.

Further we assume these operators to be total. As far as the first three operators can be expressed by the last one (using boolean expressions), we assume (without restriction of generalization) only operator "<" to be defined a priori for each type.

Let us assume the values of the types considered to be constructive objects, thus algorithms over the domains of these types can be considered. We shall say that operator "<" is *constructive* (satisfies the constructiveness "axioms") for the type $\mathbf{T}$ if

(1) there is an algorithm $\mathcal{A}$ which, given any x, $y \in \mathbf{T}$, determines whether the relation $x < y$ holds;

(2) there is an algorithm $\mathcal{B}$ which, given any x, $y \in \mathbf{T}$ such that $x < y$, determines whether there exists $z \in \mathbf{T}$ such that $x < z$ and $z < y$ and in the case of existence gives one such z;

(3) there is an algorithm $\mathcal{C}$ which, given any $x \in \mathbf{T}$, determines whether there exists $z \in \mathbf{T}$ such that $z < x$ and in the case of existence gives one such z;

(4) there is an algorithm $\mathcal{D}$ which, given any $x \in \mathbf{T}$, determines whether there exists $z \in \mathbf{T}$ such that $x < z$ and in the case of existence gives one such z.

Let us consider the most popular simple types:

– integer with operator "<";
– natural with operator "<";
– rational with operator "<"; (e.g., binary and decimal fixed point data)
– real, as treated by most common programming languages, i.e., floating point data (values are of form $n_1.n_2E + n_3$ with limited precision and limited exponent, in fact, they are rational numbers);
– charstring with operator "<" defined in one of the ways considered at the beginning of this section;
– integer subranges and enumerable types (like in Pascal) with operator "<".

It is easy to see that all these types are constructive in the abovementioned sense.

So let us assume some constructive types $\mathbf{T}_1, \ldots, \mathbf{T}_a$ to be fixed. We also assume that every value constant of these types uniquely determines the type to which it belongs.

Now let us consider the following generalization of the language $\mathbf{L}_0$, namely, the language

$$L_0^{T_1, \ldots, T_a}.$$

Programs in $L_0^{T_1, \ldots, T_a}$ like in $\mathbf{L}_0$ will have both internal and external variables. Each internal variable will be of some fixed simple type (to stress that internal variable x is of the type $\mathbf{T}$ we sometimes use the denotation $x^{\mathbf{T}}$). Again tapes will be used as external variables. We suppose that a cell of a tape can contain a value of any simple type. Thus, the value of a tape is an arbitrary finite sequence $(x_1 \ldots, x_n)$ where x_i belongs to some of the types $T_1,\ldots,T_a$. Just as before be both input and output tapes are used.

Statements in $L_0^{T_1,\ldots,T_a}$ are just the same as in $\mathbf{L_0}$. Assignments and comparisons are allowed only between the variables (and constants) of the same type. Some additional comments are necessary for input statement

$$X \rightarrow u,$$

where X is an input tape and u is an internal variable of the type **T**. Let the reading head of the tape X be on the i-th cell at the moment when the statement is executed. If the i-th cell contains a value of the type **T**, the statement is executed normally, i.e., the value of the i-th cell is assigned to the variable u and the head moves one position right (at the beginning the head was at the first cell). If the i-th cell contains a value of some other type, an error (crash) occurs and the execution of the program is halted.

A natural question arises whether previous theorems can be generalized to programs with arbitrary constructive simple types. We shall consider the analogue of Theorem 1 in some detail.

Further on by a program we understand only a closed program, i.e., a program without pending exits. Let P be such a program in $L_0^{T_1,\ldots,T_a}$ with input tapes A,B,...,C. A test $A = A^0$, $B = B^0$,..., $C = C^0$ is said to be *admissible* if the program P does not crash on this test.

A test set T is said to be *a complete test set* for a program P if

(1) it contains only admissible tests,

(2) every branch of the program executable by an admissible test is executed by some test of the set.

THEOREM 5. *Let $T_1,\ldots,T_a$ be fixed constructive types. Then there exists an algorithm constructing complete test set for every program in $L_0^{T_1,\ldots,T_a}$.*

The proof of the theorem will be similar to that of Theorem 1, only some lemmas will be more complicated.

Let **T** be a fixed constructive type with its corresponding algorithms *A, B, C, D*. We need the generalization $x < (r) < y$ of the inequality $x < y$ for $r \in \{0,1,2,\ldots\}$:

$x < (0) < y$ means $x \leq y$ (i.e., $\neg(y > x)$),

$x < (1) < y$ means $x < y$,

$x < (r) < y$ where $r \geq 2$ means that there are elements $e_1, e_2,\ldots,e_{r-1}$ of the type **T** such that $x < e_1 < e_2 < \ldots < e_{r-1} < y$.

By an inequality system N of the type **T** we understand a system

$$x_1 < (r_1) < y_1$$

$$\ldots$$

$$x_p < (r_p) < y_p,$$

where x_i, y_i are variables or constants of the type **T**.

Such a system of inequalities N (like in Section 2) is represented by a graph G_N : the vertices of the graph are labeled by variables and constants of the system N and an edge of weight r is drawn from vertex y to vertex x if there is an inequality $x < (r) < y$ in the system N. Vertex x is called constant vertex, if it corresponds to a constant in the system N and variable vertex, if it coresponds to a variable. Variable vertices with no edges issuing are called minimal ones. Variable vertices with no incoming edges are called maximal ones. Let us consider a path in the graph G_N. By weight of a path we understand, just as before, the sum of the weights of its edges.

Let us introduce some more notations. Let $x,y \in \mathbf{T}$. Let us denote

$$M(x,y)=\{ z \mid z\in \mathbf{T} \ \&\ z<x \ \&\ y<z \},$$
$$M(*,x)=\{ z \mid z\in \mathbf{T} \ \&\ x<z \},$$
$$M(y,*)=\{ z \mid z\in \mathbf{T} \ \&\ z<y \}.$$

The cardinality of the set M is denoted by |M| (it can also be infinity).
Let us define

$$x-y=\begin{cases} 0 \text{, if } x=y \\ |M(x,y)|+1 \text{ if } y<x \\ -|M(y,x)|-1 \text{ if } x<y \end{cases}$$

The "–" operator just introduced coincides with the conventional minus operator in the case when **T** is the integer type.

LEMMA 1. *An inequality system N of a type **T** has a solution if and only if its graph G_N has the following properties:*

(1) the weight of every cyclic path is equal to 0,

(2) the weight of every path leading from a constant vertex c_1 to other constant vertex c_2 does not exceed c_1-c_2,

*(3) if the type **T** has the smallest value ω, then the weight of every path leading from a constant vertex c to a minimal variable vertex does not exceed c- ω ,*

*(4) if the type **T** has the largest value Ω, then the weight of every path leading from a maximal variable vertex to a constant vertex does not exceed Ω–c,*

*(5) if the type **T** has both the smallest value ω and the largest value Ω, then the weight of every path leading from a maximal vertex x to a minimal vertex y does not exceed Ω–ω .*

Before we proceed to the proof of the lemma let us remark that the beforementioned algorithms ***A, B, C, D*** do not yield a constructive method to check the lemma conditions. Therefore, up to now the lemma has only qualitative meaning.

Now let us begin the proof.

The necessity of lemma conditions is obvious.

Let us prove the sufficiency, we assume lemma conditions (1) - (5) to be true. We search the solution by induction. On each step of the induction we assign a constant value of the type **T** to a variable vertex of G_N. We assign the constant values (i.e., replace the variable vertices by constant ones) so that the validity of lemma conditions is preserved.

To implement this idea we have to make some preparations. At first let p(x,y) denote the maximal weight of the paths leading from vertex x to vertex y.

1) Let us consider all pairs of constant vertices (c_1,c_2) where there is a path from c_1 to c_2. The second condition of lemma implies $c_2 \le c_1$. For every pair of vertices, where $p(c_1,c_2) -1 \ge 1$, we construct elements $e_1, e_2, \ldots, e_{p(c1,c2)-1}$, such that $c_2<e_1<e_2<\ldots<e_{p(c1,c2)-1}<c_1$, using algorithms ***A*** and ***B***. The existence of such elements is provided by the second condition of the lemma.

2) Let us consider all pairs (c,x) where c is a constant vertex, x is a minimal variable vertex and there is a path from c to x. For every pair of vertices, where $p(c,x) \ge 1$, we construct elements $e'_1, e'_2, \ldots, e'_{p(c,x)}$, such that $e'_1<e'_2<\ldots<e'_{p(c,x)} <c$, using algorithms ***A***, ***B*** and ***C***.

3) Let us consider all pairs (x,c) where c is a constant vertex, x is a maximal variable vertex and there is a path from x to c. For every pair of vertices, where $p(x,c) \geq 1$, we construct elements $e''_1, e''_2, \ldots, e''_{p(x,c)}$, such that $c < e''_1 < e''_2 < \ldots < e''_{p(x,c)}$, using algorithms *A*, *B* and *D*. The existence of such elements is provided by the fourth condition of the lemma.

4) Let us consider all pairs (x, y) where x is a maximal variable vertice, y is a minimal variable vertice and there is a path from x to y. For every pair of vertices we construct elements $e'''_1, e'''_2, \ldots, e'''_{p(x,y)+1}$, such that $e'''_1 < e'''_2 < \ldots < e'''_{p(x,y)+1}$, using algorithms *A, B, C,D* (and assuming that we know at least one element of each type). The existence of such elements is provided by the fifth condition of the lemma.

Now let us consider all the beforementioned elements e, e', e", e"' together with constants of the inequality system. By means of the algorihtm *A* we sort them in ascending order:

$$a_1 < a_2 < a_3 < \ldots < a_u \qquad (*)$$

The elements corresponding to constants of the inequality system are called constant elements, the other ones – auxiliary elements.

We begin to solve the inequality system N by assigning the value a_1 to all minimal variables and the value a_m to all maximal variables. This will introduce new constants in the inequality system N and its graph G_N. It is not difficult to ascertain that the introduction of such constants does not affect the truth of the lemma conditions (1) – (5). In the sequel we have, in fact, to deal only with conditions (1) and (2), the conditions (3) – (5) are used no more.

At first let us deal with vertices which belong to a cyclic path (its weight is 0 by the condition (1)). If there is a constant among them, assign the constant to all variable vertices. If all vertices of the path are variable ones, then select one variable as a representative of the path (for other variables must have the same value) and replace the cyclic path by this variable.

Let us consider a vertex z in the graph G with no constant value assigned to it in the previous steps. Let us take all constant vertices (including the ones introduced in the previous induction steps) with the paths leading from the vertices to z. We make an inductive assumption that all the values of these vertices are within the sequence (*). Hence we suppose these vertices to form a subsequence

$$a_{i1}, a_{i2}, \ldots, a_{im}.$$

of the sequence (*), i.e., every such vertex has a corresponding ordinal number i in the sequence (*). The maximal weights of paths leading from these vertices to z are denoted by $l_1, l_2, \ldots, l_m$ respectively. Let us consider the following elements of the sequence (*)

$$a_{i1-l1}, a_{i2-l2}, \ldots, a_{im-lm}$$

Let us denote by a_h the least of these elements (i.e., the element positioned leftmost in the sequence (*)).

Further we take all constant vertices (including the ones introduced in the previous induction steps) which have paths leading from z to them. Again we make an inductive assumption that values of these vertices form a subsequence

$$a_{j1}, a_{j2}, \ldots, a_{jn}$$

of the sequence (*). Let us denote the maximal weights of paths leading from z to these vertices by $r_1, r_2, \ldots, r_n$ and consider the following elements of (*)

$$a_{j1+r1}, a_{j2+r2}, \ldots, a_{jn+rn}.$$

Let a_g be the largest of these elements.

It follows from the second condition of the lemma that

$$a_g < a_h .$$

Indeed, if it were not so, it is easy to deduce that constants a_g and a_h would violate the second condition of lemma.

Let us choose any element u_i of the subsequence

$$a_g, a_{g+1}, \ldots, a_h$$

of the sequence (*) as the value z. So the vertex z becomes a constant vertex in the graph G_N. It is easy to observe that lemma conditions are preserved. Moreover, the set of values of constant vertices will not exceed the sequence (*).

Thus we continue the process until all variable vertices in G_N are replaced by constants. These constants form the solution of the system N.

This proves the sufficiency of lemma conditions (and also lemma).

The proof of sufficiency yields us an algorithm for solving inequality systems. Let us express this result as a separate lemma.

LEMMA 2. *For each constructive type T there is an algorithm which, given any inequality system N of the type T,*
(1) finds a solution if such exists,
(2) produces special indication if there is no solution.

Let us make some remarks to the proof of the second assertion of the lemma. If we consider the abovementioned algorihm for solving inequality systems more in detail, we can see that, in case Lemma 1 conditions fail, the algorithm certainly is aborted, i.e., either there are not enough elements $a_1, a_2, \ldots, a_u$ or inequality $a_g < a_h$ fails. The aborting definitely occurs after a finite number of steps. It means the algorithm can always "catch" the nonexistence of solution. So it is possible to overcome the nonconstructiveness of Lemma 1 conditions.

Now let P be a program in $L_0^{T1,\ldots,Ta}$ and $\alpha = (k_1, \ldots, k_r)$ be an initial path in this program. We define the system of inequalities corresponding to path α just as in the proof of Theorem 1. The only difference is that every occurrence of internal variable in the system will have its type ascribed, e.g., t_7^{T3}, u_0^{T1}, etc. The inequality system also contains variables X_i where X is an input tape. These variables occur only in equalities $X_i = t_j^{Te}$ where the instance of the internal variable t_j^{Te} has already the type T_e ascribed to. Relying on this equality we ascribe the same type T_e also to the variable X_i:

$$X_i^{Te}.$$

As assignments and comparisons are allowed only for variables of the same type, the inequality system $N(\alpha)$ splits into independent inequality systems according to types:

$$N(\alpha) = \{N^{T1}(\alpha), \ldots, N^{Ta}(\alpha)\}.$$

Obviously there holds

LEMMA 3. *A path α is feasible iff for each of the types T_e the corresponding inequality system $N^{Te}(\alpha)$ has a solution. Any solution of the systems $N^{T1}(\alpha), \ldots, N^{Ta}(\alpha)$ with respect to cell variables of input tapes yields a test executing the path α.*

Further we consider each of the inequality systems $N^{T1}(\alpha),\dots,N^{Ta}(\alpha)$ separately. Let $N^T(\alpha)$ be one of these inequality systems. Our aim is to define the **T**–state $S^T(\alpha)$ for a program after the execution of path α, i.e., part of the program state $S(\alpha)$ referring to the type **T**. The complete state $S(\alpha)$ is defined as $\{S^{T1}(\alpha),\dots,S^{Ta}(\alpha)\}$.

The idea for the definition of $S^T(\alpha)$ is similar to that used in the proof of Theorem 1, namely, we take the inequality systems $N^T(\alpha)$ and exclude inactive variables. However, a new problem arises: how to choose the constant c_0 used to delimit the weights of edges (see the definition of the exclusion of variable y in the proof of Theorem 1). Let us proceed as follows. Let us consider all constants of the type **T** in the program P, as well as the smallest and largest values of the type **T**, if there are such. Sort all these constants in ascending order

$$c_1, c_2,\dots, c_m.$$

Let us consider differences $c_j - c_i$. These differences can be infinite for some pairs and finite for some others. Let us consider all pairs (c_i, c_j) where the difference is finite. Let us denote the largest of the differences by C_0^T.

Now let us define the exclusion of inactive variables from the inequality system $N^T(\alpha)$ just as before, with just defined constant C_0^T playing the role of c_0. Let us recall that the constant C_0^T is used to delimit the weight of edge: if there is a weight $r > C_0^T + 1$, it is replaced by $C_0^T + 1$. It is not difficult to ascertain that after every exclusion of the variable the following assertion holds for the obtained inequality system $N'^T(\alpha)$: $N'^T(\alpha)$ satisfies the conditions of the existence of a solution from Lemma 1 iff $N^T(\alpha)$ satisfies these conditions. By the way, let us note the following easily provable proposition. Had we used some smaller constant instead of C_0^T in variable exclusion, only the following assertion would hold instead of the previous: if $N^T(\alpha)$ satisfies the conditions of solution existence from Lemma 1, then also $N'^T(\alpha)$ satisfies the conditions (but not vice versa).

Now let us define the state $S^T(\alpha)$ to be the inequality system obtained from $N^T(\alpha)$ by excluding all inactive variables. It follows from the above mentioned that an analogue of Lemma 3 from Theorem 1 holds for state $S^T(\alpha)$.

However, state $S^T(\alpha)$ cannot be used directly. The matter is that the constant C_0^T, upon which the construction of state $S^T(\alpha)$ relied, cannot be effectively found for every constructive type **T**. Therefore we do as follows. For every natural constant c we consider the state $S^{T,c}(\alpha)$, the definition of which differs from the definition of $S^T(\alpha)$ only in the point that constant c is used instead of C_0^T. By the way, if $c = C_0^T$, then $S^T(\alpha) = S^{T,c}(\alpha)$. From the abovementioned there follows

LEMMA 4. *For every constant $c \in N$ the existence of a solution for system $N^T(\alpha)$ implies the existence of a solution for system $S^{T,c}(\alpha)$ (i.e., the consistency of the state $S^{T,c}(\alpha)$). If $c \geq C_0^T$, then also the existence of a solution for the system $S^{T,c}(\alpha)$ implies the existence of a solution for the system $N^T(\alpha)$.*

It is not difficult to see that for every $c \in N$ an analogue of Lemma 4 from Theorem 1 holds for the state $S^{T,c}$.

LEMMA 5. *Let σ be a state of the type $S^{T,c}$ for the program P, α a path in the program and β a continuation of the path α. Then the equality holds:*

$$S^{T,c}(\sigma,\alpha+\beta) = S^{T,c}(S^{T,c}(\sigma,\alpha),\beta).$$

Now let us define for an arbitrary tuple of natural numbers $(c_1,\ldots,c_a)$ general state

$$S^{c1,\ldots,ca}(\alpha) = \{S^{T1,c1}(\alpha),\ldots, S^{Ta,ca}(\alpha)\}.$$

Let us emphasize that, given constants $(c_1,\ldots,c_a)$, the state $S^{c1,\ldots,ca}(\alpha)$ can be effectively constructed for an arbitrary path α. We also emphasize that the number of possible states for program P is finite for a fixed tuple $(c_1,\ldots,c_a)$.

Thus for every tuple of naturals $(c_1,\ldots,c_a)$ we can build for a program P, using states $S^{c1,\ldots,ca}(\alpha)$, its reachability graph denoted by $G^{c1,\ldots,ca}(\alpha)$. Let us consider the properties of this graph.

From Lemma 4 and other previous lemmas there follows an analogue of Lemma 6 from Theorem 1:

LEMMA 6. *For every tuple of naturals $(c_1,\ldots,c_a)$ the feasibility of an initial path α in program P implies the existence of an initial path γ in the reachability graph $G^{c1,\ldots,ca}(\alpha)$ whose projection is α. If conditions*

$$c_1 \geq C_0^{T1},\ldots, c_a \geq C_0^{Ta}$$

hold for the tuple $(c_1,\ldots,c_a)$, then the existence of an initial path γ in the reachability graph whose projection is α implies the feasibility of path α in program P.

Let us consider the covering U of the reachability graph, namely, the set of paths covering all allowed edges of the graph $G^{c1,\ldots,ca}$. A set of paths pr_U in a program is assoaciated with the set U.

From the previous lemma there follows

COROLLARY. *Every tuple of natural numbers $(c_1,\ldots,c_a)$ has a property: if U is a covering of reachability graph $G^{c1,\ldots,ca}$ for program P, then pr_U contains all feasible branches of the program. If in addition*

$$c_1 \geq C_0^{T1},\ldots, c_a \geq C_0^{Ta}, \qquad (**)$$

then all paths in pr_U are also feasible.

These lemmas show that, if we knew the constants $C_0^{T1},\ldots, C_0^{Ta}$ for the given program, we could, using Lemma 2, construct CTS for the program just the same way as in the case of Theorem 1. However, the algorithms ***A, B, C, D*** used in the definition of type constructivity do not yield a method to find these constants. Therefore much more complex actions should be performed as in the case of Theorem 1.

Initially as $c_1,\ldots,c_a$, we choose any natural numbers, e.g., $c_1 = 0,\ldots, c_a = 0$. Using these numbers we construct the reachability graph $G^{c1,\ldots,ca}$ and its covering U consisting of finite paths. Just as before we consider pr_U and for each path $\alpha \in$ pr_U construct the inequality system

$$N(\alpha) = \{N^{T1}(\alpha),\ldots,N^{Ta}(\alpha)\}.$$

Then we try to solve these inequality systems using the algorithm from Lemma 2. If the algorithm yields solutions for all paths α, then, as it is implied by the first assertion of the Corollary, these solutions will form CTS. Now let us assume that the algorithm aborts on some inequality system $N(\alpha)$. It means that there is i such that the algorithm will produce the solution inexistence indication when applied to the inequality system $N^{T_i}(\alpha)$. It follows from the definition of the reachability graph and Lemma 4 that the case is possible only for $c_i < C_0^{T_1}$. This inequality means that there are two constants c_k, c_e in program P such that $c_e - c_k < \infty$ and $c_e - c_k > c_i$. Since we know this thing, now we apply the algorithms ***A, B, C, D*** for the type T_i to all possible pairs of constants in the program and so in a finite number of steps we can construct $p \geq c_i$ elements between some pair of constants c_k and c_e, besides, by using the algorithm ***B*** we can ascertain that there are no more elements between these constants. In the next iteration step we use the number p+1 as a constant c_i. Thus with every iteration step we approximate constants $c_1,...,c_a$ to the constants $C_0^{T_1}$,..., $C_0^{T_a}$. In such a way we assure that after a finite number of steps constants $c_1,...,c_a$ can be reached such that the covering U of the reachability graph $G^{c_1,...,c_a}$ will have the required property: all $\alpha \in$ pr_U will be feasible, i.e., inequality systems $N(\alpha)$ will have solutions. These solutions will form the desired CTS.

This completes the proof of the Theorem.

Natural question arises whether we can generalize other theorems proven in the previous sections for the language $\mathbf{L_0}$ to programs in $L^{T_1,...,T_a}$ with T_1 ,..., T_a being arbitrary constructive types. Using the techniques elaborated in the previous proofs it is not difficult to obtain a positive answer to this question.

Now we return back to the base language $\mathbf{L_0}$ in the next sections. Methods developed for the language $\mathbf{L_0}$ in many cases can be transferred to wider classes of programs.

6 Programs with Stack

Let us consider a language $\mathbf{L_1}$ where a program has additional internal memory - stack. Formally $\mathbf{L_1}$ is obtained from the base language $\mathbf{L_0}$ by adding the following statements:

t→M (respectively **c→M**). The value of variable t (constant c) is added to the stack. We use the capital M to denote the stack. (Push statement).

M→t. The last element of the stack is assigned to variable t and erased in the stack. The statement has two exits: if the stack is not empty, then the exit '+' is used, otherwise use the exit '-'. In the last case the value of t is not changed. (Pop statement).

THEOREM 6. *There is an algorithm for constructing a finite complete test set for every program in* $\mathbf{L_1}$.

The proof is based on the slight modification of the notion of the program state and new lemmas about path replace. Our aim is to construct a reachability graph containing all feasible branches of the program.

Let us consider the construction of the system of inequalities $N(\alpha)$ corresponding to initial path $\alpha = (k_1, k_2, \ldots, k_r)$ for programs in $\mathbf{L_1}$. The construction is similar to that in Section 2. Additionally the initial system $N(\alpha_0)$ has inequality

$$m_0 = 0,$$

where m_0 is a variable denoting the number of stack elements. Further variables M^i with subscript are used to denote the value of the i-th stack element, and m_k are variables denoting the number of stack elements.

Now let us assume that the system of inequalities $N(\alpha_{i-1})$ is already defined. Let m_s be a variable denoting the number of stack elements after the execution of path α_{i-1}. Let us denote the value of m_s by w. Let u_l be a variable denoting the value of variable u after the execution of path α_{i-1}. Let z be the greatest subscript of all variables M with superscript w and let v be the greatest subscript of all variables M with superscript w+1. If there is no variable with superscript w or w+1, then we assume z=0 or v=0. Then we define $N(\alpha_i)$ as system obtained from $N(\alpha_{i-1})$ by adding the following inequalities:

1) If $k_i = (u \rightarrow M)$, then equalities

$$m_{s+1} = w+1 \ , \ M^{w+1}_{v+1} = u_l$$

are added. In this case new variables m_{s+1} and M^{w+1}_{v+1} are introduced. The value of variable m_{s+1} is equal to the number of stack elements.

2) If $k_i = (M \rightarrow u+)$ and $m_s > 0$, then equalities

$$m_{s+1} = w-1 \ , \ u_{l+1} = M^{w}_{z}$$

are added. New variables u_{l+1} and m_{s+1} are introduced. If $m_s = 0$, then inequalities

$$u_{l+1} < 0 \ , \ u_{l+1} > 0$$

are added to obtain contradictory inequality system.

3) If $k_i = (M \rightarrow u-)$ and if $m_s = 0$, then no inequality is added.
If $m_s > 0$, then inequalities

$$u_{l+1} < 0 \ , \ u_{l+1} > 0$$

are added to obtain contradictory inequality system.

4) If $k_i \in \mathbf{L_0}$, then we proceed the same way as defined for the language $\mathbf{L_0}$.

Let us give an example. For $\alpha = (1{:}\ A \rightarrow u+,\ 2{:}\ u \rightarrow M,\ 3{:}\ M \rightarrow t+)$ we have ineguality system

$$N(\alpha) = \begin{cases} u_0 = 0 \\ t_0 = 0 \\ m_0 = 0 \\ u_1 = A_1 \\ m_1 = 1 \\ M^1_1 = u_1 \\ m_2 = 0 \\ t_1 = M^1_1 \end{cases}$$

also in our case. So initial path α is feasible iff system $N(\alpha)$ has a solution. Now let us define state inequality system $S(\alpha)$ for our case. Internal variables with maximal subscripts and variables denoting input files are called active variables. Previous rules of variable exclusion will be used also for all variables m_s and M^i_j. Let us exclude all of them and all other inactive variables. We obtain inequality system containing only active variables and constants. The resulting system is also denoted by $S(\alpha)$ and called a *program state* after execution of path α. Easy to see that Lemma 3 from Section 2 is valid also in this case.

Let us consider a path α with the following property: the number of stack elements on path α is equal to or greater than the initial, after the execution of path α it is equal to the initial. Such path is called a *normal path.*

Let α be a normal path (there is no requirement for α to be initial) and σ be an arbitrary program state. Then we define $N(\sigma,\alpha)$ the same way as for the language $\mathbf{L_0}$. $N(\sigma,\alpha_0)$ is the same initial inequality system σ with only zero subscripts added to initial variables. The equality $m_0=0$ is also added to describe the initial status of stack. Further $N(\sigma,\alpha_i)$ is defined from $N(\sigma,\alpha_{i-1})$ and statement k_i just as before. Let us exclude inactive variables, except initial variables from $N(\sigma,\alpha)$. We obtain inequality system containing constants and internal variables with zero subscript and perhaps internal variables with another subscript. Let us replace second type subscripts of all variables by one. The reduced system is denoted by $E(\sigma,\alpha)$ and called a *path effect.*

LEMMA 1. *Let initial path α have two normal continuations β and γ with the same last statement. Let us denote $S(\alpha)$ by σ. If $E(\sigma,\beta)=E(\sigma,\gamma)$, then path $\alpha+\beta$ and path $\alpha+\gamma$ have the same feasible continuations.*

Let path δ be a continuation of path $\alpha+\beta$ or path $\alpha+\gamma$. Let us consider systems $N(\alpha+\beta+\delta)$ and $N(\alpha+\gamma+\delta)$. All variables of systems which are created on path β or γ, except those which are active at the beginning of the path δ, have no inequalities with the variables created on path δ. If we exclude all inactive variables created on path β or γ, we obtain path effect $E(\sigma,\beta)$ and path effect $E(\sigma,\gamma)$. Further we have equivalent systems of inequalities which may differ only by subscripts of the variables created on path δ. There follows the proof of Lemma.

LEMMA 2. *Let initial path α have the continuation $\beta+\gamma+\delta$ where $\beta+\gamma+\delta$ is normal path and γ also is normal path. Let states $S(\alpha)$ and $S(\alpha+\beta)$ are equal. Let path β and path γ have the same first statement and let path γ and path δ have the same last statement. If $E(S(\alpha),\beta+\gamma+\delta)=E(S(\alpha+\beta),\gamma)$, then path $\alpha+\gamma$ and path $\alpha+\beta+\gamma+\delta$ have the same feasible continuations.*

It follows from lemma condition that $E(S(\alpha),\gamma)=E(S(\alpha+\beta),\gamma)$. Then $E(S(\alpha),\gamma) = E(S(\alpha),\beta+\gamma+\delta)$. Now according to Lemma 1 path $\alpha+\beta$ and path $\alpha+\beta+\gamma+\delta$ have the same feasible continuations.This proves the lemma.

The number of the pairs (n_i,S_i), where n_i is the statement label and S_i is the program state, can be estimated by constant R_1 effectively evaluated from the given program. Also the number of quadruples (n_i, S_i, E_i, k_i), where n_i,k_i are statements labels, S_i is a state and E_i is path effect, can be estimated by constant R_2 effectively evaluated from the given program.

LEMMA 3. *For any feasible branch δ there exists a path α such that path $\alpha + \delta$ is feasible and the number of stack elements is less than R_1+R_2 on the path α.*

Let us denote by β feasible initial path to branch δ. Let us assume that the number of stack elements after the execution of β is more than R_1. Then we consider stack elements pushed on path β and not popped on path β. Let us denote by β_{k^i} the initial part of path β to the statement when the i-th abovementioned stack element is pushed and by β'_{k^i} the continuation. If we find β_{k^i} and β_{k^j}, $k^i<k^j$, where $S(\beta_{k^i})=S(\beta_{k^j})$ and first statements of β_{k^i} and β_{k^j} are the same, then path $\beta_{k^i} + \beta'_{k^j}$ is feasible. So we find feasible path β' to the branch δ where the number of stack elements after executing β' is less than R_1.

Let us denote by α the initial part of path β until maximal stack length of path β is reached and by ε the continuation of α. Let us consider the stack elements pushed on path α and popped on path ε. Let us denote by α_{k^i} the initial part of path α to statement, when the i-th stack element is pushed, and by ε_{k^i} continuation to statement, when this element is popped, and by γ_{k^i} continuation to branch δ. Every path ε_{k^i} is normal path and we consider $E(S(\alpha_{k^i}),\varepsilon_{k^i})$. If we find that path ε_{k^i} and path ε_{k^j} satisfy conditions of Lemma 2, then path $\alpha_{k^i}+\varepsilon_{k^j}+\gamma_{k^j}+\delta$ is also feasible. So we find path α with no more than R_1+R_2 stack elements used.

Before we start the construction of reachability graph we must extend the notion of the program state. We must include in the state inequality system all variables denoting the values of stack elements. So additionally the state inequality system has active variables M^1, M^2 ,...,M^t where M^i denote the value of the i-th stack element.The number of active variables denoting stack elements is equal to the value of variable m_p where m_p is variable with maximal subscript. Let us denote by $F(\alpha)$ the extended program state after the execution of initial path α. Let us denote by $F(\omega,\alpha)$ the extended program state after the execution of the path α from the extended state ω.

LEMMA 4. *Let ω be an extended state, α a path and β a continuation of path α. Then $F(\omega,\alpha+\beta)=F(F(\omega,\alpha),\beta)$.*

We can notice that inequalities generated on path β do not contain inactive variables of path α. So while constructing $F(\omega,\alpha+\beta)$ from $N(\omega,\alpha+\beta)$ we at first can exclude inactive variables generated by path α. We obtain $F(\omega,\alpha)$ as intermediate result, and the construction of $F(F(\omega,\alpha),\beta)$ from $N(F(\omega,\alpha),\beta)$ starts on equivalent inequality system. This proves the lemma.

Now we can start the construction of the reachability graph. In our case vertices of the graph are labeled by pairs (n,F), where n is a statement label and F is extended state. To construct the reachability graph we use the same algorithm as for programs in language $\mathbf{L_0}$ with one additional rule: if the number of stack elements exceeds R_1+R_2 in the state of the new vertex, then we do not construct edges from this vertex.

From the construction of the reachability graph and Lemma 3 follow

LEMMA 5. *Every initial path in the reachability graph is feasible.*

LEMMA 6. *A branch β in the program is feasible iff there is an initial path α in its reachability graph whose projection contains β.*

Complete test set is constructed from the reachability graph the same way as in case of the language $\mathbf{L_0}$. This completes the proof of Theorem 6.

7 Programs with Direct Access

Let us extend the language $\mathbf{L_0}$ by adding a new statement

RESET(X)

where X is input tape. The statement returns the input head of tape X to the beginning of the tape. By using this statement we can have the repeated reading of input tape. Let us denote the new language by $\mathbf{L_2}$.

THEOREM 7. *There exists no algorithm for constructing a finite complete test set for every program in* $\mathbf{L_2}$.

A subclass of programs in $\mathbf{L_2}$ with two input tapes with one usage of RESET for each of them is sufficient for non-existence. We consider two-tape automata by Rabin and Scott [13]. These automata may be represented by programs in base language $\mathbf{L_0}$ with two input tapes. Let us denote by $L_A \cap L_B$ the intersection of languages L_A and L_B represented by two-tape automata A and B. The problem of determination of $L_A \cap L_B$ emptiness is known to be undecidable [13]. We shall consider tapes of automata to be two input tapes of a program in $\mathbf{L_2}$. It is easy to construct a program P_{AB} using RESET statement only once for each of the tapes where STOP statement is accessible iff $L_A \cap L_B \neq 0$. Hence it follows that the emptiness of $L_A \cap L_B$ can be decided by means of a complete test set.

The previous theorem indicates that the unsolvability of CTS construction problem tends to appear readily if multiple reading of input tapes is allowed. Nevertheless it is possible to select the natural program classes with direct access by addressing to tape cells and retain the CTS problem solvability.

Further we consider a certain class of the type. In this case input and output tapes are not divided. We use both access methods for every tape. For this purpose the tape cells are addressed by numbers 1,2,3,..., and additionally to internal variables u,v,...,t we introduce a finite number of internal address variables which store tape-cell addresses. Every tape has its own address variables. We use capital letter to denote the tape and a corresponding small letter with superscript to denote the address variable. The address variables of tape A are denoted by $a^1, a^2, a^3,\dots,a^k$, those of tape B by $b^1, b^2, b^3,\dots, b^m$, etc. We say that a tape contains the sequence of integers $n_1,n_2,\dots,n_r$ if integers $n_1,n_2,\dots,n_r$ are written on the tape beginning from the first cell. As we need to modify the statements of the language $\mathbf{L_0}$ we will repeat the definition of all statements. Let A be an arbitrary tape. Let u,t be arbitrary internal variables and a^i,a^j arbitrary address variables of tape A. A program is constructed using the following statements:

1. **START.** The first statement of the program. This statement transfers heads of all tapes to the beginning and sets values of all internal and address variables to the initial value 0. A program has exactly one START statement.

2. **A → u**. The value of the scanned cell of tape A is assigned to variable u. The statement has two exits: exit "+", when the scanned cell contains a number, and exit "-", when the scanned cell is empty.This statement does not move the head on tape A. (Input statement).

3. **u → A**. The value of variable u is assigned to the scanned cell of tape A. (Output statement).

4. **NEXT(A)**. The head moves right to the next cell of tape A. (Shift statement).

5. **u → t** (respectively **c→t**). The value of variable u (constant c) is assigned to variable t. (Assignment statement).

6. **u < t** (respectively **c<t, u<c**). The statement has two exits: if the value of u (respectively c) is less than the value of t (respectively c), then exit "+" is used, otherwise use exit "-". (Comparison statement).

7. **ADR(A) → a^i**. The address of the scanned cell on tape A is assigned to the address variable a^i. (Address input statement).

8. **a^i ⇒ u** . The value of tape A cell whose address is equal to the value of variable a^i is assigned to variable u. The statement has two exits: exit "+", when the tape A cell contains an integer, and exit "-", when it is empty. (Direct access input statement).

9. **u ⇒ a^i**. The value of variable u is assigned to tape A cell whose address is equal to the value of the address variable a^i. (Direct access output statement).

10. **a^i → a^j** . The value of address variable a^i is assigned to address variable a^j Only address variables of the same tape are allowed in the statement. (Address assignment statement).

11. **STOP**.

Let us denote the language obtained in such a way by L_3

Programs in the language L_0 differ by the following constraints:

1) there is no special statement START, i.e., the exits of other statements cannot lead to START;

2) every input or output statement is directly followed by the shift statement of the corresponding tape;

3) all tapes are divided into input tapes and output tapes.

Now all these constraints are dropped.

The new statements dealing with addresses are used for all tapes. Note, however, that the address assignment statement can be applied only to address variables associated with the same tape. Removing this restriction leads to unsolvability of the problem of construction of complete test set. The same result is also obtained if we allow a comparison statement for address variables. In reality, these restrictions usually hold. The new language can be used to code the bubblesort algorithm. Fig.13 gives an example of such a program.

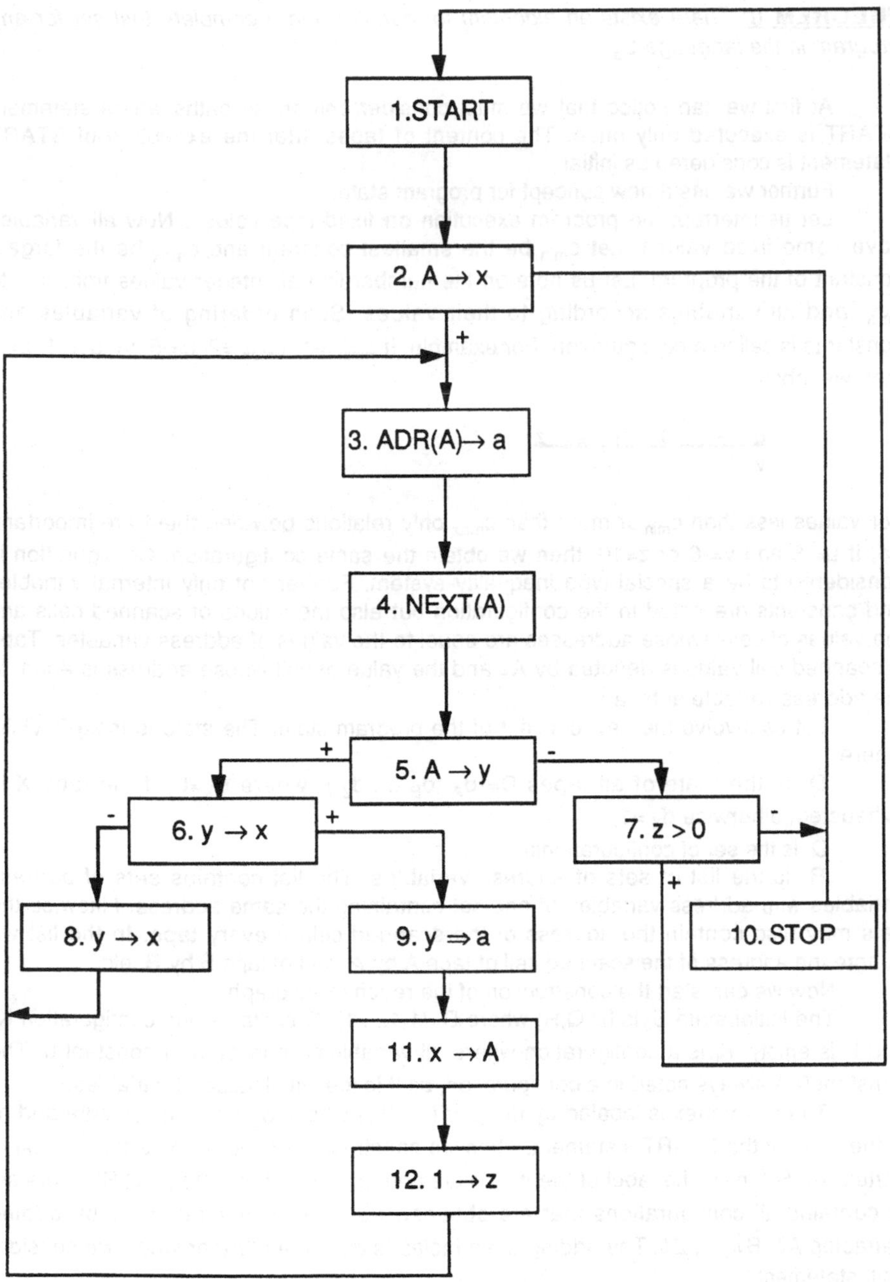
1.START
2. A → x
3. ADR(A)→ a
4. NEXT(A)
5. A → y
6. y → x
7. z > 0
8. y → x
9. y ⇒ a
10. STOP
11. x → A
12. 1 → z

Fig. 13

THEOREM 8. *There exists an algorithm for construction a complete test set for any program in the language* $\boldsymbol{L_3}$.

At first we can notice that we must consider only those paths where statement START is executed only once. The content of tapes after the execution of START statement is considered as initial.

Further we use a new concept for program state.

Let us interrupt the program execution on fixed tape values. Now all variables have some fixed values. Let c_{min} be the smallest constant and c_{max} be the largest constant of the program. Let us note on the number line all integer values from c_{min} to c_{max} and all variables according to their values. Such ordering of variables and constants is called a configuration. For example, if c_{min} =-1, c_{max} =2, u=-5, v=-5, t=1, z=7, then we obtain

```
u  -1  0  1  2  z
v         t
```

For values less than c_{min} or more than c_{max} only relations between them are important. So, if u=-6 and v=-6 or z=10, then we obtain the same configuration. Configuration is considered to be a special type inequality system. Further not only internal variables and constants are noted in the configuration but also the values of scanned cells and the values of cells whose addresses are equal to the values of address variables. Tape A scanned cell value is denoted by A↓ and the value of cell whose address is equal to the address variable a^i by a^i↓.

Let us involve the new concept of the program state. The state is triple [d,Q,R], where

D is the state of all tapes D=(d_A ,d_B ,...,d_Z), where d_X=0, if the tape X is exhausted, otherwise d_X =1,

Q is the set of configurations,

R is the list of sets of address variables. The list contains sets of address variables with address variables of one set containing the same address. Likewise the sets may also contain the address of the scanned cell of every tape. In the list we denote the address of the scanned cell of tape A by **A**, that of tape B by **B**, etc.

Now we can start the construction of the reachability graph.

The initial state S_0 is [D,Q,R] where D=(1,1,...,1), Q contains one configuration K_0 and R is empty. K_0 is a configuration where all variables are located at constant 0. The constant 0 is always noted in a configuration, as it is the initial value of variables.

The first vertex is labeled by the pair (n_0 ,S_0) where S_0 is the initial state and n_0 is the label of the START statement. Then we construct the edge from vertex (n_0 ,S_0) to vertex (n_1 ,S_1), n_1 is the label of the next statement and S_1 is the state [D,Q,R] where set Q contains all configurations that are obtained from the configuration K_0 by adding variables A↓, B↓,..., Z↓. The adding of variables is described further when we consider shift statement.

Further we define construction rules for all other statements. Let us consider an arbitrary vertex (n,S) with S being the state [D,Q,R].

1) If n = (NEXT(A)) and the statement exit leads to statement n_1, then the new vertex is (n_1 ,S_1). If d_A=1 in the state S, then state S_1 is [D,Q_1,R_1] where set Q_1 contains all configurations which can be obtained from set Q configurations by transferring or deleting variable A↓. R_1 is obtained from R by deleting **A** from all sets. In the case sets with one element appear they are also deleted.

Actually the deleting of variable A↓ from configuration means that the current scanned cell is empty.

Variable transferring means its deleting from the current point and adding to any point of configuration.

For example, if Q contains a configuration

```
0  1  2  t
___________
   u
```

and A↓ must be added, then 7 possible configurations are obtained:

```
 0 u 2 t        0 u 2 t        0 u 2 t        0 u 2 t
__________     __________     __________     __________
A↓             A↓                  A↓             A↓

0 u 2    t      0 u 2 t        0 u 2 t
__________     __________     __________
     A↓              A↓             A↓
```

If d_A=0, then state S_1 is [D,Q,R_1].

2) If n=(A→u) and the exit "-" leads to statement n_1 and exit "+" to statement n_2, then new vertices are constructed the following way. If d_A=0 in state S, then we construct an edge from vertex (n,S) to vertex (n_1,S_1) where S_1 is [D,Q,R]. If d_A=1, then let us denote by Q_1 the subset of Q where configurations contain variable A↓ and by Q_2 the set Q\Q_1. If set Q_1 is not empty, then an edge to vertex (n_2,S_2) is constructed. State S_2 is [D,Q_3,R] where configurations of set Q_3 are obtained from configurations of set Q_1 by transferring variable u to the point where variable A↓ is noted. If set Q_2 is not empty, then an edge from vertex (n,S) to vertex (n_1,S_3) is also constructed. State S_3 is [D',Q_2,R] where D' is obtained from D by setting d_A to 0.

3) If n=(u → A) and the exit leads to n_1, then the new vertex is (n_1, S_1). State S_1 is [D,Q',R] where configurations of Q' are obtained from set Q configurations by transferring A↓ to the point where variable u is noted. If list R contains a set T with **A**, then all variables of set T are also transferred to the point where variable u is noted.

4) If n=(u → v) and exit leads to n_1, then the new vertex is (n_1, S_1). State S_1 is [D,Q',R] where configurations of Q' are obtained from configurations of Q by transferring u to the point where variable v is noted.

5) If n=(u < v) and exit "-": leads to statement n_2 and exit "+" to statement n_1, then the new vertices are constructed the following way. Let us denote by Q_1 the subset of configurations from Q where u is noted on the left from v and by Q_2 the set Q\Q_1. If Q_1 is

not empty, then an edge to vertex (n_1,S_1) is constructed where S_1 is $[D,Q_1,R]$. If Q_2 is not empty, then an edge to vertex (n_2,S_2) is constructed where S_2 is $[D,Q_2,R]$.

6) If n=(ADR(A) → a^i) and the exit leads to n_1, then the new vertex is (n_1,S_1). State S_1 is $[D,Q',R']$ where configurations of Q' are obtained from set Q configurations by transferring $a^i\downarrow$ to the point where variable $A\downarrow$ is noted, if $A\downarrow$ is noted in the configuration, or by deleting $a^i\downarrow$, if $A\downarrow$ is not noted in the configuration. List R' is obtained from R by adding set $\{\mathbf{A},a^i\}$, if list R does not contain a set with **A**, or by adding a^i to the set with **A**, otherwise.

7) If n=($a^i \Rightarrow u$) and the exit "-" leads to statement n_2 and the exit "+" to statement n_1, then the new vertices are constructed the following way. Let us denote by Q_1 the subset of Q where configurations contain variable $a^i\downarrow$ and by Q_2 the set $Q\backslash Q_1$. If Q_1 is not empty, then an edge to vertex (n_1,S_1) is constructed. S_1 is $[D,Q_1',R]$ where configurations of Q_1' are obtained from set Q_1 configurations by transferring u to the point where variable $a^i\downarrow$ is noted. If Q_2 is not empty, then also an edge to vertex (n_2,S_2) is constructed,where S_2 is $[D,Q_2,R]$.

8) If n=($u \Rightarrow a^i$) and the exit leads to n_1, then the new vertex is (n_1,S_1). State S_1 is $[D,Q',R]$ where configurations of Q' are obtained from set Q configurations by transferring $a^i\downarrow$ to the point where variable u is noted. If R contains a set T with a^i, then all variables of set T are also transferred to the point where variable u is noted.

9) If n=($a^j \rightarrow a^i$) and the exit leads to n_1, then the new vertex is (n_1,S_1). State S_1 is $[D,Q',R']$ where configurations of Q' are obtained from set Q configurations by transferring $a^i\downarrow$ to the point where variable $a^j\downarrow$ is noted if the configuration contains $a^j\downarrow$. List R' is obtained from R by adding set $\{a^i,a^j\}$ if list R does not contain a^j, or by adding a^i to the set with a^i, if R contains a^j.

If the new vertex already exists, then the edge is joined to the old vertex. When no new edges can be constructed the construction of the reachability graph is finished.

In such a way we receive a lot of paths in the reachability graph. It follows from the construction of the reachability graph that for any feasible path α of the program where START statement is executed only once there exists path α' in the reachability graph whose projection is path α.

LEMMA 1. *Every initial path in the reachability graph is feasible.*

Let us denote by $\alpha=((n_0,S_0),(n_1,S_1), \ldots,(n_r,S_r))$ an arbitrary initial path in the reachability graph. Let us consider the sequence of configurations $K_0,K_1,\ldots, K_r$ where for every $j=0,\ldots,r$ K_j is a configuration from state S_j configuration set and for every $j=0,\ldots,r-1$ the configuration K_{j+1} can be obtained from K_j applying abovedescribed construction rule corresponding to the statement n_j.

Let us denote by $\alpha_i=((n_0,S_0),(n_1,S_1), \ldots,(n_i,S_i))$ the initial part of path α. Let us prove by induction on i that for every path α_i there is a test T_i such that program traverses path α_i on the test T_i and program variables satisfy configuration sequence $K_0,K_1,\ldots, K_i$.

The test T_0 is empty tapes.

If n_i is NEXT(X) and K_{i+1} contains variable X↓, then test T_{i+1} is obtained from the test T_i by adding to tape X a cell with value s that locates X↓ at the right place in the configuration K_{i+1}. Let us consider possible variable X↓ relations with other variables or constants in the configuration K_{i+1}. At first we can notice that every variable except X↓ has a fixed value that is received from a tape or is equal to some constant of program. If X↓ is located at the point where some variable is noted or the point is in interval $[c_{min}, c_{max}]$, we take the value s equal to the value of the noted variable or constant. If X↓ is located at the last point of the configuration, we take as value s the largest value of the configuration increased by one. If X↓ is transferred to the first point, we will take as value s the smallest value of the configuration decreased by one. The last case is that X↓ is located just between z and v, where z and v denote variables or constants. It is easy to see that only one of them can be equal to constant. If the difference of z and v values is less than 2, we must change the previous values of the tapes of the test T_i. If $v>c_{max}$, then we replace all values of tapes which are equal or greater than the value of v by the same value increased by one. If z is less than c_{min}, then we can decrease by one all the values of tapes equal or less than the value of z. This operation has no influence on the sequence of configurations $K_0, K_1, \ldots, K_i$ and the program traverses on the updated test T_i the same path α_i. But now the difference of z and v values is 2, and we can choose the integer value s satisfying the configuration K_{i+1}.

If K_{i+1} does not contain variable X↓ then $T_{i+1}=T_i$.

If n_i is START, then T_{i+1} is obtained by adding a cell to every tape X, such that configuration K_{i+1} contains variable X↓.

If n_i is another statement, then $T_{i+1}=T_i$.

This proves the lemma.

Now the usual algorithm constructing CTS from the reachability graph can be used. This completes the proof of Theorem 8.

8 Programs with Counters

At first, it is clear that, if we consider programs with two–way counters and comparisons between a counter and a constant, the problem of CTS construction is algoritmically unsolvable even in the case of two counters. This follows from the well–known result (see, e.g., [12]) that every recursive function can be computed by a special coding on so–called Minsky machine using only two counters Z_1 and Z_2 and statements

| $z_i + 1 \to z_i$ |, | $z_i - 1 \to z_i$ |, ← + | $z_i = 0$ | - →, | STOP |.

Therefore, we can hope at best for the solvability of CTS construction problem in the case of one–way counters. However, as the next theorem shows, the algorithmic unsolvability appears quickly also in this case.

So let us denote by $\mathbf{L_4}$ the language obtained from the base language $\mathbf{L_0}$ by adding internal variables of a new type – counters and the following statements for them:

c → Z. The value of constant c is assigned to counter Z.

Z + 1 → Z. Counter Z is incremented by 1.

Z < t. The value of counter Z is compared with the value of internal variable t. The statement has two exits: "+" and "-".

The last statement allows us to compare the value of a counter with the values of an input tape.

THEOREM 9. *There exists no algorithm for constructing a complete test system for every program in* L_4. *(The subclass of* L_4 *programs with one input tape and one counter is sufficient for the nonexistence of algorithm).*

The proof of the theorem relies on testing, by means of constructions of language L_4, whether the input tape contains a configuration sequence of some Minsky machine. More detailed it means the following. Let M be a Minsky machine with two counters Z_1 and Z_2. Let us assume the initial value y to be always assigned to the first counter Z_1. Then by a configuration sequence corresponding to the initial value y we understand the following sequence of integers

$$Z_1^0, Z_2^0, \ldots, Z_1^i, Z_2^i, \ldots,$$

where Z_1^0, Z_2^0 are the initial values of counters: $Z_1^0 = y$, $Z_2^0 = 0$, and Z_1^i, Z_2^i are the values of counters after the execution of the i–th step of machine M. For example, if machine M executes statement $Z_1+1 \rightarrow Z_1$ on the i–th step, then $Z_1^i = Z_1^{i-1}+1$ and $Z_2^i = Z_2^{i-1}$. If machine M stops on the k–th step (i.e., STOP statement is executed), then configuration sequence is terminated upon Z_1^k, Z_2^k. We shall say in this case that the configuration sequence of machine M is finite for the initial value y. We can ascertain easily that it is possible for any machine M and initial value $y \in N$ to build a program $P_{M,y}$ in L_4, such that $P_{M,y}$ reaches STOP statement only if the configuration sequence of machine M is finite for the initial value y and this sequence is written on the input tape of $P_{M,y}$. In addition the program $P_{M,y}$ uses only one counter Z. The idea of construction of $P_{M,y}$ relies on the fact that it is possible to check whether the relation t=u+1 holds by means of one counter Z (for $u \geq 0$):

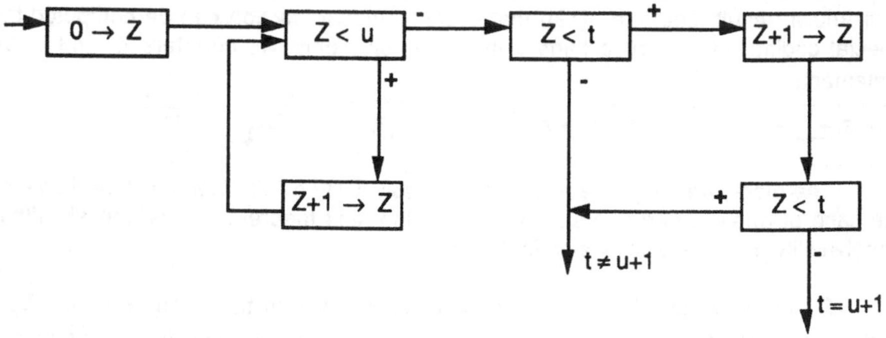

Hence it is possible to determine whether the integer sequence written on the input tape is the configuration sequence of machine M for the initial value y. Thus the halting problem for an arbitrary Minsky machine M and initial value y can be reduced to the STOP statement reachability problem for program $P_{M,y}$. Hence follows the algorithmic unsolvability of CTS construction problem for programs in $\mathbf{L_4}$.

Let us denote by $\mathbf{L_5}$ a languge differing from $\mathbf{L_4}$ only in the fact that the counter values can be compared solely with constants. It is easy to see that CTS construction problem is algorithmically solvable for programs in $\mathbf{L_5}$. The same ideas as for the proof of Theorem 1 could be used. The difference is that the counter values, if they lie between minimal and maximal constants of the program, are included in the state.

Further research is connected with finding such restrictions on counters that the solvability of CTS problem is preserved.

A.G.Tadevosjan [14] has considered the following generalization of the language $\mathbf{L_5}$ where together with the beforementioned statements of $\mathbf{L_5}$ the following statement is admitted:

$$t \rightarrow Z,$$

where t is an arbitrary internal variable. The CTS construction problem appears to be solvable also in this case.

In practice counters are mainly used for loop organisation. This is done by means of DO statement:

DO Z =1 TO r WHILE V; W; END;

where W – the body of the loop is a program block (by program block we understand part of the program consisting of $\mathbf{L_0}$ statements and, possibly, DO statements and having a single entry and a single exit), V is boolean expression constructed from comparisons of $\mathbf{L_0}$ (e.g., $(t < u)$ & $(5 < t)$), and r – the bound of the loop is an internal variable. DO statement (called also a DO–loop) is interpreted as an abbreviation of the following program block:

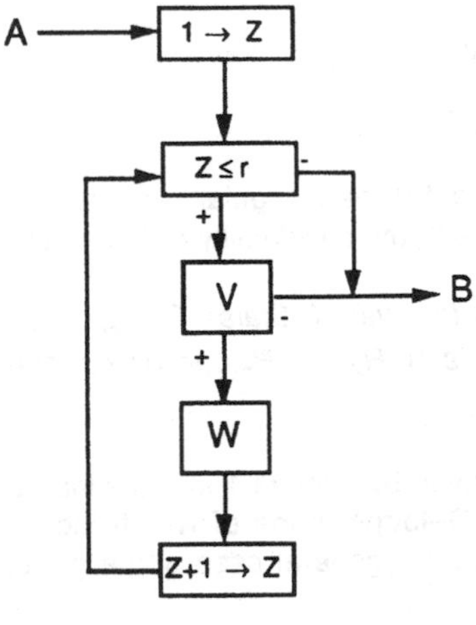

It is assumed that counter Z is used in no statements other than the above mentioned ones $Z \leq r$ and $Z + 1 \rightarrow Z$ used for loop organization.

Let us consider the programming language generated by statements of $\mathbf{L_0}$ and DO statement. There is no algorithm for constructing a CTS for every program in this language (a stronger version of Theorem 9). The proof is close to the one used for Theorem 9 except that a slightly different coding of Minsky machine configurations is used. This proof of unsolvability strongly relies on comparing the loop bound r with other internal variables. Now let us exclude this possibility.

We shall not allow the use of the loop bound r in comparisons with other internal variables and in assignments. This means that the loop bound r along with the loop organization statement $Z \leq r$ can be used only in input statement ($X \rightarrow r$), comparisons with constants ($r < c$, $c < r$) and output statements ($r \rightarrow Y$). In practice these restrictions are not essential but they usually hold for real programs. Let us note that several DO–loops can have a common bound r. The programming language generated by the base language statements and the DO statement with the above mentioned restrictions is called $\mathbf{L_6}$.

THEOREM 10. *There exists an algorithm for constructing a finite complete test set for every program in* $\mathbf{L_6}$.

A detailed proof of Theorem 10 is rather lengthy, so we shall outline only the main ideas. By a simple state we understand a state in the sense of Theorem 1, i.e., the one obtained by ignoring the statements containing counters and loop bound. Let us consider a DO–loop having no nested DO–loops in it. By entering the DO–loop in a simple state S (at entry point A) and going through all possible values of bound r we can obtain, at the exit of the loop (point B), generally speaking, distinct simple states S_1, $S_2, \ldots, S_n$. Further, for every state S_i there exists the set R_i of the value bound r for which the state S_i is reached at the exit. More precisely, $r' \in R_i$ iff for $r = r'$ there exists a feasible path through the DO–loop beginning at the point A in the state S and reaching the point B in the state S_i .The set R is said to be regular if there exists a regular expression R' in the binary alphabet {1, 0} such that for $r \geq 0$

$$r \in R \text{ iff, } \underbrace{11\ldots1}_{r} \in R'$$

and for $r < 0$

$$r \in R \text{ iff, } \underbrace{00\ldots0}_{-r} \in R'$$

The expression R' is said to be a regular representation of the set R. Regular expressions are preferable due to the decidability of the emptiness problem.

LEMMA 1. *Set R_i is regular for every i. States $S_1, S_2, \ldots, S_n$ and the corresponding regular representations of sets $R_1, R_2, \ldots, R_n$ can be constructed effectively from the DO–loop and state S.*

Theorem 10 can be proved by Lemma 1 in the simplest case when the program contains only non–nested DO–loops, none of which includes statements involving bounds of other DO–loops. In the general case some generalization of Lemma 1 is necessary.

Let us order the variables used as loop bounds in the program:

$r^1, r^2, \ldots, r^k$

Let us consider a set of strings of the type

$[r_a^1, r_b^1, r_a^2, r_b^2, \ldots, r_a^k, r_b^k,]$,

where $r_a^j \in \mathbf{N}$, $r_b^j \in \mathbf{N} \cup \{*\}$, $\mathbf{N}$ is the set of integers and * a special symbol.

A set of strings is said to be regular if it can be expressed as a finite union of cartesian products of regular set ({*} is considered to be a regular set):

$R_{a,1}^1 \times R_{b,1}^1 \times \ldots \times R_{a,1}^k \times R_{b,1}^k \cup \ldots \cup R_{a,m}^1 \times R_{b,m}^1 \times \ldots \times R_{a,m}^k \times R_{b,m}^k$,

$R_{a,1}^1, R_{b,1}^1, \ldots, R_{a,m}^k, R_{b,m}^k$ - regular sets.

The expression

$R'_{a,1}{}^1 \times R'_{b,1}{}^1 \times \ldots \times R'_{a,1}{}^k \times R'_{b,1}{}^k \cup \ldots \cup R'_{a,m}{}^1 \times R'_{b,m}{}^1 \times \ldots \times R'_{a,m}{}^k \times R'_{b,m}{}^k$,

where

$R'_{a,1}{}^1, R'_{b,1}{}^1, \ldots, R'_{a,m}{}^k \times R'_{b,m}{}^k$

are regular representations of the sets

$R_{a,1}^1, R_{b,1}^1, \ldots, R_{a,m}^k, R_{b,m}^k$,

is said to be a regular representation of the corresponding set of strings.

Let a program block with entry C and exit D be given. Let S be a simple state at point C and S_i be a simple state accessible at exit D. Let us denote by U_i the following set of strings:

$[r_a^1, r_b^1, r_a^2, r_b^2, \ldots, r_a^k, r_b^k,] \in U_i$

iff for $r^1 = r_a^1, \ldots, r^k = r_a^k$ there exists a feasible path β through the block, beginning at the point C in the state S, and reaching the point D in the state S_i, satisfying the condition: if $r_b^j = *$, then the path contains no input statements of the type "tape" $\rightarrow r^j$, if r_b^j is a number, then the path contains one or several input statements "tape"$\rightarrow r^j$ and r_b^j is a possible value of variable r^j at point D on the path β (j=1, 2, . . . , k).

LEMMA 2. *The set of strings U_i is regular for every i. The possible states $S_1, S_2, \ldots, S_n$ at the exit of the block and the corresponding regular representions of the sets $U_1, U_2, \ldots, U_n$ can be constructed effectively from the program block and state S.*

The lemma is proved by induction on the depth of nesting of loops in the block. For depth 1 Lemma 2 is a slight strengthening of Lemma 1.

Now let us consider a block path $\alpha = (k_1, k_2, \ldots, k_m)$. It differs from the usual path in that k_i can be either a $\mathbf{L_0}$ statement or a DO–loop. If k_i is a DO–loop, we fix one of the possible simple states S_i at its exit. An instance of a block path is $\alpha = (X \rightarrow a+, (D, S_i), a \rightarrow Y)$ where D is some DO–loop. Now let us define the total state $Z(\alpha)$ as a pair $(S(\alpha), W(\alpha))$ where $S(\alpha)$ is a simple state and $W(\alpha)$ is a regular expression describing all possible strings $[r'^1, \ldots, r'^k]$ of numbers acceptable at the end of the path. $W(\alpha)$ can be easily constructed using Lemma 2. It follows from the construction that for a given program the number of distinct total states is finite.

Now using arguments analogous to those used in the proof of Theorem 1 we obtain the proof of Theorem 10.

9 Programs with Real Time Counter

In this section we consider a programming language (let us call it $\mathbf{L_7}$) allowing the simulation of a comparatively wide class of real time systems. At the same time $\mathbf{L_7}$ occurs to have a solvable CTS construction problem. So we have a method for CTS construction for a certain class of real time systems (we show an example how to apply $\mathbf{L_7}$ and its CTS construction algoritm to the analysis of real time systems in the next section).

Programs in $\mathbf{L_7}$ have a finite number of input tapes (output tapes are inessential for CTS construction) and a finite number of internal variables.

The first difference of language $\mathbf{L_7}$ from $\mathbf{L_0}$ is the replacement of integers by rationals in $\mathbf{L_7}$, i.e., cells of input tapes and internal variables have rational values. Thus a test for a program in $\mathbf{L_7}$ will be a fixed assocation of rationals to cells of input tapes.

Let X be an input tape, t,u internal variables and c a rational constant. $\mathbf{L_7}$ have the same statements for these objects as $\mathbf{L_0}$:

1. **X→t**. The statement has two exits just as in $\mathbf{L_0}$; "+", if the current cell is nonempty and "-", otherwise. (Input statement).

2. **u→t** (respectively **c→t**). The value of the variable u (constant c) is assigned to the variable t. (Asignment statement).

3. **t<u**. The statement has two exits "+" and "-", determined by the result of comparison. (Comparison statement).

4. **STOP**.

Besides that every program in $\mathbf{L_7}$ can have one special internal variable z (named *real time counter*) with the following statements permitted:

5. $\mathbf{t \overset{+}{\to} z}$. The statement has two exits "+" and "-". If t>z, then the value of t is assigned to z and the exit "+" is used. If t≤z, then the value of z is not changed and the exit "-" is used. (Positive assignment statement).

The statement can be explained by means of the following block:

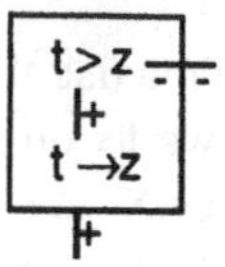

6. **z+c→t**. The value of z increased by c is assigned to the variable t. Only nonnegative rational constants c are allowed here. (Activation statement for the variable t).

When modelling real time systems the activation statements will be used to model the activation of the associated timers, the positive assignment statement will correspond to the treatment of input signals (both from outside the system and from timers).

We assume that all internal variables are set to 0 in the beginning.

We can assume without loss of generalization that constants used in the statements of type 2 and 6 are integers (a program in L_7 with arbitrary constants can be transformed to a program with integer constants by changing the scale of number line, easy to see that program logic will not be affected by the scale change).

No principial casualties would appear if rational negative constants were permitted in variable activation statements but there is no real need for it.

Let us note that if we allow normal assignment $t \to z$ instead of positive asignment, a language with algorithmically unsolvable CTS construction problem would be obtained.

The main result in the section is

THEOREM 11. *There is an algorithm constructing finite CTS for every program in* L_7.

Now let us prove the theorem.

At first for every path α we define the state $S(\alpha)$ corresponding to it, further we use the states to construct the reachability graph (as in the proofs for previous theorems).

Let us call the constants used in assignment statements *basic constants* and the ones in variable activation statements *counter constants* (0 is assumed to be both basic and counter constant by definition). The maximal and minimal basic constants are denoted by c^0_{min} and c^0_{max}, the maximal counter constant is denoted by c^1_{max} (let us remind that we assume all constants to be integers). We define $c_{max}=\max\{c^0_{max}, c^1_{max}\}$.

Let a program P have input tapes A,B,...,C, internal variables $t^1,...,t^k$ and real time counter z. Let us assume the program P to be executing on some test T, i.e., on fixed values of input tapes $A_0, B_0, ..., C_0$. If we suspend the execution at some time moment, we find that the tuple of internal variables $(z, t^1, t^2, ..., t^k)$ has a definite numeric value from $\mathbb{Q}^{k+1}$ (here $\mathbb{Q}$ is the set of rational numbers). So at the fixed moment of P execution we may consider as numeric values:

1)all basic constants of the program P,

2)all internal variables t^i and z,

3) $z, z+1, ..., z+c_{max}$ (let us call them further *active points*).

Every one of these values is located somewhere on the number line, thus defining the ordering of basic constants, internal variables and active points. Let us call this ordering an *absolute configuration* (absolute ordering) of P variables at the fixed moment.

Variables t^i and basic constants c whose values at the given moment are within segment $[z, z+c_{max}]$ are said to be *active variables* and *active constants* at this moment. Further the segment $[z, z+c_{max}]$ is called *z-interval.*

For every active variable t^i (active constant c) we define its *relative offset* t^i_Δ (c_Δ respectively) as the difference between t^i (c) and its nearest active point on the left: $t^i_\Delta = (t^i - z) - [t^i - z]$ ($c_\Delta = (c-z) - [c-z]$); here $[x]$ denotes the integer part of x.

The ordering of relative offsets of active variables and constants on number line (with number 0 included) is called the *relative configuration* (relative ordering) of P variables at the given moment.

The pair consisting of absolute and relative configurations of P variables is called *variable configuration* of P at the given moment (while working on the fixed values of input tapes $A_0, B_0, ..., C_0$).

__Example.__ If at the given moment of P execution $z=7.15$, $t^1=2.43$, $t^2=6.86$, $t^3=7.68$, $t^4=9.65$, $t^5=10.15$, $t^6=14.30$ and P has basic constants 1 and 3, $c^1_{max}=4$, then P has the following variable configuration:

$0 < 1 < t^1 < 3 < t^2 < z < t^3 < z+1 < z+2 < t^4 < t^5 = z+3 < z+4 < t^6$,

$0 = t^5_\Delta < t^4_\Delta < t^3_\Delta$.

The definition of the variable configuration at the given moment utilizes only the values of internal variables at the moment and the values of P constants. Thus, if we know a priori the values of P constants, we can likewise define the P-configuration for every tuple of k+1 rationals $(z, t^1, \dots, t^k) \in \mathbb{Q}^{k+1}$.

We define the variable configuration set for program P to be the set consisting of P-configurations corresponding to all tuples $(z, t^1, \dots, t^k) \in \mathbb{Q}^{k+1}$ where $z \geq 0$. It is easy to see that the variable configuration set $\mathcal{C}_P^{Var}$ is finite for every program P in $\mathbf{L}_7$.

Since every variable configuration is actually an inequality system, then, in case a configuration C corresponds to a tuple of variables **t**, we say that **t** *satisfies* C or **t** is one of the solutions of C.

Let k be a statement in the programm P and ε an exit of it. We define the relation $-(k,\varepsilon)\rightarrow \in \mathcal{C}_P^{Var} \times \mathcal{C}_P^{Var}$ for this statement and exit the following way:

1) if $k = (c \rightarrow t^i)$ or $k = (t^j \rightarrow t^i)$ or $k = (z+c \rightarrow t^i)$, then $C_1 -(k,\varepsilon)\rightarrow C_2$ iff the configuration C_2 can be obtained from C_1 by erasing t^i and t^i_Δ (retaining the absolute and relative ordering of all other variables and constants) and then locating them at c and c_Δ, or at t^j and t^j_Δ, or at z+c and 0 respectively (if c_Δ or t^j_Δ is undefined respectively, t^i_Δ also remains undefined);

2) if $k = (X \rightarrow t^i)$ and ε="+", then $C_1 -(k,\varepsilon)\rightarrow C_2$ holds iff C_2 can be obtained from C_1 the following way:

(i) just as before, we erase t^i and t^i_Δ in C_1;

(ii) we locate t^i at an arbitrary place in the absolute ordering of the configuration obtained;

(iii) if t^i in the absolute ordering is placed within z-interval, we locate t^i_Δ in the relative one at any place not contradicting with the place of t^i in the absolute ordering (if $t^i = t^j$ in the absolute ordering, then, certainly, $t^i_\Delta = t^j_\Delta$ in the relative one, if t^i is located so that $z+c \leq t^j < t^i < t^s \leq z+c+1$ ($c < c_{max}$), then $t^j_\Delta < t^i_\Delta < t^s_\Delta$ should hold in the relative ordering);

3) if $k = (X \rightarrow t^i)$ and ε="-", then $C_1 -(k,\varepsilon)\rightarrow C_2$ iff $C_1 = C_2$;

4) if $k = (t^i < t^j)$, or $k = (t \xrightarrow{+} z)$ and ε="-", then $C_1 -(k,\varepsilon)\rightarrow C_2$ iff C_1 does not contradict with the exit of the statement and $C_1 = C_2$;

5) if $k = (t^i \xrightarrow{+} z)$ and ε="+", then $C_1 -(k,\varepsilon)\rightarrow C_2$ holds iff C_2 can be obtained from C_1 the following way:

(i) If $t \leq z$, then C_2 does not exist.

(ii) If $t > z$, then proceed as follows:

Step 1 (deterministic).

At first we determine the mutual ordering and allocation with respect to active points of the configuration C_2 under construction for the variables and constants which are on the left (below) $z+c_{max}$ in C_1. To do this we define (calculate) for each variable t^j and basic constant c which are within segment $[\,t^i, z+c_{max}\,]$ in C_1 the value

$$\delta(t^j) = [t^j - t^i] = [t^j - z] - [t^i - z] + \Delta_{ji} \text{ where } \Delta_{ji} = 0, \text{ if } t^i_\Delta \le t^j_\Delta \text{, and } \Delta_{ji} = -1, \text{ if } t^j_\Delta < t^i_\Delta,$$

here $[t^j - z]$ and $[t^i - z]$ can be inferred from the allocation of t^j and t^i with respect to active points in the configuration C_1, the value of Δ_{ji} is determined by the relative ordering from C_1 ($\delta(c)$ is obtained in a similar way).

We retain the mutual absolute ordering of variables t^j and basic constants the same as in C_1 and move z at t^i. The location of t^j and c with respect to new active points is determined by $\delta(t^j)$ ($\delta(c)$ respectively) (if $\delta(t^j)=a$, then t^j is to be located between $z+a$ and $z+a+1$ in C_2, besides, if $t^j_\Delta = t^i_\Delta$ in C_1, then t^j must be placed just at $z+a$). If $t^i \le z+c_{max}$ in the configuration C_1, then we also insert the old value $z+c_{max}$ (we denote it further by z^0) in the configuration under construction (its location with respect to new active points is determined by $\delta(z^0) = c_{max} - [t^i - z] + \Delta_{0i}$, where $\Delta_{0i} = 0$, if $t^i_\Delta = 0$, and $\Delta_{0i} = -1$, if $t^i_\Delta > 0$).

Step 2 (deterministic).

While constructing the new relative configuration, at first we represent relative offsets only for those variables and constants which were within $[t^i, z+c_{max}]$ in the configuration C_1, as well as z^0_Δ (the relative offset of value z^0). We reorganize the relative ordering from C_1 the following way:

$$\underbrace{0 = t^i_\Delta < t^u_\Delta < \ldots t^r_\Delta}_{\text{those } t^j_\Delta \text{ which were greater than } t^i_\Delta \text{ in } C_1 \text{ are represented here in ascending order;}} < \underbrace{t^s_\Delta = z^0_\Delta}_{\text{if there was } t^s_\Delta = 0 \text{ in } C_1;} < \underbrace{t^m_\Delta < \ldots < t^k_\Delta}_{\text{those } t^j_\Delta \text{ which were less than } t^i_\Delta \text{ in } C_1 \text{ are represented here in ascending order.}}$$

Step 3 (nondeterministic).

Now we determine the place in C_2 for the variables located to the right of $z+c_{max}$ in C_1. Let us denote them in the ascending order by $t^{j_1}, t^{j_2}, t^{j_3}, \ldots, t^{j_s}$ (if two or more variables are equal, denote them by the same symbol t^{j_r}).

We allocate these variables in the same order, every one in an arbitrary admissible place in the configuration built so far. The variable $t^{j_{r+1}}$ must be allocated to the right of t^{j_r} allocated in the previous step (t^{j_1} is to be allocated to the right of z^0 (to the right of t^i if there was $t^i > z+c_{max}$ in the configuration C_1)).

For every variable t^{j_r} to be allocated we determine both its relations to the new active points (they are defined within Step 1 of the algorithm) and the place of its relative offset $t^{j_r}_\Delta$ in the relative configuration built so far (cf. the case of command $(X \to t^i)$ with exit "+" for the description of admissible locations of variable offsets).

When all variables $t^{j_1}, \ldots, t^{j_s}$ are allocated between active points or some t^{j_r} is located on the right of $z+c_{max}$ (the last active point in the configuration under construction) we delete z^0 and z^0_Δ from the obtained absolute and relative orderings, respectively, and stop the construction, retaining the mutual ordering of the variables on the right of $z+c_{max}$ the same as it was in C_1.

<u>Examples.</u> Let $C_1 = (\, 0 < 2 < z < z+1 < t^1 < z+2 < t^2 < z+3 < t^3, 0 < t^2_\Delta < t^1_\Delta \,)$;

1) if $k = (\, 2 \to t^1 \,)$, then $C_1 \text{-}(k,\varepsilon)\!\to C_2$ iff

$C_2 = (0 < t^1 = 2 < z < z+1 < z+2 < t^2 < z+3 < t^3, 0 < t^2_\Delta)$;

2) if $k = (t^1 < t^2)$ and ε="+", then C_1 -(k,ε)→ C_2 iff $C_2 = C_1$, if ε="-", then the relation holds for no C_2;

3) if $k = (t^1 \stackrel{+}{\to} z)$ and ε="+", then C_1 -(k,ε)→ C_2 holds iff C_2 is one of the following:

$0 < 2 < z = t^1 < t^2 < z+1 < t^3 < z+2 < z+3 \text{ , } 0 = t^1_\Delta < t^3_\Delta < t^2_\Delta$;

$0 < 2 < z = t^1 < t^2 < z+1 < t^3 < z+2 < z+3 \text{ , } 0 = t^1_\Delta < t^2_\Delta = t^3_\Delta$;

$0 < 2 < z = t^1 < t^2 < z+1 < t^3 < z+2 < z+3 \text{ , } 0 = t^1_\Delta < t^2_\Delta < t^3_\Delta$;

$0 < 2 < z = t^1 < t^2 < z+1 < t^3 = z+2 < z+3 \text{ , } 0 = t^1_\Delta = t^3_\Delta < t^2_\Delta$;

$0 < 2 < z = t^1 < t^2 < z+1 < z+2 < t^3 < z+3$, all possible t_Δ orderings for which there hold $t^1_\Delta = 0, t^2_\Delta > 0, t^3_\Delta > 0$;

$0 < 2 < z = t^1 < t^2 < z+1 < z+2 < t^3 = z+3 \text{ , } 0 = t^1_\Delta = t^3_\Delta < t^2_\Delta$;

$0 < 2 < z = t^1 < t^2 < z+1 < z+2 < z+3 < t^3 \text{ , } 0 = t^1_\Delta < t^2_\Delta$.

In this case the transformation algorithm after Step 2 yields the configuration
$0 < 2 < z = t^1 < t^2 < z+1 < z^0 < z+2 < z+3 \text{ , } 0 = t^1_\Delta < z^0_\Delta < t^2_\Delta$.

Inserting t^3 in it in arbitrary place to the right of z^0, we obtain the variety of the abovementioned configurations C_2.

From the definition of relation -(k,ε)→ there follows

LEMMA 1. *For every statement k and its exit ε the relation C_1-(k,ε)→C_2 holds iff there are rationals $z, t^1, \ldots, t^s$ satisfying the configuration C_1, such that the statement k can be executed at these values of variables with exit ε in a way that the tuple of variable values obtained in the result would satisfy the configuration C_2.*

Let α be an initial path in the program P. The *variable state* Q(α) corresponding to path α is defined by induction:

(1) to empty path there corresponds one element set containing the configuration with all internal variables equal to 0;

(2) if state Q(α) corresponds to path α, then for path α+(k,ε) we define Q(α+(k,ε)) $= \{ C' \in \mathcal{C}_P^{Var} \mid \exists C \in Q(\alpha): C$ -(k,ε)→ C' }.

The *state of input tapes* D(α) corresponding to path α is defined as a tuple $(d_1, d_2, \ldots, d_m)$ (m is the number of input tapes), where $d_i = 0$, if input statement from the i-th tape with exit "-" has occurred in the path, $d_i = 1$ otherwise. The *(complete) state* S(α) corresponding to path α is defined as the pair (Q(α),D(α)).

Let us note the following. If we define for an arbitrary state $\sigma = (\sigma^Q, \sigma^D)$ ($\sigma^Q \subseteq \mathcal{C}_P^{Var}$, $\sigma^D \in \{0,1\}^m$) and path α (not necessarily initial) the conditional state S(σ,α) in a way similar to S(α) (only induction basis has to be changed), we see that an analogue of Lemma 4 from Theorem 1 holds.

The complete state S(α) defined for every path α allows us to construct (in a similar way as in the proof of Theorem 1) the reachability graph for the given program P.

The vertices of the graph are pairs (n,S) where n is a statement label and S=(Q,D) is a state of the program P ($Q \subseteq \mathcal{C}_P^{Var}$, $D \in \{0,1\}^m$). For every path α+(k,ε) in the program P we draw in the graph an edge labeled by ε from (k,S(α)) to (k',S(α+(k,ε)) if there is an edge labeled by ε from k to k' in the program P. It is easy to see that the reachability graph is finite for every program P (since the set C_P^{Var} is finite).

For every initial path $v=((n_0,S_0)\varepsilon_0, (n_1,S_1)\varepsilon_1, \dots ,(n_r,S_r)\varepsilon_r)$ in the reachability graph the corresponding path $\alpha=(n_0\varepsilon_0, n_1\varepsilon_1, \dots ,n_r\varepsilon_r)$ in the program P is called the *projection* of the path v.

LEMMA 2. *An initial path α in program P is feasible iff there is an initial path v in the reachability graph of P whose projection is α (cf. Lemma 6 in Theorem 1).*

If path $\alpha=(n_0\varepsilon_0, n_1\varepsilon_1, \dots ,n_r\varepsilon_r)$ is feasible, let us consider a fixed test T which forces the execution of this path. For every j=0,1,...,r+1 we consider the configuration of program variables C_j and state of tapes D_j after the path $\alpha_j=(n_0\varepsilon_0, n_1\varepsilon_1, \dots , n_{j-1}\varepsilon_{j-1})$ while the program is executed on T. It follows from Lemma 1 and properties of D_j that there is a path $v=((n_0,S_0)\varepsilon_0, (n_1,S_1)\varepsilon_1, \dots ,(n_r,S_r)\varepsilon_r)$ with the edge ε_r leading from (n_r,S_r) to (n_{r+1},S_{r+1}) in the reachability graph, such that $S_j = (Q_j,D_j)$ and $C_j\in Q_j$ for j=0,..,r+1.

Now let us prove that for every initial path in the reachability graph the corresponding projection is feasible in the program P.

Let us choose an initial path $v=((n_0,S_0)\varepsilon_0, (n_1,S_1)\varepsilon_1, \dots ,(n_{r-1},S_{r-1})\varepsilon_{r-1})$ in the reachability graph and consider the sequence of configurations $C_0,C_1,\dots,C_{r-1}$ such that

(1) $C_j\in Q_j$ for every j=0,..r-1;

(2) C_j -(k,ε)→ C_{j+1} for every j=0,..r-2.

Let an edge labeled by ε_{r-1} leads from (n_{r-1},S_{r-1}) to (n_r,S_r) in the reachability graph, let $C_r\in Q_r$ and C_{r-1} -(k,ε)→ C_r.

For every $j\le r$ we define v_j to be the initial fragment $((n_0,S_0)\varepsilon_0,\dots, (n_{j-1},S_{j-1})\varepsilon_{j-1})$ of v. Let α_j be the projection of v_j ($\alpha_j=(n_0\varepsilon_0,n_1\varepsilon_1,\dots,n_{j-1}\varepsilon_{j-1})$)

Let us prove by induction on j that for every v_j there is a test T_j forcing the execution of P along α_j in a way that for every $s\le j$ the program variables after the path α_s satisfy the configuration C_s.

The existence of the test T_0 for empty path is obvious (test with empty input tapes A,B,...,C suffices).

The transition j → j+1 is different depending on n_j and ε_j:

1) If $n_j\in\{ c\to t^i, t^u\to t^i, z+c\to t^i\}$, or $n_j= (X\to t^i)$ and ε_j="-", we can take $T_{j+1}=T_j$.

2) If $n_j = (t^i<t^u)$, or $n_j = (t^i \overset{\pm}{\to} z)$ and ε_j="-", then it follows from the definition of -(k,ε)→ that every tuple of variables satisfying C_j forces the execution along the branch needed, once again we can take $T_{j+1}=T_j$.

3) If $n_j= (X\to t^i)$ and ε_j="+", then by the definition of reachability graph no input statement from tape X with exit "-" has occurred in path α_j. The test T_{j+1} is obtained from T_j concatenating to tape X a cell with a value that locates t^i in the configuration C_{j+1} in the appropriate place with respect to other variables and constants of the program.

4) If $n_j= (t^i \overset{\pm}{\to} z)$ and ε_j="+", we describe a method for obtaining T_{j+1} from T_j . Let us fix the values of program variables in the moment when P has executed the path α_j on the test T_j. Consider variables with the values fixed greater than $z+c_{max}$ (the list of them can also be obtained from the configuration C_j). Each of these variables has received its current value in path α_j only by means of input statement (because they are greater

than $z+c_{max}$) and has used this value in various comparison statements. So each of these values has an input tape cell corresponding to it in the test T_j. Let us update the values of cells of input tapes corresponding to the considered variables which are located below $z+c_{max}$ (or are equal to it) in the configuration C_{j+1}, in order to ensure that these variables after the execution of n_j have correct places with respect to active points and other variables' relative offsets in C_{j+1}.

It follows from the definition of relation $-(k,\varepsilon)\rightarrow$ in the case of positive assignment statement, namely, Step 3 of the algorithm, that we shall be able to update the values of tape cells preserving for the considered variables t^u the ordering and locations with respect to the old $z+c_{max}$. It means that on the new test T_{j+1} the program traverses the path $\alpha_{j+1}=\alpha_j+(n_j,\varepsilon_j)$, besides, for $s\leq j+1$, the internal variables satisfy the configuration C_s after the path α_s.

This proves the lemma.

We note that the proof of the lemma yields a constructive method how to find for a feasible path a test executing it. So, just as in the case of Theorem 1, we can build a finite CTS from the reachability graph of the program.

This completes the proof of the theorem.

Theorem 11 yields a principal possibility to build CTS for every program in $\mathbf{L_7}$. However, if a program has a large number of variables, the algorithm given in the proof can be infeasible in practice due to enormous number of variable configurations. Let us describe a principally more efficient algorithm of CTS construction for programs in $\mathbf{L_7}$ based on the usage of inequality systems.

We begin with the association (just as for programs in $\mathbf{L_0}$) of inequality system $N(\alpha)$ to every initial path α, such that

1) path α is feasible iff $N(\alpha)$ has a rational solution,

2) every solution of $N(\alpha)$ with respect to cells of input tapes yields a test on which the program executes the path α.

<u>Example.</u> Let us consider the path
$(A \rightarrow t^1 +, t^1 \overset{+}{\rightarrow} z +, z+5 \rightarrow t^2, A \rightarrow t^1 +, t^1 < t^2 +, t^1 \overset{+}{\rightarrow} z +)$.

Its inequality system is

$$\begin{cases} t_0{}^1 = t_0 = z_0 = 0 \\ t_1{}^1 = A_1 \\ t_1{}^1 > z_0 \,,\, z_1 = t_1{}^1 \\ t_1{}^2 = z_1 + 5 \\ t_2{}^1 = A_2 \\ t_2{}^1 < t_1{}^2 \\ t_2{}^1 > z_1 \,,\, z_2 = t_2{}^1 \end{cases}$$

It is easy to see that with respect to A_1 and A_2 it is equivalent to the system $0 < A_1 < A_2 < A_1 + 5$, the consistency of which assures the feasibility of the path.

Path inequality systems are used for efficient obtaining for a given path in the reachability graph a test forcing the execution of the corresponding path in the program.

The construction of the reachability graph is based on relating a set $\mathcal{U}(\alpha)=\{U_1(\alpha),...,U_r(\alpha)\}$ of certain type inequality systems $U_s(\alpha)$ to an arbitrary path α in the program. So the vertices of reachability graph are pairs $(n_i,\mathcal{U})$, where n_i is a statement label and $\mathcal{U}=\mathcal{U}(\alpha)$ for some path α. The idea of inequality systems $U_s(\alpha)$ is that the set $Q(\alpha)$ of configurations, corresponding to α, will be distributed during the graph construction in several subsets $Q_1(\alpha),Q_2(\alpha),...,Q_r(\alpha)$, such that their union coincides with $Q(\alpha)$ and each $Q_i(\alpha)$ is coded by the inequality system $U_i(\alpha)$ (actually, the state of input tapes $D(\alpha)$ is represented in every $U_s(\alpha)$ as well).

When constructing the reachability graph we use the systems consisting of inequalities of the form

(1) $a\lambda(b+c_1)$, where $\lambda\in\{>,<,\geq,\leq\}$, a and b are program internal variables or basic constants; $0\leq c_1\leq c^1{}_{max}$,

(2) $A<0$, $A>0$, where A is a program input tape (external variable).

Let us call the systems of the described form *state inequality systems*.

Let us say that a state inequality system U *codes* a pair (Q,D), where $Q\subseteq \mathcal{C}_P^{var}$, $D\in\{0,1\}^m$ (m is the number of program input tapes) if

(1) every solution of U with respect to z, $t^1,...,t^k$ satisfies at least one configuration $C\in Q$;

(2) for every configuration $C\in Q$ there are values of variables z, $t^1,...,t^k$ satisfying both C and U;

(3) for every tape A, U contains inequality $A<0$ iff $d_A=0$ in the state D; there is no inequality of the form $A>0$ in U.

Let us represent the state inequality systems as graphs (just as it was done in the case of the base language $\mathbf{L_0}$). Let all program internal variables, basic constants and input tape names serve as vertices in them. We label the edges of the graphs by weights of the form (x,ξ), where $x\in\mathbf{Z}$ and $\xi\in\{0,"+"\}$ (the comparison and the addition can be defined in the set of weights quite naturally: $(x_1,\xi_1)>(x_2,\xi_2)$ if $x_1>x_2$ or $x_1=x_2$ and $\xi_1="+"$, $\xi_2=0$; $(x_1,\xi_1)+(x_2,\xi_2)=(x_1+x_2,\xi_1+\xi_2)$, where $\xi_1+\xi_2=$ "+" if either ξ_1 or ξ_2 is "+", $0+0=0$).

Let us represent the inequalities of the system in the graph the following way:

$a\geq b+c_1$ - an edge, weighted by $(c_1,0)$ from a to b,

$a>b+c_1$ - an edge, weighted by $(c_1,"+")$ from a to b,

$a\leq b+c_1$ - an edge, weighted by $(-c_1,0)$ from b to a,

$a<b+c_1$ - an edge, weighted by $(-c_1,"+")$ from b to a.

Not difficult to prove that the state inequality system has a solution iff there is no cyclic path with positive sum of weights and no path from constant vertex c_0^1 to c_0^2 with the weight greater than $(c_0^1-c_0^2,0)$ in its graph.

We define the exclusion of a graph vertex a as replacement of all the edges leading to and from a by edges bd between other vertices b and d, such that before exclusion the graph contained both the edges ba and ad. The weight w(bd) is defined as the sum of weights w(ba)+w(ad). For every two vertices b and d we retain only that edge from b to d which has the maximum weight.

We define an edge a_1a_n with weight $w(a_1a_n)$ in the state inequality systems graph (further - state graph) *reducible* if there are vertices $a_2,...,a_{n-1}$ $(n\geq3)$, such that the graph contains edges a_ia_{i+1}, $i=1,...,n-1$ and the sum of weights $w(a_1a_2)+ ... + w(a_{n-1}a_n) \geq \geq w(a_1a_n)$.

We introduce a *reduced form* for each state graph, which can be obtained from the graph the following way:

(1) if the state graph is contradictory (i.e., it is a graph of a contradictory inequality system), replace it by the inequality systems "0>0" graph, otherwise execute (2), (3) and (4);

(2) for every cyclic path $a_1a_2,\ldots,a_na_1$ with (0,0) sum of weights, find out the ordering $a_{i_1}\lambda_1 a_{i_2}\lambda_2\ldots\lambda_{n-1}a_{i_n}$, $(\lambda_i\in\{<,\leq\})$ of vertices $a_1,a_2,\ldots,a_n$. Then replace all edges between these vertices by the edges from a_{i_s} to $a_{i_{s+1}}$ and from $a_{i_{s+1}}$ to a_{i_s} (s=1,..,n-1), weighted by $(a_{i_s}-a_{i_{s+1}},0)$ and $(a_{i_{s+1}}-a_{i_s},0)$ respectively;

(3) for every cyclic path with (0,0) weights on all its edges, gather all its vertices into one vertex;

(4) delete the reducible edges from the graph until it contains no ones.

Let us call a variable or basic constant a in a state inequality system U *very essential* if there exists an edge leading to or from a, labeled by the weight different both from (0,0) and (0,"+") in the reduced form of U graph. We denote the set of very essential variables and basic constants in U by VE(U).

Let us consider an arbitrary set V of program P variables and basic constants. We say that a state inequality system U is *complete* with respect to V if for every $a,b\in V$, such that $a\leq b<z$ holds in one of U solutions (z is the value of program real time counter), the inequalities $a\leq b$ and $b<z$ hold in every solution of U.

In other words, the complete with respect to V state inequality system must unequivocally determine the ordering of set V variables and constants which are below than z. We define U-bottom(V)=$\{a\in V|\ a<z$ in some solution of U$\}$.

Now we are able to describe the reachability graph construction algorithm.

We relate the state inequality systems' set with just one element, namely, the inequality system $0 = z = t^1 = \ldots = t^k$ to the empty path.

Assume that we have constructed the state inequality system set $\mathcal{U}(\alpha)=\{U_1(\alpha),U_2(\alpha),\ldots,U_n(\alpha)\}$ corresponding to a path α. Let us describe how to construct the set $\mathcal{U}(\alpha+(k,\varepsilon))$ corresponding to the path $\alpha+(k,\varepsilon)$.

The following cases are possible:

1) $k=(t^i \overset{+}{\rightarrow} z)$ and ε="-", or $k=(t^i<t^j)$.

Add the corresponding inequality to each of $U_s(\alpha)$.

2) $k=(c\rightarrow t^i)$ or $k=(t^j\rightarrow t^i)$, or $k=(z+c\rightarrow t^i)$.

Exclude t^i from each $U_s(\alpha)$. Add the equality $c=t^i$ ($t^j=t^i$ or $z+c=t^i$ respectively) to the obtained systems.

3) $k=(X\rightarrow t^i)$ and ε="+".

Exclude t^i from each $U_s(\alpha)$. If any of $U_s(\alpha)$ contains the inequality (X<0), add the inequality (X>0) to it.

4) $k=(X\rightarrow t^i)$ and ε="-".

If $U_s(\alpha)$ does not contain the inequality (X<0), add it to the system (s=1,..,r).

5) $k=(t^i \overset{+}{\rightarrow} z)$ and ε="+". Process every $U_j(\alpha)$ the following way:

Add the inequality $(z<t^i)$ to $U_j(\alpha)$, exclude z from the obtained system. Locate z at t^i (add the equality $z=t^i$ to the system). If the obtained system $U'_j(\alpha)$ is not complete with respect to the variables' and constants' set $VE(U'_j(\alpha))$, supplement it (by determining the ordering of variables and constants in U-bottom$(VE(U_j(\alpha)))$) in all possible ways to the complete ones, so obtaining the list $U'_{j,1}(\alpha),U'_{j,2}(\alpha),\ldots,U'_{j,p}(\alpha)$ of the complete systems

(each $U'_{j,s}(\alpha)$ is a complete system due to $VE(U'_j(\alpha))=VE(U'_{j,s}(\alpha))$.

Further process every $U'_{j,s}(\alpha)$ the following way:

Exclude from it all variables and constants being in U-bottom($VE(U_{j,s}(\alpha))$) (we have defined the exclusion of the graph vertex, it can be applied also to the constant one). Afterwards add the inequalities, determining the ordering of the set U-bottom($VE(U_{j,s}(\alpha))$) variables and constants and their relations with z, to the obtained system, so we have obtained an element of the set $U(\alpha+(k,\varepsilon))$.

The transformation of the state inequality systems in the case of the positive assignment statement with the exit "+" may be roughly considered as erasing weights on edges connecting the variables and constants which are below z (i.e., represent the past time moments) one with another and to other program internal variables and constants. However, in the general case a more sophisticated approach (like the performed one) is necessary. We note also that in the most typical cases the number of systems in $\mathcal{U}(\alpha)$ is quite small; for the most of real time systems for every α the set $\mathcal{U}(\alpha)$ consists of just one system $U(\alpha)$ which codes the set of configurations $Q(\alpha)$.

<u>Example.</u> Let us consider the path
$(A \to t^1 +, t^1 \xrightarrow{+} z +, z+5 \to t^2 , A \to t^1 +, t^1 < t^2 +, t^1 \xrightarrow{+} z +)$.

For it $\mathcal{U}(\alpha_0) = \{U(\alpha_0)\} = (0 = z = t^1 = t^2)$,

$\mathcal{U}(\alpha_1) = \{U(\alpha_1)\} = (0 = z = t^2)$,

$\mathcal{U}(\alpha_2) = \{U(\alpha_2)\} = (0 = t^2 < z = t^1)$,

$\mathcal{U}(\alpha_3) = \{U(\alpha_3)\} = (0 < z = t^1 < z+5 = t^2)$,

$\mathcal{U}(\alpha_4) = \{U(\alpha_4)\} = (0 < z < z+5 = t^2)$,

$\mathcal{U}(\alpha_5) = \{U(\alpha_5)\} = (0 < z < z+5 = t^2 , t^1 < t^2)$,

$\mathcal{U}(\alpha) = \mathcal{U}(\alpha_6) = \{U(\alpha_6)\} = (0 < z = t^1 < t^2 < z+5)$.

Using the state inequality systems sets $\mathcal{U}(\alpha)$ as states corresponding to program paths we build a reachability graph for the program likewise in the proof of Theorem 11.

<u>**LEMMA 3.**</u> *An initial path α in the given program P is feasible iff there is an initial path v in the constructed reachability graph whose projection is α.*

We note that for every path α all weights on edges of state graphs for inequality systems $U_1(\alpha),\ldots,U_r(\alpha)$ are bounded from $(-c_{max},0)$ to $(c_{max},"+")$, this ensures us about the finiteness of the constructed graph.

The proof of the lemma is based on inductive demonstration that for every path α the inequality systems $U_1(\alpha),\ldots,U_r(\alpha)$ code the pairs $(Q_1(\alpha),D(\alpha)),\ldots,(Q_r(\alpha),D(\alpha))$, respectively, where the union of configuration sets $Q_s(\alpha)$ coincides with $Q(\alpha)$.

The given construction of the reachability graph, together with the solvability of path inequality systems, form the base for the desired more efficient algorithm of CTS construction for the programs in $\mathbf{L}_7$.

At the end of the section we introduce a new programming language $\mathbf{L}'_7$ with operations over both rational and integer data types. We define the language $\mathbf{L}'_7$ as follows:

Every program in L_7' may have internal variables of two types - rationals (i.e., t^i and z) with operations of L_7 permitted and integers with permitted operations from language L_0. A type mismatch in the commands in L_7' is forbidden. Each external variable - input tape of the program has a definite type (integer or rational) as well. This determines in which system of commands the input from this tape can be used.

THEOREM 12. *There exists an algorithm constructing finite CTS for every program in* L_7'.

The proof of the theorem relies upon the construction of the reachability graph, where for every path α in the program corresponds the state $(S_0(\alpha),S_7(\alpha))$ with $S_0(\alpha)$ being the state in the sense of L_0, associated with α, but $S_7(\alpha)$ - the one in the sense of L_7.

The proof that an initial path in the program is feasible iff it is a projection of any path in the reachability graph follows from the analogous results for languages L_0 and L_7 (cf. Lemma 6 from Theorem 1, Lemma 2 from Theorem 11).

A more efficient generation of CTS for programs in L_7' can be performed by using the inequality systems, i.e., by ascribing the state $(S_0(\alpha),\mathfrak{U}(\alpha))$ to an arbitrary path α in the program.

Just as for programs in L_0 (cf. Section 4) the conditional programs can be introduced in L_7' as well (the conditions are allowed to stand for the variables of each data type separately). Likewise in Section 4 we can introduce the notions of the correct test and correct CTS for conditional programs in L_7'. Following the aforementioned ideas we can prove

THEOREM 13. *There exists an algorithm constructing finite correct CTS for every conditional program in* L_7'.

10 CTS Generation for Real Time Systems. An Example

In this section we consider a simple example how to apply the CTS generation means to real time programs.

10.1 Example Specification Language

In the current section we use a subset of specification language SDL [16] to specify the example. Now let us describe the subset.

Only one SDL process is used to describe a real time system. SDL process is a program executing in real time and communicating with the environment by means of signals. SDL process has an input queue into which the environment at certain time moments puts input signals for the process (time moment can be an arbitrary rational, time counting begins at the process start). Process input signal can have a definite number of integer valued parameters, the signal is recorded in the queue together with its parameters. We can assume for sake of simplicity that no two signals are put into the queue simultaneously. The process also has output signals, these signals are sent to the environment at certain time moments according to the process program (process diagram), as a reaction to input signals.

SDL process is a finite state machine extended by variable notion and some special statements. To be more precise, we assume that SDL process can use a finite number of internal variables, the process diagram can contain the following statements.

1. START - the beginning of the process execution. We assume that all process internal variables are initialized to 0 at the execution of START. We depict the statement in the diagram the following way:

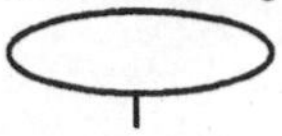

2. STATE / INPUT - the complex of statements for awaiting / reading of input signals, it has the following form in the process diagram:

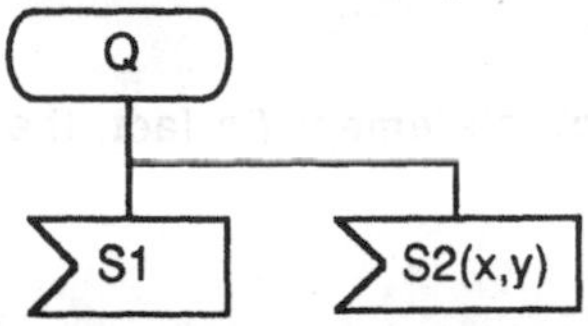

Here Q is a state name, S1 and S2 are names of signals awaited in this state, x,y are process internal variables to which the values of parameters conveyed by signal S2 are assigned at consumption (reading) of S2.

If the process has reached the state Q during the execution, it is awaiting for the arrival of some signal in the input queue. At the moment when a signal arrives the signal is consumed (and the necessary assignments of parameter values to internal variables performed). Further control flow in the diagram depends on the name of incoming signal (for the sake of clarity we assume that reaction to every possible signal is specified in every state).

3. OUTPUT - signal sending statement. It has the form:

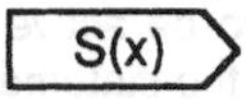

and it denotes the sending of signal to the environment at the given moment of process execution. Here S is a signal name and x is an internal variable whose value is assigned to parameter of the signal.

4. SAVE - signal save statement, it is included in STATE / INPUT complex the following way:

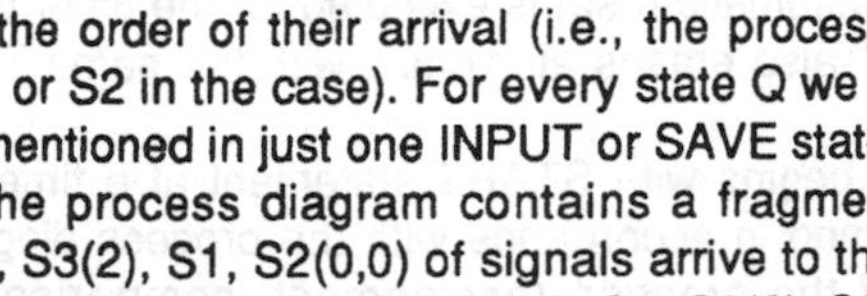

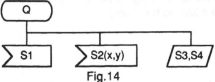

Fig.14

The location of signals S3 and S4 in SAVE statement at the state Q means that, if the process is in state Q, signals S3 and S4 are not consumed but retained in the input queue in the order of their arrival (i.e., the process waits for the arrival of some other signal, S1 or S2 in the case). For every state Q we assume that the name of every input signal is mentioned in just one INPUT or SAVE statement at this state.

If the process diagram contains a fragment (fig.15) and there the sequence S3(1), S4, S3(2), S1, S2(0,0) of signals arrive to the process queue, then these signals are consumed in the order S1, S3(1), S4, S3(2), S2(0,0) (we assume the process being in the state Q just before the arrival of signal S3(1)).

5. TASK - action statement representing assignment to internal variables of the process, e.g.,

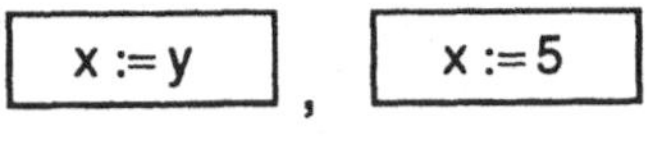

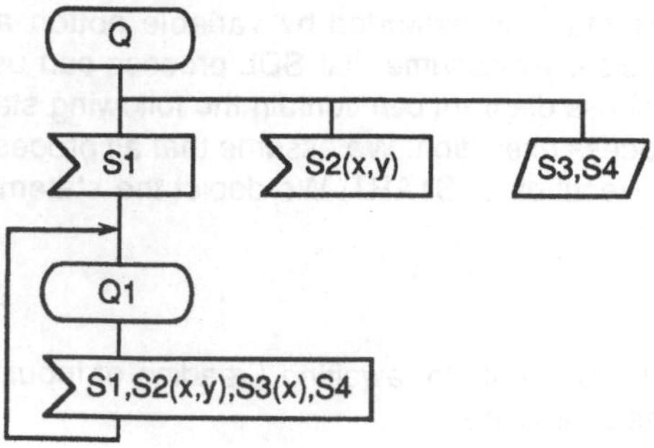

Fig.15

6. DECISION - representing variable comparison statement (in fact, the same comparison statement used in L_0):

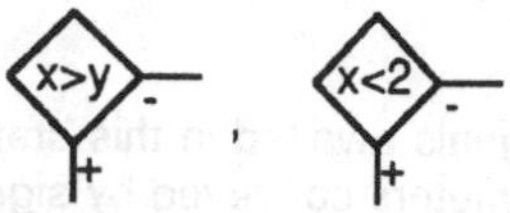

7. SET, RESET statements and timer signals.

SDL process has a predefined function *now*, at every time moment returning the numeric time value of this moment (certain nonnegative rational). Process may have a finite number of timers (informally each timer is an "alarm-clock" which can be set to send a special signal after the expiring of a definite time interval).

A timer in SDL process can be set by statement

set (now+c,T)

Here T is a timer name and c - an integer constant (a timer is said to be active after setting). The activity of the timer T, before it "rings", can be disrupted by the statement

reset (T)

When the interval of timer activity expires (i.e., c time units have passed) and it has not received the reset statement, a special signal is put into the process input queue, the signal name being the same as timer name. This signal can be consumed in a process state (a special input branch has to be added to the state):

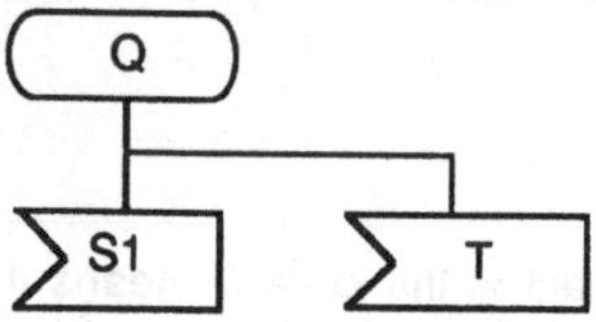

If some active timer is set, an automatic reset is executed for the timer before the new setting. The statement "reset(T)" also erases all signals with the name T from the input queue (if there are such).

The execution of the process begins with START statement at a time moment *now* =0, further processing is performed in accordance with the process diagram. We assume that all internal actions of the process (assignment, comparison, signal sending/consuming, timer setting/resetting) are performed instantaneously, so the function *now* changes its value only when the process waits for signals (or timer) in some state.

10.2 Passenger Lift Specification

We describe a control program for some kind of passenger lift by means of SDL process. The environment for the process consists of lift users and lift hardware.

A lift user can press a call button in every floor thus sending the signal S with parameter x (the floor number) to the process. Besides that the user can press the button in the lift-cage to pass the request for the lift to go to some floor; so the signal R with one parameter - the destination floor number is sent to process. In some situations the user can also generate signals FU(FloorUp) and FD(FloorDown) by leaving the lift-cage and entering it respectively (i.e., changing the status of cage floor).

The lift hardware consists of lift driving motor controlled by signals M-Up,M-Down, M-Stop, lift door motor (controlled by signals MDoor1(open the door), MDoor2 (close the door) and MDoorStop) and some sensors informing the process about the physical state of the lift. The following signals from sensors to process are considered: Z(x) - floor number x is reached, DOp(Door is Open), DC(Door is Closed).

Behaviour of the lift can be characterized by the following:

1) the lift has no memory for user requests, signals S(x),R(x) are accepted for processing only after previous request has been executed,

2) if empty lift with open door stays in some floor for more than 20 seconds, the door is being closed,

3) if the status of cage floor is changed while the door is closing (i.e., somebody has entered or left the cage), the closing of the door is interrupted and the door opens. Besides, if the door was being closed to execute some request to go somewhere, the request is canceled.

Besides the control algorithm also a partial correctness check of incoming signals is included in the specification of lift process, it will enforce tests in the generated CTS to be actually possible sequences of lift input signals. To do this in the specification language some exits are allowed to be pending for branching statements (DECISION statements, STATE/INPUT complexes). This is done in a way similar to conditional programs in Section 4.

The specification of the lift process is presented in fig. 16.1 thru 16.3.

10.3 Simulation of SDL Process by Program in L_7'

By a test for an SDL process we understand a sequence of signals which are put by environment at certain time moments into the process input queue (every signal is considered together with its parameter values). We remind that simultaneous input signals are not allowed.

If signal S1 with parameters 7 and 12 is sent to the process at moment 3, signal S2 is sent at moment 3.7 and another signal S1 with parameters 0 and -5 at 7.22, then the sequence of signals is recorded as a test for SDL process the following way:

(S1(7,12) at 3), (S2 at 3.7), (S1(0,-5) at 7.22)

A test for SDL process is said to be correct if the process never reaches pending exit while executing on the test.

We don't consider direct construction of correct CTS for SDL processes. Instead we describe a method how to simulate specifications (programs) in the described subset of SDL by conditional programs in L_7'. We also demonstrate previously described algorithm for the construction of correct CTS on lift process example.

We say that a program P(R) in L_7' simulates SDL process R if:

1) a one-to-one mapping between correct tests for process R and program P(R)

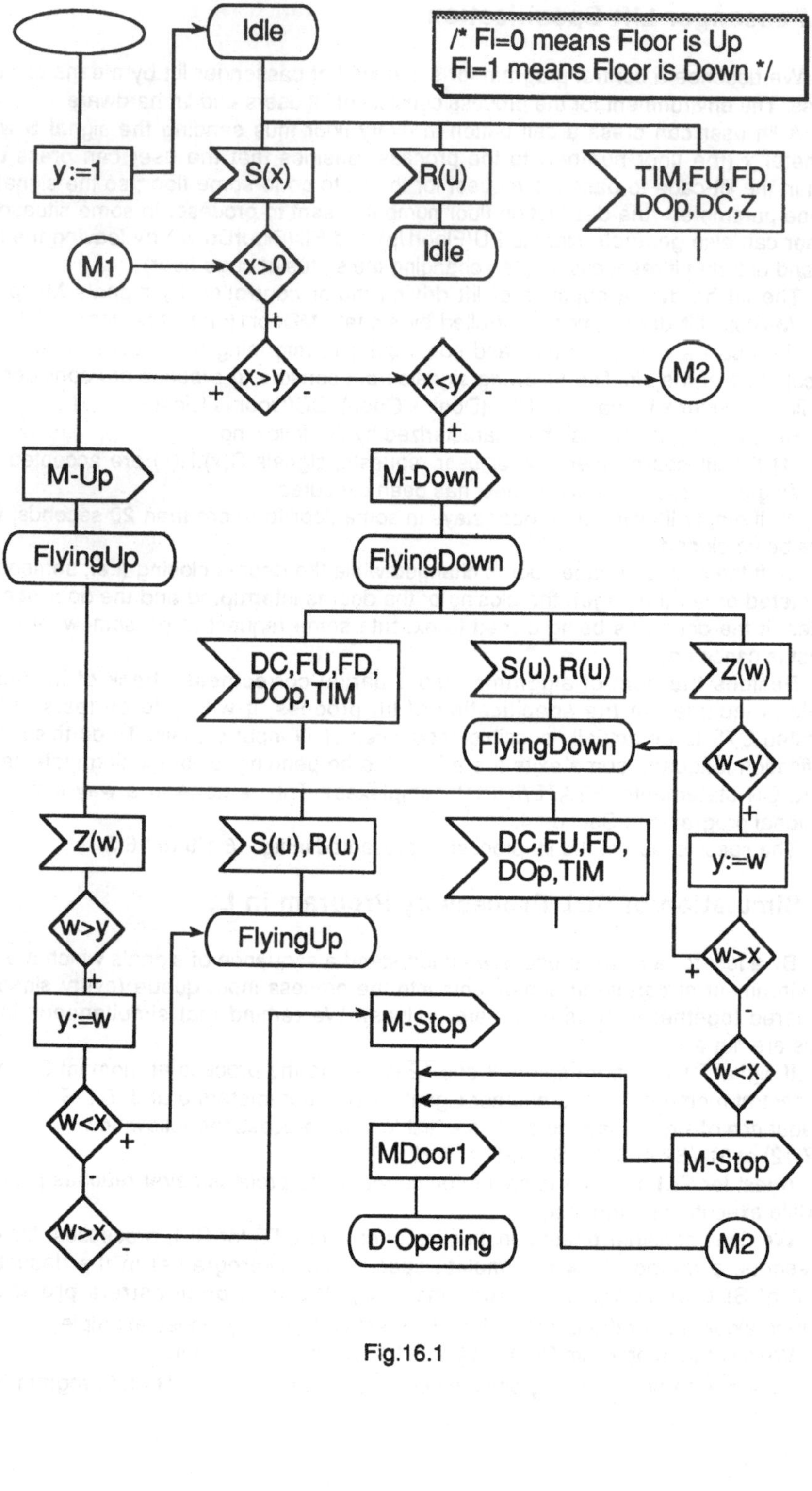
Idle
/* Fl=0 means Floor is Up
Fl=1 means Floor is Down */
y:=1
S(x)
R(u)
TIM,FU,FD,
DOp,DC,Z
Idle
M1
x>0
+
x>y
x<y
M2
M-Up
M-Down
FlyingUp
FlyingDown
DC,FU,FD,
DOp,TIM
S(u),R(u)
Z(w)
FlyingDown
w<y
y:=w
Z(w)
S(u),R(u)
DC,FU,FD,
DOp,TIM
w>y
FlyingUp
y:=w
w>x
M-Stop
w<x
w<x
MDoor1
M-Stop
w>x
D-Opening
M2

Fig.16.1

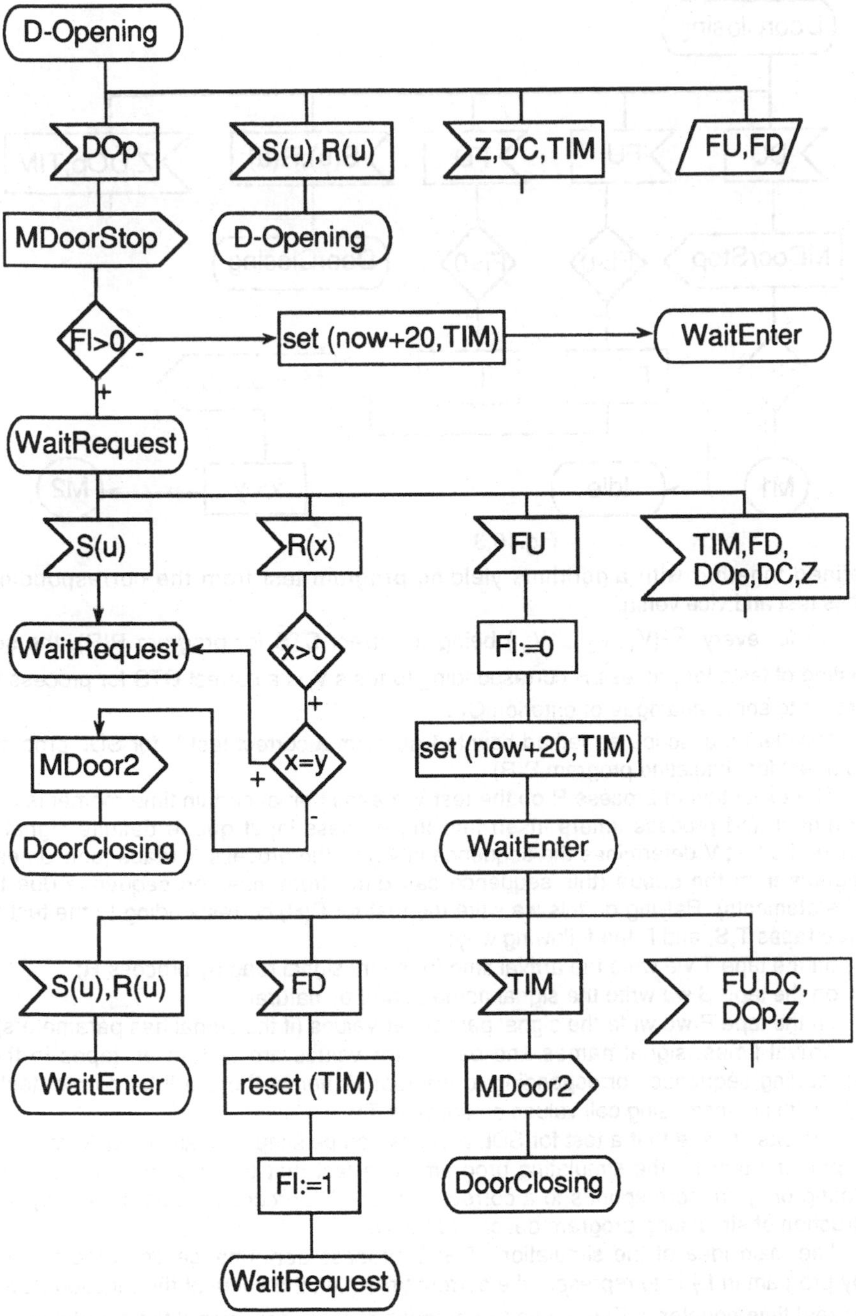
D-Opening
DOp
S(u),R(u)
Z,DC,TIM
FU,FD
MDoorStop
D-Opening
Fl>0
-
set (now+20,TIM)
WaitEnter
+
WaitRequest
S(u)
R(x)
FU
TIM,FD,
DOp,DC,Z
WaitRequest
x>0
Fl:=0
+
MDoor2
x=y
set (now+20,TIM)
+
-
DoorClosing
WaitEnter
S(u),R(u)
FD
TIM
FU,DC,
DOp,Z
WaitEnter
reset (TIM)
MDoor2
Fl:=1
DoorClosing
WaitRequest

Fig.16.2

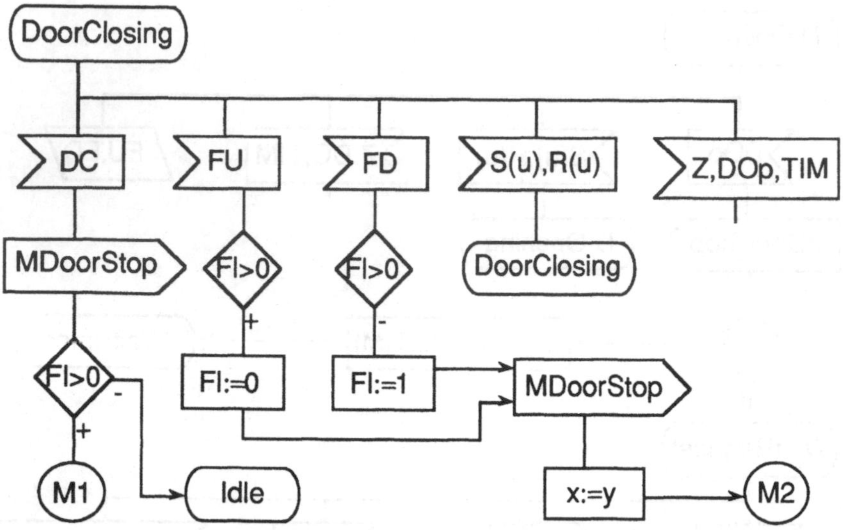

Fig.16.3

is defined together with algorithms yielding program test from the corresponding process test and vice versa,

2) for every $\mathcal{S}=(V_1, V_2, ..., V_a)$ being a correct CTS for program P(R), the set consisting of tests for process R corresponding to tests V_i is a correct CTS for process R according to some analogue of criterion C_1.

Now let us describe a method how to transform a correct test V for SDL process R into a test for simulating program P(R).

The execution of process R on the test V means that at certain time moments the environment and process timers insert into the process input queue definite signals. Likewise, the test V determines the sequence in which the process R reads (consumes) the signals from the queue (this sequence can differ from insertion sequence due to SAVE statements). Relying on this we write the test for P(R) corresponding to the test V on three tapes T,S, and P the following way:

on the tape T we write the arrival time for every signal read by process R;

on the tape S we write the signal name coded by natural;

on the tape P we write the signal parameter values (if the signal has parameters).

Arrival times, signal names and parameter values are written on tapes in the signal reading sequence corresponding to the test V (hence there will be correct tests for P(R) with not increasing cell values on the tape T).

It is easy to see that a test for SDL process can be simply obtained back from the corresponding test for the simulating program. The fact that every correct test for the simulating program corresponds to a correct test for SDL process is guaranteed by the construction of simulating program described below.

The main idea of the simulation of SDL process performance on some correct test by program in $\mathbf{L}_7^{\prime}$ is to represent the current time (i.e., the value of the function *now*) by the real time counter z. Every time the process reads a new signal the simulating $\mathbf{L}_7^{\prime}$ program reads the arrival time of this signal from tape T into variable t and assigns it to the real time counter z by means of statement $t \stackrel{+}{\to} z$ ("-" exit from this statement will be processed depending on the situation, see below).

The simulating program in L'_7 is obtained from SDL process diagram the following way:

1)START statement is transformed into the start label "—>" of the program;

2)STATE/INPUT statement complex (timer signals and SAVEs are considered later), fig.17,

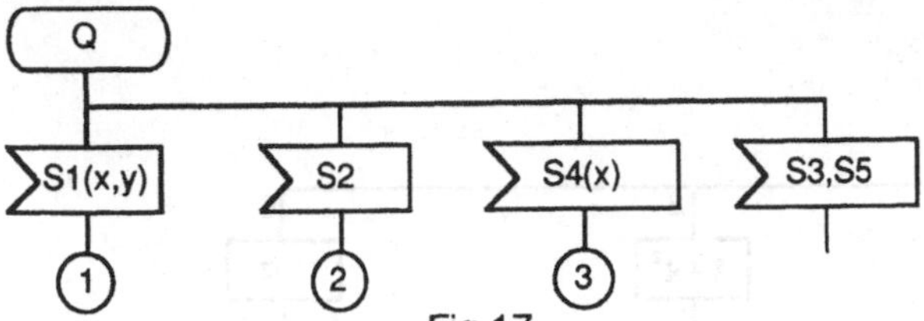

Fig.17

is transformed as shown in fig.18.

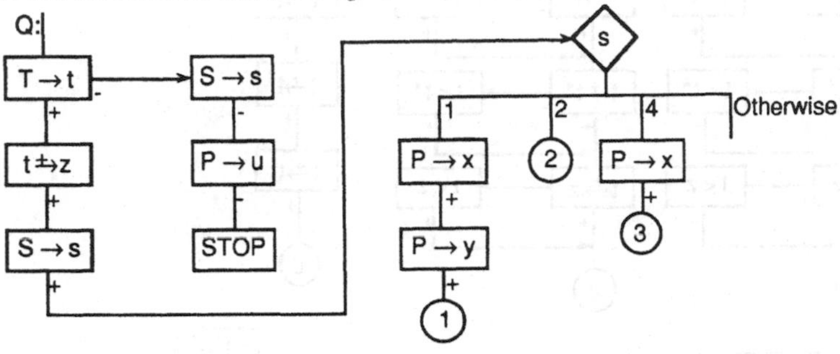

Fig.18

Here  is a normal CASE statement (easily expressible in L'_7), further on we do not show the pending OTHERWISE branch, this branch sets correctness condition upon the code of signal name contained in the corresponding tape cell (s in the example cannot assume the value either 3 or 5, or some other value different from 1,2 and 4);

3) output signals are not represented in L'_7 -program (they are inessential from CTS viewpoint);

4) internal variables are transferred to L'_7 -program without changes, only the syntactic form of variable operations is changed (see the example below);

5) if SDL process has at least one SAVE statement, then in the simulating L'_7 -program:

(i)for every signal used in at least one SAVE statement the variable t^s (s being the code of signal name) is introduced;

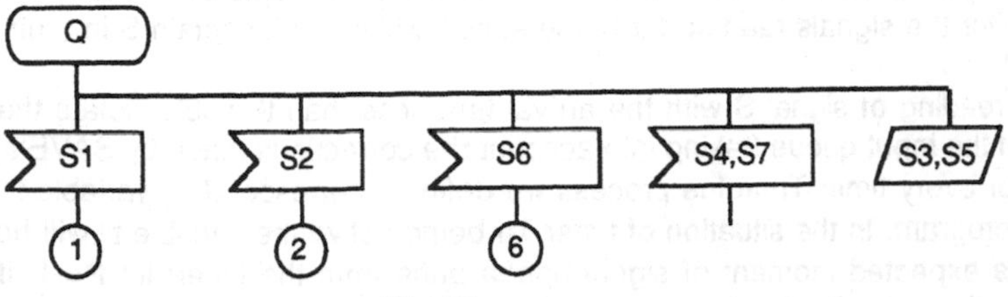

Fig.19

(ii)for every state Q in SDL process, e.g., the state shown in fig.19, (including

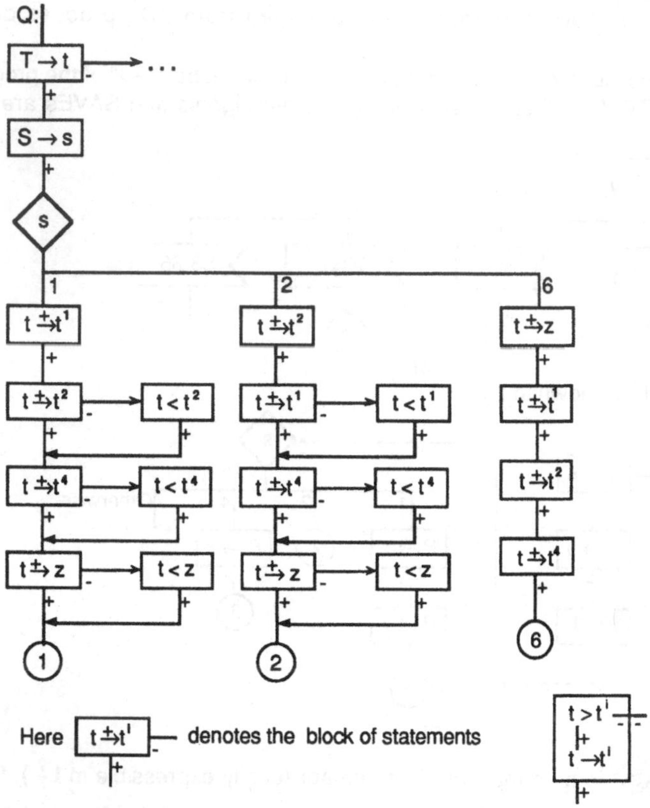

Fig.20

states without SAVE statements), if SAVE statements in the process contain, let us say, signals S1,S2,S3,S4,S5 and do not contain signals S6,S7, then the corresponding $\mathbf{L_7'}$ - fragment is transformed as shown in fig. 20.

If some signals Si,Sj,Sk appear in SAVE statements of the process always together, sole variable t^i can be defined for all of them.

If a signal S in the simulated SDL-process appears in some SAVE statement, then the arrival time of the signal, read from the input tape T, may happen to be less than the current value of z (i.e., less than the corresponding value of the function *now* in the process) because the signal could have been retained in the input queue for some time. In the given moment of execution of $\mathbf{L_7'}$ -program the value of variable t^s, corresponding to S indicates the lower bound for the arrival time of S (t^s is the largest arrival time for the signals read so far in the states which don't contain S in their SAVE statements).

The reading of signal S with the arrival time less than t^s would violate the FIFO discipline of the input queue (taking into account the corrections made by SAVE's).

6) for every timer Tn in the process we define a corresponding variable t^n in the simulating program. In the situation of timer Tn being active the variable t^n will hold the value of the expected moment of signal appearance from the timer; let t^n=-1, if Tn is inactive (for the sake of simplicity we don't consider the case when timer signals are retained by SAVE statements in SDL process, principal complications do not appear in

this case, too).

If SDL process has timers, e.g., T1 and T2, then every "-" exit from statement reading the tape T is augmented by condition expressing the inactivity of the timers:

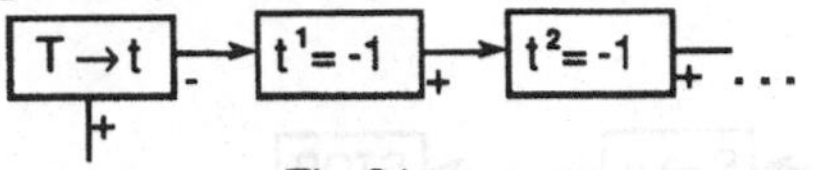

Fig.21

If input of timer signals, e.g., T3 and T4 is admissible in the state Q of the process

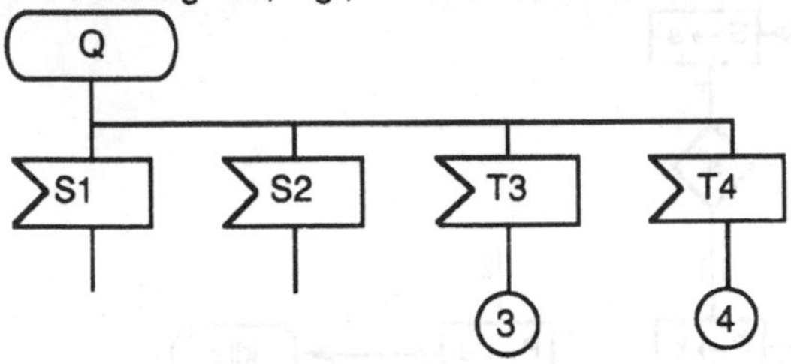

Fig.22

(we define that input of timer signal Tn is admissible in state Q if there is a path in the process diagram from START to Q such that the timer Tn remains active after the path), then the corresponding fragment (see fig. 22) is transformed in such way:

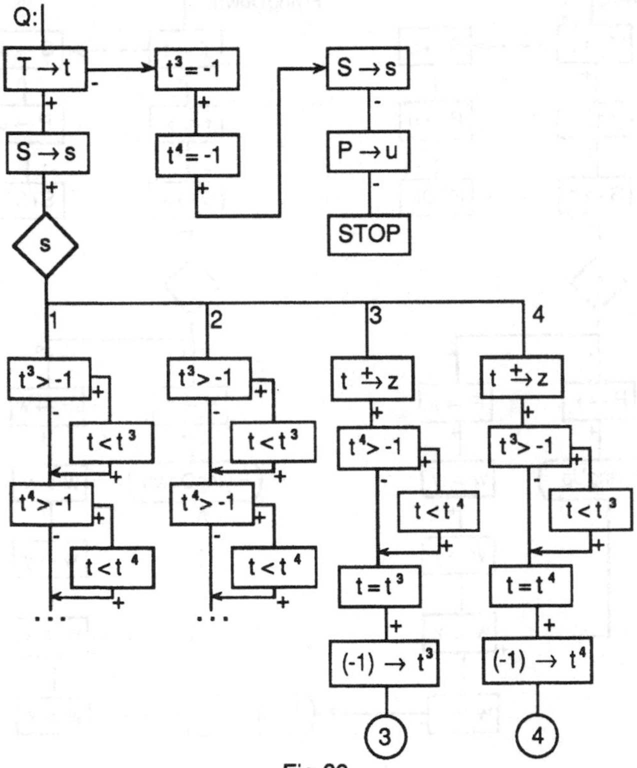

Fig.23

7) statement set(now+c,Tn) is transformed into z+c →t^n, statement reset(Tn) into (-1)→t^n.

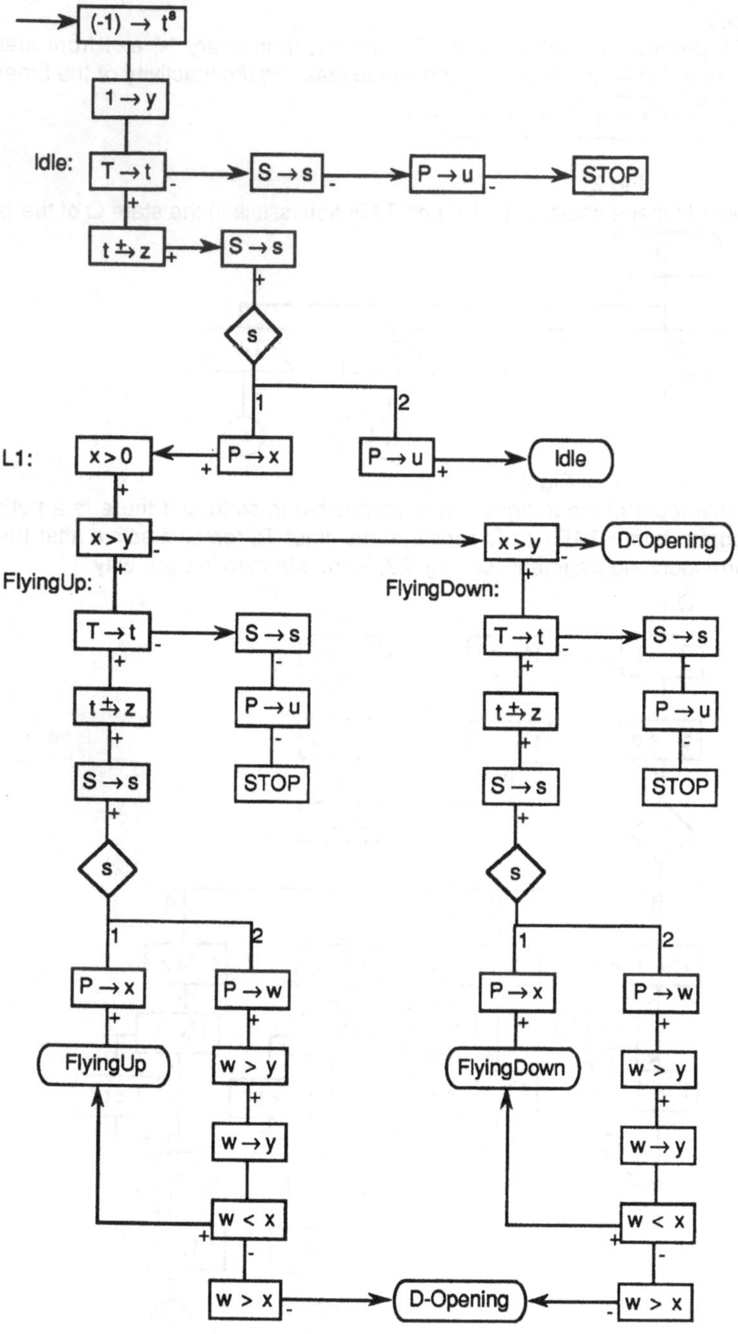

(-1) → t^s
1 → y
Idle:
T → t
S → s
P → u
STOP
t ± z
S → s
s
1
2
L1:
x > 0
P → x
P → u
Idle
x > y
x > y
D-Opening
FlyingUp:
FlyingDown:
T → t
S → s
P → u
STOP
t ± z
S → s
s
T → t
S → s
P → u
STOP
t ± z
S → s
s
1
2
P → x
P → w
FlyingUp
w > y
w → y
w < x
w > x
D-Opening
1
2
P → x
P → w
FlyingDown
w > y
w → y
w < x
w > x

Fig.24.1

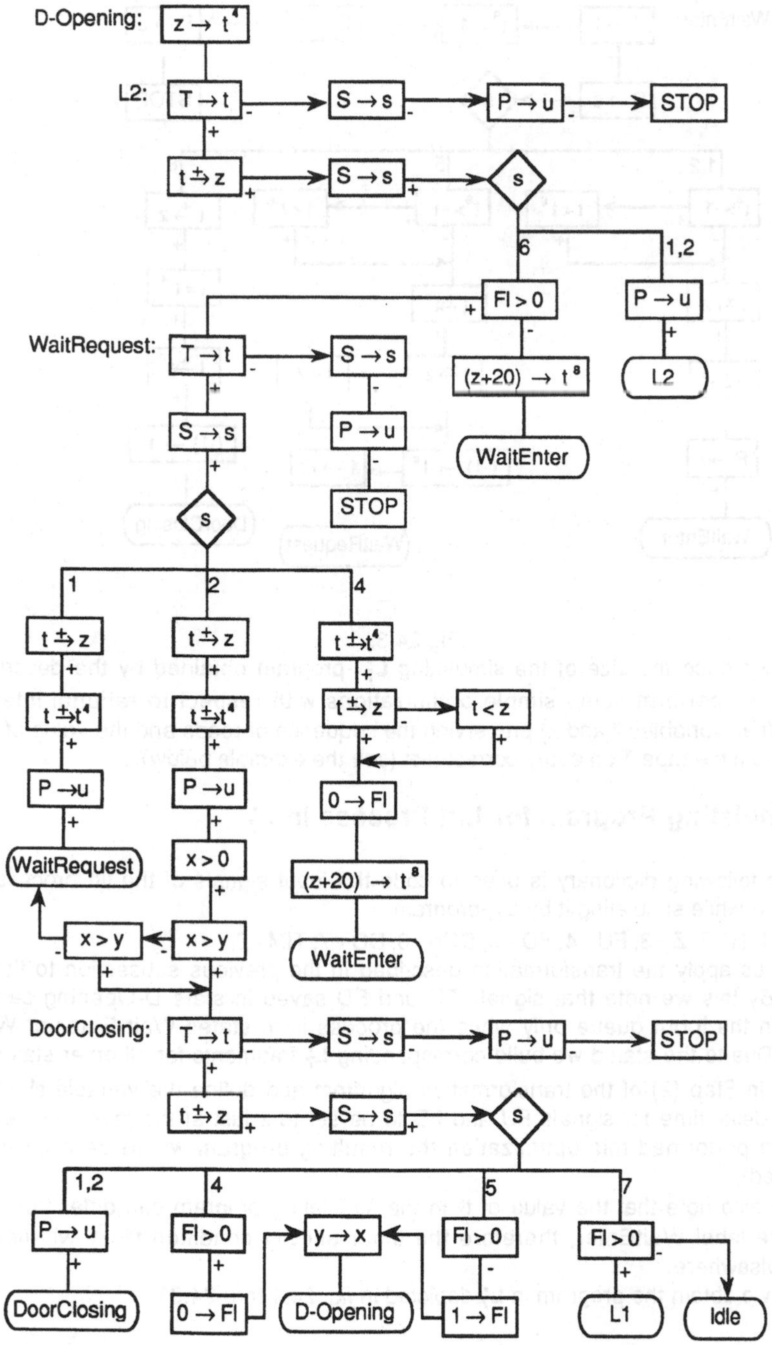
D-Opening:
z → t⁴
L2:
T → t
S → s
P → u
STOP
t ± z
S → s
s
6
1,2
Fl > 0
P → u
L2
WaitRequest:
T → t
S → s
(z+20) → t⁸
S → s
P → u
WaitEnter
STOP
s
1
2
4
t ± z
t ± z
t ± t⁴
t ± t⁴
t ± t⁴
t ± z
t < z
P → u
P → u
0 → Fl
WaitRequest
x > 0
(z+20) → t⁸
x > y
x > y
WaitEnter
DoorClosing:
T → t
S → s
P → u
STOP
t ± z
S → s
s
1,2
4
5
7
P → u
Fl > 0
y → x
Fl > 0
Fl > 0
DoorClosing
0 → Fl
D-Opening
1 → Fl
L1
Idle

Fig.24.2

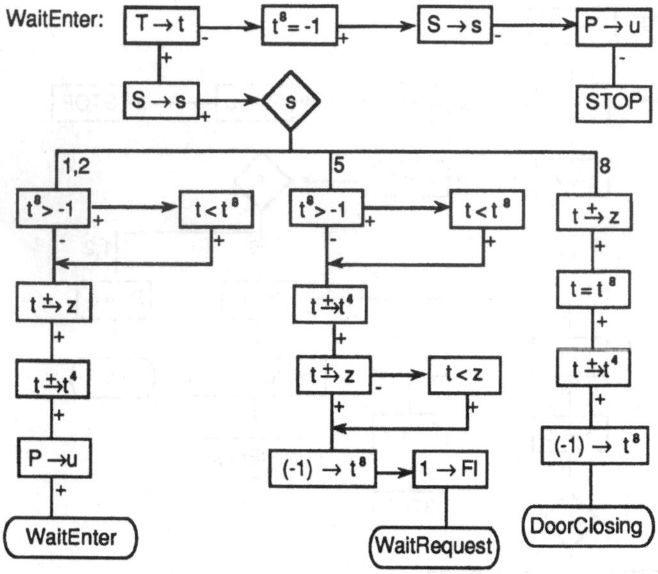

Fig.24.3

In order to reduce the size of the simulating **L'_7** -program obtained by the described algorithm we perform some simple optimizations with respect to rational internal variables (i.e., variables t^i and z) preserving the sequence of reads and the value of z at any read from the tape T on every correct test (see the example below).

10.4 Simulating Program for Lift Process in L'_7

The following dictionary is used to code the input signals of the lift process on input tape S while simulating it by **L'_7** -program:

S - 1, R - 2, Z - 3, FU - 4, FD - 5, DOp - 6, DC - 7, TIM - 8.

Let us apply the transformation described in the previous subsection to the lift process. By this we note that signals FU and FD saved in state D-Opening can be retained in the input queue only while the process is in states Wait-Enter or Wait-Request. Due to the stated we build corresponding **L'_7** fragments for all other states as described in Step (2) of the transformation algorithm and define the variable t^4 which simulates delay time for signals FU and FD to be set to z just at the label D-Opening (hadn't we performed this optimization the resulting program would be a bit more complicated).

We also note that the value of t^8 in the simulating program can differ from (-1) only at the label WaitEnter, therefore the timer activity condition t^8=-1 will not be checked elsewhere.

So we obtain the program in **L'_7** depicted in fig. 24.1 thru 24.3.

10.5 Reachability Graph for Lift Program in L'_7

The reachability graph for the lift program in **L'_7** is built using the algorithm described in the previous section, as well as some methods for reachability graph minimizing (similar to those described in Section 3 for $\mathbf{L_0}$-programs).

We define essentially located statements (ELSs) to be the statements with labels attached to them except those with label "D-Opening" (this label is located "nearly at the same place" as "L2") and "L1".

In the construction of the reachability graph we use the following states (inequality systems) corresponding to program paths:

S1 = $\{-1 = t^8 < 0 = z, y = 1, Fl = 0\}$
S2 = $\{-1 = t^8 < 0 < z, y = 1, Fl = 0\}$
S3 = $\{-1 = t^8 < 0 < z = t^4, x = y = 1, Fl = 0\}$
S4 = $\{-1 = t^8 < 0 < t^4 < z, x = y = 1, Fl = 0\}$
S5 = $\{-1 < 0 < t^4 < z < z + 20 = t^8, x = y = 1, Fl = 0\}$
S6 = $\{-1 < 0 < z = t^4 < t^8 < z + 20, x = y = 1, Fl = 0\}$
S7 = $\{-1 < 0 < z = t^4 < z + 20 = t^8, x = y = 1, Fl = 0\}$
S8 = $\{-1 = t^8 < 0 < t^4 < z, x = y = 1, Fl = 1\}$
S9 = $\{-1 = t^8 < 0 < z = t^4, x = y = 1, Fl = 1\}$
S10 = $\{-1 = t^8 < 0 = z, x = y = 1, Fl = 0\}$
S11 = $\{-1 = t^8 < 0 = z, x > y = 1, Fl = 1\}$
S12 = $\{-1 = t^8 < 0 = z, x > y > 1, Fl = 1\}$
S13 = $\{-1 = t^8 < 0 < z = t^4, x = y > 1, Fl = 1\}$
S14 = $\{-1 = t^8 < 0 < t^4 < z, x = y > 1, Fl = 1\}$
S15 = $\{-1 < 0 < t^4 < z < z + 20 = t^8, x = y > 1, Fl = 0\}$
S16 = $\{-1 < 0 < z = t^4 < t^8 < z + 20, x = y > 1, Fl = 0\}$
S17 = $\{-1 < 0 < z = t^4 < z + 20 = t^8, x = y > 1, Fl = 0\}$
S18 = $\{-1 = t^8 < 0 = z, x = y > 1, Fl = 0\}$
S19 = $\{-1 = t^8 < 0 < z, y > 1, Fl = 0\}$
S20 = $\{-1 = t^8 < 0 < z = t^4, x = y > 1, Fl = 0\}$
S21 = $\{-1 = t^8 < 0 < t^4 < z, x = y > 1, Fl = 0\}$
S22 = $\{-1 = t^8 < 0 < z, x > y > 1, Fl = 0\}$
S23 = $\{-1 = t^8 < 0 = z, 0 < x < y, Fl = 0\}$
S24 = $\{-1 = t^8 < 0 = z, 0 < x = y, Fl = 0\}$
S25 = $\{-1 = t^8 < 0 = z, 0 < x < y, Fl = 1\}$
S26 = $\{-1 = t^8 < 0 = z, 0 < x = y, Fl = 1\}$
S27 = $\{-1 = t^8 < 0 < z, x > y = 1, Fl = 0\}$

Vertices of the reachability graph are pairs (ELS label, state corresponding to program path).

Let Li and Lj be labels of ELS's, and the path β from Li to Lj contains no other ELS's. There an edge corresponding to the path β is drawn from vertex (Li,Si) to (Lj,Sj) in the graph if S(Si,β)=Sj (i.e., if the state Si is transformed into Sj by the path β according to inductive state building algorithm). The edge in the reachability graph corresponding to some path in the program will be labeled by exits of conditional statements defining the path (for the sake of brevity only exits of the statements with other exit not pending are shown in labels).

In order to make the representation of the reachability graph more compact and comprehensible we have chosen for every vertex the following kinds of paths:

1) from the vertex to stop,
2) from the vertex to itself,
3) not feasible

to be represented in special fields inside the image of the vertex. For example, the

vertex image

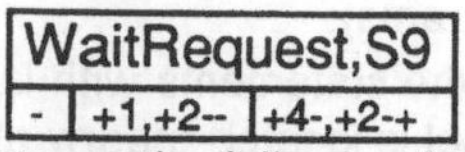

represents the following fragment of graph:

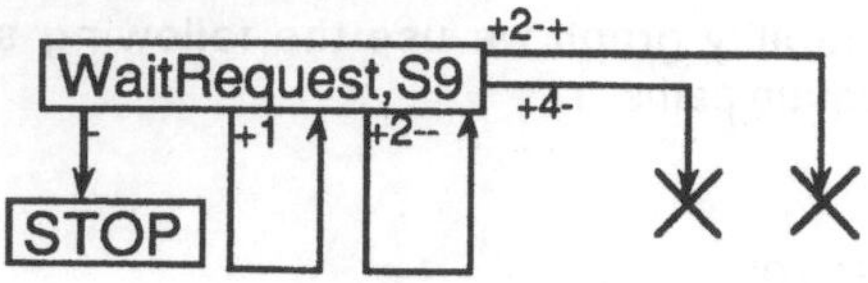

Fig.25

The constructed reachability graph is depicted in fig. 26.1 and 26.2.

During the construction of the graph a nondeterministic branching was admitted to reduce the size. Namely, while forming the inequality system S24 (S26 respectively), it is easy to see that the set of its solutions coincides with the union of solution sets for S3 and S20 (S13 and S9 respectively). Thus, instead of drawing an edge from (FlyingDown,S23) ((FlyingDown,S25) respectively) to (L2,S24) ((L2,S26) respectively) corresponding to path +3- we make a nondeterministic branching leading to both (L2,S3) and (L2,S20) ((L2,S13) and (L2,S10) respectively).

It is easy to see that nondeterministic branching causes no obstacles for finding the coverings of graph and solving corresponding inequality systems. If nondeterministic branching were not used, additional 11 states in the graph would have been necessary.

10.6 Path Inequality Systems: Example

Now let us show how to build an inequality system for some path in the lift program (being a projection of a path in the reachability graph) and find a test enforcing the execution of it.

Let us consider a path in the reachability graph v=(Idle,S1)+1+, (FlyingUp,S27)+3+, (FlyingUp,S22)+3-, (L2,S20)+6-, (WaitEnter,S15)+5+-, (WaiRequest,S14)+4-, (WaitEnter,S15)+1+, (WaitEnter,S16)+8, (DoorClosing,S18)+7-, (Idle,S19)-, STOP.

It has the following projection α in the program:

$(-1)\to t^8$, $1\to y$, $T\to t$+, $t\stackrel{\pm}{\to}z$+, $S\to s$+, s: 1, $P\to x$+, $x>0$+, $x>y$+,

$T\to t$+, $t\stackrel{\pm}{\to}z$+, $S\to s$+, s: 3, $P\to w$+, $w>y$+, $w\to y$, $w<x$+,

$T\to t$+, $t\stackrel{\pm}{\to}z$+, $S\to s$+, s: 3, $P\to w$+, $w>y$+, $w\to y$, $w<x$-, $w>x$-,

$z\to t^4$, $T\to t$+, $t\stackrel{\pm}{\to}z$+, $S\to s$+, s: 6, $Fl>0$-, $(z+20)\to t^8$,

$T\to t$+, $S\to s$+, s: 5, $t^8>-1$+, $t<t^8$+, $t\stackrel{\pm}{\to}t^4$+, $t\stackrel{\pm}{\to}z$-, $t<z$+, $(-1)\to t^8$, $1\to Fl$,

$T\to t$+, $S\to s$+, s: 4, $t\stackrel{\pm}{\to}t^4$+, $t\stackrel{\pm}{\to}z$-, $t<z$+, $1\to Fl$, $(z+20)\to t^8$,

$T\to t$+, $S\to s$+, s: 1, $t^8>-1$+, $t<t^8$+, $t\stackrel{\pm}{\to}z$+, $t\stackrel{\pm}{\to}t^4$+, $P\to u$+,

$T\to t$+, $S\to s$+, s: 8, $t\stackrel{\pm}{\to}z$+, $t=t^8$+, $t\stackrel{\pm}{\to}t^4$+, $(-1)\to t^8$,

$T\to t$+, $t\stackrel{\pm}{\to}z$+, $S\to s$+, s: 7, $Fl>0$-,

$T\to t$-, $S\to s$-, $P\to u$-, STOP.

There the following inequality system corresponds to the path α:

$z_0 = t_0 = t_0{}^4 = t_0{}^8 = 0$, $y_0 = x_0 = w_0 = Fl_0 = s_0 = 0$;

$t_1{}^8 = -1$; $y_1=1$, $t_1=T_1$; $t_1>z_0$, $z_1=t_1$; $s_1=S_1$; $s_1=1$, $x_1=P_1$; $x_1>0$; $x_1>y_1$;

$t_2=T_2$; $t_2>z_1$, $z_2=t_2$; $s_2=S_2$; $s_2=3$; $w_1=P_2$; $w_1>y_1$; $y_2=w_1$; $w_1<x_1$;

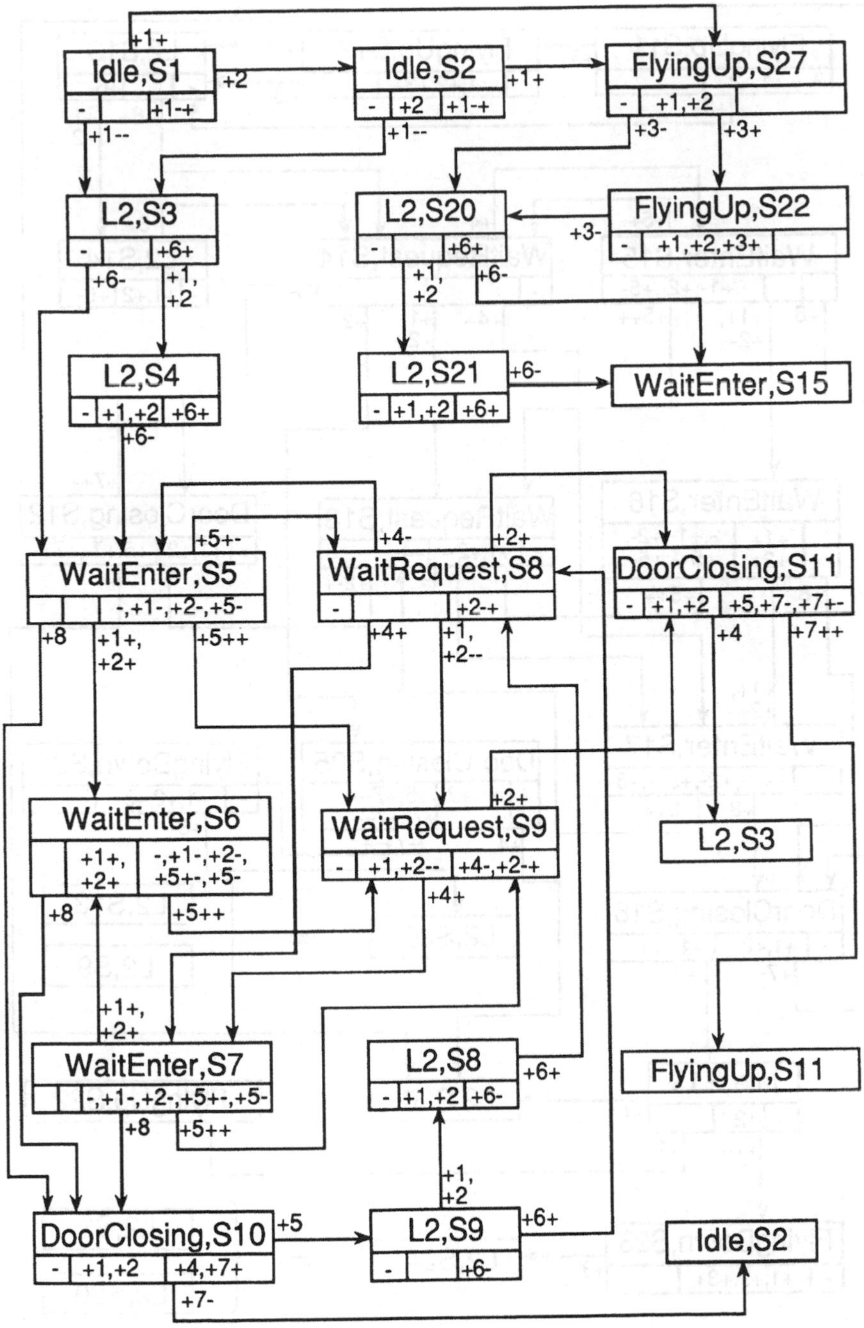
Idle,S1
Idle,S2
FlyingUp,S27
L2,S3
L2,S20
FlyingUp,S22
L2,S4
L2,S21
WaitEnter,S15
WaitEnter,S5
WaitRequest,S8
DoorClosing,S11
WaitEnter,S6
WaitRequest,S9
L2,S3
WaitEnter,S7
L2,S8
FlyingUp,S11
DoorClosing,S10
L2,S9
Idle,S2

Fig.26.1

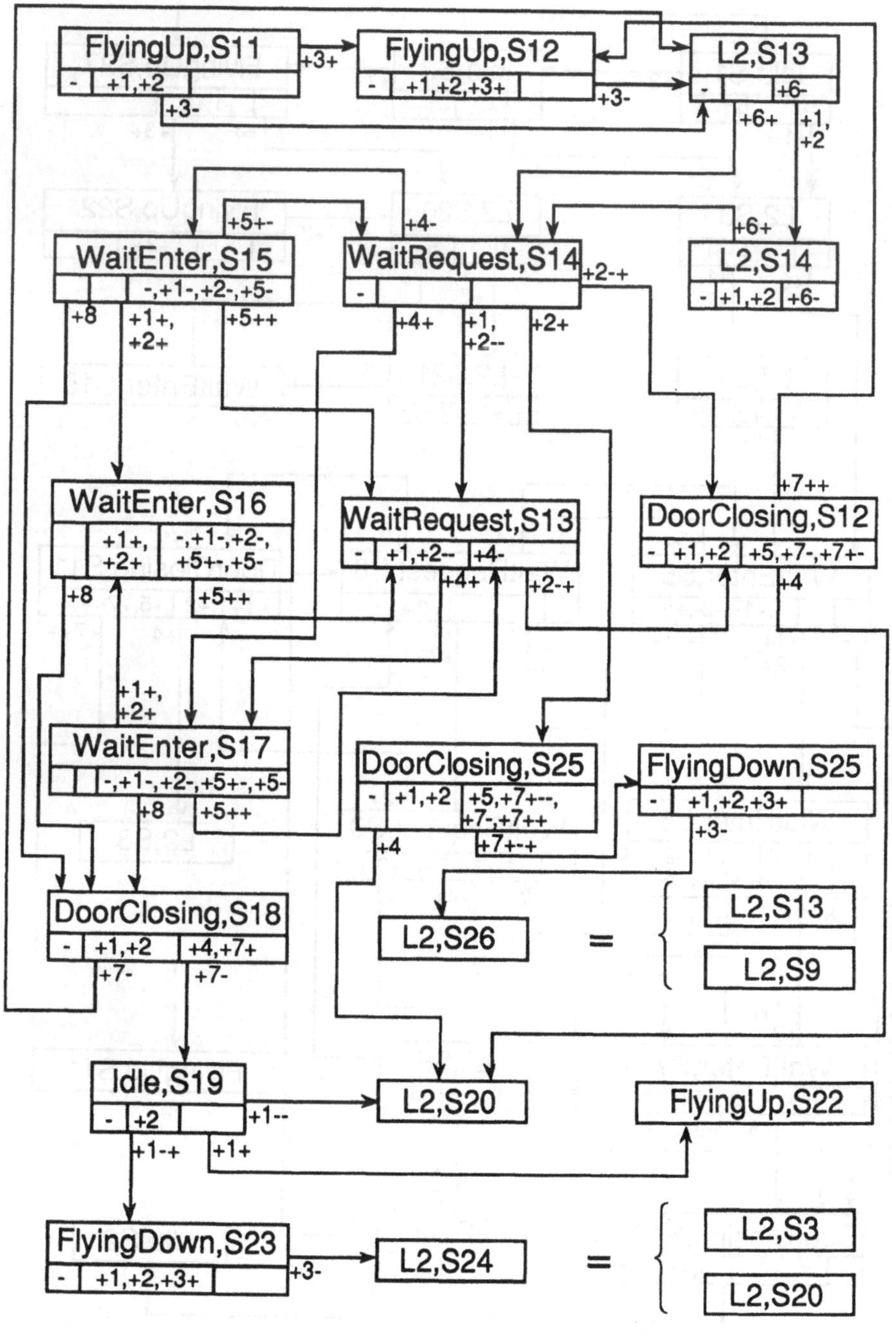
FlyingUp,S11
- +1,+2
+3+
+3-
FlyingUp,S12
- +1,+2,+3+
+3-
L2,S13
- +6-
+6+
+1, +2
WaitEnter,S15
-,+1-,+2-,+5-
+5+-
+4-
WaitRequest,S14
-
+2-+
L2,S14
- +1,+2 +6-
+6+
+8
+1+, +2+
+5++
+4+
+1, +2--
+2+
WaitEnter,S16
+1+, +2+
-,+1-,+2-, +5+-,+5-
WaitRequest,S13
- +1,+2-- +4-
DoorClosing,S12
- +1,+2 +5,+7-,+7+-
+7++
+8
+5++
+4+
+2-+
+4
+1+, +2+
WaitEnter,S17
-,+1-,+2-,+5+-,+5-
+8
+5++
DoorClosing,S25
- +1,+2 +5,+7+--, +7-,+7++
+4
+7+-+
FlyingDown,S25
- +1,+2,+3+
+3-
DoorClosing,S18
- +1,+2 +4,+7+
+7-
+7-
L2,S26
=
L2,S13
L2,S9
Idle,S19
- +2
+1--
+1-+
+1+
L2,S20
FlyingUp,S22
FlyingDown,S23
- +1,+2,+3+
+3-
L2,S24
=
L2,S3
L2,S20

Fig.26.2

$t_3=T_3; t_3>z_2, z_3=t_3; s_3=S_3; s_3=3; w_2=P_3; w_2>y_2; y_3=w_2; w_2\geq x_1; w_2=x_1;$
$t_1^4=z_3; t_4=T_4; t_4>z_3, z_4=t_4; s_4=S_4; s_4=6; Fl_0\leq 0; t_1^8=z_4+20;$
$t_5=T_5; s_5=S_5; s_5=5; t_1^8>-1; t_5<t_1^8; t_5>t_1^4, t_2^4=t_5; t_5\leq z_4; t_5<z_4; t_2^8=-1; Fl_1=1;$
$t_6=T_6; s_6=S_6; s_6=4; t_6>t_2^4, t_3^4=t_6; t_6=z_4; t_6<z_4; Fl_2=0; t_3^8=z_4+20;$
$t_7=T_7; s_7=S_7; s_7=1; t_3^8=-1; t_7<t_3^8; t_7>z_4, z_5=t_7; t_7>t_3^4, t_4^4=t_7; u_1=P_4;$
$t_8=T_8; s_8=S_8; s_8=8; t_8>z_5, z_6=t_8; t_8=t_3^8; t_8>t_4^4, t_5^4=t_8; t_4^8=-1;$
$t_9=T_9; t_9>z_6, z_7=t_9; s_9=S_9; s_9=7; Fl_2\leq 0;$
$T<0; S<0; P<0.$

With respect to the values of input tape cells $T_1,..,T_9$, $S_1,..,S_9$, $P_1,..,P_4$ it is equivalent to the following inequality system:
$0<T_1<T_2<T_3<T_4<T_7<T_8<T_9;\ \ T_3<T_5<T_6<T_7<T_8;$
$T_5<T_4;\ \ T_6<T_4;\ \ -1<T_4+20;\ T_5<T_4+20;\ T_7<T_4+20=T_8;$
$S_1=1; S_2=3; S_3=3; S_4=6; S_5=5; S_6=4; S_7=1; S_8=8; S_9=7;$
$P_1>1; P_2>1; P_2<P_3; P_3>P_2; P_3=P_1.$

From this inequality system we can obtain, for example, the following test on which lift program traverses the path
T=(1,2,3,6,4,5,7,26,27) ; S=(1,3,3,6,5,4,1,8,7) ; P=(3,2,3,0)

Computational complexity of solving path inequality systems is not considered here, we note that the special form of path inequality systems is very essential for solving algorithm.

10.7 CTS for Lift Program

Using the constructed reachability graph for every branch in the program we can
1) determine whether it is feasible,
2) if so, find a feasible path containing the branch.

Further, by solving the inequality system for the obtained path, we find a test on which the given branch is executed.

Thus, considering consecutively all branches in the program, we construct a correct CTS for the program.

Choosing a definite order of branch consideration we obtain the following correct CTS for lift program.

<u>Test N1.</u> T=(1) , S=(2) , P=(0) ;

<u>Test N2.</u> T=(1,2,3,4) , S=(1,1,2,3) , P=(3,0,0,2) ;

<u>Test N3.</u> T=(1,2,3) , S=(1,1,2) , P=(1,0,0) ;

<u>Test N4.</u> T=(1,2,3,4,5,6,7,8) , S=(1,3,6,1,2,5,1,2) , P=(2,2,0,0,0,2) ;

<u>Test N5.</u> T=(1,3,2,4,5,6) , S=(1,6,5,2,1,2) , P=(1,2,0,0) ;

<u>Test N6.</u> T=(1,2,22,23) , S=(1,6,8,5) , P=(1) ;

<u>Test N7.</u> T=(1,2,3,4,5,6) , S=(1,3,6,5,2,4) , P=(2,2,1) ;

<u>Test N8.</u> T=(1,4,2,3,24,25,26,27,28) , S=(1,6,5,4,8,5,6,2,7) , P=(1,2) ;

<u>Test N9.</u> T=(1,2,3,4,5,6,7,8,9) , S=(1,3,6,5,2,7,1,2,3) , P=(3,3,1,0,0,2) ;

<u>Test N10.</u> T=(1,2,3,4,5,6,7) , S=(1,3,6,5,2,7,3) , P=(2,2,1,1) .

To conclude the analysis of lift example we demonstrate how to transform tests from the obtained CTS into tests for the lift SDL process (as it has been explained before, these tests will form correct CTS for the process according to analogue of criterion C_1).

Test N1. (R(0) at 1).

Test N2. (S(3) at 1), (S(0) at 2), (R(0) at 3), (Z(2) at 4).

Test N3. (S(1) at 1), (S(0) at 2), (R(0) at 3).

Test N4. (S(2) at 1), (Z(2) at 2), (DOp at 3), (S(0) at 4), (R(0) at 5), (FD at 6), (S(0) at 7), (R(2) at 8).

Test N5. (S(1) at 1), (FD at 2), (DOp at 3), (R(2) at 4), (S(0) at 5), (R(0) at 6).
(Let us note the different order of signals in the corresponding L_7' test).

Test N6. (S(1) at 1), (DOp at 2), (FD at 3).
(Let us note that 4 signals were coded in the L_7' test).

Test N7. (S(2) at 1), (Z(2) at 2), (DOp at 3), (FD at 4), (R(1) at 5), (FU at 6).

Test N8. (S(1) at 1), (FD at 2), (FU at 3), (DOp at 4), (FD at 25), (DOp at 26), (R(2) at 27), (DC at 28).
(See notes at tests N5 and N6).

Test N9. (S(3) at 1), (Z(3) at 2), (DOp at 3), (FD at 4), (R(1) at 5), (DC at 6), (S(0) at 7), (R(0) at 8), (Z(2) at 9).

Test N10. (S(2) at 1), (Z(2) at 2), (DOp at 3), (FD at 4), (R(1) at 5), (DC at 6), (Z(1) at 7).

11 Conclusions

In the mid 70-ies using the ideas described in Sections 2,3,4 an experimental CTS generation system for data processing programs (the system SMOTL [8,10]) was developed at the Computing Center of Latvia University. A COBOL–like language SMOD was used as source language for SMOTL. The system SMOTL was tested on many real business data processing programs. Experiments showed that SMOTL was able to build automatically complete test sets for the described class of programs at a speed comparable to that of high level language compilers. However, business data processing programs have no sufficiently high demands for their reliability to outweigh the additional efforts of developing and using automatic test generation systems. Therefore practical research in this direction was not continued.

The situation has changed essentially in the last few years when the necessity appeared to test complicated real time systems with very high demands on reliability. Automatic generation of test cases has sufficient practical importance for programs of this class. At the same time it is clear that automatic test generation is a very hard job for these systems. Theoretical foundation of test generation for systems of the kind is considered in Section 9. Practical methods for test generation are described in the companion paper [17].

REFERENCES

[1] D.S.Alberts. The economics of software quality assurance. In Proc. AFIPS Conf. 1976, pp. 433–442.

[2] A.I.Auzins. On the Construction of complete sample systems. Dokl. Akad. Nauk SSSR, Vol. 288, No. 3, 1984, pp. 564–568 (in Russian).

[3] A.I.Auzins. Decidability of the reachability for the relational push–down automata.

Programmirovanie, No. 3, 1984, pp. 3–12 (in Russian).

[4] J.M.Barzdin, J.J.Bicevskis, and A.A.Kalninsh. Construction of complete sample system for program testing. Latv. Gosudarst. Univ. Uch. Zapiski, Vol. 210, 1974, pp. 152–187 (in Russian).

[5] J.M.Barzdin, J.J.Bicevskis, and A.A.Kalninsh. Decidable and undecidable cases of the problem of Construction of the complete sample system. Latv. Gosudarst. Univ. Uch. Zapiski, Vol. 210, 1974, pp. 188–205 (in Russian).

[6] J.M.Barzdin, J.J.Bicevskis, and A.A.Kalninsh. Construction of complete sample system for correctness testing. Lecture Notes in Computer Science, Vol. 32, Springer-Verlag, 1975, pp. 1–12.

[7] J.M.Barzdin and A.A.Kalninsh. Construction of complete sample system for programs using direct access files. Latv. Gosudarst. Univ. Uch. Zapiski, Vol. 233, 1975, pp. 123–154 (in Russian).

[8] J.J.Bicevskis. Automatic construction of sample systems. Programmirovanie, No. 3, 1977, pp. 60–70 (in Russian).

[9] J.M.Barzdin, J.J.Bicevskis, and A.A.Kalninsh. Automatic construction of complete sample systems for program testing. In Proc. IFIP Congress, 1977, North-Holland, 1977, pp. 57–62.

[10] J.Bicevskis, J.Borzovs, U.Straujums, A.Zarins, and E.F.Miller. SMOTL–a system to construct samples for data processing program debugging. IEEE Transactions on Software Enqineering, SE–5, No. 1, 1979, pp. 60–66.

[11] E.F.Miller, Jr. Program testing technology in the 1980s. In Tutorial: Software Testing and Validation Techniques, 1978, pp. 399–406.

[12] M.L.Minsky. Finite and infinite machines. Prentice–Hall, Englewood Cliffs, N.Y., 1967.

[13] M.O.Rabin and D.Scott. Finite automata and their decision problems. IBM J. of Research and Development, vol. 3, No. 2, 1959, pp. 114–125.

[14] A.G.Tadevosjan. Decidable cases of the problem of construction of a complete sample system. Kibernetika, No. 6, 1985, pp. 41–44 (in Russian).

[15] K.C.Tai. Program testing complexity and test criteria. IEEE Trans. Software Engineering, SE–6, No. 6, 1980, pp. 531–538.

[16] CCITT Specification and Description Language (SDL), Recomendation Z. 100, 1988.

[17] J.Barzdins, J.Borzovs, A.Kalnins, I.Medvedis. Automatic construction of test sets: practical approach, this volume.

AUTOMATIC CONSTRUCTION OF TEST SETS: PRACTICAL APPROACH

Juris Borzovs, Audris Kalniņš, Inga Medvedis

Institute of Mathematics and Computer Science
The University of Latvia
Raiņa Bulv. 29, Riga 226250, Latvia

Abstract. The problem of symbolic execution and test generation is considered both for sequential and concurrent programs. Practical methods for test construction for the given program path are presented.

1. Introduction

Computer program testing (i.e., program execution on different input values - tests) remains an essential basis of program correctness decision. It is accepted that testing is not capable of program correctness proving (except cases when program is executed on all possible input values), nevertheless, in practice, if program gives correct outputs on sufficiently large amount of tests, confidence of its correctness becomes psychologically very strong.

As test generation is rather labor-consuming and quite often rather subjective, already tens of years ago trials were performed to automate this process [1,2]. One possible approach to the solution of the problem is test generation by means of symbolic execution of program paths and the following solution of path conditions (which mainly are systems of equalities and inequalities over program input parameters) obtained by symbolic execution.

Since 70-ies rather many experimental systems have been developed on the basis of the before mentioned approach [3-11]. In the second half of the 80-ies this approach has experienced the revival in the application of testing of specifications of large program systems (especially telecommunication) [12-14,28,29].

This paper deals with automated test generation methods for sequential programs and protocol specifications written in SDL language [15,16]. In both cases symbolic execution of programs is used.

The paper consists of two major parts. Part 2 deals with sequential programs. The notion of symbolic execution is formalized here. Sequential subset of SDL (equivalent to large part of Pascal) is described and an example of program is given. Correct symbolic execution is defined for this subset of SDL and demonstrated on the program example. A heuristic method for solving equations (path conditions) obtained as the result of symbolic execution of program path is presented, thus yielding a practical method to generate a test executing a selected program path.

In Part 3 the approach is extended to concurrent programs. Correct symbolic execution is extended to all major concurrency concepts of SDL. The method is demonstrated on a realistic example - sliding window protocol in SDL, test generation procedure based on symbolic execution is shown for selected paths. Moreover, a heuristic method is presented for path selection (according to criterion C1) based on state concept related to that used for theoretical approach to test generation [17]. The method ensures the generation of test set executing all branches for the sliding window example in a reasonable time. A more sophisticated heuristic test generation method supposed to work efficiently on comparatively large SDL systems is also outlined.

Part 2 has been written by J.Borzovs and I.Medvedis. It contains results obtained by the authors at various times [10, 21, 22]. Part 3 has been written by A.Kalniņš and it contains new results.

2. Symbolic execution and test generation for sequential programs

Symbolic execution of programs is a wide area per se and has various applications. In this paper we restrict ourselves to the use of symbolic execution for feasibility condition description for program paths and test generation for a path based on these conditions.

Our approach to test generation by means of symbolic execution can be applied to a class of programming languages characterized by the following properties. These are block structured procedural languages with strong typing. A typical representative of this class is Pascal together with its newest derivatives like Modula-2, Turing, etc. Some restrictions, nevertheless, are present. We exclude direct memory management (pointers and related operations), calls of external procedures and functions as black boxes (with no source text available), nondeterministic functions (like random number generators).

Languages of the considered class have common property that the main control unit is a procedure with formal input parameters and declaration part defining local variables and their types. Procedure body consists of statements (assignments, conditionals, etc.) which can be represented both in conventional textual form and in flowchart like form.

Symbolic execution can be defined by our methods for any language of the class described. To do this a special symbolic execution language correlated to the given programming language must be designed. In this paper we describe only symbolic execution of SDL - in Part 2 for its sequential subset (equivalent in fact to large Pascal subset), in Part 3 we expand this definition to concurrent aspects of SDL.

2.1 Formalization of Symbolic Execution of Program Path

In order to define formally symbolic execution we must describe more precisely some notions present in any programming language L of the considered language class.

1. All data types permitted in the programming language L are denoted by T_1, T_2, T_3,.... If the language L permits only predefined types, then the number of the types used is finite. If the language L has type defining facilities (like **Array** [1..10] **Of** Integer in Pascal), then the number of possible types is infinite. Nevertheless we assume that syntax and semantics definition of the language L determines uniquely the complete type list T_1, T_2, ... and type declaration in a program is only a way to select one of these types. The domains of types (i.e., sets containing possible values of the variables of the type) are denoted by D_1, D_2, D_3, ... If the language L has type naming facilities like

```
Type Seqno = Integer;
     List  = Array[1..10] Of Seqno;
Var  Buf : List;
```

in Pascal, the corresponding <u>ground type</u> containing no intermediate program defined identifiers and having the same domain (**Array**[1..10] **Of** Integer for variable Buf in the example) is used to denote the type of variable in our discussions. A program independent list of possible ground types T_1,T_2,... can actually be defined for Pascal like languages (in a way similar to that used further for SDL subset).

2. We assume type T_1 to correspond to normal Boolean data type, so D_1 = {True,False}.

3. Every program P in the language L has a certain number n of variables. Each variable has a name and a certain type (from the list $T_1, T_2, \ldots$). If program P has variables $X_1, \ldots, X_n$, then the corresponding types are denoted by $T^P_{x_1}, T^P_{x_2}, \ldots T^P_{x_n}$ and domains by $D^P_{x_1}, \ldots, D^P_{x_n}$.

4. A certain number of the program variables are input parameters, i.e., variables containing program input data. We assume the first m variables $X_1, \ldots, X_m$ to be the parameters.

5. The body of program P consists of statements, each of them having one or more exits (e.g., If-statement normally has two exits), all statements are somehow labelled. A sequence (S_1e_1, S_2e_2, ..., S_ke_k) is called a path if S_1 is the first statement of the program and if exit e_i of statement S_i determines S_{i+1} as the next statement to be executed. If statement S_i has only one exit or the exit is uniquely determined by some other syntactic means, e_i will not be given explicitly.

Now let us describe the symbolic execution of programs in the language L.

The <u>symbolic</u> <u>language</u> SL corresponding to the programming language L is defined as:

1. Many-sorted signature $\sum$ defined over the same (ground) types $T_1, T_2, \ldots$ used in the programming language L. A special type T_0 with only one value undef in its domain D_0 is introduced (this value is used to denote undefined variable values). The signature contains function symbols $f_1, f_2, \ldots$ and for every function symbol f_i its argument types and result type are specified

f_i: T_{i_1}, ..., T_{i_k} ---> T_{i_0}

(including zero argument constant functions) .No function f_i is defined over T_0, only constant function Undef has T_0 as value type.

2. An interpretation I of functions symbols $f_1, f_2, \ldots$ from signature $\sum$.

The main objects considered in the language SL are terms. Terms in SL are well-typed expressions composed of function symbols and typed variables in normal sense. Terms are used to describe the behaviour of programs in L. Though it is not required formally, function symbols $f_1, f_2, \ldots$ and their interpretation I normally isclosely related to functions used in the language L itself or in its semantics description.

A term in SL is said to be a <u>predicate term</u> if its range is D_1= {True,False}.

We say that a term T <u>conforms</u> with a program P if all variables occurring in the term T are also input parameters of the program P and the type of the variable determined by its occurrence in the term T coincides with the type specified for the variable in the program P. If the language L uses type naming, then variable having some type in program P must have the corresponding ground type in term T (domains are the same!). Conformance informally means that term T is defined for the same entities which are processed by program P.

By <u>symbolic execution</u> (of programs in the language L) we understand an algorithm which, given a program P in the language L and a path α in P, produces:

1) a predicate term PC conforming with the program P,

2) for each variable $x_i (i=1,\dots,n)$ of program P a term T_{x_i} conforming with program P such that range of T_{x_i} according to signature Σ coincides with the value range of x_i determined by its type (or the range is D_0={Undef}).

The predicate term PC is called <u>path condition</u>, the terms $T_{x_1},\dots,T_{x_n}$ associated with variables - <u>system of symbolic values</u>, and both of them together <u>symbolic state</u>.

Symbolic execution is said to be <u>correct</u> if it produces for every program P in the language L and for every path α in P a symbolic state such that, for all parameter values of program P $a_1 \in D^P_{x_1}$, $a_2 \in D^P_{x_2}, \dots, a_m \in D^P_{x_m}$, there holds:

1) path condition $PC(a_1,a_2,\dots,a_m)$=true iff the program P executed on parameter values $a_1,\dots,a_m$ traverses the path α,

2) if term T_{x_i} is associated with variable $x_i (i=1,\dots, n)$ according to the system of symbolic values and the value of the instantiated term $T_{x_i}(a_1,\dots,a_m)$ is z_{x_i}, then after the program P has traversed the path α on parameter values $a_1,a_2,\dots,a_m$, variable x_i contains the same value z_{x_i}; if T_{x_i} = Undef, then variable x_i has no value assigned on path α.

So informally path condition is an assertion on parameter values of program P in order to force the execution of this path. Path condition actually accumulates the information from the conditional statements (If, Case,...) traversed in the path . Some assertions to prevent from overflow-like errors are also accumulated in path condition. In test generation applications path condition is used to find parameter values (i.e., a test) forcing the execution of the path.

To summarize the above mentioned we can say that symbolic execution definition for some programming language L requires three tasks to be done:

1. symbolic language corresponding to L must be defined,
2. symbolic execution algorithm must be constructed,
3. correctness of symbolic execution must be proved.

In practice the majority ofmost attention usually is paid to symbolic execution algorithm, nevertheless, the two other items are important as well.

The next sections are devoted to symbolic execution definition for a certain programming language.

2.2 Programing Language

In this section we consider a simple sequential programming language. Constructions of the language we denote in traditional SDL [15,16] graphical form, adhering completely to SDL syntax, although many typical SDL language constructions (such as state, signal, timer...) do not occur. The considered subset of SDL functionally do not exceed the capability of Pascal language, therefore, in order to improve readability, sometimes we present translation of SDL construction in Pascal terminology.

This simple sequential programming language is used to demonstrate symbolic execution and test generation algorithms later on. We stress that the scope of the language constructions could be substantially wider from the point of view of our methods. However, we shall consider only those language constructions having been used in examples.

In this part test generation methods are demonstrated on separate SDL procedure. In SDL language the procedure has textual and graphic parts. Textual part contains the description of procedure formal parameters, types and variables. Graphic part describes data manipulations and control flow. Further we describe this language more precisely.

Data type definitions

1. Our language has three predefined data types: Integer, Boolean and Real associated with usual operations:

```
Newtype Integer
    Literals 0,1,2,3,... ;
    Operators
        "+"   : Integer, Integer -> Integer ;
        "-"   : Integer, Integer -> Integer ;
        "mod" : Integer, Integer -> Integer ;
        "="   : Integer, Integer -> Boolean ;
        "/="  : Integer, Integer -> Boolean ;
        "<"   : Integer, Integer -> Boolean ;
        ">"   : Integer, Integer -> Boolean ;
        "<="  : Integer, Integer -> Boolean ;
        ">="  : Integer, Integer -> Boolean ;
Endnewtype Integer;
Newtype Boolean
    Literals True, False;
    Operators
        "NOT" : Boolean -> Boolean ;
        "AND" : Boolean, Boolean -> Boolean ;
        "OR"  : Boolean, Boolean -> Boolean ;
        "="   : Boolean, Boolean -> Boolean ;
        "/="  : Boolean, Boolean -> Boolean ;
Endnewtype Boolean ;
Newtype Real
    Literals ...
    Operators
        "+"   : Real, Real -> Real ;
        "-"   : Real, Real -> Real ;
        "="   : Real, Real -> Boolean ;
        "/="  : Real, Real -> Boolean ;
        "<"   : Real, Real -> Boolean ;
        ">"   : Real, Real -> Boolean ;
        "<="  : Real, Real -> Boolean ;
        ">="  : Real, Real -> Boolean ;
Endnewtype Real
```

2. Subranges of Integer type with the following declaration:

```
Syntype Mytype=Integer
     Constants First : Last ;
Endsyntype Mytype ;
```

According to SDL semantics the behaviour of the subrange type is the same as the behaviour of the Integer type with the only difference that during the assignment of a value to subrange type variable (and in some other special cases) the range check of the value is performed.

3. Enumerated type with the following declaration:

```
Newtype Mytype
     Literals Lit1, Lit2, Lit3 ... ;
Endnewtype Mytype ;
```

For these types only the following equality relations are defined:

```
"="   : Mytype, Mytype -> Boolean ;
"/="  : Mytype, Mytype -> Boolean ;
```

4. Records (structs) with fields of any type mentioned above:

```
Newtype Mytype
     Struct
        Field1  Type1;
        Field2  Type2; ...
Endnewtype Mytype
```

5. Arrays with integer subscripts and values of any type mentioned above (including structs):

```
Newtype Mytype
     Array (Type1, Type2)
Endnewtype Mytype;
```

Here Type1 - type of index, Type2 - type of value.

Ground types corresponding to the introduced SDL types will be described in Section 2.3.

Statements of textual part

Along with type declarations textual part may also contain the following statements.

1. Procedure heading which is the first statement in every procedure specifying its name and describing its formal parameters:

```
Procedure Myproc
      Fpar
          In       Parameter1  Type1, ...
          In/Out   Parameter2  Type2, ...
```

Types Type1, Type2... must be defined outside the procedure or must be predefined.

2. Declarations of variables:

```
DCL
    Var1  Type1,
    Var2  Type2 ... ;
```

In the case of embedded procedures usual visibility rules are valid.

Statements of graphic part

1. Procedure start:

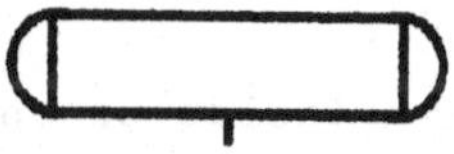

2. Procedure termination:

3. Assignment statement:

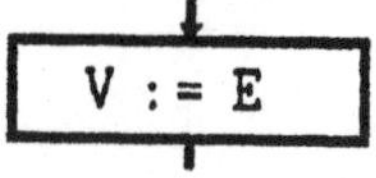

Here V is either name of variable, element of array A(I), structure element S!F or element of array of structures S(I)!F. Symbol E denotes expression of appropriate type in the usual sense.

4. Decision statement:

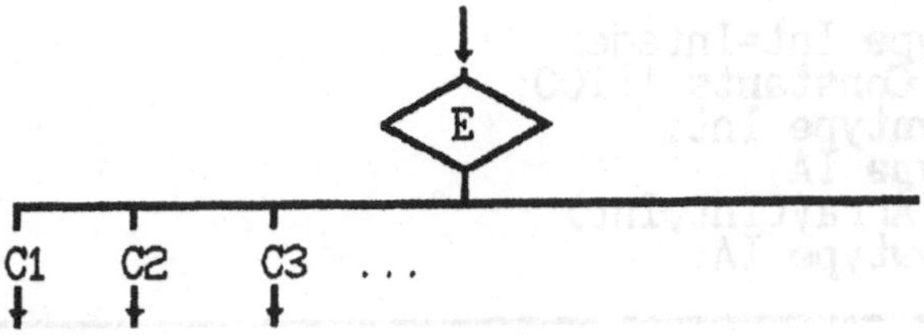

where E is expression of scalar type (except Real) and C1,C2,C3 ... - constants of the same type.

5. Procedure call:

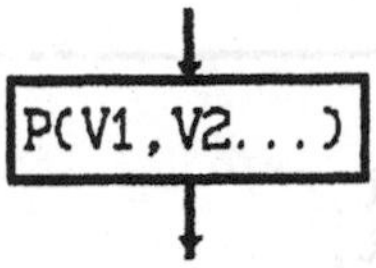

where P - name of procedure; V1, V2 ... - variables or expressions of appropriate type.

Example of Sequential Program

Let us consider a program FIND [19] which is often used to demonstrate different techniques of verification and testing.

Input of the program FIND is integer array A, its length N and some integer F. The purpose of the program is to find the element of array A whose value is F-th in the order of magnitude and to rearrange the array in such a way that this element is placed in A(F) and, furthermore, all elements with subscripts lower than F have lesser values and all elements with subscripts greater than F have greater values. Thus on completion of the program the following relationship holds:

A(1), A(2), ... A(F-1) <= A(F) <= A(F+1), ... A(N)

```
Syntype Int=Integer
    Constants 1:100;
Endsyntype Int;
Newtype IA
    Array(Int,Int)
Endnewtype IA;

Procedure Find
    Fpar
       In/Out A   IA,
       In     N   Int,
              F   Int;

    Dcl
           K   Int,
           L   Int,
           I   Int,
           J   Int,
           R   Int,
           W   Int;
```

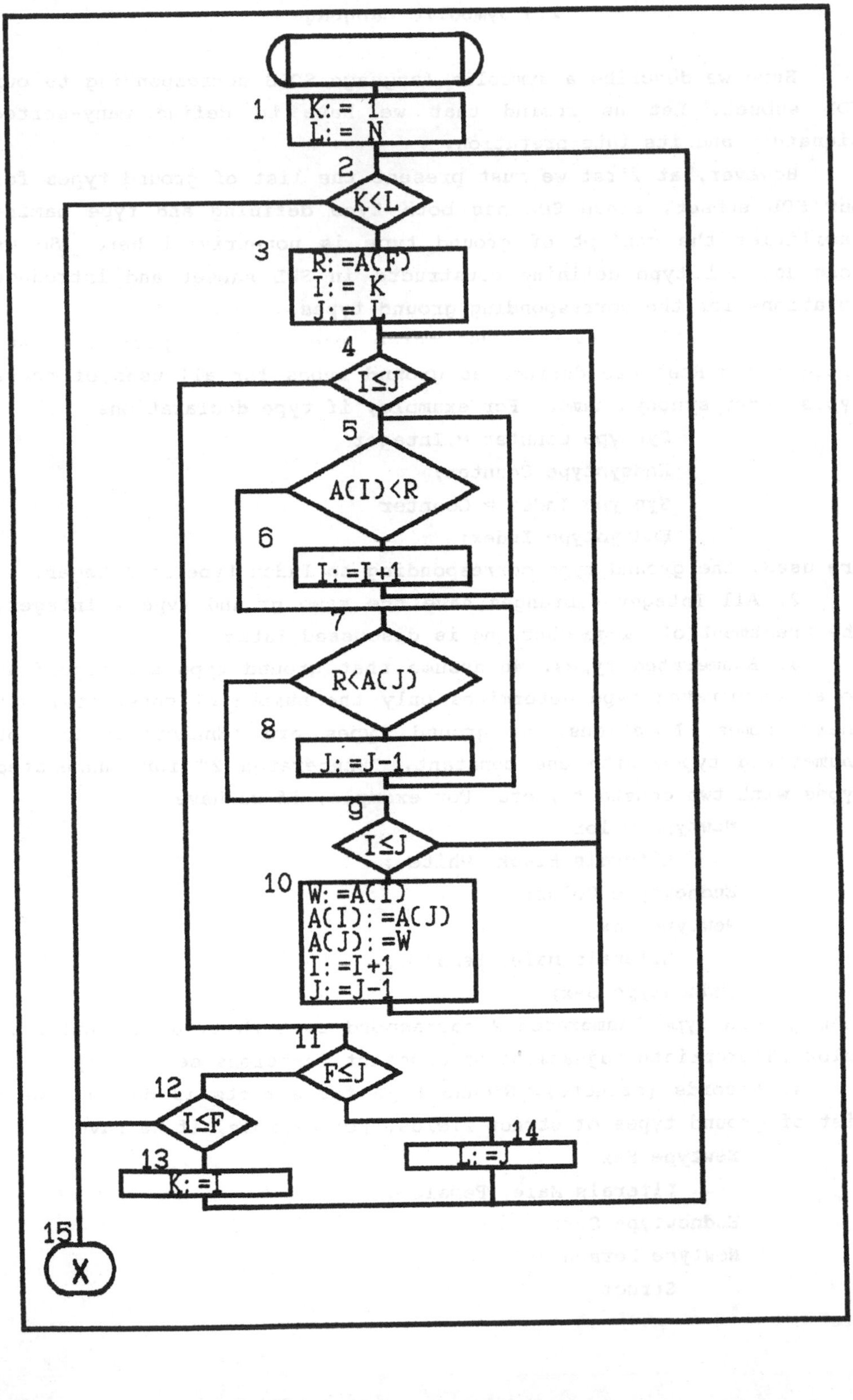
1
K: = 1
L: = N
2
K<L
3
R: =A(F)
I: = K
J: = L
4
I≤J
5
A(I)<R
6
I: =I+1
7
R<A(J)
8
J: =J-1
9
I≤J
10
W: =A(I)
A(I): =A(J)
A(J): =W
I: =I+1
J: =J-1
11
F≤J
12
I≤F
13
K: =I
14
L: =J
15
X

2.3 Symbolic Language

Here we describe a symbolic language SDLS corresponding to our SDL subset. Let us remind that we have to define many-sorted signature and its interpretation.

However, at first we must present the list of ground types for our SDL subset. Since SDL has both type defining and type naming facilities the concept of ground type is non-trivial here. So we consider all type defining constructs in SDL subset and introduce notations for the corresponding ground types.

1. Predefined types. The three predefined types: Boolean, Integer and Real are defined as ground types for all uses of these types under synonym names. For example, if type declarations

```
Syntype Counter = Integer
Endsyntype Counter;
Syntype Index = Counter
Endsyntype Index;
```

are used, the ground type corresponding to Index type is Integer.

2. All Integer subranges have the same ground type - Integer. The treatment of range checking is discussed later.

3. Enumerated types. We assume that ground type corresponding to an enumerated type determines only the number of constants, not their names. Notations for ground types are "Enumerated 1" for enumerated types with one constant, "Enumerated 2" for enumerated types with two constants, etc. For example, if we have

```
Newtype Color
     Literals Black, White ;
Endnewtype Color;
Newtype Sex
     Literals Male, Female ;
Endnewtype Sex;
```

then ground type Enumerated 2 correspond to both type Sex and type Color (Appropriate adjustment of constant functions see later).

4. Records (structs). Ground type for structs is defined as a list of ground types of struct fields. For example, if we have

```
Newtype Sex
     Literals Male, Female ;
Endnewtype Sex;
Newtype Person
     Struct
```

```
        Sex_of_Person  Sex;
        Age_of_Person  Integer ;
    Endnewtype Person;
```

then the ground type corresponding to type Person is Struct (Enumerated 2, Integer).

5. **Arrays.** Ground type for arrays defines the range of index and ground type of components. For example, if we have

```
    Syntype Index=Integer
        Constants 1:100 ;
    Endsyntype Index;
    Newtype Table
        Array(Index, Real)
    Endnewtype Table;
```

then the ground type of Table is Array(1:100, Real).

This completes the list of ground types (cf. $T_1, T_2, \ldots$ in 2.1). Domains corresponding to ground types follow straightforwardly from the language definition so they are discussed no more.

Now let us introduce function symbols of SDLS signature. The interpretation is described only for those functions where it is not obvious. Function symbols mainly are based on the operators introduced in our programming language (+, -, =, /=,...), and they use the same infix notation. However, most of the operators in our language are overloaded (i.e., defined for various data types simultaneously). Therefore SDLS contains derived function symbols for each of the ground types. So we have functions +, -, mod, =, /=... for Integer type; ¬, &, ∨, $=_{Boolean}$, $/=_{Boolean}$ for Boolean type and $+_{Real}$, $-_{Real}$, $=_{Real}$, $/=_{Real}$,... for Real type.

Four new groups of function symbols are introduced for complex data types (arrays and structs). They are based on functions used in SDL semantics definition.

1. Functions of extraction of value of array element $extract_T(a,i)$, where T - ground type of array as described above. These functions have array as the first argument and array index as the second one. Function yields value of corresponding array element.

2. Functions of modification of array $modify_T(a,i,v)$, where T - ground type of array, a - array, i- index of element and v- new value of element. Function yields a new array differing from the array a in the modified element i.

3. Functions of extraction of value of structure element

$extract_T(s,i)$. Functions yield the i-th element in structure s.

4. Functions of modification of structure element $modify_T(s,i,v)$. Functions yield a new structure with the value of the i-th element set to v.

In order to describe array operations adequately we assume that the first argument (array) of the function $modify_T$ can assume both values from the domain determined by type T and special value Undef of type T_0. (We could be completely formal in this case and introduce an auxiliary function $Undefarray_T$: T_0--> T, but this would make array expressions more awkward). Thus the interpretation of $modify_T$ is extended in a natural way, so that, e.g., the term
$extract_{Array(1:10,Integer)}(Modify_{Array(1:10,Integer)}(Undef,1,3),1)$,
has value 3.

The domain of modify function for structs is extended in a similar way.

The signature of SDLS also contain functions with zero arguments or constants. The same notations for constants as in SDL are used (of course, excluding overloading by means of ground type postfixes). So, e.g., the signature contains constants 1,2,3,... for Integer type, True and False for Boolean type and $1_{Real}, 2_{Real}, 3_{Real}, \ldots$ for Real type. New constant notations are introduced for enumerated types (in accordance with the corresponding ground type definitions). So the type Enumerated 2 has two constants $1_{Enumerated2}$, $2_{Enumerated\ 2}$. Constant notations adopted in SDL are used for arrays and structs, for example, $(.1,2,3.)_{Array(1:3,Integer)}$ or $(.1,18.)_{Struct(Enumerated2,Integer)}$.

This concludes the definition of the symbolic language SDLS. Unfortunately, terms in this language look very lengthy. For example, if we use data types from the program FIND, a correct term would be $extract_{Array(1:100,Integer)}(A,F)$. To make terms more readable we introduce a new notation system called the <u>derived</u> symbolic language. In this language as function and constant postfixes we do not use ground type notations but corresponding type names from the program declarations. So the beforementioned term in the derived symbolic language is $extract_{IA}(A,F)$. This is no more a correct term in the signature of SDLS, since there is no function $extract_{IA}$ in it and it can't be introduced unambiguously because identifier IA can designate various types in different programs. However, if we consider pairs <type declarations in program, term in derived language>, evidently there is an algorithm yielding an equivalent term in SDLS for such a pair. For this reason we use the derived language without any special indication.

2.4 Algorithm of Symbolic Execution of Program Path

The aim of symbolic execution of program path is to obtain correct symbolic state.

Assume that a program path is given. In the case of procedure call program path contains also the corresponding sequence of statements of the called procedure. We shall show how to build symbolic state traversing the given path statement by statement.

Procedure Start

If symbolic execution begins with the given procedure, then variables - input parameters are assigned terms consisting of single variable, namely, the parameter itself. The rest of procedure variables are assigned undefined values (i.e., term Undef). The path condition is assigned term True.

If, on the contrary, we have reached this statement from other procedure, then, according to the range of accessibility of variable names, those pairs of variables are determined whose values are the same in the caller procedure and in this one. Formal parameters are assigned the same symbolic values as actual parameters in the caller procedure have (or terms formed by call statement). Local variables are assigned Undef values.

In both cases, if some of the input parameters are of subrange type, we also add (by means of & function) appropriate range checking predicate (such as N >= 1 & N <= 100) to the path condition.

Assignment Statement

The execution of assignment statement consists of value extraction of expression operands, calculation of value of expression and, the last, assignment of calculated value to the variable located in the lefthand side of the statement.

1. Extraction of values.

Due to the correspondence of names and values within the system of symbolic values of current symbolic state we find symbolic values of variables contained in the righthand side of the statement.

If the considered variable is an element of array or record (struct), then we must form a new term using functional symbols of extract type. We also add predicates to the path condition to ensure that the range of indexes for the array is not violated.

For constants contained in the righthand side their ground types are determined (according to SDL typing rules for expressions) and the corresponding constant denotations are found.

2. Calculation of value of expression.

Taking previously obtained operand terms and functional symbols associated with corresponding operations (with correct type postfixes found) we construct a new term. If any of the operands has Undef as symbolic value, the resulting term is also Undef.

3. Assignment of value.

If the lefthand side of the statement contains scalar variable (or whole array), then the latter is assigned the newly obtained term in the system of symbolic values. If the variable is of subrange type, we add range checking predicate to the path condition, too.

If, on the contrary, the lefthand side contains array or record element, then the term of the modified value is constructed by means of modify function and this new value is assigned to the corresponding variable (i.e., array or record) in the system of symbolic values. We also enhance the path condition to ensure that the range of indexes is not violated.

Procedure Call

Here we remind that program path contains also corresponding sequences of statements of called procedures, and we permit only calls of procedures whose texts are available.

Therefore the next statement of the path is procedure start statement of the called procedure, and the given statement will be executed when we determine the binding of actual and formal parameters of procedure statement. If actual parameter is an expression, the corresponding term is formed as in assignment statement.

Decision Statement

As in the case of assignment statement we extract values of operands (terms) and construct the resulting term. If its type is Boolean, then such decision statement is called If statement, otherwise, Case statement.

In case of If, if the path proceeds along True-exit, the newly constructed term (simultaneously it is also a predicate term) is added to the path condition by means of & function. If the path proceeds along False-exit, we form negation of the previous term by means of ¬ function and add it to the path condition.

In the case of Case a new predicate term is constructed by the help of function = (equality) with the above mentioned term as the first argument, but the second argument is the constant assigned to the corresponding exit of the statement in the program. This last predicate term is added to the path condition.

Procedure Exit

Local variables of the procedure are removed from the system of symbolic values.

This concludes the definition of symbolic execution. It remains to formulate the following assertion:

The symbolic execution defined in this section is correct for SDL subset described in Section 2.2.

The proof of this assertion is a little bit lengthy and is left to very patient readers.

We just note that formally correctness refers only to the basic form of symbolic language. As far as this form can be uniquely restored from the derived form and program declarations the derived form is also correct in some sense and henceforth only this form is used (sometimes omitting type qualifiers for owerloaded functions at all, if they can be uniquely restored from the context).

Simplifier of Symbolic State

Whenever a new term is assigned to any variable or a new predicate is added to path condition we try to simplify this symbolic value or path condition. Our simplifier is rather primitive and is mainly designed to find and calculate constant subterms in expressions. The simplifier is able to perform the following transformations:

1. Find out and calculate numerical and enumerated subterms composed of constants. Term ((1+x)+1)+1, for example, is reduced to x+3.

2. Find out and calculate subterms composed of array-type constants. Simplify array-type terms according to the following rules:

$extract_T(modify_T(A,i,x),i) \rightarrow x$

$modify_T(modify_T(A,i,x),i,y) \rightarrow modify_T(A,i,y)$

If i /= j then $extract_T(modify_T(A,i,x),j) \rightarrow extract_T(A,j)$

. . .

Here T - type of array; A - array-type term; i,j,x,y - scalar terms.

3. Simplify record-type terms the same way as arrays.

4. Reduce predicate terms to normal form. We define the normal form as conjunction P_1 & P_2 & ... P_n. Here P_i - elementary relations in form E op F , where E and F are numerical (enumerated) type terms and op is one of the operations =, /=, >, ... Our normal form is a special case of the conjunctive normal form and, of course, arbitrary predicate term can't be reduced to such a form. Nevertheless, in order to simplify material presentation, we discuss predicate terms only in normal form.

5. Simplify elementary relations (i.e., E > F & E < F -> False).

6. Calculate constant predicate terms (i.e., P & False -> False).

It should be noted that in this section we give only examples of simplification rules, not a complete list of them.

2.5 Example of Symbolic Execution of Program Path

Here we do not analyze particular methods of program path selection, although one of them actually is used to select program paths to be executed (the fundamental principle is to proceed along those feasible branches having been selected less frequently; in the case of several equal variants a generator of pseudo random numbers is used).

We apply symbolic execution to the program FIND mentioned in Section 2.2, namely, to path :

(1,2,3,4,5,6,5,7,9,10,4,5,7,8,7,9,4,11,14,2,3,4,5,6,5,7,
9,10,4,11,12,15).

After symbolic execution of procedure start statement the symbolic state is as follows:

System of symbolic values	Path condition
A = A	N >= 1 & N <= 100 &
N = N	F >= 1 & F <= 100 &
F = F	$extract_{IA}$(A,1) >= 1 &
K = undef	$extract_{IA}$(A,1) <= 100 &
L = undef	. . .
I = undef	$extract_{IA}$(A,100) >= 1 &
J = undef	$extract_{IA}$(A,100) <= 100
R = undef	
W = undef	

Parameters of the procedure are assigned terms consisting of single term variable, all other program variables are assigned undef term and the path condition consists of range checking predicates. Further for the sake of brevity we demonstrate only changes of symbolic state. If some term can be simplified by our simplifier, we show the result of the simplification (especially it refers to the range checking predicates).

After statement 1 (K:=1; L:=N) the symbolic state is changed as follows:

System of symbolic values	Path condition
K = 1	No changes
L = N	

After statement 2 (If K<L true exit):

No changes	1 < N

After statement 3 (R:=A(F); I:=K; J:=L):

R = $extract_{IA}$(A,F)	No changes
I = 1	
J = N	

After statement 4 (I<=J true exit):

no changes	no changes (1 <= N is reduced by simplifier)

We conclude the example by showing the symbolic state at the end of the given path. We use the following shorthand denotation:
$B = \text{modify}_{IA}(\text{modify}_{IA}(A,2,\text{extract}_{IA}(A,N)),N,\text{extract}_{IA}(A,2))$
The resulting symbolic state is as follows:

System of symbolic values

$A = \text{modify}_{IA}(\text{modify}_{IA}(B,2,\text{extract}_{IA}(B,N-2),$
$\quad N-2,\text{extract}_{IA}(B,2))$
$N = N$
$F = F$
$K = 1$
$L = N-2$
$I = 3$
$J = N-3$
$R = \text{extract}_{IA}(B,F)$
$W = \text{extract}_{IA}(B,2)$

Path condition

$\text{extract}_{IA}(A,1) < \text{extract}_{IA}(A,F)$ &
$\text{extract}_{IA}(A,2) >= \text{extract}_{IA}(A,F)$ &
$\text{extract}_{IA}(A,F) >= \text{extract}_{IA}(A,N)$ &
$4 <= N$ &
$\text{extract}_{IA}(A,3) >= \text{extract}_{IA}(B,F)$ &
$\text{extract}_{IA}(B,F) < \text{extract}_{IA}(B,N-1)$ &
$\text{extract}_{IA}(B,F) >= \text{extract}_{IA}(B,N-1)$ &
$5 > N$ &
$F <= N-2$ &
$\text{extract}_{IA}(A,1) < \text{extract}_{IA}(B,F)$ &
$\text{extract}_{IA}(A,N) >= \text{extract}_{IA}(B,F)$ &
$\text{extract}_{IA}(B,F) >= \text{extract}_{IA}(B,N-2)$ &
$F > N - 3$ &
$3 > F$

2.6 Method for Solving Path Conditions

In the result of the symbolic execution of program path we obtain path condition $PC(x_1 \ldots x_n)$, where x_i - scalar, array or record type variable. In order to find a test case which forces this path to be executed we must solve PC as a system of equalities (inequalities). The fact that PC is reduced to normal form is irrelevant for our solution algorithm; it is used only to simplify the explanation.

Before we begin solving the path condition we, first, free it from variables and functions of record type. It can be done easily because we can assume that record fields are independent variables or arrays (if array of records). Next we separate the given path condition into independent components $PC(x_1 \ldots x_n) = P_1(x_1 \ldots x_l)$ & $P_2(x_{l+1} \ldots x_j)$ & ..., where P_k and P_l have no common variables. After that we begin to solve these independent components.

Our method (see method of segments in [22]) is in fact exhaustive search algorithm which is improved by a number of heuristics. These heuristics are based on the study of real-life programs and are proved to be useful in test generation systems [10,22].

First let us sketch pure exhaustive search algorithm:

```
1 Procedure Resolve(P:Path_condition);
2    Select X - any variable or element of array in P;
3    For C := all possible values of X do
4        Q := P with X fixed to C;
5        Simplify Q;
6        If Q = True
7           Then System solved;
8        If Q /= True & Q /= False
9           Then Resolve(Q);
10   End
11 End Resolve;
```

To fix the value of X to C in step 4 we simply replace X by constant C or, in the case when X is an element of array (i.e., A(I)), we replace A by modify(A,I,X). In step 5 the above described simplification procedure is used to determine how successful our fixations were.

This algorithm, of course, can solve any path condition, but it is extremely impractical. After the improvements the algorithm becomes much faster, but it is not able to solve some very complex path conditions. Nevertheless, inability to solve some path condition is not dangerous for test generation system. It may lead (and even then not always) only to test systems with lower quality.

We discuss heuristics related to the three steps of the given algorithm.

First, in step 2 we select the next variable to be fixed. In practice the sequence in which we fix variables is very important for the speed-up of algorithm [8].

Second, in step 3 we try all possible values of the given variable. Yet, most of these values are not useful a priori [10].

Third, when values are fixed in step 3, first of all we must try those values that are more likely to be solutions of path condition.

Let us discuss these three heuristics separately.

Selection of Next Variable

The following criteria are used to select the next variable to be fixed:

1. Select only scalar variables or elements of arrays that are addressed in path condition with constant index (i.e., if path condition contains extract(A,5), then we are allowed to fix A(5)). It is easy to see that this criterion can never lead us to a situation when none of the variables can be selected.

2. If criterion 1 leaves some freedom for selection, we find in path condition the elementary relation containing the least number of variables and we fix one of these variables (according to criterion 1). It allows us to simplify the path condition as early as possible.

3. If criterion 2 also leaves some freedom, we select a variable with the smallest set of admissible values (see below).

Set of Admissible Values

With every variable in path condition we associate a set of admissible values, namely, some segment [a,b], such that no value outside the segment can act as solution of the given path condition. We do not worry if some value inside the segment can never be solution of the system, but we are interested to keep these segments as small as possible.

For Boolean and Enumerated variables we discuss only two types of sets of admissible values: "any value (no limitations)" and "only one value C admitted". Further these sets of admissible values we call segments.

Before we begin to solve the path condition we find initial segments of variables. After fixation of every new value we revise them. First, we can set up initial segments according to the declaration of variable (for example, if the variable is a subrange). Second, a very valuable source of information is the user of the test generation system. Single remark, such as: "I am interested only in the case when all variables are less than 10", can significantly improve the performance. Third, the source of initial segments can be input/output formats, the use of variable in some language constructs, etc.

The most interesting procedure of our algorithm is reduction of segments with respect to the path condition. The aim of this procedure is to make our segments as small as possible. We apply this procedure any time when a new value of variable is fixed (after step 5). For example, if the current path condition is x+y<z & x>2 and all variables are of integer type with equal segments [1,9], we are able to reduce the segment of x to [3,7], the segment of y to [1,5] and the segment of z to [5,9]. Reduction of segments is based on simple properties of arithmetic operations and relations. For example: "If the segment of x is [a1,a2], the segment of y is [b1,b2] and the value of x+y must be in segment [c1,c2], then the segment of x can be reduced to [max(a1,c1-b1), min(a2,c2-b1)], the segment of y can be reduced to [max(b1,c1-a2),min(b2,c2-a1)] but the value of x+y must be in the segment [max(c1,a1+b1),min(c2,a2+b2)]". Or another example: "If the segment of x is [a1,a2] and path condition contains relation x=b, then the segment of x can be reduced to [b,b]".

With iterative application of these local reductions we can propagate improvements through entire path condition. The algorithm of propagation is not quite trivial and includes some new heuristics for performance improvement, yet we do not discuss it in detail.

Selection of Values

It is possible that even after segment reduction exhaustive search is not useful. For that reason we first try to fix some outstanding values of variable: 1) both ends of segment, 2) those values within the segment that appear in the program text as constants, 3) one arbitrary point between every two values mentioned above. These rules (like our algorithm as a whole) are very simple but they work on real-life programs.

Example of Test Generation

Now we demonstrate how the path condition produced at the end of the previous section can be solved by our methods. It is easy to see that this path condition is only roughly simplified but we do not need a stronger simplifier because our method of segments can take into account all relations between variables.

We begin with the setup of initial segments. According to the declarations, segments of all variables (i.e., N, F and A) are set to [1,100]. The second step is the reduction of segments. During reduction the segment of N is improved to [4,4], the segment of F to [2,2] but segments of A are not significantly improved. Now we must fix a value of one of the variables. It was suggested that scalar variables must be fixed first, so we can fix N to 4 (no choice).

Next we perform the simplification and the reduction of segments once more. Then, the same way, we fix F to 2 and after just another simplification and reduction of segments get the following results:

Path condition:

$extract_{IA}(A,1) < extract_{IA}(A,2)$

$extract_{IA}(A,1) < extract_{IA}(A,4)$

$extract_{IA}(A,2) >= extract_{IA}(A,4)$

$extract_{IA}(A,3) > extract_{IA}(A,4)$

Segments:

$extract_{IA}(A,1)$ [1,98]

$extract_{IA}(A,2)$ [2,100]

$extract_{IA}(A,3)$ [3,100]

$extract_{IA}(A,4)$ [2,99]

Now one element of A is to be fixed. All elements are accessed with constant indexes and three of them have segments of equal size (i.e., 1-st, 3-rd and 4-th). Let us assume that we select the 3-rd element at random and fix it to 3 (the left end of the segment). This time the following reduction of segments is not trivial, nevertheless, it is very successful:

$extract_{IA}$(A,1)   [1,1]
$extract_{IA}$(A,2)   [2,100]
$extract_{IA}$(A,4)   [2,2]

So we proceed until the system is solved. It should be noted that during the solution of this system we are never forced to step back and fix a variable repeatedly. The resulting test is as follows:

A = (.1,2,3,2.)
N = 4
F = 2

If one tries to build a test for the same path manually, he probably will get a slightly different array A = (.1,4,3,2.) and will expect the procedure FIND to exchange the 2-nd and the 4-th elements. The test we have built is not so natural but it shows a significant drawback of the procedure FIND - although input array has been already partially sorted the procedure wastes time to exchange equal elements of the array.

Our path selection method coupled with the above mentioned test generation algorithm produce the following set of tests:

A = (.1,2,3,2.)	A = (.1.)	A = (.1,3,2,4.)
N = 4	N = 1	N = 4
F = 2	F = 1	F = 2

2.7 Abstract Data Types and Symbolic Execution

So far we have considered only programs with predefined data types. As we know, when new data types are introduced in SDL, their semantics is specified by means of axioms. So let some new types $t_1,t_2,\ldots$ with new operators $o_1,o_2,\ldots$ of some fixed signatures be given. The new operators are just included in the definition of symbolic functional term. (Now the formal definition of symbolic execution language changes for program to program even for the basic form of the language). The main problem is how to cope with a widened class of terms while simplifying symbolic values and solving path conditions. So we request axioms for new types and operators to be respecified as term rewriting system (TRS) rules [23,27]. The TRS should be as good as possible - confluent and terminating.

TRS describing the new types is supplied to the simplifier. As we see from the general description of the simplifier (2.4), its basic action (simplifying arithmetic, logic, array and struct terms) could also be in fact described by means of TRS (though not always with a unique normal form, due to commutative rules). So the new and basic rules are merged together making a single TRS for both old and new types. So the simplifier tries to simplify any symbolic value of a variable using this TRS as far as possible. Boolean terms in path conditions are simplified in the same way. In this paper we limit ourselves to the case when path conditions involving new types can be simplified by means of TRS to relations containing only predefined types (and boolean True or False in the best case). So the solver is not supposed to find values of new types $t_1, t_2, \ldots$(except for trivial cases: any value and the value which has to be equal to some constant (literal) of new type).

Conditional rules in TRS (like in OBJ2 [24,27]) are also allowed, conditions should contain equalities (or inequalities) for predefined types, in particular, integers. If types and operators are generic, corresponding rules are also considered generic.

Let us consider an example: a new type queue of integers (it is used in a more general manner in Part 3). Let it have literal qnew and operators

```
qadd:integer, queue --> queue
qfirst: queue --> integer
qrest: queue --> queue.
```

Then a standard form of TRS for this queue would be

```
qfirst (qadd (x, qnew)) --> x
qfirst (qadd (x1, qadd (x2, q))) --> qfirst (qadd (x2, q))
qrest (qnew) --> qnew
qrest (qadd (x,qnew)) --> qnew
qrest(qadd(x1,qadd(x2,q)))-->qadd(x1,qrest(qadd(x2,q)))
```

It can be simply deduced from the signatures that x, x1, x2

stand for integers, q for queue.

If we have a program fragment (with variable q1 declared as queue)

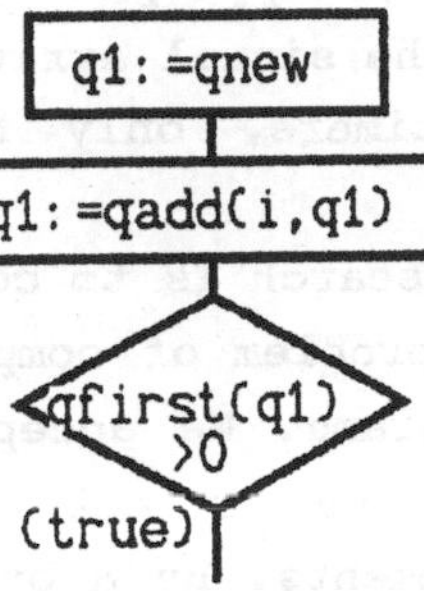

then we have at its symbolic execution:

q1=qnew (after statement1)

q1=qadd (i_1, qnew) (after statement2)

The true exit of the decision yields condition

qfirst (qadd(i_1,qnew))>0

which is reduced by simplifier (using the first rule for queues) to

$i_1>0$

(a condition completely manageable by the solver).

3. Symbolic Execution and Test Generation for Concurrent Programs

3.1 General Principles of Test Generation for Communicating Processes

In this part we consider symbolic execution and automatic test generation for real time programs in the specification language SDL. Our investigations are demonstrated for a subset of SDL including all essential concepts of the language used to describe parallel processes. We consider open systems having one or more channels from environment to system (and possibly some channels to environment). A system can contain one or more blocks, a block can contain one or more processes, procedures are also permitted. Dynamic creation of process instances is not included and all signals are assumed to be sent via channels and signalroutes. Each process is assumed to have only one instance, interprocess communication is solely by signals, viewing/revealing and export/import are not considered. We also don't consider enabling conditions and continuous signals.

A test for an SDL system is a completely ordered sequence of input signals (including their parameter values) sent from environment to system through appropriate channels. If there are timers in the system, also the signal arrival times are fixed in the test (if there are no timers, only the order of signals is significant).

The main goal of our research is to construct complete test set (CTS) for an SDL system. A problem of completeness criterion arises just as for sequential programs. We accept the same criterion C1, nonetheless this time its use is not so obvious, besides, its definition requires some comments. By a branch in an SDL process we understand either an input branch starting from signal input statement or a conventional program branch starting from decision statement (or START statement). A branch ends at nextstate, decision or stop statement. Criterion C1 requires every feasible branch in every process to be executed at least once. Let us remark that sometimes more stringent criteria taking into account the concurrent nature of SDL processes are used, however, there is no such one widely adopted.

All our research in SDL area is demonstrated on a popular protocol example, namely, the sliding window protocol [25,26]. At first we describe the example itself. Then we define the symbolic execution of a path in SDL system (defining at first the path itself in some reasonable way). We explain how to construct and solve path inequalities like in Sections 2.4 - 2.6. A method for constructing (potentially infinite) execution tree similar to ACT used in [14] is given. A heuristic state-based approach to construct CTS using an initial segment of this tree is briefly described, CTS for the sliding window example can be built by means of this approach. To improve the performance of CTS construction algorithms we outline the main ideas of a more sophisticated approach which uses the symbolic execution of separate processes more deeply and allows to construct CTS for this example (and even more realistic protocols) while keeping the search in reasonable limits acceptable for practice.

3.2 Sliding Window Protocol Example

Sliding window protocol is a popular error recovery technique used in many real protocols at data link layer. At first we present its informal description taken from [25].

3.2.1 Overview

The sliding window protocol supports unidirectional message flow from transmitter to receiver with positive acknowledgement sent back on each transfer. Windows are used for flow control in both transmitter and receiver. The protocol operates over a medium which may lose, reorder or corrupt messages and acknowledgements. It is assumed that corruption of messages can be reliably detected by protocol using checksums sent with messages.

3.2.2 Sequence Numbering

The transmitter sends a sequence number with each message. A sequence number is unbounded and is incremented for each new message. The first message transmitted is given sequence number 1.

The receiver sends an Acknowledgement when it receives a message. The Acknowledgement carries a sequence number which refers to the last message successfully transferred to the receiving user. If an Acknowledgement has to be sent before a successful reception (e.g., the first message was corrupted), it is given sequence number 0.

3.2.3 Transmitter Behaviour

The transmitter maintains a window of sequence numbers as shown in Figure 3.1.

This gives the lowest sequence number for which an Acknowledgement is awaited, and the highest sequence number so far used. The window size is limited to the value tws.

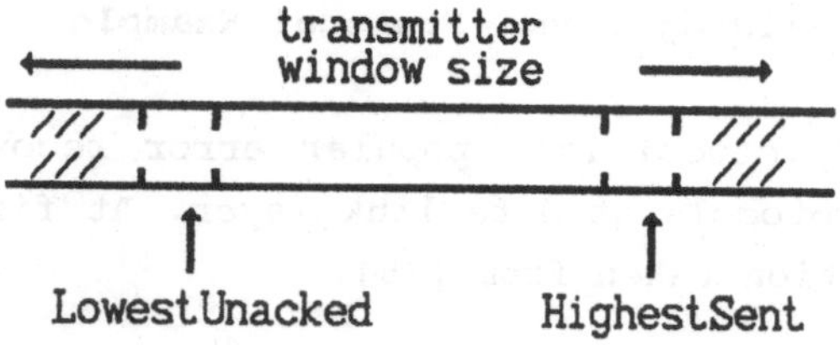

Figure 3.1. Transmitter Window Parameters

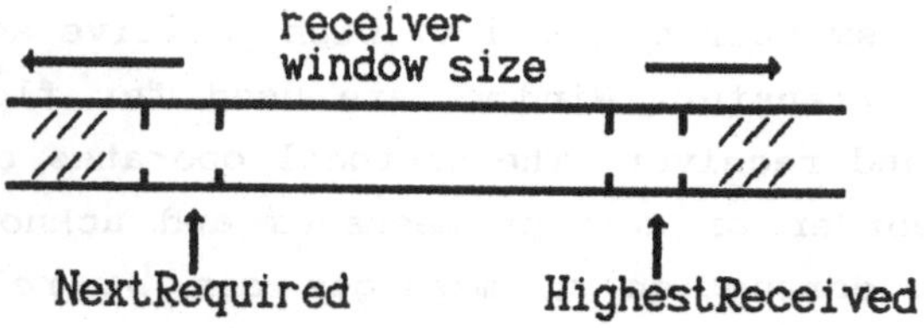

Figure 3.2. Receiver Window Parameters

The transmitter behaves initially as (a) below, and then loops doing (b), (c) and (d) where possible:

(a) LowestUnacked is set to 1 and HighestSent to 0

(b) If the current window size (HighestSent-LowestUnacked+1) is less than tws, then a message with the next sequence number (HighestSent+1) may be transmitted. In this case, HighestSent is incremented, and a timer for that message is started.

(c) If an Acknowledgement is received which is not corrupted and whose sequence number is not less than LowestUnacked, then all timers for messages up to and including that sequence number are cancelled. In this case, LowestUnacked is set to the sequence number following the acknowledged one.

(d) If a time-out occurs, then the timers for all messages transmitted after the timed-out one are cancelled. All these timed-out messages are retransmitted (in sequence, starting with the earliest) and have timers started for them.

3.2.4 Receiver Behaviour

The receiver maintains a window of sequence numbers as shown in Figure 3.2.

This gives the lowest sequence number which is awaited NextRequired and the highest sequence number which has been received. The window size is limited to the value rws.

The receiver behaves initially as (a) below, and then loops doing (b) and (c) where possible.

(a) NextRequired is initialized to 1

(b) If a message is received which is not corrupted, which has not already been received and which lies within the current receive window (NextRequired +rws-1), then all messages from NextRequired up to but not including the first unreceived message are delivered to the receiving user. (There may be no such messages if there is a gap due to misordering). In this case, NextRequired is set the sequence number of the next message to be delivered to the receiving User.

(c) If a message is received under any circumstances, an Acknowledgement giving the last delivered sequence number (NextRequired-1) is returned.

3.2.5 SDL Description of Protocol

SDL description of the protocol is also taken from [25]. Some obvious errors are corrected and medium description is slightly changed to adapt it for testing purposes.

The description consists of three blocks representing sender, receiver and medium. Both protocol user supplying data for sender and user consuming data from receiver are located in the environment. The sending user supplies data via channel ut by signals UDTreq, the receiving one gets data via channel ur by signals UDTind. The sender forms messages from each data unit (signal MDTreq) and passes them to medium via channel mt, acknowledgements (MAKind) are received from medium via the same channel.Conversely, the receiver gets messages from medium (MDTind) and puts acknowledgements (MAKreq) onto it via bidirectional channel mr.

The Sender_entity block contains one process Transmit performing all sending actions. Each message (MDTreq) sent contains the generated sequence number, user data (of some unspecified type Udata) and cyclic range check computed by function dcheck. Data in transmitter window (i.e., sent but not acknowledged) are represented by queue mq, the current window limits are held in variables lu and hs. Time-out management is accomplished by setting indexed timer tim with the corresponding seqno parameter for every message sent (and resetting it when acknowledgement arrives). The timer parameter also shows which timer instance has expired (and which messages are to be resent respectively). The time-out value is some constant delta. When the window contains maximum number of messages, the process enters the second state window_closed.

The receiver_entity block contains one process Receiver. The Next-Required sequence number is held in nr, message data received out of order (within window) are held in the array recbuf, the boolean array already_rec (of the same size) records which messages have arrived (but have not been delivered to the user yet).

The medium block contains processes MsgMan and AckMan managing the message and acknowledgement queues respectively. Message queue actions (normal transfer of message, loss of first message, reordering of messages in queue, corruption of the first message) are controlled by corresponding orders from system tester (signal MsgContr) sent from the environment. We note that in [25] the equivalent signals are generated randomly.

In the case of normal transfer the medium actually performs only signal renaming (from MDTreq to MDTind) while retaining the same parameters. Message corruption is performed by special function corrm. Acknowledgement queue manager performs the same way.

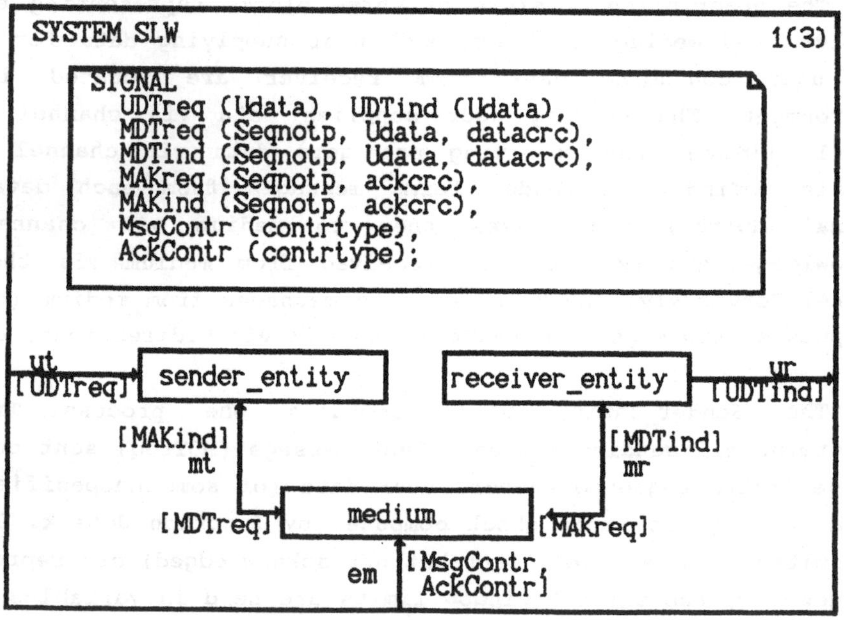

```
SYSTEM SLW                                                    2(3)

NEWTYPE Udata
ENDNEWTYPE Udata;

SYNTYPE Seqnotp=INTEGER
ENDSYNTYPE Seqnotp;

NEWTYPE datacrc
OPERATORS dcheck: Seqnotp, Udata → datacrc
/*builds crc field for a given pair of sequence
number and userdata in data message */
ENDNEWTYPE datacrc;

NEWTYPE ackcrc
 OPERATORS acheck: Seqnotp → ackcrc
/* builds crc field for a sequence number in ack-
nowledgement */
ENDNEWTYPE ackcrc;

NEWTYPE contrtype
  LITERALS norm, lose, reord, corr;
/* tester control options for medium action */
ENDNEWTYPE contrtype;

SYNONYM tws NATURAL = EXTERNAL;
SYNONYM rws NATURAL = EXTERNAL;
SYNONYM delta REAL  = EXTERNAL;
/* external parameters of the system */

 GENERATOR queue (TYPE item);
 LITERALS qnew;
 OPERATORS
       qadd: item, queue → queue;
      qfirst: queue → item;
      qrest: queue →  queue;
      qdelete: integer,queue → queue;
      qreplace: item, queue → queue;
      qempty: queue → BOOLEAN;
AXIOMS
qfirst(qnew)== ERROR!;
qfirst(qadd(x,qnew))== x;
qfirst(qadd(x1,qadd(x2,q)))==qfirst(qadd(x2,q));
qrest(qnew)==qnew;
qrest(qadd(x,qnew))==qnew;
qrest(qadd(x1,qadd(x2,q)))==qadd(x1,qrest(qadd(x2,
                                                 q)));

qempty(qnew);
NOT(qempty(qadd(x,q)));
qdelete(i,q)==IF i=0 THEN q
              ELSE qdelete (i-1,qrest(q))FI;
qreplace(x1,qadd(x2,qnew))==qadd(x1,qnew);
qreplace(x1,qadd(x2,qadd(x3,q)))==
        qadd(x2,qreplace(x1,qadd(x3,q)));
/*replaces the first element of queue by new value*/
 ENDGENERATOR queue;
```

```
SYSTEM SLW                                                    3(3)

  NEWTYPE message
        STRUCT
          seq Seqnotp;
          dat Udata;
          dc datacrc;
  ADDING
  OPERATORS
              corrm: message ⟶  message;
/* message corruption procedure */
   AXIOMS
    NOT (dcExtract!(corrm(m))=dcheck(seqExtract!
          (corrm(m)),datExtract!(corrm(m))));
/* every corruption is reliably detected by dcheck*/
    ENDNEWTYPE message;

 NEWTYPE acknow
      STRUCT
        seq seqnotp;
        ac ackcrc;
 ADDING
 OPERATORS
      corra: acknow ⟶ acknow;
 AXIOMS
  NOT(acExtract!(corra(a))=acheck(seqExtract!
                              (corra(a))));
  ENDNEWTYPE acknow;
SYNTYPE rsn=INTEGER
         CONSTANTS 0:rws-1
         ENDSYNTYPE rsn;
```

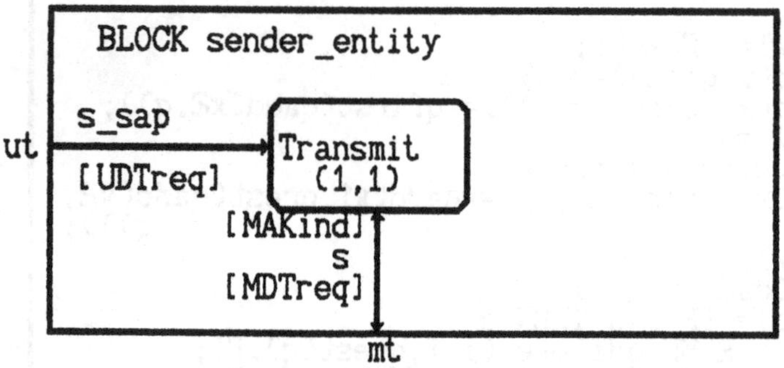

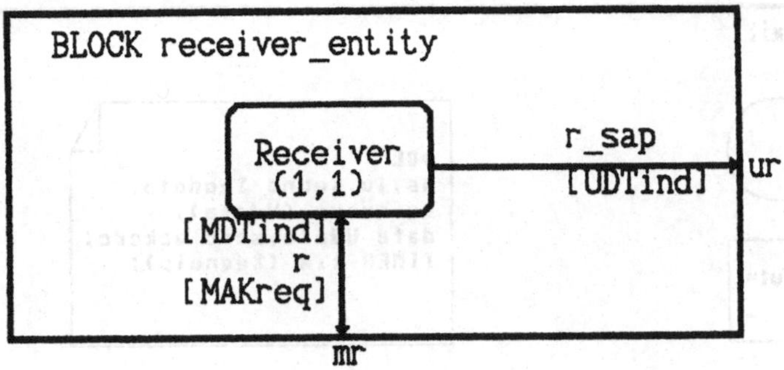
BLOCK receiver_entity
Receiver
(1,1)
r_sap
[UDTind]
ur
[MDTind]
r
[MAKreq]
mr

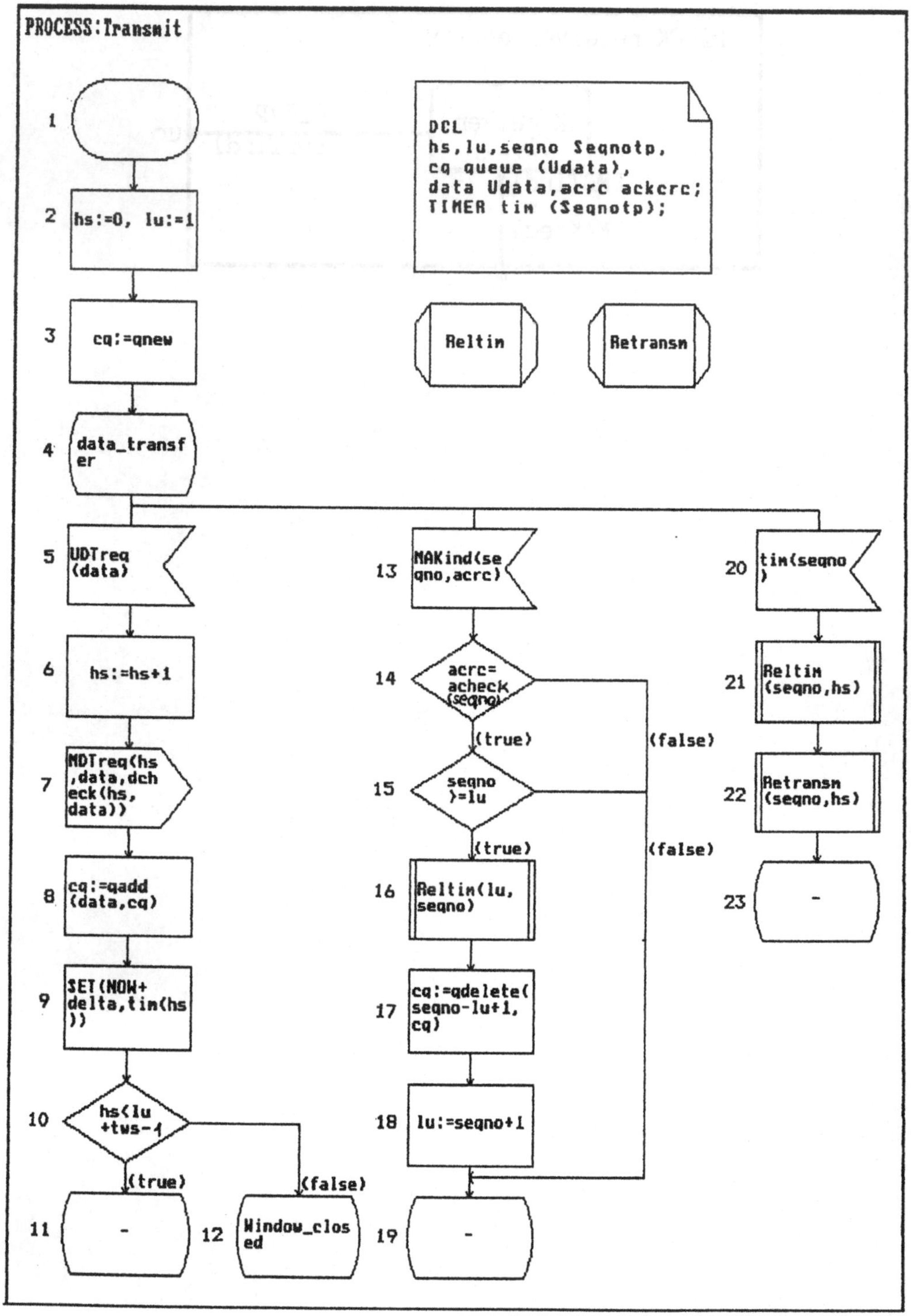
PROCESS:Transmit
DCL
hs,lu,seqno Seqnotp,
cq queue (Udata),
data Udata,acrc ackcrc;
TIMER tim (Seqnotp);
Reltim
Retransm
1
2
hs:=0, lu:=1
3
cq:=qnew
4
data_transfer
5
UDTreq
(data)
6
hs:=hs+1
7
MDTreq(hs
,data,dcheck(hs,
data))
8
cq:=qadd
(data,cq)
9
SET(NOW+
delta,tim(hs
))
10
hs<lu
+tws-1
(true)
(false)
11
-
12
Window_closed
13
MAKind(seqno,acrc)
14
acrc=
acheck
(seqno)
(true)
(false)
15
seqno
>=lu
(true)
(false)
16
Reltim(lu,
seqno)
17
cq:=qdelete(
seqno-lu+1,
cq)
18
lu:=seqno+1
19
-
20
tim(seqno
)
21
Reltim
(seqno,hs)
22
Retransm
(seqno,hs)
23
-

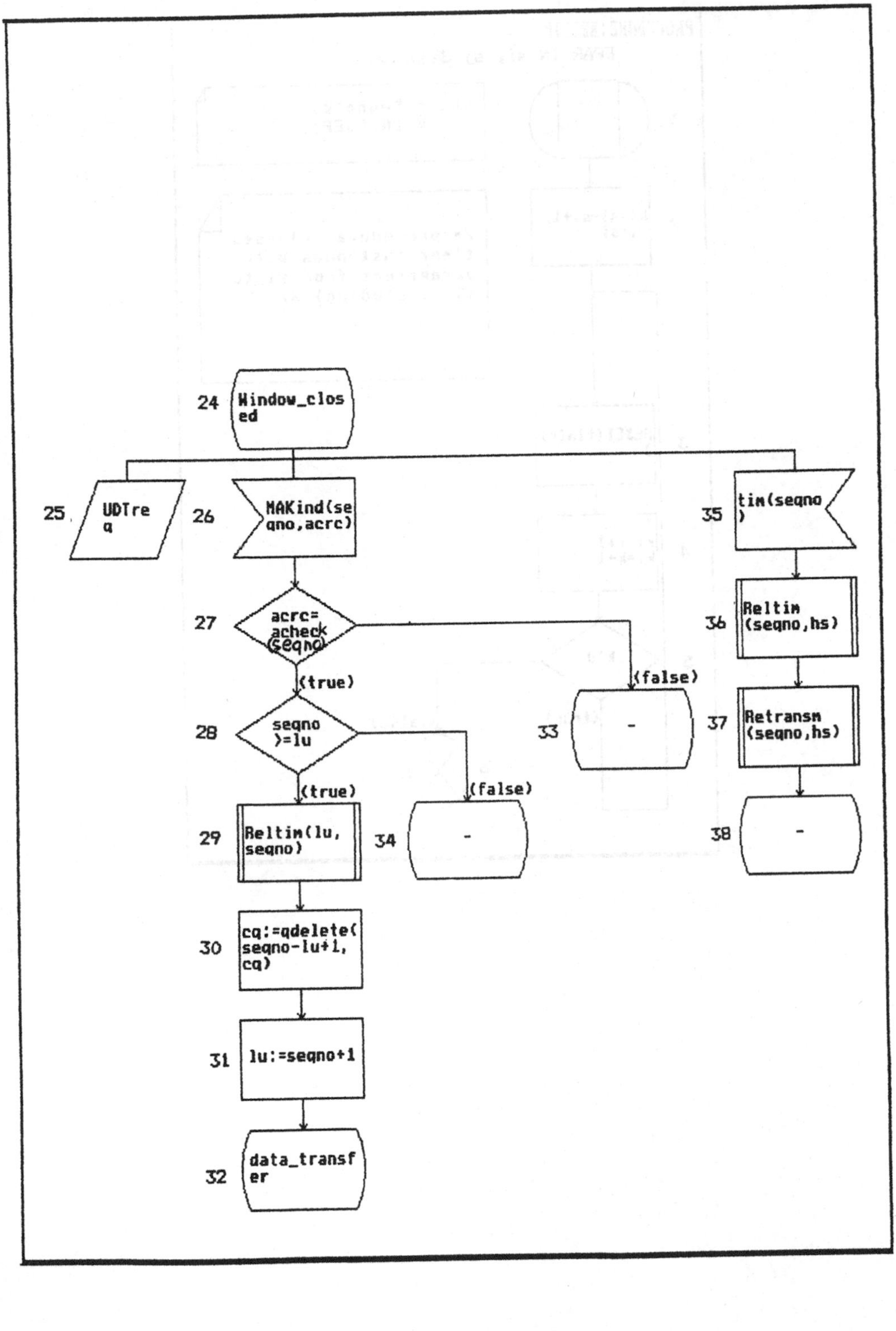

24 Window_closed
25 UDTreq
26 MAKind(seqno,acrc)
27 acrc=acheck(seqno)
(true)
(false)
28 seqno>=lu
(true)
(false)
29 Reltim(lu, seqno)
30 cq:=qdelete(seqno-lu+1, cq)
31 lu:=seqno+1
32 data_transfer
33 -
34 -
35 tim(seqno)
36 Reltim(seqno,hs)
37 Retransm(seqno,hs)
38 -

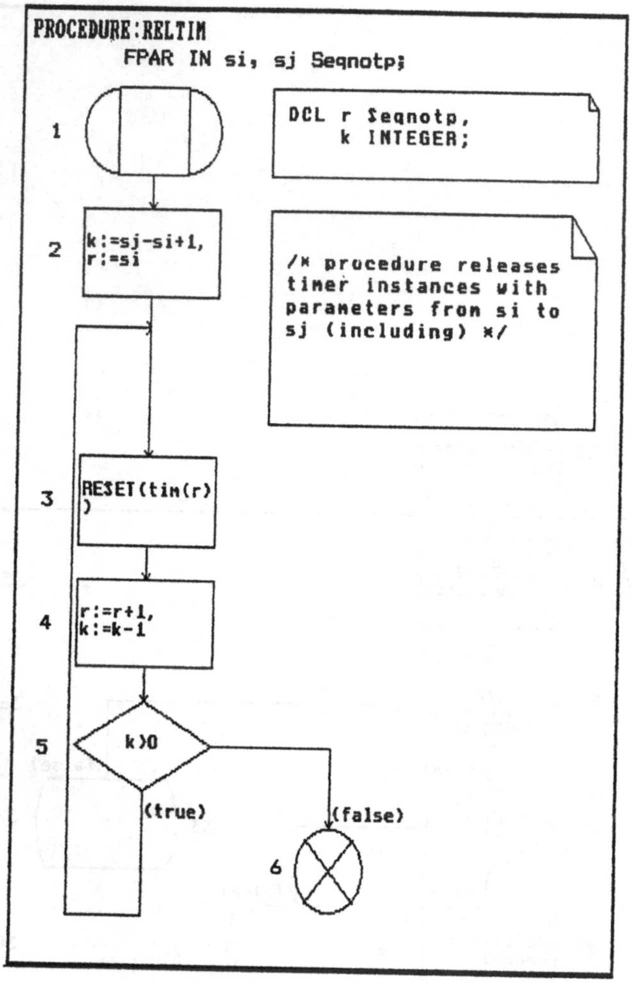
PROCEDURE:RELTIM
FPAR IN si, sj Seqnotp;
DCL r Seqnotp,
k INTEGER;
1
2
k:=sj-si+1,
r:=si
/* procedure releases timer instances with parameters from si to sj (including) */
3
RESET(tim(r))
4
r:=r+1,
k:=k-1
5
k>0
(true)
(false)
6

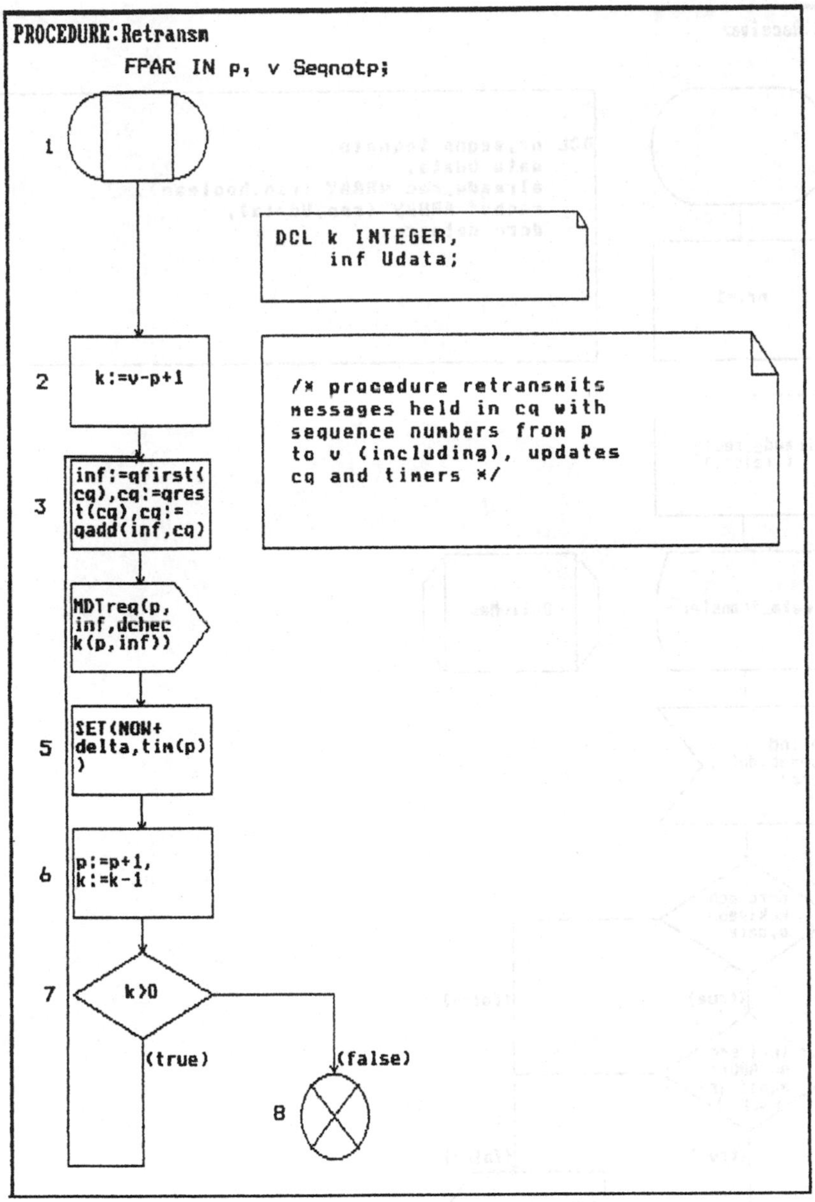
PROCEDURE:Retransm
FPAR IN p, v Seqnotp;
DCL k INTEGER,
inf Udata;
/* procedure retransmits messages held in cq with sequence numbers from p to v (including), updates cq and timers */
1
2
k:=v-p+1
3
inf:=qfirst(cq),cq:=qrest(cq),cq:=qadd(inf,cq)
MDTreq(p,inf,dcheck(p,inf))
5
SET(NOW+delta,tim(p))
6
p:=p+1,
k:=k-1
7
k>0
(true)
(false)
8

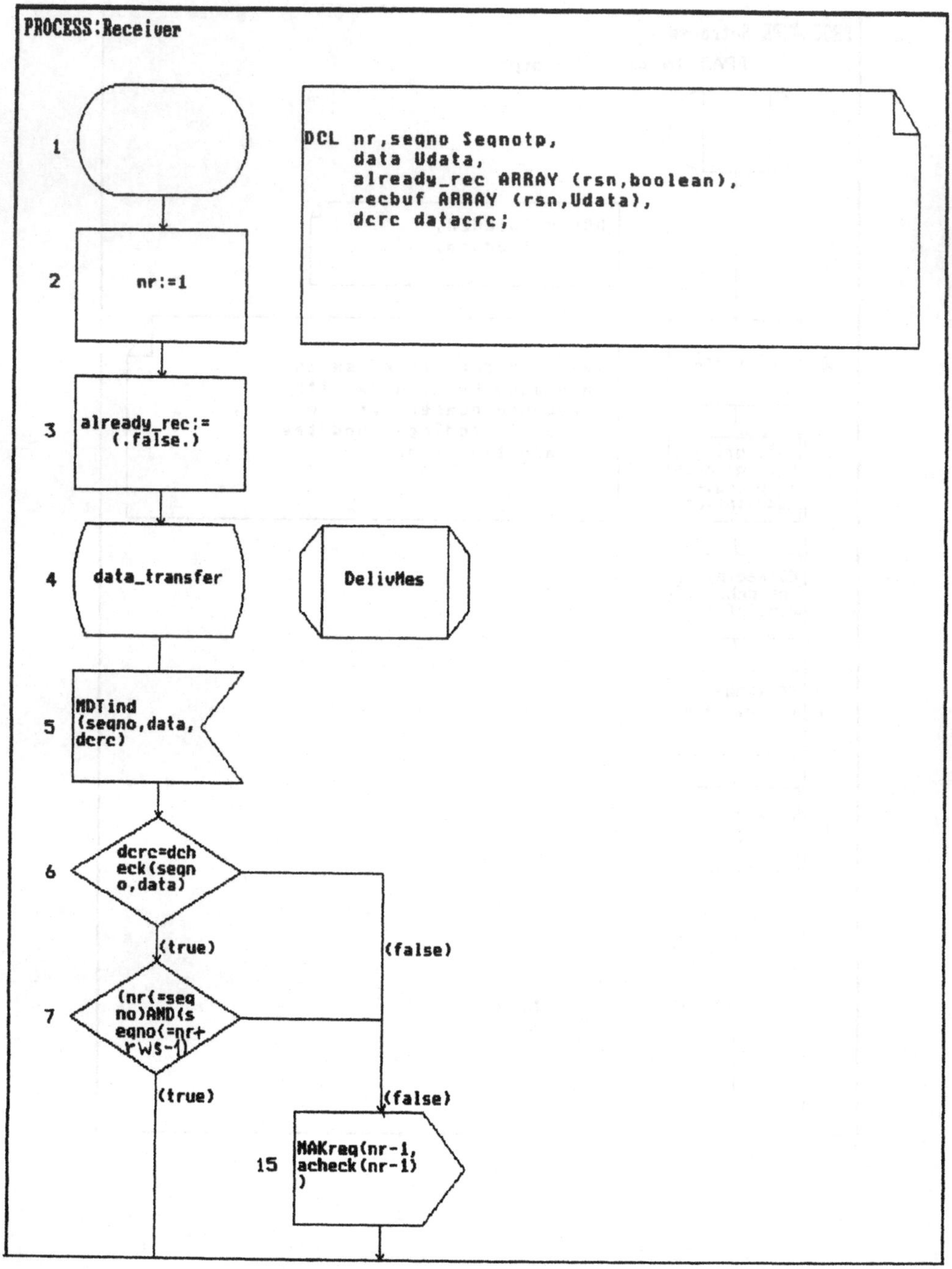
PROCESS:Receiver
1
DCL nr,seqno Seqnotp,
data Udata,
already_rec ARRAY (rsn,boolean),
recbuf ARRAY (rsn,Udata),
dcrc datacrc;
2
nr:=1
3
already_rec:=
(.false.)
4
data_transfer
DelivMes
5
MDTind
(seqno,data,
dcrc)
6
dcrc=dch
eck(seqn
o,data)
(true)
(false)
7
(nr(=seq
no)AND(s
eqno(=nr+
rws-1)
(true)
(false)
15
MAKreq(nr-1,
acheck(nr-1)
)

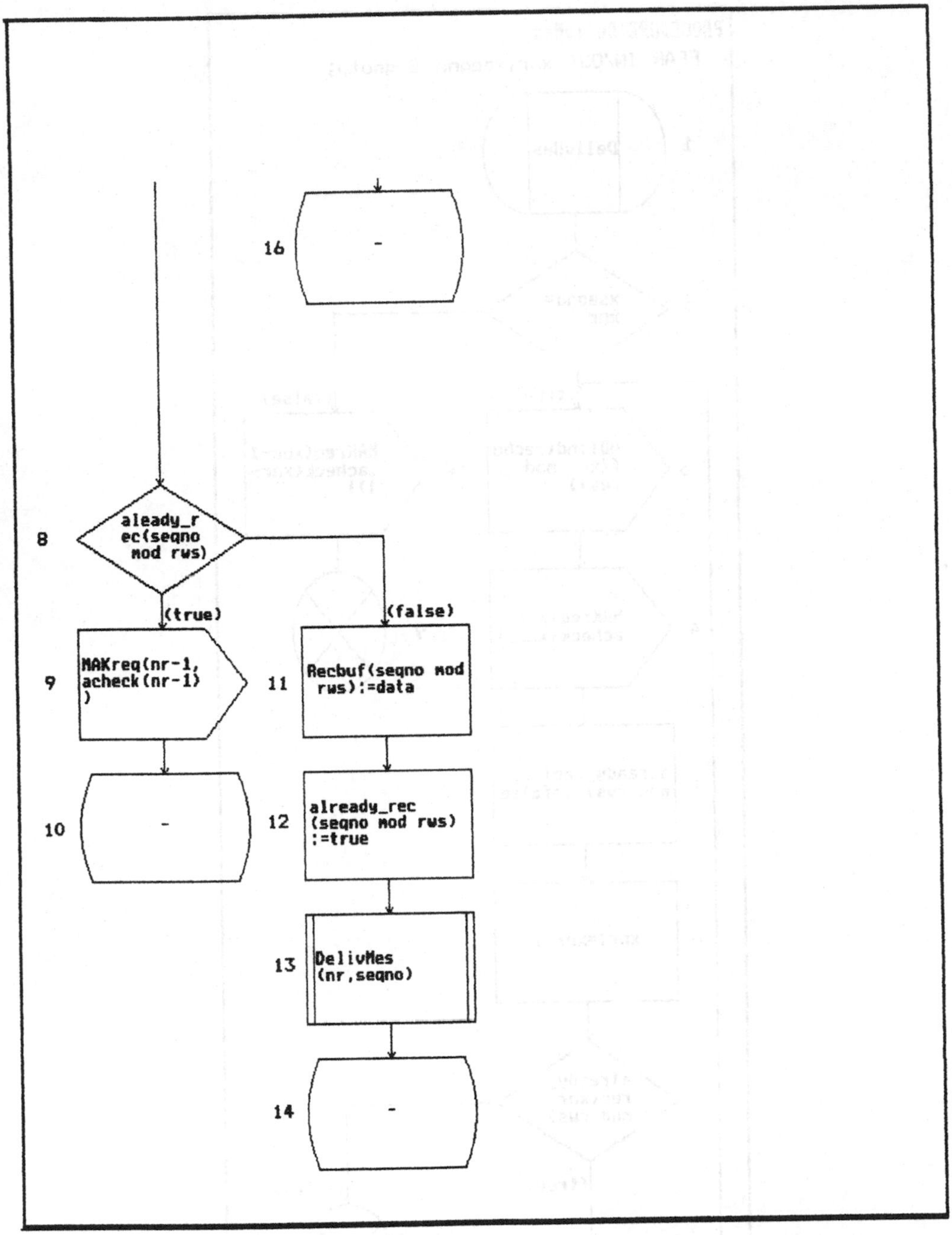
16
-
8
aleady_r
ec(seqno
mod rws)
(true)
(false)
9
MAKreq(nr-1,
acheck(nr-1)
)
11
Recbuf(seqno mod
rws):=data
10
-
12
already_rec
(seqno mod rws)
:=true
13
DelivMes
(nr,seqno)
14
-

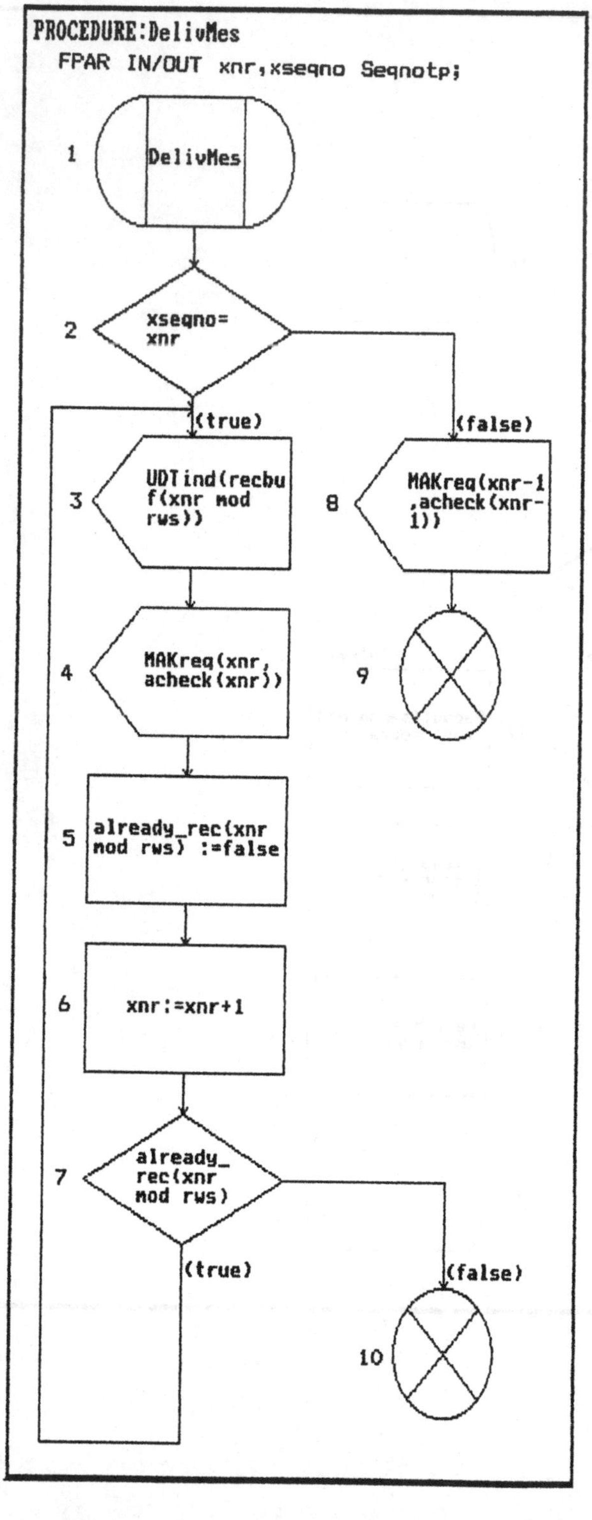
PROCEDURE:DelivMes
FPAR IN/OUT xnr,xseqno Seqnotp;
1
DelivMes
2
xseqno=
xnr
(true)
(false)
3
UDTind(recbu
f(xnr mod
rws))
8
MAKreq(xnr-1
,acheck(xnr-
1))
4
MAKreq(xnr,
acheck(xnr))
9
5
already_rec(xnr
mod rws) :=false
6
xnr:=xnr+1
7
already_
rec(xnr
mod rws)
(true)
(false)
10

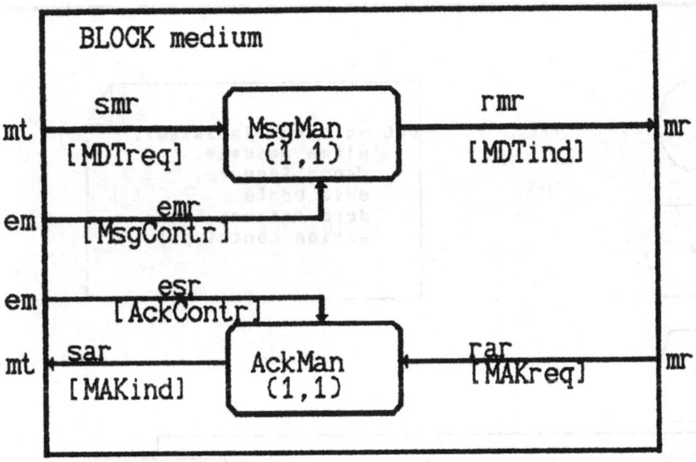
BLOCK medium
mt
smr
[MDTreq]
MsgMan
(1,1)
rmr
[MDTind]
mr
em
emr
[MsgContr]
em
esr
[AckContr]
mt
sar
[MAKind]
AckMan
(1,1)
rar
[MAKreq]
mr

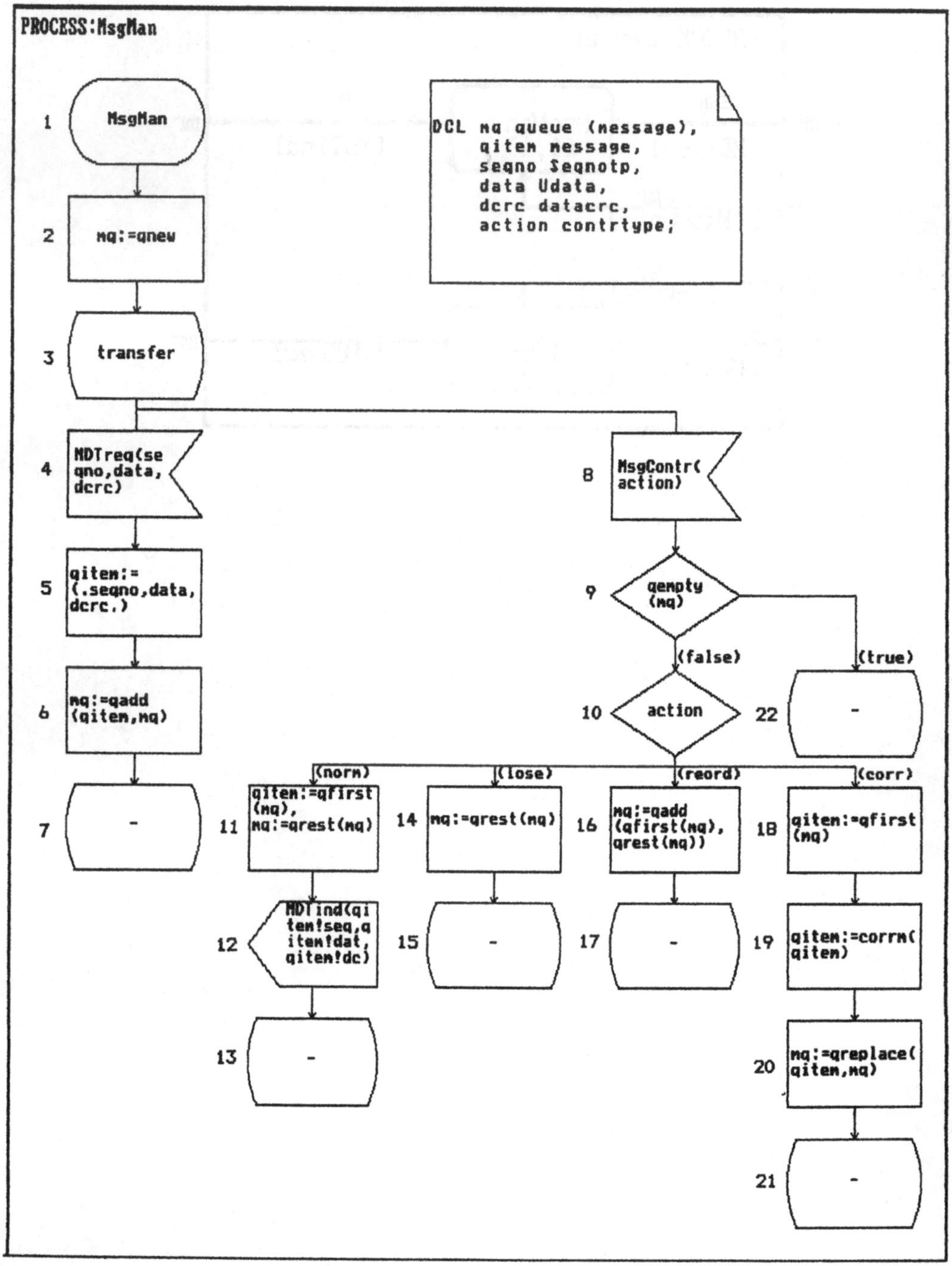
PROCESS:MsgMan
1
MsgMan
DCL mq queue (message),
qitem message,
seqno Seqnotp,
data Udata,
dcrc datacrc,
action contrtype;
2
mq:=qnew
3
transfer
4
MDTreq(seqno,data,dcrc)
8
MsgContr(action)
5
qitem:=(.seqno,data,dcrc.)
9
qempty (mq)
(false)
(true)
6
mq:=qadd (qitem,mq)
10
action
22
-
(norm)
(lose)
(reord)
(corr)
7
-
11
qitem:=qfirst (mq), mq:=qrest(mq)
14
mq:=qrest(mq)
16
mq:=qadd (qfirst(mq), qrest(mq))
18
qitem:=qfirst (mq)
12
MDTind(qitem!seq,qitem!dat,qitem!dc)
15
-
17
-
19
qitem:=corrm(qitem)
13
-
20
mq:=qreplace(qitem,mq)
21
-

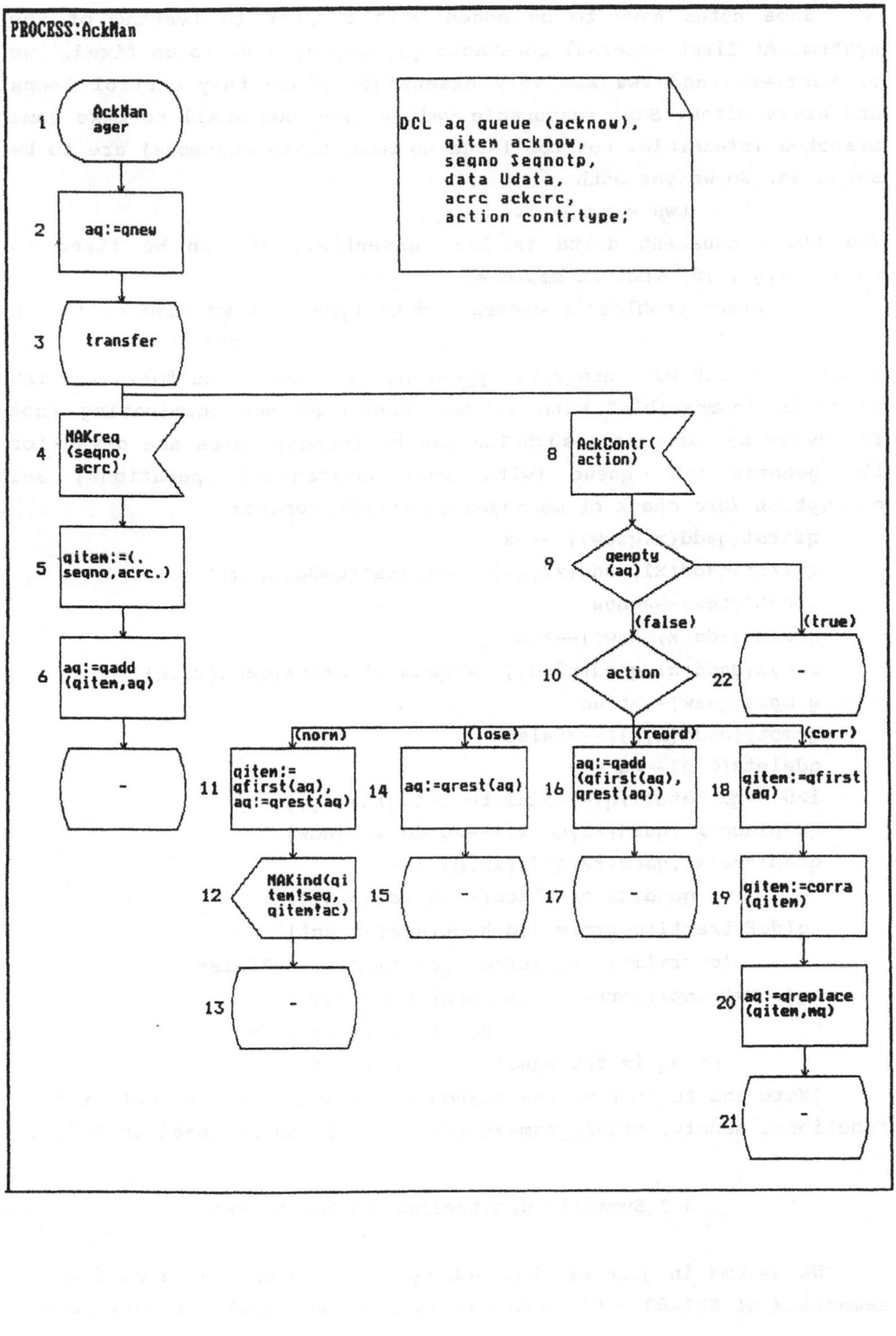

PROCESS:AckMan

1 AckMan ager

2 aq:=qnew

3 transfer

DCL aq queue (acknow),
    qitem acknow,
    seqno Seqnotp,
    data Udata,
    acrc ackcrc,
    action contrtype;

4 NAKreq (seqno, acrc)

5 qitem:=(. seqno,acrc.)

6 aq:=qadd (qitem,aq)

—

8 AckContr(action)

9 qempty (aq)

(false)   (true)

10 action   22 —

(norm)   (lose)   (reord)   (corr)

11 qitem:= qfirst(aq), aq:=qrest(aq)

14 aq:=qrest(aq)

16 aq:=qadd (qfirst(aq), qrest(aq))

18 qitem:=qfirst (aq)

12 NAKind(qi tem!seq, qitem!ac)

15 —

17 —

19 qitem:=corra (qitem)

13 —

20 aq:=qreplace (qitem,nq)

21 —

Some notes have to be added with respect to testing of the system. At first external constants (synonyms) have to be fixed. Two of them:-tws and rws are very essential, since they control loops and array sizes. Some reasonable values (not too small to make some branches infeasible, not too large to make tests enormous) are to be selected. So we set both

tws = rws = 3.

The third constant delta is less essential, it can be fixed to value, e.g., 10, when it matters.

The other problem is abstract data types. As we have explained in 2.7, axioms should be replaced by some TRS to make the simplifier work with new data types. So we present the following TRS which is "compatible" with axioms, confluent and terminating (not for every set of axioms such TRS can be found). Rules are given for the generic type queue (with some nonstandard operations) and corruption /crc check of messages (acknowledgements)

```
qfirst(qadd(x,qnew)) -->x
qfirst(qadd(x1,qadd(x2,q)))-->qfirst(qadd(x2,q))
qrest(qnew)-->qnew
qrest(qadd(x,qnew))-->qnew
qrest(qadd(x1,qadd(x2,q)))-->qadd(x1,qrest(qadd(x2,q)))
qempty(qnew)-->true
qempty(qadd(x,q))-->false
qdelete(0,q)-->q
i>0 =>qdelete(i,q)-->qdelete(i-1,qrest(q))
qreplace(x1,qadd(x2,qnew))-->qadd(x1,qnew)
qreplace(x1,qadd(x2,qadd(x3,q)))-->
          qadd(x2,qreplace(x1,qadd(x3,q)))
eq(dcExtract!(corrm(m)),dcheck(seqExtract!
       (corrm(m)),datExtract!(corrm(m))))-->false
eq(acExtract!(corra(a)),acheck(seqExtract!
                        (corra(a))))-->false
       /* eq is the equality relation */
```

(Here and further we use standard SDL syntax for struct extract functions, namely, <field_name>Extract!, not the one used in 2.3.).

3.3 Semantic Constraints on SDL Subset

We assume in general that SDL system is executing according to semantics of SDL-88 [15]. However, some inessential limitations and changes are introduced to make the description of process of test generation more understandable. These changes are inessential for the example considered and, as we hope, for protocol specification in general.

First, no two events in the whole system are assumed to be simultaneous, thus the events can be completely ordered in time. Actually, we make an even stronger assumption that only one transition from state to state occurs in the whole system at a given moment of time, the transition is always completed before another one takes place.

Second, all SDL actions including signal sending inside the system are assumed to be executing zero time. Thus, if a signal is sent from one process to other (including sending via channel), the receiving process is ready to operate just after the sending process has completed its transition, no time advancement occurs at that operation. Time is advanced only at reception of every signal from environment, and at active timer "firing".

Third, "internal" signals have priority before the signals from environment, i.e., whilst some process queue is nonempty (except the case when all existing signals are saved in the current state), no signal from environment is permitted.

The abovementioned semantic restrictions allow to assume that the whole system is executing under the control of some nondeterministic scheduler, which chooses at random an active process (i.e., a process with nonempty queue containing nonsavable signals) and activates it for one transition.If no process is active, the scheduler allows either an environment signal to arrive or an active timer to "fire" (if there is such). At the very beginning of execution the scheduler activates the initial transitions of all processes one after another.

The semantics considered is very appropriate for test generation and deterministic testing in general. To confirm practical reasonability of it we note that deterministic testing of a protocol specification makes similar assumptions as a rule [13,14]. If there are time-consuming operations in process diagrams (making zero time unrealistic), explicit timing should be introduced. We recommend delay (delta) statement for this purpose (it is in fact a macro call for the following macrodefinition:

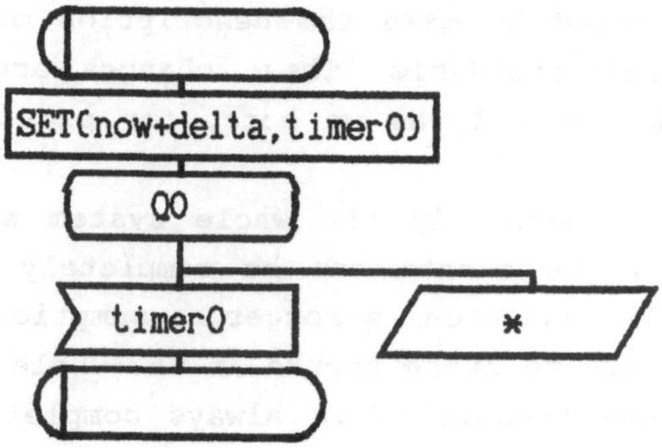

which is completely within our SDL subset.)

Signal propagating delays along "real channels" should actually be described explicitly as testing environment controlled medium description processes in the system (e.g., MsgMan and AckMan processes in our example) in order to make delay dependencies actually testable.

3.4 Symbolic Execution of SDL Programs (many communicating processes)

Now, as we have discussed our semantic restrictions of SDL system behaviour, we can define the symbolic execution of a path in SDL system.

At first we have to explain what is a path in a concurrent system like SDL. We rely strongly on our semantic restrictions and the notion of the nondeterministic scheduler. Informally, a path is a particular execution trace of an SDL system. To be more formal, a <u>path</u> is a sequence of <u>transition</u> <u>segments</u> where each transition segment is a path from state to state (start to state, state to exit) (containing no state inside) in some process. If the path contains a procedure call, a path fragment inside the called procedure body has to follow immediately (separated into several transition segments if states are entered).If transition segments A1,A2,... referring to the same process P are singled out from path, then Ai must lead to the same state Si from which Ai+1 begins. Pseudo - transition segments (save for an environment signal, implicit transition, i.e., signal consumption in a state where it is not awaited) are also admitted in the path where they are possible according to SDL semantics. Some additional choices refining the path will be described in the course of symbolic execution.

If the order of transition segments in the path were chosen at random, it might be highly probable that SDL semantics were violated, e.g., consumption of a signal would be required when no signal has been sent to the process. Therefore the notion of an admissible path is introduced. Informally an <u>admissible path</u> is one which complies with finite automata properties of SDL semantics and the scheduling principles described above, e.g., a signal can be consumed only if there is such in the corresponding queue, a timer can "fire" only after it has been set, etc. The admissibility of a path can be checked formally, but this check can be performed only along with the symbolic execution of the path. On the other hand, symbolic execution is defined only for admissible paths. We define a joint procedure for admissibility check and symbolic execution of a given path. The procedure is halted when the path is not admissible. Let us point out that admissibility does not imply feasibility, it is only a prerequisite for it.

Now let us describe the admissibility check and symbolic execution algorithm. The admissibility check is defined in the form of admissibility rules to be applied to the current symbolic state. Let an SDL system S containing processes P1,P2,...,Pn be given and α be a path in S. Two new "implicit" variables Q(P) and T(P) are introduced for every process P, and the symbolic values of these variables are maintained. Informally, Q(P) is the signal queue for process P, and T(P) is its active timer set. Symbolic values of Q(P) are finite sequences of symbolic values of signals denoted as <S1,...,Sk>, values of T(P) are sets of symbolic values of timers {T1,...,Te}.

Let us begin with the description of admissibility check and symbolic execution for SDL systems without timers (as we have mentioned before, the symbolic execution and test generation is simpler in that case). So the variable T(P) will not be used for a while.

Symbolic execution is performed for every SDL statement, while admissibility check is performed only at the beginning of transition segment, i.e., when interpreting its state and input (or save) statements. In the beginning of the algorithm Q(P) are empty for all P, i.e., they contain empty signal sequence < >. Let us assume that α contains transition segments $A_1^{i_1}$, $A_2^{i_2}$, $A_3^{i_3}$,..., from processes Pi_1,Pi_2,Pi_3,..., respectively. For the moment we are interested in initial paths only, so the first admissibility rule is that $A_1^{i_1}, A_2^{i_2}, \ldots, A_n^{i_n}$ must be transition segments corresponding to start transitions (up to the first state) of all processes P1,...,Pn (in an arbitrary order), no other admissibility rules are imposed on start transitions.

Now let us define symbolic execution of SDL statements within a transition segment. Symbolic value system and path conditions are defined just as for sequential subset of SDL considered in Part 2. Symbolic execution of assignment, decision, call and procedure statements is retained just the same way. Let us remind only that each process has its own variables, thus symbolic value system contains symbolic values of variables for each process. As far as there are no input parameters for an SDL system, the only initial symbolic values used are parameter values for signals entering from environment (ENV signals for short). If the i-th instance of ENV signal S with, let's say, two parameters of types T1 and T2 is received, the symbolic values of these parameters are denoted by S_i^1 and S_i^2 (their types T1 and T2 are determined uniquely by the declaration of signal S), the whole symbolic value of signal instance is denoted by $S(S_i^1, S_i^2)$.

Let us define symbolic execution of output statement, for example,

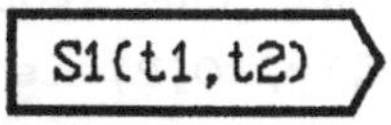

where t1 and t2 are some expressions. Let us assume that we are within transition segment in process P1 and signal S1 is sent to process P2 (signal destination can be determined statically, i.e., from declarations in our subset of SDL). At first expressions t1 and t2 are evaluated symbolically in the context of P1 (i.e., its symbolic variable values are substituted), let the resulting terms be t_1^s and t_2^s . Then the symbolic value of signal $S1(t_1^s, t_2^s)$ is constructed. This value is added to the right end of signal sequence contained in Q(P2). For example, now the symbolic value of Q(P2) might be $<S1(t_3^s, t_4^s), S3, S1(t_1^s, t_2^s)>$, i.e., the signal queue is coded in a normal way, the end of the queue being on the right.

The state (better to say, next state) statement concluding the transition segment has no effect on any symbolic value. There can be no other SDL specific statements within transition segment (except timer management postponed until later and input statement in the beginning of transition, to be considered next).

Now let us consider state and input (and save) statements. At first let us describe the admissibility rules. It follows from our scheduling principle that there can be two different situations in the whole system, namely, the one when queues Q(Pi) are nonempty for some of the processes P_i (and contain signals not saved in the current state) and the other when all queues Q(Pi) are empty (or contain only saved signals). Let us consider the first situation (let us call it "internal input"). If the current transition segment refers to process P1 and starts with state ST1 followed by input of S2, then admissibility rules require the signal S2 to be in the queue Q(P1) ready for consumption. More precisely it means that symbolic value of Q(P1) either has S2 as its first element (i.e., it is of the form < S2(t^s), S3, ...>) or contains S2 preceded only by signals saved in the state ST1 (i.e., the value of Q(P1) is, e.g., <S3,S4,S2(t^s)> where there is "save S3,S4" statement at state ST1). Implicit transition (or, in other words, the deletion of signal) is permitted when the signal in Q(P1) ready to be consumed is neither on input nor save list at state ST1. Let us note also that if several processes have signals in their queues ready for consumption, anyone of them can be selected for the current transition segment (our scheduler was assumed to be nondeterministic). No transition involving ENV signals is permitted in this situation.

Now, if the second situation takes place (we call it "external input"), a transition segment involving ENV signal input should follow. It can be a normal transition segment containing input of ENV signal S for some process P in state ST. There can also be a pseudo transition when ENV signal is saved in the queue Q(P) (if there is save symbol for S at state ST). Let us note that timer transitions are also treated as external input but they will be considered later.

Now let us define symbolic execution of state - input part. State statement has no effect on symbolic execution. Let us consider input statement, for example,

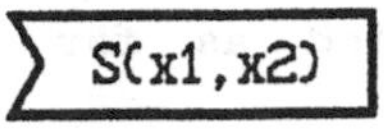

(in state ST in process P).

The symbolic value of the signal is taken (let it be S(t^s_1,t^s_2)), and symbolic values of parameters are assigned to corresponding variables, e.g., x1 assumes symbolic value t_1^s. In the case of "internal input" the symbolic value of signal is obtained from the symbolic value of queue, i.e., the signal instance to be consumed is found in the corresponding signal sequence and after assignment this instance is deleted from the queue. In the case of "external input", as it was described earlier, new symbolic signal value $S(S_i^1, S_i^2)$ is generated (i is the number of instance of signal S sent from the environment). In the case of saving an ENV signal its symbolic value is added to the end of queue; implicit transition means the discarding of symbolic signal value.

Let us remark that generation of symbolic values for queues and signal consumption could be formalized by some TRS (using conditional rules), but we think this would add no clarity to our explanation.

Before proceeding to an example we note that a "very short" form of symbolic language is used to improve readability (type postfixes omitted at all, trivial path conditions from range checks not included).

Let us show an example of symbolic execution of a path in our system SLW. Although actually it is a system with timers, we ignore them for a moment (omitting the setting statement 9). To indicate a path we use numeric labels of statements preceded by the first letter of process name (T for Transmit, R for Receiver, M for MsgMan,A for AckMan). Exits of decision statements are not indicated explicitly (they can be deduced from the next statement label). So, let us consider an initial path
T1,T2,T3,T4,R1,R2,R3,R4,M1,M2,M3,A1,A2,A3,T4,T5,T6,T7,T8,
T10,T11,M3,M4,M5,M6,M7.

The presence of start transitions (T1,T2,T3,T4,...) for all processes in the beginning of the path was required by admissibility rules (certainly, the order is inessential). As initial transitions contain no statements of "genuine SDL", the symbolic execution proceeds the same way as in Part 2.

So we present the symbolic state after the path T1,T2,T3,T4,R1,R2,R3,R4,M1,M2,M3,A1,A2,A3 at once. All symbolic values are shown to be simplified as far as possible by the simplifier described in 2.4

<u>Transmit</u>	<u>Receiver</u>	<u>MsgMan</u>	<u>AckMan</u>
hs=0	nr=1	mq=qnew	aq=qnew
lu=1	already_rec= (.false,false,false.)	qitem=undef	qitem=undef
cq=qnew	Q(Receiver)=<>	action=undef	action=undef
seqno=undef	recbuf=undef	Q(MsgMan)=<>	Q(AckMan)=<>
data=undef			
acrc=undef			
Q(Transmit)=<>			

Path condition: true

Some variables with undef values are not shown.

Statements T4,T5,...T11 form the first nontrivial transition segment (in the process Transmit). It conforms to admissibility rules since all queues are empty and "external input" occurs (namely, ENV signal UDTreq enters). After statement T5 the symbolic value of variable data is updated

$$data = UDTreq_1^1$$

(a new symbolic initial value has been generated, involving the first instance of UDTreq).

Statement T6 also updates one value

hs=1.

Statement T7 updates the queue value of process MsgMan, since channels and routes direct the signal MDTreq to this process

$Q(MsgMan)=<MDTreq(1,UDTreq_1^1,dcheck(1,UDTreq_1^1))>$.

Statement T8 adds the following

$C_q=Qadd(UDTreq_1^1,qnew)$.

Decision statement T10 adds no path condition since its value 1<1+3-1 is reduced to true by simplifier, the "true" exit implicitly assumed in the path is valid. Statement T11 closes the transition by returning to state Data-transfer.

Now let us consider the second transition segment M3,M4,M5,M6,M7. As the queue Q(MsgMan) is nonempty (the other queues being empty), this is the only transition segment permitted by admissibility rules in this situation. The statement M4 updates the values of variables mentioned in this input statement

seqno=1

$data=UDTreq_1^1$

$dcrc=dcheck(1,UDTreq_1^1)$.

Statement M5 forms new struct value

$qitem=(.1,UDTreq_1^1,dcheck(1,UDTreq_1^1))$.

After M6 we have

mq=(qadd((.1,$UDTreq_1^1$,dcheck(1,$UDTreq_1^1$).),qnew).

The final symbolic state after the path is:

<u>Transmit</u>

hs=1
lu=1
cq=qadd($UDTreq_1^1$,qnew)
seqno=undef
data=$UDTreq_1^1$
acrc=undef
Q(Transmit)=<>

<u>MsgMan</u>

mq=qadd((.1,$UDTreq_1^1$,dcheck(1,$UDTreq_1^1$).),qnew)
qitem=(.1,$UDTreq_1^1$,dcheck(1,$UDTreq_1^1$).)
action=undef
Q(MsgMan)=<>

<u>Receiver</u>

nr=1
already_rec=(.false,false,false.)
recbuf=undef
Q(Receiver)=< >

<u>AckMan</u>

aq=qnew
qitem=undef
action=undef
Q(AckMan)=<>

The path condition remains true.

The path occurs to be both admissible and feasible.

Now let us consider the general case when timers are used. In this case the active timer set T(P) is maintained during the symbolic execution for every process P and admissibility rules for timers rely on this set. The initial value of T(P) is empty set {}. Timer instances (or, more precisely, symbolic values of timers) are added to the set by SET statements. The symbolic value of the timer consists of its name followed by the symbolic value of time moment to which the timer is set (and symbolic values of parameters, if there are such), for example, tcon(t^s), tim(t_1^s,1). The set T(P) contains at most one instance of each timer in the process P (in the case of timers with parameters, one instance for each distinct value of parameters).

Admissibility rule for timers says that "timer transition" (i.e., transition starting with timer input) is permitted only in "external input" situation if the corresponding timer instance is in T(P) for process P under consideration. To define the symbolic execution of time involving statements, a new, real valued variable NOW is introduced (one for the whole system). The initial value of NOW is 0, and it contains the symbolic value of system time at every moment (as demanded by SDL semantics).

Basic "reference points" for time counting are times of arrival of ENV signals. Every instance of signal S sent from the environment has associated its symbolic arrival time value S_1^T (i is the instance number just as for initial values of parameters). Values of the form S_1^T (for all ENV signals) play the role of initial symbolic values for time counting. When the input of ENV signal S is executed, the symbolic value of NOW is set to S_1^T. The old symbolic value of NOW (i.e., before the new assignment, let us denote this value by NOWold) is used to add a new inequality

$$NOWold < S_1^T$$

to path condition. The inequality expresses the fact that according to our modifications of SDL semantics a new ENV signal cannot be simultaneous with some previous event in the system. The saving of ENV signal advances NOW in the same way.

For example, if we consider the previous example as a system with timers (in fact, it is such), then after statement T5 the value of NOW is

$$NOW=UDTreq_1^T$$

and the inequality $0<UDTreq_1^T$ is added to path condition (the previous value of NOW was the initial value 0).

Next we consider the symbolic execution of SET statement. This statement has the form SET(t,tim), where t is an expression of type real (as a rule, in the form NOW+t_1, t_1 can also be an expression of type real but often is a constant) and tim is a timer name. At first the symbolic value of t (denoted by t^s) is obtained. Then the symbolic value of timer tim(t^s) is added to T(P), where P is the current process.

If there already is an instance of tim in T(P), the old instance is removed. For a timer with parameters the action is similar. Let us consider SET statement SET(t, tim1(p_1)). At first we assume that expression p_1 can be reduced to some constant C_1(of the corresponding type) when computing its symbolic value p_1^s. Then tim1(C_1) acts in fact as an independent timer. We also assume instances of tim1 in T(P) having the same property that their parameters are reduced to constants. So symbolic value tim1(t^s,C_1) is added to T(P), and, if there is an instance tim1(t'^s; C_1) with the same constant parameter in T(P), the previous one is deleted.Let us return to our example and restore statement T9, omitted at first.

Let us remind that before T9 the value of NOW is $UDTreq_1^T$ and HS=1. Then after statement T9 we have a timer value

tim($UDTreq_1^T$+delta,1)

and T(Transmit) assumes value

{tim($UDTreq_1^T$+delta,1)}.

Now we have to consider the most general case when either the parameter value p_1^s for the timer tim1 to be set cannot be reduced to constant by simplifier or T(P) already contains an instance of tim1 with non-constant parameter. Let us assume the instances of tim1 in T(P) to be

tim1(t_1,q_1), tim1(t_2,q_2),...,tim1(t_k,q_k)

(q_i are symbolic values of the parameter).

In this moment path refinement is done. The following cases are possible here - either the new symbolic value of the parameter p_1^s coincides with one of the existing values, say, q_j, or p_1^s is a new value. Path refinement means an a priori choice of one of the possibilities (it is reasonable to call this choice a path refinement because admissibility of timer transitions later on the path depends on the choice). If the first case is chosen, tim1(t^s,p_1^s) is added to T(P), tim1(t_j,q_j) is removed, and besides that equality

$$p_1^s = q_j$$

is added to path condition. If the second case is chosen, tim1(t^s,p_1^s) is added to T(P) and inequalities

$$p_1^s \neq q_1, \ldots, p_1^s \neq q_k$$

are added to path condition.

The symbolic execution of RESET statement is similar. The corresponding instance of the timer is simply removed from T(P) when the timer has no parameters or all parameters of timer instances (i.e., their symbolic values) can be reduced to a constant. In general case for timer resetting with parameters a similar path refinement is made and corresponding equalities (inequalities) are added to path condition.

The using of timers involves additional timing constraints in path condition. So, when active timer set T(P) is nonempty for at least one of the processes P, additional inequalities are to be added to path condition at ENV signal input. The new symbolic value of NOW (namely, S_i^T if signal S is consumed the i-th time) has to be less than the value of time held in any instance of active timer, so inequalities

$$S_i^T < t_j$$

are added to path condition for symbolic value of time t_j held in any active timer instance in any of $T(P_i)$.

Let us consider an example. We extend the path considered in the previous example (with statement T9 reinserted) the following way:

T1,T2,T3,T4,R1,R2,R3,R4,M1,M2,M3,A1,A2,A3,T4,T5,T6,T7,T8,
T9,T10,T11,M3,M4,M5,M6,M7,T4,T5,T6,T7,T8,T9,T10,T11.

We describe completely the symbolic execution of the second occurrence of T5. We have before it

hs=1

$T(Transmit)=\{tim(UDTreq_1^T+delta,1)\}$

$NOW=UDTreq_1^T$

The execution of T5 gives

$NOW=UDTreq_2^T$

and two new inequalities in the path condition

$UDTreq_1^T<UDTreq_2^T$

$UDTreq_2^T<UDTreq_1^T+delta$

After the second occurrence of T9 we have

$T(Transmit)=\{tim(UDTreq_1^T+delta,1),tim(UDTreq_2^T+delta,2)\}$

The last item to be described is the symbolic execution of timer "firing". In process P the symbolic execution of timer input, i.e., statement

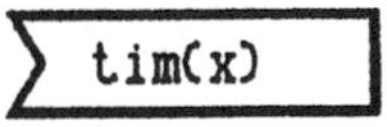

,

invokes the following actions. At first an instance of timer tim is selected in T(P), let it be $tim(t^s,p^s)$ (for timers without parameters, it is the only instance of the timer, its existence is guaranteed by admissibility rules). The act of timer instance selection again is a path refinement. Then the symbolic value of NOW is set to t^s, the selected timer instance is excluded from T(P) and x assumes the value p^s. New inequalities expressing the fact that time is nondecreasing and the timer with the least time value should "fire" the first are added to path condition. So inequalities

$NOWold \le t^s$

and

$t^s \le t_j$

for all symbolic values of time t_j held in any (remaining) active timer instance in any of $T(P_i)$. Inequalities are nonstrong this time because two timers can be set on the same time moment.

Now we give an example of timer "firing" which is the continuation of the previous example with the following two transitions added:

M3,M4,M5,M6,M7,T4,T20,T21,RL1,RL2,RL3,RL4,RL5,
RL3,RL4,RL5,RL6,T22,...

(RL stands for RelTim).

The "internal input" transition M3...M7 is implied by admissibility rules (the queue Q(MsgMan) is nonempty). This occurrence of the transition is similar to the first one and affects only variables in process MsgMan, so it is not described. We start the description with T20. The previous example shows that before it there holds

$NOW=UDTreq^T_2$
$T(Transmit)=\{tim(UDTreq^T_1+delta,1),tim(UDTreq^T_2+delta,2)\}$
$hs=2,$

all queues are empty. So T20 is admissible, we can select the timer instance to "fire". We choose the first one. After the execution of T20 we have

$NOW=UDTreq^T_1+delta$
$T(Transmit)=\{tim(UDTreq^T_2+delta,2)\}$
$seqno=1$

The following inequalities are added to the path condition

$UDTreq^T_2 \le UDTreq^T_1+delta$
$UDTreq^T_1+delta \le UDTreq^T_2+delta$

Just the last inequality shows that our choice of timer instances is the only possible one to obtain a feasible path (and corresponds to reasonable behaviour of timers). Had we selected the second instance, we have had contradicting inequalities in path condition

$UDTreq^T_1 < UDTreq^T_2$ and
$UDTreq^T_2+delta \le UDTreq^T_1+delta,$

the fact obviously noticed by our inequality solver. The next statement T22 calls the procedure RelTim, so after statements RL1,RL2 we have

k=2

r=1

si=1

sj=2,

After RL3

$T(Transmit)=\{tim(UDTreq_2^T+delta,2)\}$

(no instance to reset actually). The path chosen in RelTim is the only feasible one in the given context, after second occurrence of RL3

T(Transmit)={ }

(because r=2 this time). So we can continue the execution, the path occurs to be feasible.

The defined timing inequalities have the property that path condition has a solution with respect to arrival times of ENV signals (i.e., the variables in the form Si_j^T) iff all events along the path can be allocated in time so that they comply with the details of SDL semantics laid out in Section 3.3. We could formulate this result as a theorem, had our description of symbolic execution been more formal.

We conclude this section by one more example, namely, we show the symbolic execution of another extension of the path considered in the first example. So we consider the path

T1,T2,T3,T4,R1,R2,R3,R4,M1,M2,M3,A1,A2,A3,T4,T5,
T6,T7,T8,T9,T10,T11,M3,M4,M5,M6,M7,M3,M8,M9,M10,
M11,M12,M13,R4,R5,R6,R7,R8,R11,R12,R13,D1,D2,D3,
D4,D5,D6,D7,D10,R14,A3,A4,A5,A6,A7,A3,A8,A9,A10,
A11,A12,A13,T4,T13,T14,T15,T16,RL1,RL2,RL3,RL4,RL5,
RL6,T17,T18,T19.

(Prefix D stands for procedure DelivMes, RL for RelTim).
This path corresponds to complete successful sending of one message from transmitter to receiver and successful acknowledgment sending vice versa. Active use of TRS to simplify symbolic values is demonstrated on the path. From the first example we know the symbolic state after M7:

<u>Transmit</u>

hs=1	$T(Transmit)=\{tim(UDTreq_1^T+delta,1)\}$
lu=1	Q(Transmit)=< >
$cq=qadd(UDTreq_1^1,qnew)$	

data=$UDTreq_1^1$
acrc=undef
seqno=undef

<u>MsgMan</u>

mq=qadd((.1,$UDTreq_1^1$,dcheck(1,$UDTreq_1^1$).),qnew)
qitem=(.1,$UDTreq_1^1$,dcheck(1,$UDTreq_1^1$).)
action=undef
T(MsgMan)={ }   Q(MsgMan=< >

<u>Receiver</u>

nr=1
already_rec=(.false,false,false.)
recbuf=undef
T(Receiver)={ }   Q(Receiver)=< >

<u>AckMan</u>

aq=qnew   T(AckMan)={ }
qitem=undef   Q(AckMan)=< >
action=undef

NOW=$UDTreq_1^T$

Path condition

$0<UDTreq_1^T$

External input in M3, M8 is obviously admissible.

We have after it

action = $MsgContr_1^1$

NOW = $MsgContr_1^T$,

path condition is augmented by

$UDTreq_1^T < MsgContr_1^T$

$MsgContr_1^T < UDTreq_1^T + delta$

From M9 with exit "false" we have condition

not(qempty(qadd((.1,$UDTreq_1^1$,dcheck(1,$UDTreq_1^1$).),qnew)),which is obviously reduced by a single TRS rule application to not(false)=true. So the feasibility of the selected path is not violated, no path condition is added.

Statement M10 (with exit norm implied) gives path condition

$MsgContr_1^1$ =Norm

After M11 we have

qitem= qfirst(qadd((.1,$UDTreq_1^1$,dcheck(1,$UDTreq_1^1$).),qnew))

evidently reduced by TRS to

qitem=(.1,$UDTreq_1^1$,dcheck(1,$UDTreq_1^1$).)

(namely the reduced value is fixed in symbolic value system), similarly the new value of mq is reduced to mq=qnew.

Statement M12 augments the queue of Receiver

$Q(Receiver)=<MDTind(1,UDTreq_1^1,dcheck(1,UDTreq_1^1))>$

Further a nonempty queue for Receiver makes R4, R5 be the sole admissible continuation. After R5 we have in Receiver

seqno =1

data =$UDTreq_1^1$

dcrc =$dcheck(1,UDTreq_1^1)$.

The exit true in statement R6 is, in fact, implied ($dcheck(1,UDTreq_1^1)=dcheck(1,UDTreq_1^1)$ is reduced to true by the simplifier).

The chosen exit in the next two statements is also implied, for both

(1<= 1) AND (1<=1+3-1)

and

not(extract((.false,false,false.),1 mod 3))

reduces to true.

Statements R11 and R12 make

recbuf=modify(undef,1,$UDTreq_1^1$)

already_rec=modify((.false,false,false.),1,true)).

In the procedure DelivMes we have after D1

xnr =1

xseqno=1,

which implies the chosen exit of D2 (parameters are in/out, so the changed values are returned to nr, seqno). D3 sends signal

UDTind ($UDTreq_1^1$) to environment.

We can continue the symbolic execution of the path in the same way. All remaining decisions in the path uniquely reduce to true (except one in process AckMan which gives path condition

$AckContr_1^1$=Norm). Admissibility rules uniquely determine the chosen internal transitions.

So we end the path with the following values (only the essential ones are given)

<u>Transmit</u>	<u>MsgMan</u>	<u>Receiver</u>	<u>AckMan</u>
hs=1	mq=qnew	nr=2	aq=qnew
lu=2		already_rec=	
cq=qnew		=(.false,false,false.)	

All sets T and queues Q are empty, NOW=$AckContr_1^T$,

final path condition is

$0<UDTreq_1^T$

$UDTreq_1^T < MsgContr_1^T$

$MsgContr_1^T < UDTreq_1^T + delta$

$MsgContr_1^1 = norm$

$MsgContr_1^T < AckContr_1^T$

$AckContr_1^T < UDTreq_1^T + delta$

$AckContr_1^1 = norm.$

The path is obviously feasible. The path condition requires only the arrival times of three ENV signals to be ordered properly, taking into account also the time-out interval delta. So the following ENV signal sequence UDTreq(data1),MsgContr(norm),AckContr(norm) with arrival times 1,2,3 (if delta is assumed to be, e.g., 10) is a test executing the chosen path (value of data1 is inessential).

So it is easy to ascertain that for every feasible path in the SLW example trivially solvable path conditions can be obtained. Due to this the corresponding ENV signal sequence (with their arrival times fixed) can be generated which actually forces the execution of the path.

3.5 Path Selection for Test Generation - Simple Approach

As we have seen in the previous section, it is logically easy (though a little bit lengthy) to find a test (ENV signal sequence) forcing the execution of a given feasible path. In order to obtain CTS for the system SLW it would be necessary to fix some path selection strategy. However, the paths considered in the previous section show a special feature of the system SLW (and this feature is common to many protocol and similar programs). Namely, the choice of feasible path continuations in decision statements is uniquely determined (i.e., a sole exit is feasible). The only exceptions are decisions relying upon ENV signal parameters. So the only free choice is the choice of ENV signal to be received (including parameters for signals to MsgMan and AckMan). The analysis of timing inequalities show that actually two things are significant - the order of arrival of ENV signals and whether the current ENV signal arrives before the time-out period has expired (for the timer set earliest). So the following choices are available at every "external input" point (in parenthesis the shorthand notation for the choice is presented):

input of UDTreq (U),

input of MsgContr with parameter values norm (MN), lose (ML), reorder (MR), corrupt (MC),

input of AckContr with parameter values norm (AN), lose (AL), reorder (AR), corrupt (AC),

no ENV signal until the timer tim fires (T).

If we fix the ENV input string, the internal behavior of the system (and consequently, the path traversed in process bodies) is uniquely determined. As we have seen in the previous section, admissibility rules sometimes exclude T choice. The possible choices can be summarized in the following potentially infinite tree (if complete symbolic state remains unchanged after the choice, we cut off the tree after the branch). We call this tree an external signal tree (EST) (fig.3.3).

Any feasible branch in process bodies is executed somewhere in the tree. However, there is no good means to find out where exactly the point is in the tree. For example, to execute the branch R8, R9, R10, a path of length 7 in the tree is necessary (this branch seems to be the most "hidden").

As we see, the branching coefficient for the tree is 10 (excluding few first vertices), so direct exhaustive search of nearly 10^6 vertices would not be very efficient. State based theoretical methods from [17] are not directly applicable to the example (because of potentially unlimited queues), thus some heuristic methods are necessary to limit the search.

We outline briefly one such heuristic idea which uses the state notion as in [17], however, in a more heuristic sense. We recall the notions of essential variable and essentially located statement (ELS) introduced in [10,17], Section 3.

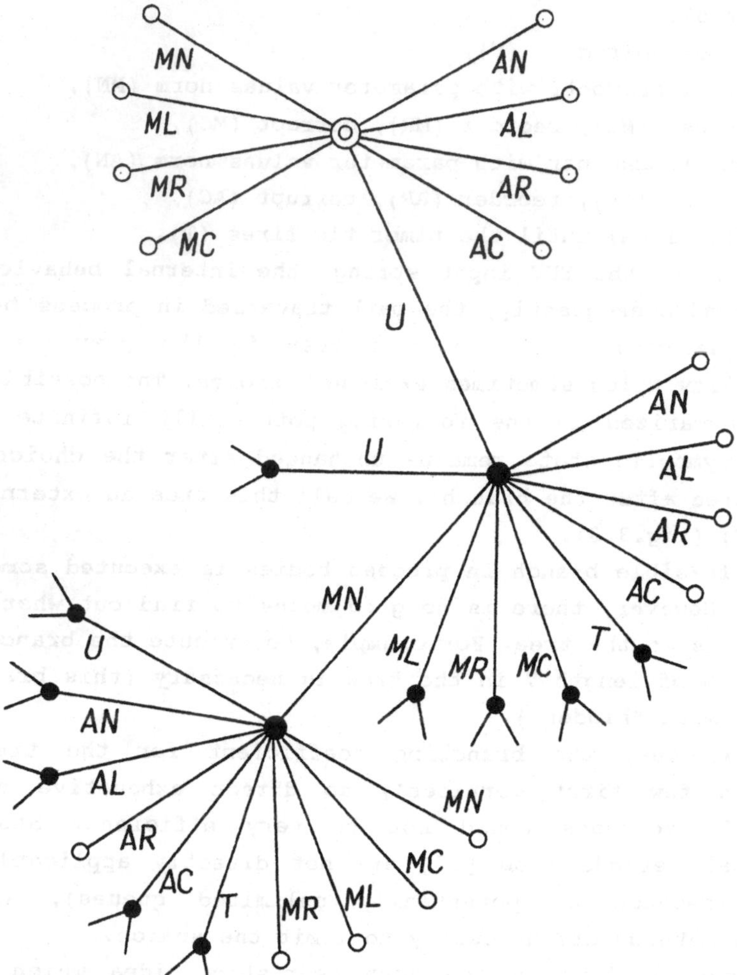

Figure 3.3. External Signal Tree

A comparatively simple analysis shows that there can be no unbounded loops within transition segments in our example. Moreover, only a bounded sequence of "internal" transition segments can follow an ENV signal input or timer firing. So we can choose the inputs of ENV and timer signals as ELS. Thus, essential variables are associated only with transitions corresponding to ENV and timer signals.

So, in a more pragmatic approach , we can say that a variable in a process is essential if it is used in decision statement and is not reassigned from ENV input to its usage in a decision (actually, for SLW example this requirement is equivalent to the formal one used in [17]. The variables affecting path admissibility are also considered essential. As we consider only external inputs as ELS, signal queues are not essential (they are always empty at these inputs), however timer sets are essential. So the following variables occur to be essential in our example: hs, lu, nr, already_rec, mq, aq, T(Transmit). Some additional arguments show that for elements of queues (mq and aq) only the sequence numbers and corrupted/not corrupted property is essential, so these elements can be reduced to pairs (s, 'n'|'c') in our state concept. For timer sets only the sequence numbers held as parameters are essential (the ordering of time moments is implied). So a reduced heuristic state containing only reduced values of essential variables is attached to each node of EST. And, as usually, the tree is cut off at state repetition, however, the finiteness of the set of states is not achieved this way. Some more stringent heuristic cut-off rules can be given, specific to this example, guaranteeing the finiteness of state set (e.g., replacing the counter values hs, lu, nr by some differences in state comparisons and estimating maximum lengths of mq, aq). A simpler heuristic approach is based on fact that all branches actually are reachable for hs, lu, nr and queue lengths not exceeding 4. So the estimated number of EST nodes to be searched for CTS building is approximately 1000 (cutting off nodes with variable values or queue lengths exceeding 4 and stopping the search when all branches have been reached). The introduced state concept actually also supports symbolic execution of each path, so the outlined approach can be used in tools generating CTS (a tool generating CTS for this example could be implemented on IBM PC). Essential variable selection and cut-off rules for states would be user supplied for such tool. The heuristic state approach is practically acceptable for test generation for medium size protocols. A more efficient idea applicable to large systems is outlined in the next section.

To conclude the theme on signal tree we have to mention that EST is similar to asynchronous communication tree (ACT) used in [12,14]. ACT contains also signals from system to environment but our approach allows to find them as well (see signal UDTind in symbolic execution example). So the symbolic execution method allows to construct ACT also for protocols whose functioning depends essentially upon some data processing.

3.6 A More Intelligent Approach to Test Generation

As we have seen in the previous section, CTS can be generated on the basis of symbolic execution approach. However, though there are 34 branches (all feasible) in our example system, the state oriented approach requires considerable search (of ≈1000 states). When a human is asked to generate a test executing some branch he performs, as a rule, some backward search from the specified branch trying to find out gradually some meaningful considerations on input data (signals in our case) finally leading to some test case.

The same idea can also be used for automatic test generation. We outline it briefly on some example. So let us assume we have to generate a test executing branch D7, D3, D4, D5, D6, D7 (in procedure Delivmes in process Receiver). So for a moment we assume the process Receiver with its procedures to form a separate system (with corresponding declarations updated). So the signal MDTind is an ENV signal for the modified system, its parameters are treated as input values.

Now we try to find a feasible path containing the branch D7, D3,... . As one process is in fact a sequential program, heuristic methods from [21] can be applied. The shortest path containing the branch is R1, R2, R3, R4, R5, R6, R7, R8, R11, R12, R13, D1, D2, D3, D4, D5, D6, D7, D3,... , however, this path occurs to be infeasible (during the symbolic execution the solver founds the path condition contradictory). So by some (not described here) reasonable heuristic the next (by length) path is found, namely,

R1,R2,R3,R4,R5,R6,R7,R8,R11,R12,R13,D1,D2,D8,D9,R14,R4,R5,
R6,R7,R8,R11,R12,R13,D1,D2,D3,D4,D5,D6,D7,D3,D4,D5,D6,D7,...

The symbolic execution of the path gives the following path

condition (no timing conditions included, as there are no timers)

$MDTind_1^3$=dcheck($MDTind_1^1$, $MDTind_1^2$)

$1 \le MDTind_1^1$ & $MDTind_1^1 \le 3$

$\neg(MDTind_1^1=1)$

$MDTind_2^3$=dcheck($MDTind_2^1$,$MDTind_2^2$)

$1 \le MDTind_2^1$ & $MDTind_2^1 \le 3$

extract(modify((.false,false,false.),$MDTind_1^1$mod3,true),
$MDTind_2^1$mod3)=false

$MDTind_2^1=1$

extract(modify(modify(modify((.false,false,false.),
$MDTind_1^1$mod3,true),$MDTind_2^1$mod3,true),1,false),2)=true

The solver is able to find from the path condition unique values for numeric parameters of signals: $MDTind_1^1=2$, $MDTind_2^1=1$. The values of two other parameters are bound only by the conditions

$MDTind_1^3$=dcheck($MDTind_1^1$, $MDTind_1^2$) (*)

$MDTind_2^3$=dcheck($MDTind_2^1$, $MDTind_2^2$)

These two conditions can be treated as preconditions for the process Receiver. Thus our solver can be extended so that it can be used not only for finding test values but also for generating preconditions from path conditions (we can also consider this process as a special kind of simplification).

Now we return to the whole system and find out (statically from declarations) that signal MDTind can come only from process MsgMan. Then we consider MsgMan alone in a similar manner with both MDTreq and MsgContr treated as ENV signals. However, this time the aim is different, namely, we have to find a path in MsgMan with the specified postcondition, namely, two instances of MDTind are sent with fixed values of the first parameter 2 and 1 respectively, in addition parameters are bound by (*). Using similar heuristics for path finding, the shortest path is found

M1,M2,M3,M4,M5,M6,M7,M3,M4,M5,M6,M7,M3,M8,M9,M10,M11,M12,
M13,M3,M8,M9,M10,M11,M12,M13,

which satisfies the given postcondition.

The postcondition and path condition from symbolic execution of the path together yield:

$MDTreq_1^1=2$

$MDTreq_2^1=1$

$MDTreq_1^3$=dcheck($MDTreq_1^1$, $MDTreq_1^2$)

$MDTreq_2^3$=dcheck($MDTreq_2^1$, $MDTreq_2^2$)

$MsgContr_1^1$=norm

$MsgContr_2^1$=norm

(see how postconditions are transformed by symbolic execution into preconditions). The order of ENV signals is

$MDTreq_1$,$MDTreq_2$,$MsgContr_1$,$MsgContr_2$ (timing again is unessential). As far as only the last two signals are true ENV signals from the system point of view, the search has to be continued to obtain two input signals MDTreq from Transmit with the first four equalities as postconditions. However similar analysis of Transmit yields the postcondition to be unfeasible - because under no circumstances sequence MDTreq(2,...) MDTreq(1,...) can issue from Transmit. So another path in MsgMan (with another postcondition arising for Transmit) must be found conforming with its own postcondition. The next (by length) path is the path induced by input signals $MDTreq_1$, $MDTreq_2$, $MsgContr_1$(Reord), $MsgContr_2$(Norm), $MsgContr_3$(Norm). This path gives the postcondition for Transmit with the first two equations modified

$MDTreq_1^1$=1

$MDTreq_2^1$=2

(and equations three and four remaining the same).

This is a completely "acceptable" postcondition for Transmit. The corresponding path is induced by (this time true) ENV signals $UDTreq_1$, $UDTreq_2$. So the complete sequence of ENV signals for the system is

$UDTreq_1$, $UDTreq_2$, $MsgContr_1$(Reord), $MsgContr_2$(Norm), $MsgContr_3$(Norm).

(or U, U, MR, MN, MN in terms of EST)

The complete ordering of signals is found substituting intermediate signals by ENV signal sequences generating these signals (likewise nonterminals are substituted by terminals in grammars). Timing conditions remain to be added to specify the test completely (the most stringent of them requesting that arrival times of all ENV signals are less than $UDTreq_1^T$+delta).

The search space for the method outlined is some tens of paths in the example considered (if powerful heuristics is used for path selection in one process). We also note that several branches in the "terminal" process (this time Receiver) can be searched for simultaneously, so reducing the complete search space for CTS even more. So, similarly we can find that ENV signal sequence activating our "champion" branch R8,R9,R10 is (in terms of EST)

U, U, T, ML, MN, ML, MN

Maybe to find the latter path it would be more effective to consider at first Receiver alone and then Transmit and MsgMan together. Our estimate is that some hundreds of paths have to be considered to find CTS, a value completely acceptable for the example. So we hope a tool can be built using the approach outlined constructing CTS for pretty large protocols (and we hope also for large parts of electronic exchanges). However, such a tool would require some methods of reasoning on processes and pre/postconditions not completely formalized here.

We note only that the transformation of path postcondions to its preconditions by means of symbolic execution bears some resemblance to the methods used in program verification.

4 Conclusions

The results in both parts show that automatic test case generation has reached the status where practical implementations yielding acceptable results for programs of considerable size are possible. Certainly, such test generation systems would be complicated enough and will use the precise and heuristic methods described in the paper as well as some other ones. The main problem requiring some additional solutions is the path selection for traversing deeply "hidden" branches. In the theoretical approach the main principle used in path selection was state concept. Its modifications have proved their fitness also in a heuristic setting, however much work remains to be done to select appropriate heuristic state concepts for various classes of programs. One possible approach would be the attachment of formal comments by program authors to guide the automatic system in the right direction.

Acknowledgements

The authors would like to thank Prof. Jānis Bārzdiņš for the setting of the problem and valuable suggestions. They also wish to thank their colleagues at the Software Research and Development Department for help in the preparation of the paper.

References

1. Sauder R.L. General Test Data Generator for COBOL. - AFIPS Conference Proceedings, SJCC, 1962, pp. 317-323.

2. Hanford K.V. Automatic Generation of Test Cases. - IBM Systems Journal, 1970, vol. 9, No. 4, pp. 242-257.

3. Balzer R.M. EXDAMS - Extendable Debugging and Monitoring System. - In: Proc. 1969 SJCC, Montvale, N.Y., 1969, pp. 567-580.

4. Bārzdiņš J.M., Bičevskis J.J., Kalniņš A.A. Construction of Complete Sample Systems for Correctness Testing. - In: Mathematical Foundations of Computer Science, Berlin: Springer, 1975, pp. 1-12.

5. Howden W.E. Methodology for the Generation of Program Test Data. - IEEE Trans. Comput., vol C-24, pp. 554-559.

6. Clarke L.A. A System to Generate Test Data and Symbolically Execute Programs. - IEEE Trans. Software Eng., 1976, vol. SE-2, No. 3, pp. 215-222.

7. King J.C. Symbolic Execution and Program Testing. - CACM, 1976, vol. 19, No. 7, pp. 385-394.

8. Ramamoorthy C.V., Ho S.B.F., Chen W.T. On the Automated Generation of Program Test Data. - IEEE Trans. Software Eng., 1976, vol. SE-2, No. 4, pp. 293-300.

9. Pravilschikov P.A. Test Generation for Programs. - Avtomatika i Telemekhanika, 1977, No. 5, pp. 147-160 (In Russian).

10. Bičevskis J., Borzovs J., Straujums U., Zariņš A., Miller E.F. Jr. SMOTL - a System to Construct Samples for Data Processing Program Debugging. - IEEE Trans. Software Eng., 1979, vol. SE-5, No. 1, pp. 60-66.

11. Pozin B.A. A Method of Structural Test Generation for Programs. - Programmirovanie, 1980, No. 2, pp. 62-69 (In Russian).

12. Hogrefe D. Automatic Generation of Test Cases from SDL

Specifications. - In: SDL Newsletter, 1988, No. 12, pp. 34-52.

13. Kristoffersen F. Conformance Testing Based on SDL Specifications. - In: SDL'89: The Language at Work, North-Holland, 1989, pp. 257-266.

14. Bromstrup L., Hogrefe D. TESDL - Experience with Generating Test Cases from SDL Specifications. - In: SDL'89: The Language at Work, North-Holland, 1989, pp. 267-280.

15. CCITT : Specification and Description Language (SDL). Recommendations Z.100. - CCITT Blue Book, 1988, 199 p.

16. Saracco R., Smith J.R.W., Reed R. Telecommunication Systems Engineering Using SDL. - North-Holland, 1989, 633 p.

17. Auziņš A., Bārzdiņš J., Bičevskis J., Čerāns K., Kalniņš A. Automatic Construction of Test Sets: Theoretical Approach. - This volume.

18. Wirth N. Systematic Programming. - Prentice-Hall, 1973.

19. Hoare C.A.R. Algorithms 65; FIND. - CACM, 1961, vol 4, No. 1, p. 321.

20. Hoare C.A.R. Proof of Programm FIND. - CACM, 1971, vol. 14, No. 1, pp. 39-45.

21. Borzovs J.V., Urtāns G.B., Shimarov V.A. Program Path Selection for Test Generation. - Upravlayuschie Sistemi i Mashini, 1989, No. 6, pp. 29-36 (In Russian).

22. Borzovs J.V., Medvedis I.E., Urtans G.B. The Segment Method for the Solution of Systems of Equalities and Inequalities at Test Generation for Program Validation. - Upravlayuschie Sistemi i Mashini, 1990, No. 2, pp. 49-58 (In Russian).

23. Huet G., Oppen D. Equations and Rewrite Rules: a Survey. - In: Formal Languages: Perspectives and Open Problems, Academic Press, N.Y., 1980.

24. Futatsugi K., Goguen J.A., Jouannaud J.P., Meseguer J. Principles of OBJ'2. - In: Proceedings of Principles of Programming Languages, ACM, 1985.

25. Guidelines for the Application of Estelle, Lotos and SDL, Draft Manual. - CCITT, Geneva, 1988, 347 p.

26. Stenning N.V. A Data Transfer Protocol. - Computer Networks, 1976, No. 1, pp. 99-110.

27. Bergstra J.A., Heering J., Klint P. (ed.) Algebraic Specification. - ACM Press, N.Y., 1989, 397 p..

28. Sato F., Katseryama K., Mizuno T. TENT: Test Sequence Generation Tool for Communication Systems. - In: FORTE'89, Proceedings of 2nd Int. Conf. on Formal Description Techniques, North Holland, 1990, pp. 1-6.

29. Chan W.Y.L., Vuong S.T., Ito M.R. On Test Sequence Generation for Protocols. - In: Proceedings of the IFIP WG 6.1 Nineth Int. Workshop on Protocol Specification, Testing and Verification, 1989, North Holland, 1989.

AGGREGATE APPROACH FOR SPECIFICATION, VALIDATION, SIMULATION AND IMPLEMENTATION OF COMPUTER NETWORK PROTOCOLS

Henrikas Pranevitchius

Kaunas University of Technology

Faculty of Informatics

V.Juro 50, Kaunas, 2330028

Lithuania

ABSTRACT

The application of aggregate approach for the formal description, validation, simulation and implementation of computer networks protocols is considered in the paper. With this approach the above mentioned design stages can be executed using a single mathematical scheme. The method of reachability states is used for the validation of protocol general properties, while individual characteristics are analysed by the invariant method which enables to verify the correctness of the invariant by protocol formal description. Aggregative mathematical schemes are used in the specification languages AGREGAT-84 and ESTELLE/AG applied in creating protocol analysing systems simulation and validation of protocols. Protocol automated implementation method based on the specification language ESTELLE/AG is presented. Formal description and results of alternating -bit protocol validation and simulation as its speciffication in AGREGAT 84 and Estelle/Ag are presented for illustration.

Introduction

The main function of computer networks software is providing interaction of information processes realized in a distributed and, as a rule, non - homogenous mediumm. The main part of this software, namely, detailed system agreement and rules of interaction, realized in computer networks is called the protocol.

Complication and distributed character of protocols increase the probability of errors in protocol design. This concerns semantic errors in particular. Therefore in the process of the design of reliable software for distributed systems a number of measures must be taken to investigate the compliance of the software with the estabilished technical requirements.

A full cycle of protocol design is shown in fig.1. In the first stage,applying generally accepted standards (if such exist), requirements are estabilished and protocol functioning characteristics are determined.

Protocol design stages	Investigation tasks
I. Development of the user's request and the criteria of the protocol functioning effectiveness	
↓	
II. Development of protocol informal specification	
↓	
III. Development of service and protocol formal specification	Validation
↓	↗
IV. Protocol analysis	→ Simulation
↓	
V. Protocol implementation	→ Testing

Fig.1 Basic stages of protocol design.

The second stage is the informal description of the protocol algorithm. In the third stage formal specifications of the service and the protocol are made. In the fourth stage the protocol analysis task is determined. In the last stage protocol programs are worked out.

The chart of protocol design in fig.1 shows that it is desirable to have all the stages of the design based on one protocol specification language.

The paper will present methods of formal description (specification), validation, simulation and programm implementation based on aggregative mathematical schemes.

In the first chapter the architecture of distributed computer systems interaction is presented. The protocol and service concepts are discussed. The requirements for protocol specification languages and protocol validation and verification problems are formulated.

In the second chapter the aggregate definition and the controlling sequences method for the aggregate formal description are presented. The interrelation between protocol specifications, used in validation and simulation, is shown. As an illustration of an alternating-bit protocol aggregative specification as a three - aggregate system is presented. A validation technique of individual properties of protocols by the invariant approach, applying aggregative models for their specification is proposed. The technique comprises the method of forming protocol invariant based on the event representation of protocol functioning and graphs of the symbolic states. The principles of invariant proof and an example of alternating-bit protocol invariant formation are given there too.

Short charasteristics of the protocol-analysing systems for validation and simulation based on the specification languages

AGREGAT-84 and ESTELLE/AG are given. The alternating-bit protocol validation and simulation results are presented.

Alternating-bit protocol specification in the ESTELLE/AG language, which is a further development of the language AGREGAT-84 is presented. Automated protocol implementation technique for the specification language ESTELLE/AG is described. The proposed automated implementation technique determines the components of the protocol programm implementation and their place in the operational system.

1. Methods of Formal Description and Analysis Correctnes of Protocols

The hierarchy principle is one of the main architectural concepts, applied in the development of distributed computer systems. According to this principle every level supplies the next, higher in hierarchy, one with a service (a set of means for the definite functions of the given quality). In its turn, in the process of functioning, every level uses the service of the lower in hierarchy one. The number of services is chosen resulting from the service, supplied by the data transfer means (lower level), demands of the systems applied (service of the higher level) and limitations of the complexity of every level developed.

Model OSI will be considered as an example of level subdivision. The model consists of seven levels. The lower levels - physical, channel and network - supply data transfer service through communication network, the examples of which can be channel switching or package switching networks. The next, transport level, supplies the interaction of data transfer network users. The three higher levels - session, presentation and application are linked with virtualization of operational environment of every computer system. In additation to the universal interaction means these levels supply standard network service (file transmission, remote task starting and control, virtual terminal servicing, electronic mail etc.).

After having subdivided the architecture into levels, we face the task of describing the service supplied by every level. Such descriptions are necessary to be able to develop coordinated in the architectural framework requirements for every level, and to show, after having finished the design, that every level provides the requested service.

The service description allows to consider the potocol level as a "black box", the behaviour if which is of an abstract character and is determined in terms of input and output signals (events). The interaction of the user with the protocol level is realized through special access points (SAP)to the service . Service specification determines only the types and sequence of the data exchanged through SAP, leaving the determination of the control formats and interaction mechanisms to the judgement of the programmer.The data exchanged are called service data elements (SDE) in this case.

The work of any level can be formally represented as interacting protocol objects, whose functioning provides the required service. These objects are the users of the adjacent levels and the suppliers of service to the higher level. Thus, the interaction of one level objects is possible only when the lower level service is applied.

Protocol specification is of a more concrete character than service description. The protocol object is influenced in its functioning by signals of four types: higher level SDE, lower level SDE, inner events of the level (e.g. timer) and SDE from the object - partner. Some preliminary assumptions about the inner structure of the protocol object are made. Besides, the object can be decomposed into individual modules.

In the area of communication protocol design so - called formal description techniques are used to describe the behaviour of systems. Various models, mathematical schemes such as automatic models, Petri nets and their various modifications, the apparatus of the calculus of communicating systems, temporal logic ect. Creation of protocol specification languages is based on the use of an appropriate mathematical scheme.

The main requirements for protocol specification languages are:

1. Formality - the language must be based on a strict mathematical scheme.

2. Accessibility - the language constructions must exclude ambiguities and uncertainties.

3. ISO orientation - the language must be convenient for expressing the notations fixed by the specifications of the International Organization for Standards.

4. Basis for implementation. The language must provide a good basis for protocol programm implementation.

5. Time reflection - the language must contain a means for the description of sequencing the timing of the events.

6. Reflection of non - determinism - in case of simultaneous occurrence of several events the language must allow not to take into account their sequence. Occurrence sequence must be considered in the protocol programm implementation.

7. Reflection of spontaneous transitions - the language must contain a means for the description of the cause of internal events occurrence in the protocol entities.

8. Validation and verification possibilities. Specification must allow to investigate protocol correctness.

9. Simulation possibilities. Specification must serve as a basis for protocol simulation.

10. Independence from implementation. Specification must contain only the protocol algorithm without going into details of its programm implementation.

11. Data abstraction. The language must contain facilities for determining data types and operations with them.

At present the most widely used protocol specification languages are ESTELLE |Este87|, LOTOS |Loto87|, SDL |SDL87| which have been proposed as standards for the specification of OSI protocols and services. The formal nature of specifications allows application of partially automated methods for the validation of specifications, the implementation process and the systematic testing of the resulting implementations |Boch87a|.

Intuitively protocol correctness is understood as protocol compliance with the set requirements, i.e. the correspondence of the protocol to the purpose set by the developer. Thus protocol correctness is a relative concept: the protocol can be correct in relation to the set requirements. Protocol correctness determination is usually called corretness analysis or validation.

The requirements, set by the protocol contain all the properties of protocols, whose presence increase the reliability of protocols in computer networks. They can be general to the whole class of the protocols under investigation and individual, charasteristic of the given protocol under investigation.Choosing this or that point of the properties under investigation leads to the division of the validation task into two types. Validation methods of the first type are those controlling general properties of protocols. Validation methods of the second type are those allowing to state the matching of protocol specification and individual requirements to the protocol.

General properties of protocols include:

1. Boundedness, which means that in protocol functioning the number of

messages in every channel between the protocol objects does not exceed the channel capacity.

2. State ambiquities freeness, i.e. absence of protocol entity, one state of which can coexist with several states of another (protocol object) in void transmission medium.

3. Absence of overspecification,e.g., absence of the description of non-arrived messages processing.

4. Completeness meaning that the reception of all the possible messages is foreseen in the protocol specification.

5.Static deadlock freeness meaning that the protocol never gets into a state without an output.

6. Dynamic deadlock freeness meaning that the protocol never gets into non-effective cycles with useless exchange of the same messages. Absence of cycles with impossible output as well as absence of tempoblocking are distinguished, i.e. absence of non-effective cycles, with possible outputs resulting from the wrong choice of protocol parameters (most often the duration of time-outs).

7. Termination (or cyclic behaviour) meaning that the protocol provides the requested services in the finite time (i.e. the protocol always reaches the final state).

By the given definition of validation the concept of protocol correctness is expressed by the protocol and the request matching. There can be no universal answer to the question what the correctness of an algorithm, or protocol in particular, is. It can be differently formulated for algorithms of different types and purposes. In determining protocol correctness, some aspect of protocol functioning reliability is expressed. The following statements can serve as examples of different definitions of matching:

- protocol specification possesses definite general properties;
- protocol request and specifications are equivalent (observed equivalence);

- the protocol is partially or fully correct;

- for protocols and requests, specified by logical statements, the matching is determined as the truth of the statements being determinated.

Protocol validation methods are classed into three groups: 1. analysis of states; 2. logical proof of correctness; 3. hybrid methods.

The essence of the states method is the use of the global state which is understood as a joint state of the protocol objects and the transmitting environment providing object interaction. Then a graph of reachability states is worked out which is presented in the form of an oriented graph, the vertices of which are the global states of the protocol and the archs indicate the possible transitions from one state to another. In working out the graph the initial and final states must be specified. The resulting states graph is used for the analysis of definite protocol properties as some of them are closely linked with the graph structure. The given validation method allows to investigate protocols general properties. The given method yields to automation easily this being one of its advantages. Its main shortcoming is the fast growth of global states sets with the increase in protocol complication. Therefore, even with automated systems, the described method can be used only for validation of simple protocols or separate parts of complicated protocols.

The logical proof aproach consists in forming statements that will reflect the desired correctness properties and the proof of their implementation in the system functioning. This approach allows to check any properties that can be presented as statements.The main shortcoming of the approach is the dificulty of the formation of invariants reflecting the desired protocol properties. In |Pran88| protocol validation technique based on aggregative models is presented. Besides protocol invariant forming technique is presented.

Application of the calculus communicating systems |Mil80| in terms of the principles of algebraic transformations is the most prospective approach in the solution of protocol verification problem, i.e. verification of service specification correspondence to protocol.

Hybrid methods of validation are based on simultaneous use of logical proof and reachability states, analysis.

2. Application of Aggregative Approach and Method of Controlling Sequences for Formal Protocol Description

In the application of the aggregative approach for protocol formalization the protocol is represented as a set of interacting piece - linear aggregates (PLA). The PLA is taken as an object defined by a set of states Z, input signals X and output signals Y. The aggregate functioning is considered in a set of time moments $t \in T$. The state $z \in Z$, the input signals $x \in X$ and the output signals $y \in Y$ are considered to be time functions. Apart from these sets, transition H and output G operators must be known as well.

The state $z \in Z$ of the piece - linear aggregate is the same as the state of a piece-linear Markoff process, i.e.:

$$z(t)=(\nu(t),Z_{\nu}(t)), \tag{1}$$

where $\nu(t)$ - a discrete state component taking on a countable set of values;

$Z_{\nu}(t)$- a continuous component having $z_{\nu 1}(t),z_{\nu 2}(t),\ldots,z_{\nu k}(t)$ coordinates.

When no inputs exist the state of the aggregate changes in the following manner:

$$\nu(t)=\text{const}, \qquad \frac{dz_{\nu}(t)}{dt} = -\alpha_{\nu} ,$$

where $\alpha_{\nu} = (\alpha_{\nu 1},\alpha_{\nu 2},\ldots,\alpha_{\nu k})$ - is a constant vector.

The state of the vector can change in two cases only : when an input signal arrives in the aggregate or when a continuous component acquires a definite value. Theoretical basis of piece - linear aggregates is their representation as piece - linear Markoff processes. The exact definition of piece-linear processes is given in |Pran82a1.

As an example a one channel system will be considered in the form of a piece - linear aggregate.

The state of the aggregate is the following :

$$Z(t) = (\nu(t),\ z_{\nu 1}(t),\ z_{\nu 2}(t)),$$

where $\nu(t)$ - is the number of requests present in the system at the moment t,

$z_{\nu 1}(t)$ - is the time duration after which the requests will arrive in the system,

$$z_{\nu 2}\ \tau \begin{cases} \text{is not determined, if } \nu(t)=0, \\ \neq 0, \text{ if } \nu(t)\neq 0, \end{cases}$$

$z_{\nu 2}(t)$ - is the time duration after which the service ends.

Time variation of the coordinates $\nu(t), z_{\nu 1}(t)$ and $z_{\nu 2}(t)$ is shown in fig.2. The requests arrive in the system at the moments t_1, t_2, t_5. The moments t_3, t_4 correspond to the completion of the request servicing. The height of each jump of the coordinate $z_{\nu 1}(t)$ equals the time interval of the arrival of every next request in the system. The jumps of the coordinate $z_{\nu 2}(t)$ equal the time of servicing one request.

The coordinates $z_{\nu 1}(t)$ and $z_{\nu 2}(t)$ in the time intervals $[t_m, t_{m+1}]$, when m = 0,1,2,... vary according to the following equation

$$\frac{dZ_{\nu i}(t)}{dt} = -1,\ i = 1,2.$$

At the moment when $Z_{\nu i}(t)$, i = 1,2, becomes zero the state of the system is changed.

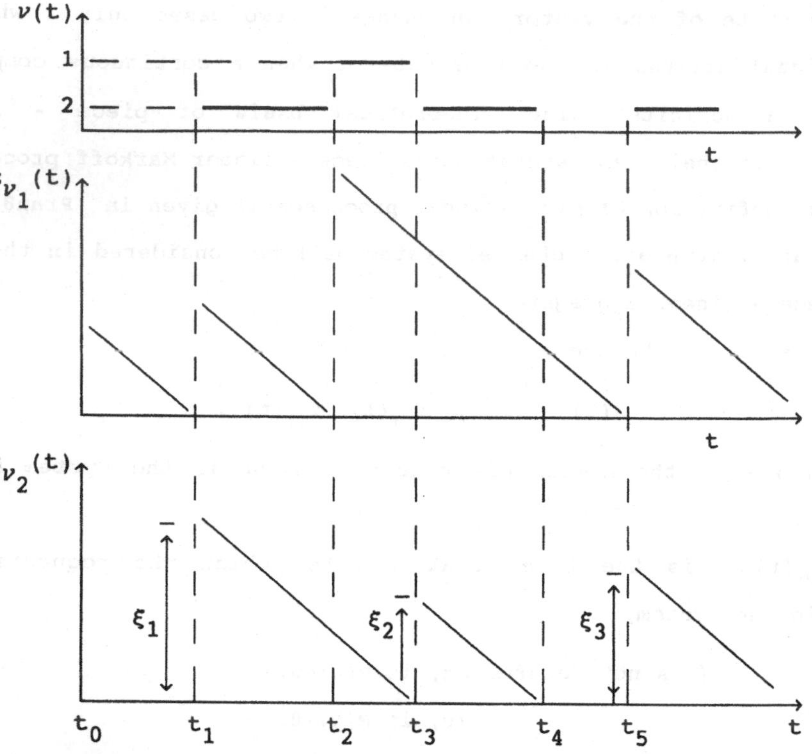

Fig.2. Time variation of the coordinates of a piece-linear aggregate.

The procedure of the formal description of piece-linear aggregates by method of controlling sequences is discused in this chapter. The essence of the method lies in the fact that system functioning is determined by controlling sequences having clear physical meaning and by algorithms, describing system control by means of input sequences, and controlling algorithms enable to construct recurrent expressions for the description of piece-linear aggregate functioning.

Let us consider an aggregate as a system with N input and M output poles. Input signals $x_1, x_2, \dots, x_N \in X$ arrive at the input poles, here the signals $x_i \in X_i, i=\overline{1,N}$ are treated as elementary ones, X_i is a set of elementary signals. In the general case and elementary signal is of a vector structure $x_i=\{x_i^1, x_i^2, \dots, x_i^{r_i}\}$,- i.e. can be described by several quantities, each of which has a value from some set X_i^j, so that $x_i^j \in X_i^j$, $j=\overline{1,r_i}$.

Thus a set of elementary signals coming to the i-th pole of the aggregate,is:

$$X_i = X_i^1 * X_i^2 * \ldots * X_i^{r_1}, \quad i=\overline{1,N}.$$

A set of the aggregate input signals is presented as a union of sets X_i:

$$X = \bigcup_{i=1}^{N} X_i .$$

A set of output signals has an analogical structure:

$$Y=\{y_1, y_2, \ldots, y_M\}, \quad y_l=\{y_l^1, y_l^2, \ldots, y_l^{S_l}\} \in Y_l,$$

$$y_l^k \in Y_l^k, \quad l=\overline{1,M}, \quad k=\overline{1,S_l}.$$

A set of elementery output signals taken from the l-th pole:

$$Y_l = Y_l^1 * Y_l^2 * \ldots * Y_l^{S_1}, \quad l=\overline{1,M},$$

and a set of output signals is of the form:

$$Y = \bigcup_{l=1}^{M} Y_l .$$

Aggregate functioning is examined on a set of time moments $T=(t_0, t_1, \ldots t_m, \ldots)$ at which one or several events take place, resulting in the aggregate state alternation. The set of events E which may take place in the aggregate is divided into two non-intersecting subsets $E'= E' \cup E''$. The subset $E' = \{e_1', e_2', \ldots, e_N'\}$ comprises classes of events (or simply events) e_i', $i=\overline{1,N}$ resulting from the arrival of input signals from the set $X=\{x_1, x_2, \ldots x_N\}$. The class of events $e_i'=\{e_{ij}', j=1,2,3,..\}$, where e_{ij}' - is an event from the class of events e_i' taking place the j-th time since the moment t. The events from the subset E′ are called external events. A set of aggregate input signals is unambiguously reflected in the subset E′ i.e. $X \to E'$. The events from the subset $E''=\{e_1'', e_2'', \ldots, e_f''\}$ are called internal events where $e_i''=\{e_{ij}'', j=1,2,3,\ldots\}$, $i=\overline{1,f}$ are the classes of the aggregate internal events. Here f determines the number of operations taking place in the aggregate. The events in the set E" indicate the end of the operations taking place in the aggregate.

The events of the subsets E′ and E" are called the basic evolutional events of the aggregate. The main evolutional events are sufficient for unambiguous determination of the aggregate evolution. Apart from the basic evolutional events auxiliary evolutional events can be considered, which are simultaneous to the basic ones and determine the start of the operations.

Additional events, associated with the gathering of statistics, determination of the steady state,the end of system functioning simulation ect. are introduced in the aggregate. Let a set of additational events be denoted E"′. The events from the subset E"′ are internal too. Let the additional events, having no impact on the evolutional ones, be called auxiliary events.

In accordance with the input subsets of events, a set of time moments T is divided into two subsets: T′- a subset of input signals arrival, T" - a subset of internal events occurence. Moreover T=T′∪ T".

For every class of events e''_i from the subset E" control sequoences are specified $\{\xi_j^{(i)}\}$,where $\xi_j^{(i)}$-the duration of the operation which is followed by the event $e''_{i,j}$, as well as event counters $\{r(e''_i,t_m)\}$, $i=\overline{1,f}$, where $r(e''_i,t_m)$ - is the number of events from the class e''_i having taken place in the time interval $[t_0,t_m]$.

For the determination of the moments of the start and the end of the operations use the variables $\{S(e''_i,t_m)\}$, $\{W(e''_i,t_m)\}$, $i=\overline{1,f}$, so called control sums are introduced, where $S(e''_i,t_m)$ - the time moment of the start of the operation followed by an event from the class e''_i. This time moment is indeterminate if the operation has not started; $W(e''_i,t_m)$ - the time moment of the end of the operation followed by an event from the class e''_i. This variable is called control sum. In case of no-priority operations the control sum $W(e''_i,t_m)$ is determined in the following way:

$$W(e_i'',t_m)=\begin{cases} S(e_i'',t_m)+\xi^{(1)}_{r(e_i'',t_m)+1} & \text{,if at the moment } t_m \text{ an} \\ \text{operation is taking place, which is followed} & \\ \text{by the event } e_i''; & \\ \infty \text{ - in the opposite case.} & \end{cases}$$

The infinity symbol (∞) is used to denote the undefined values of the variables.

The control sum definition presented above is used in simulation. When aggregative models are used for protocol formalization and correctness analysis, the control sums can be determined in a simplified way:

$$W(e_i'',t_m) = \begin{cases} < \infty, \text{ if at the moment } t_m \text{ an operation is} \\ \text{taking place , followed by the event } e_i''; \\ \infty\text{- in the oppsite case.} \end{cases}$$

Control sums determine only the conditions for the events after the moment t_m while the event occurrence moments are not determined.

Let us specify the meaning of the coordinates of the aggregate state (I). The discrete component of the state $\nu(t_m)=\{\nu_1(t_m),\nu_2(t_m),\ldots,\nu_p(t_m)\}$ - presents the protocol state, i.e. counters of transmitted and received information, readiness for information transmission etc.

$z_\nu(t_m)=(W(e_1'',t_m),W(e_2'',t_m),\ldots,W(e_f'',t_m))$ - control coordinates specifying the moment of evolutional events occurrence.

The control coordinates $z_\nu(t_m)$ are continuos. The control coordinate $W(e_i'',t_m)$ corresponds to every event e_i'' from the subset of events E", while always $W(e_i'',t_m)\geq t_m$.

The state coordinates $z(t_m)$ can change their values only at discrete time moments t_m, m=1,2,3,..., of event occurrence, remaining fixed or changing linearly at some speed in every interval $[t_m,t_{m+1}]$,

$m=0,1,2,\ldots$, where t_0- the initial moment of system functioning.

When the state of the system is known $z(t_m)$, $m=0,1,2,\ldots$, the moment t_{m+1} of the following event is determined by the moment of input signal arrival in the aggregate or by the equation:

$$t_{m+1} = \min_i\{W(e_i'',t_m)\},\ 1\le i\le f.$$

The class of the next event e_{m+1} is specified by the input signal, if an input signal arrives at the time moment t_{m+1} or is determined by the control coordinate having the minimum value at the moment t_m, i.e. the coordinate $W(e_i'',t_m)$ having become minimal, $e_{m+1}\in E''$.

The new aggregate state is stated by the operator H.

$$z(t_{m+1})=H[z(t_m),e_i],e_i \in E'\cup E''.$$

The output signals y_i from the set of output signals $Y=\{y_1,y_2,\ldots,y_m\}$, can be generated by the aggregate only at the moments of events from the subset E' and E". The operator G determines the content of the output signals:

$$y=G[z(t_m),e_i],\qquad e_i\in E'\cup E'',\qquad y\in Y.$$

Further transition and output operators will be denoted $H(e_i)$ and $G(e_i)$.

Let us consider an aggregate system, comprising K aggregates, including the environmental ones. Let the k-th aggregate contain N_K input and M_K output poles. The general number of communication channels, transmitting information between the aggregates, will be denoted L.

Let us assume the matrix $R=||r_{ji}||$, $i=\overline{1,L}$, $j=\overline{1,2}$ of input poles, the meaning of its elements being: r_{1i}- the number of the aggregate receiving input signals from the i-th communication channel; $r_{1i}=1,2,\ldots,K$; r_{2i}- the number of the input pole of the aggregate r_i, incidental to the i-th channel, $1\le r_{2i}\le N_r$.

The inputs of the aggregates are specified by the matrix $H=||h_{ij}||$, $i=\overline{1,K}$, $j=\overline{1,\max\{M_K\}}$, $1\le k\le K$, where h_{ij}- the number of the channel incidental to the j-th output pole of the i-th aggregate $1 \le h_{ij} \le L$.

The matrices R and H determine unambiguously the address of all the output signals of all the aggregates in the system.

Only one signal can be transmited through every channel, which is an output of one aggregate and an input of another. In view of the fact, that an aggregate system is a closed one, i.e. no outside signals arrive and no signals are generated, occurrence of input signals in the aggregates result from the occurrence of internal events in one of the aggregates of the aggregate system.

The set of events, possible in the aggregate system, is the union of subsets of internal event taking place in every aggregate, i.e.:

$$E = \bigcup_{k=1}^{K} E_k'',$$

where E_k''- a set of events taking place in the k-th aggregate.

A set of time moments at which the events from the set E take place is:

$$T = \bigcup_{k=1}^{K} T_k'',$$

where T_k''- is a set of time moments at which the internal events of the k-th aggregate take place.

The next time moment t_{m+1}, at which the events from the set E take place, is determined in the following way.

$$t_{m+1} = \min_k \min_r (W_k(e_r'', t_m) \cup W_k(e_r''', t_m)), \quad 1 \le k \le K, e_r'' \in E_k'', \; e_r''' \in E_k'''.$$

3. Aggregative Model of the Alternating - Bit Protocol

A half - duplex version of the alternating-bit protocol is analysed below. The aggregative model consists of three aggregates: A_1 is a sender, A_2 is an unreliable data transmission medium and A_3 is a receiver. The structural scheme of the aggregative model is given in fig.3.

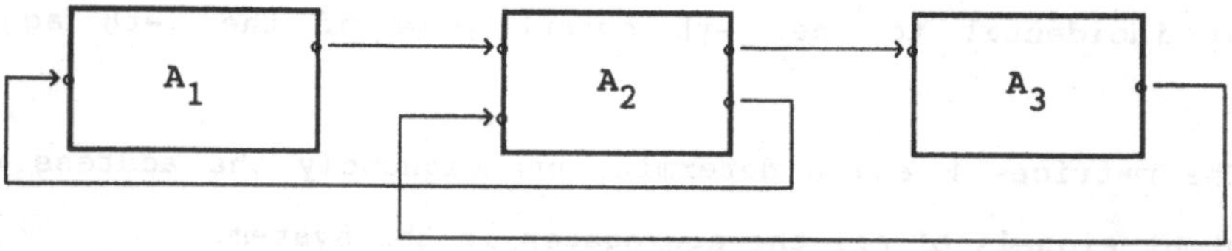

Fig.3. Structural scheme of the aggregative model of the protocol.

Mathematical description of the aggregates follows.

Aggregate A_1.

1. Input signal $X = (B)$, in which B is the value of the alternating-bit in the acknowledgement.

2. Output signal $Y = (B)$, in which B is the value of the alternating-bit in the frame being transmitted.

3. Set of events.

$E' = \{e'_{11}\}$, in which e'_{11} means that the signal X has been received.

$E" = \{e"_{11}, e"_{12}\}$, in which $e"_{11}$ means that the frame has been formed and sent out, $e"_{12}$ indicates the timer expiration (time-out).

4. Controling sequences of events :

$$e"_{11} \Rightarrow \{\eta_{1j}\}_{i=1}^{\infty} \quad , \; e"_{12} \Rightarrow \{\tau_1\}_{i=1}^{\infty} \quad ,$$

in which η_{1j} is the time of the j-th frame formation, τ_1 = const is the duration of the time-out interval.

5. Aggregate state:

$\nu(t_m) = \{ PSK(t_m), Bit1(t_m)\};$

$z_\nu(t_m) = \{ W(e"_{11}, t_m), W(e"_{12}, t_m)\},$

in which $PSK(t_m)$ is the number of the acknowledgements received, $Bit1(t_m)$ is the value of the alternating-bit in the last frame, which has already been sent out or formed, $W(e"_{11}, t_m)$ is the moment of time at which the formation of the frame is completed, $W(e"_{12}, t_m)$ is the moment of time at which the time-out is over.

6. Parameters:

P_{11} is a distortion probability of the acknowledgement, RND(1) is a random value uniformly distributed in the range |0,1|.

7. Initial state:

$z(t_0) = \{0,1,\eta_{11},\infty\}$.

8. Transition and output operators:

$H(e'_{11})$: IF $(B=Bit1(t_m))\wedge(P_{11}<RND(1))$

THEN

BEGIN

$Bit1(t_{m+1})=\overline{Bit1(t_m)}$;

$PSK(t_{m+1})=PSK(t_m)+1$;

$W(e''_{11},t_{m+1})=t_m+\eta_{1j}$;

END

ELSE

$W(e''_{11},t_{m+1})=t_m+\eta_{1j-1}$;

$W(e''_{12},t_{m+1})=\infty$;

$H(e''_{11})$: $W(e''_{11},t_{m+1})=\infty$;

$W(e''_{12},t_{m+1})=t_m+\tau_1$;

$G(e''_{11})$: $Y=(Bit1(t_m))$;

$H(e''_{11})$: $W(e''_{11},t_{m+1})=t_m+\eta_{1j-1}$;

$W(e''_{12},t_{m+1})=\infty$;

Agregate A_2 .

1. Input signals:

X1=(B), in which B is the value of the alternating-bit in the frame being transmitted; X2=(B), in which B is the value of the alternating- bit in the acknowledgement being transmitted. The signal X1 arrives from the sender, while X2 - from the receiver.

2. Output signals:

Y1=(B), in which B is the value of the alternating-bit in the acknowledgement being transmitted, X2=(B), in which B is the value of the alternating-bit in the frame being transmitted.

3. Set of events:

$E'=\{e'_{21},e'_{22}\}$, in which e'_{21} means the arrival of the signal X1 (from A_1), e'_{22} -the arrival of the signal X2 (from A_2).

$E"=\{e"_{21},e"_{22}\}$, in which $e"_{21}$ means that the acknowledgement has been transmitted, $e"_{22}$ means the arrival of the frame at the receiver.

4. Controlling sequences:

$e"_{21} \Rightarrow \{ \xi_{1j} \}_{j=1}^{\infty}$, in which ξ_{1j} is the transmission time of the j-th acknowledgement,

$e"_{22} \Rightarrow \{ \xi_{2j} \}_{j=1}^{\infty}$, in which ξ_{2j} is the transmission time of the j-th frame.

5. State of the aggregate A_2.

$\nu(t_m)=Bit2(t_m)$,

$z_{\nu}(t_m)=\{W(e"_{21},t_m),W(e"_{22},t_m)\}$,

in which $Bit2(t_m)$ is the value of the alternating-bit of the frame/acknowledgement being transmitted, $W(e"_{21},t_m)$ is the moment of time at which the acknowledgement will be transmitted (i.e. it will arrive at the sender), $W(e"_{22},t_m)$ is the moment of time at which the frame will be transmitted (i.e. it will arrive at the receiver).

6. Parameters:

P_{21} is a frame loss probability, P_{22}-is an acknowledgement loss probability, RND(2) is a random value uniformly distributed in the range |0,1|.

7. Initial state:

$z(t_0)=\{ 0,\infty,\infty \}$.

8. Transition and output operators:

$H(e'_{21})$: IF $W(e"_{21},t_m)=\infty \wedge W(e"_{22},t_m)=\infty$

```
        THEN
          BEGIN
            Bit2(t_{m+1})=B;
            IF P_{21}≥RND(2)
              THEN
                W(e"_{22},t_{m+1})=∞
              ELSE
                W(e"_{22},t_{m+1})=t_m+ξ_{2j}
        END;
H(e'_{22}):   IF W(e"_{22},t_m)=∞ ∧ W(e"_{21},t_m)=∞
          THEN
            BEGIN
              Bit2(t_{m+1})=B;
              IF P_{21}≥RND(2)
                THEN
                  W(e"_{21},t_{m+1})=∞
                ELSE
                  W(e"_{21},t_{m+1})=t_m+ξ_{1j}
        END;
H(e"_{21}):   W(e"_{21},t_{m+1})=∞;
G(e"_{21}):   Y1=(Bit2(t_{m+1}));
H(e"_{22}):   W(e"_{22},t_{m+1})=∞;
G(e"_{22}):   Y2=(Bit2(t_{m+1}));
```

Aggregate A_3.

1. Input signal X(B), in which B is the value of the alternating-bit in the frame being received.

2. Output signal Y=(B), in which B is the acknowledgement being transmitted.

3. Set of events:

$E'=\{ e'_{31}\}$, in which e'_{31} means the arrival of the signal X (frame arrival), $E''=\{ e''_{31}\}$, in which e''_{31} means that the acknowledgement has been formed and sent out.

4. Controlling sequences:

$e_{31} \Rightarrow \{ \eta_{3j}\}_{j=1}^{\infty}$, in which η_{3j}- is the duration of the j-th acknowledgement formation.

5. State of the aggregate A_3:

$\nu(t_m)=\{KSK(t_m),Bit3(t_m)\}$,

$z_{\nu}(t_m)=\{W(e''_{31},t_m)\}$,

in which Bit3(t) is the value of the alternating-bit in the last acknowledgement, $KSK(t_m)$is the number of the frames received , $W(e''_{31},t_m)$ is the moment of time by which the acknowledgement will have been formed and sent out.

6. Parameters:

P_{31} is a frame distortion probability, RND(1) is the same as in the aggregate A_1.

7. Initial state:

$z(t_m)=\{0,0,\infty\}$.

8. Transmission and output opertors:

```
H(e'31):   IF W(e"31,tm)=∞ THEN
            IF (B≠Bit3(tm))^(P31<RND(1))
              THEN
            BEGIN
                  KSK(tm+1)=KSK(tm)+1;
                  Bit3(tm+1)=B;
                  W(e"31,tm+1)=tm+η3j
             END
           ELSE
             W(e"31,tm+1)=tm+η3j-1;
H(e"31):  W(e"31,tm+1)=∞ ;
```

$G(e''_{31})$: $Y=Bit3(t_{m+1})$);

4. Invariant Approach for Aggregative Model Validation

4.1. Invariant Analysis Technique

The invariant analysis technique is viewed below. A System invariant (I) is an assertion which describes correct system functioning and it must remain true in spite of the events taking place and system transition from one state to another. The essence of the method is as follows: assertions are formulated in relation to the program variables (in this case to the coordinates of the aggregative model) so as to express the requirements for protocol functioning. These assertions are joined together by logical operations to construct one or some system invariants, whose invariantability is proved by means of a deductive system and mathematical induction. The asserations from which the invariant is constructed may represent the following requirements:

1. The user gets the information undistorted.
2. Messages arrive at the user in the sequence they have been sent.

Specific protocol properties are described by extra assertions.

There is a program fragment, viz. transition and output operators, for every event in aggregative description. The system state is determined by the values of coordinates. Transition from one system state to another results from the occurrence of events and an appropriate alteration in coordinates, which happens due to the execution of the program fragment related to the event. Thus the system functioning can be defined as a sequence of events, i.e. execution of a sequence of program fragments. These fragments make up the total sequence of operators which alter system coordinates in time. Values of logical assertions used in the invariant may change only when an event occurs. Since any event may take place only if certain condition are met, the invariant is proved with the help of enabling conditions of events which are predicates on system coordinates. The enabling condition of event is determined by the values of continuous system coordinates, i.e. a particular event may take place if the corresponding continuous coordinate is of a finite value. Such a predicate is constructed for every event and its value is true only in case the system state is such that the event can take place. We can prove that I is a system invariant if the following assertion is true |Pran88|.

<u>Assertion</u>. The following steps are sufficient to prove that I is a system invariant:

1. Proving that I is true for the initial system state.
2. Proving that the following assertion is true:

$$\forall\ e_i : \{EP_i \wedge I\}\ P_i\ \{I\}\ ,\ i=1,2,\ldots,n$$

in which EP_i is the enabling condition of the event e_i, P_i is a program fragment related to the event e_i, n - is the number of events.

4.2. Method for System Invariant Formulation

On the grounds of a conceptual model we can describe system functioning by an event sequence, which can be represented by the graph G(V), in which V is a set of vertices, $A=[a_{ij}]$ is a adjacency matrix. In this case $V=\{e_1,e_2,\ldots e_n\}$, in which e_i is i-th event, n is the number of events. $(e_ie_j)\neq(e_je_i)$, which means that the graph is oriented.

$$a_{ij} = \begin{cases} 1, & \text{if the event } e_j \text{ can occur after } e_i; \\ 0, & \text{in other cases.} \end{cases}$$

System coordinates are altered by every event corresponding to the program fragment related to it and transition from one state to another takes place, the alteration depending on both the probabilistic system characteristics and the system state before the event.

<u>Definition</u>. The set of states which the system may enter after the event e_i is called the i-th set of possible states (symbolic state) (SS_i).

$$SS_i = \{z \in Z \mid (\exists z')((z' \in Z) \wedge EP_i(z') \wedge (z = H_i(z', P)))\}$$

in which Z is a set of all possible system states, $EP_i(z')$ is an enabling predicate' of the event e_i in the state z', P is a set of probabilistic parametres of the system, H_i is a transition operator determining a new system state when the event e_i occurs.

The system is in the symbolic state SS_i only if it is in the state z and $z \in SS_i$. On the grounds of this SS_i definition every event e_i is related to the symbolic state SS_i, therefore replacing the set of vertices V in the graph G(V) by $V' = \{SS_1, SS_2, \ldots, SS_n\}$, while the adjacency matrix A remains unchanged, we obtain the graph of symbolic states G(V') which describes system operation by means of determining possible sets of states and transitions from one symbolic state to another. In some cases G(V') may be modified according to a conceptual model, which means that in order to reveal some special properties of the particular model the set of possible states SS_i may be divided into several sets of states $SS_{i_1}, SS_{i_2}, \ldots, SS_{i_m}$, on condition that $SS_i = \bigcup_{j=1}^{m} SS_{i_j}$ (thus the number of states with in the set of possible states is reduced in order to express the protocol properties more precisely), besides, if the differences between some sets of possible states are inessential to the researcher analysing the model, these sets $SS_{i_1}, SS_{i_2}, \ldots, SS_{i_q}$ can be united into a new one $SS_{NEW} = \bigcup_{j=1}^{q} SS_{i_j}$. The system invariant I is constucted on the assumption that the system must be in some symbolic state SS_i at any moment of its operation. In order to construct I a defining predicat formulated for every SS_i.

<u>Definition.</u> The predicate P_i defining SS_i is a predicate, which expresses restrictions on the system coordinates of the states which

can be in SS_i.

The I sructure is as follows:

$$I = \bigvee_{i=1}^{n} P_i$$

in which n is the number of the symbolic states. The P_i sructure is:

$$P_i = \bigwedge_{i=1}^{m} K_{ij}$$

in which K_{ij} is the j-th predicate expresing restrictions related to SS_i, on one if possible, or some coordinates, m is the number of predicates K_{ij}, for SS_i. If the user is not interested in the value of a certain coordinate, it may be not restricted by any of the predicates K_{ij}. Every K_{ij} is formulated on the grounds of the conceptual model by means of the variables of the formal model description. In the above methods of I formulation, the event graph is constructed by the first step for the following reasons:

1. Usualy, it is natural for the user to imagine the system as a sequence of events and not that of symbolic states, therefore transition from the conceptual model to the event graph and from the latter to the graph of symbolic states is more natural than generating the graph of symbolic states from a conceptual model.

2. It is easier to generate all K_{ij} on the grounda of a conceptual model if one keeps in mind both the graph of symbolic states and the event graph.

The above methods are of a general character. As has been mentioned above, it is nesesary to know the event graph to be able to use them. The event graph determination is usually difficult, unless there are restrictions on the probabilistic parameters of the protocol. Often, however, we can determine restrictions on probabilistic protocol parameters and then we will know the event graph obtained without restrictions. In such a case event enabling conditions (and therefore enabling predicate) must be modified in accordance with the protocol specification and the restrictions mentioned above.

4.3 Analysis of the Sequence of Symbolic States

The proof of the invariant formulated by the given methods provides that the system will be in one of the defined possible states at any moment of its functioning. More detailed and precise requirements for system operation can be expressed with the help of such an invariant, rather than of an ordinary one, if the number of symbolic states is more than 1. The described invariant facilitates correspondence analysis between the sequence of symbolic states determined by the researcher and the sequence generated by the formal specification of the protocol. Based on the conceptual model, symbolic states, to one of which the system may proceed after the event, are determined for every event in order to specify a desirable sequence of symbolic states. It means the set PIS_i, which is a set of predicate indices, is determined for every e_i.

Numbers of the predicates P_j (j meaning the predicate number), which determine the symbolic states, the transition to one of which is caused by the event, are elements of the set. The correspondence between the sequence of the simbolic states specified by the researchers and the sequence generated by a formal model is checked in the following way: when proving I, for every event of all j, for which P_j is true after the event e_i the set PIS'_i is generated and the relation $PIS_i = PIS'_i$ is checked for every i.

4.4. Invariant Forming Example

We will present the invariant of the alternating-bit protocol, the formal description of which is presented in paragraph 3.

The protocol will be analyzed under the condition that time-out is possible only when either packet or acknowledgement has been lost. It follows from the formal analysis of the protocol that time $\xi_{2j}+\xi_{1j}+\eta_{3j}$ is spent for the transmission of the j-th packet and the formation and transmission of the j-th acknowledgement. The protocol will be analyzed under the condition that the probability of timer duration above the maximum value of the sum $\xi_{2j}+\xi_{1j}+\eta_{3j}$ equals one, i.e.

$$P(\tau_1=const>max(\xi_{2j}+\xi_{1j}+\eta_{3j}))=1.$$

Definition of selected symbolic states follows. SS_0- frame formation is taking place after the time-out or after the reception of the acknowledgement, SS_1- frame has been sent out, the receiver is waiting for the frame, and the sender is waiting for the acknowledgement, SS_2- the frame has been received and an acknowledgement is being formed, SS_3-the acknowledgement has been sent out, the sender is waiting for the acknowledgement, and the user is waiting for another frame.

We formulate auxiliary predicates which will be used to formulate predicates for defining symbolic states.

E11: $W(e''_{11},t_m)\neq\infty$ - a frame is being formed,

E12: $W(e''_{12},t_m)\neq\infty$ - the timer has started,

E21: $W(e''_{21},t_m)\neq\infty$ - an acknowledgement is being transmitted,

E22: $W(e''_{22},t_m)\neq\infty$ - the frame is being transmitted,

E31: $W(e''_{31},t_m)\neq\infty$ - the acknowledgement is being formed,

RK: $PSK(t_m)=KSK(t_m)$ - the number of acknowledgement received undistorted is equal to the number of frames received undistorted. From the conceptual model, it is obvious that a frame is necessary in this case.

RP: $PSK(t_m)-1=KSK(t_m)$ - the number of acknowledgements received undistored is less by one in comparison with the number of frames received undistored, which means an acknowledgement is nesessary.

EG:$Bit1(t_m) \neq Bit3(t_m)$ - the number of the last-formed frame and that of the acknowledgement differ. From the conceptual model it follows, that in case of EG, the transmitted frame should be accepted by the receiver, while the transmitted acknowledgement should be ignored by the sender, and in case of $\overline{EG}$, the transmitted acknowledgement should be accepted by the sender, while the transmitted frame should be ignored by the receiver.

SK:$Bit1(t_m)=Bit2(t_m)$ - the data with an alternating bit equal to the alternating bit of tho laot-formed frame are being transmitted.SP:$Bit3(t_m)=Bit2(t_m)$ - the data with an alternating bit equal to the alternating bit of the last-formed acknowledgement are being transmitted.

We formulate predicates defining symbolic states of the protocol as follows.

The symbolic state SS_0. Frame formation is taking place, therefore E11 is true, but the timer has not started ($\overline{E12}$) while an acknowledgement or a frame must not be transmitted and acknowledgement formation can not take place ($\overline{E21} \wedge \overline{E22} \wedge \overline{E31}$). From the conceptual model it follows that RKVRP is true at any time of the protocol functioning, because the number of frames received undistored can only be equal or/more by one the number of acknowledgements received undistotred, but frame formation is taking place in the symbolic state SS_0 and therefore RK being true (i.e. a frame is needed), EG must be true for the frame to be received, while RP being true (i.e. an acknowledgement is needed), $\overline{EG}$ must be for the frame being formed to be ignored by the receiver. From the stated above, it means that $(RK \wedge EG) \wedge (RP \wedge \overline{EG})$ must be true in SS_0. Thus the predicate defining the symbolic state SS_0 will be as follows:

$$P_0: E11 \wedge \overline{E12} \wedge \overline{E21} \wedge \overline{E22} \wedge \overline{E31} \wedge (RK \wedge EG) \vee (RP \wedge \overline{EG})).$$

Predicates for other symbolic states are specified analogically:

$P_1: \overline{E11} \wedge E12 \wedge \overline{E21} \wedge \overline{E31} \wedge ((RK \wedge EG) \vee (RP \wedge \overline{EG})) \wedge SK$,

$P_2: \overline{E11} \wedge E12 \wedge \overline{E21} \wedge \overline{E22} \wedge E31 \wedge ((RK \wedge EG) \vee (RP \wedge \overline{EG}))$,

$P_3: \overline{E11} \wedge E12 \wedge \overline{E22} \wedge \overline{E31} \wedge ((RK \wedge EG) \vee (RP \wedge \overline{EG})) \wedge SP$.

The protocol invariant will be $I = P_0 \vee P_1 \vee P_2 \vee P_3$.

Proof of the invariant corectness. Resulting from the composition of aggregates the alternating - bit protocol will be described by the aggregate whose state is:

$$\upsilon(t_m)=\{PSK(t_m),Bit1(t_m),Bit2(t_m),KSK(t_m),Bit3(t_m)\};$$

$$Z_\upsilon(t_m)=\{W(e''_{11},t_m),W(e''_{12},t_m),W(e''_{21},t_m),W(e''_{22},t_m),W(e''_{31},t_m)\}.$$

Initial state:

$$Z(t_0)=(0,1,0,0,0,\eta_{11},\infty,\infty,\infty,\infty).$$

A set of events: $E=\{e_1,e_2,e_3,e_4,e_5\}$, where e - corresponds to the events e''_{11} and e'_{21}, e_2- corresponds to the events e''_{22} and e'_{31}, e_3- e''_{31} and e'_{22}, e_4- e''_{21}, and e'_{11}, e''_{12} will be denoted by e_5.

The events $e_1,e_2,\ldots,e_5$ denote: e_1- completion of packet formation, e_2- completion of packet transmission, e_3- completion of acknowledgement formation, e_4- completion of acknowledgement transmission, e_5- end of time-out.

Using the conceptual model, the graph of events and global states, the sets PIS_i can be constructed for every event e. After the event e_1 the system can pass to the symbol state SS_1 only, therefore $PIS_1=\{1\}$.

Correspondingly:

$$PIS_2=\{2\},\ PIS_3=\{3\},\ PIS_4=\{0\},\ PIS_5=\{0\}.$$

Hence,from the mathematical model the predicates of event possibility are formed:

$$EP_1:\ W(e''_{11},t_m)\neq\infty\ ,$$

$$EP_2:\ W(e''_{22},t_m)\neq\infty\ ,$$

$$EP_3:\ W(e''_{31},t_m)\neq\infty\ ,$$

$$EP_4:\ W(e''_{21},t_m)\neq\infty\ .$$

From the end of time - out condition:

$$EP_5: (W(e''_{21},t_m)=\infty)\wedge(W(e''_{22},t_m)=\infty)\wedge(W(e''_{12},t_m)\neq\infty),$$

that is $EP_5=\overline{E21}\wedge\overline{E22}\wedge E12$.

Proof of the invariant for the event e_1. $EP_1\wedge I$ must be true before the event e_1 (i.e. $E11\wedge I$). It follows that $E11\wedge\overline{E12}\wedge\overline{E21}\wedge\overline{E22}\wedge\overline{E31}\wedge(RK\wedge EG)_\vee(RP\wedge\overline{EG})$ is true before the event e_1. After the event e_1 the coordinates of the system change in the following way (from the formal description):

$$W(e''_{11},t_{m+1})=\infty \text{ , } W(e''_{12},t_{m+1})=t_m+\tau_i \text{ ,}$$

$Bit2(t_{m+1})=B$, but $B=Bit1(t_m)$, as B - the signal from the sender, it follows that $Bit2(t_{m+1})=Bit1(t_{m+1})$.

In case $P_{21}\geq RND$, $W(e''_{22},t_{m+1})=\infty$ and if $P_{21}<RND$, then $W(e''_{22},t_{m+1})\neq\infty$. The other coordinates of the system do not change. Therefore after the event e_1 the expression $E11\wedge E12\wedge E21\wedge E31\wedge(RK\wedge EG)_\vee(RP\wedge EG)\wedge SK$ will be true.

It follows from this expression that the predicate P_1 is true and therefore I is true.

$1\in PIS_1$, therefore e_1 will transfer the system to the symbolic state possible for the event e_1.

In the same way the invariant trueness for the other events is proved.

5. Protocol Analysis System PRANAS

Protocol analysing system PRANAS is based on the use of aggregative mathematical schemes for specification, validation and simulation |Pran 85|.

Protocol specification is realised in the language AGGREGAT 84 based on the aggregative approach and controlling sequences method. On the basis of this description the preprocessor generates a program model for validation and simulation, depending on the research type chosen.

The preprocessor implements the analysis and translation of the protocol formal description in the language AGREGAT 84 into the program model in the language FORTRAN for a validation and simulation experiment.

The validation model constructed by the translator is described in the form of pocedure in the language FORTRAN for the generation program and the analysis of reachability graph.

After completing the construction of the reachability graph, the program analyzes it, and verifies the following characteristics of protocols: 1) boundness; 2) absence of redundancy in specification; 3) completeness; 4) absence of static deadlocks; 5) absence of dynamic deadlocks; 6) termination.

The programm of the simulation model, constructed by the translator, realizes the eventual method of simulation of protocol functioning. The standard programm modules are used for the simulation of accidental values, and outputting the results of modelling.

To build a validation protocol, some changes are introduced in the protocol specification. The main of them is that in the given case continuous coordinates can acquire only two values: 0 or 1. A continuous coordinate takes the value 0 if at the given moment an operation followed by an event determined by the given coordinate, is not active. And, on the contrary, if at the given moment an operation, followed by an event, is active, the value of the continuous coordinate equals 1. On account of protocol elements distortion and disappearance, additional continupus coordinates must be introduced. For alternating-bit protocol the coordinates W11, W21, W22 and W31, used in the aggregative specification and explained earlier, are replaced by the coordinates W111, W112, W211, W212, W221, W222, W311, W312, where W111 - packet formation on receiving a non-distorted response; W112 - packet formationon receiving a distorted response; W211 - the statement has been transmitted to the channel and will not be lost; W212 - the statment has been transmittaed to the channel and will be lost; W221 - packet has been transmitted to the channel and will not be lost; W222 - the packet transmitted to the channel and will be lost; W311 - a non-distorted packet received; W312 - a distorted packet received.

Fig.4. presents the reachable states of the alternating-bit protocol for the cases when the initial state PSK=0, Bit1=1, W111=1, W12=0, W112=1; Bit2=0, W211=0, W221=0, W212=0, W222=0; Bit3=0, W311=0, W312=0.

The final state:PSK=1,Bit1=1, W111=1, W12=0, W112=1; Bit2=0, W211=0,W221=1,W221=0, W212=0, W222=1; Bit3=1, W311=0, W312=0.

The numbers of the vertices the protocols can pass to are indicated in the graph of reachable states. For example, from the 19 vertex, transition to the vertices 13, 7, 8, and 22 are possible.

```
[   1 ]  <A1> 0 1 / 101 <A2> 0 / 0000 <A3> 0 / 00
⇒   2\    3\
[   2 ]  <A1> 0 1 / 010 <A2> 1 / 0101 <A3> 0 / 00
⇒   4\    5\   6\
[   3 ]  <A1> 0 1 / 010 <A2> 0 / 0000 <A3> 0 / 00
⇒   1\
[   4 ]  <A1> 0 1 / 101 <A2> 1 / 0101 <A3> 0 / 00
⇒   2\    2\   7\   8\
[   5 ]  <A1> 0 1 / 010 <A2> 1 / 0000 <A3> 1 / 11
⇒   7\    9\  10\
[   6 ]  <A1> 0 1 / 010 <A2> 1 / 0000 <A3> 0 / 11
⇒   8\   11\  12\
[   7 ]  <A1> 0 1 / 101 <A2> 1 / 0000 <A3> 1 / 11
⇒  13\    5\  14\  15\
[   8 ]  <A1> 0 1 / 101 <A2> 1 / 0000 <A3> 0 / 11
⇒  16\    6\  17\  18\
[   9 ]  <A1> 0 1 / 010 <A2> 1 / 1010 <A3> 1 / 00
⇒  14\    0\  15\
[  10 ]  <A1> 0 1 / 010 <A2> 1 / 0000 <A3> 1 / 00
⇒  15\
[  11 ]  <A1> 0 1 / 010 <A2> 0 / 1010 <A3> 0 / 00
⇒  17\    1\   0\
[  12 ]  <A1> 0 1 / 010 <A2> 1 / 0000 <A3> 0 / 00
⇒  18\
[  13 ]  <A1> 0 1 / 010 <A2> 1 / 0101 <A3> 1 / 11
⇒  19\    5\   6\  20\  20\
[  14 ]  <A1> 0 1 / 101 <A2> 1 / 1010 <A3> 1 / 00
⇒   9\    9\   0\  15\
[  15 ]  <A1> 0 1 / 101 <A2> 1 / 0000 <A3> 1 / 00
⇒  20\   10\
[  16 ]  <A1> 0 1 / 010 <A2> 1 / 0101 <A3> 0 / 11
⇒  21\    5\   6\   2\   2\
[  17 ]  <A1> 0 1 / 101 <A2> 0 / 1010 <A3> 0 / 00
⇒  11\   11\   1\   0\
[  18 ]  <A1> 0 1 / 101 <A2> 1 / 0000 <A3> 0 / 00
⇒   2\   12\
[  19 ]  <A1> 0 1 / 101 <A2> 1 / 0101 <A3> 1 / 11
⇒  13\   13\   7\   8\  22\  22\
[  20 ]  <A1> 0 1 / 010 <A2> 1 / 0101 <A3> 1 / 00
⇒  22\    5\   6\
[  21 ]  <A1> 0 1 / 101 <A2> 1 / 0101 <A3> 0 / 11
⇒  16\   16\   7\   8\   4\   4\
[  22 ]  <A1> 0 1 / 101 <A2> 1 / 0101 <A3> 1 / 00
⇒  20\   20\   7\   8\
```

Fig.4. Reacheble states graph.

Protocol analysing system PRANAS has been further developed. At pressent a protocol analysing system PRANAS-2 has been developed which uses the specification language ESTELLE/AG. The largest sructural unit of the language ESTELLE/AG is specification. The specifisation consists of modules, which are communicated by channels. In special cases the specification may consist of a single module. The channel is used for the exchange of information between the modules. The unit of exchange is the primitive. The set of primitives transmitted by channels, their sructure and direction of transmission are described by determining the type of the channel. Every type of module determined by its header describes a definite piece-linear aggregate. The set of input and output signals of the aggregate is determined by connecting the corresponding types of channels. The set of external events of the aggregate makes up the moments of arriving of primitives at the points of interaction.

A discrete component of the aggregate state is described in the section of description of variables and a continuous component is described in the section of description of operation so that a definite operation conforms to every continuous component. The set of internal events makes up the moments of the completion of operation performance. The initialization of an aggregate is determined by the initial setting, and its evolution - by the description of transmissions. The specification sructure is determined by modules, which form it, and by method of their connection. The syntax of some used elements of the language PASCAL is extended by additational means enabling to determine the actions over operations.

The system consists of the following software tools:

- the tool translating the protocol specification into a validation model;
- the tool for reachability graph construction and analysis;
- the tool translating the protocol specification into a simulation model;
- the tool executing simulation experiments and statistically processing the simulation results obtained.

For illustration specification of an alternating-bit protocol by means of the specification language ESTELLE/AG is presented |Pran 87|. In fig.5. the alternating -bit protocol sructure is presented. After fig.5. protocol specification using ESTELLE/FG language is presented.

In fig.6. the dependence of the average packet transmission time from the sender to the receiver with the acknowledgement of the relation t/T, where T - the time-out duration; $t=t_{21}+t_{22}+t_{31}$, where t_{21} -average time of the acknowledgement transmission; t_{22} - average time of the packet transmission from the sender to the receiver; t_{31} - average time of the acknowledgement formation. In simulation the packet transmission and acknowledgement time, as well as the time of the acknowledgement formation, were considered to be random values distributed according to the exponential law with the average values t_{22}, t_{21}, and t_{31} respectively. It was also considered that $P_{11}=P_{21}=P_{22}=P_{31}=P$. The simulation was carried out at $t_{21}=t_{22}= 0.1$; $t_{31}= 0.05$, and the two values P=0.1 and P=0.01. Duration of simulation 5000.

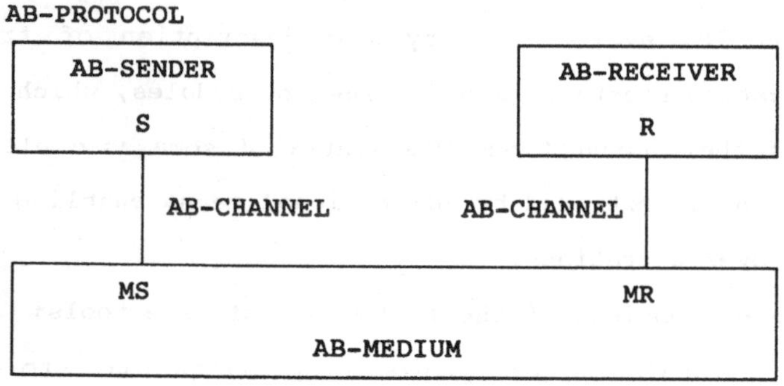

Fig 5. Alternating - bit protocol structure.

```
secification AB-PROTOCOL;
type BIT-TYPE = 0..1;
channel AB-CHANNEL(SM,RM);
  by SM, RM:
     BIT(B: BIT-TYPE);
module AB-SENDER-TYPE;
  ip S: AB-CHANNEL(SM);
end;
body AB-SENDER-BODY for AB-SENDER-TYPE;
```

```
var Bit-1: BIT-TYPE;
  Psk:   integer;
op
  PAC-form;
  TIMER;
function Ack-Corrupt: boolean;
primitive;
initialize
   begin
      Bit-1 := 1; Psk := 0;
      cancel TIMER;
      start PAC-form
   end;
trans
when S.BIT
   begin
     cancel TIMER;
     start PAC-form;
     if B = Bit-1 and not Ack-Corrupt then
       begin
         Psk := Psk + 1;
         Bit-1 := ((Bit-1)+1) mod 2
       end
   end;
when eop.PAC-from
   begin
     start TIMER;
     output S.PAC(Bit-1)
   end
when eop.TIMER
   begin
     start PAC-form;
   end
end;
module AB-MEDIUM-TYPE;
  ip MS: AB-CHANNEL(SM);
     MR: AB-CHANNEL(RM);
end;
body AB-MEDIUM-BODY for AB-MEDIUM-TYPE;
var Bit-2: BIT-TYPE;
op
  ACK-send;
  PAC-send;
function Packet-Lost: boolean;
primitive;
function Ack-Lost: boolean;
primitive;
initialize
   begin
     Bit-2 := 0;
     cancel
   end;
trans
when MS.BIT
   begin
     if not active ACK-send then
       begin
         Bit-2 := B;
         if Packet-Lost then cancel else start PAC-send
       end
```

```
    end;
 when MR.BIT
    begin
      if not active PAC-send then
        begin
          Bit-2 := B;
          if Ack-Lost then cancel else start ACK-send
        end
    end;
 when eop.ACK-send
    begin
      output MS.ACK(bit-2)
    end;
 when eop. PAC-send
    begin
      output MR.PAC(Bit-2)
    end
 end;
 module AB-RECEIVER-TYPE;
   ip R: AB-CHANNEL(RM);
 end;
 body AB-RECEIVER-BODY for AB-RECEIVER-TYPE;
 var Bit-3: BIT-TYPE;
   Ksk:   integer;
 op
   ACK-form;
 function Packet-Corrupt: boolean;
 primitive;
 initialize
    begin
      Bit-3 := 0; Ksk := 0;
      cancel ACK-from
    end;
 trans
 when R.BIT
    begin
      start ACK-form;
      if B <> Bit-3 and not Packet- COrrupt then
        begin
          Ksk := Ksk + 1;
          Bit-3 := B
        end
    end;
 when eop.ACK-from
    begin
      output R.ACK(Bit-3)
    end;
 modvar
   AB-SENDER: AB-SENDER-TYPE;
   AB-MEDIUM: AB-MEDIUM-TYPE;
   AB-RECEIVER: AB-RECEIVER-TYPE;
 initialize
    begin
   init AB-SENDER with AB-SENDER-BODY;
   init AB-MEDIUM with AB-MEDIUM-BODY;
   init AB-RECEIVER with AB-RECEIVER-BODY;
   connect AB-SENDER.S to AB-MEDIUM.MS;
   connect AB-RECEIVER.R to AB-MEDIUM.MR
    end
 end.
```

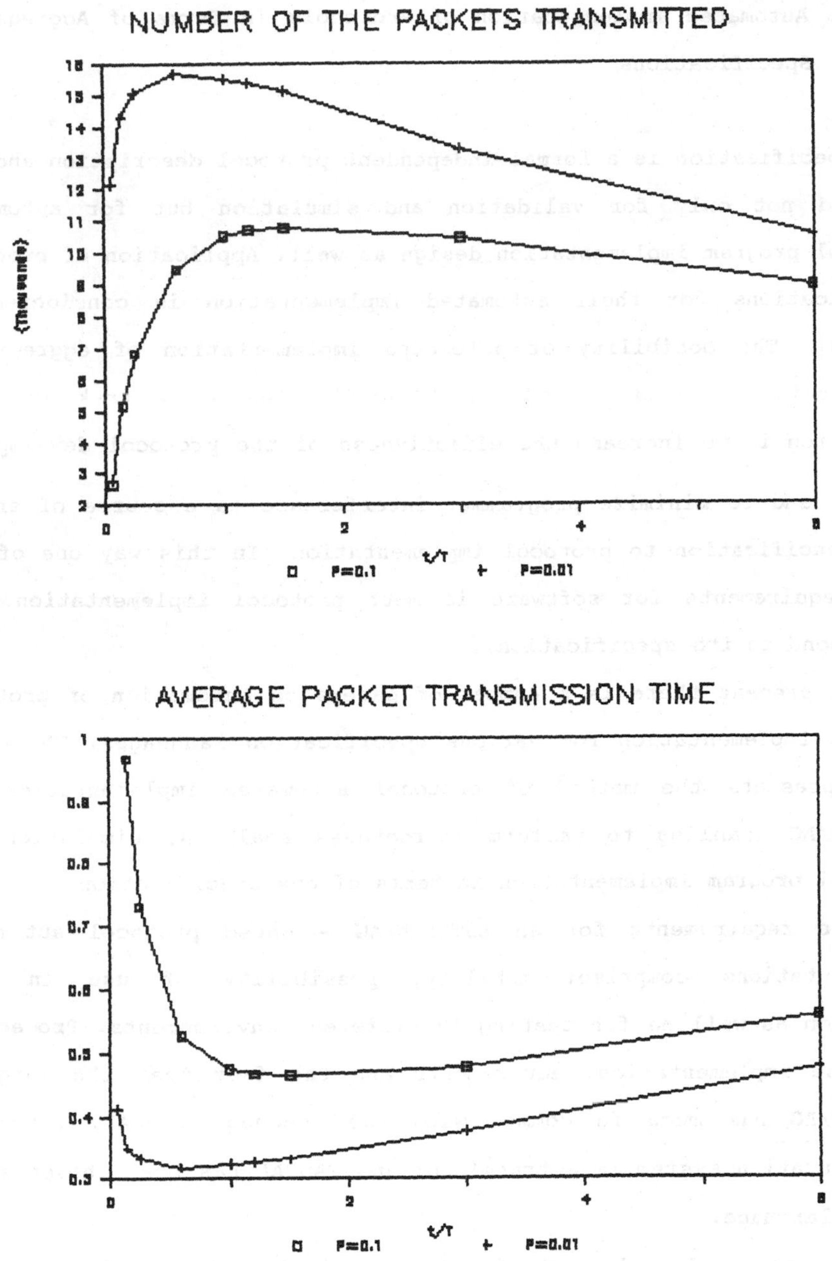

Fig.6. Simulation results.

6. Automated Implementation of Protocols in Terms of Aggregative Specifications

Specification is a formal independent protocol description and can be used not only for validation and simulation but for automated protocol program implementation design as well. Application of protocol specifications for their automated implementation is considered in |Boch84|. The posibility of automated implementation of aggregative specifications is discussed in |Pran89|. The main task of such automation is to increase the effectivness of the protocol development process and to minimize programmer interference as a source of errors from specification to protocol implementation. In this way one of the main requirements for software is met: protocol implementation must correspond to its specification.

At present there is a number of papers on automation of protocol program implementation for various specification languages. The given paper presents the method of protocol automated implementation for ESTELLE/AG enabling to perform correctness analysis, simulation and protocol program implementation in terms of one specification.

The requirements for an ESTELLE/AG - based protocol automated implementations comprise: mobility, possibility of use in real operation as well as for testing in different environments. Proceeding from the implementation requirements and the fact that the language ESTELLE/AG has much in common with the language PASCAL, automated implementation system is a translator and PASCAL has been chosen as an object language.

The proposed technique of automated implementation includes the following stages: 1. construction of operation - control algorithm; 2.determination of the automated implementation sructure: determination of the protocol implementation components and their place in the operational system; formalization of the interaction of the components of protocol implementation and their interaction with protocols of contiguous levels; 3. formalization of translation of specifications into the object language (PASCAL) by means of attributive grammars and development of automated implementation systems in terms of attributive grammar.

Protocol specification does not contain any information on the ways of interaction of protocol implementation with the operational system and the protocols of contiguous levels. Therefore,it should be mentioned that protocol implementation can not be obtained completly automaticaly in terms of specification.

Protocol implementation can be divided into two parts: algorithmic (AL) and system dependent (SD). AL is a program in the language PASCAL, automatically generated in terms of the specification, expresses the protocol algorithm; it must be mobile and computer - independent, as the specification itself, and open to the connecting of modules of SD part. The system - dependent part is developed in the usual way (i.e. non automated) and is dependent on the operational system, in which the protocol will function, and the details of the given implementation. It provides interaction of the protocol implementation with the protocols of contiguous levels and the operational system, as well as the control of the low level data structures.

The protocols receive signals from contiguous levels asynchronially, therefore the determination of the way of interaction between the protocol automated implementation and the protocols of contiguous levels, and its formalization are important.

In fig.7. the composition of protocol automated implementation is presented |Pran 89|. Here AL - the algorithm part of automated implementation; SD - system dependent part; LMS - list of module states; QIS - queue of input signals; QEIS - queue of external input signals; QFO - queue of finished operations; OSS - procedures providing operational system service; PIS - processor of input signals; PIO1, PIO2,...,PION - program implementation operations; UP - unspecified procedures; AP1, AP2 - auxiliary procedures, implementing individual operators of the specification language; POS - processor ofyoutput signals. The modules - are the procedures corresponding to the specification ones. Event scheduler is the controlling program of the whole protocol implementation. PIS operates asynchronically and on receiving a signal from the contiguous level protocol makes a record in QEIS. Any operation having been completed a record is made in QFO. A record in QIS is realized by procedures in transmitting the signal to another internal module.

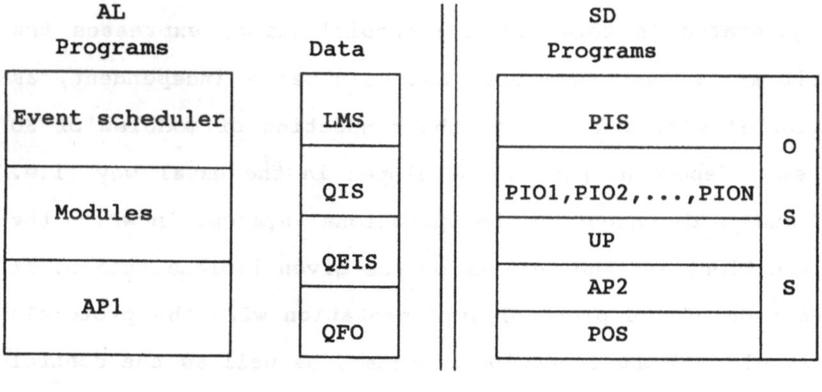

Fig.7. Structure of automated implementation of protocol's.

In fig.8. an AR structure with parallel realization of operations, representing the place of AR in the operational system, is shown. The processor of input signals is an asynchronous progrm (ASP). The event scheduler jointly with the procedures of modules, non-specified procedures (NSP), auxiliary procedures (AP1,AP2), processor output signals (POS) and procedures providing service of the operational system (SOS) make up the main task of protocol program implementation. Implementations of operations (OP1,OP2,...,OPN) act as the main task. The position of the components AR in the operational system is determined by such terms as asynchronous program, main task, subtask, which can be used in any multiprogram operational system. The proposed system is sufficiently universal relative to operational systems.

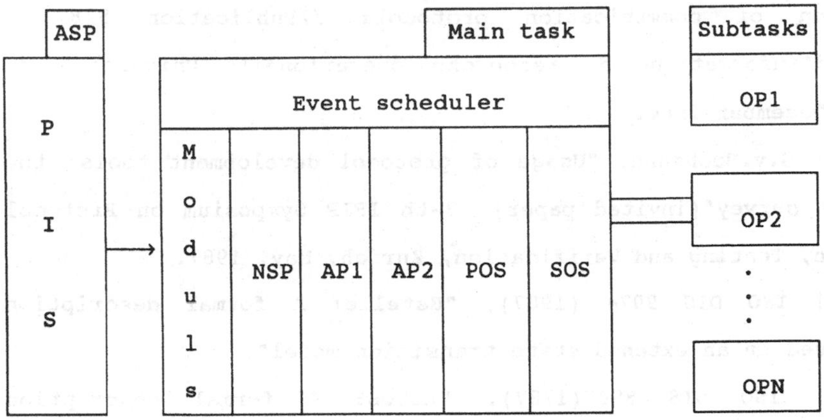

Fig.8. Stucture of AR with parallel execute operations.

Conclusion

The paper shows that aggregative mathematical schemes can be successfully applied for the solution of the main problems of protocol design, i.e. specification, validation, simulation and program implementation, using a single protocol specification. Specification languages AGREGAT-84 and ESTELLE/AG based on the application of aggregative mathematical schemes have been created as well as validation and simulation systems for the given specification languages. Use of simulation in protocol analysis allows to determine optimal protocol parameters (e.g. timer duration, the number of repetitions) which is particulary import for effective functioning of protocols.

Simulation makes protocol tempoblocking analysis possible, while this cannot be done by reachability states techniques.

References

|Boch84| G.v.Bochmann, G.Gerber, J.M.Serre. Semiautomatic implementation of communication protocols //Publication 518. - Department d'informatique de recherche operationelle Universite de Montreal. - December 1984.

|Boch87| G.v.Bochmann, "Usage of protocol development tools: the results of a survey"(invited paper), 7-th IFIP Symposium on Protocol Specification, Testing and Verification, Zurich, May, 1987.

|Este87| ISO DIS 9074 (1987), "Estelle: A formal description technique based on an extened state transition model".

|Loto87| ISO DIS 8807(1987), "LOTOS: A formal description technique".

|Mil80| R.Milner, A calculus of communicating systems, Lecture Notes in Computer Science, Vol. 92, 1980.

|Pran82a| H.Pranevitchius, " Models and methods for computer system investigation ", Mokslas, Vilnius, 1982, 228p., (in Russian).

|Pran82b| H.Pranevitchius and N.Listopadskis, "Aggregative approach application for formal specification and modeling of protocols", Acad. Sci. USSR, Moscow, 1982, 63p., (in Russian).

|Pran83| H.Pranevitchius⊥ and A.Chmieliauskas, "Correctness analysis and performance predication of protocols using aggregative approach and control sequences method", Acad. Sci. USSR, Moscow, 1983, 32p., (in Russian).

|Pran85| H.Pranevitchius, A.Chmieliauskas⊥ V.Pilkauskas, "Protocol

simulation and verification in PRANAS", Packet Switching Networks, ESTI, Riga, 1985, p.209- 231, (in Russian).

|Pran87| H.Pranevitchius and A.Chmieliauskas. ASPECT- language for specification services and protocols. XII-th cconference of computer networks. Moscow - Odesa, 1987, p.76-81. (in Russian).

|Pran88| H.Pranevitchius and A.Panevezys, "Proof of correctness technique for aggregative models of protocols", IFAC/IMAC Symp. on distributed intelligence systems, Varna, 1988, p.100-105.

|Pran89| H.Pranevitchius and A.Panevezys, " Automated implementation of protocols in terms of aggregative specifications ", Automatic and Computer Technic, Riga, 1989, p.17-22, (in Russian).

|SDL87| CCITT S6 XI, Recomendation Z.100(1987).

A COMPOSITIONAL PROOF SYSTEM FOR DISTRIBUTED PROGRAMS

Kastytis GEČAS

Institute of Mathematics and Informatics
Lithuanian Academy of Sciences
232600, Vilnius, Akademijos 4, Lithuania

Abstract. The current paper deals with the issues of axiomatic semantics of communication primitives in distributed programs. As a sample language we use a certain class of distributed programs with a synchronous mode of communication regarded as standard. A compositional proof system dealing with partial correctness of distributed programs is presented. The correctness of formalization is justified by proving the system to be sound and relatively complete. The proof is based on the given operational semantics. We also consider the structure of interrelation predicates – global invariants of distributed programs. This is done in order to get insight into the correspondence between communication modes and proof systems which define axiomatic semantics of distributed programs.

Introduction

The proof of program correctness was firstly intended as a posteriori technique for a verification of programs. Unfortunately, these hopes have not come true because of the undecidability of certain problems. Though practical verification is of a great interest (see, for example [11]), now it is understood that proof systems for proving properties of programs have to be used in a program design process as a technique to define programming language semantics.

Usually such a kind of semantics is called axiomatic. The main idea in this approach is to consider axioms and proof rules for proving program correctness (more rigorously, theorems deduced using them) as meanings of various programming language constructs. We are interested in an axiomatic semantics of communicating sequential processes. Here we revise and extend our previous paper [4].

One of the aims of this paper is to present a firm, formal foundation for such a semantics. With that end in view, on the whole we have to consider the main phenomenon in distributed programs, that of communication. It has to be supplied with adequate tools for a description of communication, separately from termination, sequential composition, nondeterminism, nesting and other operational phenomena of distributed programming. Therefore we investigate the simplest possible subset of communicating sequential processes. Once the basic intuition behind communication was captured formally, the axiomatic semantics became clear as well.

In order to support the program design process, the axiomatic semantics ought to be reflected by it. The program design has its own requirements. For instance, any large system must be organized so that it can be understood and modified. This issue is very important for concurrent and distributed systems because of their inherent complexity.

A top–down way of the design has proved to be an effective approach to achieve the above requirement. In its turn,the top–down approach determines certain properties of syntax and semantics for programming languages to be used. In particular, a modularization, one of the main principles in top–down design, causes extra restrictions on the form of correctness proofs in the axiomatic semantics. A proof of correctness of programs has to be compositional.

Compositionality means that the proof of correctness of the entire program must rely only upon the proof of correctness of its components (see [8] for a survey on the subject). While we consider Hoare logics, that is, proof systems dealing with partial correctness of programs, compositionality can be defined in the following way:

The compositional Hoare logics is a proof system where any deducible assertion $\{P\}p\{Q\}$ is deduced solely from the assertions of the components of program p.

The classical Hoare logics for structured sequential programs [6] is compositional, whereas most of proof systems for parallel, including distributed programs are not. This is caused by the conditions used as assumptions in certain inference rules. Noninterference [10], cooperation [1] might be the examples of such context conditions. Such rules used so far may be regarded as metarules where assumptions are proofs of assertions, not assertions themselves.The rules with context conditions contradict the compositionality, and consequently, the simplicity of proof systems in question.

If one defines the axiomatic semantics for the programs involving communication, then compositionality of proof systems becomes of vital importance. This claim may be explained as follows.

Since proof rules define the meaning of program constructs, compositionality is a necessary condition for semantics to be flexible. For instance, various meanings of statements may be assigned simply by selecting appropriate proof rules. This is especially important as various communication mechanisms are adopted in distributed programs [5, 9]. Compositionality allows us to separate the definitions of statements and the definitions of communication itself. So we may fix a syntax of the distributed programs, and then consider semantical issues related with the communication. In this paper synchronous communication (rendezvous mode) is regarded as standard. We describe an axiomatic and operational semantics for the distributed programs with standard communication. Given this "standard" semantics, we investigate what and how proof rules have to be changed in order to axiomatize other communication modes.

Section 1 defines syntax for distributed programs, a certain subset of communicating sequential processes [7].

In Section 2 we describe an axiomatic semantics of the programming language under consideration. We present a proof system for the inference of Hoare formulae like: $\{P\}p\{Q\}$, expressing partial correctness of program p with respect to assertions P and Q [4]. An assertion language is that of first–order arithmetics extended by trace variables for communication histories and appropriate functions and predicates. A similar proof system is presented in [13] without formal justification.

The main feature of the proof system is that of compositionality achieved by introduction of special predicates defined on history variables. The predicates, called here interrelation predicates, are intended to reflect a joint behaviour of communicating processes. The interrelation predicate is a special form of global invariant of distributed program introduced in [1].

In order to define the validity of Hoare formulae,we propose an operational semantics (in Section 3). Its definition is presented in axiomatic way as in [12]. The semantics distinguishes itself by an explicit use of communication histories as components of execution states.

Soundness and relative completeness of the presented proof system is shown in Section 4. Thus, the presented axiomatization may be regarded as an adequate description of the standard communication mode. We should emphasize that through compositionality the proof is carried out straightforwardly by induction on a structure of programs(compare with [1] where a proof like this is indirect).

In Sections 5 and 6 we consider the structure of interrelation predicates. This allows to get insight into the structure of proof systems corresponding to various mechanisms of communication in distributed programs.

1. Language of distributed programs.

We consider a CSP-like [7] language, which is an abstract, simplified version of the distributed programming language PROSTOR [5]. As PROSTOR was intended to be used for functional applications, the programming language under consideration has also only determinate sequential statements. It is its main difference from CSP.

To reason about the properties of programs formally, we have to define all syntactic and semantic domains in a rigorous way. Henceforth we fix a formal language $\mathcal{L}^0$ of first-order predicates with signature $\{<, =, +, \times, 0, 1\}$ demanding all the variables, expressions, and formulae in programs to belong to $\mathcal{L}^0$.

In the sequel we use the following denotations.

B, a set of Boolean expressions ranged over by b,

$Var = \{x, y, z, \ldots\}$, a set of variables,

$Expr$, a set of terms ranged over by e,

$Names = \{L, \ldots\}$, a set of process names disjoint with Var,

Bop, a set of basic statements ranged over by op. Basic statements are:

ε, null (**skip**) statement,

$x := e$, an assignment statement,

$L \leftarrow e$, an output statement "Send (a value of) e to (a process with a name) L". Note that $L \leftarrow e$ is another notation of CSP's statement $L!e$.

$L \rightarrow x$, an input statement "Assign the value sent by (the process named) L to a variable x" (written $L?x$ in CSP).

The set of *sequential programs* Seq_prog ranged over by $p, q, \ldots$ is generated by the following rule:

$p ::= p; q \mid \textbf{if } b \textbf{ then } p \textbf{ else } q \mid \textbf{while } b \textbf{ do } p \mid op.$

A *parallel program* p is defined by the rule:

$$p ::= L_1 :: p_1 \| \ldots \| L_n :: p_n, \qquad L_i \in Names, \quad i = \overline{1, n}.$$
$$p_i \in Seq\_prog,$$

A sequential program p_i with $i \in \{1, \ldots, n\}$ in a parallel program p will be called ith process with a coordinate i and name L_i.

We assume $Proc\_var, In\_names, Out\_names$ assignments defined by induction on the syntactic structure to be given. By $Proc\_var(p), In\_names(p), Out\_names(p)$

we denote, respectively, sets of process variables, names of processes from which the data is received, and names of processes to which the data is sent.

A ***distributed program*** is a parallel program in which processes have disjoint names, disjoint sets of variables, and communicate strictly between themselves, i.e., we allow, for the sake of simplicity, only one-level parallel communication without selfcommunication.

Formally, we say that a parallel program $L_1 :: p_1 \| \ldots \| L_n :: p_n$ is a ***distributed program*** if

1. $L_i \neq L_j \iff i \neq j, \quad i,j = \overline{1,n}$.
2. $Proc\_var(L_i :: p_i) \cap Proc\_var(L_j :: p_j) = \emptyset$ for all $i,j = \overline{1,n}$, such that $i \neq j$.
3. $In\_names(L_i :: p_i) \cup Out\_names(L_i :: p_i) \subseteq \{L_1, \ldots, L_n\} \backslash L_i$.

In the sequel the set *Prog* will denote a set of distributed programs.

Considering an informal semantics for the contructs of the language *Prog* the classical meaning of all sequential statements is adopted. As mentioned above we regard a synchronous communication as standard and fix it till Section 5. Thereby communication may only happen when both primitives, output statement $L_j \leftarrow e$ from ith process, and input statement $L_i \rightarrow x$ from jth process, are ready for an execution. Otherwise, they have to wait for one another. The result of their joint execution is the same as performing an assignment $x := e$.

2. Axiomatic semantics of distributed programs.

In axiomatic semantics the meaning of constructs of the programming language is described using partial correctness formulae, or Hoare formulae. A formula $\{P\}p\{Q\}$ has the following meaning:

If an assertion P is true before the execution of program p then an assertion Q will be true after it, if and when p terminates. The assertion P (Q) is called a pre–condition (respectively, a post–condition).

A ***partial correctness theory*** of program p is a set of formulae pairs (P, Q) where P, Q are the formulae of some formal assertion language, and $\{P\}p\{Q\}$ are the theorems. The logic semantics is given for programming language by associating with each program its partial correctness theory. The axiomatized theory of partial correctness will be called axiomatic semantics.

In this section we define a proof system ABC which describes the axiomatic semantics of the language *Prog*.

As discussed in various papers on axiomatic semantics of parallel programs, we need auxiliary variables (variables which are not originally presented in programs) for describing the semantics. These variables are often arithmetical. In a converse approach adopted here, the variables that range over communication histories (introduced in [3]) are used. Such variables will be called history variables. In order to use history variables in assertions, we have to extend a language $\mathcal{L}^0$ from Section 1. This extension will be called $\mathcal{L}$.

Let $C = \{c^1, c^2, \ldots\}$ be a set of ***(communication) history variables*** such that $C \cap (Var \cup Names) = \emptyset$.The values of these variables will be finite sequences over a set defined below. We require C to be included in the assertion language. In order to deal with the sequences the signature of $\mathcal{L}$ have to include the corresponding function and predicate symbols, too. Though we are not interested in their full their description, however, we assume symbols $\circ, \Lambda, \sqsubseteq$ are included in the signature. They are interpreted as a concatenation of finite sequences, an empty sequence, and a relation of prefix, respectively. The reader who is interested in a concrete language of this kind is referred to [14].

In the following we shall use the sign of equality sign in different meanings understandable from the context.

We now define the values of history variables.

At first recall the definitions of $\mathcal{L}^0$ and *Prog*.The program variables and expressions from *Expr* are assumed to be assigned nonnegative integer values. By the definition of output and input statements the values communicated by processes in distributed programs are natural numbers, too. Therefore the set of communicated values is considered to be equal to the set of natural numbers $\mathcal{N}$ ranged over by n.

Let $p = L_1 :: p_1 \| \ldots \| L_n :: p_n$ be a distributed program. We associate with each process p_i the only history variable c^i. The value of such a variable is a sequence of *communication records* $(i,j;v)$ and/or $(j,i;v)$ with $i,j \in \overline{1,n}$ and $v \in \mathcal{N}$. A communication record $(i,j;v)$ $((j,i;v))$ of ith communication history corresponds to an output (respectively, to an input) of value v from ith process to jth process.

A formal system ABC for proving Hoare formulae consists of axioms and inference rules defined below. All the axioms and rules A–1—A–8 are actually axiom schemes parameterized by the coordinates of processes containing definable statements. Each variable free in assertions is either local to the process or history variable of the process. Similar restrictions apply to rule C–1 whenever the program is sequential. Assertions P_i, Q_i in rule B–1 contain no free variables nonlocal to process $L_i :: p$. A formula $P^{x,y}_{e_1,e_2}$ denotes an assertion obtained from P through a substitution of all the occurrences of free variables x and y by corresponding expressions e_1 and e_2.

Axioms and proof rules A–1—A–7, except A–3 and A–4 are classic [6] and thus need no additional motivation.

A - 1:

$$\{P\}\ \varepsilon\ \{P\}$$

A - 2:

$$\{P^x_e\}\ x := e\{P\}$$

A - 3:

$$\{P^{c^i}_{c^i \circ (i,j;e)}\}\ L_j \leftarrow e\ \{P\}$$

To understand the axiom, consider an output statement $L_j \leftarrow e$ belonging to ith process. The axiom states that it has no effect on any program variable. But whenever an output action had taken place, a history of communication of process must change. Or, in our terms, a new communication record has to be appended to the previous trace of records. Thus, the entire effect of an execution of the output statement is much the same as of an assignment $c^i := c^i \circ (i,j;e)$, provided c^i were a variable of the ith process.

A - 4:

$$\{\forall v\ P^{x,c^i}_{v,c^i \circ (j,i;v)}\}\ L_j \rightarrow x\ \{P\}$$

Input and output statements are similar, so are the corresponding axioms. However, according to the purpose of an input statement, its target variable ought to be assigned some value received from another process. But executing the statement alone does not determine certain input value. Actually, any feasible value can be received. In such a case the communication history may have more than one successor, each recording a different input value. The situation is resolved by universally quantifying the precondition of the input statement.

A - 5:

$$\frac{\{P\&b\}\ p\ \{Q\} \quad \{P\&\neg b\}\ q\ \{Q\}}{\{P\}\textbf{if}\ b\ \textbf{then}\ p\ \textbf{else}\ q\ \{Q\}}$$

A - 6:

$$\frac{\{P\}\ p\ \{R\} \quad \{R\}\ q\ \{Q\}}{\{P\}\ p; q\ \{Q\}}$$

A - 7:

$$\frac{\{P\&b\}\ p\ \{P\} \quad P\&\neg b \supset Q}{\{P\}\textbf{while}\ b\ \textbf{do}\ p\ \{Q\}}$$

A - 8:

$$\frac{\{P\}\ p\ \{Q\}}{\{P\}\ L :: p\ \{Q\}}$$

The rule A–8 is the only way to reason about the properties of entire processes of distributed programs. It states that the correctness of a process is completely determined by the correctness of its program.

As mentioned above, proof systems for parallel programs had to be faced by the following problem: how to deduce partial correctness of the entire distributed program using the proofs for processes.

To solve this problem in a compositional way, we introduce a specific predicate on communication histories, called the ***interrelation predicate*** $\mathcal{B}(c^1, \ldots, c^n)$:

$$\mathcal{B}(c^1, \ldots, c^n) \equiv \exists c\ \forall i\ 1 \leqslant i \leqslant n\ c|_i = c^i,$$

where communication history sequence $c|_i$ is obtained from a sequence c by deleting all the communication records without i as first or second coordinate. Sequence c is called the ***global*** communication history of histories $c^1, \ldots, c^n$.

B - 1.

$$\frac{\{P_i\&c^i = \Lambda\}\ L_i :: p_i\ \{Q_i\} \qquad i = \overline{1,n}}{\{\mathop{\&}\limits_{j=1}^{n} P_i\}\ L_1 :: p_1 \| \ldots \|\ L_n :: p_n \{\mathop{\&}\limits_{i=1}^{n} Q_i \& \mathcal{B}(c^1, \ldots, c^n)\}}$$

In the proposed proof system communication histories are local to processes and can't be changed by other ones. Thus we are offered to prove the correctness of each process in isolation, and then deduce the correctness of the entire distributed program. Rule B–1 states that the processes of the distributed program started with empty histories in preconditions P_i will terminate (if it is the case!) in the resulting global state satisfying the interrelation predicate. Moreover, as we'll see in the proof of Lemma 1 in Section 4 the interrelation predicate holds before and after each occurrence of communication while executing distributed programs. Usually, a predicate which has this property is called a global invariant of the program (see [1]).

On the other hand, the interrelation predicate is the only place in the suggested proof system where certain communication mechanism is presupposed. Therefore the predicate of this type may be regarded as a formal description of the communication mechanism.

We conclude a presentation of the proof system with a rule of consequence or a *cut-rule.*

C - 1.

$$\frac{P \supset P' \; \{P'\}\; p \; \{Q'\} \; Q' \supset Q}{\{P\}\; p\; \{Q\}}$$

It should be emphasized that through composionality cut-rule C-1 may be eliminated. It is possible to replace it by specialized cut rules. It is sufficient to add to rules A-6 and B-1 pure logical implication-type premises. A full proof is straightforward, and it is omitted here.

3. Operational semantics for distributed programs.

To substantiate a claim that the interrelation predicate $\mathcal{B}$ expresses the essence of synchronous communication, we prove that a proof system ABC is sound and relatively complete with respect to an operational semantics for distributed programs. In this section we provide such a semantics. The semantics is described in terms of transitions between configurations of programs. Specifically, the sequences of configurations determined by feasible transitions are to be assigned to a distributed program so defining its operational meaning. On the strength of the meaning we then define formally the validity of Hoare formulae.

Now we present some preliminaries.

To simplify the semantics, we assume that Boolean expressions in the statements **if–then–else** and **while–do** are quantifier–free formulas of $\mathcal{L}^0$. The right-hand sides of assignment statements as well as the value expressions in output statements are assumed to be terms in $\mathcal{L}^0$ as well.

Let

A^* be a set of all the finite sequences over a set A with a distinguished element Λ for an empty sequence.

σ be a mapping from Var to $\mathcal{N}$, called the *memory state*,

δ be a mapping from $C = \{c^1, \ldots, c^i \ldots\}$ to $(\mathcal{N} \times \mathcal{N} \times \mathcal{N})^*$, called the *history state.*

Then an ordered pair $s = < p, \sigma >$ or triple $s = < p, \sigma, \delta >$ is called the *configuration* of p. The letter S stands for a set of configurations of programs in *Prog*.

One may consider a configuration as a snapshot of the execution of the program. That is, the memory state associates integer values with the variables of the considered, to be executed program , whereas the history state assigns communication histories to the history variables. Therefore a pair of the memory state and the history state in a configuration constitutes an integral entity to be called the *program state.* Note that in configurations the history states are optional; they do not restrict and predetermine possible execution steps of distributed programs. Nevertheless, it is convenient to us them explicitly, thereby simplifying the definition of transition relation (compare with

[1]) and also the definition of truth of assertions. In the set of configurations we distinguish *initial* configurations $< p, \sigma >$ and *final* ones $< \varepsilon, \sigma, \delta >$. Informally speaking, the initial configurations are those before any step of execution of the program, thereby, before any attempt of communication. Therefore an initial configuration $< p, \sigma >$ may be identified with an empty history configuration $< p, \sigma, \delta^{\Lambda} >$, where $\delta^{\Lambda}(c^i) = \Lambda$ for all i. Similarly, we make no difference between a final configuration $< \varepsilon, \sigma, \delta >$ and its program state. Usually we use the notation $< \sigma, \delta >$ for the configurations of this kind. The notation S_F stands for a set of final configurations.

Because the sets of variables of processes in the distributed programs are disjoint, and there is one–to–one correspondence between processes and history variables, the program states may be legally expressed in a handy form of tuples.

We say a configuration $< p_1 \| \cdots \| p_n, \sigma, \delta >$ is *distributed* if

$\sigma_i = \sigma|_{Proc\_var(p_i)}$,

$\delta_i = \delta(c^i) \in \Delta^i =_{df} ((\{i\} \times \{1, \ldots, n\} \times \mathcal{N}) \cup (\{1, \ldots, n\} \times \{i\} \times \mathcal{N}))^*$.

Note that history states in the distributed configurations may be replaced by their values. Therefore we shall write $< \vec{p}, \sigma_1, \ldots, \sigma_n, \delta_1, \ldots, \delta_n >$ or $< \vec{p}, \vec{\sigma}, \vec{\delta} >$ for the distributed configurations. We also assume that all the configurations of the distributed programs are the distributed ones. We also use a notation $< p, \sigma_i, \delta_i >$ in order to stress that p is a component of the ith process. In either case when the syntax is not so important, we use a previous notation $< p, \sigma, \delta >$, too.

Let M stand for a model of the assertion language $\mathcal{L}$ (see Sect. 1), an extension of the standard model M^0 of $\mathcal{L}^0$. Thereby this interpretation includes standard values (natural numbers) for non–history variables in $\mathcal{L}$. In addition, we have finite sequences in M as a domain of values of history variables. From now on we consider only the models of this kind and denote a set of them by $\mathfrak{M}$. While the values of variables are to be given by states, the values of terms and formulae we define in the following, standard way.

If e is a term of $\mathcal{L}$ with integer variables $x_1, \ldots, x_n$ and history variables $c_1, \ldots, c_n$, then a value of e in program state (σ, δ) is obtained by evaluating

$$e[\sigma(x_1)/x_1, \ldots, \sigma(x_n)/x_n, \delta_1/c^1, \ldots, \delta_m/c^m],$$

i.e., the term obtained from e by a simultaneous substitution of values $\sigma(x_1), \ldots, \sigma(x_n)$ and $\delta_1, \ldots, \delta_m$ for variables $x_1, \ldots, x_n$ and $c^1, \ldots, c^m$, respectively. Similarly, we may define $P(\sigma, \delta)$ where P is a formula of $\mathcal{L}$. Then we say that formula P *is true in a state* (σ, δ) *in model* M (denoted $(\sigma, \delta) \models_M P$). In order to reason about the programs in initial configurations, we consider formulae of $\mathcal{L}^0$ which are true in a memory state σ in model M^0 as true in a program state $(\sigma, \delta^{\Lambda})$ in the model M. We also say that a formula is true in model M if it is true in all the program states of M.

Now we are ready to define an operational semantics for the distributed programs. Meanings of the statements in *Prog* are specified by transition inference systems. We distinguish two types of transitions: immediate transitions and their "closures", simply called the transitions.

By an *immediate transition* relation we mean a binary relation $\rightarrow \subseteq S \times S$ such that $\forall s \in S_F \; \forall s' \in S \; (s, s') \notin \rightarrow$, where S_F stands for a set of final configurations.

We write $s \rightarrow s'$ if $(s, s') \in \rightarrow$.

A triple $(S, S_F, \rightarrow)$ is called the *transition system* and is denoted by the letter S.

A transitive and reflexive closure of the direct transition relation specifies the *transition* relation of the system denoted by $\rightarrow^*$.

Hence, $s \rightarrow^* s'$ iff there exists a sequence of configurations $\gamma = s_0, \ldots, s_n$, called the *computation,* such that $s = s_0, s_i \rightarrow s_{i+1}, \ (i = \overline{1, n-1}), s_n = s'$.

We say that γ *confirms* the transition $s \rightarrow^* s'$.

Intuitively, a transition between the configurations

$$< p, \sigma, \delta > \rightarrow^* < p', \sigma', \delta' >$$

expresses a possibility to execute the program p starting in a program state (σ, δ) and resulting in a program state (σ', δ') with the remaining, to be executed program p'. Immediate transitions are devoted to capture the elementary steps of execution while composite actions cause sequences of such steps.

On the whole, possible transitions are determined by the structure of programs and the memory state. Some programs in certain states can't be executed. In such a case corresponding configurations may have no successors. Recall that the final configurations have this property by the definition of an immediate transition relation. Of course, it is not accidental. Transitions, ending in final configurations, do reflect normally terminating processes of execution of the program. Such transitions are called *terminating* as well as computations confirming them.

Now we specify an immediate transition relation for the programs in *Prog*. By virtue of the structured syntax of *Prog* the definition may be presented in the axiomatic way [12].

We define axioms like: $s \rightarrow s'$ and inference rules

$$\frac{s_1 \rightarrow s_1' \quad s_2 \rightarrow s_2'}{s \rightarrow s'}$$

All the program states in the configurations are supplied with a subscript i, a coordinate of the process containing the considered statements.

The following axioms concern transitions between the configurations of sequential statements. With rule X–8 for the sequential composition and rule X–9 for processes added, they constitute a full description of transition relation between the configurations of sequential programs. Note that an inference of transitions of that kind may be accomplished individually. As a result, transitions (and also computations) of processes are independent of each other.

X - 1. $< x := e, \sigma_i, \delta_i > \rightarrow < \varepsilon, \sigma_i[\sigma_i(e)/x], \delta_i >$,
where $\sigma[v/x]$ stands for a state σ' which is equal to σ, except $\sigma'(x) = v$.

X - 2. $<$ **if** b **then** p **else** $q, \sigma_i, \delta_i > \rightarrow < p, \sigma_i, \delta_i >$, if $\sigma \models_M b$,

X - 3. $<$ **if** b **then** p **else** $q, \sigma_i, \delta_i > \rightarrow < q, \sigma_i, \delta_i >$, if $\sigma \models_M \neg b$,

X - 4. $<$ **while** b **do** $p, \sigma_i, \delta_i > \rightarrow < p;$ **while** b **do** $p, \sigma_i, \delta_i >$, if $\sigma \models_M b$,

X - 5. $<$ **while** b **do** $p, \sigma_i, \delta_i > \rightarrow < \varepsilon, \sigma_i, \delta_i >$, if $\sigma \models_M \neg b$.

The axioms for communication statements are the only ones where history states are modified. Each action of output and input appends one record to the corresponding communication history. Note the main difference between axioms X–6 and X–7. Because of the nondeterministic nature of an input action executed alone the configuration of the input statement in X–7 has a countable number of successive final configurations – each for a distinct input value.

X – 6. $< L_j \leftarrow e, \sigma_i, \delta_i > \rightarrow < \varepsilon, \sigma_i, \delta_i \circ (i, j; e(\sigma_i)) >$

X – 7. $< L_j \rightarrow x, \sigma_i, \delta_i > \rightarrow < \varepsilon, \sigma_i[v/x], \delta_i \circ (i, j; v) >$ for any $v \in \mathcal{N}$

X – 8.

$$\frac{< p, \sigma_i, \delta_i > \rightarrow < p', \sigma_i', \delta_i' >}{< p; q, \sigma_i, \delta_i > \rightarrow < p'; q, \sigma_i', \delta_i' >}$$

The above inference rule states that it is possible to execute p and then q, if it is possible to execute p alone. Incidentally, the effect of execution on the program states is the same.

X – 9.

$$\frac{< p, \sigma_i, \delta_i > \rightarrow < p', \sigma_i', \delta_i' >}{< L_i :: p, \sigma_i, \delta_i > \rightarrow < L_i :: p', \sigma_i', \delta_i' >}$$

According to the rule, an execution of the individual process of the distributed program is determined only by its sequential program. Of course, not all the transitions being inferred in this way will cause transitions between the configurations of the entire distributed program.

Such cases are described by the following rules. The first one deals with an execution without communication as reflected in communication histories being unchanged.

Y – 1.

$$\frac{< L_i :: p, \sigma_i, \delta_i > \rightarrow < L_i :: p', \sigma_i', \delta_i' > \quad \delta_i = \delta_i'}{< \vec{p}, \vec{\sigma}, \vec{\delta} > \rightarrow < \vec{p}[p_i'/p_i], \vec{\sigma}[\sigma_i'/\sigma_i], \vec{\delta} >},$$

where $\vec{p}[p_i'/p_i]$ denotes a substitution of process p_i by process p_i'.

The following is an inference rule for communication. It is a bit unusual as it has no direct reference to communication statements. But as we shall see later in the proofs, it appears that the similarity of communication histories is a suitable condition for a proper inference.

By ***similar*** communication histories we mean the histories with the last communication records to be equal.

Y–2.

$$\frac{\begin{array}{c}< p_i, \sigma_i, \delta_i > \rightarrow < p_i', \sigma_i', \delta_i' > \\ < p_j, \sigma_j, \delta_j > \rightarrow < p_j', \sigma_j', \delta_j' >\end{array}}{s \rightarrow s[p_i'/p_i, p_j'/p_j, \sigma_i'/\sigma_i, \sigma_j'/\sigma_j, \delta_i'/\delta_i, \delta_j'/\delta_j]},$$

provided histories δ_i and δ_j are similar, and $s =< p_1 \| \ldots \| p_n, \sigma_1, \ldots, \sigma_n, \delta_1, \ldots, \delta_n >$.

In the sequel we call the above transition inference system T.

Now we are able to define an operational meaning of the programs we consider. To do this, assign to a program the set of its terminating transitions.

Relying on the operational semantics, we now are able to interpret Hoare formulae:

A formula $\{P\}\ p\ \{Q\}$ is *true* (in a model M), written $\models_M \{P\}\ p\ \{Q\}$, if the following implication holds:

$$\forall(\sigma,\delta)\ (\sigma',\delta')((\sigma,\delta)\models_M P \text{ and } <p,\sigma,\delta>\rightarrow^*<\sigma',\delta'>\Rightarrow(\sigma',\delta')\models_M Q)$$

4. Proof of soundness and completeness.

We precede proof of soundness of ABC with the following main lemma. As was mentioned above, not all computations of processes which might be inferred cause computations of the entire distributed program. The lemma below describes a close relationship between computations of distributed programs and interrelation predicates – the validity of the interrelation predicate is necessary and sufficient for mixing local process computations to yield a global one.

Lemma 1. *Let $\vec{p} = p_1\|\ldots\|p_n$ be a distributed program, and let $(\vec{\sigma},\vec{\delta})$ be a program state, in which the interrelation predicate $\mathcal{B}(c^1,\ldots,c^n)$ holds. Then the following are equivalent:*

1. $<\vec{p},\vec{\sigma},\vec{\delta}>\rightarrow^*<\vec{p}',\vec{\sigma}',\vec{\delta}'>$.
2. $<p_i,\sigma_i,\delta_i>\rightarrow^*<p_i',\sigma_i',\delta_i'>$ for all $i=\overline{1,n}$ and $(\vec{\sigma}',\vec{\delta}')\models_M \mathcal{B}(c^1,\ldots,c^n)$.

Proof. The proof of implication (1) $\Rightarrow$ (2) goes by induction on the length l of the computation, confirming the transition $<\vec{p},\vec{\sigma},\vec{\delta}>\rightarrow^*<\vec{p}',\vec{\sigma}',\vec{\delta}'>$.

For coinciding configurations, when $l=0$, the implication is trivial.

Let an induction hypothesis for $l=L\geqslant 0$ hold, and the length of computation be equal to $L+1$. There is the last but one configuration s such that

$$<\vec{p},\vec{\sigma},\vec{\delta}>\rightarrow^* s \qquad s\rightarrow<\vec{p}',\vec{\sigma}',\vec{\delta}'>.$$

We may apply the hypothesis to the first transition . Since the second one has to be inferred either by rule Y–1 or by rule Y–2, there exist corresponding either one or two immediate transitions of processes. Because the other processes do no transition, now there follows the existence of computations confirming the transitions of processes.

To finish the proof, it is sufficient to show that the interrelation predicate still holds in the last program state $<\vec{\sigma}',\vec{\delta}'>$.

Let us consider both specified cases of inference.

If the rule Y–1 was applied, then no communication history was changed during the transition. Since the interrelation predicate has free only history variables, it follows that $<\vec{\sigma}',\vec{\delta}'>\models_M \mathcal{B}$.

In the case of rule Y–2, immediate transitions of both communicating processes end in configurations with similar communication histories, that is, having the same last members.

Any immediate transition, inferable by rule Y–2, is inferable either from axiom X–6 or X–7. In both cases the communication history is extended by one communication record. Thus, the following statement holds.

Lemma 2. *Whenever $<p,\sigma_i,\delta_i>\rightarrow<p,\sigma_i',\delta_i'>$ with $\delta_i\neq\delta_i'$, then $\delta_i'=\delta_i\circ a$ for some communication record a.*

Applying this lemma to both premises of Y–2, we have that only two among communication histories are changed during the considered transition; both are extended by the same communication record. By the definition of $\mathcal{B}(c^1, \ldots, c^n)$, the truth of $\mathcal{B}$ in the program state of s implies that $\mathcal{B}$ is true in $< \vec{\sigma}', \vec{\delta}' >$. Thus, we have proved (1) $\Rightarrow$ (2).

For (2) $\Rightarrow$ (1), consider (2). By the definition of $\mathcal{B}(c^1, \ldots, c^n)$, the truth of $\mathcal{B}$ in program states $(\vec{\sigma}, \vec{\delta})$ and $(\vec{\sigma}', \vec{\delta}')$ implies an existence of global communication histories, say, δ and δ', respectively.

Notice that condition (2) itself does not impose any restriction on the interconnection of the global histories. Fortunately, one may always choose δ' such that δ is a prefix of δ'. This issue is of vital importance for the proof of (2) $\Rightarrow$ (1) and the whole lemma, because then we may use an induction on the difference of lengths of global histories instead of an induction on the length of all process computations. The proof of the statement is given in the Appendix.

On the strength of the above we may assume that $\delta \sqsubseteq \delta'$. Let $l = |\delta'| - |\delta|$ be a difference of lengths of the global communication histories δ, δ'.

If $l = 0$, then $\delta = \delta'$. So, there was no communication steps in the computation. By the definition of the interrelation predicate, the communication histories of processes must coincide, too:

$$\delta_i = \delta|_i = \delta'|_i = \delta'_i.$$

Thus, $\vec{\delta} = \vec{\delta}'$. Applying Y–1 (rule Y–2 is not applicable) to all immediate transitions in computations

$$< p_i, \sigma_i, \delta_i > \rightarrow \ldots \rightarrow < p'_i, \sigma'_i, \delta'_i >, \quad i = \overline{1,n},$$

we deduce the desired transition (1)

$$< \vec{p}, \vec{\sigma}, \vec{\delta} > \rightarrow \ldots \rightarrow < \vec{p}', \vec{\sigma}', \vec{\delta} > .$$

Let now $l > 0$, and let the last member of sequence δ' be equal to $(i, j; v)$. Then the last members of histories δ_i and δ_j coincide in the state $(\vec{\sigma}', \vec{\delta}')$ and are equal to $(i, j; v)$. By definition, history states δ'_i and δ'_j are similar.

Further, since $\delta \neq \delta'$, in both process computations

$$< p_i, \sigma_i, \delta_i > \rightarrow \ldots \rightarrow < p'_i, \sigma'_i, \delta'_i >,$$

$$< p_j, \sigma_j, \delta_j > \rightarrow \ldots \rightarrow < p'_j, \sigma'_j, \delta'_j >,$$

there have to be immediate transitions, where history states were changed.

For the last ones we apply rule Y–2.

Using the induction hypothesis for the preceding transitions and rule Y–1 for the subsequent ones, we obtain the entire transition

$$< \vec{p}, \vec{\sigma}, \vec{\delta} > \rightarrow^* < \vec{p}', \vec{\sigma}', \vec{\delta}' > .$$

This concludes the proof. $\square$

The proved lemma shows that the interrelation predicate is true in all the program states during the computation of the distributed program. But for the proof of soundness and relative completeness a weaker statement is sufficient. To define it, we need an additional concept.

We say that a history predicate $\mathcal{F}$ which holds on empty histories is a *semantic invariant* of the transition system $\mathcal{S}$ if for any distributed program the following are equivalent:

1. $<\vec{p},\vec{\sigma},\vec{\delta}^{\Lambda}>\rightarrow^{*}<\vec{\sigma}',\vec{\delta}'>$.
2. $<p_i,\sigma_i,\Lambda>\rightarrow^{*}<\sigma_i',\delta_i'>$ and $(\delta_1',\ldots,\delta_n')\models_M \mathcal{B}$.

Thus, semantic invariants are true only in the initial and final configurations of terminating transitions. It is obvious that the above lemma implies the following statement.

Invariant lemma. *Interrelation predicate $\mathcal{B}$ is a semantic invariant of $\mathcal{S}$.*

Now we are able to prove the soundness theorem (Theorem 1).

A proof system is *sound* (in model M) if all the provable formulae are true in M. In order to consider the soundness of ABC alone, we assume the sound (in model M) proof system, say, D, for pure logical formulae of $\mathcal{L}$ to be given.

Theorem 1. $\models_M \{P\}p\{Q\}$ *whenever* $\vdash_{\mathrm{D,ABC}} \{P\}p\{Q\}$.

Proof. Having fixed an arbitary model M (therefore, we omit the subscript M), it is sufficient to check the truth of axioms A–1—A–4 in model M and the preservation of truth by inference rules. This could be done in analogy to the proof of soundness in [2]. The only extra case is rule B–1 for distributed programs.

We wish to show that

$$\{\mathop{\&}_{i=1}^{n} P_i\}\ \vec{p}\ \{\mathop{\&}_{i=1}^{n} Q_i\&\mathcal{B}\}$$

is true, provided $\models \{P_i\&c^i=\Lambda\}\ p_i\ \{Q_i\}$ for all i.

Let $\vec{\sigma}$ be a memory state such that $\vec{\sigma}\models \mathop{\&}_{i=1}^{n} P_i$, and let a terminating computation

$$<\vec{p},\vec{\sigma}>=<\vec{p},\vec{\sigma},\vec{\delta}^{\Lambda}>\rightarrow\ldots\rightarrow<\vec{\sigma}',\vec{\delta}'>$$

be inferred in T.

According to Lemma 1, transitions of computations of processes

$$<p_i,\sigma_i,\Lambda>\rightarrow\ldots\rightarrow<\sigma_i',\delta_i'>,\quad i=\overline{1,n}$$

are to be inferred, and the interrelation predicate $\mathcal{B}$ is true in $(\vec{\sigma}',\vec{\delta}')$. Combining this fact with the premises of the rule, we have that the conclusion is true. This concludes the proof of Theorem 1. □

In the sequel we also use Corollary of Theorem 1.

Let $\mathcal{F}$ be a predicate on communication histories, which is true on empty histories. Replace $\mathcal{B}$ in proof rule B–1 by $\mathcal{F}$ and denote the rule by B–$1_{\mathcal{F}}$. A proof system with B–$1_{\mathcal{F}}$ instead of B–1 is called ABC$_{\mathcal{F}}$. The predicate defined in this way is called a *syntactic invariant* of the proof system. It is straightforward to prove that proof rule B–$1_{\mathcal{F}}$ is deducible in ABC provided $\mathcal{F}$ is implied by $\mathcal{B}$. So, any provable in ABC$_{\mathcal{F}}$ formula is provable in ABC as well. Hence, the following statement holds.

Corollary. *Let $\mathcal{F}$ be a syntactic invariant of* ABC$_{\mathcal{F}}$ *which is implied by $\mathcal{B}$. Then proof system* ABC$_{\mathcal{F}}$ *is sound.*

Now we proceed with the discussion of the completeness issues of ABC. A proof system is called *complete*, if all true formulae are deducible in it.

Because of its richness, as full predicate logic and arithmetics are included, the assertion language $\mathcal{L}$ has no recursive axiomatization. Therefore we consider the relative completeness [2] of the proof system ABC.

To provide the proof of relative completeness, we need the concept of strong postcondition.

By a ***strong postcondition*** $post(P,p)$ corresponding to a program p and an assertion P, we mean the following predicate:

$$(\sigma', \delta') \models_M post(P,p) \iff \text{there is a program state } (\sigma, \delta) \text{ such that}$$
$$(\sigma, \delta) \models_M P \text{ and } < p, \sigma, \delta > \to^* < \sigma', \delta' >$$

We remark here that the definition is ambiguous in reference to the programs under consideration. There are two types of the programs in *Prog*: sequential and distributed, so are two specific forms of the definition. They differ in a nature of the considered program states, and consequently, in free variables used for the formulation of strong postconditions as described below.

For distributed programs, program states on both sides of the equation have to be distributed as well. Otherwise, if sequential programs are considered, then program states are subscripted by a coordinate of the process which contains the considered sequential program. For example, if p belongs to process p_i, then the corresponding program states are (σ_i, δ_i) and (σ_i', δ_i').

We prefer the previous definition as it unifies both cases. The concrete form may be easily understood from the context.

By the definition, for an arbitrary program p and formula P we have

$$\models \{P\}\ p\ \{post(P,p)\}.$$

Fix now an arbitrary model M from $\mathfrak{M}$. We demand to hold two assumptions about the formulae of assertion language $\mathcal{L}$. The first assumption is equivalent to an existence of a complete non-axiomatizable system for the formulae of $\mathcal{L}$. We use the second one in the sequel as a hypothesis though it is not difficult to prove it. For the proof one may exploit the simple observation that history sequences may be coded by natural numbers. By the operational semantics, the programs in *Prog* describe partial recursive functions which are expressible in $\mathcal{L}$. So are the predicates. The proof is straightforward but rather longwinded, and thus it is omitted here.

1. Completeness assumption. All true in M formulae of $\mathcal{L}$ are the axioms of proof system ABC.

2. Expressiveness assumption. For any $P \in \mathcal{L}$ and $p \in Prog$, the strong postcondition $post(P,p)$ is expressible by the formula of $\mathcal{L}$.

Now we shall prove relative completeness of ABC. The relativity here means "relative to particular model M".

Theorem 2. *Let assumption 1 and 2 hold. Any true in M formula $\{P\}p\{Q\}$ is provable in ABC.*

Proof. We proceed by induction on the structure of program p.

Note that through the compositionality of our proof system a pure induction on a structure of programs is enough to establish completeness (compare with [1] where the proof like this is more complicated).

The proof of the claim for sequential and communication statements is much the same as in [2], where the completeness proof is done for sequential programs. So we omit it here.

An extra and crucial step is in the case of a distributed program, that is, when $p = p_1 \| \ldots \| p_n$.

Given

$$\models \{P\} p_1 \| \ldots \| p_n \; \{Q\}, \tag{4.1}$$

we have to prove

$$\vdash \{P\} p_1 \| \ldots \| p_n \; \{Q\}, \tag{4.2}$$

Assume (4.1), and let $(P_1, \ldots, P_n)$ be the list of predicates such that

$$\sigma_i \models_M P_i \;\; (i = \overline{1,n}) \iff (\sigma_1, \ldots, \sigma_n) \models_M P \tag{4.3}$$

Recall that P has no communication history variables, and a truth of P in memory state $\vec{\sigma}$ amounts to the truth of it in program state $(\vec{\sigma}, \vec{\delta}^{\Lambda})$ with all the histories empty.

As mentioned above for arbitrary formula R_i in $\mathcal{L}$ and program p in *Prog*

$$\models_M \{R_i\} \; p_i \; \{post(R_i, p_i)\} \tag{4.4}$$

In the sequel we are interestered in a particular case, when $R_i = \widehat{P}_i \& c^i = \Lambda$, where $\widehat{P}_i$ $(i = \overline{1,n})$ are formulae in $\mathcal{L}$ which express predicates P_i.

According to the induction hypothesis, any true Hoare formula for the sequential program is provable in ABC. Thus, (4.4) is provable as well.

$$\vdash_{\text{ABC}} \{\widehat{P}_i \& c^i = \Lambda\} \; p_i \; \{post(\widehat{P}_i \& c^i = \Lambda, p_i)\} \tag{4.5}$$

Having proved (4.5) for arbitrary i, we may apply rule B–1, and we get

$$\vdash_{\text{ABC}} \{\mathop{\&}_{i=1}^{n} \widehat{P}_i\} \; p_1 \| \ldots \| p_n \; \{\mathop{\&}_{i=1}^{n} post(R_i, p_i) \& \mathcal{B}(c^1, \ldots, c^n)\} \tag{4.6}$$

To prove (4.2), now it is sufficient to show

$$\models_M P \supset \mathop{\&}_{i=1}^{n} \widehat{P}_i \tag{4.7}$$

and

$$\models_M \mathop{\&}_{i=1}^{n} post(R_i, p_i) \& \mathcal{B}(c^1, \ldots, c^n) \supset Q. \tag{4.8}$$

The proof of (4.7) is trivial according to the definition of formulae $\widehat{P}_i$.

To prove (4.8), we show

$$\models_M \mathop{\&}_{i=1}^{n} post(R_i, p_i) \& \mathcal{B}(c^1, \ldots, c^n) \supset \mathrm{post}(P, \vec{p}) \tag{4.9}$$

and

$$\models_M post(P, \vec{p}) \supset Q. \tag{4.10}$$

An implication (4.10) holds by the definition of strong postconditions.

Analogously, by the definition of postconditions, if for some program state $(\vec{\sigma}', \vec{\delta}')$

$$(\vec{\sigma}', \vec{\delta}') \models_M \mathop{\&}_{i=1}^{n} post(R_i, p_i) \& \mathcal{B}(c^1, \ldots, c^n), \tag{4.11}$$

then there exists a program state $(\vec{\sigma}, \vec{\delta})$ such that

$$(\sigma_i, \delta_i) \models_M \widehat{P}_i \& c^i = \Lambda \tag{4.12}$$

and

$$< p_i, \sigma_i, \delta_i > \rightarrow^* < \sigma_i', \delta_i' > \qquad \text{for every } i.$$

This is possible only if $\vec{\delta} = \Lambda, \ldots, \Lambda$.

According to Lemma 1, (4.11) and (4.12) together imply

$$< \vec{p}, \vec{\sigma}, \vec{\delta} > \rightarrow^* < \vec{\sigma}', \vec{\delta}' > \tag{4.13}$$

and

$$< \vec{\sigma}, \vec{\delta} > \models_M P \tag{4.14}$$

By (4.13) and (4.14), $< \vec{\sigma}', \vec{\delta}' > \models_M post(P, \vec{p})$. So, we have proved (4.9).

Finally, applying the completeness assumption to (4.7), (4.9), (4.10), and combining the proved formulae in $\mathcal{L}$ with (4.6), by cut rule C–1, we get (4.2). □

5. Structure of the interrelation predicate

Theorems 1 and 2 of Sect.4 together imply an adequacy of an interrelation predicate $\mathcal{B}$ for an axiomatization of global invariant of synchronous communication. However, to verify the distributed programs it is often sufficient to use global invariants weaker than the interrelation predicate. The way of their definition relies heavily on certain weaker variants of interrelation predicates. On the other hand, we are interested in the nature of global invariants corresponding to the communication mechanisms different to synchronous. Intuitively, the synchronous communication is a most restrictive mode, and the interrelation of communication histories is the strongest requirement on communication.

In order to get more insight in an axiomatization of communication, in this section we concentrate on the structure of interrelation predicates.

Before we proceed to the proofs, let us define some technical details and terminology. In order to get the section self-contained, certain definitions of Sect.2 and 3 are revised, too. For convenience, in the sequel we identify history variables with the values they denote. Though we restrict ourselves with natural numbers as the values communicated by the processes, all the considerations equally apply to any set of the communicated values.

Let $\mathcal{N}$ be a set of natural numbers, and let for arbitrary $n \in \mathcal{N}, n > 0$,

$$\Delta = (\{1,\dots,n\} \times \{1,\dots,n\} \times \mathcal{N})^*$$

be a set of communication histories, ranged over by δ.

Then, for $i \in \{1,\dots,n\}$

$$\Delta^i = ((\{i\} \times \{1,\dots,n\} \times \mathcal{N}) \cup (\{1,\dots,n\} \times \{i\} \times \mathcal{N}))^*,$$
$$\Delta^i_{in} = (\{i\} \times \{1,\dots,n\} \times \mathcal{N})^*,$$
$$\Delta^i_{\mathrm{out}} = (\{1,\dots,n\} \times \{i\} \times \mathcal{N})^*.$$

Additionally, we define the following projection mappings

$$Out : \Delta \times \{i\} \to \Delta^i_{out},$$
$$In : \Delta \times \{i\} \to \Delta^i_{in},$$
$$| : \Delta \times \{i\} \to \Delta^i,$$

where an input from ith process history $In(\delta, i)$ (respectively, an output to ith process history $Out(\delta, i)$, and a projection $\delta|_i$) is obtained by deleting all the members of sequence δ without i as a first (respectively, second, and either first or second) argument.

Finally, a prefix of sequence δ ending in a member a will be denoted by $\delta[a]$.

Recall the definition of the interrelation predicate:

Communication histories $(\delta_1,\dots,\delta_n)$, $\delta_i \in \Delta^i$, $(i = \overline{1,n})$, are *interrelated* iff there exists history $\delta \in \Delta$ such that

$$\delta|_i = \delta_i, \qquad i = \overline{1,n}.$$

Our main concern is about the controversy between the local and global requirements in the interrelation predicate. By a local requirement we mean a relationship among individual communication histories or even among their members, independently of the rest of the list. Here we are interested to state local conditions as weak as possible. With that end in view we introduce an idea of a pairwise interrelation of communication histories.

Communication histories $(\delta_1,\dots,\delta_n)$, $\delta_i \in \Delta^i$, $(i = \overline{1,n})$, are *pairwise interrelated* if for every i and j such that $1 \leqslant i,j \leqslant n$, $i \neq j$,

$$Out(\delta_i, j) = In(\delta_j, i). \tag{5.1}$$

Proposition. *The pairwise interrelation is strictly weaker than*

$$\delta_i|_j = \delta_j|_i \qquad i,j = \overline{1,n}. \tag{5.2}$$

Proof. Since (5.2) $\Rightarrow$ (5.1) is satisfied by the definition of projection mappings, it is sufficient to show nonequivalence of (5.1) and (5.2).

For counterexample, consider

$$\delta_i = (j,i;x) \circ (i,j;y) \circ (i,j;z),$$

$$\delta_j = (i,j;y) \circ (i,j;z) \circ (j,i;x).$$

Histories δ_i and δ_j are pairwise interrelated, but $\delta_i|_j = \delta_i \neq \delta_j = \delta_j|_i$. □

We are going to describe the global condition on histories which in conjunction with the local pairwise interrelation is equivalent to the interrelation.

First, we consider a matching of communication records in communication histories of distinct processes. The matching is defined in terms of coincidence of communication records. Since one communication record in one communication history may coincide with several records in another one, we require, additionally, to take into consideration an input–output history. It seems that the matching defined below is a historical analog of the "semantic match" introduced in [1].

Second, by gluing all the matching members of histories, we construct the communication graph of histories, thus describing time dependencies of overall communication in the distributed program.

And finally, we establish that an acyclicity of the graph is the very global condition we require.

Consider two communication histories $\delta_i \in \Delta^i$ and $\delta_j \in \Delta^j$ with $i \neq j$, and a pair of their coinciding members. According to the definition of the sets of histories, two members of histories, one of δ_i, the other of δ_j, coincide only if both have the form: $(i,j;v)$ for some $v \in \mathcal{N}$.

We say that members a and b of respective histories $\delta_i \in \Delta^i$ and $\delta_j \in \Delta^j$ *match* if

1. $a = b$,
2. $Out(\delta_i[a], j) = In(\delta_j[b], i)$ whenever $a = (i,j;v)$.

A member of history is called *matching* if it has the matching pair in another history.

Now we are prepared to construct communication graphs.

Let $(\delta_1, \ldots, \delta_n)$ be a list of communication histories with $\delta_i \in \Delta^i$, $(i = \overline{1,n})$. Assign to each history δ_i a trivial directed graph, that is, a chain $G^0(\delta_i)$ whose nodes are identified with the communication records and whose arcs correspond to the precedence relation in history sequences.

A directed graph is a *communication graph* $G = G(\delta_1, \ldots, \delta_n)$ if it is obtained by gluing all the matching nodes of graphs $G^0(\delta_1), \ldots, G^0(\delta_n)$ and preserving all the incident arcs.

Examples of communication graphs are presented on Fig.1 and 2 (nodes conctructed by gluing are placed in double–line boxes).

Lemma 3. *If communication histories* $(\delta_1, \ldots, \delta_n)$, *with* $\delta_i \in \Delta^i$ $(i = \overline{1,n})$, *are pairwise interrelated, then all their members are matching.*

Proof. Assume the contrary. Then there exists some nonmatching member, say, $a = (i,j;v)$ in history δ_i. By definition, it belongs to $Out(\delta_i, j)$. It follows from the pairwise interrelation that $Out(\delta_i, j) = In(\delta_i, j)$ and, in particular, $Out(\delta_i[a], j) =$

$In(\delta_j[a], i)$ for some prefix $\delta_j[a]$. The last member of $\delta_j[a]$ matches a, so a contradiction is derived. □

$$\delta_1 = (1,2;x) \circ (1,3;y)$$
$$\delta_2 = (1,2;x) \circ (2,3;y)$$
$$\delta_3 = (3,2;z) \circ (2,3;y)$$

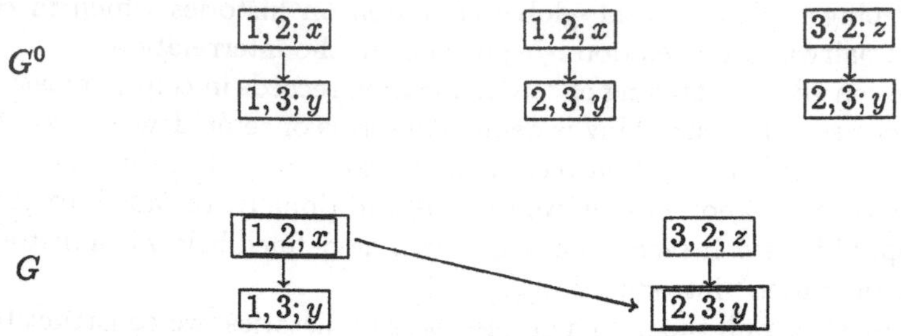

Figure 1.

$$\delta_1 = (1,2;x) \circ (3,1;z), \qquad \delta_2 = (2,3;y) \circ (1,2;x),$$
$$\delta_3 = (3,1;z) \circ (2,3;y), \qquad \delta_4 = (5,4;y) \circ (4,5;y),$$
$$\delta_5 = (5,4;y) \circ (4,5;z)$$

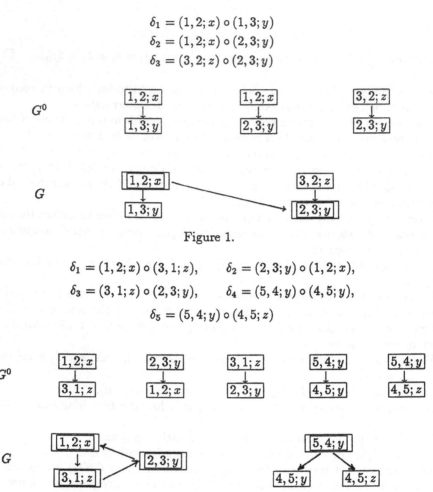

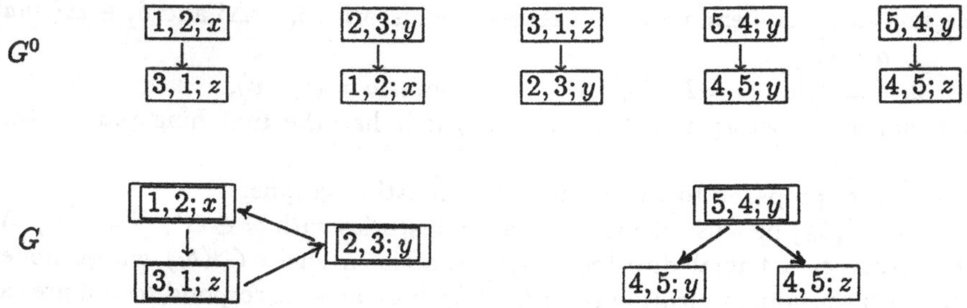

Figure 2.

Lemma 3 implies the following statement.

Lemma 4. *Let u be the number of nodes of communication graph $G(\delta_1, \ldots, \delta_n)$, and m be the number of all the nodes of graphs $G^\circ(\delta_1), \ldots, G^\circ(\delta_n)$. Then $u = m/2$, provided communication histories $(\delta_1, \ldots, \delta_n)$ are pairwise interrelated.*

Now we prove the main result of the section.

Theorem 3. *Communication histories $(\delta_1, \ldots, \delta_n)$ with $\delta_i \in \Delta^i$ $(i = \overline{1,n})$ are interrelated iff they are pairwise interrelated and the communication graph $G(\delta_1, \ldots, \delta_n)$ is acyclic.*

Proof. In the right direction, the proof proceeds by induction on the length $|\delta|$ of global communication history δ whose existence is implied by the interrelation assumption.

Assume $|\delta| = 1$ and $\delta = (i,j;v)$ for some $i,j \in \{1,\ldots,n\}$, $v \in \mathcal{N}$. Then the interrelation of histories implies

$$\delta|_k = \delta_k = \Lambda \text{ for any } k \neq i,j,\ 1 \leqslant k \leqslant n$$

and

$$\delta_i = \delta_j = (i,j;v).$$

Now the pairwise interrelation of histories is trivially satisfied, because the only nonempty output and input histories are those of δ_i and δ_j :

$$Out(\delta_i, j) = (i,j;v) = In(\delta_j, i).$$

Obviously, histories δ_i and δ_j match, and the corresponding communication graph $G(\delta_1,\ldots,\delta_n)$ consists of the only node.

Suppose further that the claim holds for any interrelated histories $(\delta_1,\ldots,\delta_n)$, whose global history δ has the length $N \geqslant 1$.

Assume global history δ with $|\delta| = N+1$, and $\delta = \delta' \circ (i,j;v)$ for some $\delta' \in \Delta$, $i,j \in \{1,\ldots,n\}$, $v \in \mathcal{N}$. Then by the definition of interrelation there exist prefixes δ'_i and δ'_j such that

$$\delta_i = \delta'_i \circ (i,j;v),\ \ \delta_j = \delta'_j \circ (i,j;v).$$

Assume communication histories δ_i and δ_j within the list $(\delta_1,\ldots,\delta_n)$ are replaced by their prefixes δ'_i and δ'_j. Here the new tuple of the histories is written $(\delta_i{}', \delta_j{}', \ldots)$ instead of $(\delta_1,\ldots,\delta'_i,\ldots,\delta'_j,\ldots,\delta_n)$. It is easy to see that the interrelation of communication histories has to be preserved under such a replacement. By the induction hypothesis, histories $(\delta'_i, \delta'_j, \ldots)$ are pairwise interrelated, and the communication graph $G' = G(\delta'_i, \delta'_j, \ldots)$ is acyclic.

Since

$$Out(\delta_i, j) = Out(\delta'_i, j) \circ (i,j;v) = In(\delta'_j, i) \circ (i,j;v) = In(\delta_j, i)$$

and

$$In(\delta_i, j) = In(\delta'_i, j) = Out(\delta'_j, i) = Out(\delta_j, i),$$

communication histories $(\delta_1,\ldots,\delta_n)$ are pairwise interrelated, too.

Hence, the last members of δ_i and δ_j match, and corresponding last nodes of graphs $G^\circ(\delta_i)$ and $G^\circ(\delta_j)$ can be glued.

So, if we add the node $(i,j;v)$ and the corresponding incoming arcs to the graph G', then we obtain graph $G = G(\delta_1,\ldots,\delta_n)$. Since G' is acyclic, and the added node has no outcoming arcs, G has no cycles, too. This concludes the proof in a left–to–right direction.

Now suppose communication histories $(\delta_1,\ldots,\delta_n)$ are pairwise interrelated, and the communication graph is acyclic.

We shall prove the interrelation of the histories by induction on $l = |\delta_1| + \ldots + |\delta_n|$, the total length of communication histories. Note that by Lemma 4, l is even.

If $l = 2$, then by Lemma 3 there exist strictly two nonempty and coinciding histories of unit length. Then the existence of desired global history immediately follows.

Assume now that the sufficiency claim holds for the communication histories whose length $l = N \geqslant 2$. Let $(\delta_1, \ldots, \delta_n)$ be the list of pairwise interrelated histories with acyclic communication graph $G = G(\delta_1, \ldots, \delta_n)$ and $l(\delta_1, \ldots, \delta_n) = N + 2$.

The acyclicity of G implies the existence of its node, say, $u = (i, j; v)$, without outcoming arcs. According to the definition of communication graphs and Lemma 3, every node of G is obtained by gluing some two nodes of graphs $G^{\circ}(\delta_1), \ldots, G^{\circ}(\delta_n)$.

Let a and b be the members of respective histories δ_i and δ_j, yielding the node u. Then a and b have to be the last members of histories δ_i and δ_j, respectively.

To establish the last claim, observe simply that any existing subsequent member would yield an outcoming arc of u thus contradicting its definition. Therefore, there exist prefixes δ_i' and δ_j' such that

$$\delta_i = \delta_i' \circ (i, j; v), \quad \delta_j = \delta_j' \circ (i, j; v).$$

It is obvious that histories $(\delta_i', \delta_j', \ldots)$ are pairwise interrelated.

Delete now u from G with all its incoming arcs and denote the resulting graph by G'. By construction, G' is acyclic as well as G. Moreover, G' coincides with the communication graph $G(\delta_i', \delta_j', \ldots)$. So we may apply the induction hypothesis. It follows that there exists the global history δ such that

$$\delta|_l = \delta_l \quad \text{for } l \neq i, j$$

and

$$\delta|_i = \delta_i', \quad \delta|_j = \delta_j'.$$

Since $(i, j; v)$ is the last member of sequences δ_i and δ_j,

$$\delta \circ (i, j; v)|_l = \delta_l \quad \text{for} l = \overline{1, n}.$$

Thus, the communication history $\delta \circ (i, j; v)$ is the global one required for the interrelation. This concludes the proof of Theorem 3. □

6. Invariants of distributed programs

Having proved Theorem 3 we now concentrate on the role of pairwise interrelation and other invariants of distributed programs.

Recall from Section 4 how interrelation predicates are replaced by other ones yielding new proof systems. If we denote by $\mathcal{B}^0$ the formula by which the pairwise interrelation is expressed, then by Corollary of Theorem 1 the proof system $\mathrm{ABC}_{\mathcal{B}^0}$ is sound. So we have

Theorem 4. $\vdash_{\mathrm{ABC}_{\mathcal{B}^0}} \{P\}p\{Q\} \quad \Longrightarrow \quad \models \{P\}p\{Q\}.$

Assume now that one needs to describe rigorously the distributed programs which use some specific communication mechanism while the syntax of communication statements is the same as we consider. The order of requests for input and output and their relationship has to be reflected properly in any such description. We adhere to the opinion that an interaction of processes has to be expressed in an explicit way, in particular, by means of communication histories. To justify this opinion, consider the interrelation and pairwise interrelation predicates.

Firstly, according to the interpretation of communication histories, their elements, communication records, correspond to the requests for input or output in the processes of distributed programs. The pairwise interrelation means that for any two processes p_i and p_j the number and order of requests for input from p_j in p_i amounts to the number and order of requests for output to p_i in p_j, and vice versa. For any rational communication mode, this demand is a necessary one. It seems that the pairwise interrelation is the weakest condition on communication. Any violation of it contradicts our intuitive comprehension of pairwise communicating processes. Stated as a pairwise interrelation predicate, the demand assumes a simple and elegant form.

On the other extreme, a very restricted mode of communication, synchronous, is properly described by the interrelation predicate. As $\mathcal{B}^0$ is implied by $\mathcal{B}$, it seems that any rational invariant of communication is somewhere in between these extreme demands. Therefore, it could be stated as a conjunction of $\mathcal{B}^0$ and some other predicate on communication histories. The rest of the section is devoted to reveal this idea.

Now we present some auxiliary definitions.

Given transition system $\mathcal{S}$ and transition inference system X, we say that $\mathcal{S}$ is *specified by* X if the immediate transition relation of $\mathcal{S}$ is defined by X. The system $\mathcal{S}$ specified by X is called $\mathcal{S}_X$. For example, $\mathcal{S}_T$ is the transition system presented in Section 3. We also say that transition system $\mathcal{S}_X$ is *simulated* by transition system $\mathcal{S}_Y$ if every terminating transition inferred in X has to be inferred in Y as well. Formally, for any $s \in S$, $s' \in S_F$

$$s \rightarrow_X^* s' \Rightarrow s \rightarrow_Y^* s'.$$

For clarity, the denotation of truth of Hoare formulae will be supplied by the superscript showing in what system transitions are inferred. For example, $\models^X \{P\}p\{Q\}$. Here the subscript suggesting an arbitrary, but fixed model M is omitted as usual. Then we say that Hoare formula $\{P\}p\{Q\}$ is true *relative to* X.

Theorem 5. *If transition system $\mathcal{S}_Y$ simulates transition system $\mathcal{S}_X$, then $\models^X \{P\}p\{Q\}$ whenever $\models^Y \{P\}p\{Q\}$.*

Proof. Assume the contrary. Then there exist the formula $\{P\}p\{Q\}$ which is true relative to Y and is false relative to X.

By the definition of the truth of Hoare formulae, there exist program states (σ, δ) and (σ', δ') such that $(\sigma, \delta) \models P$, $< p, \sigma, \delta > \rightarrow_X^* < \sigma', \delta' >$, and $(\sigma', \delta') \models \neg Q$. By simulation, $< p, \sigma, \delta > \rightarrow_Y^* < \sigma', \delta' >$. According to the truth of considered Hoare formula relative to Y, it follows that $(\sigma', \delta') \models Q$.

The obtained contradiction shows the statement of the theorem. □

Let $\mathcal{B}$ implies $\mathcal{F}$ and $\mathcal{S}_X$ simulates $\mathcal{S}_T$, then statements of Theorem 1, 2, 4, and 5 may be described as follows.

$$\vdash_{\mathrm{ABC}_{\mathcal{F}}} \{P\}p\{Q\} \Rightarrow \vdash_{ABC} \{P\}p\{Q\}$$
$$\Updownarrow$$
$$\models^{X} \{P\}p\{Q\} \Rightarrow \models^{T} \{P\}p\{Q\}$$

Figure 3.

The lacking relation between the provability in $\mathrm{ABC}_{\mathcal{F}}$ and the truth relative to X is described by the following Theorem 6.

To formulate it, we need some auxiliary concepts.

We say that a final configuration $s \in S_F$ is *reachable* in transition system $\mathcal{S}_X$ if there exists the computation ending in s with an initial configuration $< p, \sigma, \delta^{\Lambda} >$, that is,

$$< p, \sigma, \delta^{\Lambda} > \rightarrow^{*}_{X} s.$$

We say that a predicate is *reachable* in $\mathcal{S}_X$ if every program state in which it is true is reachable in $\mathcal{S}_X$. Thus, the reachable predicates are those "calculated" by programs we consider.

Lemma 5. *Interrelation predicate $\mathcal{B}$ is reachable in $\mathcal{S}_T$.*

Proof. The proof proceeds by induction on the length of global history whose existence is implied by $\mathcal{B}$. The details of the construction of desired initial configuration are straigtforward, and so the proof is omitted here. □

Revise now the definition of semantic invariant of Section 4.

We say that history predicate $\mathcal{F}$ which holds on empty communication histories is a *semantic invariant* of transition system $\mathcal{S}_X$ if for any distributed program the following are equivalent:

1. $< \vec{p}, \vec{\sigma}, \vec{\delta}^{\Lambda} > \rightarrow^{*}_{X} < \vec{\sigma}', \vec{\delta}' >$.
2. $< p_i, \sigma_i, \Lambda > \rightarrow^{*}_{X} < \sigma'_i, \delta'_i >$ and $(\delta'_1, \ldots, \delta'_n) \models \mathcal{F}$.

We now prove Theorem 6 which justifies the addition of a new arrow to the diagram on Figure 3 in a particular case. The arrow shows the implication between the provability in $\mathrm{ABC}_{\mathcal{F}}$ and the truth relative to $\mathcal{S}_X$.

Theorem 6. *If $\mathcal{S}_X$ simulates $\mathcal{S}_T$, and $\mathcal{F}$ is a semantic invariant of $\mathcal{S}_X$, then*

1. $\mathcal{B}$ implies $\mathcal{F}$,
2. $\mathrm{ABC}_{\mathcal{F}}$ is sound.

Proof. At first, we prove (1).

Let $(\vec{\sigma}, \vec{\delta})$ be the program state in which $\mathcal{B}$ is true. According to Lemma 5, the state is reachable in $\mathcal{S}_T$. Thus, we have some terminating transition inferred in T which ends in $< \vec{\sigma}, \vec{\delta} >$. By simulation, the same transition may be inferred in X.

Since $\mathcal{F}$ is the semantic invariant of $\mathcal{S}_X$, then $\mathcal{F}$ is true in $(\vec{\sigma}, \vec{\delta})$. This settles the statement (1).

Using (1), (2) follows easily from Corollary of Theorem 1. □

Having proved the above theorem, we may add the corresponding arrow to the diagram. The opposite arrow means the relative completeness of the proof system with the syntactic invariant $\mathcal{F}$. If $\mathcal{F}$ is also the semantic invariant, that is, if the analog of Invariant lemma of Section 4 holds, then the proof of completeness might follow the lines of reasoning as in Theorem 2. For each concrete proof system the proof has to be individual. This is because not only proof rule B–1 may be replaced by other rules in order to capture properly the meaning of certain communication mechanism.

The theorems proven above explain the significance of the simulation while considering semantical issues of communication in the distributed programs.

Firstly, it is straighforward to show the consistency between the operational semantics and the axiomatic one for the distributed programs with the communication mechanisms whose operational meaning is definable by transition systems which simulate $\mathcal{S}_T$. The consistency is understood here as the soundness and relative completeness of the proof systems in question.

Secondly, by means of the simulation of transition systems one may formally do scribe certain natural ordering among the communication mechanisms. That is, the synchronous mode of communication is the strongest one; it causes the largest possibility of deadlocks performing distributed programs. Other, more "liberal" communication mechanisms ought to "simulate" the synchronous one as, for example, an asynchronous communication does.

In summary, the class of transition systems related by simulation is of vital importance while we consider the semantics for the distributed programs, especially, for the programs with varied mode of communication. The construction of interrelation predicates and proof systems for the concrete, non-synchronous communication modes is a worth-while domain for further investigation.

Appendix

Lemma. *Let* $<\vec{p},\vec{\sigma},\vec{\delta}>$ *and* $<\vec{p}',\vec{\sigma}',\vec{\delta}'>$ *be configurations such that*

$$(\vec{\sigma},\vec{\delta}) \models \mathcal{B}, \tag{1}$$

$$(\vec{\sigma}',\vec{\delta}') \models \mathcal{B}, \tag{2}$$

$$< p_i, \sigma_i, \delta_i > \rightarrow^* < p_i', \sigma_i', \delta_i' > \quad \textit{for any } i. \tag{3}$$

Then every global history of $\delta_1, \ldots, \delta_n$ may be extended to the global history of $\delta_1', \ldots, \delta_n'$.

Proof. Let δ and δ' be arbitrary global histories of $\delta_1, \ldots, \delta_n$ and $\delta_n', \ldots, \delta_n'$, respectively. Their existence is implied by (1) and (2).

If δ is the prefix of δ', then the lemma is proved.

Assume the contrary. Then neither δ nor δ' is empty. We shall reconstruct the global history δ' in order to get the new one whose prefix would be δ.

Consider aforementioned global histories δ and δ'. By their definition, $\delta|_i = \delta_i$ and $\delta'|_i = \delta_i'$ for $i = \overline{1,n}$. It follows from Lemma 2 of Section 4 that for any i δ_i is the prefix of δ_i' provided (3) holds.

Thus, for any i $\delta|_i$ is a prefix of δ_i'.

Projections $\delta|_i$ and $\delta'|_i$, where $i = \overline{1,n}$, are all among the possible projections of δ and δ'. Moreover, every element of global histories δ and δ' must fall under some projection. Thus, every element of δ is the element of δ' as well. Unfortunately, the order of common elements in both sequences may differ. The elements of δ which are not linearly ordered by the projection mappings may be transposed in δ'.

Taking into account the above, δ' may be specified as follows.

Assume $\delta = a_1 \ldots a_m$. Then there exist sequences $\gamma_1, \ldots, \gamma_{m+1}$ and the permutation of sequence δ, say, $b_1 \ldots, b_m$ such that

$$\delta' = \gamma_1 b_1 \gamma_2 \ldots \gamma_m b_m \gamma_{m+1}.$$

Now we claim that $\widehat{\delta} = a_1 \ldots a_m \gamma_1 \ldots \gamma_{m+1}$ is the global history of $\delta'_1, \ldots, \delta'_n$ as well as δ'.

We prove the claim by the construction of the sequence of histories $\delta^{(1)}, \ldots, \delta^{(m)}$ each of which is the global history of $\delta'_1, \ldots, \delta'_n$. The lth constructed history $\delta^{(l)}$, $l = \overline{1,m}$, will be the global history with first l elements of the global history δ as its first elements. So, $\delta^{(m)}$ would be the required global history, and we would conclude the proof.

Consider now a_1, the first element of δ. Assume that $a_1 = (i, j; v)$ for some v, and b_k is its image in δ'. According to the definition of projections, we have

$$\delta'|_i = (\gamma_1 b_1 \ldots \gamma_k)|_i \circ a_1 \circ (\gamma_{k+1} \ldots \gamma_{m+1})|_i$$

and

$$\delta|_i = a_1 \circ (a_2 \ldots a_n)|_i.$$

Hence, $(\gamma_1 b_1 \ldots \gamma_k)|_i = \Lambda$. The same equality holds for the projection $|_j$. Because $a_1|_l = \Lambda$ for any $l \neq i, j$, we may transpose $\gamma_1 b_1 \ldots \gamma_k$ with b_k and still be preserved the orderings of projections.

So, the sequence

$$\delta^{(1)} = a_1 \gamma_1 \ldots \gamma_k \gamma_{k+1} \ldots \gamma_{m+1}$$

will be the global history of communication histories $\delta'_1, \ldots, \delta'_n$.

One can construct by the same way

$$\delta^{(2)} = a_1 a_2 \gamma_1 \ldots \gamma_k \gamma_{k+1} \ldots \gamma_s \gamma_{s+1} \ldots \gamma_{m+1},$$

and so on.

This conclude the proof of the lemma. □

Acknowledgements

In the first place my acknowledgements are due to A.A. Letichevskij from the Institute of Cybernetics in Kiev, Ukraine, for introducing me into the field of semantical problems of distributed programming language PROSTOR. And also, this work would not have been done without their support and works.

I would like to thank my colleagues from the Institute of Mathematics and Informatics of the Lithuanian Academy of Sciences, in particular Regimantas Pliuškevičius, for helpful conversations and continuous encouragement to do this work.

Thanks are also due to Dines Bjørner, and their colleagues from Denmark Technical University for helpful discussions on the subject of the paper during my visit in Copenhagen.

REFERENCES

1. Apt K.R. (1983). Formal justification of a proof system for communicating sequential processes *Journal of the ACM* **30**, No. 1, pp. 197 - 216.
2. Cook S.A. (1978). Soundness and completeness of an axiom system for program verification *SIAM J. Comput.* **7**, No. 1, pp.70 - 90.
3. Francez N., Hoare C.A.R., Lehmann D.J.,de Roever W.P. (1979). Semantics of nondeterminism, concurrency, and communication *Journal of Computer and System Sciences* **19**, No. 3, pp.290 - 308.
4. Gečas K. (1988). An axiom system for proving properties of simple multimodular programs *Kibernetika (Kiev)* No. 2 pp. 33-38. (in Russian)
5. Gorochovskij S.S.,Kapitonova J.V.,Letichevskij A.A.,Molchanov I.N., Pogrebinskij S.B. (1984). Algorithmic language MAJAK *Kibernetika* , No. 3, pp.54 - 74. (in Russian)
6. Hoare C.A.R. (1969). Axiomatic basis for computer programming *Comm. of ACM* **12**, No. 10, pp. 576-580
7. Hoare C.A.R. (1978). Communicating sequential processes *Comm. of the ACM* **21**, No. 8, pp.666 - 677.
8. Hooman J., de Roever W.P. (1986). The quest goes on: a survey of proofsystems for partial correctness of CSP *Lect. Notes Comp. Sci.* **224**, pp. 343-395
9. Letichevskij A.A., Godlevskij A.B., Doroshenko A.E., Krivoj S.L. (1983). A semantics of data communication in simple multimodular programs *Programmirovanie* , No. 5, pp. 3 - 11. (in Russian)
10. Levin G.M., Gries D. (1981). A proof technique for communicating sequential processes *Acta Informatica* **15**, No. 2, pp. 281 - 302.
11. Nepomnyashchij V.A. (1986). On problem-oriented program verification *Programmirovanie* No. 1, pp. 3-13. (in Russian)
12. Plotkin G.D. (1983). An operational semantics for CSP In: *Formal Descriptions of Programming Consepts*, North-Holl., Amsterdam pp. 199-223
13. Soundararajan N. (1984). Axiomatic semantics of communicating sequential processes *ACM Trans. Progr. Lang. Sys.* **6**, No. 4, pp.647 - 662.
14. Zwiers J.,de Roever W.P.,van Emde Boas P. (1985). Compositionality and concurrent networks: soundness and completeness of a proofsystem *Lect. Notes in Comp. Sci.* **194**, pp.509 - 519.

INVESTIGATION OF FINITARY CALCULUS FOR A DISCRETE LINEAR TIME LOGIC BY MEANS OF INFINITARY CALCULUS

Regimantas PLIUŠKEVIČIUS

Institute of Mathematics and Informatics
Lithuanian Academy of Sciences
Akademijos 4, Vilnius, 232600, Lithuania

Abstract. A method for the investigation of undecidable and noncompact temporal logic is presented. It begins with a construction of a Gentzen-like calculus containing some infinitary rules reflecting semantics of the temporal logic. Some semantic (e.g., completeness) and proof theoretical (e.g., cut elimination) properties for this infinitary calculus are proved. The main part of the method consists of reducing an arbitrary derivation in the infinitary restricted calculus into the cut-free derivation in the finitary calculus (in short reduction of the infinitary calculus to the finitary one). As the infinitary rules are similar to the ω-induction rule the method is called the ω-reduction. The method allows: 1) to construct a finitary calculus with efficient proof-theoretical properties and 2) to prove the completeness theorem for the considered restricted first order temporal logic.

Introduction.

Temporal logics are a formalism for reasoning about a changing world. So far as the concept of time is directly built into the formalism, temporal logics has been widely used as suitable bases of formal techniques for the analysis, specification and development of concurrent computing systems; temporal logics can serve directly as a programming (PROLOG-like) language.

There are several different types of deductive systems known as: (a) Hilbert-Frege style systems, (b) natural deduction systems, (c) Gentzen-type sequent calculi, (d) tableau systems, (e) resolution-type (computer oriented) systems. We shall consider the Gentzen-type sequent calculi because such calculi are more close to resolution-type systems than axiom (or Hilbert-Frege) style or natural deduction systems (tableau systems are essentially a variant of the sequential calculi). The soundness and completeness of various resolution procedures can be proved in the evident way through explicit translations between resolution refutations and Gentzen-type calculus. In turn the resolution-type systems serves as bases for the interpreters of a logic programming systems.

The temporal logic has close similarity with the formalized (Peano) arithmetic. That is, according to the results of Gődel, Peano arithmetic is incomplete in the sense that some true statements are unprovable, and it remains incomplete upon the addition of any effective valid rule of inference. On the other hand, it becomes complete upon the addition of the noneffective ω-rule: if $A(0), A(1), A(2), \ldots$, then $\forall x A(x)$. It is the same situation in the case of first order linear temporal logic. As it follows from [1, 2, 12] a finitary first order calculus of a linear temporal logic is incomplete. And what is more in [3] it is proved (using D.Scott idea) that already first order linear time logic with unary predicate symbols only is incomplete, because the Peano arithmetic can be imbedded in this logic. It becomes complete [5] upon the addition of the infinitary rule: if $A, \bigcirc_1 A, \bigcirc_1\bigcirc_1 A, \ldots$, then $\Box_1 A$, where $\bigcirc_1$ and $\Box_1$ are future temporal operators "next" and "always". The similarity of the linear temporal logic with Peano arithmetic appears also in noncompactness property. For example, let $T = \{A, \bigcirc_1 A, \bigcirc_1\bigcirc_1 A, \ldots\}$ is the infinite set, then it is obvious that the formula $\Box_1 A$ is a semantic consequence of the set T ($T \models \Box_1 A$), but it does not exist a finite subset T^* of the set T such that $T^* \models \Box_1 A$. In spite of the noncompactness property completeness of many decidable temporal logics (mainly propositional ones) has been proved. Therefore a problem arises to find a method of constructing a complete finitary calculus (with efficient proof–theoretical properties) for undecidable and noncompact restricted first order temporal logic. The noncompactness of the temporal logic makes a suggestion to apply infinitary rules for investigation the properties of (both undecidable and decidable) temporal logics. The infinitary rule establishs a link between model theory and proof theory. The use of infinitary rules for temporal operators allows not only reflect the semantics of temporal operators naturally but also to construct a sequential calculus for the considered temporal logic with the following important property: the complexity of premises in each rule of inference is less (or equal) than that of the conclusion in this rule of inference. Using these several important properties (such as completeness and cut elimination) of first order linear infinitary temporal logics (with "next" and "always") have been proved in [5]. The possibility of reduction of an arbitrary derivation in the infinitary calculus into the cut–free derivation in the finitary calculus may serve as a simple and natural criterion of completeness of corresponding finitary calculus. The reduction enables us to obtain the finitary calculus with effective proof–theoretical properties. Since infinitary rules for temporal operators are similar to the ω–rule the proposed method will be called the ω–reduction method. In the ω–reduction method the main problem is to find some way for searching a formula $\mathcal{R}$ (called invariant formula, i.e., such formula that $\models \mathcal{R} \supset \bigcirc_1 \mathcal{R}$) in the finitary rule of inference ($\rightarrow \Box_1$).

The main new results of the paper: (1) an infinitary sequential calculus $G_{LS\omega}$ is constructed for a first order symmetric linear temporal logic with the future temporal operators $\bigcirc_1$ (next), $\Box_1$ (always) and the past time temporal operators $\bigcirc_2$ (previous), $\Box_2$ (always previously); (2) the completeness and cut elimination theorems for $G_{LS\omega}$ is proved semantically; (3) structural cut elimination theorem (providing some structural characterization of derivations not increasing during the elimination procedure) for infinitary calculus $G_{LS\omega k}$ (equivalent to $G_{LS\omega}$) is proved syntactically; (4) a complete infinitary calculus $G_{L\omega}$ and a finitary calculus G_L (with efficient proof–theoretical properties) are constructed for a restricted first order nonsymmetric linear temporal logic (i.e., containing only temporal operators $\bigcirc_1$ and $\Box_1$) and the proof of the completeness and cut elimination theorem for G_L is based on the reduction of $G_{L\omega}$ to G_L; (5) some sufficient condition the formula to be invariant (in the finitary succedent rule ($\rightarrow \Box_1$) for operator "always") is presented; (6) the alternation properties in the calculi $G_{L\omega}$, G_L (allowing to decrease the complexity of the given sequent and to separate undecidable part from decidable one of the given sequent) is founded.

Organization of the paper: in the first section infinitary sequential calculus $G_{LS\omega}$ is described; in the second section the completeness and cut elimination theorems for $G_{LS\omega}$ are proved; in the third section structural cut elimination for $G_{LS\omega k}$ are founded; in the fourth section the infinitary and finitary calculi $G_{L\omega}$, G_L for the restricted first order nonsymmetric linear temporal logic and reduction of $G_{L\omega}$ to G_L is described; in the fifth section reduction of $G_{L\omega}$ to G_L is described; in the sixth section some applications and extensions of the ω–reduction method are presented. This paper is extended and improved version of [9].

I thank to G.Mints and H.Luckhardt for valuable discussions.

§1. Description of the infinitary calculus $G_{LS\omega}$ for the first order symmetric linear temporal logic.

We shall consider so–called pure (i.e., without function symbols) first order language for symmetric linear temporal logic consisting of the following classes of symbols:

1) Variables:

1.1) free variables denoted by $a, b, c, d, \ldots$ (possibly with subscripts);

1.2) bound variables denoted by $x, y, z, w, \ldots$ (possibly with subscripts);

2) m–ary ($m \geqslant 0$) relation symbols: $P, Q, R, \ldots$ (possible with subscripts);

3) Logical symbols: $\neg, \wedge, \vee, \supset, \forall, \exists$;

4) Temporal symbols: $\circ_1, \Box_1, \circ_2, \Box_2$;

5) Auxiliary symbols: (,) (parentheses) and, (comma).

0–ary relation symbols are used as propositional variables.

Let P be a m–ary relation symbol and $a_1, \ldots, a_m$, be free variables, then $P(a_1, \ldots, a_m)$ is called an atomic formula. Suppose S, x, t are arbitrary expressions. Then $S[t/x]$ will stand for the result obtained from S substituting the expression t in S for all occurrences of x. If $x \notin S$, then S and $S[t/x]$ coincide. Let us define the notion of a formula:

1) Every atomic formula is a formula.

2) If A and B are formulas, then $(A \supset B)$, $(A \vee B)$, $(A \wedge B)$, (σA) (where $\sigma \in \{\neg, \circ_1, \circ_2, \Box_1, \Box_2\}$) are formulas.

3) If A is a formula, a is a free variable and x is a bound variable not occurring in A, then $\forall x A[x/a]$ and $\exists x A[x/a]$ are formulas.

In the following we shall omit parentheses whenever the meaning is evident from the context. For example $\neg A \wedge \circ_1 B$ is abbreviation for $(\neg A) \wedge (\circ_1 B)$. The other logical and temporal symbols such as $\equiv$ (equivalence), $\Diamond_1$ (eventually), $\Diamond_2$ (sometime previously) can be introduced by the usual definitions: $A \equiv B$ will stand for $(A \supset B) \wedge (B \supset A)$, $\Diamond_i A$ will stand for $\neg \Box_i \neg A$ $(i = 1, 2)$.

To obtain a cut free and invertible calculus for the considered temporal logic let us introduce formulas with indices (denoted by A^i and certifying the truth value of A in the i–th moment of time). The indexed formulas in the modal logic $S5$ have been introduced in [4]. In [5] for linear temporal logic the indexed formulas are used in the form $J^k A$ (where J plays the role of temporal symbol "next"). In [7] and here the index method is extended for the symmetric linear temporal logic. It should be stressed that index method provides (for some nonclassical logics) a method for constructing cut–free and invertible calculi with the rules of inference allowing "local" transformation with

nonlogical operators (with logical operators as well). For nonclassical logics with complicated semantics a "nonlocal" transformation with nonlogical operators or an analytic cut may be applied. Therefore index method does not provide anything like a universal proof–theoretic approach to modal, temporal, and dynamics logics. Nevertheless, when it does work, it works very well. The formulas A^i are defined as follows:
1) $(E^i)^{\rho k} := E^{i\rho k}$ where E is an atomic formula, i is zero (which is identified by an empty word) or any integer, k is any natural number, $\rho \in \{+,-\}$;
2) $(A \odot B)^k := A^k \odot B^k$, $\odot \in \{\supset, \wedge, \vee\}$;
3) $(\sigma A)^k := \sigma A^k$, $\sigma \in \{\neg, \Box_1, \Box_2, \forall x, \exists x\}$;
4) $(\circ_i A)^k := \circ_i A^{\rho k}$, where $\rho = +$ if $i = 1$ and $\rho = -$, if $i = 2$.

Any formula with index also will be called a formula.

A sequent is an expression of the form $\Gamma \to \Delta$, where Γ, Δ are arbitrary multisets of formulas (i.e., the order of formulas in Γ, Δ is disregarded). Here $\to$ is a new formal symbol. Γ and Δ are called the antecedent and succedent, respectively. The sequent $A_1, \ldots, A_n \to B_1, \ldots, B_m$ has the same meaning as the formula $A_1 \wedge \ldots \wedge A_n \supset B_1 \vee \ldots \vee B_m$; when $m = 0$, then the sequent $A_1, \ldots, A_n \to$ has the meaning as the formula $A_1 \wedge \ldots \wedge A_n \supset F$ (where F is any false formula), when $n = 0$, then the sequent $\to B_1, \ldots, B_m$ has the meaning as the formula $B_1 \vee \ldots \vee B_m$.

A rule of inference is an expression of the form

$$\frac{S_1, S_2, \ldots, S_n, \ldots}{S},$$

where $S_1, S_2, \ldots, S_n, \ldots$ $(n \geqslant 1)$ is a finite or infinite set of sequents $S_1, S_2, \ldots, S_n, \ldots$, (called premises of the rule of inference), S is a sequent (called conclusion of the rule of inference).

The calculus $G_{LS\omega}$ has the following axiom and rules of inference:
Axiom: $\Gamma, A \to \Delta, A$.
Rules of inference:

$$\frac{\Gamma, A \to \Delta, B}{\Gamma \to \Delta, (A \supset B)}(\to\supset) \qquad \frac{\Gamma \to \Delta, A; \;\; \Gamma, B \to \Delta}{\Gamma, (A \supset B) \to \Delta}(\supset\to)$$

$$\frac{\Gamma \to \Delta, A; \;\; \Gamma \to \Delta, B}{\Gamma \to \Delta, (A \wedge B)}(\to \wedge) \qquad \frac{\Gamma, A, B \to \Delta}{\Gamma, (A \wedge B) \to \Delta}(\wedge \to)$$

$$\frac{\Gamma \to \Delta, A, B}{\Gamma \to \Delta, (A \vee B)}(\to \vee) \qquad \frac{\Gamma, A \to \Delta; \;\; \Gamma, B \to \Delta}{\Gamma, (A \vee B) \to \Delta}(\vee \to)$$

$$\frac{\Gamma, A \to \Delta}{\Gamma \to \Delta, \neg A}(\to \neg) \qquad \frac{\Gamma \to \Delta, A}{\Gamma, \neg A \to \Delta}(\neg \to)$$

$$\frac{\Gamma \to \Delta, A[b/x]}{\Gamma \to \Delta, \forall x A}(\to \forall) \qquad \frac{A[t/x], \forall x A, \Gamma \to \Delta}{\forall x A, \Gamma \to \Delta}(\forall \to)$$

$$\frac{\Gamma \to \Delta, A[t/x], \exists x A}{\Gamma \to \Delta, \exists x A}(\to \exists) \qquad \frac{A[b/x], \Gamma \to \Delta}{\exists x A, \Gamma \to \Delta}(\exists \to)$$

$$\frac{\Gamma \to \Delta, A^{k\rho 1}}{\Gamma \to \Delta, \circ_i A^k}(\to \circ_i) \qquad \frac{\Gamma, A^{k\rho 1} \to \Delta}{\Gamma, \circ_i A^k \to \Delta}(\circ_i \to)$$

$$\frac{\Gamma \to \Delta, A; \;\; \Gamma \to \Delta, \circ_i A; \ldots; \;\; \Gamma \to \Delta, \circ_i^k A; \ldots}{\Gamma \to \Delta, \Box_i A}(\to \Box_{i\omega})$$

$$\frac{\Gamma, A, \circ_i \Box_i A \to \Delta}{\Gamma, \Box_i A \to \Delta}(\Box_i \to)$$

$$\frac{\Gamma \to \Delta, A; \;\; A, \Pi \to \Omega}{\Gamma, \Pi \to \Delta, \Omega}(\text{cut})$$

The notation $\circ_i^k A$ in the rule of inference $(\to \Box_{i\omega})$ denotes $\overbrace{\circ_i \ldots \circ_i}^{k \text{ time}} A$ $(k \geqslant 0,\ i = 1,2)$; in the rules of inference $(\to \circ_i)$, $(\circ_i \to)$ $(i = 1,2)$ $\rho = +$, if $i = 1$ and $\rho = -$, if $i = 2$; in the rules of inference $(\forall \to)$, $(\to \exists)$ t is an arbitrary free variable; in the rules of inference $(\to \forall)$, $(\exists \to)$ b (called eigenvariable of the rule of inference) does not occur in the conclusion of the rule of inference.

Remark 1.1. (a) The examination of the possibility to prove the true sequent $S = E \to \circ_1 \circ_2 E$ (where E is an atomic formula) shows that it is impossible to prove the sequent S without cut, if we do not use rules emploing indices. (b) The rule of inference $(\to \Box_{i\omega})$ can be written briefly in following way

$$\frac{\{\Gamma \to \Delta, \circ_i^k A\}_{k \in \omega}}{\Gamma \to \Delta, \Box_i A},$$

where ω denote the set of natural numbers (i.e., $k \in \omega$ means that $k \in \{0, 1, \ldots\}$).

We can write a general form for any rule of inference (except (cut)) of $G_{LS\omega}$ as follows:

$$\frac{\Gamma, \Xi_1^0, \nabla_{11} \to \Delta, \nabla_{12}, \Xi_2^0; \ldots; \Gamma, \Xi_1^0, \nabla_{n1} \to \Delta, \nabla_{n2}, \Xi_2^0; \ldots}{\Gamma, \Xi_1 \to \Delta, \Xi_2}(j),$$

where $n \in \{1, 2, \ldots\}$ when $(j) = (\to \Box_{i\omega})$ and $n \in \{1, 2\}$ for the other rules of inference; Ξ_1 (Ξ_2) is the formula (called the principal formula) from the conclusion of the rule of inference containing the introduced logical or temporal symbol; $\Xi_i^0 = \Xi_i$, when $j \in \{(\forall \to), (\to \exists)\}$ and $\Xi_i^0 = \varnothing$ for the other rules of inference (Ξ_i^0 is called the quasiprincipal formula); ∇_{n1} (∇_{n2}) consists of the formulas (called the side formulas) arising from the principal formula of the rule of inference; ∇_{n1} (∇_{n2}) is an immediate ancestor of Ξ_1 (Ξ_2); Ξ_1 (Ξ_2) is an immediate descendant of the ∇_{n1}, ∇_{n2}; Γ, Δ consists of the formulas called the extra formulas. In the rule of inference (cut) the formula A is called the cut formula, formulas from $\Gamma, \Delta, \Pi, \Omega$ are called extra formulas. For example, in the rule of inference $(\Box_i \to)$ the formula $\Box_i A$ is the principal formula, formulas $A, \circ_i \Box_i A$ are side formulas, Γ, Δ are multisets of the extra formulas.

Derivations in $G_{LS\omega}$ are built in a usual (for the sequential calculi with ω–rule) way, i.e., in the form of an infinite tree, besides each branch of this tree is finitary. As $G_{LS\omega}$ has the infinitary rule of inference $(\to \Box_{i\omega})$ all derivations containing some applications of the rule of inference $(\to \Box_{i\omega})$ are informal. For example, let us build in $G_{LS\omega}$ the derivation of the sequent $\bigcirc_1\Box_1 A \to \Box_1\bigcirc_1 A$:

$$\dfrac{\cdots \quad \dfrac{\dfrac{\dfrac{A^1,\ldots,A^{k+1},\bigcirc_1\Box_1 A^{k+1} \to A^{k+1}}{\cdots}(\bigcirc_1 \to),(\Box_1 \to)}{\bigcirc_1\Box_1 A \to A^{k+1}}}{\dfrac{\cdots}{\bigcirc_1\Box_1 A \to \bigcirc_1^{k+1} A}}(\to \bigcirc_1) \quad \cdots}{\bigcirc_1\Box_1 A \to \Box_1\bigcirc_1 A}(\to \Box_{1\omega})$$

It is obvious that all branches for each k $(k = 0, 1, \ldots)$ are finitary. By the given derivation D of a sequent S and by the given sequent S_1 from D we can easily define all ancestors in S_1 of some formula S. For example let us consider the derivation given above. Then all the formulas $A^1, \ldots, A^{k+1}, \bigcirc_1\Box_1 A^{k+1}$ from the antecedent of the axiom are ancestors of the formula $\bigcirc_1\Box_1 A$ from antecedent of the end–sequent of the given derivation. On the other hand the formula $\bigcirc_1\Box_1 A$ is the descendant of any formula $A^1, \ldots, A^{k+1}, \bigcirc_1\Box_1 A^{k+1}$ from the antecedent of the axiom. As the derivations in $G_{LS\omega}$ are constructed in the form of infinitary tree the height of the derivations in $G_{LS\omega}$ is evaluated by ordinals. Every natural number is an ordinal; ω is the ordinal following all natural numbers, ε_0 is the first ordinal following the ordinals $\omega, \omega^\omega, \omega^{\omega^\omega}, \ldots$ Ordinals less than ε_0 are those which can be written as exponential polynomials in ω with finite ordinal coefficients. The "natural sum" (denoted by #) of two ordinals gives the correct ordinal. For example let $\alpha = \omega^{\omega^1+1} + 1$, $\beta = \omega^{\omega^{\omega^{1+1+1}+1}} + \omega^{\omega^1} + \omega^1$, then $\alpha\#\beta = \omega^{\omega^{\omega^{1+1+1}+1}} + \omega^{\omega^1+1} + \omega^{\omega^1} + \omega^1 + .1$.

Let S is a sequent from a given derivation in $G_{LS\omega}$, D is a derivation of S. The height of the derivation D of the sequent S (denotes by $O(D)$) is defined as follows. If S is an axiom, then $O(D) = 1$. Let S is a conclusion of a rule of inference with k premises, then $O(D) = \sup_{i<k}(O(D_i) + 1)$, where D_i are derivations of the premises of the given rule of inference.

Let I, I_1, I_2 be arbitrary calculi, then the notation $I \vdash S$ means that sequent S is derivable in I; the notation $I_1 \vdash S_1 \Rightarrow I_2 \vdash S_2$ means that the derivability S_1 in I_1 implies the derivability S_2 in I_2. Then the derivation of S_1 in I_1 is called the given derivation and the derivation of S_2 in I_2 is called the resulting derivation. The notation I^{cf} will denote a calculus, obtained from I by dropping the rule of inference (cut). The rule of inference (j) is called derivable in a calculus I if it is possible to build the derivation of the conclusion of the (j) from the premises of the (j) using the axioms and rules of inferences of I. The rule of inference (j) is called admissible in I if adding the (j) does not extend the set of provable sequents in I. For example, the following rules of inference are derivable in $G^{cf}_{LS\omega}$:

$$\frac{\Gamma \to \Delta, A}{\Gamma \to \Delta, \neg\neg A}(\to \neg\neg) \qquad \frac{\Gamma, A \to \Delta}{\Gamma, \neg\neg A \to \Delta}(\neg\neg \to)$$

$$\frac{\Gamma, A \to \Delta, B; \quad B, \Gamma \to \Delta, A}{\Gamma \to \Delta, (A \equiv B)}(\to\equiv)$$

$$\frac{\Gamma \to \Delta, A, B;\ \ \Gamma, A, B \to \Delta}{\Gamma, (A \equiv B) \to \Delta}(\equiv\to)$$

$$\frac{\Gamma, \bigcirc_i \Box_i \neg A \to \Delta, A}{\Gamma \to \Delta, \Diamond_i A}(\to \Diamond_i)$$

$$\frac{\Gamma, A \to \Delta;\ \ \Gamma, \bigcirc_i A \to \Delta; \ldots; \Gamma, \bigcirc_i^k A \to \Delta; \ldots}{\Diamond_i A, \Gamma \to \Delta}(\Diamond_i \to)$$

The cut and following "structural" rules of inference are admissible in $G_{LS\omega}$ (for a proof see in §3):

$$\frac{\Gamma \to \Delta}{\Pi, \Gamma \to \Delta, \Omega}(W)(\text{weakening})$$

$$\frac{\Gamma \to \Delta, A, A}{\Gamma \to \Delta, A}(\to C) \quad \frac{A, A, \Gamma \to \Delta}{A, \Gamma \to \Delta}(C \to)(\text{contraction})$$

The rule of inference (j) of a calculus I is called invertible if the derivability in I of the conclusion of the (j) implies the derivability in I of each of premises of the (j). As will be shown in the section 3 all the rules of inference of $G^{cf}_{LS\omega}$ are invertible. The rules of inference (W) and (cut) are not invertible.

Let (i) is any rule of inference. Usually (i) is applied to get the conclusion of (i) from the premises of (i). Sometimes (for example constructing the derivation from bottom to top) it is convenient to apply (i) to get the premises of (i) from the conclusion of (i). Then instead of " application of (i)" we have the "antiapplication of (i)". In the case when (i) is invertible the antiapplication of (i) preserves deducibility.

§2. Completeness of $G_{LS\omega}$.

In this section we shall consider semantic basis of the temporal logic under consideration and prove (using Schütte's method of reduction trees) completeness theorem for $G_{LS\omega}$. The cut elimination theorem is a corollary of the completeness theorem as formulated below.

A model M over which a formula of temporal logic under consideration is interpreted is a pair $< I, V >$, where I is a triple $< D, Z, \leqslant>$ (called a frame), V is a valuation function; D is a non-empty set (the set of values of free individual variables), Z is a set of all integers, $\leqslant$ is the usual order relation on Z. The valuation function (in short: valuation) V is defined as follows:

1) if a is a free variable then $V(a)$ is an element of D;

2) if P is a m-ary relation symbol then $V(P) \in D^m \times Z$ (i.e., the valuation V defines the value of m-ary predicate symbol at time point $k \in Z$).

The concept "A is valid in $M =< I, V >$ at time point $k \in Z$" (in symbols, $M, k \models A$) is defined as follows:

1) $M, k \models P^l(a_1, \ldots, a_m) \iff < V(a_1), \ldots, V(a_m), k + l > \in V(P)$.

2) $M, k \models \neg A \iff M, k \not\models A$.

3) $M,k \models A \supset B \iff M,k \not\models A$ or $M,k \models B$.

4) $M,k \models A \wedge B \iff M,k \models A$ and $M,k \models B$.

5) $M,k \models A \vee B \iff M,k \models A$ or $M,k \models B$.

6) $M,k \models \circ_1 A^l \iff M,k+1 \models A^{l+1}$.

7) $M,k \models \circ_2 A^l \iff M,k-1 \models A^{l-1}$.

8) $M,k \models \Box_1 A \iff \forall l(l \in \omega)\ M,k+l \models A$,

9) $M,k \models \Box_2 A \iff \forall l(l \in \omega)\ M,k-l \models A$,

10) $M,k \models \forall x A \iff$ for every valuation V' which differs from V at most with respect to b, $< I, V' >, k \models A[b/x]$.

11) $M,k \models \exists\, x\, A \iff$ for some valuation V' which differs from V at most with respect to b, $< I, V' >, k \models A[b/x]$.

A formula A is valid in a model M (in symbols $M \models A$) if for each time point $k \in Z$ and each valuation $V, M, k \models A$. A sequent S is valid in $M =< I, V >$ at time point $k \in Z$ (in symbols $M,k \models S$) if either there exists a formula A in the antecedent of the S, such that $M,k \not\models A$ or there exists a formula B in the succedent of the S, such that $M,k \models B$. A formula A is universally valid if $\forall M\ M \models A$. A sequent S is universally valid if $\forall M$ and $\forall k\ M,k \models S$.

To prove the completeness of $G_{LS\omega}$ let us introduce the "symmetric" calculus $G_{LS\omega k}$ obtained from $G_{LS\omega}$ replacing the rule of inference $(\Box_i \to)$ by the following one:

$$\frac{\Gamma, \circ_i^k A, \Box_i A \to \Delta}{\Gamma, \Box_i A \to \Delta}(\Box_i^k \to) \quad (k \in \omega)$$

Remark 2.1. The rules of inference $(\to \Box_{i\omega}), (\Box_i^k \to)$ contain the side formulas of the same form, namely, $\circ_i^k A, (k \in \omega)$ (contrary to the pair rules of inference $(\to \Box_{i\omega}), (\Box_i \to)$ of $G_{LS\omega}$). The same is true for other pairs of rules of inference in $G_{LS\omega k}$. Therefore $G_{LS\omega k}$ has the traditional Gentzen calculi property, that of symmetry.

Lemma 2.1. $G_{LS\omega} \vdash S \Rightarrow G_{LS\omega k} \vdash S$.

Proof. The derivability of the rule of inference $(\Box_i \to)$ in $G_{LS\omega k}$ (and therefore the Lemma 2.1) follows from the fact that $G_{LS\omega k} \vdash \Box_i A \to A \wedge \circ_i \Box_i A$.

Theorem 2.1 (soundness of $G_{LS\omega}, G_{LS\omega k}$).
Let $I \in \{G_{LS\omega}, G_{LS\omega k}\}$. If $I \vdash S$ then S is universally valid.

Proof. The theorem is easily proved by induction on $O(D)$, where D is a given derivation.

Lemma 2.2. Let S be a sequent, then either $G^{cf}_{LS\omega k} \vdash S$, or there is a model M in which S is not valid for some time point $k \in Z$.

Proof. To prove the Lemma 2.2. we apply the method of Schütte, i.e., we construct for any sequent S a tree $T(S)$ (possibly having a infinite branch) called a reduction tree for S. From $T(S)$ we shall obtain either a proof of S in $G^{cf}_{LS\omega k}$ or a model in which S is not valid. $T(S)$ contains a sequent at each node and is constructed in stages as follows.

Stage 0: let us write S at the bottom of the tree.

Stage $k (k > 0)$:

Case 1. Each topmost sequent is an axiom, then stop.

Case 2. Otherwise the reduction rules are applied to any sequent $\Pi \to \Omega$ which has been obtained in stage $k - 1$. These rules correspond to the rules of inference of $G_{LS\omega k}$. We shall describe only the rules of reduction, corresponding the rules of inference $(\to \bigcirc_2), (\to \Box_2), (\Box_2^k \to)$.

1) Let $\Pi \to \Omega = \Pi \to \Omega', \bigcirc_2 A_1^{k_1}, \ldots, \bigcirc_2 A_n^{k_n}$, let $\bigcirc_2 A_1^{k_1}, \ldots, \bigcirc_2 A_n^{k_n}$ be all the formulas in Ω of the form $\bigcirc_2 A^l$. Then write down the sequent $\Pi \to \Omega', A_1^{k_1-1}, \ldots, A_n^{k_n-1}$ above the sequent $\Pi \to \Omega$ (rule of the right reduction of $\bigcirc_2$).

2) Let $\Pi \to \Omega = \Pi', \Box_2 A_1^{k_1}, \ldots, \Box_2 A_n^{k_n} \to \Omega$, let $\Box_2 A_1^{k_1}, \ldots, \Box_2 A_n^{k_n}$ be all the formulas in Π of the form $\Box_2 A^l$. Then write down the sequent $\Pi', A_1^{k_1}, \ldots, A_1^{k_1-h}, \ldots, A_n^{k_n-1}, \ldots, A_n^{k_n-h}, \Box_2 A_1^{k_1}, \ldots, \Box_2 A_n^{k_n}$ above the sequent $\Pi \to \Omega$ where h is the stage of the reduction (rule of the left reduction of $\Box_2$).

3) Let $\Pi \to \Omega = \Pi \to \Omega', \Box_2 A_1, \ldots, \Box_2 A_n$ and let $\Box_2 A_1, \ldots, \Box_2 A_n$ be all the formulas in Ω of the form $\Box_2 A$. Then write down all the sequents of the form $\Pi \to \Omega', \bigcirc_2^{k_1} A_1, \ldots, \bigcirc_2^{k_n} A_n$, where $k_i \in \omega (1 \leqslant i \leqslant n)$ (rule of the right reduction of $\Box_2$). Then take all possible (i.e., ω^n) combination of k_i.

Other rules of reduction are formulated analogously. The collection of those sequents which are obtained by the above reduction process, together with the partial order obtained by this process, is the reduction tree $T(S)$. A sequence (finite or infinite) $S_0, S_1, S_2, \ldots$ of sequents in $T(S)$ is called a branch of the tree if (1) $S_0 = S$; (2) S_{i+1} stands immediately above S_i; (3) if the sequence is finite, say $S_1, \ldots, S_n$, then S_n is axiom. If each branch of $T(S)$ ends with an axiom, then one can construct the proof in $G^{cf}_{LS\omega k}$ of the sequent S in an obvious way. Let us consider the case when in $T(S)$ there is an infinite branch $S = \Gamma_0 \to \Delta_0, \Gamma_1 \to \Delta_1, \ldots, \Gamma_i \to \Delta_i, \ldots$ such that no $\Gamma_i \to \Delta_i$ is an axiom. Let Γ_a denote the set of atomic formulas included in $\Gamma_0, \Gamma_1, \ldots, \Gamma_i, \ldots$ and Δ_a denote the set of atomic formulas included in $\Delta_0, \Delta_1, \ldots, \Delta_i, \ldots$. Then $\Gamma_a \bigcap \Delta_a = \varnothing$. For every atomic formula E let us define the model M in such way that $M \vDash E$ if $E \in \Gamma_a$ and $M \nvDash E$ if $E \in \Delta_a$.

Now we shall prove the following

Proposition (*). Let A be any formula, then $M \vDash A$ if $A \in \bigcup\{\Gamma_i : i \in \omega\}$ and $M \nvDash A$ if $A \in \bigcup\{\Delta_i : i \in \omega\}$.

Proof. Let $t(A)$ is the number of occurrences of logical symbols and temporal symbols $\Box_1, \Box_2$ in A, $g(A)$ is the number of occurrences of logical symbols and all temporal symbols (i.e., $\bigcirc_1, \bigcirc_2, \Box_1, \Box_2$) in A. The proof of the proposition (*) is carried out by the induction on $\omega \cdot t(A) + g(A)$ (i.e., by the double induction $< t(A), g(A) >$). When A is an atomic, the proposition (*) follows from the definition of M. Let as consider the case when $A = \Box_2 B$ (other cases are examined analogously). Let $\Box_2 B \in \cup\Gamma_i$, then according to the rule of the left reduction of $\Box_2$ we have that $B, \bigcirc_2 B, \ldots, \bigcirc_2^i B, \ldots \in \cup\Gamma_i$. From the induction hypothesis, $M \vDash B, M \vDash \bigcirc_2 B, \ldots, M \vDash \bigcirc_2^i B, \ldots$. Therefore $M \vDash \Box_2 B$. If $A \in \cup\Delta_i$, then $\exists i$ such that $\Box_2 B \in \Delta_i$ and according to the rule of the right reduction of $\Box_2$ we have that $\bigcirc_2^k B \in \Delta_j$ for some k and $j > i$. From the induction hypothesis, $M \not\models \bigcirc_2^k B$. Therefore, $M \not\models \Box_2 B$.

This completes the proof of the proposition (*) and the lemma 2.1.

Theorem 2.2. (Completeness and cut elimination for $G_{LS\omega k}$). If a sequent S is universally valid, then $G_{LS\omega k}^{cf} \vdash S$.

Proof: follows from Lemma 2.1.

Remark 2.2. It is possible to prove the equivalence of the rule of inference $(\to \Box_{i\omega})$ with so called the constructive ω-rule of inference $(\to \Box_{i\omega}^{con})$ in which the existence of a constructive method of obtaining a proof of the sequent $\Gamma \to \Delta, \bigcirc_i^k A$ is required, when k is given (e.g. [10]). Therefore the completeness of the calculus $G_{LS\omega k}^{\prime cf}$ (obtained from $G_{LS\omega k}^{cf}$ replacing the rule of inference $(\to \Box_{i\omega})$ by the $(\to \Box_{i\omega}^{con})$) can be proved.

To prove that $G_{LS\omega k}^{cf} \vdash S \Rightarrow G_{LS\omega}^{cf} \vdash S$ let us introduce some auxiliary calculus $G_{LS\omega kd}$, obtained from $G_{LS\omega k}$ replacing the rule of inference $(\Box_i^k \to)$ by the following one:

$$\frac{\Gamma, \bigcirc_i^k A, \bigcirc_i \Box_i A, \Box_i A \to \Delta}{\Gamma, \Box_i A \to \Delta}(\Box_i^{kd} \to)(k \in \omega)$$

Lemma 2.3. $G_{LS\omega k}^{cf} \vdash S \Rightarrow G_{LS\omega kd}^{cf} \vdash S$.

Proof. The admissibility of the structural rule of inference (W) holds for $G_{LS\omega kd}^{cf}$ (the proof is the same as Lemma 3.2 below). Using this fact the admissibility of the rule of inference $(\Box_i^k \to)$ in $G_{LS\omega kd}^{cf}$ is proved.

Let $G_{LS\omega od}$ be the special case of the calculus $G_{LS\omega kd}$ when $k = 0$.

Lemma 2.4. $G_{LS\omega od} \vdash \Gamma, \; \bigcirc_i^k A, \bigcirc_i \Box_i A, \; \Box_i A \to \Delta \Rightarrow G_{LS\omega od} \vdash \Gamma, \Box_i A \to \Delta$.

Proof. By induction on $O_1 \cdot k + O(D)$ (where $O_1 > O(D)$, D is given derivation) and using the admissibility of the structural rule of inference (W) in $G_{LS\omega od}$.

Lemma 2.5. $G_{LS\omega kd}^{cf} \vdash S \Rightarrow G_{LS\omega od} \vdash S$.

Proof. Using Lemma 2.4.

Lemma 2.6. $G_{LS\omega od}^{cf} \vdash S \Rightarrow G_{LS\omega}^{cf} \vdash S$.

Proof. The rule of inference $(\Box_i^{od} \to)$ is derivable in $G_{L\omega}^{cf}$. Indeed, by applying $(\Box_i \to)$ and $(C \to)$ (which is admissible in $G_{L\omega}^{cf}$, see Lemma 3.4, below) we get the conclusion of $(\Box_i \to)$.

Lemma 2.7. $G_{LS\omega k}^{cf} \vdash S \Rightarrow G_{LS\omega}^{cf} \vdash S$.

Proof: follows from Lemmas 2.3, 2.5, 2.6.

Theorem 2.3. (completeness of $G_{LS\omega}$). If a sequent S is universally valid, then $G_{LS\omega}^{cf} \vdash S$.

Proof: follows from Theorem 2.2. and Lemma 2.7.

Theorem 2.4. (cut elimination for $G_{LS\omega}$). $G_{LS\omega} \vdash S \Rightarrow G_{LS\omega}^{cf} \vdash S$.

Proof: follows from Lemma 2.1, Theorems 2.1, 2.2 and Lemma 2.7.

§3. Structural elimination theorem for $G_{LS\omega k}$.

It is well known (e.g. [11]) that cut elimination enormously increases the height of the given derivation. Here we shall prove the theorem claiming not only the possibility of cut elimination from the derivation in $G_{LS\omega k}$ but also providing some structural characterization of derivations not increasing during the elimination procedure (therefore the theorem is called structural elimination theorem). In [8] the structural elimination theorem was proved for the first order modal logic $S5$.

In this section by I we denote the calculi $G^{cf}_{LS\omega}, G^{cf}_{LS\omega k}$. A derivation in the calculus I will be called atomic if all the axioms are of the form $\Gamma, E \to \Delta, E$, where E is an atomic formula. Through the section D means a given atomic derivation, D_1 means resulting one in I.

Lemma 3.1. An arbitrary derivation in the calculus I may be transformed into an atomic one.

Proof. By induction on $t(A)$, where $t(A)$ is the temporal complexity of the formula A defined by the number of occurrences of logical symbols and temporal symbols $\Box_1, \Box_2$ in A from the axiom $\Gamma, A \to A, \Delta$.

Let us introduce the notion of structural complexity of atomic derivations in I. Two formulas will be called compatible if they coincide up to renaming of free variables. The pairs $< A, (i) >, < B, (i) >$ will be called compatible if A, B are compatible and if they are the principal formulas of an application of the same rule of inference (i). The structural complexity of an atomic derivation D in calculus I is defined as (and denoted by $C(D)$) a set of incompatible pairs $< A, (i) >$, where A is the principal formula of rule of inference (i) in D.

Let the notation $I \vdash_D S$ stand for the derivation D of S in I.

Lemma 3.2. $I \vdash_D S \Rightarrow I \vdash_{D_1} S[b/a]$, where b is any free variable, $C(D) = C(D_1)$, $O(D) = O(D_1)$.

Proof: follows from the possibility of renaming an eigenvariable (from D) if this eigenvariable coincides with the free variable b.

Lemma 3.3. (admissibility of the structural rule (W) in I). $I \vdash_D \Gamma \to \Delta \Rightarrow I \vdash_{D_1} \Pi, \Gamma \to \Delta, \Omega$ and $C(D) = C(D_1)$, $O(D) = O(D_1)$.

Proof. By induction on $O(D)$, using Lemma 3.2.

Lemma 3.4 (invertibility of the rules of inference of I). Let (j) be a rule of inference of I; S be the conclusion; S_1 be any premise of (j). Then $I \vdash_D S \Rightarrow I \vdash_{D_1} S_1$, and also $O(D_1) \leqslant O(D)$, $C(D_1) \subseteq C(D)$. Moreover, if D does not contain applications of the rule of inference $(\to \Box_{i\omega})$, then $O(D_1) < O(D)$.

Proof. By induction on $O(D)$; when $(j) \in \{(\Box_i^k \to), (\to \exists)\}$ the Lemma 3.2 is applied.

Lemma 3.5 (admissibility of $(\to C), (C \to)$ in I). (a) $I \vdash_D \Gamma \to \Delta, A, A \Rightarrow I \vdash_{D_1} \Gamma \to \Delta, A$; (b) $I \vdash_D \Gamma, A, A \to \Delta \Rightarrow I \vdash_{D_1} \Gamma, A \to \Delta$, besides, $C(D_1) \subseteq C(D)$.

Proof. By induction on $O_1 \cdot t(A) + O(D)$, where $O_1 > O(D), t(A)$ is a temporal complexity of the formula A (see Lemma 3.1). Let us consider the case (b), when $I = G^{cf}_{LS\omega}, A = \Box_1 B$ (other cases are considered analogously). Let the end of the given derivation D be of the form:

$$D \left\{ \frac{D' \{\Gamma, \Box_1 B, B, \bigcirc_1 \Box_1 B \to \Delta}{\Gamma, \Box_1 B, \Box_1 B \to \Delta} (\Box_1 \to) \right.$$

From the definition of $O(D)$ we have that $O(D') < O(D)$; by applying Lemma 3.4 we get the derivation D'^* of the sequent $\Gamma, B, \bigcirc_1 \Box_1 B, B, \bigcirc_1 \Box_1 B \to \Delta$ from the derivation D' of the sequent $\Gamma, \Box_1 B, B, \bigcirc_1 \Box_1 B \to \Delta$, besides $O(D'^*) \leqslant O(D') < O(D)$, $C(D'^*) \subseteq C(D') \subsetneq C(D)$. Therefore from the induction hypothesis (since $O(D'^*) < O(D)$, $t(\bigcirc_1 \Box_1 B) = t(\Box_1 B)$) we get the derivation D^{**} of the sequent $\Gamma, B, B, \bigcirc_1 \Box_1 B \to \Delta$, besides $C(D^{**}) \subseteq C(D)$. As $t(B) < t(\Box_1 B)$, then by induction hypothesis we get the derivation D'_1 of the sequent $\Gamma, B, \bigcirc_1 \Box_1 B \to \Delta$, besides $C(D'_1) \subseteq C(D)$. From the D'_1 we get the desired derivation D_1 of the sequent $\Gamma, \Box_1 B \to \Delta$ with the help of the rule of inference $(\Box_1 \to)$, besides $C(D_1) \subseteq C(D)$.

A derivation in the calculus I is called pure if for every application of the rules of inference $(\to \forall)$, $(\exists \to)$ the eigenvariable of this application occurs only in the sequents located higher than this application.

Lemma 3.6. An arbitrary derivation D in the calculus I may be transformed into a pure derivation D_1 with the same end sequent, and $C(D) = C(D_1)$, $O(D) = O(D_1)$.

Proof. Follows from a possibility of renaming the eigenvariables of an application of the rules of inference $(\to \forall)$, $(\exists \to)$ without changing the structural complexity of resulting derivation.

Lemma 3.7. Let $G^{cf}_{LS\omega k} \vdash_{D_1} S_1 = \Gamma \to \Delta, A$ and $G^{cf}_{LS\omega k} \vdash_{D_2} S_2 = A, \Pi \to \Omega$. Then $G^{cf}_{LS\omega k} \vdash_{D^*} \Gamma, \Pi \to \Delta, \Omega$ and $C(D^*) \subseteq C(D)$. Here D is a derivation obtained by (cut) from the pure atomic derivations D_1, D_2 of the sequents S_1, S_2, and D^* is the pure resulting derivation of the sequent $\Gamma, \Pi \to \Delta, \Omega$.

Proof. By induction on $O_1 \cdot t(A) + O(D_1) \# O(D_2)$, where $t(A)$ is temporal complexity (see Lemma 3.1) of the cut formula A; $O_1 > O(D_1) \# O(D_2)$. Let us consider the case when $A = \Box_i B$ $(i = 1, 2)$ and the end of the given derivation is the following:

$$D \left\{ \frac{D_1 \left\{ \frac{D_1^k \{\{\Gamma \to \Delta, \bigcirc_i^k B\}_{k \in \omega}}{\Gamma \to \Delta, \Box_i B} (\to \Box_{i\omega}) \right. \quad D_2 \left\{ \frac{D'_2 \{\bigcirc_i^l B, \Box_i B, \Pi \to \Omega}{\Box_i B, \Pi \to \Omega} (\Box_i^l \to) \right.}{\Gamma, \Pi \to \Delta, \Omega} (\text{cut}) \right.$$

Let us apply (cut) to the derivations D_1, D'_2. As $O(D_1) \# O(D'_2) < O(D_1) \# O(D_2)$, by the induction hypothesis we can obtain the pure derivation D_3 of the sequent $\Gamma, \bigcirc_i^l B, \Pi \to \Delta, \Omega$ in $G^{cf}_{LS\omega k}$, besides $C(D_3) \subseteq C(D)$. Further, let us choose from the derivations D_1^k such that $k = l$ and apply (cut) to the derivations D_1^l, D_3. As $t(\bigcirc_i^l B) < t(\Box_i B)$ by the induction hypothesis we can obtain the pure derivation D'

of the sequent $\Gamma, \Gamma, \Pi \to \Delta, \Delta, \Omega$ in $G^{cf}_{LS\omega k}$, besides $C(D') \subseteq C(D)$. Finally, applying Lemma 3.5 to the derivation D' we can obtain the desired derivation D^* of the sequent $\Gamma, \Pi \to \Delta, \Omega$ in $G^{cf}_{LS\omega k}$. It is obvious that $C(D^*) \subseteq C(D)$.

Other cases are considered analogously.

Theorem 3.1. (Structural cut elimination theorem for $G_{LS\omega k}$). $G_{LS\omega k} \vdash_D S \Rightarrow G^{cf}_{LS\omega k} \vdash_{D_1} S$, besides $C(D_1) \subseteq C(D)$.

Proof. Follows from Lemmas 3.6, 3.7.

Let us define the notion of a ω–subformula of an arbitrary formula of symmetric linear temporal logic under consideration. The set of ω–subformulas of a formula is inductively defined as follows. An atomic formula has exactly one ω–subformula, i.e., the formula itself. The ω–subformulas of $\neg A$ are the ω–subformulas of A and $\neg A$ itself. The ω–subformulas of $A \odot B (\odot \in \{\supset, \wedge, \vee\})$ are the ω–subformulas of A and of B and $A \odot B$ itself. The ω–subformulas of $\circ_i A$ $(i = 1, 2)$ are the ω–subformulas of $A^{\rho 1}$ (where $\rho = +$, if $i = 1$ and $\rho = -$, if $i = 2$) and $\circ_i A$ itself. The ω–subformulas of $\Box_i A$ are the subformulas of $\circ_i^k A$ $(k \in \omega)$ and $\Box_i A$ itself. The subformulas of $\forall x A$ or $\exists x A$ are the subformulas of any formula of the form $A[b/x]$, where b is an arbitrary free variable and the formula $QxA (Q \in \{\forall, \exists\})$ itself.

Lemma 3.8. (ω–subformula property for $G_{LS\omega k}$). Let D be any derivation in $G^{cf}_{LS\omega k}$ of a sequent S, then all the formulas which occur in D are ω–subformulas of the formulas in the S.

Proof. Follows from the definitions of $G^{cf}_{LS\omega k}$ and ω–subformula.

Remark 3.1. From Lemma 2.1, Theorem 3.1 and Lemma 2.7 we obtain the syntactic proof of cut elimination theorem for $G_{LS\omega}$.

§4. Description of the infinitary calculus $\mathbf{G_{L\omega}}$ and the finitary one $\mathbf{G_L}$ for the restricted first order nonsymmetric linear temporal logic.

From now on we consider only the restricted first order linear temporal logic. For the sake of simplicity we shall also consider only temporal operators for future. Instead of $\circ_1, \Box_1$ we shall use notations $\circ$ ("next") and $\Box$ ("always"). Therefore the rules of inference $(\to \circ_1), (\circ_1 \to), (\to \Box_{1\omega}), (\Box_1 \to)$ will be denoted by $(\to \circ), (\circ \to), (\to \Box_\omega), (\Box \to)$ respectively. Besides for the sake of simplicity from the language under consideration we shall omit the existential quantifier. Therefore the expression $\exists x A$ will denote the formula $\neg \forall x \neg A$.

Let P be any part of a given formula A (this part may be a formula, logical or temporal symbol, relation symbol or variable). The positive and negative parts of A are defined as follows: (1) an occurrence of P is a positive part of the same occurrence of P; (2) if P is a positive (negative) part of B, then P is a negative (respectively, positive) part of $\neg B$; (3) if P is a positive (negative) part of B or of C, then P is a positive (respectively, negative) part of $B \odot C$, where $\odot \in \{\wedge, \vee\}$; (4) if P is a positive (negative) part of B, then P is a positive (respectively, negative) part of σB, where $\sigma \in \{\forall x, \circ, \Box\}$; (5) if P is a positive (negative) part of B, then P is a positive (respectively, negative) part of $C \supset B$, and a negative (respectively, positive) part of

$B \supset C$. Let $S = A_1, \ldots, A_n \to B_1, \ldots, B_m$, and P is any part of S, then P in S is a positive or negative part of the sequent S according as (1) it is a positive (respectively, negative) part of B_i $(1 \leqslant i \leqslant m)$, or (2) it is a negative (respectively, positive) part of A_i $(1 \leqslant i \leqslant n)$. For example, in $\forall x \bigcirc P(x) \to \bigcirc \forall x P(x)$ first (from the left) occurrences of the symbols $\bigcirc, \forall x$ are negative, the second occurrence of the same symbols are positive.

Let us define the notion of temporal–propositional formula (shortly: (T–P)–formula). (1) Any propositional variable (possibly with indices) is (T–P)–formula. (2) If A, B are (T–P)–formulas, then $A \odot B$, (where $\odot \in \{\supset, \wedge, \vee\}$) is (T–P)–formula. (3) If A is (T–P)–formula then σA (where $\sigma \in \{\urcorner, \bigcirc, \Box\}$ is (T–P)–formula.

Let us define objects under consideration in a finite calculus G_L. A sequent S containing positive occurrences of $\Box$ will be called the singular regular sequent if either S does not contain negative occurrences of $\Box$ or (1) all negative occurrences of $\Box$ are in the scope of positive ones and (2) all formulas of the form $\Box A$ in S are (T–P)–formulas. A sequent S containing both positive and negative occurrences of $\Box$ (which do not occur in the scope of positive occurrence of $\Box$) will be called ordinary regular if (1) all formulas of the form $\Box A$ contained in S are (T–P)–formulas; (2) $\mathrm{var}(\forall x C) \cap \mathrm{var}(\Box B) = \varnothing$, where $\mathrm{var}(\forall x C)$ is the set of propositional variables occurring in negative occurrences of the formulas of type $\forall x C$, besides C containes $\bigcirc$(next) and/or indices and does not contain $\Box$; $\mathrm{var}(\Box B)$ is the set of propositional variables occurring in occurrences of the formulas of type $\Box B$ in S. The sequent S will be called regular if S is either singular regular or ordinary regular. The sequent S will be called strong regular if S does not contain any positive occurrences of $\Box$.

Let $G_{L\omega}$ be a calculus, obtained from $G_{LS\omega}$ by dropping the rules of inference $(\to \bigcirc_2), (\bigcirc_2 \to), (\to \Box_{2\omega}), (\Box_2 \to), (\to \exists), (\exists \to)$. It is obvious all the statements from sections 2, 3 concerning the calcúlus are true for $G_{L\omega}$. Let G_L be the calculus where objects under consideration are regular or strong regular sequents and postulates (i.e., axiom and rules of inference) are obtained from $G_{L\omega}$ replacing the rule of inference $(\to \Box_\omega)$ by the following ones:

$$\frac{\Gamma \to \Delta}{\sqcap, \Gamma^1 \to \Delta^1, \Theta}(+1)$$

$$\frac{\Gamma, \Box\Omega \to \Delta, R; \quad R \to \bigcirc R; \quad R \to A}{\sqcap, \Gamma, \Box\Omega \to \Theta, \Delta, \Box A}(\to \Box_1)$$

$$\frac{\Gamma \to \Delta, A; \quad \Gamma \to \Delta, \bigcirc\Box A}{\Gamma \to \Delta, \Box A}(\to \Box_2)$$

$$\frac{S_1; \ldots; S_n}{\Gamma, \Box\Omega \to \Delta, \Box A_1, \ldots, \Box A_n}(\to \Box_3)$$

where $S_1 = \Box\Omega \to A_1, \Box A_2, \ldots, \Box A_n; \ldots; S_n = \Box\Omega \to \Box A_1, \ldots, \Box A_{n-1}, A_n$; The rule of inference $(\to \Box_1)$ satisfies the following conditions:
(1) $\Gamma, \Box\Omega \to \Delta \in INV = \{S_1 = \Gamma_1, \Box\Omega \to \Delta_1; \ldots; S_n = \Gamma_n, \Box\Omega \to \Delta_n\}$; this set (for construction of the set INV see section 5) will be called an invariant set and INV must satisfy the following conditions:

(1.1) $\Box\Omega$ does not contain indices;

(1.2) $\forall i\ (1 \leqslant i \leqslant n) IN \vdash \Gamma_i, \Box\Omega \to \Delta_i, \circ(\bigvee_{i=1}^{n} (\Gamma_i^{\wedge} \wedge \neg\Delta_i^{\vee}))$, where IN is the calculus obtained from G_L by dropping the rules of inference $(\to \Box_1), (\to \Box_3), (\to \forall), (\forall \to)$; the notation $\Pi^{\wedge}(\Pi^{\vee})$ means conjunction (disjunction, respectively) of the formulas from Π.

(2) the formula R (called invariant formula) has the form $\bigvee_{i=1}^{n} (\Gamma_i^{\wedge} \wedge \neg\Delta_i^{\vee}) \wedge (\Box\Omega)^{\wedge}$. In the rules of inference $(\to \Box_1)$, $(\to \Box_2)$ the principal formula $\Box A$ does not contain indices. In the rule of inference $(+1)$ (and below) A^1 means B^{k+1}, where $A = B^k$ $(k \geqslant 0)$.

Remark 4.1.(a) Γ_i, $\neg\Delta_i$ occurring in the invariant formula R are constructed from some subformulas of the formulas from Ω (see section 5 below). (b) It is obvious that the calculus IN is incomplete (with respect to the semantics described in the section 2). IN serves as some axiomatic characterization of invariant formula R in $(\to \Box_1)$. (c) We can verify the usefulness of $(\to \Box_3)$ by considering the following formulas:
1) $\Box\Diamond\Box A \equiv \Diamond\Box A$;
2) $\Box(\Box A \supset \Box B) \vee \Box(\Box B \supset \Box A)$;
3) $\Diamond A \wedge \Diamond B \supset \Diamond(A \wedge B) \vee \Diamond(A \wedge \Diamond B) \vee \Diamond(B \wedge \Diamond A)$;

Lemma 4.1. $G_{Lw}^{cf} \vdash A_1^{k_1}, \dots, A_n^{k_n} \to B_1^{k_1}, \dots, B_m^{k_m} \Rightarrow G_{Lw}^{cf} \vdash A_1^{k_1+l}, \dots, A_n^{k_n+l} \to B_1^{k_1+l}, \dots, B_m^{k_m+l}$ $(l \in \omega)$.

Proof. By induction on the height of a given derivation.

Lemma 4.2. In the calculus G_{Lw}^{cf} the following rule of inference is admissible:

$$\frac{\Gamma \to \Delta}{\circ\Gamma \to \circ\Delta}(\circ).$$

Proof. By Lemma 4.1 we have $G_{Lw}^{cf} \vdash \Gamma^1 \to \Delta^1$; then applying rules of inference $(\to \circ), (\circ \to)$ we have $G_{Lw}^{cf} \vdash \circ\Gamma \to \circ\Delta$.

Lemma 4.3. In $G_{L\omega}$ the following rule of inference

$$\frac{\Gamma \to \Delta, R; \quad R \to \circ R; \quad R \to A}{\Gamma \to \Delta, \Box A}(\to \Box)$$

(where R is an arbitrary formula) is admissible.

Proof. Starting from the middle premise of $(\to \Box)$ by induction on n we get that $G_{L\omega} \vdash R \to \circ^n R$ $(n \in \omega)$. Hence, by using left and right premises of $(\to \Box)$, the Lemma 4.2, (cut) and by $(\to \Box_\omega)$, we get that $G_{L\omega} \vdash \Gamma \to \Delta, \Box A$.

Lemma 4.4. In $G_{L\omega}$ the rule of inference $(\to \Box_2)$ is admissible.

Proof. Follows from the Lemma 4.3, taking $R = A \wedge \circ\Box A$.

Lemma 4.5. The following rule of inference is admissible in $G_{L\omega}$

$$\frac{S_1; \dots; S_n; S_{n+1}}{\Gamma \to \Delta, \Box A_1, \dots, \Box A_n}(\to \Box_2^*),$$

where

$$S_1 = \Gamma \to \Delta, A_1, \Box A_2, \ldots, \Box A_n;$$

$$\cdots$$

$$S_n = \Gamma \to \Delta, \Box A_1, \ldots, \Box A_{n-1}, A_n;$$

$$S_{n+1} = \Gamma \to \Delta, \bigcirc\Box A_1, \ldots, \bigcirc\Box A_n.$$

Proof. By induction on n, applying the Lemma 4.4, $G_{L\omega} \vdash \Box A \to \bigcirc\Box A$ and (cut).

Lemma 4.6. In $G_{L\omega}$ the rule of inference $(\to \Box_3)$ is admissible.

Proof. At first we shall prove that the following rule of inference is admissible in $G_{L\omega}$:

$$\frac{S_1; \ldots; S_n}{\Box\Omega \to \bigcirc^k A_1, \Box A_2, \ldots, \Box A_n}(\to \Box_3^k),$$

where $k \in \omega$, $S_1 = \Box\Omega \to A_1, \Box A_2, \ldots, \Box A_n; \ldots; S_n = \Box\Omega \to \Box A_1, \ldots, \Box A_{n-1}, A_n$.

The admissibility is proved by induction on k. If $k = 0$, then S_1 coincides with the conclusion of $(\to \Box_3^k)$. Let $k > 0$. Then by the induction hypothesis we have that $G_{L\omega} \vdash \Box\Omega \to \bigcirc^{k-1} A_1, \Box A_2, \ldots, \Box A_n$. Using the admissibility in $G_{L\omega}^{cf}$ of the rules of inference $(\bigcirc)$ and (W) (see Lemma 4.2, 3.2) and applying $(\Box \to)$ we can get $G_{L\omega} \vdash S'_n = \Box\Omega \to \bigcirc^k A_1, \bigcirc\Box A_2, \ldots, \bigcirc\Box A_n$. Using that $G_{L\omega} \vdash \Box A_1 \to \bigcirc^k A_1$ from the premises $S_2, \ldots, S_n$ of $(\to \Box_3^k)$ by the (cut) we get that $G_{L\omega} \vdash S'_1 = \Box\Omega \to \bigcirc^k A_1, A_2, \Box A_3, \ldots, \Box A_n; \ldots; G_{L\omega} \vdash S'_{n-1} = \Box\Omega \to \bigcirc^k A_1, \Box A_2, \ldots, \Box A_{n-1}, A_n$. Applying the Lemma 4.5 to the sequents $S'_1, \ldots, S'_{n-1}, S'_n$ we get that $G_{L\omega} \vdash \Box\Omega \to \bigcirc^k A_1, \Box A_2, \ldots, \Box A_n$ $(k \in \omega)$, i.e., the conclusion of $(\to \Box_3^k)$. Then applying $(\to \Box_\omega^k)$, (W) to the conclusion of $(\to \Box_3^k)$ we obtain the conclusion of $(\to \Box_3)$.

Theorem 4.1. $G_L \vdash S \Rightarrow G_{L\omega} \vdash S$.

Proof. Follows from the Lemmas 4.3, 4.4, 4.6.

Lemma 4.7. An arbitrary derivation in G_L^{cf} may be transformed into an atomic one, i.e., all the axioms are of the form $\Gamma, E \to \Delta, E$, where E is atomic formula

Proof. Analogously as in the Lemma 3.1. In the case of the axiom $\Box A \to \Box A$, the rule of inference $(\to \Box_3)$ is applied.

Remark 4.2. Let G_L^* be the calculus, obtained from G_L replacing $(\to \Box_1), (\to \Box_2), (\to \Box_3)$ by $(\to \Box)$ (see Lemma 4.3). Then the sequent $\Box A \to \Box A$ shows that for G_L^* Lemma 3.1 fails.

Lemma 4.8. The rule of inference (W) is admissible in G_L^{cf}.

Proof. By induction on the height of a given derivation.

Lemma 4.9. The rule of inference $(\to \Box_2)$ is invertible in G_L^{cf}.

Proof. By induction on the height of a given derivation.

§5. Reduction of $G^{cf}_{L\omega}$ to G^{cf}_{L}.

Let $J' \in \{G'_{L\omega},\ G'_L\}$ be the calculus obtained from $J \in \{G_{L\omega},\ G_L\}$ by adding the structural rule of inference (W).

Lemma 5.1 $J^{cf} \vdash S \iff J'^{cf} \vdash S$.

Proof. Follows from Lemmas 3.3, 4.8.

Let $G'^{cf}_{L\omega} \vdash S = \Gamma \to \Delta,\ \Box A$, then the explicitly shown occurrence of $\Box A$ will be called nonessential if $\Box A$ is not a descendant of any formula, except principal formulas of an application of (W). Notation $(\to \Box_\omega)\,[D]$ will mean the number of different applications of $(\to \Box_\omega)$ in atomic derivation D. Any two applications of $(\to \Box_\omega)$ will be called different if the principal formulas in these applications are either different (formulas of the type $\bigcirc^k A, \bigcirc^l A$ and formulas distinguished by indices and free variables are considered as coincident) or coincide but have different descendants.

Lemma 5.2 (a) Let $G'^{cf}_{L\omega} \vdash \Gamma \to \Delta,\ \Box A$ and let the explicitly shown occurrence of the formula $\Box A$ be nonessential in the given atomic derivation D, then $G'^{cf}_{L\omega} \vdash \Gamma \to \Delta$ and $(\to \Box_\omega)\,[D_1] = (\to \Box_\omega)[D]$;
(b) Let $G'^{cf}_{L\omega} \vdash_D \Gamma \to \Delta,\ \Box A$ and let the explicitly shown occurrence of the formula $\Box A$ be a descendant of the principal formula of an application of $(\to \Box_\omega)$ in the given atomic derivation, then $G'^{cf}_{L\omega} \vdash_{D_1} \Gamma \to \Delta,\ \bigcirc^k A\ (k \in w)$ and $(\to \Box_\omega)[D_1] < (\to \Box_\omega)[D]$.
Proof. By induction on $O(D)$.

The notion of a subformula of an arbitrary formula of nonsymmetric linear temporal logic under consideration is obtained from the notion of ω–subformula (see section 3) replacing the clauses concerning temporal operators by following: the subformulas of $\bigcirc A$ are the subformulas of A^1 and $\bigcirc A$ itself; the subformulas of $\Box A$ are the subformulas of A, formula $\bigcirc\Box A$ and $\Box A$ itself.

Now we shall set a canonical forms of ordinary regular sequents and singular regular sequents. A ordinary regular sequent S will be called primary if $S = \Sigma_1,\ \sqcap^1_1,\ \Box\Omega^1_1,\ \forall\bar{x}\Xi \to \Sigma_2,\ \sqcap^1_2,\ \Box\Omega^1_2,\ \Box\nabla$, where $\Sigma_i\,(i = 1,2)$ is empty set or consists of a formulas which not contain $\bigcirc, \Box$ and indices; $\sqcap_i\,(i = 1,2)$ is empty set or consists of atomic formulas (possible with indices), $\Omega_i\,(i = 1,2)$, ∇ consists of (T–P)–formulas, besides ∇ does not contain indices; $\forall\bar{x}\Xi$ is empty set or consists of formulas of the form $\forall x B_i,\ (1 \leqslant i \leqslant n)$ where B_i contain $\bigcirc$(next) and/or indices and do not contain $\Box$, besides $\forall i\,(1 \leqslant i \leqslant n)\text{var}(\forall x B_i) \cap \text{var}(\Omega^1_1) = \varnothing$. If instead of $\Box\Omega^1_1$ in S there is the multiset $\Box A^{i_1}_1, \ldots, \Box A^{i_n}_n$, where some of $i_j = 0\ (1 \leqslant j \leqslant n)$, then such ordinary regular sequent S will be called quasiprimary.

A singular regular sequent S will be called primary, if $S = \sqcap_1 \to \sqcap_2, \Box\nabla$, where $\Box \notin \sqcap_i\,(i = 1,2)$; ∇ consists of formulas which either do not contain negative occurrences of $\Box$ or ∇ contains negative occurrences of $\Box$ and then ∇ consists of (T–P)–formulas.

Let us define the notion of critical occurrences of a formula B in ordinary regular sequent S, which will be marked by B^+.

1. Let $\Box B$ occur negatively in S and let this occurrence of the formula $\Box B$ be not controlled by positive occurrence of the symbol $\Box$ in S, then $\Box^+ B$.

2. Let B occur in $\Box^+ A \in S$, where $B \in \{P^i, \Box D\}$ (P^i is propositional variable, possibly with index i) and let this occurrence of B be not controlled by positive occurrence of $\Box$ in S, thenB^+. We shall mark critical occurrences when $S = \Gamma \to \Delta, \Box A$

and S is the conclusion of the lowest application of $(\to \Box_w)$ (in given atomic derivation of S) and the selected occurrence of the formula $\Box A$ is the principal formula of this application. The invariant set (defining the invariant formula R in the rule of inference $(\to \Box_1)$) is constructed from critical occurrences of formulas (see below). The sequent S with marked critical occurrences of formulas will be called marked and denoted by S^+. Let us define the rank of the sequent S^+, denoted by $r(S^+)$. First we define the rank of an arbitrary formula A of the sequent S, denoted by $r(A)$. (a) $r(A^+) = 0$. (b) Let $A \neq A^+$, then (1) $r(A) = 1$ if A is an atomic formula; (2) $r(A) = r(B) + r(C) + 1$, if $A = B \odot C$, $\odot \in \{\supset, \wedge, \vee\}$; (3) $r(A) = r(B)+1$, if $A = \sigma B$, $\sigma \in \{\circ, \urcorner\}$; (4) $r(A) = 0$, if $A = \Box B$. Let $S^+ = A_1, \ldots, A_n \to A_{n+1}, \ldots, A_{n+m}$, then $r(S^+) = \sum_{i=1}^{n+m} r(A_i)$.

The notion of a deduction of some sequents in calculus I is obtained from the notion of a derivation in I by rejecting the requirement that each vertex (i.e. initial sequent) must be an axiom. Let some vertices of a deduction be sequents $S_1, \ldots, S_n$. In such case we shall say that we can construct a deduction of a sequent S from the sequents $S_1, \ldots, S_n$.

Lemma 5.3. Let S is regular sequent and let $G'^{cf}_{Lw} \vdash S^+$, then we can construct a deduction V in G'^{cf}_{Lw} of the sequent S^+ from the primary sequents $S_1^+, \ldots, S_n^+$, besides

1) $G'^{cf}_{Lw} \vdash S_1^+, \ldots, G'^{cf}_{Lw} \vdash S_n^+$;

2) V does not contain applications of the rules of inference $(\to \Box_w), (\forall \to)$; besides each formula of the form $\Box A^i$ $(i > 0)$ from antecedent of S_k^+ $(1 \leqslant k \leqslant n)$ is ancestor of the principal formula $\Box A^{i-1}$ of the application of $(\Box \to)$ in V;

3) $O(D_i) \leqslant O(D)$, where D is a given atomic derivation, D_i $(1 \leqslant i \leqslant n)$ is a derivation of the sequent S_i^+;

4) $(\to \Box_w)[D_i] \leqslant (\to \Box_w)[D]$;

5) $r(S_i^+) < r(S^+)$, if $r(S^+) > 0$ and $r(S_i^+) = r(S^+)$, if $r(S^+) = 0$.

Proof. By using the invertibility of the rules of inference of G^{cf}_{Lw}, except $(\to \Box_w), (\forall \to)$ (see Lemma 3.4.).

The expression $\Gamma, \Gamma_{11}^k, \ldots, \Gamma_{n1}^k \to \Delta, \Gamma_{12}^k, \ldots, \Gamma_{n2}^k$ $(k \in w)$ will be called metasequent, k will be called metaindex. For example metasequent $\Gamma \to A^k$ $(k \in w)$ means the infinite set of sequents $\Gamma \to A$, $\Gamma \to A^1, \ldots, \Gamma \to A^i, \ldots$. Each metasequent may be interpreted as the sequent arising from the sequent $S = \Gamma \to \Delta, \Box A_1, \ldots, \Box A_n$. where Γ_{ij}^k $1 \leqslant j \leqslant 2$, $1 \leqslant i \leqslant n$ consists of ancestors of $\Box A_i$ in some derivation of S in G'^{cf}_{Lw}. Therefore the metasequent $\Gamma, \Gamma_{11}^k, \ldots, \Gamma_{n1}^k \to \Delta, \Gamma_{12}^k, \ldots, \Gamma_{n2}^k$ plays the same role as the sequent $\Gamma \to \Delta$, $\Box A_1, \ldots, \Box A_n$ and all definitions (and lemmas) about sequents hold if we replace sequents by metasequents.

Following by S.Kleene we shall introduce the notion of product of sequents (metasequents) S_1, S_2. Let $S_1 = \Gamma \to \Delta$, $S_2 = \sqcap \to \Theta$ then $S_1 \cdot S_2 = \Gamma, \sqcap \to \Delta, \Theta$.

Let us denote by (A_w) the following "metarule" of inference

$$\frac{S}{S_i} \quad (i = 1 \text{ or } i = 2),$$

where $S = S' \cdot X$, and S' is a primary ordinary regular sequent, i.e. $S' = \Sigma_1, \sqcap_1^1, \Box\Omega_1^1, \forall \bar{x} \Xi \to \Sigma_2, \sqcap_2^1, \Box\Omega_2^1, \Box\nabla$, besides $\Omega_1 \neq \emptyset$, $\Omega_2, \nabla \neq \emptyset$; $X = \Gamma_{11}^k, \ldots, \Gamma_{n1}^k \to \Gamma_{12}^k, \ldots, \Gamma_{n2}^k$

(i.e. X is metasequent corresponding to the sequent of the form $\rightarrow \Box A_1, \ldots, \Box A_n$); X consists of (T-P)-formulas. $S_1 = \Sigma_1, \sqcap_1^1, \forall \bar{x} \Xi \rightarrow \Sigma_2, \sqcap_2^1$; $S_2 = S_2' \cdot X$, where $S_2' = \sqcap_1^*, \Box\Omega_1 \rightarrow \sqcap_2^*, \Box\Omega_2, \Box\nabla$, where $\sqcap_i^* \subseteq \sqcap_i$ $(i = 1, 2)$, $\sqcap_i^*$ consists of propositional variables occurring in $\Omega_1, \Omega_2, \nabla, X$. When $X = \varnothing$, then instead of metarule (A_w) we have the corresponding rule, denoted by (A).

Lemma 5.4. The metarule (A_w) (rule(A)) of inference is admissible in $G_{Lw}^{\prime cf}$.

Proof. By induction on $O(D)$ (by using Lemma 5.3), where D is a given derivation of S, we can easily prove the admissibility of (A_w) in $G_L^{\prime cf}$. From this follows the admissibility of (A).

Remark 5.1. By virtue of decidability of the propositional linear temporal logic an application of the rule of inference (A) is decidable .

Let S^+ is an ordinary regular marked sequent and let $G_{Lw}^{\prime cf} \vdash S^+$. Let us introduce the notion of n–th ($n \geqslant 0$) resolvent of a sequent S^+ (denoted by $\mathfrak{R}^n(S^+)$). $\mathfrak{R}^n(S^+)$ is a set of some sequents and when $n = 0$ then $\mathfrak{R}^n(S^+) = \{S^+\}$. Let $S_i^+ \in \mathfrak{R}^k(S^+)$, then $\mathfrak{R}^{k+1}(S^+)$ is defined by the following tree:

$$D_i \left\{ D_i' \left\{ \begin{array}{ccc} \overline{\phantom{S_{i1}^+}}\,(\bar{A}) & & \overline{\phantom{S_{in}^+}}\,(\bar{A}) \\ S_{i1}^+ & \ldots & S_{in}^+ \\ & \mid & \\ & S_i^+ & \end{array} \right. \right.$$

where the part D_i' is primary deduction of S_i^+ (see Lemma 5.3), reducing S_i^+ to the primary sequents $S_{i1}^+, \ldots, S_{in}^+$, $(\bar{A})$ means antiapplication of (A). The vertices of the tree D_i of the form $\Gamma, A \rightarrow \Delta, A$ will be called closed, the others–nonclosed. The set of nonclosed vertices of the tree D_i will be called a resolvent of the sequent S_i^+ and will be denoted by $\mathfrak{R}(S_i^+)$. $\mathfrak{R}^{k+1}(S^+) = \bigcup_i \mathfrak{R}(S_i^+)$ for all $S_i^+ \in \mathfrak{R}^k(S_i^+)$.

For example if $S^+ = P_1, P_2^1, \Box^+\Omega \rightarrow \Box A$ (where $\Box^+\Omega = \Box^+(\urcorner(\circ P_1^+ \vee \circ P_2^+) \vee \circ(\circ P_1^+ \vee \circ P_2^+)))$, then $\mathfrak{R}(S^+) = \mathfrak{R}^1(S^+) = \{P_2, P_1^{+1}, \Box^+\Omega \rightarrow \Box A;\ P_2, P_2^{+1}, \Box^+\Omega \rightarrow \Box A\}$. $\mathfrak{R}^2(S^+) = \{P_1^+, P_1^{+1}, \Box^+\Omega \rightarrow \Box A;\ P_1^+, P_2^{+1}, \Box^+\Omega \rightarrow \Box A;\ P_2^+, P_1^{+1}, \Box^+\Omega \rightarrow \Box A;\ P_2^+, P_2^{+1}, \Box^+\Omega \rightarrow \Box A\}$.

Let us introduce the notion of a deduction tree of n–th resolvent of a sequent S^+ (denoted by $D\mathfrak{R}^n(S^+)$). It consists of subtrees D_i by which $\mathfrak{R}^n(S^+)$ is constructed. From the construction of $D\mathfrak{R}^n(S)$ it follows that each non–closed vertex of $D\mathfrak{R}^n(S^+)$ is either primary or quasiprimary and $D\mathfrak{R}^n(S^+)$ is infinite in general. In spite of this it will be shown that $D\mathfrak{R}^n(S^+)$ has some periodic structure. Instead of $D\mathfrak{R}^n(S^+)$ we shall usually write $D\mathfrak{R}(S^+)$. Let $S_i^+ = \Gamma^+, \Box^+\Omega \rightarrow \Delta^+, \Box\nabla$ is a nonclosed vertex of $D\mathfrak{R}(S^+)$ and Γ^+, Δ^+ consists of propositional variables and/or formulas of the form $\Box^+B$, besides all formulas from Γ^+, Δ^+ are subformulas of formulas from Ω and Ω is not indexed. Then such S_i^+ will be called Ω–saturated sequent. If all vertices of $D\mathfrak{R}(S^+)$ are either closed or Ω–saturated then such $D\mathfrak{R}(S^+)$ will be called Ω–saturated and denoted by $D_\Omega\mathfrak{R}(S^+)$.

Lemma 5.5. Let S^+ is an ordinary regular sequent and let $G_{Lw}^{\prime cf} \vdash S^+$, then it is possible to construct $D_\Omega\mathfrak{R}(S^+)$.

Proof. By induction on $r(S^+)$, using Lemmas 5.3, 5.4.

Lemma 5.6. Let $G'^{cf}_{Lw} \vdash S^+ = \Gamma^+, \Box^+\Omega \to \Delta^+, \Box\nabla$, where S^+ is Ω-saturated, let $\mathfrak{R}(S^+) = \{S^+_1, \ldots, S^+_n\}$. Then $\forall i (1 \leqslant i \leqslant n)$ S^+_i is Ω- saturated.

Proof. Follows from the definition of $\mathfrak{R}(S^+)$ and Ω-saturated sequent.

Let $S^+_1 = \Gamma^+, \Box^+\Omega \to \Delta^+, \Box\nabla$ and $S^+_2 = \Pi^+, \Box^+\Omega \to \theta^+, \Box\nabla$ be Ω-saturated sequents. Then $S^+_1 = S^+_2$ ($S^+_1 \neq S^+_2$), if $\{\Gamma^+, \Box^+\Omega\} \to \{\Delta^+, \Box\nabla\}$ and $\{\Pi^+, \Box^+\Omega\} \to \{\theta^+, \Box\nabla\}$ coincide ($\{\{\Gamma^+, \Box^+\Omega\} \to \{\Delta^+, \Box\nabla\}$ disagree with $\{\Pi^+, \Box^+\Omega\} \to \{\theta^+, \Box\nabla\}$, respectively). Let $D_\Omega\mathfrak{R}(S^+)$ have been constructed. It will be called complete (and denoted by $CD_\Omega\mathfrak{R}(S^+)$) if it is not possible to construct any new nonclosed vertex of the $D_\Omega\mathfrak{R}(S^+)$.

Lemma 5.7. Let $G'^{cf}_{Lw} \vdash S^+ = \Gamma^+, \Box^+\Omega \to \Delta^+, \Box\nabla$, where S^+ is Ω-saturated, then it is possible to construct $CD_\Omega\mathfrak{R}(S^+)$.

Proof. From the finiteness of the set of subformulas of formulas from Ω follows that the set of different Ω-saturated sequents is finite. Therefore for constructive proof of the Lemma let us indicate the test to end the process of constructing $CD_\Omega\mathfrak{R}(S^+)$. That is, let us stop the constructing of $CD_\Omega\mathfrak{R}(S^+)$, when for each vertex S_i of $D_\Omega\mathfrak{R}(S^+)$ there exists S_j such that $S_i = S_j$ and S_j is bellow S_i in the same branch. The existence of such situation follows from the finiteness of the set of different Ω-saturated sequents.

Lemma 5.8. Let $S^+ = \Gamma^+, \Box^+\Omega \to \Delta^+, \Box\nabla_1, \Box\nabla$ be Ω-saturated sequent, let $S^+_i = \Pi^+_{i1}, \Box^+\Omega \to \Pi^+_{i2}, \Box\nabla_1, \Box\nabla$ $(1 \leqslant i \leqslant n)$ be any nonclosed vertex of $CD_\Omega\mathfrak{R}(S^+)$, let $X = \Gamma^k_{11}, \ldots, \Gamma^k_{m1} \to \Gamma^k_{12}, \ldots, \Gamma^k_{m2}$ be the metasequent arising from the sequent $\to \Box\nabla_1$, where $\nabla_1 = A_1, \ldots, A_m$; let $G'^{cf}_{Lw} \vdash S'^+_i = S''^+_i \cdot X$, where $S''^+_i = \Pi^+_{i1}, \Box^+\Omega \to \Pi^+_{i2}, \Box\nabla$. Then either (a) $G'^{cf}_{Lw} \vdash S^* \cdot X$, where $S^* = \Box^+\Omega \to \Box\nabla_1, \Box\nabla$ or $\forall i\,(1 \leqslant i \leqslant n)$ either (b_1) there exists $j\,(1 \leqslant j \leqslant m)$ such that $G'^{cf}_{Lw} \vdash \Pi^+_{i1}, \Gamma^k_{j1}, \Box^+\Omega \to \Pi^+_{i2}, \Gamma^k_{j2}$ or (b_2) there exists a formula $\Box A \in \Box\nabla$ such that $G'^{cf}_{Lw} \vdash \Pi^+_{i1}, \Box^+\Omega \to \Pi^+_{i2}, \Box A$, besides the explicitly shown occurrence of the formula $\Box A$ is the principal formula of an application of $(\to \Box_w)$.

Proof. By induction on $O(D)$ using Lemma 5.6.

Lemma 5.9. Let $S^+ = \Gamma^+, \Box^+\Omega \to \Delta^+, \Box\nabla$ be Ω-saturated sequent, let $S^+_i = \Pi^+_{i1}, \Box^+\Omega \to \Pi^+_{i2}, \Box\nabla$ $(1 \leqslant i \leqslant n)$ be any nonclosed vertex of $CD_\Omega\mathfrak{R}(S^+)$, then either (a) $\forall i\,(1 \leqslant i \leqslant n)$ there exists a formula $\Box A \in \Box\nabla$ such that $G'^{cf}_{Lw} \vdash S'^+_i = \Pi^+_{i1}, \Box^+\Omega \to \Pi^+_{i2}, \Box A$, besides the selected occurrence of the formula $\Box A$ is principal formula of an application of $(\to \Box_w)$ or (b) $G'^{cf}_{L} \vdash \Box^+\Omega \to \Box\nabla$.

Proof. Follows from Lemma 5.8.

Lemma 5.10. (The sufficient condition the formula to be invariant). Let S_i is the same as S'^+_i in Lemma 5.9, then $IN \vdash R \to \circ R$, where IN is the calculus obtained from G'^{cf}_{L} by dropping $(\to \Box_1)$, $(\to \Box_3)$, $(\to \forall)$, $(\forall \to)$, $R = \bigvee_{i=1}^{n} (\Pi^{+\wedge}_{i1} \wedge \neg \Pi^{+\vee}_{i2}) \wedge (\Box^+\Omega)^\wedge$.

Proof. Let $\mathfrak{R}(S_i) = \{S_{i1}, \ldots, S_{im}\}$. Let us consider the deduction V_i of S_i from $S_{i1}, \ldots, S_{im}$. To prove the Lemma we shall transform V_i to derivation D_i in IN of the sequent $S'_i = \sqcap^+_{i1}, \Box^+\Omega \to \sqcap^+_{i2}, \bigcirc R$. Let us consider any antiapplication of rule of inference (A) in V_i:

$$\frac{S'_i}{S^*_{ij} = \Sigma^+_1, \sqcap^{+1}_{i1j}, \Box^+\Omega^1 \to \Sigma^+_2, \sqcap^{+1}_{i2j}, \Box A}(\bar{A}),$$

where $l = 1$ or $l = 2$; $S'_1 = \Sigma^+_1, \sqcap^{+1}_{i1j} \to \Sigma^+_2, \sqcap^+_{i2j}$; $S'_2 = \sqcap^+_{i1j}, \Box^+\Omega \to \sqcap^+_{i2j}, \Box A$. As $\Box \notin S'_1$, then $G'^{cf}_L \vdash S'_1$. Applying (W) to S'_1 we get that $G'^{cf}_L \vdash S'^*_{ij} = \Sigma^+_1, \sqcap^{+1}_{i1j}, \Box^+\Omega^1 \to \Sigma^+_2, \sqcap^{+1}_{i2j}, \bigcirc R$. Let us consider the case when $l = 2$. By Lemma 5.6 $S'_2 = S_{ij} = \sqcap^+_{i1j}, \Box^+\Omega \to \sqcap^+_{i2j}, \Box A$ $(1 \leqslant j \leqslant m)$ is the Ω–saturated sequent. Because of S_i (as follows from the Lemma's condition) is any nonclosed vertex of $CD_\Omega\mathfrak{R}(S)$ we have that $\forall i (1 \leqslant i \leqslant n)\ \forall j (1 \leqslant j \leqslant m)\ \exists\, i' (1 \leqslant i' \leqslant n)$ such that $\sqcap^+_{i1j} = \sqcap^+_{i'1}$ and $\sqcap^+_{i2j} = \sqcap^+_{i'2}$. Therefore with the help of $(\to \vee)$, $(\to \wedge)$, $(\urcorner \to)$ we get that $IN \vdash S''_2 = S'_{ij} = \sqcap^+_{i1j}, \Box^+\Omega \to \sqcap^+_{i2j}, R$. Applying (+1), $(\to \bigcirc)$, (W) to S''_2 we get that $G'^{cf}_L \vdash S'^*_{ij}$. In the part of deduction V_i which is bellow (above) any antiapplication of (A) we substitute formula $\bigcirc R$ (R respectively) for selected occurrence of the formula $\Box A$. Then instead deduction V_i $(1 \leqslant i \leqslant n)$ we get $IN \vdash S'_i = \sqcap^+_{i1}, \Box^+\Omega \to \sqcap^+_{i2}, \bigcirc R$. Applying rules of inference $(\wedge \to)$, $(\urcorner \to)$, $(\vee \to)$ to all S'_i $(1 \leqslant i \leqslant n)$ we get that $IN \vdash R \to \bigcirc R$.

Lemma 5.11. Let $G'^{cf}_{Lw} \vdash S^+$, $D\mathfrak{R}(S^+)$ be a deduction tree of a resolvent of the ordinary regular sequent S^+, all the vertices of which are provable in G'^{cf}_L, then $G'^{cf}_L \vdash S^+$.

Proof. The proof is carried out by induction on $(\to \Box_w)[D]$ (see above). Let Y/X be antiapplication of (A) in $D\mathfrak{R}(S^+)$, where $X = \Sigma_1, \sqcap^1_1, \Box\Omega^1_1, \forall\bar{x}\Xi \to \Sigma_2, \sqcap^1_2, \Box\Omega^1_2, \Box\nabla_1, \Box\nabla_2$, where $\Box\nabla_1$ consists of formulas which are nonessential in D, $\Box\nabla_2$ consists of formulas which are principal formula in an application of $(\to \Box_w)$ in D. Then by Lemma 5.2 (a) we have that $G'^{cf}_{Lw} \vdash X' = \Sigma_1, \sqcap^1_1, \Box\Omega^1_1, \forall\bar{x}\Xi \to \Sigma_2, \sqcap^1_2, \Box\Omega^1_2, \Box\nabla_2$, besides $(\to \Box_w)[D_1] = (\to \Box_w)[D]$, where D_1 is derivation of X'; $Y = S_1 = \Sigma_1, \sqcap^1_1, \forall\bar{x}\Xi \to \Sigma_2, \sqcap^1_2$, or $Y = S_2 = \sqcap^*_1, \Box\Omega_1 \to \sqcap^*_2, \Box\Omega_2, \Box\nabla_2$ where $\sqcap^*_i \subseteq \sqcap_i$ $(i = 1, 2)$. If $Y = S_1$ then $G'^{sf}_L \vdash X$. It follows from (Y) by (W). Let us consider the case when $Y = S_2$. Applying to S_2 (+1), $(\to \bigcirc)$, (W) we get that $G'^{cf}_L \vdash Y' = \Sigma_1, \sqcap^1_1, \Box\Omega^1_1, \forall\bar{x}\Xi \to \Sigma_2, \sqcap^1_2, \Box\Omega^1_2, \bigcirc\Box\nabla_2$. For simplicity let us consider the case when $\nabla_2 = A_1, A_2$ (if $\nabla_2 = A_1, \ldots, A_n$ $(n > 2)$, then we must repeat the process described below). By Lemma 5.2 (b) from X' we get that $G'^{cf}_{Lw} \vdash X^* = \Sigma_1, \sqcap^1_1, \Box\Omega^1_1, \forall\bar{x}\Xi \to \Sigma_2, \sqcap^1_2, \Box\Omega^1_2, A_1, \Box A_2$, besides $(\to \Box_w)[D_2] < (\to \Box_w)[D]$, where D_2 is the derivation of X^*. Therefore by induction hypothesis we get that $G'^{cf}_L \vdash X^*$. Applying to X^* (with respect to $\Box A_2$) the invertability of $(\to \Box_2)$ (see Lemma 4.9) we get that $G'^{cf}_L \vdash X'^* = \Sigma_1, \sqcap^1_1, \Box\Omega^1_1, \forall\bar{x}\Xi \to \Sigma_2, \sqcap^1_2, \Box\Omega^1_2, A_1, \bigcirc\Box A_2$. Applying $(\to \Box_2)$ to X'^* and Y' we get that $G'^{cf}_L \vdash Y'' = \Sigma_1, \sqcap^1_1, \Box\Omega^1_1, \forall\bar{x}\Xi \to \Sigma_2, \sqcap^1_2, \Box\Omega^1_2, \Box A_1, \bigcirc\Box A_2$. Again applying Lemma 5.2. (b) and induction hypothesis to X' (with respect to $\Box A_2$) we get that $G'^{cf}_L \vdash X'' = \Sigma_1, \sqcap^1_1, \Box\Omega^1_1, \forall\bar{x}\Xi \to \Sigma_2, \sqcap^1_2, \Box\Omega^1_2, \Box A_1, A_2$. Applying $(\to \Box_2)$ to X'', Y'' we get that $G'^{cf}_L \vdash X'$ and by (W) from X' we get that $G'^{cf}_L \vdash X$.

Lemma 5.12. Let $G'^{cf}_{Lw} \vdash S = \Gamma^+, \Box^+\Omega \to \Delta^+, \Box\nabla$, where S is Ω–saturated sequent, then $G'^{cf}_{L} \vdash S$.

Proof. By induction on $(\to \Box_w)[D]$, where D is given atomic derivation. By Lemma 5.9 either (1) $G'^{cf}_{Lw} \vdash \Box^+\Omega \to \Box\nabla$ or (2) $\forall i (1 \leqslant i \leqslant n)$ $G'^{cf}_{Lw} \vdash S'_i = \sqcap^+_{i1}, \Box^+\Omega \to \sqcap^+_{i2}, \Box A$ $(*)$, where $\Box A \in \Box\nabla$ and S'_i is the same as in Lemma 5.9. In case (1) we get $G'^{cf}_{L} \vdash S$ using Lemma 5.2, induction hypothesis and $(\to \Box_3)$. Let us consider case (2). We shall prove that $G'^{cf}_{L} \vdash S'_i$ $(1 \leqslant i \leqslant n)$ $(**)$. To prove $(**)$ we shall prove that

$$IN \vdash \sqcap^+_{i1}, \Box^+\Omega \to \sqcap^+_{i2}, R \tag{1}$$

$$IN \vdash R \to \bigcirc R \tag{2}$$

$$G'^{cf}_{L} \vdash R \to A, \tag{3}$$

where IN is the calculus defined in §4, $R = \bigvee_{i=1}^{n} (\sqcap^{+\wedge}_{i1} \wedge \urcorner \sqcap^{+\vee}_{i2}) \wedge (\Box^+\Omega)^\wedge$.
Validity of (1)follows from the form R with the help of the rules of inference $(\to \vee), (\to \wedge), (\to \urcorner)$. Validity of (2) follows from Lemma 5.10. Let us establish the validity of (3). Applying to $(*)$ Lemma 5.2 (b) and induction hypothesis we have that $\forall i (1 \leqslant i \leqslant n)$ $G'^{cf}_{L} \vdash \sqcap^+_{i1}, \Box^+\Omega \to \sqcap^+_{i2}, A$ $(3'_i)$. Applying to $(3'_i)$ $(1 \leqslant i \leqslant n)$ $(\urcorner \to), (\wedge \to), (\vee \to)$ we get (3). Applying $(\to \Box_1)$ to (1), (2), (3) we get $(**)$. Applying to $(**)$ Lemma 5.11 we get that $G'^{cf}_{L} \vdash S$.

Lemma 5.13. Let $G'^{cf}_{Lw} \vdash S$, where S is an ordinary regular sequent, then $G'^{cf}_{L} \vdash S$

Proof. By induction on $(\to \Box_w)[D]$, where D is a given atomic derivation. It is sufficient to consider the case when S is the conclusion of the lowest application of $(\to \Box_w)$ in D. The case when $S = \Box\Omega \to \Box\nabla$ is considered as case (1) in Lemma 5.12. If $S \neq \Box\Omega \to \Box\nabla$, then apply Lemmas 5.5, 5.12, 5.11.

Lemma 5.14. Let us $G'^{cf}_{Lw} \vdash S$, where S is strong regular sequent, then $G'^{cf}_{L} \vdash S$.

Proof. Then $(\to \Box_w)[D] = 0$ and therefore $G'^{cf}_{L} \vdash S$.

Let us call the metasequent S primary singular regular metasequent if $S = S^* \cdot X$, where S^* is a primary singular regular sequent, X is metasequent, corresponding to the singular regular sequent $\to \Box A_1, \ldots, \Box A_n$ Let us denote by (A_{1w}) the following metarule of inference

$$\frac{S}{S_i} \quad (i = 1 \text{ or } i = 2),$$

where S is a primary singular regular metasequent, $S_1 = \sqcap_1 \to \sqcap_2$; $S_2 = X \cdot S_0$, where $S_0 = \to \Box\nabla$. When $X = \varnothing$, then $(A_{1w}) = (A_1)$.

Lemma 5.15. The metarule (rule) of inference (A_{1w}) ((A_1), respectively) is admissible in G'^{cf}_{Lw}, besides $(\to \Box_w)[D_1] \leqslant (\to \Box_w)[D]$, where D is a given atomic derivation, D_1 is the resulting one.

Proof. By induction on $O(D)$ (see Lemma 5.4).

Remark 5.2. Let us denote by (A_1^*) the following rule of inference

$$\frac{S}{S'}$$

where S is a primary singular regular sequent (i.e. $S = \sqcap_1 \to \sqcap_2, \Box B_1, \ldots, \Box B_n$) and S does not contain negative occurrences of $\Box$, S' is either $\sqcap_1 \to \sqcap_2$ or $\exists i$ $(1 \leqslant i \leqslant n)$ such that $S' = \to \Box B_i$. Analogously as in Lemma 5.15 we can proof admissibility of (A_1^*) in $G_{L\omega}^{\prime cf}$.

Lemma 5.16. Let $G_{Lw}^{\prime cf} \vdash S$, where S is singular regular sequent, then $G_L^{\prime cf} \vdash S$.

Proof. By induction on $(\to \Box_w)[D]$. By the Lemma 5.3 we can construct deduction of the sequent S from the sequent $S_1, \ldots, S_n$, where S_i $(1 \leqslant i \leqslant n)$ is a primary singular regular sequent, besides $G_{Lw}^{\prime cf} \vdash S_i$ and $(\to \Box_w)[D_i] \leqslant (\to \Box_w)[D]$, where D_i is the derivation of $S_i = \sqcap_1 \to \sqcap_2, \Box\nabla$, where $\Box \notin \sqcap_1, \sqcap_2$. With a help of the antiapplication of the rule of inference (A_1) to S_i we get either (1) $G_{Lw}^{\prime cf} \vdash S_{i1} = \sqcap_1 \to \sqcap_2$ or (2) $G_{Lw}^{\prime cf} \vdash S_{i2} = \to \Box\nabla$. As $\Box \notin \sqcap_i$ $(i = 1,2)$, in the case (1) we have $G_L^{\prime cf} \vdash S_{i1}$. In the case (2)applying to S_{i2} Lemma 5.2(b), the induction hypothesis and $(\to \Box_3)$ we get that $G_L^{\prime cf} \vdash S_{i2}$. For proving the Lemma it remains to replace the antiapplication of (A_1) by the applications of rules of inference of $G_L^{\prime cf}$. It may be done analogously as in Lemma 5.11.

Theorem 5.1. Let $G_{Lw}^{cf} \vdash S$, where S is a regular or strong regular sequent, then $G_L^{cf} \vdash S$.

Proof. Follows from Lemmas 5.1, 5.13, 5.14, 5.16.

§6. Some properties of the calculus G_L and some possible extensions of the presented ω–reduction method.

Theorem 6.1. (completeness and cut elimination for G_L). Let S is either regular or strong regular and S is universally valid, then $G_L^{cf} \vdash S$.

Proof. Follows from Theorems 2.3, 5.1.

Theorem 6.2. (alternating properties for G_L^{cf})
(a) Let S is a primary ordinary regular sequent, i.e. $S = \Sigma_1, \sqcap_1^1, \Box\Omega_1^1, \forall\bar{x}\Xi \to \Sigma_2, \sqcap_2^1, \Box\Omega_2^1, \Box\nabla$, then from $G_L^{cf} \vdash S$ follows either (1) $G_L^{cf} \vdash \Sigma_1, \sqcap_1^1, \forall\bar{x}\Xi \to \Sigma_2, \sqcap_2^1$ or (2) $G_L^{cf} \vdash \sqcap_1^*, \Box\Omega_1 \to \sqcap_2^*, \Box\Omega_2, \Box\nabla$, where $\sqcap_i^* \subseteq \sqcap_i$ $(i = 1,2)$ and $\sqcap_i^*$ consists of propositional variables occurring in Ω_i, ∇;
(b) Let S is a primary singular regular sequent, i.e. $S = \sqcap_1 \to \sqcap_2, \Box\nabla$, where $\Box \notin \sqcap_i$ $(i = 1,2)$, then from $G_L^{cf} \vdash S$ follows either (1) $G_L^{cf} \vdash \sqcap_1 \to \sqcap_2$ or (2)$G_L^{cf} \vdash \to \Box\nabla$. Besides if S does not contain negative occurrences of $\Box$ and $\Box\nabla = \Box A_1, \ldots, \Box A_n$, then instead of (2) we have that $\exists i$ $(1 \leqslant i \leqslant n)$ such that $G_L^{cf} \vdash \Box A_i$;
(c) Let $S = \Sigma_1, \sqcap_1^1 \to \Sigma_2, \sqcap_2^1$, where Σ_1, Σ_2 does not contain $\bigcirc$, $\Box$ and indices, $\sqcap_1^1, \sqcap_2^1$ consists of (T–P)–formulas without $\Box$, then from $G_L^{cf} \vdash S$ follows either (1)$G_L^{cf} \vdash \Sigma_1 \to \Sigma_2$ or (2)$G_L^{cf} \vdash \sqcap_1 \to \sqcap_2$.

Proof. Parts (a), (b) follows from Theorem 4.1, Lemmas 5.3, 5.15, Remark 5.2 and Theorem 5.1. Part (c) is proved by induction on the height of given derivation.

Remark 6.1. (a) Let $S = \rightarrow \Box A_1, \ldots, \Box A_n$ where $A_1, \ldots, A_n$ does not contain negative occurrences of $\Box$. Then as follows from Theorem 6.2.(b) we get that $G_L^{cf} \vdash S \Rightarrow G_L^{cf} \vdash\rightarrow \Box A_i$ for some i $(1 \leqslant i \leqslant n)$. This property is some analogy of a disjunctive property for G_L^{cf}. The sequent $\rightarrow \Box(\Box A \supset \Box B), \Box(\Box B \supset \Box A)$ shows that the disjunctive property for an arbitrary sequents of the form $\rightarrow \Box A \vee \Box B$ fails for linear temporal logic. (b) It has been proved in [6] that interpolation property fails for propositional linear temporal logic. Let $S = \rightarrow A \supset B$ is strong regular sequent or singular regular not containing negative occurrences of $\Box$. Then by the help of Theorems 5.3, 6.2(b) it is not difficult to prove that S has interpolation property, i.e. from $G_L^{cf} \vdash\rightarrow A \supset B$ follows that there exists such the formula C that (1) $G_L^{cf} \vdash\rightarrow A \supset C$, $G_L^{cf} \vdash C \supset B$ and (2) $\mathrm{var}(C) \subseteq \mathrm{var}(A) \cap \mathrm{var}(B)$, where $\mathrm{var}(D)$ means predicate symbols occurring in D.

As it was shown in the introduction it is not possible to reduce the derivation of an arbitrary sequence in G_{Lw} to G_L. However it is possible to extend the notion of regular sequences, i.e. there is a possibility to generalize the described w-reduction method "in depth". For example, let us call sequent S ordinary regular if S can be reduced by the help of 1) equivalent replacements (including for example $\sigma\forall x\, A \equiv \forall x \sigma\, A$, where $\sigma \in \{\bigcirc, \Box\}$) and 2) substitutions by propositional variables for formulas of type $\forall x \Box A$ to such sequent S^* that 1)S^* is ordinary regular (in sense of §4) and 2) $G_{Lw}^{cf} \vdash S^*$. Example of such sequent is following sequent $S = \Box(\neg\forall x \neg\neg\Box E(x) \supset \neg\forall x \bigcirc\Box E(x)) \rightarrow \Box\forall x E(x), \Box\neg\forall x \Box E(x)$, which can be reduced (as described above) to the sequent $S^* = \Box(\neg P \supset \neg\bigcirc P) \rightarrow P, \Box\neg P$. The described above w-reduction for the case of nonsymmetric linear logic (with the operators "next" and "always") can be generalized in "width", i.e. for the temporal logic containing other temporal operators and nonlinear temporal logics. For this purpose it is necessary: (1) to construct a sound and complete cut-free sequential calculus J_w^{cf} for the considered temporal logic; (2) to determine an alternation property (or properties) for $J_w^{*cf} \subseteq J_w^{cf}$; (3) using (2) to do the reduction from J_w^{*cf} to the corresponding finitary calculus J^{*cf}. Usually to construct sound and complete cut-free infinitary sequential calculus is rather ordinary. For example it is not difficult to prove completeness of a calculus $G_{L\sqcup w}^{cf}$ (for the nonsymmetric linear temporal logic with $\bigcirc$(next) and $\sqcup$(until)) obtained from G_{Lw}^{cf} replacing the $(\rightarrow \Box_w)$, $(\Box \rightarrow)$ by the following ones:

$$\frac{\{\Gamma \rightarrow \Delta,\ U_k\}_{k \in w}}{\Gamma \rightarrow \Delta,\ A \sqcup B}\ (\rightarrow \sqcup_w),$$

where $U_0 = B \vee A$, $U_k = B \vee \bigcirc U_{k-1}$ $(k = 1, 2, \ldots)$.

$$\frac{(A \vee B), (B \vee \bigcirc(A \sqcup B)), \Gamma \rightarrow \Delta}{A \sqcup B,\ \Gamma \rightarrow \Delta}\ (\sqcup \rightarrow)$$

It should be stressed that sometimes realization of w-reduction may be done "from up to bottom", i.e., realizing the elimination of the upper application of temporal w-rule for a corresponding temporal operator (contrary to the described in §5 way "from bottom to up"). Then it is not necessary to construct "splitting" succedent rule of inference for a corresponding "inductive" temporal operator (analogous to the rule of inference ($\rightarrow \Box_3$)) but the "invariant set" for corresponding temporal operator must be extended. For example, for the calculus $G^{*cf}_{L\sqcup}$ it is sufficient to have only one succedent rule for the operator $\sqcup$ of the following form:

$$\frac{\Gamma \rightarrow \Delta, R; \quad R \rightarrow B, \bigcirc R; \quad R \rightarrow A, B}{\Gamma \rightarrow \Delta, A \sqcup B} (\rightarrow \sqcup),$$

where R consists of Boolean combination some subformulas of any occurrence (not only negative ones) of formulas of type $C \sqcup D$ in the conclusion.

REFERENCES

1. M. Abadi, *The power of temporal proofs*, Proceedings of the second Annual IEEE Symposium on Logic in Computer Science, (1987), 123–130.
2. H. Andreka, I. Nemeti, I. Sain, *On the strenghth of temporal proofs*, Preprint of Math.Institute of the Hungarian Academy of Science, Budapest, (1989), 1–22.
3. D. Gabbay, *Decidability of some intuitionistic predicate theories*, Journal of Symbolic Logic, Vol.37, No.2, (1972), 579–587.
4. S. Kanger, *Provability in logic*, Acta Universiatis Stockholmiensis, Stockholm Studies in Philosophy, Vol.1, (1957).
5. H. Kawai, *Sequential calculus for a first order infinitary temporal logic*, Zeitschr. fur Math. Logic und Grundlagen der Math., Vol.74, (1987), 423–432.
6. L.L.Maksimova, *Interpolation, Beth's property and temporal logic "tomorrow"*, (in Russian), Preprint No.90 of Math. Institute of Sibirian Division of the USSR Academy of Sciences, Novosibirsk, (1989), 3–25.
7. R. Pliuškevičius, *Structural analytical indexal deduction for Kamp's tense logic* (in Russian), Mathematical Logic and its applications, Issue 5, Vilnius, (1987), 76–84.
8. R. Pliuškevičius, *Structural elimination theorem for functional modal logic S5*, (in Russian), Mathematical Logic and its applications, Issue 5, Vilnius, (1987), 85–91.
9. R. Pliuškevičius, *Investigation of finitary calculi for temporal logics by means of infinitary calculi*, Proc. Conf. MFCS'90.
10. J.R. Shoenfield, *On a restricted ω-rule*, Bulletin de L'Academie Polonaise Des Sciences, Vol.7, No.7, (1959), 405–407.
11. R. Statman, *Bounds for proof-search and speed-up in the predicate calculus*, Ann. Math. Logic, Vol.15, (1978), 225–287.
12. A. Szalas, *Concerning the semantic consequence relation in first-order temporal logic*, Theoretical Computer Science, Vol.47, (1986), 329–334.

RIGAL -
a Programming Language for Compiler Writing

Mikhail AUGUSTON
Institute of Mathematics and Computer Science
The University of Latvia
Rainis boulevard 29, Riga, Latvia, SU - 226250

Abstract. A new programming language for compiler writing is described. The main data structures are atoms, lists and trees. The control structures are based on advanced pattern matching. All phases of compilation, including parsing, optimization and code generation, can be programmed in this language in short and readable form. Sample compiler written in RIGAL is presented.

1. Introduction

Programming language RIGAL is intended to be a tool for parsing(context checking, diagnosing and neutralization of errors included), for code optimization, code generation, static analysis of programs, as well as for the programming of preprocessors and convertors.

Almost all the systems envisaged to solve compiler construction problems contain means to describe context-free grammar of the source language. Earlier systems, like the Floyd - Evans language, [1] present tools to work with stack, which is used for parsing. Parsing methods for limited grammar classes are implemented in the languages and systems of later generations (usually LL(1) or LR(1)).

Such systems as YACC (Johnson [2]), CDL-2 (Koster [3]), SHAG (Agamirzyan [4]) and many others make use of synchronous implementation of parsing and different computations, e.g., formation of tables, context checking, etc. Usually these actions are performed by call of semantic subroutines, written in some universal programming language (e.g., in Pascal or C).

Attribute grammars advanced by Knuth [5] have greatly influenced development of systems for compiler construction. Systems, like, SUPER (Serebryakov [6]), ELMA (Vooglaid, Lepp, Lijb [7]), MUG2 (Wilhelm [9]) are based on the use of attribute grammars not only for parsing, but for code generation as well.

Pattern matching is a convenient tool for programming of parsing, optimization and code generation. The REFAL programming language [10], acknowledged for translator writing, may serve as a good example.

Vienna method for defining semantics of programming languages [11] suggests the usage of labelled trees in order to present the abstract syntax of programs. Representation of compilation intermediate results in the tree form has become usual (see [12]).

Dependence of control structures in the program from data structures used for program's work is one of the basic principles in programming. The recursive descent method could be considered to be the application of dependence principle.

The above mentioned ideas and methods were taken into account when creating RIGAL language.

The language possesses few basic notions. Data structures contain atoms, lists and trees. Advanced mechanism of pattern matching lies at the basis of control structures.

The fact that RIGAL is a closed language makes RIGAL distinctive. That means that almost all the necessary computations and input-output could be executed by internal means and there is no need to use external semantic subroutines. Therefore the portability of RIGAL programs to other computers is increased.

Means for work with trees, different patterns including, enable both programming of parsing algorithms and optimization phases and code generation as well. The language supports design of multipass translators. Trees are used as intermediate data.

The language allows to split the program into small modules (rules) and presents various means to arrange interaction of these modules. Pattern matching is used for parameter passing.

RIGAL supports attribute translation scheme and easy

implementation of synthesized and inherited attributes is possible. The problem of global attributes is solved by usage of special references.

Lexical analysis is a separate task and requires special language facilities for description as it is, for example, in LEX/YACC [2] system. In the current implementation of RIGAL two scanners are included that accept lexics of Pascal and RIGAL.

2. Implementation

RIGAL was designed and implemented in the Computing Center of Latvia University in years 1987-1988. The first implementation was for PDP-11 in RSX-11.

At the present stage RIGAL interpreter has been developed and optimizing compiler RIGAL -> Pascal has been implemented by means of RIGAL itself. The interpreter and the compiler have been ported to VAX/VMS and IBM PC AT /MS DOS environments.

3. Lexical Rules

The text of RIGAL program is a sequence of tokens - atoms (e.g., identifiers and integers), keywords (e.g., *if, return*), special symbols (e.g., +, ##), names of variables and rules (e.g., $A, #L). Tokens may be surrounded by any number of blanks. A comment is any string of symbols that begins with two consecutive symbols '-' (minus). The end of the comment is the end of the line. For example,

```
#Sum    -- rule for addition of two numbers
      $N1   -- the first number
      $N2   -- the second number
   / return  $N1 + $N2 /    -- return of the result
##
```

4. Data

4.1 Atoms

An atom is a string of symbols. If the atom is an identifier (the first symbol is a letter followed by letters or digits or underscore symbols), in the text of RIGAL program it could be written directly: AABC total_number x25

Numerical atoms are integers, for instance, 2, 187, 0, -25

In other cases the atom is quoted: '+' ':=' '1st'

Some identifiers are reserved as keywords in RIGAL. If they are used as RIGAL atoms, they should be quoted. For example, 'if', 'return'. Besides, any atom, which is an identifier, also can be quoted - ABC and 'ABC' represent one and the same atom.

It should be noted that 25 and '25' are different atoms, the latter is just a string of symbols '2' and '5'.

Two special atoms are distinguished in the language.

NULL - this atom is frequently yielded as a result of different operations, if something was incorrect in the process of computations. This atom also represents an empty list, an empty tree and Boolean value "false".

T - usually this atom is yielded by logical operations and represents value "true".

4.2 Variables

The name of a variable must begin with the symbol $, followed by an identifier. Value can be assigned to a variable, for example, by the help of assignment statement: $E := A

In this case the atom A becomes value of the variable $E.

In RIGAL variables have no types, the same variable may have an atom, a list or a tree as a value in different time moments.

4.3 Lists

Ordered sequences, i.e., *lists* can be composed from atoms and from other lists and trees, as well. A special function - *list constructor* serves for list formation. For instance, (. A B C .) forms a list of three atoms A, B and C.

Arguments of the list constructor may be expressions. The sample $E := (. (. 8 14 7 .) (. A B .) .) could be rewritten as follows:

$A := (. 8 14 7 .); $B := (. A B .); $E := (. $A $B .);

Separate elements of the list can be selected by indexing. Hence, $B [1] is atom A, $A [2] is atom 14, $E [2] is list (. A B .), but $E [10] is atom NULL

If the value of the index is a negative number, for instance -N, then the N-th element, beginning from the end of the list, is selected. For example, $A [-1] is atom 7.

The necessity to add one more element to the list is quite common. Operation !. is envisaged for this purpose.

Example. (. A B .) !. C yields the list (. A B C .)

To link two lists in a new list the operation !! is applied (list concatenation). For instance, (. A B .) !! (. C D .) yields (. A B C D .).

4.4 Trees

Tree constructor is used to create a tree. For example,

<. A : B, C : D .>

One can imagine tree as a graph, the nodes and arches of which are marked by some objects.

Objects before ':' in the tree constructor are named *selectors*. In the given implementation solely atoms, which are identifiers (except NULL), may serve as selectors. In the graphical representation selectors correspond to arches of the graph. All selectors of one and the same level in the tree must be different.

Any object - atom, list or tree, except atom NULL, may correspond to terminal nodes of the graph ("leaves" of the tree). Hence, multilayer trees can be built. For instance,

<. A : B, C : <. D : E, F : G .> .>

Pair "selector : object" in the tree is named *branch* of the tree. Branches are unordered in the tree.

Likewise for the list constructor, the tree constructor may be described by expressions (in both selector and object places), for instance,

$X := D; $B := (. 2 8 .);

$C := <. A : <. M : K .>, $X : '+' , E : $B .>;

Select operation serves to extract the tree component. It is in the following form: *tree . sel* , where *tree* is the expression, whose value must be some tree, but *sel* is the expression, whose value must be an atom-identifier.

Consequently, $C . A is the tree <. M : K .> ,
$C . D is the atom '+' , $C . E is the list (. 2 8 .) ,
$C . E[2] is the atom 8 , $C . A . M is the atom K

If there is no branch with a given selector in the tree, then the result is NULL: $C . W is atom NULL.

Operation of the tree "addition" is performed as well: T1 ++ T2 , where T1 and T2 are trees. Tree T2 branches are added to the tree T1 one by one. If in the tree T1 there already exists a branch with the same selector, the branch is substituted by a new one. Therefore, the operation "++" is not commutative.

It should be pointed out that the tree constructor is computed from left to right, i.e., <. s1 : a1, s2 : a2, s3 : a3 .> gives the same result as the expression

((NULL ++ <. s1 : a1 .>) ++ <. s2 : a2 .>) ++ <. s3 : a3 .>

5. Expressions

Operations = and <> serve for the comparison of objects. The result of the comparison is either T ("true") or NULL ("false").

Atoms are matched directly, for instance, a = b gives NULL, 25 = 25 gives T, 17 <> 25 gives T.

Lists are considered equal iff they contain equal number of components and if these components are equal respectively.

Trees are considered equal iff they contain equal number of branches and if one of the trees contains the branch "S : OB", then the other tree also contains the branch "S : OB1" and OB = OB1.

Arithmetical operations +, -, *, *div, mod* are assigned for numerical atoms. The essence of these operations is similar to those in Pascal. The result of an arithmetical operation is a numerical atom. Atom NULL is also admitted as the argument of arithmetical operation, in this case integer 0 is supposed to be its value. Under matching these atoms are considered different, i.e., NULL = 0 gives NULL.

Besides the operations = and <> numerical values could be compared by the help of >, <, >= and <=.

Logical operations *and, or* and *not* usually are applied under conditions in conditional statements. Their arguments may be arbitrary objects. If the object differs from NULL, it is supposed to have the value "true" in a logical operation. Atom NULL represents the "false" value. The result of a logical operation always is either T or NULL.

In order to make complex hierarchic objects (trees and lists of complex structure) more visual and to improve the work of pattern matching, trees and lists may be labelled. A name is an atom opposed to the root node of the tree or the whole list. Labelling operation is written the following way:

A :: OB

where A is an atom , OB is an object (a tree or a list). For example, Add_op :: <. arg1 : 5, arg2 : 4 .>

The execution order of operations in the expression is controlled by parentheses "(" and ")". Priority is assigned to every operation, and, if the execution order is not defined by parentheses, operations are executed according to their priorities - beginning with the higher and proceeding to the lower.

Operations are listed in decreasing order of priorities (some operations will be discussed later).

1) Rule call, list constructor, tree constructor, *last*

2) Selector ".", index "[]", ::

3) *not,* unary -

4) *, *div, mod*

5) !. , !! , ++ , +, binary -

6) = , <> , > , < , >= , <=

7) *and*

8) *or*

Binary operations of the same priority are executed from left to right, while unary operations from right to left.

5.1 Accumulative Assignment Statements

It is quite often that working with a list or a tree elements are added step by step, thus the growing object is retained in the same variable. Therefore short form of assignment statement has been introduced. For the operations !. , !! , ++ and + statements of the form $X := $X *op* Expr can be written as $X *op* := Expr .

5.2 Semantics of Variables

In the implementation of RIGAL every object - atom, list or tree has a descriptor. It is a special data structure that contains some information about this object: the value of atom, the number of elements and pointers to elements for lists and trees. Variables have pointers to object descriptors as values.

Statement $X := OB assigns to the variable $X a pointer to the descriptor of object OB. After the execution of the statement $Y := $X both variables $X and $Y contain pointers to the same object OB.

Operations !.:= , !!:= , +:= and ++:= change the descriptor of their first argument, i.e., have a side effect. Sometimes it can be undesirable. For example,

```
$A := (. 3 17 .); $B := $A;  $B !.:= 25;
```

The value of $B becomes list (. 3 17 25 .), but operation

!.:= has added element 25 immediately to the list (. 3 17 .), and the descriptor of this list is changed. As the value of the variable $A was a pointer to this descriptor, then after the execution of the statement $B !.:= 25 the value of the variable $A is changed, too.

To prevent this, we must have a copy of the object, to which $A refers to before assigning it to $B. Built-in rule #COPY(OB) is used for this purpose. It makes a copy of the descriptor of the object OB.

Now we can write a "safe" call of the operation !.:= in such a way: $A := (. 3 17 .); $B := #COPY($A); $B !.:= 25;

As a result $B takes the value (. 3 17 25 .), but $A remains equal to (. 3 17 .). The same effect can be obtained after execution of statements $A := (. 3 17 .); $B := $A !. 25;

6. Rules

The concept of rule is analogous to concepts of procedure and function in conventional languages, such as Pascal or C.

First of all, by the help of a rule we can check, whether an object or a sequence of objects complies with some grammar. For this purpose rule has a pattern. Objects, assigned under rule call (*arguments of the rule*), are matched with the pattern. If there is a necessity, some operations could be executed, for instance, computations and input-output operations, simultaneously with rule arguments and pattern matching.

Rule that is called can compute and return back some value (object),i.e., it can be used as function.

Depending on the result of rule arguments and pattern matching, the rule call ends with success or failure. Thus the rule call could be used in another rule patterns.

6.1. Simple Patterns

Definition of the rule begins with the indication of the name of the rule in the form of #LLL , where LLL is an atom-identifier. In the most common case the pattern is indicated after the name of the rule. Rule definition ends with symbol '##'. For instance,

#L1 A B ##

In this case the pattern consists of atoms A and B. Call of the rule #L1 takes place, for instance, the following way :

#L1 (A B)

The sequence of objects - atoms A and B, is assigned as rule arguments.

After rule call the argument and pattern matching begins. The first argument - atom A is matched with the first pattern, which is also an atom. These atoms are equal, so their matching is successful. After that the next object from the sequence of arguments - atom B and the next pattern, also atom B, are matched. Their matching is also successful, therefore, the call of the rule #L1 is successful, too.

#L1(A C) call fails, because the second argument - atom C was not successfully matched with the pattern - atom B.

#L1(A) call fails, as there is no object for the second pattern with which it could be matched successfully.

But #L1(A B C) call is successful, as the third rule argument - atom C was not demanded by any pattern and matching of the first two rule arguments was successful.

Arbitrary atoms, both non-numerical and numerical, may be described as patterns.

Such operations as assignment statements, input - output and others may be indicated before the pattern, after it and between patterns. These statements are quoted in the pair of symbols '/' . If there is a necessity to write several statements within the pair '/' , these statements are separated by the symbol ';' .

A group of statements is executed in the rule pattern, if matching of the previous pattern with the corresponding rule arguments was successful.

The value returned by the rule is worked out by statement *return* . It has the following form: *return expression*.

Simultaneously this statement completes the execution of the rule.

Example.

#L2 'begin' 'end' / *return* 'The pair begin-end' / ##

Rule call is illustrated in the following example.

$A := #L2 ('begin' 'end'); As a result the atom 'The pair begin-end' is assigned to the variable $A.

If *return* statement is not described in the rule, then the NULL value is returned.

If the rule call ends in failure, then usually value NULL is returned, although in case of failure, it is possible to work out the returned value, which is not NULL; for this purpose statement *return* must be used in *onfail*-operations (see sect.6.3.).

Variable could be used as pattern. It is matched with one object (atom, list or tree) from the sequence of rule arguments. Matching always ends in success, and as a side effect the variable obtains this object as value. For example,

#L3 $A $B / *return* (. $B $A .)/ ##

After the call $X := #L3 (1 2) the variable $X obtains as value (. 2 1 .)

The rule pattern, in its turn, may refer to some rule (recursively, as well). Then the subsequence of the calling rule arguments become arguments of rule - pattern. If the call of the rule - pattern is successful, then matching of further patterns of the calling rule with the remaining arguments proceeds. If the call of the rule - pattern fails, then the pattern matching of the calling rule fails, too. For example,

#L4 A #L5 D ##

#L5 B C ##

Then the call #L4(A B C D) is successful, but the call #L4(A E F D) is unsuccessful.

There is a number of built-in rules in the language (see section 11.). For instance, #NUMBER is successfully matched with a numerical atom and returns it as a value, other arguments fail and return NULL. #IDENT is successfully matched with atom - identifier and returns it as value.

6.2. Assignment in Patterns

Every pattern, when successfully matched with the corresponding rule argument, returns some value. The value of atom pattern coincides with this atom, the value of variable pattern coincides with the value obtained by this variable as a result of matching with the arguments. The value of rule pattern is defined by statement *return* in this rule.

If the matching ends in failure, the pattern usually returns value NULL.

These values, returned by patterns, can be assigned at once to some variable. It is enough to write the name of the variable and the assignment symbol ':=' before the pattern element.
Example.

```
#L6   $A  $R := #L7  / return  (. $A .) !! $R /  ##
#L7   $B  $C   / return  (.  $B  $C .) /   ##
```

After execution of the statement $X := #L6 (1 2 3) the value of $X will be (. 1 2 3 .)

Symbols of accumulative assignment '!.:=' , '!!:=' , '++:=' and '+:=' can be used instead of ':=' in patterns .

Therefore, we can rewrite the previous example the following way:

```
#L6_1  $R !.:= $A    $R !!:= #L7_1  / return  $R /  ##
#L7_1  $M !.:= $B    $M !.:=  $C    / return  $M /  ##
```

It should be noted that all variables in the rule are initialized by value NULL, so the value of the expression NULL !. $A that equals to (. $A .) is assigned to the variable $R by the first application of the pattern $R !.:= $A in #L6_1.

Patterns of the type $N := #NUMBER or $ID := #IDENT are used very often, therefore, following defaults are introduced in the language. If the first letter of the variable name is N, then this variable, having been used as pattern element, will have a successful matching only with a numerical atom, in other cases matching ends in failure, and variable obtains value NULL. If the first letter of the name of the variable is I, this variable is matched successfully only with an atom-identifier.

6.3 Rule Branches. Onfail Operations

Several groups of patterns may be united in one rule.

The first group of patterns is applied to the rule arguments first. If matching of this group of patterns with the arguments is successful, the rule call is successful. But if matching has failed, transition to the next group of patterns takes place, and it is matched with the same arguments. It goes on until some group of rule patterns is matched with the arguments successfully. If not a single pattern group matches successfully with rule arguments, the rule call ends in a failure.

Such alternative pattern groups are called *rule branches*, and, when writing the rule, they are separated by the symbol ';;'.

If the branch fails, the execution of its patterns and statements is abandoned at the place, where branch pattern failed, and control is transferred to the next branch (if there is one) or the whole rule fails (if the current branch is the last one in the rule). Still there is a possibility to execute some operations before exit from the branch.

Onfail operation is a sequence of statements, written at the end of the branch and delimited from patterns and branch statements by keyword *onfail*.

If *onfail*-statements are described in the branch, then in case of branch failure, control is transferred to them and statements, given in *onfail*-unit , are executed. So, in case of branch failure, causes of failure can be analyzed and message can be output. Statement *return* can be executed in *onfail* operations, as well. Then exit from the rule takes place (with failure), and some other value than NULL can be returned.

6.4 Special Variables

Special variable without name $ denotes the first rule

argument matched by a rule pattern.

The value of special variable **$$** equals to the value of current rule argument, to which current rule pattern is applied.

7. Compound Patterns

Lists, sequences of elements in lists and trees can be analyzed by patterns. Nesting of patterns practically is unlimited. It is allowed to insert statements before, after and within any pattern.

7.1 List Pattern

List pattern is written in the rule the following way:

(. S1 S2 ... SN .)

where S1, S2, ..., SN are patterns . For instance,

#L8 (. $E1 $E2 .) ##

Pattern of the rule #L8 is matched successfully with any list, containing precisely two elements. Such call is successful:

#L8((. (. 1 2 .) <. A : B .> .))

But the following calls end in failure.

#L8(A B) - because pattern will be applied to the first argument, i.e., to atom A.

#L8((. 13 .)) - because the argument is one element list.

In case of success the list pattern yields value that can be assigned to some variable. This value coincides with the whole list, to which the pattern was applied.

7.2 Iterative Pattern of Sequence

In RIGAL the following pattern is defined for sequence recognition: (* S1 S2 ... SN*) , where S1 , S2, ... SN are some patterns. This pattern describes the repetition of enclosed sequence of patterns zero or several times.

Rules with a variable number of arguments can be defined by

iterative pattern of sequence. For example,

```
#Sum  (*   $S +:= $N   *)  / return $S /  ##
```

This rule is used for summing up any amount of numbers.

#Sum(2 5 11) = 18 and #Sum(3) = 3

Iterative pattern is very often used within list pattern. For instance, the following rule counts the number of list elements.

```
#Length (. / $L := 0 / (*  $E / $L +:= 1 / *) .) / return $L / ##
```

Samples of rule call.

#Length((. A B C .)) = 3 and #Length(NULL) = 0

Iterative pattern (+ S1 S2 ... SN +) is analogous to the pattern (* ... *), but assigns the repetition of enclosed pattern sequence one or several times.

In the iterative pattern of sequence the element delimiter is indicated in the form of

(* S1 S2 ... SN * *Delimiter*) or (+ S1 S2 ... SN + *Delimiter* +)

Atom or name of the rule may serve as *Delimiter* .

Example. Analysis of a simple Algol-like declaration. A fragment of variable table coded in a tree form is returned as a result.

```
#Declaration   $Type := ( integer ! real)
               (+ $Id  / $Rez ++:= <. $Id : $Type .> / + ',')
      / return $Rez /    ##
```

Call #Declaration (real X ',' Y) returns value

<. X : real, Y : real .>

It should be noted that the pattern (* $E * ',') differs from the pattern (* $E ',' *) in the point that the presence of atom ',' is obligatory in the second pattern at the end of sequence.

7.3 Patterns for Alternative and Option

The choice of several possible patterns is written the following way: (S1 ! S2 ! ... ! SN)

Patterns S1 , S2 , ... , SN are applied one by one from left to right, until one of them succeeds.

In case of success alternative pattern yields value. It coincides with the value of the successful pattern within the alternative and may be assigned by some variable.

Example. Simple arithmetic expression parsing. When successful, an expression tree is returned, which can be regarded as an intermediate form for the next compilation phases.

```
#Expression    $A1 := #Term
        (* $Op := ( '+' ! '-' )  $A2 :=-#Term
           / $A1 := <. op : $Op , arg1 : $A1 , arg2 : $A2 .> / *)
        / return $A1 /    ##
#Term   $A := ( $Id  ! $Num ) / return $A /  ;;
        '('  $A := #Expression ')'  / return $A /    ##
```

The call #Expression(X '-' Y '+' 7) returns the value

```
<. op: '+', arg1: <. op: '-', arg1: X, arg2: Y .>, arg2: 7 .>
```

In RIGAL we may write a rule that matches successfully with an empty sequence of arguments: #empty ##

Now the pattern for option can be written down: (S ! #empty)

In short form this issue may be written down in RIGAL the following way: [S]

where S is some pattern or pattern sequence. Pattern [S] always ends in success.

7.4 Tree Pattern

Tree pattern checks, whether the object is a tree with fixed structure. By means of this pattern access to the components of the tree is obtained. The tree pattern is described the following way:

```
<. Sel1 : Pat1, Sel2 : Pat2, ... , SelN : PatN  .>
```

where Sel1, Sel2, ... SelN are atoms-identifiers, but Pat1, Pat2, ... PatN are patterns.

If the object, to which the tree pattern is applied, is not a tree, then the application of the pattern fails at once. If there is the selector Sel1 in the tree, then the pattern Pat1 is applied to the corresponding object. If there is no selector Sel1 in the tree or the application of Pat1 has failed, the whole pattern also fails.

If matching the first branch was successful, branch matching of the pattern 'Sel2 : Pat2' , etc. begins.

Hence, pattern branches are applied to the tree in the same order as they are written in the pattern. Therefore, the order of tree traversing may be controlled. It is possible to have reiterative visit of branches (if selectors are repeatedly described in the tree pattern) or omission of branches (if corresponding selectors are not given in the pattern).

In case of success the tree pattern returns the value, which coincides with the whole object - a tree, to which the pattern was applied, irrespective of presence of all tree selectors in the pattern or absence of some.

Example. Let us suppose expression tree to be formed like in the above example. The task is to traverse the tree and return a list that represents the Polish postfix form of this expression.

```
#Postfix_form  <. arg1: $Rez := #Postfix_form,
                  arg2: $Rez !!:= #Postfix_form,
                  op:   $Rez !.:= $Op   .>   / return $Rez /  ;;
               $Rez := ( $Id ! $Num )  / return (. $Rez .) /  ##
```

The call #Postfix_form(<. op: '-', arg1: X, arg2: <. op: '+', arg1: Y, arg2: 5 .> .>) returns the value (. X Y 5 '+' '-' .)

Some branches in the tree pattern may be described as optional, in this case they are enclosed in brackets '[' and ']' . If there is no selector of optional branch in the argument tree, its pattern is omitted and transition to next pattern branch takes place. If there is a selector of the type in the argument tree, the pattern branch is developed as usual.

7.5 Iterative Tree Pattern

The simplest form of iterative tree pattern is the following:

```
<* $Var : P *>
```

where $Var is some variable, and P is a pattern.

A loop over the tree is performed by the help of this pattern. All selectors of the argument tree are assigned to the variable $Var one by one. The pattern P is applied to each object, which corresponds in the argument tree to the current selector in the variable $Var. If even one application of the pattern P fails, the whole iterative tree pattern fails. For example,

```
#Variable_table  <* $Id : $E := ( integer ! real )
                 / $R !.:= (. $Id  $E .)/  *>  / return $R /  ##
```

Call example.

```
#Variable_table( <. X : integer, Y : real, Z : real .> ) =
     (. (. X  integer .) (. Y  real .) (. Z  real .)  .)
```

Sometimes, performing a loop over the tree, some branches should be updated in a special way. For this purpose iterative tree pattern with distinguished branches is used.

```
<* Sel1 : Pat1, Sel2 : Pat2, ..., SelN : PatN, $Var : P *>
```

where Sel1, Sel2, ... SelN are atoms-identifiers; Pat1, Pat2, ... PatN are patterns, i.e., like elements in simple tree pattern; $Var is a variable, but P is a pattern, as in simple case of iterative tree pattern.

The pattern is applied to the argument tree the following way. First of all distinguished pattern branches 'Sel : Pat' are developed. Their matching with branches of the argument tree happens exactly the same way as with simple tree pattern. Then the element '$Var : P' is applied to other branches of the argument tree the same way as in simple iterative tree pattern.

Some distinguished branches can be optional, for this purpose they are enclosed in brackets '[' and ']'. Semantics is the same as in the case of simple tree pattern.

Example. Let it be a tree of arbitrary size. In some of its subtrees there is the selector LABEL, to which numerical atom is attached. All these numbers over the whole tree must be collected in a list, and the list must be returned as result.

```
#Label_list
 <*  [ LABEL : $Result !.:= $N ],
       $S   : $Result !!:= #Label_list  *> / return  $Result / ;;
```

$E ##

The rule has two branches. Traversing of the tree and its subtrees is described in the first branch. The resulting list is formed in the variable $Result. The traversing of subtrees is carried out by the help of recursive call of the rule #Label_list. The second branch of the rule consisting of just one pattern $E is applied at the leaves of the tree. The pattern matches successfully with any object and the whole branch returns value NULL, which is accepted as empty list at the previous level of recursion.

Call sample. #Label_list (<. A: <. LABEL: 5, B: abc .>, LABEL: 17, D: 25 .>) = (. 17 5 .)

7.6 Names of Lists and Trees in Patterns

The assignment of names was discussed in Section 5.

In list and tree patterns we can have matching of list and tree names with the described values or simply get these names in the described variable. For this purpose the name may be indicated before list or tree pattern: atom :: pattern

If the atom described in the pattern coincides with the name of the list (or tree), to which the pattern is applied, the application of the pattern to the argument begins. If it does not, other pattern elements are not applied and the pattern fails.

To obtain access to the name of the argument, instead of atom we must indicate the variable, in which the name is assigned as value.

7.7 Patterns of Logical Condition Testing

Pattern of the type: S' (*expression*)

works the following way. First of all the expression is evaluated. If its value differs from NULL, the pattern is successful. The value of the matched argument is returned as the value of the pattern, if matching was successful. If the value of the expression equals to NULL, the pattern fails and returns NULL.

The value of special variable $$ in the expression of S-pattern equals to the value of the argument, to which S-pattern is applied.

The skip of token sequence until the nearest symbol ';' is described by the pattern: (* S' ($$ <> ';') *)

Let under parsing a case is accentuated when the assignment statement is in the form of X := X + E , where X is a variable, and E is an expression. This case could be described by pattern of the type: $Id ':=' S' ($$ = $Id) '+' #Expression

Pattern of the type: V' (*expression*)
works similar to S-pattern, yet in case of success no advancing along the sequence of rule arguments takes place, so the next pattern element is applied to the same argument.

This pattern is useful for context condition check.
Example. The pattern S' (#NUMBER($$) *and* ($$ > 7)) may be substituted by a sequence of patterns $Num V'($Num > 7)

8. Statements

8.1 Assignment Statement

In the left side of assignment statement a variable may be indicated, which is followed by an arbitrary number of list indexes and/or tree selectors. For example,
$X := (. A B C .); $Y := <. D : E, F : G .>;

After assignment $X[2] := T the value of $X is (. A T C .) .

After assignment $Y.D :=17 the value of $Y is <.D :17, F:G .>

The execution of the statement $Y.A := T yields the run time error message. The necessary result is obtained the following way: $Y ++:= <. A : T .> . The branch is deleted by assigning an empty object to the corresponding selector: $Y.D := NULL;

8.2 Conditional Statement

Conditional statement has the following form:

if expression -> statements

Then branches may follow (it is not compulsory)

elsif expression -> statements

Conditional statement ends with keyword *fi*.

In conditional statement branches expressions are computed one by one, until a value different from NULL is obtained. Then the statements described in this branch are executed.

8.3 Fail Statement

Fail statement finishes the execution of the rule branch with failure.

Example. In order to repair errors in parsing process, the sequence of tokens should be skipped quite frequently, for instance, until semicolon symbol. It is done the following way.

```
#statement    ...          ;; -- branches for statement analysis
     (* #Not_semicolon  *)   ';'  -- no statement is recognised
##
#Not_semicolon  $E / if  $E = ';' -> fail  fi/  ##
```

8.4 Loop Statements

Statement of the type

forall $VAR *in* expression *do* statements *od*

loops over a list or a tree.

The value of the expression must be either a list or a tree. Value of the current list element (if the loop is over the list) or value of the current selector (if the loop is over the tree) is assigned to the loop variable $VAR one by one. Statements, describing body of the loop, may use the current value of the variable $VAR.

Loop statement of the type

loop statements *end*;

repeats statements of the loop body, until one of the statements - *break, return* or *fail* is not executed.

8.5 Rule Call

If a rule is called just to execute statements described in it, and value returned by the rule is not necessary, the rule call is written down as statement. It is analogous to procedure call in traditional programming languages. Success/failure of the rule and value returned by it is disregarded in such a call.

9. Input and Output

9.1 Save and Load Statements

Objects created by RIGAL program (atoms, lists, trees) can be saved in the file and loaded back to the memory.

Statement *save* $Var file-specification unloads the object, which is the value of the variable $Var to the file with the given specification. File, formed by *save* statement, contains precisely one object (atom, list or tree).

We can load the object from the file in the memory having executed statement: *load* $Var file-specification

9.2 Text Output

To output texts (messages, generated object codes, etc.) several text files can be opened in the RIGAL program. The text file FFF is opened by statement: *open* FFF file-specification File-specification may be an expression. It presents the name of the file on the device.

Statement of the type

```
FFF << Expr1  Expr2  ...  ExprN
```

outputs a sequence of atoms to the file FFF. Values of expressions Expr1, Expr2, ... are either atoms or lists consisting of objects, different from trees.

This statement outputs atoms as sequences of symbols to the text file, inserting a blank after every atom. Atoms in the list are output in the same order as they are in the list.

Example. FFF << A B 12 ;

A string of characters is output in the text file FFF the following way: "A B 12 "

Symbol @ in the sequence of expressions of output statement switches over to other output mode of blanks separating atoms. By default at the beginning of execution of text output statement the output mode with blanks is on.

Example. FFF << A B @ C D 25 @ E F 57 ;

The following string of characters is output to the text file

"A B CD25E F   57"

Statement of the type FFF << ... always begins output with the beginning of a new record. Output statement of the type FFF <] ... continues output in the current record.

By the help of the statement of the type

Print expression

the value of atom, list or tree can be output in a readable form on the display, disc or on the printer. It is useful when debugging RIGAL programs.

10. Program Structure

Program written in the RIGAL language consists of the main program and rules. The main program text must be at the beginning of the RIGAL program text, but the text of the rules is written afterwards. Main program, as well as rule, begins by the name indication in the form of #main_program_name, then statements are described, separated by symbols ';' . The end of the main program is marked by the symbol '##'.

Usually operations that deal with the initial object loading, rule call and unloading of created objects in the files are concentrated in the main program. Therefore, main program has no pattern elements or arguments of its own.

When RIGAL is used for parsing, text file with the input information first is updated by scanner, which transforms it into a list of tokens. Thus rules describing required parsing can be applied to this list. Intermediate results of the RIGAL program, for instance, abstract syntax trees obtained by parsing can be unloaded in the file by the help of *save* statement. They are unloaded so, that other RIGAL programs (for instance, those, which implement phase of code generation in compilers) can load them as input data. Sample of main program is given in Section 12.4.

Rules can be written down after main program in any order.

10.1 Local Variables

There are no special variable declarations in RIGAL. The fact that a variable is used in some statement, pattern or expression implies that the variable is defined as local variable of the rule or the main program.

For recursive rule calls local rule variables are pushed in a stack, so, that every active rule instance has its own set of local variables.

All variables are initialized by the NULL value, when the corresponding rule or the main program is called and when the execution of rule branch starts.

10.2 References to Variables of Other Rules

The construction of RIGAL makes it possible to obtain access from the rule to local variables of another rule. It has the following form: *last* #L $X

This reference denotes the value of the variable $X in the last (in time) and still active instance of the rule #L. Such references can be used in left and right sides of assignment statement.

If at the moment of evaluation of the expression *last* #L $X there is no active instance of the rule #L, the value of the expression *last* #L $X equals NULL. If such *last* #L $X is in the left side of assignment statement, the statement is disregarded (and run time error message is output). By the help of *last* we may refer to both rule and main program variables.

10.3 Attribute Grammars and RIGAL Global Attributes

There is a close analogy between attribute grammar and RIGAL program. Rules in RIGAL correspond to grammar nonterminals, and variables - to attributes.

In attribute grammars the greatest part of attributes are used as transit attributes. To avoid this global attributes are introduced in the attribute grammar implementations. The usage of *last* references solves this problem in RIGAL.

Implementation of both synthesized and inherited attributes is possible as it is demonstrated in the following scheme.

```
#LA  ... ... ...
     assigns value to the attribute $A
     calls #LB       ... ... ...     ##
#LB  ... ... ...
     $B1 := last #LA $A -- uses the inherited attribute $A from #LA
     calls #LC
      -- after this call the value of the attribute $C
      -- from #LC is assigned to the synthesized attribute $B2
     ... ... ...        ##
#LC  ... ... ...
     assigns value to the attribute $C
     last #LB $B2 := $C    -- the value is assigned to the
                           -- synthesized attribute $B2 of #LB
     ... ... ...           ##
```

11. Built-in Rules

There is a number of built-in rules in the language. These rules implement functions, the implementation of which is impossible or ineffective by other language means.

Call of built-in rules is written down the same way as call of rules defined by the user itself. Along with the value a built-in rule yields success or failure hence, built-in rules are used as patterns.

There are predicates such as #ATOM(E), #NUMBER(E), #IDENT(E), #LIST(E) and #TREE(E).

The built-in rule #LEN(E) returns numerical atom as value. If E is an atom, then for non-numerical atoms it returns the number of atom symbols. For numerical atoms this rule returns the number of significant digits plus 1, if the atom is a negative number. #LEN(NULL) equals 0, #LEN('ABC') equals 3, #LEN(-185) equals 4.

If E is a list, then #LEN(E) returns the number of list elements, but, if E is a tree, then it returns the number of tree branches.

#EXPLODE(E). If E is an atom, then it succeeds and returns one character atom list that represents the value E 'decomposed' in separate characters. If E is a numerical atom, only significant digits are present.

Examples. #EXPLODE(X25) yields (. 'X' '2' '5' .).
#EXPLODE(-34) yields (. '-' '3' '4' .).

#IMPLODE(E1 E2 ... EN). This rule yields the concatenation of atoms or lists E1, E2, ..., EN in a new, non-numerical atom.

Examples. #IMPLODE(A B 34) equals 'AB34'.
#IMPLODE(25 (. A -3 .)) equals '25A-3'.

#CHR(N). The rule returns an atom, which consists of just one ASCII character with the code N (0 <= N <= 127).

#ORD(A). Returns an integer, which is an internal code of the first character of the nonnumerical atom A.

For instance, #ORD(A) = 65, #ORD(ABC) = 65.

#PARM(T) . Returns list of parameters which was assigned when the whole program called for execution.

#DEBUG(E). If E equals the atom 'RULES', then, as soon as the rule is called, information concerning calls of the rules (both user defined and built-in rules) and their execution results will be output. The call #DEBUG(NORULES) stops the debugging of the rules.

12. Sample Compiler

Compiler for the TOYLAN language, which is a very simple programming language, is discussed in the following units. Compiler works in two passes. The first phase is parsing and construction of the program's intermediate form as abstract syntax tree. The second phase is code generation.

Description of input and intermediate language grammars by means of RIGAL is presented. Thus formalized compiler documentation (admitting checking on a computer) is obtained.

12.1 TOYLAN Language

The description of TOYLAN syntax can be regarded as description of acceptable sequences of tokens. Atoms represent lexical elements of TOYLAN program: keywords, identifiers, constants, operation signs, delimiters. The context free grammar of TOYLAN can be described in the form of RIGAL program.

```
#PROGRAM        'PROGRAM' $Id
                (* #DECLARATION ';' *)  (+ #STATEMENT + ';' )  ##
#DECLARATION    ('INTEGER'!'BOOLEAN')    (+ $Id  + ',')        ##
#STATEMENT      ( #ASSIGNMENT       !  #INPUT      !
                  #OUTPUT           !  #CONDITIONAL  )         ##
#ASSIGNMENT     $Id ':='  #EXPRESSION                          ##
#INPUT          'GET' '(' (+ $Id  + ',') ')'                   ##
#OUTPUT         'PUT' '(' (+ #EXPRESSION + ',') ')'            ##
#CONDITIONAL    'IF' #EXPRESSION    'THEN' (+ #STATEMENT + ';')
                ['ELSE' (+ #STATEMENT + ';' )]    'FI'         ##
#EXPRESSION     #SUM       [  '='  #SUM  ]                     ##
#SUM            #FACTOR    (*  '+'  #FACTOR   *)               ##
#FACTOR         #TERM      (*  '*' #TERM      *)               ##
#TERM           $N ;; -- numeric constant
                ('TRUE' ! 'FALSE' ) ;; -- Boolean constants
                $Id;; -- variable
                '(' #EXPRESSION ')'                            ##
```

Context conditions are the following:

1) all variables used in statements and expressions must be declared,

2) one and the same variable name should not be declared twice,

3) left and right parts of assignment statement must be of the same type,

4) operands of input-output statements must be of the type INTEGER.

All variables of the type INTEGER have initial value 0, and all variables of the type BOOLEAN have initial value FALSE.

12.2 Intermediate Form of Program. Abstract Syntax Tree

Special languages to represent intermediate results of compilation are used in compiler building practice. For instance, P-code for PASCAL compilers and language DIANA [8] for ADA.

The result of the first phase of the TOYLAN compiler is a tree. Let's call it abstract syntax tree. Along program components it contains some semantic attributes, for instance, types of expressions. One of the most significant attributes is table of variables, obtained as a result of parsing of the TOYLAN program declarations.

The structure of abstract syntax tree of the TOYLAN program is described by the following rules.

```
#S_PROGRAM
     'PROGRAM'::<. NAME : $Id,
                   DECLARATIONS : #S_DECLARATIONS ,
                   STATEMENTS   : (.(* #S_STATEMENT *).) .>     ##
#S_DECLARATIONS       -- variables table
     <* $Id : ( INTEGER ! BOOLEAN )  *>                          ##
#S_STATEMENT
     ASSIGNMENT :: <. LEFT  : $Id,
                      RIGHT : #S_EXPRESSION   .>   ;;
```

```
    INPUT :: (. (* $Id *) .)    ;;
    OUTPUT :: (. (* #S_EXPRESSION *) .)       ;;
    CONDITIONAL :: <. COND : #S_EXPRESSION,
                      THEN : (.(* #S_STATEMENT *).),
                      [ ELSE : (.(* #S_STATEMENT *).)] .>    ##
#S_EXPRESSION
    COMPARE :: <. ARG1 : #S_EXPRESSION, ARG2 : #S_EXPRESSION,
                  TYPE : BOOLEAN     .>  ;;
    ADD :: <. ARG1 : #S_EXPRESSION, ARG2 : #S_EXPRESSION,
              TYPE : INTEGER         .>  ;;
    MULT :: <. ARG1 : #S_EXPRESSION,  ARG2 : #S_EXPRESSION,
               TYPE : INTEGER        .>  ;;
    <. VARIABLE : $Id , TYPE      : ( INTEGER ! BOOLEAN ) .>    ;;
    <. CONSTANT : $N ,  TYPE      : INTEGER .>     ;;
    <. CONSTANT : ( 0 ! 1) , TYPE : BOOLEAN .>             ##
```

12.3 Target Language BAL

The goal of the TOYLAN compiler is to obtain program text in a low level language BAL. This language is a simplified model of assembler languages. The memory of BAL-machine is divided into separate words. Every word may contain an integer, besides, there are work registers R0, R1, R2, ... of the word size each. Let us suppose the number of registers to be unlimited, in order to eliminate the problem of optimal register usage during generation phase.

Command of BAL   ABC: DEFWORD   N

reserves a word in the memory and imbeds integer N in it. We can refer to this word in other commands by name ABC.

Commands of BAL have two operands which are described by the name of memory word, by the name of register or by the literal of the type =NNN, where NNN is an integer. Commands can be marked by labels.

1) MOV A1,A2 This command moves memory word A1 to memory word A2.
2) LOAD RI,A Loading of word A into register RI.

3) SAVE RI,A Unloading of the contents of register RI into memory word A.

4) ADD RI,A or ADD RI,RJ The sum of operands is imbedded in RI.

5) MULT RI,A or MULT RI,RJ Multiplication of operands is imbedded in RI.

6) COMPARE RI,A or COMPARE RI,RJ If operand values are equal, it is 1 that is imbedded in RI, if they are not equal, 0 is imbedded.

7) BRANCH RI,M If the value of RI is equal to 0, then transfer to the command marked by label M takes place, otherwise, to the next command.

8) JUMP M Unconditional transfer to the command marked by label M.

9) EOJ Completes the execution of the BAL program.

10) READ A Reads the integer from standard input device and imbeds it in word A.

11) WRITE A or WRITE RI Outputs the integer from memory word or from register to standard output device.

12) NOP An empty statement.

12.4 Main Module of Compiler

The main program of the TOYLAN compiler contains calls of the first and second compilation phases and file opening statements.

```
#TOYLAN_COMPILER
    open REP 'TI:';  --message file is connected with the screen
    load $LEXEMS 'A.S'; -- a list of tokens is loaded from the
                    -- file A.S, where it was imbedded by scanner
    $S_TREE := #A_PROGRAM($LEXEMS);
    -- 1st  phase; result of parsing - abstract syntax tree - is
    -- imbedded in the variable $S_TREE; during parsing messages
    -- about discovered errors in file REP can be output.
    if $S_TREE -> open GEN 'A.BAL'; -- if the tree is created,
         -- then file is opened to output the generated BAL text
              #G_PROGRAM($S_TREE) -- 2nd phase - code generation
    elsif T -> REP << errors are discovered  fi;
```

```
REP << end of compilation            ##
```

The compilation listing that contains source text and error messages is not envisaged in the TOYLAN compiler. Formation of the listing can be a separate phase.

12.5 Parsing Phase

The rule #A_PROGRAM carries out parsing of tokens list, checks context conditions, generates error messages and builds abstract syntax tree of TOYLAN program.

Patterns of the rule #A_PROGRAM and of the rules subordinate to it, actually, coincide with patterns of the rule #PROGRAM and with the associated rules that describe context free grammar of the TOYLAN language. Just operations to check context conditions, to output error messages and to construct abstract syntax tree are added.

In our parser diagnostics is based on the following principles. First of all, "panic" reaction to an error should be avoided and several messages concerning one and the same error should not be output (though, we can't manage it always), secondly, error neutralization is transition to the analysis of the next statement, i.e., skip of tokens until the nearest symbol ';'.

```
#A_PROGRAM      -- the rule is applied to the list of tokens
    (. PROGRAM  $Id
        (*  $DECL++:= #A_DECLARATION  ';' *)
                --formation of variables table
        (+  $STATEMENTS !.:= #A_STATEMENT   + ';' )
                --formation of statements list
    .)  / return 'PROGRAM' :: <. NAME : $Id,
                                 DECLARATIONS : $DECL ,
                                 STATEMENTS : $STATEMENTS .>/ ##
#A_DECLARATION      $TYPE := ( INTEGER ! BOOLEAN )
   (+ $Id /if last #A_PROGRAM $DECL.$Id or $REZ.$Id ->
            REP << VARIABLE $Id DOUBLE DEFINED  fi;
```

```
          $REZ++:= <.$Id : $TYPE .>/  + ',' ) / return $REZ / ##
#A_STATEMENT   $REZ := ( #A_ASSIGNMENT ! #A_INPUT !
                  #A_OUTPUT ! #A_CONDITIONAL )   / return $REZ / ;;
     (* $A!.:=S'($$ <> ';' ) *)      -- skip until nearest ';'
                / REP << UNRECOGNIZED STATEMENT $A /          ##
#A_ASSIGNMENT  $Id  ':=' / $LPType := last #A_PROGRAM $DECL .$Id;
        if not $LPType  -> REP << VARIABLE $Id IS NOT DEFINED fi /
   $E:= #A_EXPRESSION
         /if $LPType <> $E . TYPE ->
               REP<< LEFT AND RIGHT SIDE TYPES ARE DIFFERENT
                   IN ASSIGNMENT STATEMENT fi;
     return ASSIGNMENT::<. LEFT: $Id, RIGHT: $E .> /
 onfail if $LPType  -> REP<< WRONG EXPRESSION IN ASSIGNMENT  fi ##
#A_INPUT       GET '('
    (+ $E !.:= $Id  /if  last #A_PROGRAM $DECL.$Id <> INTEGER ->
             REP << $Id IN STATEMENT GET IS NOT OF THE TYPE INTEGER
                      fi / + ',' ) ')' / return INPUT :: $E /   ##
#A_OUTPUT   PUT  '(' (+  $C := #A_EXPRESSION  / $E !.:= $C;
               /if  $C . TYPE  <> INTEGER ->
         REP << OPERAND OF PUT STATEMENT IS NOT OF THE TYPE INTEGER
                fi /   + ',' ) ')'/ return OUTPUT :: $E /       ##
#A_CONDITIONAL      'IF' $BE := #A_EXPRESSION
     /if $BE . TYPE <> BOOLEAN ->
               REP<< CONDITION IS NOT OF BOOLEAN TYPE fi /
                   'THEN' (+ $P1 !.:= #A_STATEMENT + ';' )
        [ 'ELSE' (+ $P2 !.:= #A_STATEMENT + ';' ) ]        'FI'
    / return CONDITIONAL :: <. COND : $BE , THEN : $P1 ,
                          ELSE : $P2  .> /              ##
#A_EXPRESSION      $A := #A_SUM   [  '=' $B := #A_SUM
    / $A := COMPARE::<. ARG1 : $A, ARG2 : $B, TYPE : BOOLEAN.>/ ]
     / return $A /         ##
#A_SUM   $A := #A_FACTOR    (* '+' $B := #A_FACTOR
         / $A := ADD::<. ARG1: $A, ARG2: $B, TYPE: INTEGER .>/ *)
     / return $A /         ##
#A_FACTOR  $A := #A_TERM     (* '*' $B := #A_TERM
```

```
        /$A := MULT::<. ARG1: $A, ARG2: $B, TYPE: INTEGER .>/ *)
     / return $A /              ##
#A_TERM
     $N   / return <. CONSTANT : $N , TYPE : INTEGER .>;;
   ( ( TRUE / $K :=1/ ) ! ( FALSE / $K :=0 / ) )
                  /return <. CONSTANT: $K, TYPE: BOOLEAN .>/  ;;
     $Id  / $X:= last #A_PROGRAM $DECL.$Id;
         if not $X  ->  REP << VARIABLE $Id IS NOT DECLARED
         elsif T -> return <. VARIABLE: $Id, TYPE: $X .> fi / ;;
     '(' $E := #A_EXPRESSION ')' / return $E /           ##
```

12.6 Code Generation Phase

Code generation is performed when traversing abstract syntax tree.

To avoid possible conflicts between variable names in the TOYLAN program and register names (of the type RNNN) and labels (of the type LNNN) in the object program, variable names are substituted by standard names of the type VARNNN.

```
#G_PROGRAM      / $LABEL := 0 /   --global variable $LABEL serves
                                  --to generate unique labels.
  PROGRAM::<.DECLARATIONS: $TAB := #TABLE_OF_NUMBERS,
              --creation of the table of unique variable numbers
            STATEMENTS: (.(* #G_STATEMENT *).) / GEN << 'EOJ' /,
            DECLARATIONS : #G_DECLARATIONS     .>        ##
#TABLE_OF_NUMBERS <* $Id: $TYPE /$N :=$N+1; $T++:=<. $Id: $N.>/ *>
                    /return $T/      ##
#G_STATEMENT ( #G_ASSIGNMENT ! #G_INPUT !
               #G_OUTPUT     ! #G_CONDITIONAL )        ##
#G_ASSIGNMENT    ASSIGNMENT::<. LEFT: $Id := $NAME,
  RIGHT :( ( <. VARIABLE: $Id1:=#NAME .>
               /GEN << MOV @ $Id1 ',' $Id / ) !
          ( <. CONSTANT : $N .> /GEN << MOV @ '=' $N ',' $Id /) !
          ( $NREG := #G_EXPRESSION
               /GEN << 'SAVE' @ 'R' $NREG ',' $Id / ) )  .>    ##
```

```
#G_INPUT  INPUT::(. (* $Id := #NAME /GEN << READ $Id / *) .)   ##
#G_OUTPUT       OUTPUT :: (. (*
     ( ( <. VARIABLE : $Id := #NAME .> /GEN << WRITE $Id / ) !
       ( <. CONSTANT : $N .> /GEN << WRITE @ '=' $N / )  !
       ( $NREG := #G_EXPRESSION /GEN << WRITE @ 'R' $NREG /) )
                                *) .)                          ##
#G_CONDITIONAL       CONDITIONAL ::
      <. COND : $NREG := #G_EXPRESSION
            / $LABEL1 :=#NEW_LABEL(); $LABEL2 :=#NEW_LABEL() /,
         THEN    : / GEN << BRANCH @ 'R' $NREG ',L' $LABEL1 ) /
                  (. (* #G_STATEMENT *) .)
               / if $.ELSE -> GEN << JUMP @ 'L' $LABEL2 fi;
                                GEN << @ 'L' $LABEL1 ': NOP' / ,
       [ ELSE : (. (* #G_STATEMENT *) .)
               / GEN << @ 'L' $LABEL2 ': NOP' / ]       .>   ##
#G_EXPRESSION  --returns the number of the register containing
               --result of the evaluation of expression
    / $NREG := 0 / -- number of the first accessible register
    $REZ := #G_EXPR / return $REZ /     ##
#G_EXPR       ( <. VARIABLE: $ID :=#NAME .>  !
                <. CONSTANT: $N / $ID := #IMPLODE('=' $N)/ .>)
             / $REG := #COPY( last #G_EXPRESSION $NREG ) ;
                GEN << 'LOAD' @ 'R' $REG ',' $ID  ;
                last #G_EXPRESSION $NREG + := 1; return $REG /  ;;
         $OP::<. ARG1 : $R1 := #G_EXPR, ARG2 : $R2 := #G_EXPR .>
          / GEN << $OP @ 'R' $R1 ',R' $R2 ; return $R1 /    ##
#G_DECLARATIONS
<* $ID: $TYPE /$ID1 := #NAME($ID); GEN<< $ID1 ':' DEFWORD 0 /*> ##
#NEW_LABEL      --auxiliary rule
     /last #G_PROGRAM  $LABEL+:=1;
      return #COPY (last #G_PROGRAM $LABEL )/               ##
#NAME      $ID  --returns standard name of the variable $ID in $TAB
     / return #IMPLODE( VAR  last #G_PROGRAM $TAB.$ID)/     ##
```

13. Conclusions and Future Work

As it was demonstrated above, RIGAL supports syntax-oriented style of compiler design. Programs written in RIGAL are well-structured and it is easy to read and debug them.

Our experience [13] proves that the optimizing RIGAL compiler in VAX/VMS environment makes it possible to implement production quality compilers for high level languages.

RIGAL can be considered as yet another language prototyping tool in the sense of [14], because it allows the designer to develop an experimental translator in short period of time.

Besides interpreter for debugging purposes and optimizing compiler RIGAL support system includes a cross-referencer, which helps to avoid misuse of global variables.

In order to improve static and dynamic type checking, variable type descriptions in the form of formal comments would be added to the language.

Taking in account that control structures of RIGAL program are very close to input data structures, it seems promising to develop automatic and semiautomatic methods for test example generation for the given RIGAL program.

References

[1] A.Aho, J.Ullman. The theory of parsing, translation and compiling// Prentice-Hall, Inc. Englewood Cliffs,N.J. 1972. - vol.1,2.

[2] S.C.Johnson. YACC - Yet Another Compiler Compiler // Bell Laboratories, Murray Hill,N.J., 1978, A technical manual.

[3] C.H.Koster. Using the CDL Compiler Compiler// Lecture Notes in Computer Science, Vol.21, Springer-Verlag, Berlin, 1977.

[4] I.R.Agamirzyan. Compiler Design Technological Support System SHAG. // Space mechanics algorithms, Leningrad, vol. 79, 1985, pp.1-53., (in Russian).

[5] D.E.Knuth. Semantics of context-free languages// Mathematical

Systems Theory, 2, 2, 1968, pp.127-146.

[6] V.A.Serebryakov. Methods of Attribute Translation.// In: Programming Languages, Moscow, "Nauka", 1985, pp.47-79, (in Russian).

[7] A.O.Vooglaid, M.V.Lepp, D.B.Lijb. Input Languages of the ELMA System.// Proceedings of the Tallinn Polytechnical Institute, #524, 1982, pp.79-96, (in Russian).

[8] The intermediate language DIANA : Design and Implementation// Lecture Notes in Computer Science, Vol.180, Springer-Verlag, Berlin, 1984.

[9] R.Vilhelm. Presentation of the compiler generation system MUG2 : Examples, global flow analysis and optimization// Le point sur la compilation, INRIA, 1978, pp.307-336.

[10] Basic REFAL and its implementation on computers.// CNIPIASS, Moscow, 1977, (in Russian).

[11] P.Lucas. Formal definition of programming languages and systems // IFIP Congress , 1971.

[12] M.Ganapatti, C.N.Fisher, J.L.Hennessy. Retargetable compiler code generation// ACM Computing Survays, 14(4), 1982.

[13] J.Barzdin, A.Kalnins, M.Auguston, SDL tools for rapid prototyping and testing.// in SDL'89 : The language at work, ed. O.Faergemand and M.M.Marques, North-Holland, 1989, pp.127-133.

[14] R.Herndon, V.Berzins, The realizable benefits of a language prototyping language.// IEEE Transactions on Software Engineering , vol.14, No 6, June 1988, pp.803-809.

COMPLEXITY OF PROBABILISTIC VERSUS DETERMINISTIC AUTOMATA

Rūsiņš Freivalds
Institute of Mathematics and Computer Science
The University of Latvia
Raina bulvāris 29
Riga, Latvia

1. INTRODUCTION

The paper contains several results showing advantages of probabilistic automata over deterministic ones. The advantages always are of one kind, namely, the complexity of probabilistic automata turns out to be considerably smaller. The paper contains both new results and results already published in the USSR (though, hardly these results are known outside the USSR).

The economy of computer resources (computation time, memory, etc.) is studied in this paper, comparing computation by probabilistic and deterministic machines. Both from theoretical and applications aspect the most interesting part of the problem is the possibility of such an economy in computation of explicitly defined natural functions with probability as close to 1 as possible. Nevertheless until recently this part of the problem was the most hard and the least explored. The power of probabilistic machines was proved only in two cases: 1) when the probability of the correct result is high but the concept of computation is rather artificial, 2) for recognition of explicitly defined specific languages but for non-isolated cut-points, i.e. with probability exceeding 1/2 only by unboundedly small numbers.

Every theorem on power of probabilistic machines in this survey consists of two parts. The first part asserts that the language under consideration is recognizible by a probabilistic machine. The second part shows that no deterministic machine can do this. We organize the paper according to the methods used in the proofs of the first parts of theorems. The proofs of the second parts use various techniques with no unifying idea.

The types of automata and machines used in the paper are well-known in the literature. Precise definitions can be found in [Hen 77].

2. A LEMMA FOR JOINING COUNTERS

When designing efficient probabilistic algorithms for simple computational devices sometimes the algorithms can be presented as a procedure involving large number of counters, and the number of the counters depends on the input word. This section contains a lemma that can be used to justify the correctness of the probabilistic algorithm.

Let N denote the set of all non-negative integers, Z denote the set of all integers and X denote an arbitrary set.

Let $n \in N$. Let P be a function $X \to \{0,1\}$ and F be a function $X \times \{1,2,\ldots,n\} \to Z$. We call the pair of functions $\langle P,F \rangle$ dispersive if for all $x \in X$ the following holds:

1) $P(x)=1 \to (\forall u,v \in \{1,2,\ldots,n\})\ (F(x,u)=F(x,v))$,

2) $P(x)=0 \to (\forall u,v \in \{1,2,\ldots,n\})\ (u \neq v \to (F(x,u) \neq F(x,v)))$.

Let $n \in N$, $k(x)$ be a function $X \to N$, and for every $i \in \{1,2,\ldots,k(x)\}$ a dispersive pair of functions $(P_i : X \to \{0,1\};\ F_i : X \times \{1,2,\ldots,n\} \to Z)$. We denote the family $\{F_1,F_2,\ldots,F_n\}$ by F. We consider the following random value $S_F(x)$. For arbitrary $i \in \{1,2,\ldots,k(x)\}$ a random number y_i is taken which is distributed equiprobably in $\{1,2,\ldots,n\}$ and every y_i is statistically independent from all the other y_j. Then

$$S_F(x) = \sum_{i=1}^{k(x)} F_i(x,y_i).$$

LEMMA 2.1. For arbitrary $x \in X$, if $\prod_{i=1}^{k(x)} P_i(x)=1$ then there is a $z \in Z$ such that $S_F(x)=z$ with probability 1, and if $\prod_{i=1}^{k(x)} P_i(x)=0$ then there is not a single z such that the probability of $S_F(x)=z$ would exceed $1/n$.

PROOF. The first assertion is evident. To prove the second assertion we assume that for some x, $i \in \{1,2,\ldots,k(x)\}$ it holds $P_i(x)=0$. Then the values $\{F_i(x,1),F_i(x,2),\ldots,F_i(x,n)\}$ are pairwise distinct. The total $S_F(x) = \sum_{j=1}^{k(x)} F_j(x,y_j)$ includes $F_i(x,y_i)$ and y_i is independent from all the rest of y_j. Hence the total $S_F(x)$ can equal z for no more than one of the n possible values y_i.

3. THREE-HEAD PROBABILISTIC FINITE AUTOMATA VERSUS MULTI-HEAD DETERMINISTIC ONES

Some languages can be recognized by multi-head finite automata. For these languages the minimum number of heads is a complexity measure. It was proved in **FREIVALDS** (1979) that for arbitrary k>0 there is a language which can be recognized by probabilistic 2-head finite automaton with probability $1-\varepsilon$ fot arbitrary $\varepsilon>0$ but which is not recognizable by any deterministic k-head finite automaton. In this Section another advantage of probabilistic multi-head finite automata is proved. A language is described which can be recognized by a probabilistic 3-head finite automaton but no deterministic multi-head finite automaton can recognize this specific language.

On the other hand, I risk to conjecture that 2-head of a probabilistic automaton do not suffice for such an advantage:

CONJECTURE 1. If a language is recognized by a probabilistic 2-head finite automaton with probability $1-\varepsilon$ for arbitrary $\varepsilon>0$ then the language is recognized by a deterministic multi-head finite automaton as well.

We describe a language W. To describe it we introduce the types of blocks A(b), B(m,k), C(m,k), D(n,i), $E_b(i,k)$.

$$A(b):\ 0^b 2 0^{2^1} 1 0^{2^2} 1 0^{2^3} 1 \ldots 1 0^{2^{b-1}} 2 0^{2^b};$$

$$B(m,k):\ 0^m 2 \underbrace{0^{m^{k-1}} 1 0^{m^{k-1}} 1 \ldots 1 0^{m^{k-1}} 2 0^{m^{k-1}}}_{m \text{ times}} 2 0^{m^k};$$

$$C(m,k):\ 0^x 3B(m,1)3D(m,3)3\ldots 3B(m,k-1)4B(m,k);$$

$$D(n,i):\ \underbrace{0^i 1 0^i 1 \ldots 1 0^i 2 0^i}_{n \text{ times}}$$

$$E_b(i,k):\ C(1,k)4D(1^k,i)4C(2,k)4D(2^k,i)4\ldots$$

$$...4C(2^b-1,k)4D((2^b-1)^k,i)5C(2^b,k)5D((2^b)^k,i);$$

$$\text{code}_b(i_1,i_2,...,i_b,j_b,...,j_2,j_1):\ A(b)7E_b(i_1,1)6E_b(i_2,2)6...$$
$$...6E_b(i_{b-1},b-1)7E_b(i_b,b)7E_b(j_b,b)6E_b(j_{b-1},b-1)6...$$
$$...6E_b(j_2,2)7E_b(j_1,1);$$

$$W' = \{x|x\in\{0,1,2,3,4,5,6,7\}^* \ \&\ (\exists\ b\geq 2,i_1,i_2,...,i_b,j_b,...,j_2,j_1)$$
$$(x=\text{code}_b(i_1,i_2,...,i_b,j_b,...,j_2,j_1))\}$$

$$W = \{x|x\in\{0,1,2,3,4,5,6,7\}^* \ \&\ (\exists\ b\geq 2,i_1,i_2,...,i_b)$$
$$(x=\text{code}_b(i_1,i_2,...,i_b,i_b,...,i_2,i_1))\}$$

THEOREM 1. (1) For arbitrary $\varepsilon>0$ there is a probabilistic 3-head finite automaton which recognizes the language W accepting every word in W with probability 1 and rejecting carry word in W with probability $1-\varepsilon$. (2) No deterministic multi-head finite automaton can recognize W.

PROOF. (1) Let b_0 be the least value of b for which $b/2^b<\varepsilon$, and let d be a power of 2 for which $d>1/\varepsilon$. The computation is started by the head h_1 going through the subword 0^b of the block A(b) and deciding whether or not $b\geq b_0$. Note that it suffices to read only the first b_0+1 letters of the subword.

The processing of the input word is different for large and small values of b.

If b is small, i.e. $b/2^b\geq\varepsilon$ then the input word $x\in W$ can be represented as a concatenation of words $z_1 0^{l_1} z_2 0^{l_2} z_3 0^{l_3} z_4 .. z_1 0^{l_t}$, where t is a constant, $z_1,z_2,...,z_t$ are fixed words in $\{0,1,2,3,4,5,6,7\}^*$ and these words begin with letters differing from 0. Additionally, there is a binary relation R_b completely defined by the parameter b such that $(i,j)R_b \Rightarrow l_i=l_j$.

Two heads h_1 and h_2 suffice to process the word for small values of b. The leading head h_1 does all the reading from the tape. The head h_2 reads nothing. It position on the tape is used to simulate a counter. The content of the counter equals the distance between the heads multiplied to a constant factor plus residue modulo this factor kept in the internal memory of the automaton.

The correctness of $z_1,z_2,...,z_z$ is checked by the finite automaton while reading the input. The checking of all the equalities $l_i=l_j$ where it is needed is done in a probabilistic way by using the counter. We define the following family of dispersive pairs of functions.

$$P_{ij}(x) = \begin{cases} 1, & \text{if } l_i=l_j \\ 0, & \text{if } l_i \neq l_j \end{cases}$$

$$F_{ij}(x,y) = y(l_i-l_j).$$

The pair (P_{ij},F_{ij}) is in the family iff $(i,j)\in R_b$. Let $F=\{F_{ij}\}_{(i,j)\in R_b}$. The probabilistic automaton for every $(i,j)\in R_b$ produces a random number $y_{ij}\in\{1,2,\dots,d\}$ being independent of all the other random numbers and adds $F_{ij}(x,y_{ij})$ to the counter. The input word is accepted iff at the end the counter is empty. The correctness of the algorithm follows from Lemma 1.

If b is large, i.e. $b/2^b<\varepsilon$ then the processing of the input word is more complicated. The processing consists of 3 separate actions:

1) testing whether $x\in W'$,
2) choice of a random number a $(1\le a\le 2^b)$,
3) testing whether $a^1 i_1+a^2 i_2+\dots+a^b i_b=a^1 j_1+a^2 j_2+\dots+a^b j_b$.

The leading head h_1 reads the input word. The head h_2 simulates the counter. This counter is used to perform the actions 1) and 3). The head h_3 is used to perform the action 2).

To perform the action 1), first, correctness of the structure of the input word is tested (the structure can be desaibed by means of a special regular language W" such that W'⊂W"), and, second, $S_F(x)$ is acumulated in the counter where F is the following family of functions.

$F_1(x,y)=y(x_1{}^1-x_2{}^1-1)$ where $x_1{}^1$ is the number of zeros in the subword 0^b in A(b), and $x_2{}^1$ is the number of subwords consisting of zeros between the symbols 2 in the block A(b).

$F_2(x,y)=y(x_1{}^2-x_2{}^2)$ where $x_1{}^2$ is the number of zeros in the first subword 0^{2^b} consisting of zeros after the second symbol 2 in the block A(b), and $x_2{}^2$ is the number of blocks C(u,1) in the block $E_b(i_1,1)$.

$F_{3,u}(x,y)=y(2x_1{}^{3,u}-x_2{}^{3,u})$, $(1\le u\le b-1)$ where $x_1{}^{3,u}$ is the number of zeros in the u-th subword 0^{2^u} of zeros after the first symbol 2 in the block A(b), and $x_2^{3,u}$ is the number of zeros in the (u+1)-th subword $0^{2^{u+1}}$ of zeros after the first symbol 2 in the block A(b).

$F_{y,u,v,w,z}(x,y)=y(x_1^{y,u,v,w,z}-x_2^{y,u,v,w,z}+2)$, $(1\le z\le 2,\ 1\le w\le b,\ 1\le v\le w,\ 1\le u\le 2b)$ where $x_1^{y,u,v,w,z}$ is the number of zeros in the first substring 0^u of zeros in the block B(u,v) in C(u,w) either in $E_b(i_w,w)$, if z=1, or in $E_b(j_w,w)$, if z=2, and $x_2^{y,u,v,w,z}$ is the number of subwords of zeros in the same block B(u,v) in C(u,w) in $E_b(i_w,w)$, if z=1, or in $E_b(j_w,w)$, if z=2.

$F_{5,u,v,w,z,t}(x,y)=y(x_1^{5,u,v,w,z,t}-x_2^{5,u,v,w,z,t})$, $(1\le z\le 2,\ 1\le w\le b,\ 1\le v\le w,\ 1\le u\le 2^b, 2\le t\le u)$ where $x_1^{5,u,v,w,z,t}$ is the number of zeros in the t-th subword of zeros in the block D(u,v) un C(u,w) either in $E_b(i_w,w)$, if z=1, or in $E_b(j_w,w)$, if z=2, and $x_2^{5,u,v,w,z,t}$ is the number of zeros in the (t+1)-th subword of zeros in the block B(u,v) in C(u,w) either in $E_b(i_w,w)$, if z=1, or in $E_b(j_w,w)$, if z=2.

$F_{6,u,v,w,z}(x,y)=y(x_1^{6,u,v,w,z}-x_2^{6,u,v,w,z})$, $(1\le z\le 2,\ 1\le w\le b,\ 1\le v\le w,\ 2\le u\le 2^b)$ where $x_1^{6,u,v,w,z}$ is the number of zeros between the first and the third symbol 2 in the block B(u,v) in C(u,w) either in $E_b(i_w,w)$, if z=1, or in $E_b(j_w,w)$, if z=2, and $x_2^{6,u,v,w,z}$ is the number of zeros in the first subword of zeros after the third symbol 2 in the block B(u,v) in C(u,w) either in $E_b(i_w,w)$, if z=1, or in $E_b(j_w,w)$, if z=2.

$F_{7,u,v,w,z}(x)=y(x_1^{7,u,v,w,z}-x_2^{7,u,v,w,z})$, $(1\le z\le 2,\ 1\le w\le b,\ 1\le v\le w-1,\ 1\le u\le 2^b)$ where $x_1^{7,u,v,w,z}$ is the number of zeros in the first after the third symbol 2 subword of zeros in the block B(u,v) in C(u,w) either in $E_b(i_w,w)$, if z=1, or in $E_b(j_w,w)$, if z=2, and $x_2^{7,u,v,w,z}$ is the number of zeros in the second subword of zeros in the block B(u,v+1) in C(u,w) either in $E_b(i_w,w)$, if z=1, or in $E_b(j_w,w)$, if z=2.

$F_{8,u,v,w,z}(x,y)=y(x_1^{8,u,v,w,z}-x_2^{8,u,v,w,z})$, $(1\le z\le 2,\ 1\le w\le b,\ 1\le v\le w-1,\ 1\le u\le 2^b)$ where $x_1^{8,u,v,w,z}$ is the number of zeros in the first subword of zeros in the block B(u,v) in C(u,w) either $E_b(i_w,w)$, if z=1, or in $E_b(j_w,w)$, if z=2, and $x_2^{8,u,v,w,z}$ is the number of zeros in the first subword of zeros in the block

$B(u,v+1)$ in $C(u,w)$ either in $E_b(i_w,w)$, if $z=1$, or $E_b(j_w,w)$, if $z=2$.

$$F_{9,u,w,z}(x,y)=y(x_1^{9,u,w,z}-x_2^{9,u,w,z}), \quad (1\le z\le 2,\ 1\le w\le b,\ 1\le u\le 2^b)$$

where $x_1^{9,u,w,z}$ is the number of zeros in the last subword of zeros in the block $B(u,w)$ in $C(u,w)$ either in $E_b(i_w,w)$, if $z=1$, or in $E_b(j_w,w)$, if $z=1$, and $x_2^{9,u,w,z}$ is the number of zeros in the first subword of zeros either in the block $D(u^w,i_w)$ in $E_b(i_w,w)$, if $z=1$, or in the block $D(u^w,j_w)$ in $E_b(j_w,w)$, if $z=2$.

$$F_{10,u,w,z,t}(x,y)=y(x_1^{10,u,w,z,t}-x_2^{10,u,w,z,t}), \quad (1\le z\le 2,$$

$1\le w\le b$, $1\le u\le 2^b$, $1\le t\le u^w-1$) where $x_1^{10,u,w,z,t}$ is the number of zeros in the t-th subword of zeros either in the block $D(u^w,i_w)$ in $E_b(i_w,w)$, if $z=1$, or in $D(u^w,j_w)$ in $E_b(j_w,w)$, if $z=2$, and $x_2^{10,u,w,z,t}$ is the number of zeros in the (t+1)-th subword of zeros either in the block $D(u^w,i_w)$ in $E_b(i_w,w)$, if $z=1$, or in the block $D(u^w,j_w)$ in $E_b(j_w,w)$, if $z=2$.

$$F_{11,u,w,z}(x,y)=y(x_1^{11,u,w,z}-x_2^{11,u,w,z}), \quad (1\le z\le 2,\ 1\le w\le b,$$

$1\le u\le 2^b-1$) where $x_1^{11,u,w,z}$ is the number of zeros in the first subword of zeros either in the block $D(u^w,i_w)$ in $E_b(i_w,w)$, if $z=1$, or in the block $D(u^w,j_w)$ in $E_b(j_w,w)$, if $z=2$, and $x_2^{11,u,w,z}$ is the number of zeros in the first subword of zeros either in the block $D((u+1)^w,i_w)$ in $E_b(i_w,w)$, if $z=1$, or in the block $D((u+1)^w,j_w)$ in $E_b(j_w,w)$, if $z=2$.

$$F_{12,u,w,z}(x,y)=y(x_1^{12,u,w,z}-x_2^{12,u,w,z}+1), \quad (1\le z\le 2,\ 1\le w\le b,$$

$1\le u\le 2^b-1$) where $x_1^{12,u,w,z}$ is the number of zeros in the second sibword of zeros in the block $C(u,w)$ either in $E_b(i_w,w)$, if $z=1$, or in $E_b(j_w,w)$, if $z=2$, and $x_2^{12,u,w,z}$ is the number of zeros in the second subword of zeros in the block $C(u+1,w)$ either in $E_b(i_w,w)$, if $z=1$, or in $E_b(j_w,w)$, if $z=2$.

$$F_{13,u,w,z}(x,y)=y(x_1^{13,u,w,z}-x_2^{13,u,w,z}), \quad (1\le z\le 2,\ 1\le w\le b,$$

$1\le u\le 2^b-1$) where $x_1^{13,u,w,z}$ is the number of zeros in the first subword of zeros in the block $C(u,w)$ either in $E_b(i_w,w)$, if $z=1$, or in $E_b(j_w,w)$, if $z=2$, and $x_2^{13,u,v,w,z}$ is the number of zeros in the first subword of zeros in the block $C(u+1,w)$ either in $E_b(i_w,w)$, if $z=1$, or in $E_b(j_w,w)$, if $z=2$.

$F_{14,w,z}(x,y)=y(x_1^{14,w,z}-x_2^{14,w,z})$, $(1\le z\le 2,\ \ 1\le w\le b-1)$ where $x_1^{14,w,z}$ is the number of zeros in the first subword of zeros either in $E_b(i_w,w)$, if z=1, or in $E_b(j_w,w)$, if z=2, and $x_2^{14,w,z}$ is the number of zeros in the first subword of zeros either in $E_b(i_{w+1},w+1)$, if z=1, or in $E_b(j_{w+1},w+1)$, if z=2.

$F_{15}(x,y)=y(x_1^{15}-x_2^{15})$, where x_1^{15} is the number of zeros in the first subword of zeros in the input word, and x_2^{15} is the number of blocks $E_b(i_w,w)$, in the input word up to the third symbol 7.

$F_{16}(x,y)=y(x_1^{16}-x_2^{16})$, where x_1^{16} is the number of zeros in the first subword of zeros in the input word, and x_2^{16} is the number of blocks $E_b(j_w,w)$, in the input word after the third symbol 7.

$P_1(x),P_2(x),P_3(x),\ldots,P_{16}(x)$ equal 1 if $F_1(x,y),F_2(x),F_3(x),\ldots,F_{16}(x)$, respectively, are equal 0, and they equal 0, otherwise.

We denote the family of functions $\{F_1,F_2,\ldots,F_{16}\}$ by F.

The head h_2 simulates a counter accummulating the value $S_F(x)$. The machine starts with an empty counter. Hence, the head h_2 coincides with h_1. To start the computation of an arbitrary function $F_\delta \in F$, a random number $y_\delta \in \{1,2,\ldots,d\}$ is chosen. Suppose, $F_\delta(x,y)=y(x_1^\delta-x_2^\delta)$ where x_1^δ is the number of symbols from a set M_1, and x_2^δ is the number of symbols from a set M_2. Then in response to reading a symbol from M_1 by the head h_1, the content of the counter is increased by y_δ. In response to reading a symbol from M_2, the content of the counter is decreased by y_δ. While simulating the counter by the head h_2, the following relation between the content of the counter and the distance between the heads h_1 and h_2 is kept: the content equals 54 d times the distance plus the residue modulo 54 d (which is stored in the internal memory of the automaton).

The number of pairs $<P_i,F_i>$ can be unboundedly large but the finite memory of the automaton does not prevent it from the counting up the total $S_F(x)$ since the automaton never needs to compute simultaneonsly more than two functions from any subfamily $\{F_{3,u}(x,y)\}$, $\{F_{5,u,v,w,z,t}(x,y)\}$, $\{F_{7,u,v,w,z}(x,y)\}$, $\{F_{8,u,v,w,z}(x,y)\}$, $\{F_{10,u,w,z,t}(x,y)\}$, $\{F_{11,u,w,z}(x,y)\}$, $\{F_{12,u,w,z}(x,y)\}$, $\{F_{13,u,w,z}(x,y)\}$, $\}F_{14,w,z}(x,y)\}$, and it never needs more than one function from any subfamily $\{F_{4,u,v,w,z}(x,y)\}$, $\{F_{6,u,v,w,z}(x,y)\}$, $\{F_{9,u,w,z}(x,y)\}$. Hence at no moment the automaton keeps more than 26 random numbers $y_\delta \in \{1,2,\dots,d\}$. For the functions from $\{F_{3,u}(x,y)\}$ sometimes the automaton add 2 y_δ to the content of the counter. We see that the content is never changed by a number exceeding 27d.

To perform the action 2) the head h_3 starts with finding the block $E(i_1,1)$. While the head h_1 goes through the block A(b), at moments when h_1 reads the first symbol 2 and all the symbol 1 (i.e. before every subword $0^{2^1}, 0^{2^2}, \dots, 0^{2^{b-1}}$) the automaton uses the random number generator and it produces a random bit r. If this bit corresponding to the subword 0^{2^i} equals 1 then the head h_3 is moved 2^i blocks $D(j,i_1)$ ahead (one block $D(j,i_1)$ per one zero in 0^{2^i}). If the bit r equals 0 then the head h_3 is not moved. Thus the generation of all these r's ends in moving h_3 to a random block $D(a,i_1)$ where the values $a \in \{1,2,3,\dots,2^b\}$ are equiprobable.

To perform the action 3) the numbers $i_1,i_2,..,i_b,j_b,..,j_2,j_1$ are read by the head h_3. The block $D(a,i_1)$ contains $a^1\ i_1$ zeros. The number $a^1\ i_1$ is added to the counter. Next, while h_1 traverses the block $E_b(i_2,2)$ and hence meets 2^b blocks $D(1^2,i_2)$, $D(2^2,i_2),\dots,D((2^b)^2,i_2)$, the head h_3 goes through 2^b blocks of type D, reaches the block $D(a^2,i_1)$ and adds the number of zeros in $D(a^2,i_1)$ (being equal $a^2.i_2$) to the content of the counter. Then, while h_1 traverses the block $E_b(i_3,3)$, thr head h_3 goes through 2^b blocks of type D, reaches the block $D(a^3,i_3)$ and adds $a^3.i_3$ to the content of the counter, etc. After reaching the block $E_b(j_b,b)$ by h_1, the head h_3 goes to the block $D(a^b,b)$ and from this moment on the numbers $a^b.j_b, a^{b-1}.j_{b-1},\dots,a^1.j_1$ are subtracted (not added). In total, the action 3) results in adding $a^1.i_1+a^2.i_2+\dots+a^b.i_b-a^bj_b-\dots-a^2.j_2-a^1.j_1$ to the content of the counter.

The automaton ends its work after performing the actions 1), 2), 3). If the counter is empty at this moment then the input word is accepted, otherwise it is rejected.

In order to prove the probability of the right result, we first note that random numbers y_σ and a are chosen to be statistically independent.

If $x \in W$ then for all possible choices of random numbers the counter is empty at the end and the input word is accepted. If $x \in W' \setminus W$ then $S_F(x)=0$ and at the end the counter contains

$$a^1 i_1 + a^2 i_2 + \ldots + a^b i_b - a^b j_b - \ldots - a^2 j_2 - a^1 j_1 .$$

Taking into account the properties of Vandermonde determinant it may be proved that no more than b-1 out of 2^b possible values of a allow equality

$$a^1 (i_1 - j_1) + a^2 (i_2 - j_2) + \ldots + a^b (i_b - j_b) = 0$$

if not all $i_1=j_1, i_2=j_2, \ldots, i_b=j_b$. In the beginning of our proof we made a distinction between large and small values of b, and for large values of b the probability of the error $b/2^\varepsilon < \varepsilon$.

Now we consider $x \notin W'$. Lemma 2.1 asserts that for arbitrary fixed value a the probability P_a of $S_F(x)$ being -

$$(a^1 i_1 + \ldots + a^b i_b - a^b j_b - \ldots - a^1 j_1)$$

does not exceed ε. Since a is chosen independently of y_o, the total probability of error equals the mean value of p_a for all a's and it does not exceed ε.

(2) Let g>2. We will prove that if an arbitrary deterministic (and even nondeterministic) g-head 1-way finite automaton accepts all words in W with the parameter b equal g^8 then it accepts at least one word not in W.

Let n be sufficiently large integer (we make this restriction precise below in the proof). By the definition of W, the word $x \in W$ is completely described by the parameters b, $i_1, i_2, \ldots, i_b$. We fix a finite subset $S_o \subset W$ consisting at all the words $x \in W$ for which $b=g^8$ and

$$i_1 + i_2 + \ldots + i_{g^6} = n ,$$

$$i_{g^6+1} + i_{g^6+1} + \ldots + i_{2g^6} = n ,$$

$$\ldots\ldots\ldots$$

$$i_{b-g^6+1} + i_{b-g^6+2} + \ldots + i_b = n .$$

We divide the word x into the following nonintersecting subwords:

$$W_1 = A(b) 7 E_b(i_1, 1) 6 E_b(i_2, 2) 6 \ldots 6 E_b(i_{g^6}, g^6),$$

$$W_2=6E_b(i_{g^6+1},g^6+1)6E_b(i_{g^6+2},g^6+2)6\ldots 6E_b(i_{2g^6},2g^6),$$

- - - - - - - - -

$$W_{g^2}=6E_b(i_{b-g^6+1},b-g^6+1)6E_b(i_{b-g^6+2},b-g^6+2)6\ldots 7E_b(i_b,b),$$

$$W_{g^2+1}=7E_b(i_b,b)6\ldots 6E_b(i_{b-g^6+2},b-g^6+2)6E_b(i_{b-g^6+1},b-g^6+1),$$

- - - - - - - - -

It is easy to see that

$$\text{card}(S_o) = \binom{n+g^6-1}{g^6-1}^{g^2}$$

Configuration of the g-head automaton at a fixed moment is a (g+1)-tuple $(\sigma,p_1,\ldots,p_g)$ where σ is internal state of the automaton and p_i is the index of the tape square observed by the head h_i. The type of the configuration is a g-tuple $(q_1,\ldots,q_g)$ where q_i is the index j of the subword W_j observed by the head h_i.

If the automaton is nondeterministic then we fix one possible accepting path of computation for every $x\in S_o$. Let $c_1(x)$, $c_2(x),\ldots,c_t(x)$ be the sequence of the configurations. Let $d_1(x),\ldots,d_l(x)$ be the subsequence obtained by taking $d_1(x)=c_1(x)$ and all $c_i(x)$ such that type $(c_i(x)) \neq$ type $(c_{i-1}(x))$. The subsequence $d_1(x),\ldots,d_l(x)$ is called the schema of the computation.

Let S be the number of the states. Since $l<g\,(2g^2-1)+1$, the number of possible schemes do not exceed $O(n^{2g^4})$.

We divide S_o into subsets with respect of the schema. The cardinality of the largest subset (we denote it by S_1) is no less than

$$\binom{n+g^6-1}{g^6-1}^{g^2} \Big/ O\left(n^{2g^4}\right) .$$

We denote the schema corresponding to S_1 by $\hat{d}_1,\ldots,\hat{d}_l$.

We say that the subword W_i correspond to W_{2g^2-i+1}. If one of the $\binom{g}{2}$ pairs of heads at some moment is placed on a pair of corresponding subwords W_i and W_{2g^2-i+1} then at no moment they are placed on another pair of corresponding subwords W_j and W_{2g^2-j+1}, $j\neq i$. Since there are more corresponding pairs of subwords than pairs of heads there is at least one pair of subwords (W_i, W_{2g^2-i+1}) which is never simultaneously observed by any pair of heads. Knowing the schema we can reconstruct such an i. Let l be such an i for the schema $\hat{d}_1,\ldots,\hat{d}_1$.

We divide S_1 further into subsets with respect to the values of $W_1,\ldots,W_{l-1},W_{l+1},\ldots,W_{2g^2-1},W_{2g^2-l+2},\ldots,W_{2g^2}$ (all W_j are taken except W_l and W_{2g^2-l+1}). The largest of these subsets is denoted by S_2. It contains

$$\frac{\binom{n+g^6+1}{g^6-1}^{g^2}}{o\left(n^{2g^4}\right)\binom{n+g^6+1}{g^6-1}^{g^2-1}} = \frac{\binom{n+g^6+1}{g^6-1}}{o\left(n^{2g^4}\right)} = o\left(n^{g^6-2g^4-1}\right)$$

words. When we started to prove (2) we announced that n is sufficiently large integer and promised to make this statement precise. Now we have suitable terms for the precision. Namely, we demand that n is large enough such that S_2 contains at least two different words. Let these words be, respectively,

$X = W_1 \ldots W_{l-1}\, X_l\, W_{l+1} \ldots W_{2g^2-1}\, X_{2g^2-l+1}\, W_{2g^2-l+2} \ldots W_{2g^2}$,

$Y = W_1 \ldots W_{l-1}\, Y_l\, W_{l+1} \ldots W_{2g^2-1}\, Y_{2g^2-l+1}\, W_{2g^2-l+2} \ldots W_{2g^2}$,

Now we consider the following word:

$Z = W_1 \ldots W_{l-1}\, X_l\, W_{l+1} \ldots W_{2g^2-1}\, Y_{2g^2-l+1}\, W_{2g^2-l+2} \ldots W_{2g^2}$.

We will prove that the multi-head automaton assumed to accept all words in W accepts the word Z as well. Indeed, we consider the sequences of the configurations $\{c_i(x)\}$, $\{c_i(y)\}$ and construct admissible sequence $\{c_i(z)\}$. To do this, we divide the given sequences into blocks of configurations such that the first (and only the first) configuration in every block is from the schema $\hat{d}_1,\ldots\hat{d}_1$. To construct $\{c_i(z)\}$ we take the blocks in which no head reads the subword Y_{2g^2-l+1}, from $\{c_i(x)\}$ and we take the blocks in which at least one head reads Y_{2g^2-l+1}, from $\{c_i(y)\}$. Note that at no moment a pair of heads reads X_l and Y_{2g^2-l+1} simultaneously but all the subwords of w type are in x and y as well. Hence the automaton cannot distinguish z from x or from y and accepts it along with x and y.

4. TWO-COUNTER PROBABILISTIC AUTOMATA VERSUS MULTI-COUNTER DETERMINISTIC ONES

We considered a language W in Section 3 and proved that it can be recognized by a 3-head probabilistic finite automaton but cannot be recognized by a multi-head deterministic finite automaton. Counter automata (with one one-way head) differ from multi-head finite automata rather much. Nonetheless the same language W can distinguish capabilities of multi-counter probabilistic and deterministic automata (Theorem 4.1). Later in Theorem 4.2 we consider a still more complicated language and get a wider gap in complexity.

THEOREM 4.1. (1) For arbitrary $\varepsilon>0$ there is a probabilistic 1-way 3-counter automaton which recognizes the language W in real time accepting every word in W with probability 1 and rejecting every word in $\overline{W}$ with probability $1-\varepsilon$. (2) No deterministic 1-way multi-counter automaton can recognize W in real time.

PROOF. (1) Like in Theorem 3.1 we consider seperately the work of the automaton for large values of b ($b/z^b<\varepsilon$) and for small values of b.

For small values of b the proof of Theorem 3.1 contains an algorithm for a probabilistic automaton with 1 counter, and a description how to modify this algorithm to get a 2-head finite automaton. Our proof involves the same 1-counter automaton without any modifications.

For large values of b the processing of the input word consists of actions 1), 2), 3) described in the proof of Theorem 3.1.

The action 1) is already described in terms of a counter automaton. It remains to note additionally that this action can be performed in real time.

The action 2) and, hence, the action 3) in our case is organized in a different way. While the head h_1 (now it is the only head) reads the block A(b), a random number a (produced in the same way) is recorded by the second counter. When h_1 traverses $E_b(i_1,1)$, the content of the second counter is used to find the block $D(a^1,i_1)$. Since the value of a will be needed many times more, it should not be lost. Therefore whenever a unit is subtracted from the content of the second counter, it is immediately added to the content of the third counter. When the second counter becomes empty, the third counter contains a, they change the roles and the automaton is ready to search for the block $D(a^2,i_2)$, etc.

(2) Assume from the contrary that there such an automaton exist. We denote the number of its counters by k and the number of states by S.

Let n be a sufficiently large positive integer. We consider a finite set S_0 of words in W. For all these words the parameter b equals 2k+1 but $i_1,i_2,\ldots,i_b$ take all possible values from the set $\{1,2,3,\ldots,n\}$. Then card $(S_0)=n^{2k+1}$. The length of the words in S_0 does not exceed c_k n, where c_k depends on k but not on n.

Configuration of a k-counter automaton at a definite moment is a (k+1)-tuple $(\sigma,p_1,\ldots,p_k)$ where σ is the state of the automaton, and p_i is the content of the i-th counter. Note that in t steps the content of a counter can enlarge at most for t units. Hence, a real-time automaton can have no more than $S\ (c_k\ n)^k$ different configurations on words in the set S_0.

For arbitrary $x\in S_0$ we fix an admisible sequence of instructions performed by the automaton on x such that the automaton accepts x. (This fixation makes sense only if the automaton is nondeterministic. If it is deterministic then only one such a sequence is possible). For arbitrary $x\in S_0$ we consider the configuration of the automaton on x, provided the fixed sequence of performed instructions, at the moment when the head reads the third symbol 7 of the word (this is the center of the word).

Now we make precise the requirement for n. It should be large enough to ensure $n^{2k+1} > S\ (c_k\ n)^k$. Then S_0 contains at least two different words x and y for which the abovementioned configurations coincide. We construct a new word z from the given x and y, taking the head of the word x (up to the third symbol 7) and the tail of the word y (from the third symbol 7). The word z is not in W but the automaton accepts it along with y. Contradiction.

Modifying the language W, it is possible to strengthen the assertion (1) in Theorem 4.1 replacing the probabilistic 3-counter automaton by a 2-counter one, keeping (2) untouched at the same time. We present here only the essence of the improvement.

For the new language the blocks A(b), B(m,k), C(m,k), D(n,i) are defined precisely as for W.

$$E_b(i,k) : C(1,k)5D(1^k,i)5C(2,k)4D(2^k,i)4\ldots$$
$$\ldots 4C(2^b-1,k)4D((2^b-1)^k,i)5C(2^b,k)5D((2^b)^k,i);$$

$$F_b(i,k) : C(2^b,k)5D((2^b)^k,i)5C(2^b-1,k)4D((2^b-1)^k,i)4\ldots$$
$$\ldots 4C(2,k)4D(2^k,i)5C(1,k)5D(1^k,i);$$

$$code_b(i_1,i_2,\ldots,i_{2b},j_{2b},\ldots,j_2,j_1) : A(b)7E_b(i_1,1)6F_b(i_2,2)6$$
$$E_b(i_3,3)6F_b(i_4,4)6\ldots 6E_b(i_{2b-1},2b-1)7F_b(i_{2b},2b)7$$
$$E_b(j_{2b},2b)6F_b(j_{2b-1},2b-1)6\ldots 6E_b(j_4,4)6F_6(j_3,3)6$$
$$E_b(j_2,2)7F_b(j_1,1).$$

$$V=\{x \ / \ x\in\{0,1,2,3,4,5,6,7\}^* \ \& \ (\exists b>2,i_1,i_2,\ldots,i_{2b})$$
$$(x=code_b(i_1,i_2,\ldots,i_{2b},i_{2b},\ldots,i_2,i_1))\}.$$

THEOREM 4.2. (1) For arbitrary $\varepsilon>0$ there is a probabilistic 1-way 2-counter automaton which recognizes the language V in real time accepting every word in V with probability 1 and rejecting every word in $\overline{V}$ with probability $1-\varepsilon$. (2) No deterministic 1-way multi-counter automaton can recognize V in real time.

5. OTHER APPLICATIONS OF LEMMA 2.1.

Lemma 2.1 is a useful tool that allows us to use multiple random choices provided they are statistically independent. Some more profound results on probabilistic algorithms are proved as well which are a bit outside our topic. We note here two results of this kind.

Undecidability of the emptiness problem for languages recognizable by probabilistic 2-head 1-way finite automata was proved by the author in 1980 (English version see in [Fre 83]).

INPUT: an infinite sequence of probabilistic 2-tape 1-way finite automata all of which recognize the same language L; the automata accept every pair of words in L with probability 1 and reject every pair in $\overline{L}$ with probabilistic 2/3, 3/4, 4/5,..., respectively.

PROPERTY: L is empty.

It is known that a projection of a language recognized by a deterministic multihead 1-way finite automaton to one of its tapes is a regular language. A similar result holds also for nondeterministic automata but not for probabilistic ones. In the latter case the projection, of course, is a recursively enumerable language as a projection of a recursive language. It turns out that one can say no more.

THEOREM 5.1. Given arbitrary recursively enumerable language L of strings in a finite alphabet, there is a language K of triples of words such that: 1) L is the projection of K to the first tape, 2) given arbitrary $\varepsilon>0$, there is a probabilistic 3-tape 1-way finite automaton which accepts every triple of words in K with probability 1 and rejects every triple of strings in $\overline{K}$ with probability $1-\varepsilon$.

Only for recursive languages L it may be possible to replace the language K of triples of words by a language K′ of pairs of words.

6. PROBABILISTIC RECOGNITION OF PALINDROMES

The methods considered above could prove advantages of probabilistic machines over their deterministic counterparts only for 1-way machines. Now we consider a new method. Suppose, it is needed to compare two objects (strings, matrices, polynomials) whether or not they are identical. Instead of full scale comparison we propose to consider a large set of simple functions defined on these objects, to pick one function at random and compute its value on the two given objects. If the objects are really identical then the obtained values coincide. The set of functions should be chosen to ensure that for every pair of nonidentical objects most of these functions expose their distinctness.

The author proved his first theorem by this method in 1975. It was known [Bar 65] that palindromes cannot be recognized by deterministic 1-head off-line Turing machines in less time than const n^2. It turned out [Fre 75] that probabilistic machines can have less running time (see Theorem 6.1 below). This theorem and the proof have been published in several modifications (see also [Fre 77], [Fre 83]). For the sake of brevity, we include only a brief sketch of proof here. On the other hand, the first lower bound for probabilistic Turing machines ([Fre 75], {Fre I 79]) seems never having been published in English. Hence it is included here in full detail (Theorem 6.2 below).

THEOREM 6.1. For arbitrary $\varepsilon>0$, there is a probabilistic 1-head off-line Turing machine recognizing palindromes with probability $1-\varepsilon$ in const n log n time.

SKETCH OF PROOF. The input word x itself and its reversion are interpreted as binary notations of numbers $\bar{x},\bar{y}$. They are compared modulo a small random prime number. For this, a random string $m\in\{0,1\}^d$, $d=\lceil\log_2 c\ |x|\rceil$ where c is an absolute constant obtained from theory-of-numbers considerations. If the string turns out to represent a prime number $\bar{m}$, it is tested whether $\bar{x}\equiv\bar{y}$ (mod $\bar{m}$) holds. The result of this test is the output of the probabilistic machine. If $\bar{m}$ is not a prime number, a new string m is generated, and so on. The proof of the estimate of the running time and the probability of the correct result involve Çebiáev theorem on density of prime numbers.

THEOREM 6.2. Let $\varepsilon<1/2$ and a probabilistic 1-head off-line Turing machine recognize palindromes in $\{0,1\}^*$ with probability $1-\varepsilon$ in time $t(x)$. Then there is a $c>0$ such that $t(x)>c.|x|.\log_2|x|$ for infinitely many words x.

PROOF. Let the machine $\mathfrak{M}'$ recognize palindromes. We can assume that $\mathfrak{M}'$ always starts on the leftmost symbol of the input word.

We modify $\mathfrak{M}'$ to get an additional property. The new machine $\mathfrak{M}$ at first marks the leftmost and the rightmost nonempty symbols of the input word. Then $\mathfrak{M}$ simulates the work of $\mathfrak{M}'$ keeping precise records of where the most extreme ever visited squares of the tape are. When the simulation ends because $\mathfrak{M}'$ has produced the result, the new machine ends its work by walking through all the used part of the tape in a special state $q_{(0)}$ or $q_{(1)}$, respectively. This way, the running time has increased at most by $O(|x|)$ but the machine has acquired a new important property: every nonempty crossing sequence allows to reconstruct the result. It suffices to prove the Theorem for the machine $\mathfrak{M}$ only.

We call a palindrome special if its length equals 0 modulo 3, and the central third part consists of zeros only. The set of squares on the tape corresponding to this central third part is called the central zone.

Let n be on arbitrary integer. We consider the work of $\mathfrak{M}$ on the special palindromes of length 3n. The set of all these special palindromes is denoted by S_n.

Let $\mathfrak{M}$ recognize palindromes with probability 1-ε in time t(x). We define the function σ(n) such that

$$n\,(\sigma(n)-1) < \max_{|x|=3n} t(x) < n\,\sigma(n),$$

where the maximum is taken over all the special palindromes of length 3n. To prove the Theorem, it suffices to show that $\sigma(n) > O(\log_2 n)$.

We consider admissible sequences of instructions corresponding to the given machine $\mathfrak{M}$ and the given input word x. All possible admissible sequences of instructions of $\mathfrak{M}$ on $x \in S_n$ can be divided into two subsets:

a) "good", i.e. producing the result 1 in no more than n σ(n) steps,

b) "bad", i.e. all the other possible sequences.

Note that there can be only finitely many "good" sequences, while infinitely many "bad" ones are possible.

Knowing the program of the machine and the probabilities of the random number generator (which is equiprobable and Bernoulli type), it is casy to compute the probability of each admissible sequence of instructions. The total probability of the "good" sequences for every $x \in S_n$ exceeds 1-ε.

Consider

$$\sum_{\substack{\rho \text{ being} \\ \text{"good"} \\ \text{sequence}}} p_\rho \sum_{t=1}^{n\,\sigma(n)} \sum_{\substack{i \in \text{central} \\ \text{zone}}} X(\rho,i,t) \tag{6.2.1}$$

where p_ρ is the probability of the sequence ρ of instructions of $\mathfrak{M}$ on the given $x \in S_n$, and

$$X(\rho,i,t) = \begin{cases} 1, & \text{if, when performing the t-th instruction in the sequence } \rho\text{, the head crosses the point } i; \\ 0, & \text{if otherwise.} \end{cases}$$

On the one hand, the innermost sum does not exceed 1, and hence the total (6.2.1) does not exceed $n\,\sigma(n)$. On the other hand, all sums in (6.2.1) are finite. Hence

$$\sum_{i \in \text{central zone}} \left(\sum_{\rho \text{ being "good" sequence}} p_\rho \sum_{t=1}^{n\,\sigma(n)} X(\rho,i,t) \right) < n\,\sigma(n)$$

and for arbitrary $x \in S_n$ it is possible to fix a point $i_o(x)$ in the central zone such that

$$\sum_{\rho \text{ being "good" sequence}} p_\rho \sum_{t=1}^{n\,\sigma(n)} X\left(\rho, i_o(x), t\right) < \sigma(n).$$

We will refer this $i_o(x)$ as the checkpoint of x.

The formula above contains the internal sum

$$\sum_{t=1}^{n\,\sigma(n)} X\left(\rho, i_o(x), t\right)$$

expressing the number of times when the head crosses $i_o(x)$ at the sequence of instructions ρ . All the members in the sum are nonnegative. Hence for arbitrary $\delta>0$ it is true that the probability, for the given $\mathfrak{M}$ and x, of the event when simultaneously 1) the sequence ρ is "good", and 2) the length of the crossing sequence in the checkpoint exceeds $1/\delta\ \sigma(n)$, does not exceed δ.

Hence, for arbitrary $\delta>0$ it is true that the probability of the event, for the given $\mathfrak{M}$ and x, when simultaneously 1) the result is correct, and 2) the length of the crossing sequence in the checkpoint does not exceed $1/\delta\ \sigma(n)$, is no less than $1-\varepsilon-\delta$. In particular, the abovementioned is true for $\delta=1-2\varepsilon/4$.

To define the notions "the leftside probability of the crossing sequence", "the rightside probability of the crossing sequence", we consider the following procedure γ for the given $x \in S_n$, checkpoint $i_o(x)$ and crossing sequence $\tau=+q(1)\ q(2)\ \ldots\ q(2r-1)$ where $q(2r-1)=q_{(1)}$.

The procedure starts with simulation of the work of $\mathfrak{M}$ on x. The simulation continues uninterrupted until the head crosses the checkpoint. If at the given sequence of instructions $\mathfrak{M}$ comes to the checkpoint in the state q(1) then the simulation is temporarily interrupted, the state replaced by q(2), the head returned through the checkpoint into the square of the tape bordering the checkpoint on the left side, and then the simulation is continued. If $\mathfrak{M}$ comes to the checkpoint for the first time in a state different from q(1) then the procedure stops without result.

If the head comes to the checkpoint (from the left) for the second time in the state q(3) then the head is returned automatically in the state q(4) (if the head comes to the checkpoint in a state different from q(3) then the procedure stops without result), etc.

If this way the procedure reaches a moment when the head is going to cross the checkpoint from the left to the right for the r-th time in the state q(2r-1) then the procedure comes to an accepting end.

The probability of the abovedescribed procedure with the given $\mathfrak{M}$, x, $i_o(x)$ and τ is called the leftside probability of the crossing sequence τ in $i_o(x)$ for $\mathfrak{M}$ and x.

The rightside probability is defined in a similar way (only the simulation is performed on the part of the tape to the right from the checkpoint).

It is easy to see that the leftside and rightside probabilities are nonnegative numbers not exceeding 1 and their product equals the probability of the event "given $\mathfrak{M}$, x, $i_o(x)$, the crossing sequence of $\mathfrak{M}$ and x at $i_o(x)$ equals τ". (Note that we use here the assumption $q(2r-1)=q_{(1)}$, in the general case the product expresses the event "the crossing sequence has an initial fragment τ").

Let x′ and x" be two different words from S_n. Let x′′′ be a word consisting of the head (up to the checkpoint $i_o(x')$) of the word x′ and the tail (after the checkpoint $i_o(x")0$ of the word x". The word x''' may be of length different from 3n but, any case, x''' is not a palindrome.

We denote by $\tau_1,\tau_2,\tau_3,\ldots$ all possible crossing sequences allowing acception of the input word. We assume that the crossing sequences are ordered in increasing length.

We denote by $\xi_1', \xi_2', \xi_3',\ldots$ the leftside probabilities of the crossing sequences $\tau_1,\tau_2,\tau_3,\ldots$ for x' in $i_o(x')$. We denote by $\eta_1', \eta_2', \eta_3',\ldots$ the rightside probabilisties of the crossing sequences $\tau_1,\tau_2,\tau_3,\ldots$ for x' in $i_o(x')$. We denote by $\xi_1'', \xi_2'', \xi_3''$, ... the leftside probabilities of $\tau_1,\tau_2,\tau_3,\ldots$ for x" in $i_o(x")$.

We denote by s the index of the crossing sequence τ_s such that all the crossing sequences $\tau_1,\tau_2,\ldots,\tau_s$ and only these crossing sequences have the properties: 1) they lead to the acception of the input word, and 2) their length does not exceed $4/1-2\varepsilon\ \sigma(n)$. It is easy to see that

$$s < 2^{O(\sigma(n))} ,$$

$$\xi_1'\eta_1' + \xi_2'\eta_2' + \ldots > 1-\varepsilon ,$$

$$\xi_1'\eta_1' + \xi_2'\eta_2' + \ldots + \xi_s'\eta_s' > 1-\varepsilon - 1-2\varepsilon/4 = 3-2\varepsilon/4 \qquad (6.2.2)$$

The probabilities of the crossing sequences in $i_o(x')$ for $\mathfrak{M}$ and x''' being $\tau_1,\tau_2,\tau_3,\ldots$, respectively, are $\xi_1''\eta_1'$, $\xi_2''\eta_2'$, $\xi_3''\eta_3',\ldots$ The input word x''' is not a palindrome. Hence

$$\xi_1''\eta_1' + \xi_2''\eta_2' + \ldots + \xi_s''\eta_s' + \ldots < \varepsilon .$$

All the terms in the left part of the inequality are nonnegative. Hence

$$\xi_1''\eta_1' + \xi_2''\eta_2' + \ldots + \xi_s''\eta_s' < \varepsilon$$

Subtracting this from (6.2.2) we get

$$(\xi_1' - \xi_1'')\eta_1' + (\xi_2' - \xi_2'')\eta_2' + \ldots + (\xi_s' - \xi_s'')\eta_s' > 3-6\varepsilon/4$$

Hence

$$\xi_1' - \xi_1'' + \xi_2' - \xi_2'' + \ldots + \xi_s' - \xi_s'' > 3-6\varepsilon/4 \qquad (6.2.3)$$

The S-tuple

$$\vec{\xi}(x) = (\xi_1, \xi_2, \ldots, \xi_s)$$

of the leftside probabilities of the crossing sequences $\tau_1, \tau_2, \ldots, \tau_3$ of x in its checkpoint can be understood as a point in an s-dimensional unit cube. The inequality (6.2.3) shows that the points corresponding to distinct special palindromes from S_n should be distant in the metrics

$$\rho(\vec{\xi}(x'), \vec{\xi}(x'')) = \xi_1' - \xi_1'' + \xi_2' - \xi_2'' + \ldots + \xi_s' - \xi_s'' .$$

Around arbitrary point $(\xi_1^o, \xi_2^o, \ldots, \xi_s^o)$ corresponding a special palindrome from S_n we circumscribe a body

$$\xi_1 - \xi_1^o + \xi_2 - \xi_2^o + \ldots + \xi_s - \xi_s^o < 1\text{-}2\varepsilon/4 .$$

It follows from (6.2.3) that these bodies do not intersect. The volume of every such body equals

$$\frac{\left(\frac{1-2\varepsilon}{4}\right)^S}{S!} \, 2^S$$

All they are situated in an S-dimensional cube with the side length

$$1 + 2\,\frac{1-2\varepsilon}{4} = \frac{3-2\varepsilon}{2}$$

Hence, the number of the distinct special palindromes in S_n does not exceed

$$\frac{\left(\frac{3-2\varepsilon}{2}\right)^S (S!)}{\left(\frac{1-2\varepsilon}{4}\right)^S \, 2^S} = 2^{O(s \log_2 s)}$$

Hence

$$2^n < 2^{O(s \log_2 s)}$$

$$S > O\left(\frac{n}{\log_2 n}\right)$$

On the other hand,

$$S < 2^{O(\sigma(n))}$$

Hence

$$O\left(\frac{n}{\log_2 n}\right) < 2^{O(\sigma(n))}$$

and

$$\sigma(n) > O(\log_2 n) .$$

7. BOOLEAN CIRCUITS WITH MEMORY

M.O.Rabin [Rab 63] considered language recognition by probabilistic finite automata and found an essential property of such recognition which influences the practical meaningfulness of this process. This property is cut-point's being isolated.

The most natural way to define what does it mean when a probabilistic automaton $\mathfrak{A}$ recognizes a language L with cut-point λ, is as follows. The automaton $\mathfrak{A}$ accepts arbitrary input word x with the probability p(x). We say that $\mathfrak{A}$ accepts x, if $p(x)>\lambda$ (a version of the definition: if $p(x)>\lambda$), and $\mathfrak{A}$ rejects x, if otherwise.

For practical purposes such a "recognition" is somewhat dubious because it may be hard to distinguish by a statistical experiment between x′ and x" such that $p(x')=\lambda+\delta'$ and $p(x")=\lambda-\delta"$ where δ' and $\delta"$ are very small. We have a different case when for the given automaton there is a positive constant δ_o (called isolation radius) such that for all x, either $p(x)>\lambda+\delta_o$ or $p(x)<\lambda-\delta_o$. Then it is easy to calculate how many times the experiment should be repeated to get the result with the needed probability.

M.O.Rabin [Rab 63] proved that languages recognized with isolated cut-point by probabilistic finite automata are recognized by deterministic finite automata as well. On the other hand, the complexity of the deterministic automaton can be higher.

More precisely, M.O.Rabin proved that a deterministic finite 1-way automaton needs no more than $(1+r/\delta)^{m-1}$ states to recognize a language recognized by a probabilistic finite 1-way automaton with m-states and isolation radius δ. As another result in [Rab 63], a probabilistic automaton with 2 states and cut-points $\{\lambda_t\}$ was constructed such that the corresponding deterministic finite automaton needs no less than t states.

This way, it was shown that complexity of a probabilistic finite automaton cannot be characterized merely by the number of states. At least the isolation radius is to be taken into consideration.

We return once more to the last mentioned theorem by Rabin. A sequence $L=\{L_t\}$ of languages was constructed such that the corresponding deterministic automata are to have no less than

$D_L(t)=t$ states. Unfortunately, the first mentioned theorem by Rabin gives us an exagerated estimate $R_L(t)=(1+r/\delta)^{m-1}=3^t$.

It was an open problem: either to lower $R_L(t)$ or to construct a better sequence of languages for which

$$R_L(t) = O\left(3^{D_L(t)}\right)$$

The estimate $R_L(t)$ was somewhat lowered in [Paz 66] and [GM 78]. Unfortunately, these improvements did not influence even the exponent 3 in $3^{D_L(t)}$. For the first time $3^{D_L(t)}$ was replaced by a function growing less rapidly in [Fre 82]. Namely, it was replaced by a function growing less rapidly than any exponent but growing more rapidly than any polynomial.

This Section contains further improvements of the abovementioned theorem. A.A.Lorenc [Lor 86] in his invited talk at the USSR National Symposium on probabilistic automata, Kazan, 1983 turned everybodies attention to the fact that in all the results of the considered type either very small isolation radia are used or very complicated probabilities of transition among the states of the automaton are used. Any case, if the probabilistic finite automata are represented by Boolean circuits with 2-argument Boolean gates, 1-bit memory elements and the simplest random number generators producing zeros and ones equiprobably by Bernoulli scheme, i.e. independently, then the probabilistic circuit is no less complicate than the deterministic one.

A.A.Lorenc proposed to construct a sequence of languages $B=\{B_t\}$ such that in the probabilistic Boolean circuit with memory: 1) the cut-point is 1/2, 2) the isolation radius does not depend on t and is reasonably large (for instance, 1/4), 3) the complexity of the probabilistic circuit turns out to be essentially smaller than the complexity of every deterministic Boolean circuit with memory representing the same language. In fact, a more realistic complexity measure for probabilistic finite automata is considered.

In our results in this Section the Boolean circuit with memory has one input and one output. The input and output alphabets are {0,1}. At the first step the first input symbol is read, at the second step the second input symbol is read, etc. At any step the automaton claims to output the result of whether or not the input word read up to this moment in the language represented by the automaton.

We will compare complexity of circuits over basis $\mathfrak{A}$ versus basis $\mathfrak{B}$. Basis $\mathfrak{A}$ consists of the 2-argument conjunction, the 2-argument disjunction, the 1-argument negation (these elements have no delay in time), and 1-argument memory element which outputs at any moment the value of its input read at the previous moment. Basis $\mathfrak{B}$ contains all the mentioned elements, and it contains additionally a special 0-argument element the output of which equals 1 with probability 1/2, and 0 with probability with 1/2, and outputs at any moment are statistically independent of the outputs at other moments. Hence, circuits over $\mathfrak{A}$ are deterministic and circuits over $\mathfrak{B}$ are probabilistic.

We say that the circuit recognizes the language L with isolated cut-point λ and isolation radius δ if the circuit accepts every $x \in L$ with probability no less than $\lambda+\delta$, and the circuit accepts every $x \notin L$ with probability not exceeding $\lambda-\delta$.

We consider the sequence of languages $D=\{D_t\}$. The language D_t consists of one word only, namely, $0^{2^t}1$.

ASSERTION 7.1. Arbitrary (deterministic) Boolean circuit with memory over basis $\mathfrak{A}$, which recognizes the language D_t has at least t+1 elements of memory.

PROOF. Immediate.

THEOREM 7.2. For arbitrary t there is a (probabilistic) Boolean circuit with memory over basis $\mathfrak{B}$ which recognizes the language D_t with the cut-point 1/2, and isolation radius 1/4. The circuit has 1 simplest random element, O(log t) memory elements and O(t/log t) Boolean elements.

PROOF. Following the traditional notation in number theory textbooks (e.g. [Bu 60]) we denote the increasing sequence of all prime numbers by $p_1, p_2, p_3, \ldots$ $(p_1=2,\ p_2=3,\ p_3=5, \ldots)$ Çebiáev function $\Phi(x)$ is the sum of natural logarithms of all prime numbers not exceeding x. $\Phi(x) = \sum_{p<x} \ln p$.

We introduce auxiliary function F(t) equal to $p_1\, p_2\, p_3 \cdots p_t = e^{\Phi(p_t)}$. Note that if a positive integer x does not exceed F(t) then x has no more than t distinct prime divisors. The function

$\Pi(x)$ denotes the number of distinct primes not exceeding x.

P.L.Çebiáev [Çeb 44] proved that there are positive numbers a,b,c,d such that:

$$ax < \quad (x) < bx \; ,$$

$$c \frac{x}{\ln x} < \Pi(x) < d \frac{x}{\ln x} \; ,$$

$$\frac{1}{d}\, t \ln t < p_t < \frac{2}{c}\, t \ln t \; .$$

Hence F(t) has the order of magnitude

$$(\mathrm{const})^{t \ln t}$$

It is well-known that

$$\lim_{k\to+\infty} \left(1 - \frac{1}{k}\right)^{k} = \frac{1}{e} \; .$$

Let f and g be large positive integers such that

$$\lim_{k\to\infty} \left(1 - \frac{1}{k}\right)^{fk} < \frac{1}{64} \quad , \quad \lim_{k\to\infty} \left(1 - \frac{1}{k}\right)^{k/g} > \frac{7}{8} \; .$$

Hence there is a k_o such that for arbitrary $k>k_o$

$$\left(1 - \frac{1}{k}\right)^{fk} < \frac{1}{64} \qquad (7.2.1)$$

$$\left(1 - \frac{1}{k}\right)^{k/g} > \frac{7}{8} \qquad (7.2.2)$$

Let l be a large positive integer such that $F(l)>2^t$. Surely, $F(l)<2^{t+1}$. Hence

$$t = O(l \log l)$$

By r we denote the number $\lceil \log_2 p_{4l+5} \rceil$, and by S we denote $2^{r+1} - 1$. It follows from Çebiáev theorems that p_{4l+5} and S have the order of magnitude t, and $r = \log_2 t + O(1)$.

By u we denote the nearest complete power of 2 exceeding 2t. Surely, $u < 4t$.

Let w be a positive solution of the equation

$$g\,(2^t - u)\,/\,w = 2^w$$

and $v = \lceil w \rceil$. Then

$$(2^t-u)/v < (2^t-u)/w = 2^w/g < 2^v/g \qquad (7.2.3)$$

Hence $w = t - o(t)$ and for large t

$$\frac{2^t-u}{w} < \frac{3}{2}\left(\frac{2^t-u}{v}\right).$$

Since $v < w+1$, we have $2^v < 2^{w+1}$. Hence for large t

$$\frac{2^v}{g} < 3\,\frac{2^t-u}{v} \qquad (7.2.4)\ .$$

It follows from (7.2.2) that

$$\left(1-\frac{1}{2^v}\right)^{2^v/g} > \frac{7}{8}\,.$$

Taking into account (7.2.3), we have

$$\left(1-\frac{1}{2^v}\right)^{\frac{2^t-u}{v}} > \frac{7}{8} \qquad (7.2.5)$$

It follows from (7.2.1) that

$$\left(1-\frac{1}{2^v}\right)^{f2^v} < \frac{1}{64}\,.$$

Taking into account (7.2.4), we have for large t

$$\left(1-\frac{1}{2^v}\right)^{fg3(2^t-u)/v} < \left(1-\frac{1}{2^v}\right)^{fg\,2^v/g} < \frac{1}{64}\,,$$

$$\left(1-\frac{1}{2^v}\right)^{fg(2^t-u)/v} < \frac{1}{4} \qquad (7.2.6)$$

The formulation of the assertion in our Theorem is only asymptotic. Hence it suffices to prove it only for large t. We prove the Theorem for large t such that: 1) $\frac{f}{c}\, r \ln s < t-1$; 2) $F(l+1) > fgF(l)$; 3) $\ln s > c\, k_o$; 4) $u < 2^t$; 5) (7.2.6) holds.

The circuit in demand consists of 6 blocks.

The block 1 is a counter up to the number u. One memory element is fixed in this block. This element is supposed to have as its output for the first u moments the value 0 and after that the value 1. The block ends its work after producing the first 1. Such a block can be constructed using no more than $\lceil \log_2 u \rceil = \log_2 t + O(1)$ memory elements and $O(\log t)$ Boolean instantaneous elements.

The blocks 2 and 3 work in parallel with 1 but completely independent from 1 . First 2 starts, and after 2 has ended, 3 starts.

The block 2 is designed to choose a random prime number $m<s$. The block has $r+1$ memory elements. One of these elements is used to signal the end of the work of the block 2 . All the remaining r memory elements are used to memorize outputs of the only random elements during r moments in row. After that a Boolean circuit consisting of $\frac{2^r}{r} + O\left(\frac{2^r}{r}\right)$ instanteous elements tests whether or not the obtained r-digit number is prime. The abovementioned number of elements in the circuit suffices for arbitrary Boolean function. (It follows from a theorem by O.B.Lupanov [Lup 63]). If <u>prime</u> then the block 2 ends and produces 1 in the special memory element. If <u>not prime</u> then a new r-digit random number is generated in r steps, the primality tested, etc. We remind that $r=\log t+O(1)$, $2^r/r=O(t/\log t)$.

The block 3 starts only after the block 2 has ended. It is designed to find the residue modulo m (produced by the block 2) of 2^t-u. More precisely, the residues of 2^t and of u are found seperately and then their difference is found. To compute these residues, first the residues of $2^1,2^2,2^3,2^4,\ldots$ modulo m are computed. For this the block has 4 sets of memory elements: two sets each consisting of r elements are used to record the residues ($r=\log_2 t+O(1)$), one set of $\lceil \log_2 t \rceil$ elements is to record first t, then $t-1$, $t-2,\ldots$, and one set of $\log_2 u$ elements is to record u, $u/2$, $u/4,\ldots$ In total, the block 3 has $O(\log t)$ memory elements and $O(\log t)$ instanteous Boolean elements.

The block 4 starts immediately after the block 1 has ended. This block does not check whether the blocks 2 and 3 have ended but the parameters of the circuit are chosen such that with high probability blocks 2 and 3 end before the block 1. The block 4 is designed to compute the residue modulo m of the number of zeros read from the input during the work of this block, provided that no other symbols have been read from the input. The block 4 ends when the first symbol 1 is read from the input. The block has $r=\log_2 t+O(1)$ memory elements. These elements store an r-digit binary number expressing the residue modulo m of the number of zeros read from the input up to the moment. Whenever this number reaches m, i.e. it equals m recorded by memory elements in the block **2** , the residue is automatically returned to 0.

The block **5** also starts immediately after the block **1** has ended. This block is designed to enable the circuit at special moments (namely, at moments equal 0 modulo v) to enter with small probability 2^{-v} a special rejecting state in which the circuit remains forever and rejects all the continuations of the considered input word. For this purpose, the block **5** has $2+\lceil\log_2 v\rceil<\log_2 t+O(1)$ memory elements. One memory element serves to signal of transition to the special rejecting state. $\lceil\log_2 v\rceil$ elements make a counter modulo v. At every moment the block considers the symbol received from the random element of the circuit. If during one cycle between two adjacent moments of empty counter all the outputs of the random element equal 0 (to check this, one more memory element is needed) then the circuit enters the special rejecting state. If not, the normal work of the circuit continues.

The block **6** works after the first symbol 1 has been read from the input. If the block **5** has produced the signal of the special rejecting state then the circuit rejects all the continuations of the word. If at the moment when the first 1 is read from the input the block **1** has ended its work and the residue of the number of zeros read from the input during the work of **4** coincides with the result of the block **3** then the input word is accepted and the circuit is prepared to reject any continuation of this word. If the results of **3** and **4** differ then the circuit rejects the input word. The block **6** does not contain new memory elements and it has O(log t) instanteous Boolean elements.

We have followed the number of elements in the circuit. Now we will prove the correctness.

The block **3** works no more than t+1 steps. Now we estimate the probability of the event "the block **2** completes its work in no more than t-1 steps". The work of this block consists of cycles the length of which equals r. Cycle is resultative if a prime number m is generated. Out of all s possible and equiprobable numbers the number of primes is $\Pi(s)$. Hence the probability to generate a prime number is $\Pi(s)/s$. By Çebiáev's theorem, $\Pi(s)>c\ s/\ln s$. The probability to have generated, only compound numbers in the first $(f \ln s)/c$ cycles equals

$$\left(1 - \frac{\Pi(s)}{s}\right)^{\frac{f \ln s}{c}} < \left(1 - \frac{c}{\ln s}\right)^{\frac{f \ln s}{c}}$$

which, due to (7.2.1), does not exceed 1/64. Since we prove the Theorem only for large n such that $\frac{f}{c}$ r ln s < t-1, we may predect that with probability 63/64 the block **2** will work no more than t-1 steps, and the blocks **2** and **3** in total no more than 2^t steps, and, hence, the block **1** will end first.

If the input word $0^n1 \in D_t$, i.e. if $n=2^t$ then the word will be accepted, provided two conditions: 1) the blocks **2** and **3** end the work before the block **1** (the probability of this event is no less that 63/64), and 2) the block **5** does not enter the special rejecting state. To calculate the probability of 2), we note that the work of the block **5** consists of $2^t/v$ cycles and the probability of entering the special state equals 2^{-v}. The probability to avoid this state equals

$$\left(1 - \frac{1}{2^v}\right)^{2^t/v}$$

which, by (7.2.5), exceeds 7/8. Hence, the input word is accepted with probability

$$\frac{63}{64}\ \frac{7}{8} > \frac{3}{4}$$

Let $n \neq 2^t$ and $n > f\ g\ 2^t$. It follows from (7.2.6) that the block **5** enters the special rejecting state with probability exceeding 3/4.

Let $n \neq 2^t$ and $n < f\ g\ 2^t$. Then $n < f\ g\ F(l)$ and $n < G(l+1)$. We only increase the estimate for the probability of error if we pay no attention to the possibility for the block **5** to enter the special rejecting state and if we pay no attention to the possibility that the block **1** end the work before the blocks **2** and **3** . We will show that no less than 3/4 of all possible values of m are such that $n \not\equiv 2^t \pmod{m}$ and $n-u \not\equiv 2^t-u \pmod{m}$. Indeed, the congruence $n \equiv 2^t \pmod{m}$ holds only if m divide $|n-2^t|$. The number $|n-2^t|$ does not exceed F(l+1), and, hence, it has no more than l+1 distinct prime divisors. The number m is chosen equiprobably among $p_1, p_2, p_3, \ldots, p_{4l+5}$. Hence, no more than 3/4 choices for m will show that $0^n1 \notin D^t$.

THEOREM 7.3. For arbitrary t there is a (probabilistic) Boolean circuit with memory over basis $\mathfrak{B}$ which recognizes the language D_t with the cut-point 1/2, and isolation radius 1/4. The circuit has 1 simplest random element, $O((\log t)^2)$ memory elements and $O((\log t)^2)$ Boolean elements.

PROOF. Like the circuit in the proof of Theorem 7.2, this circuit consists of 6 blocks. The purpose of the blocks is the same. What the circuits differ in is the following. The circuit in Theorem 7.2 produced one prime modulo m and compared the number of zeros with the standard modulo this m but the new circuit does not test primality. It takes a bundle of random modulos and compares the number of zeros with the standard modulo all these m. The bundle is taken large enough (namely, $\lceil (f \ln s)/c \rceil = O(\log t)$ random modulos) to ensure at least one prime modulo in this bundle with high probability.

The blocks **1** and **5** completely equal their counterparts in the proof of Theorem 7.2.

The block **2** in $r \lceil (f \ln s)/c \rceil$ steps generate $\lceil (f \ln s)/c \rceil$ random r-digit numbers m.

The blocks **3** and **4** consist of $\lceil (f \ln s)/c \rceil$ copies of the corresponding block in the proof of Theorem 7.2, one per a value of m.

The block **6** perform the same functions as its counterpart in the proof of Theorem 7.2.

Theorems 7.2 and 7.3 try to minimize distinct complexity measures for Boolean circuits with memory. In Theorem 7.3 the total number of elements is much less than in Theorem 7.2 but in Theorem 7.2 the number of memory elements is smaller than in Theorem 7.3. The trade-off between these two complexity measures in this context is still an open problem.

8. SPACE COMPLEXITY OF 1-WAY TURING MACHINES

Finite automata are too much restricted to be a realistic model of computers. Unrestricted Turing machines and their generalizations are hard for proving lower bounds of complexity. A nice compromise is the notion of 1-way Turing machine. They are reasonably powerful, and, on the other hand, allow nontrivial lower bounds of complexity.

This survey, of course, cannot include all the results on advantages of probabilistic machines over their deterministic counterparts. Nevertheless, there was a recent advancement for space complexity of 1-way Turing machines. In [KF 90] an open problem was solved.

If a language L is recognized by a deterministic 1-way Turing machine in O(log n) space then L is regular [SHL 65]. In [Fre 83_1] it was shown that nonregular languages can be recognized with arbitrarily high probability by a loglog n - bounded 1-way Turing machines as well. (This theorem is repeated as our Theorem 8.2).

All the results in this Section on advantages of probabilistic machines are based on the following lemma. It shows that for any two nonequal natural numbers N′ and N", there are many reasonably small prime modulos m such that $N' \neq N''$ (mod m). Probabilistic algorithms in this Section are based on the possibility to take such a prime modulo m at random.

Let $P_1(l)$ be the number of primes not exceeding $2^{\lceil \log_2 l \rceil}$, $P_3(l,N',N'')$ be the number of primes not exceeding $2^{\lceil \log_2 l \rceil}$ and not dividing $|N'-N''|$, and $P_3(l,n)$ be the maximum of $P_2(l,N',N'')$ over all $N'<2^n$, $N''<2^n$, $N' \neq N''$.

LEMMA 8.1. ([3]) Given any ε>0, there is a natural number c such that

$$\lim_{n\to+\infty} \frac{P_3(cn,c)}{P_1(cn)} < \varepsilon .$$

PROOF. Let $p_1,p_2,\ldots,p_k$ be all the primes that divide $Z=|N'-N''|<2^n$. Since Z>k!, we have k<O(n/log n). By Çebiáev's theorem on the density of primes (see [Bu 60]), the first $\lceil k/\varepsilon \rceil$ primes do not exceed c n for a suitable constant c.

We define a language $S\subset\{0,1,2,3,4,5\}^*$. Let bin(i) denote a string representing i in the binary notation (the first symbol of bin(i) being 1).

We start to describe how the strings in S can be generated. An arbitrary integer k is taken and the following string is considered

bin(1) 2 bin(2) 2 bin(3) 2 ... 2 bin(2k).

Next, every symbol in the substrings bin(k+1), bin(k+2), ..., bin(2k) is preceded by one arbitrary symbol from {3,4}. If the obtained string in $\{0,1,2,3,4\}^*$ is denoted by x then the language S contains the string x5x. Every string in S is obtained by this procedure.

THEOREM 8.1. (1) Given any $\varepsilon>0$, there is a log n-space bounded probabilistic 1-way Turing machine which accepts every string in S with probability 1 and rejects every string in $\bar{S}$ with probability $1-\varepsilon$.

(2) Every deterministic 1-way Turing Machine recognizing S uses at least const. n space.

PROOF. (1) The head of string w is its initial fragment up to the symbol 5. The tail of w is the rest of the string.

The probabilistic machine performs the following 11 actions to recognize whether or not the given string w is in S:

1) it checks whether the projection of the head of w to the subalphabet {0,1,2} is a string of the form

bin(1) 2 bin(2) 2 ... 2 bin($2k_1$)

for an integer k_1;

2) it checks whether the projection of the tail of w to the subalphabet {0,1,2} is a string of the form

bin(1) 2 bin(2) 2 ... 2 bin($2k_2$)

for an integer k_2;

3) it checks whether $k_1=k_2$;

4) it counts the number k_3 of the substrings bin(1), bin(2), ..., bin(k_3) in the head of w where no symbol from {3,4} are inserted;

5) it checks whether $k_1=k_3$;

6) it counts the number k_4 of the substrings bin(1), bin(2), ..., bin(k_4) in the tail of w where no symbols from {3,4} are inserted;

7) it checks whether $k_2=k_4$;

8) using generator of random numbers it generates a string in $\{0,1\}^{cl}$ where c is the constant from Lemma 8.1, and l is the lenght of bin($2k_3$). The generated string m ($1<m<2^{cl}$) is tested for primality. If m is not prime, a new string bin(m) is generated, tested for primality, and so on;

9) it regards the projection y of the head of w to the subalphabet {3,4} as binary notation of a number N_1 ($0<n_1<2^{|y_1|}-1$) and calculates the remainder m_1 obtained by dividing N_1 to m;

10) it regards the projection y of the tail of w to the subalphabet {3,4} as binary notation of a number N_2 ($0<N_2<2^{|y_2|}-1$) and calculates the remainder m_2 obtained by dividing N_2 to m;

11) it checks whether $m_1=m_2$.

The string w is accepted if all the checks result positively. Otherwise w is rejected.

The actions 1)-11) can be performed in log w space. Lemma 8.1 implies the correctness of the result with the needed probability.

(2) If $w\in S$ then its projection to the subalphabet {3,4,5} is of the form y5y, where $y\in\{3,4\}^*$ and $|y|>\lfloor\frac{w}{6}\rfloor - 2\log_2|w|$. Hence a linear space bound linear in |w| for deterministic one-way Turing machines is evident.

The language S is similar to S but it is defined in a more complicate way.

Let the strings $x=x_1x_2\ldots x_u$ and $y=y_1y_2\ldots y_v$ in $\{0,1\}^u$ and $\{0,1\}^v$, respectively, be considered, and either u=v or u+1=v. We use join (x,y) to denote the string $x_1y_1x_2y_2 \ldots$.

We define a map Z: $\{0,1\}^* \to \{0,1,2,3,4,5\}^*$. At first, the given $w\in\{0,1\}^*$ is transformed into w', substituting every symbol 0 in w by 3 and every 1 by 4. We denote the total number of symbols in the strings bin(t+1), bin(t+2), ..., bin(2t) by s(t). Let l be an integer such that $s(l-1)<|w|\le s(l)$. Then z(w) can be obtained from the string

bin(1) 2 bin(2) 2 bin(3) 2 ... 2 bin(2l)

inserting symbols from {3,4,5} so that every symbol in the substrings bin(l+1), bin(l+2), ..., bin(2l) is preceded by one symbol from {3,4,5} and the projection of the obtained string to the subalphabet {3,4,5} equals the w'555 ... .

The language S consists of all possible strings of the form z(join(bin(1),bin(2))) 6 z(join(bin(2),bin(3))) 6 z(join(bin(3), bin(4))) 6 ... 6 z(join(bin(2k-1),bin(2k))).

THEOREM 8.2. (1) Given any $\varepsilon>0$, there is a loglogn-space bounded probabilistic 1-way Turing machine which accepts every string in S with probability 1 and rejects every string in S with probability $1-\varepsilon$. (2) Every deterministic 1-way Turing machine recognizing S uses at least const. logn space.

PROOF is similar to the proof of Theorem 8.1. The main additional idea in the proof of (1) is to perform all the needed (probabilistic) comparisons whether the substrings bin(i) correspond one to another in the fragment

... 6 z(join(bin(i-1),bin(i))) 6 z(join(bin(i),bin(i+1))) 6 ...

independently, i.e. by using another choice of a random modulo. If the given string is in S then all the many comparisons end in positive with probability 1. If there is at least one discrepancy then the comparisons end in negative with probability $1-\varepsilon$.

It is possible to extend Theorems 8.1 and 8.2 for "natural" space complexities f(n) between log n and loglogn. On the other hand, the method used above does not permit to construct nonregular languages recognizable by probabilistic 1-way Turing machines in o(loglogn) time. Now we proceed to prove Theorem 8.3 which shows that if a language L is recognized by probabilistic 1-way Turing machine in o(loglogn) space then L is regular. The result may seem trivial since Trakhtenbrot [Tra 74] and Gill [Gi 74] have proved theorems showing that determinization of probabilistic Turing machines increase space complexity no more than exponentially, and it is known from [SHL 65] that if a language L is recognized by a deterministic 1-way Turing machine in o(logn) space then L is regular. Unfortunately, the situation is more complicate since no function o(logn) is space constructible by deterministic 1-way Turing machines. Hence the argument by Trakhtenbrot and Gill is not applicable. Our proof is nonconstructive. We do not present an algorithm for determinization of probabilistic 1-way Turing machines.

Theorem 8.2 gave an example of a nonregular language recognizable in o(log log n) space by a probabilistic one-way Turing machine.

On the other hand, as proved in [SHL 65], no deterministic one-way Turing machine can recognize nonregular languages in o(log n) space. R.Freivalds [Fre 83_1] proved that recognition of a language in o(log log n) space by a probabilistic one-way Turing machine with probability 2/3 implies regularity of the language.

A modification of this theorem says that regularity of a language is implied as well its recognition with any probability $p>1/2$ by a probabilistic one-way Turing machine which never exceeds a space bound $S(n)=o(\log \log n)$ whatever random options are taken by the probabilistic Turing machine.

It was formulated explicitly in [Fre 83_1] as an open problem, to eliminate the abovementioned restriction (either $p\geq 2/3$ or space bound $S(n)=o(\log \log n)$ for all random options). In spite of many attempts, this problem turned out to be very hard. We solve it only [KF 90] by considering a notion of n-similar pairs of words and proving the crucial Lemma 2 which, we believe, may be of some interest itself.

It is interesting to note that for two-way machines there is no minimal nontrivial space complexity such that capabilities of probabilistic and deterministic machines differ only starting from this complexity. Theorem 9.1 below shows that there is a nonregular language which can be recognized by probabilistic two-way finite automata with arbitrary probability $1-\varepsilon$ $(\varepsilon>0)$.

We remind the reduction theorem by M.O.Rabin [Rab 63]. Let X be a finite set, and $L\subseteq X^*$ be a language. The words $w', w''\in X^*$ are called equivalent with respect to the language L if

$$(\forall w\in X^*)\ (w'w\in L) \Leftrightarrow (w''w\in L).$$

By weight (L) we denote the number of the classes of equivalence with respect to the language L (language L is regular if weight $(L)<\infty$).

M.O.Rabin proved the following theorem. If a language L is recognized by a finite probabilistic 1-way automaton with k states with probability $1/2+\delta$ then weight $(L)\leq(1+1/\delta)^{k-1}$.

(In fact, M.O.Rabin formulated his theorem in a slightly more general form. Any case, it follows from this theorem that finite probabilistic automata with isolated cut-point recognize only regular languages).

Let X be a finite set, $L\subseteq X^*$ be a language and $n\geq 0$ be an integer. The words $w',w''\in X^{\leq n}$ are called n-similar with respect to the language L if

$$(\forall w\in X^{*})(w'w\in X^{\leq n} \& w''w\in X^{\leq n}) \Rightarrow (w'w\in L \Leftrightarrow w''w\in L).$$

To denote this relation we use

$$w' \quad w''(L,X^{\leq n}).$$

Rank $r_{sim}(l,X^{\leq n})$ is the cardinality of the maximal subset of $X^{\leq n}$ such that all words in the subset are pairwise non-n-similar with respect to L.

We say that a probabilistic automaton recognizes the initial n-fragment of L with probability $1/2+\delta$ if the automaton accepts every word in $X^{\leq n}\cap L$ with probability no less than $1/2+\delta$ and accepts everyword in $X^{\leq n}\setminus L$ with probability not exceeding $1/2-\delta$.

The proof of Rabin's theorem proves the following lemma as well.

LEMMA 8.2. If a finite probabilistic automaton with k states recognizes the initial n-fragment of $L\subseteq X^{*}$ with probability $1/2+\delta$ $(\delta>0)$ then

$$r_{sim}(L,X^{\leq n})\leq(1+1/\delta)^{k-1}.$$

Below we prove the crucial technical lemma.

LEMMA 8.3. If a language $L\subseteq X^{*}$ is nonregular then for infinetely many n

$$r_{sim}(L,X^{\leq n})\geq\lfloor(n+3)/2\rfloor.$$

Rather many textbooks on automata and formal language theory contain the following definition.

Let X be a finite set and $L\subseteq X^{*}$ be a language. The words $w',w''\in X^{*}$ are called equivalent with respect to L if

$$(\forall w\in X^{*})(w'w\in L \Leftrightarrow w''w\in L).$$

We denote this equivalence by $w' \quad w''(L)$. For every $n\in N$ the relation (L) divides $X^{\leq n}$ into a certain number of classes of the equivalence. The number of these classes is denoted by $r_{reach}(L,X^{\leq n})$ and called the rank of n-reachability of the language L.

For arbitrary $n\in N$ the words $w',w''\in X^{*}$ are called n-indistinguishable with respect to L if

$$(\forall w\in X^{\leq n})(w'w\in L \Leftrightarrow w''w\in L).$$

This property is denoted by $w' \quad w''(L,X^{\leq n})$.

The relation $(L,X^{\leq n})$ again is an equivalence type relation, and the rank of n-indistinguishability $r_{indist}(L,X^{\leq n})$ is the number of the equivalence classes of X^* for this relation.

Note that the relation of n-similarity (see Section 1 for the definition) is not an equivalence type relation. Nevertheless this relation has useful properties rather close to equivalence type relations:

$$(\forall w \in X^{\le n})(w\ w(L,X^{\le n})), \tag{8.1}$$

$$(\forall w',w'' \in X^{\le n})(w'\ w''(L,X^{\le n}) \Leftrightarrow w''\ w'(L,X^{\le n})) \tag{8.2}$$

$$(\forall w,w',w'' \in X^{\le n})(|w| \le \max\{|w'|,|w''|\} \& w\ w'(L<X^{\le n}) \& \\ \& w\ w''(L,X^{\le n}) \Rightarrow (w'\ w''(L,X^{\le n})), \tag{8.3}$$

$$(\forall w,w',w'' \in X^{\le n})(w'\ w''(L,X^{\le n}) \& |w'w| \le n \& \\ \& |w''w| \le n) \Rightarrow (w'w\ w''w(L,X^{\le n})). \tag{8.4}$$

We consider the functions $n \to r_{reach}(L,X^{\le n}), n \to r_{indist}(L,X^{\le n}), n \to r_{sim}(L,X^{\le n})$ in this Section. Note that these functions are nondecreasing.

EXAMPLE 8.1. Prefix of a word is a subword containing the first symbol of the given word (or it is the empty subword). We consider a language $L \subseteq \{0,1\}^*$ defined by the following property. All words in L contain a prefix in which the number of zeros strictly exceeds the number of ones. Fig.1 shows the diagram of a finite deterministic one-way automaton recognizing the initial n-fragment of L. The initial state of the automaton is q_1, the only accepting state is q_{accept}. The total number of the states is $1+\lfloor (n+2)/2 \rfloor = \lfloor (n+4)/2 \rfloor$.

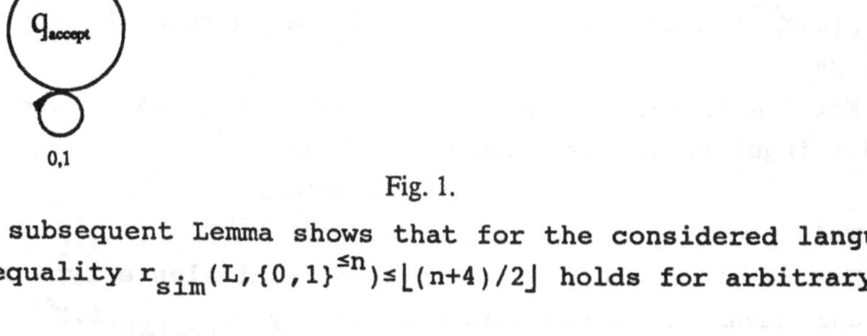

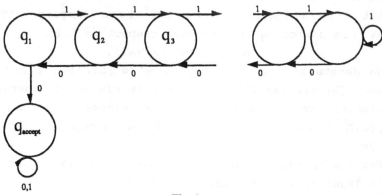

Fig. 1.

The subsequent Lemma shows that for the considered language L the inequality $r_{sim}(L,\{0,1\}^{\le n}) \le \lfloor (n+4)/2 \rfloor$ holds for arbitrary n.

LEMMA 8.4. Let X be a finite set, $L \in X^*$ be a language, $n \in N$. The rank $r_{sim}(L,X^{\le n})$ equals the number of states of the minimal finite deterministic one-way automaton recognizing the initial n-fragment of L.

PROOF. We consider the case $n=0$ seperately. Evidently, $r_{sim}(L,X^{\le n})=1$. On the other hand, the minimal automaton recognizing the initial 0-fragment (either containing e or not containing it) needs no more than one state. Hence, Lemma holds for $n=0$.

Let $n>0$. Since L and n are fixed for the rest of the proof, we replace $w' \quad w''(L,X^{\le n})$ by $w' \quad w''$. We call a word $w \in X^{\le n}$, being short if there exists no word $w' \in X^{\le n}$ such that $|w'|<|w|$ and $w' \quad w$.

We denote $r_{sim}(L,X^{\le n})$ by r. We take r pairwise non-n-similar words $w_1, w_2, \ldots, w_r$ from $X^{\le n}$ (Their existence is implied by the definition of r). For every $i \in \{1,\ldots,r\}$ we fix a word w_i' as the shortest word with the property $w_i' \quad w_i$.

(If several words of the same minimum length exist, we take one of them). Clearly $|w_i'| \le |w_i|$.

Now we prove that w_i' is short. (Had been equivalence type relation, this would be trivial). Assume the contrary.

Then for some $w_i'' \in X^{\le n}$ there holds $|w_i''|<|w_i'|$ and $w_i'' \quad w_i'$.

Since $|w_i'| \le \max\{|w_i|,|w_i''|\}$, $w_i' \quad w_i$, $w_i' \quad w_i''$, it follows from (3) that $w_i \quad w_i''$. Contradition, since w_i' is the shortest among the words n-similar to w_i. Hence, all the words w_i' $(i=1,2,\ldots,r)$ are short.

Now we prove that for distinct i,j the words w_i' and w_j'' are non-n-similar. Assume the contrary, namely, assume $w_i' \quad w_j'$. From this and $|w_i'| \le \max\{|w_i|,|w_j'|\}$, and (3) it follows $w_j' \quad w_i$. Now we make the same type conclusion from $w_j' \quad w_j$, $|w_j'| \le \max\{|w_i|,|w_j|\}$, and (3). We get $w_i \quad w_j$. Contradiction.

Thus all the words $w_1', w_2', \ldots, w_r'$ are short and pairwise non-n-similar with respect to L. Assume from the contrary that there is a finite deterministic one-way automaton with less than r states recognizing the initial n-fragment of L. Then there are distinct i,j such that w_i' and w_j' move the automaton from the initial state to the same current state. But then the automaton cannot distinguish between w_i' and w_j'. Hence for arbitrary $w \in X^*$ either both $w_i'w$ and $w_j'w$ are accepted or the two words are both rejected. We have

$$(\forall w \in X^*)(w_i'w \in X^{\le n} \,\&\, w_j'w \in X^{\le n}) \Rightarrow (w_i'w \in L \Leftrightarrow w_j'w \in L).$$

Hence $w_i' \;\; w_j'$. Contradiction.

To conclude the proof it remains to construct a finite deterministic one-way automaton with r states for recognition of the initial n-fragment of L. Since $\{w_1', w_2', \ldots, w_r'\}$ is a maximal set of pairwise non-n-similar words, for arbitrary $w \in X^{\leq n}$ there is an i such that $w \;\; w_i'$. Hence, for some i, it holds $e \;\; w_i'$.

From the shortness of w' if follows $w_i' = e$. For the sake of brevity, we assume $w_1' = e$.

We define the map $\varphi: \{q_1, q_2, \ldots, q_r\} \times X \rightarrow \{q_1, q_2, \ldots q_r\}$ as follows. If $i \in \{1,2,\ldots,r\}$, $|w_i'| \leq n-1$, $v \in X$ then $\varphi(q_i, v)$ is defined to be q_j such that $w_i'v \;\; w_j'$. (Such a value j exists because $w'v \in X^{\leq n}$). If several distinct j with this property are found, we take one of them. For those pairs (i,v) where $|w_i'| = n$ the value $\varphi(q_i, v)$ is not really needed and we define, for example, $\varphi(q_i, v) = q_i$.

We consider the automaton $\mathfrak{A}$ with the set of states $Q = \{q_1, \ldots, q_r\}$, the initial state q_1, the set of accepting states $S = \{q_i \mid w_i' \in L\}$ and the map φ.

We extend the map φ to the domain $Q \times X^*$ in the standart way. Let $\varphi(q_i, w)$ be used to denote the state of $\mathfrak{A}$ into which $\mathfrak{A}$ is moved after reading w, provided it has been in q_i initially. By induction over the length of w we prove

$$(\forall w \in X^{\leq n}) \varphi(q_1, w) = q_i \Rightarrow w \;\; w_i'. \qquad (8.5)$$

Since $\varphi(q_1, e) = q_1$, $e = w_1' \;\; e$ then for $w = e$ the property (8.5) holds. Let (8.5) hold for the words of length k (k<n). We will prove (8.5) for arbitrary word $wv \in X^{\leq n}$ where $w \in X^k$, $v \in X$. Let $\varphi(q_1, w) = q_i$. By the assertion of induction, $w \;\; w_i'$. Since the word w_i' is short, $|w_i'| \leq |w| = k < n$. Hence, $w_i'v \in X^{\leq n}$. It follows fron (8.4) that $wv \;\; w_i'v$. Let $\varphi(q_i, w) = q_j$, i.e. $w_i'v \;\; w_j'$.

Since $w_i'v \;\; wv$, $w_i'v \;\; w_i'v \;\; w_j'$, $|w_i'v| \leq \max\{|wv|, |w_j'|\}$, it follows from (8.3) that $wv \;\; w_j'$. Taking into consideration $\varphi(q_1, wv) = \varphi(\varphi(q_1, w), v) = \varphi(q_i, v) = q_j$ we have the property (8.5) for the word wv. This concludes the proof of (8.5).

Let $w \in X^{\leq n}$ and $\varphi(q_1, w) = q_j$. It follows from (8.5) that $w \;\; w_j'$ and this implies $(w \in L) \Leftrightarrow (w_j' \in L)$. Hence, $(q_j \in S = \{q_i \mid w_i' \in L\}) \in L \Leftrightarrow (w_j' \in L) \Leftrightarrow (w \in L)$. Hence, the automaton $\mathfrak{A}$ recognizes the initial n-fragment of the language L.

LEMMA 8.5. If a language $L \subseteq X^*$ is nonregular then

$$\lim_{n\to\infty} r_{sim}(L, X^{\leq n}) = \infty.$$

PROOF. If L is nonregular then there is an infinite set of words pairwise nonequivalent with respect to L. Let c be an arbitrary positive integer. Let $w_1, w_2, \ldots, w_c \in X^*$ be pairwise noneequivalent, i.e. $1 \le i < j \le c \Rightarrow w_i \neq w_j(L)$. For every pair $w', w'' \in X^*$ such that $w' \quad w''(L)$ there is a n_0 such that $(\forall n \ge n_0) w.' \quad w''(L, X^{\le n})$. We take n_0 to be large enough to ensure for all $n > n_0$, $1 \le i < j \le c$ the property $w_i \quad w_j(L, X^{\le n})$. Then for $n > n_0$ it holds $r_{sim}(L, X^{\le n}) \ge c$. It implies $\lim_{n\to\infty} r_{sim}(L, X^{\le n}) = \infty$.

Now we are ready to prove the crucial Lemma 8.3.

PROOF OF LEMMA 8.3. Assume the contrary. Then there is $n_0 > 0$ such that for all integers $n > n_0$ it holds $r_{sim}(L, X^{\le n}) \le \lfloor (n+3)/2 \rfloor - 1 = \lfloor (n+1)/2 \rfloor$. By Lemma 8.5 $\lim_{n\to\infty} r_{sim}(L, X^{\le n}) = \infty$.

Hence there is a $m > n_0$ such that $r_{sim}(L, X^{\le m+1}) > r_{sim}(L, X^{\le m})$.

Let $\mathfrak{A}_m$ and $\mathfrak{A}_{m+1}$ be the minimal finite deterministic one-way automata recognizing, respectively, the initial m- and m+1-fragments of the language L. By Lemma 8.4 they have, respectively $r_{sim}(L, X^{\le m})$ and $r_{sim}(L, X^{\le m+1})$ states. Since $r_{sim}(L, X^{\le m}) < r_{sim}(L, X^{\le m+1})$, it follows that $\mathfrak{A}_m$ recognizes the initial m-fragment of L, but not the initial m+1-fragment. Hence, the shortest word accepted by one of the automata $\mathfrak{A}_m$, $\mathfrak{A}_{m+1}$, but rejected by the other one, is of the length m+1. In another words, $\mathfrak{A}_m$ and $\mathfrak{A}_{m+1}$ are not equivalent but they are indistinguishable on the $X^{\le m}$. Two nonequivalent automata can be distinguished by a word of length no more than the sum of the numbers of the states minus one ([KAP 85], Theorem 2.10). Hence, $m+1 \le r_{sim}(L, X^{\le m}) + r_{sim}(L, X^{\le m+1})$, i.e.

$$r_{sim}(L, X^{\le m}) + r_{sim}(L, X^{\le m+1}) \ge m+2.$$

This contradicts our assumption.

$$r_{sim}(L, X^{\le m}) \le \lfloor (m+1)/2 \rfloor, \quad r_{sim}(L, X^{\le m+1}) \le \lfloor (m+2)/2 \rfloor$$

Example 1 shows that the bound $\lfloor (n+3)/2 \rfloor$ is nearly optimal. Note that for $r_{reach}(L, X^{\le n})$ and $r_{indist}(L, X^{\le n})$ bounds are quite different: if L is nonregular then for all n, $r_{reach}(L, X^{\le n}) \ge n+1$, and $r_{indist}(L, X^{\le n}) \ge n+1$ (Corollaries of Theorem 2.13 in [TB 72]).

THEOREM 8.3. If a language L is recognized by a probabilistic one-way Turing machine with probability $1/2+\delta$ ($\delta>0$) in $g(n)=o(\log\log n)$ space then L is regular.

PROOF. Let the input alphabet of the probabilistic machine $\mathfrak{M}$ be X, the work-tape alphabet be Y and the set of states be $Q=\{q_1,\ldots,q_k\}\cup\{q_{accept},q_{reject}\}$, where q_1 is the initial state. Without loss of generality we assume that $\mathfrak{M}$ can enter the states q_{accept} or q_{reject} only when the head on the input tape observes the symbol $\#\notin X$.

Configuration of $\mathfrak{M}$ at any moment (but the final moment) is triple (q,u,l) where $q\in Q\setminus\{q_{accept},q_{reject}\}$ is the current state, $u\in Y^*$ is the content of the work-tape, $l\in\{1,2,\ldots,|u|\}$ is the current position of the head on the work-tape. Configuration of $\mathfrak{M}$ at the final moment consists of the state 1_{accept} or q_{reject} only.

For arbitrary $n\in N$ we denote by C_n the cet of all configurations of the type

$$(Q\setminus\{q_{accept},q_{reject}\})\times Y^{\leq g(n)}\times\{1,\ldots,g(n)\}.$$

It follows from the properties of $\mathfrak{M}$ that for arbitrary $w\in X^{\leq n}\cap L$ (respectively, for arbitrary $w\in X^{\leq n}\setminus L$) the probability of the following event is no less than $1/2+\delta$ (respectively, does not exceed $1/2=\delta$): all the configurations during the processing of w by $\mathfrak{M}$ (but the final moment) belong to C_n and $\mathfrak{M}$ ends in q_{accept}. We denote the probability of this event by $h_{n,w}$.

Let the head on the input tape observe atbitrary symbol $x\in X$ and the current configuration be $(q',u',l')\in C_n$. We associate with this moment a period of work of $\mathfrak{M}$ onwards from this moment until one of the two events take place:

1) the head on the input tape moves right;
2) $\mathfrak{M}$ enters a configuration outside C_n.

We denote by

$$p_n(x,(q',u',l'),\text{infinity})$$

the probability of the associated period lasting infinitely long time. By

$$p_n(x,(q',u',l'),\text{full})$$

we denote the probability of the associated period ending in a configuration outside C_n (i.e. in a configuration $(q",u",l")$ where $|u"|>g(n)$). For arbitrary triple $(q",u",l")\in C_n$ we denote by

$$p_n(x,(q',u',l'),(q",u",l"))$$

the probability of the associated period ending in moving the head on the input tape, and in this moment $\mathfrak{M}$ finding itself in the configuration (q",u",l").

Now we consider the associated period for arbitrary configuration $(q',u',l')\in C_n$ where the head on the input tape observes #. In this case we associate a period of work of $\mathfrak{M}$ until one of the events take place:

1) the input word is accepted or rejected;
2) $\mathfrak{M}$ enters a configuration (q",u",l") where $|u"|>g(n)$.

We denote by

$$p_n(\#,(q',u',l'),\text{infinity})$$

the probability of the associated period lasting infinitely long time. By

$$p_n(\#,(q',u',l'),\text{full})$$

we denote the probability of the associated period ending in a triple (q",u",l") where $|u"|>g(n)$. By

$$p_n(\#,(q',u',l'),q_{accept}),$$
$$p_n(\#,(q',u',l'),q_{reject})$$

we denote the probabilities of the acceptation and rejection, respectively, at the end of the associated period.

Additionally for arbitrary $z\in X\cup\{\#\}$ we define $p_n(z,q_{accept},\text{stop})=p_n(z,q_{reject},\text{stop})=1$,

$$p_n(z,\text{infinity},\text{infinity})=p_n(z,\text{full},\text{full})=p_n(z,\text{stop},\text{stop})=1$$

Let n be arbitrary positive integer. Consider finite probabilistic one-way automaton $\mathfrak{A}_n$ in alphabet $X\cup\{\#\}$ with the set of states

$$S_n=C_n\cup\{\text{infinity},\text{full},q_{accept},q_{reject},\text{stop}\},$$

the initial state $(q_1,\Lambda,1)$ where Λ is the empty symbol q_{accept} is the only accepting state. The automaton $\mathfrak{A}_n$ works as follows. When $\mathfrak{A}_n$ in the state $s'\in S_n$ reads from the input an arbitrary symbol $z\in X\cup\{\#\}$, the automaton $\mathfrak{A}_n$ moves to the state $s"\in S_n$ with the probability $p_n(z,s',s")$. It is easy to see that the automaton $\mathfrak{A}_n$ accepts arbitrary word w#, where $w\in X^{\le n}$, with probability $h_{n,w}$. Every word not of the form w#, where $w\in X^*$, is rejected by $\mathfrak{A}_n$. Since

$$(w\in X^{\le n}\cap L) \Rightarrow h_{n,w}\ge 1/2+\delta,$$
$$(w\in X^{\le n}\setminus L) \Rightarrow h_{n,w}\le 1/2-\delta,$$

the automaton $\mathfrak{A}_n$ recognizes the initial (n+1)-fragment of the language $L\#=\{w\#|w\in L\}$ with probability $1/2+\delta$. Hence by Lemma 8.2, for arbitrary $n \in N$ it holds

$$r_{sim}(L\#,(X\cup\{\#\})^{\le n+1}) \le (1+1/\delta)^{|S_n|}.$$

On the other hand, when $n \to \infty$ we have $g(n)=o(\log \log n)$,

$$|S_n| \le |Q\backslash\{q_{accept},q_{reject}\}| \cdot |Y^{\le g(n)}| g(n)+5=o(\log n),$$

$(1+1/\delta)^{|S_n|}=o(n)$. Hence, for sufficiently large n

$$r_{sim}(L\#,(X\cup\{\#\})^{\le n+1}) \le (1+1/\delta)^{|S_n|} < n/2.$$

It follows from Lemma 8.3 that the language L# is regular. Hence L is as well regular.

9. SPACE COMPLEXITY OF 2-WAY TURING MACHINES

M.O.Rabin [Rab 57] and J.C.Shepherdson [She 59] considered deterministic 2-way finite automata (2-FA) and proved that they recognize only regular languages. Nondeterministic and even alternating 2-FA also accept only regular languages [LLS 78]. However we prove below that for arbitrary $\varepsilon>0$ the nonregular language $\{0^n1^n\}$ can be recognized by a probabilistic 2-FA with probability $1-\varepsilon$. Had the recognizability of this language been proved by the method of invariants, we would have also a nondeterministic 2-FA recognizing $\{0^n1^n\}$ but nondeterministic 2-FA recognize only regular languages. The same reason causes a positive probability of error for strings in the complement of the language.

THEOREM 9.1. For arbitrary $\varepsilon>0$ there is a probabilistic 2-way finite automaton recognizing the language $A=\{0^n1^n\}$ with probability $1-\varepsilon$.

PROOF. Let $c(\varepsilon)$ and $d(\varepsilon)$ be large natural numbers such that

$$2\left(\frac{1}{2}\right)^{d(\varepsilon)}<\varepsilon \ , \qquad \left(\frac{2^{c(\varepsilon)}}{1+2^{c(\varepsilon)}}\right)^{d(\varepsilon)}>1-\varepsilon.$$

Let the input string x be of the form 0^n1^m. The automaton processes alternately the block of zeros and the block of ones. One processing of a block is a series of options when $c(\varepsilon)$ random symbols 0 or 1 are produced per every letter in the block. We call the processing to be positive if all the results are 1, and negative otherwise. If the length of the block is n, then the probability of a positive processing of it is $2^{-n\,c(\varepsilon)}$.

We interpret a processing of an ordered pair of blocks as a competition. A competition where one processing is positive and the other is negative, is interpreted as a win of the block processed positively.

To recognize the language the automaton helds competitions until the total number of wins reaches $d(\varepsilon)$. If at this moment the two blocks have at least one win each, then x is accepted, otherwise it is rejected.

If the competitions are held unrestrictedly, then one of the blocks wins with probability 1. If $n\neq m$ then the probability of the win by the shortest block relates to the probability of the win by the longest block at least as $2^{c(\varepsilon)}:1$. Our choice of $c(\varepsilon)$ and $d(\varepsilon)$ ensures that the probability of error does not exceed ε both in the case $n=m$ and in the case $n\neq m$.

Now we consider a more complicate language being the Kleene star of the language $\{0^n1^n\}$.

$$A^*=\{0^{n_1}1^{n_1}0^{n_2}1^{n_2}\ldots0^{n_k}1^{n_k} \mid k=0,1,2,\ldots;\ n_1,\ldots,n_k=1,2,\ldots\}$$

THEOREM 9.2. For arbitrary $\varepsilon>0$ there is a probabilistic 2-way finite automaton recognizing the language A^* with probability $1-\varepsilon$.

PROOF. The basic difficulty arises from the following obstacle. The algorithm in the proof of Theorem 9.1 yields the right answer with a guaranteed probability 1 neither for strings in A nor for strings in $\bar{A}$. The number k can be large, and therefore recognition of each fragment $0^{n_i}1^{n_i}$ with a high fixed probability does not suffice to obtain the right answer about whether the string is in A^* or not with a high enough probability.

Let δ be a real number $(0<\delta<1)$, and $d(\varepsilon)$ a natural number such that

$$2\left(\frac{1}{2}\right)^{d(\varepsilon)} < \varepsilon,$$

$$(1-\delta)^{d(\varepsilon)} > 1-\varepsilon.$$

Let $\mathfrak{A}(\delta)$ be the automaton recognizing the language A from the proof of Theorem 9.1. We shall use $\mathfrak{A}(\delta)$ as a part of the automaton to be constructed. We describe the performance of our new automaton on a string of the form

$$0^{n_1}1^{m_1}0^{n_2}1^{m_2}\dots0^{n_k}1^{m_k} \qquad (9.1)$$

The main idea of the proof reminds the idea of the proof of Theorem 9.1, and consists in organizing "competitions" (in the sense of that proof) between the string (9.1) and the string

$$0^{n_1}1^{n_1}0^{n_2}1^{n_2}\dots0^{n_k}1^{n_k}. \qquad (9.2)$$

Macroprocessing of the string (9.1) (or 9.2)) is a series of applications of the algorithm $\mathfrak{A}(\delta)$ to each fragment $0^{n_i}1^{m_i}$ of the string (or to fragment $0^{n_i}1^{n_i}$). The macroprocessing is positive if $\mathfrak{A}(\delta)$ has accepted all the fragments $0^{n_i}1^{m_i}$.

Macrocompetition is a pair of macroprocessings: each of the strings (9.1) and (9.2) is processed once. A macrocompetition where one string is processed positively and the other is processed negatively is counted as a win for the positively processed string. The macrocompetitions are repeated until the total number of wins reaches $d(\varepsilon)$.

Let a_i denote (for $i=1,2,\dots,k$) the probability with which the automaton $\mathfrak{A}(\delta)$ accepts the string $0^{n_i}1^{m_i}$. The similar probability for $0^{n_i}1^{n_i}$ is denoted by b_i. The probability of a positive macroprocessing of strings (9.1) and (9.2), is $a_1 \cdot a_2 \dots a_k$, and $b_1 \cdot b_2 \dots b_k$, respectively. It is important for us that, if $n_i=m_i$, then $a_i=b_i \geq 1-\delta$, and if $n_i \neq m_i$, then $a_i<\delta$ and $b_i \geq 1-\delta$. Hence, if $n_i=m_i$ for all $1 \leq i \leq k$, the probabilities of positive macroprocessing for both strings are equal. If $n_i \neq m_i$ for at least one i, then

$$\frac{a_1 \cdot a_2 \dots a_k}{b_1 \cdot b_2 \dots b_k} < \frac{\delta}{1-\delta}$$

10. AUTOMATA ON TREES

The method of the proof of Theorem 9.2 is rather powerful. It can be used for more complicated types of automata where capabilities of probabilistic automata proved by this method are a bit unexpected.

We consider 3-way automata walking on binary trees. In cotrast to other definitions of automata on trees, there is only one copy of the automaton, and no duplication of the automaton is allowed. The automaton may choose among 3 possible direction: up, down-to-the-left, down-to-the-right. The automaton starts at the root of the binary tree (which is the uppermost vertice of the tree). The tree is finite. Every leaf is at a finite distance from the root. The automaton can walk as much time as it wishes. When the automaton decides to stop, it produces the output value "yes" or "no". Such an automaton can be used to decide properties of finite binary trees (languages of trees).

We denote by D the following language. It consists of all uniform finite binary trees, i.e. all the leaves are at the same distance from the root. It is easy to see that no such deterministic finite automaton can decide uniformity of trees. In contrast to this we have the following theorem.

THEOREM 10.1. For arbitrary $\varepsilon>0$ there is a probabilistic finite automaton walking on finite binary trees which recognizes the language B with probability $1-\varepsilon$.

PROOF. Finite binary tree is uniform if and only if for arbitrary vertice a of the tree the lengths of the two following paths are equal: 1) the path starting from a and going, first, down-to-the-right, and then down-to-the-left, down-to-the-left, down-to-the-left,..., 2) the path starting from a and going, first, down-to-the-left, and then down-to-the-right, down-to-the-right,...

The essence of the probabilistic algorithm completely coincides with that in the proof of Theorem 9.2.

REFERENCES

[Bar 65] J.M.Barzdin. Complexity of recognition of palindromes by Turing machines. Problemy kibernetiki, 15 : 245-248, 1965 (Russian).

[Bu 60] A.A.Bukhshtab. Number theory. Uchpedgiz, 1960(Russian)

[Čeb 44] P.L.Čebišev. On prime numbers. In: Opera omnia, 1: 191-207, Gosgiz (Moscow), 1944.

[Fre 75] R.Freivalds. Fast computation by probabilistic Turing machines. Teorija algoritmov i programm. 2: 201-205, 1975 (Russian).

[Fre 77] R.Freivalds. Probabilistic machines can use less running time. Information Processing'77 (Proc. IFIP Congress'77), 839-842, 1977.

[Fre 79] R.Freivalds. Speeding of recognition of languages by usage of random number generators. Problemy kibernetiki, 36: 209-224 (Russian).

[Fre 79_1] R.Freivalds. Recognition of languages by finite probabilistic multitape and multihead automata. - Problemy peredachi informacii, 15: 99-106, 1979 (Russian).

[Fre 82] R.Freivalds. On increase of the number of states in determinization of finite probabilistic automata. - Avtomatika i vychislitelnaja tehnika, No.3, 39-42, 1982 (Russian).

[Fre 83] R.Freivalds. Methods and languages to prove the power of probabilistic machines. Information Processing'83 (Proc. IFIP Congress'83), 157-162, 1983.

[Fre 83_1] R.Freivalds. Space and reversal complexity of probabilistic one-way Turing machines. Lecture Notes in Computer Science, 158: 159-169, 1983.

[GM 78] N.Z.Gabbasov and T.A.Murtazina. Improvement for the bound in the reduction theorem by Rabin. Algorithms and automata, Kazan University Press, 7-10, 1978 (Russian).

[Gi 74] J.T.Gill III. Computational complexity of probabilistic Turing machines. Proc. 6th ACM Symposium on Theory of Computation, 91-95, 1974.

[Hen 77] F.Hennie. Introduction to Computability. Addison Wesley, 1977.

[KF 90] J.Kaņeps and R.Freivalds. Minimal nontrivial space complexity of probabilistic one-way Turing machines. Lecture Notes in Computer Science. 452: 355-361, 1990.

[KAP 85] V.B.Kudrjavcev, S.V.Aleshin, A.S.Podkolzin.

Introduction into Theory of Automata. Nauka, Moscow, 1985 (Russian).

[LLS 78] R.E.Ladner, R.J.Lipton and L.J.Stockmeyer. Alternating pushdown automata. Proc. IEEE Symp. on Foundations of Computer Science, 92-106, 1978.

[Lor 86] A.Lorencs. The problems of structural analysis of probabilistic automata and transformers of probabilistic distributions. - In: Probabilistic automata and applications. Kazan University Press, 16-22, 1986 (Russian).

[Lup 63] O.B.Lupanov. On synthesis of some classes of control systems. Problemy kibernetiki, 10: 88-96, 1963 (Russian).

[Paz 66] A.Paz. Some aspects of probabilistic automata. Information and Control, 9: 26-60, 1966.

[Rab 57] M.O.Rabin. Two-way finite automata. Summaries of Talks Presented at the Summer Institute of Symbolic Logic (Cornell Univ., 1957), 2nd ed. Comm. Res. Div., Inst. Defense Anal., Princeton, N.J., 366-369, 1960.

[RS 59] M.O.Rabin and D.Scott. Finite automata and their decision problems. IBM Journal of Research and Development, 6: 230-245, 1963.

[Rab 63] M.O.Rabin. Probabilistic automata. Information and Control, 6: 230-244, 1963.

[She 59] J.C.Shepherdson. The reduction of two-way automata to one-way automata. IBM Journal of Research and Development, 3:198-200, 1959.

[SHL 65] R.E.Stearns, J.Hartmanis and P.M.Lewis II. Hierarchies of memory limited computation. In: Proc. IEEE Symp. on Switching Circuit Theory and Logical Design, 179-190, 1965.

[TB 72] B.A.Trakhtenbrot and J.M.Barzdin. Finite Automata (Behaviour and Synthesis). North-Holland, 1972.

[Tra 74] B.A.Trakhtenbrot. Notes on complexity of computation by probabilistic machines. In: Research in Mathematical Logic and Theory of Algorithms, Comp. Ctr. Acad. Sci. USSR, Moscow, 1974 (Russian).

About the Authors

Mikhail Auguston has graduated from the University of Latvia in 1971 where he studied mathematics. He joined the Computing Centre of the University of Latvia as Research Scientist in 1971.

He has taken part in the design and implementation of the language for file processing, in the design of interpreter for PL/1 program testing, in the design of testbed environment for assembler level language for PDP-11 computers. He is the author of 28 scientific articles and coauthor of the textbook on PL/1. He received PhD from the Institute of Cybernetics in Kiev in 1983.

He is currently Leading Research Scientist at the Institute of Mathematics and Computer Science of the University of Latvia. Dr.M.Auguston's research interests are in the programming languages design and implementation and program validation.

Andrejs Auziņš was born in Latvia in 1959. He graduated from the University of Latvia in 1982 where he studied mathematics. He received PhD from Moscow University in 1987 for the study "Solvable Cases of Complete Test System Generation for Programs with Direct Access Methods". Dr.A.Auziņš's recent scientific activities are concerned with the compiler for language SDL. He is Senior Research Associate at the Institute of Mathematics and Computer Science of the University of Latvia.

Jānis Bārzdiņš was born in Latvia in 1937. He graduated from the University of Latvia in 1959, received PhD (1966) and DSc (1976) in mathematics from the Institute of Mathematics in Novosibirsk.

Since 1966 he has been with the Institute of Mathematics and Computer Science of Latvia University (former Computing Centre of Latvia State University). He has developed new inductive synthesis and automatic test generation methods, has supervised several software design projects. He is a coauthor of a book on finite automata and several books on specification and programming languages. He is currently the Head of Software Research and Development Department of the Institute of Mathematics and Computer Science and Professor at the Department of Physics and Mathematics of the University of Latvia.

His current research interests include inductive synthesis of programs, specification languages and automatic test generation methods.

Guntis Bārzdiņš graduated from the University of Latvia in 1986. In 1989 he finished postgraduate studies at the Computing Centre of the Siberian Division of the Academy of Sciences in Novosibirsk, with thesis "Inductive Synthesis of Term Rewriting Systems" and joined the Institute of Mathematics and Computer Science of the University of Latvia.

During postgraduate studies under supervising of Acad.A.P.Ershov he worked in the field of partial evaluation. His latest works are related with inductive synthesis of programs from examples. He is the author and coauthor of 7 scientific articles.

He is currently Research Scientist at the Research Institute of Mathematics and Computer Science of the University of Latvia. G.Bārzdiņš's research interests are in program synthesis by means of partial evaluation and induction from examples.

Jānis Bičevskis was born in 1946, graduated from the University of Latvia in 1970, received PhD from Kiev Institute of Cybernetics, Ukranian Academy of Sciences, in 1979. Since 1972 he has published more than 40 papers on program testing. He has participated in design and implementation of data management systems. He is currently the Head of Discrete Mathematics and Programming Department at the University of Latvia. His research interests include the theory of program testing and verification, programming languages, programming methodology, sorting methods and system software.

Juris Borzovs was born in Finland in 1950. He graduated from the University of Latvia in 1973, received PhD in computer science from the Research Institute of Mathematics, Byelorussian Academy of Sciences, Minsk, in 1989.

From 1973 to 1979 he was with the Department of Software Research and Development, since 1980 he has been the Head of the Department of Computer Technology at the Institute of Mathematics and Computer Science of the University of Latvia. He has participated in the design and implementation of several data management systems, telecommunication subsystems, experimental systems of automatic test case generation. His research interests include the theory of program testing and verification, programming methodology and system software.

Dr.J.Borzovs is a member of the American Mathematical Society.

Alvis Brāzma was born in Latvia in 1959. He graduated from the University of Latvia in 1982 where he studied mathematics. He received PhD from Moscow University in 1987 for the study "Inductive Synthesis of Dot Expressions". Dr.A.Brāzma's recent scientific activities are concerned with studies of different models of inductive synthesis and learning theory. Since 1989 he is Senior Research Associate at the Institute of Mathematics and Computer Science of the University of Latvia. He is the author and coauthor of 10 scientific articles.

Kārlis Čerāns was born in Latvia in 1965. He received MSc degree in mathematics from the University of Latvia in 1988. Currently he is a postgraduate student of computer science at the Institute of Mathematics and Computer Science of Latvia University. His research interests include automatic test case generation and analysis of real-time systems, inductive inference and theory of learning, complexity of boolean functions, teaching methods of mathematics and computer science.

Rūsiņš Freivalds was born in Cesvaine, Latvia, in 1942. He graduated from the University of Latvia in 1965, received PhD from the Institute of Mathematics in Novosibirsk (under B.A.Trakhtenbrot) in 1971, Dsc from Moscow University in 1985. Since 1971 Prof.R.Freivalds has been with the Institute of Mathematics and Computer Science, the University of Latvia (former Computing Centre, up to 1990, of Latvia University).

Prof.Freivalds has given invited talks on his research in computational complexity and inductive inference at conferences in USA, Japan, etc., served in program committees of international conferences. Member of the EATCS (1979). His another interest is computer education which has resulted in educational TV shows, books published in more than a million copies and in a text serialized in a nationwide newspaper for teachers of the USSR.

Kastytis Gečas was born in Lithuania in 1955. He graduated from the University of Vilnius in 1978, received PhD in mathematical cybernetics from Kiev University in 1987. He is Senior Researcher at the Department of

Mathematical Logic and Theory of Algorithms at the Institute of Mathematics and Informatics of the Lithuanian Academy of Sciences. His research interests include formal semantics of parallel and distributed programming languages, particularly, axiomatic, logics of programs, verification of programs, temporal logics.

Audris Kalniņš was born in Riga, Latvia, in 1942. Studied mathematics at the University of Latvia. Received PhD (1971) in applied mathematics from the Institute of Mathematics, Novosibirsk.

He joined the Computing Centre of the University of Latvia as Research Scientist in 1965. He has worked in the areas of automatic test generation, specification languages and other aspects of program testing. Now he is leading the design of SDL support environment for telecommunications systems design.

He is currently the Head of Software Engineering Division at the Institute of Mathematics and Computer Science of Latvia University. His research interests are in program testing and software development methods based on specification languages.

Efim B. Kinber was born in 1949. Studied mathematics at the University of Latvia. Graduated from Latvia University in 1971. Received PhD from the Leningrad Division of Steklov Institute of Mathematics in 1971. He is currently Associate Professor at the Institute of Mathematics and Computer Science of Latvia University. His recent scientific interests are concerned with inductive inference, syntactical inductive synthesis of programs, decision problems.

Inga Medvedis was born in Riga, Latvia, in 1957. He received MSc degree in mathematics from the University of Latvia in 1981. Currently he is a postgraduate student of computer science. His research interests include specification languages for real-time systems and automatic generation of test cases.

Merik Meriste was born in 1950, graduated in applied mathematics from the University of Tartu and received PhD in computer science from the Institute of Cybernetics of the Estonian Academy of Sciences in Tallinn.

Dr.M.Meriste is Senior Scientific Researcher and Lecturer in computer science at the University of Tartu in Estonia. His resarch interests include compiler construction, object-oriented programming systems, programming methodology and programming languages.

Grigorii Efroimovich Mints was born in Leningrad in 1939, graduated from Leningrad University in 1961 and obtained PhD in 1965. In 1961 he obtained a post with the Leningrad Division of Steklov Institute of Mathematics and in 1985 joined the Institute of Cybernetics at the Estonian Academy of SCiences in Tallinn. He is the author of more than 150 papers on logic and of more than 2500 reviews of books and papers, and an active member of the Leningrad School of Proof Theory. He participated in the development of automated proof search programs and investigated constructive mathematical analysis, proof theory of classical and intuitionistic systems, relations between programming systems and logical calculi.

Jaan Penjam was born in 1955, graduated in applied mathematics from the University of Tartu and received PhD in computer science from the Institute of Cybernetics of the Estonian Academy of Sciences, in 1984.

He is curently a head of department at the Institute of Cybernetics, Tallinn, Estonia. His research interests include compiler construction, language processing, automatic program synthesis and logic programming.

Regimantas Pliuškevičius was born in Lithuania in 1937. He graduated from Vilnius University in 1961 and obtained PhD in 1967 from the Leningrad Division of Steklov Institute of Mathematics. From 1961 up to now he is currently working at the Institute of Mathematics and Informatics of the Lithuanian Academy of Sciences. He is the Head of the Mathematical Logic Group of the institute. His research interests include proof theory of non-classical logics and their applications to computer science, mainly to program verification and logic programming. He is one of collecting editors of the new international journal "Applied Non-classical Logics".

Kārlis Podnieks graduated from the University of Latvia in 1971 and joined the Computing Centre of the University (since 1990 - the Institute of Mathematics and Computer Science), where he carried out research in computer science under the supervision of prof.J.Bārzdiņš. He received PhD from the Computing Centre of the Academy of Sciences of USSR, Moscow, in 1979 for a study of inductive inference of recursive functions. Dr.K.Podnieks has also obtained results in mathematical logic (so called double -incompleteness theorem).

Henrikas Pranevitchius graduated from Kaunas Polytechnic Institute, Faculty of Radio Engineering, in 1964. He received PhD of technical sciences in cybernetics from Kaunas Polytechnic Institute in 1970 and the degree of Doctor of Science in cybernetics and computer science from Riga Electronics and Computer Institute in 1984.

Since 1964 he has been with Kaunas Polytechnic Institute. He is currently Professor of Control Systems Department at Kaunas Polytechnic Institute and the Head of the Department, and editor-in-chief of the journal "Computers and Simulation". He has published over 150 papers and the monogram "Models and Methods from Computer Systems Analysis". His research interests include computer networks protocol specification, validation, testing, simulation and simulation of complex systems.

Tanel Tammet was born in 1965, studied applied mathematics at Tartu University during 1983-1988. From 1988 Junior Research Scientist at the Institute of Cybernetics in Tallinn, from 1989 a PhD student at the same institute under the supervision of professor Grigori Mints. Up to now has studied decision strategies of the resolution method and finite model building for classical predicate calculus. He is also interested in automating correctness proofs and program synthesis.

Enn H. Tyugu studied engineering at Tallinn Technical University and computer science at Leningrad Technical University. Received PhD (1965) and DSc (1973) in computer science. Full member of the Estonian Academy of Sciences since 1987.

He developed the method of structural synthesis of programs. He has written books on program synthesis and knowledge based programming. He is also the author of several intelligent CAD systems and knowledge based programming environments.

His current interests are in semantics of declarative languages, knowledge based programming and intelligent CAD software development.

Lecture Notes in Computer Science

For information about Vols. 1–420
please contact your bookseller or Springer-Verlag

Vol. 421: T. Onodera, S. Kawai, A Formal Model of Visualization in Computer Graphics Systems. X, 100 pages. 1990.

Vol. 422: B. Nebel, Reasoning and Revision in Hybrid Representation Systems. XII, 270 pages. 1990 (Subseries LNAI).

Vol. 423: L.E. Deimel (Ed.), Software Engineering Education. Proceedings, 1990. VI, 164 pages. 1990.

Vol. 424: G. Rozenberg (Ed.), Advances in Petri Nets 1989. VI, 524 pages. 1990.

Vol. 425: C.H. Bergman, R.D. Maddux, D.L. Pigozzi (Eds.), Algebraic Logic and Universal Algebra in Computer Science. Proceedings, 1988. XI, 292 pages. 1990.

Vol. 426: N. Houbak, SIL – a Simulation Language. VII, 192 pages. 1990.

Vol. 427: O. Faugeras (Ed.), Computer Vision – ECCV 90. Proceedings, 1990. XII, 619 pages. 1990.

Vol. 428: D. Bjørner, C.A.R. Hoare, H. Langmaack (Eds.), VDM '90. VDM and Z – Formal Methods in Software Development. Proceedings, 1990. XVII, 580 pages. 1990.

Vol. 429: A. Miola (Ed.), Design and Implementation of Symbolic Computation Systems. Proceedings, 1990. XII, 284 pages. 1990.

Vol. 430: J.W. de Bakker, W.-P. de Roever, G. Rozenberg (Eds.), Stepwise Refinement of Distributed Systems. Models, Formalisms, Correctness. Proceedings, 1989. X, 808 pages. 1990.

Vol. 431: A. Arnold (Ed.), CAAP '90. Proceedings, 1990. VI, 285 pages. 1990.

Vol. 432: N. Jones (Ed.), ESOP '90. Proceedings, 1990. IX, 436 pages. 1990.

Vol. 433: W. Schröder-Preikschat, W. Zimmer (Eds.), Progress in Distributed Operating Systems and Distributed Systems Management. Proceedings, 1989. V, 206 pages. 1990.

Vol. 434: J.-J. Quisquater, J. Vandewalle (Eds.), Advances in Cryptology – EUROCRYPT '89. Proceedings, 1989. X, 710 pages. 1990.

Vol. 435: G. Brassard (Ed.), Advances in Cryptology – CRYPTO '89. Proceedings, 1989. XIII, 634 pages. 1990.

Vol. 436: B. Steinholtz, A. Sølvberg, L. Bergman (Eds.), Advanced Information Systems Engineering. Proceedings, 1990. X, 392 pages. 1990.

Vol. 437: D. Kumar (Ed.), Current Trends in SNePS – Semantic Network Processing System. Proceedings, 1989. VII, 162 pages. 1990. (Subseries LNAI).

Vol. 438: D.H. Norrie, H.W. Six (Eds.), Computer Assisted Learning – ICCAL '90. Proceedings, 1990. VII, 467 pages. 1990.

Vol. 439: P. Gorny, M. Tauber (Eds.), Visualization in Human-Computer Interaction. Proceedings, 1988. VI, 274 pages. 1990.

Vol. 440: E. Börger, H. Kleine Büning, M.M. Richter (Eds.), CSL '89. Proceedings, 1989. VI, 437 pages. 1990.

Vol. 441: T. Ito, R.H. Halstead, Jr. (Eds.), Parallel Lisp: Languages and Systems. Proceedings, 1989. XII, 364 pages. 1990.

Vol. 442: M. Main, A. Melton, M. Mislove, D. Schmidt (Eds.), Mathematical Foundations of Programming Semantics. Proceedings, 1989. VI, 439 pages. 1990.

Vol. 443: M.S. Paterson (Ed.), Automata, Languages and Programming. Proceedings, 1990. IX, 781 pages. 1990.

Vol. 444: S. Ramani, R. Chandrasekar, K.S.R. Anjaneyulu (Eds.), Knowledge Based Computer Systems. Proceedings, 1989. X, 546 pages. 1990. (Subseries LNAI).

Vol. 445: A.J.M. van Gasteren, On the Shape of Mathematical Arguments. VIII, 181 pages. 1990.

Vol. 446: L. Plümer, Termination Proofs for Logic Programs. VIII ,142 pages. 1990. (Subseries LNAI).

Vol. 447: J.R. Gilbert, R. Karlsson (Eds.), SWAT '90. 2nd Scandinavian Workshop on Algorithm Theory. Proceedings, 1990. VI, 417 pages. 1990.

Vol. 448: B. Simons, A. Spector (Eds.), Fault Tolerant Distributed Computing. VI, 298 pages. 1990.

Vol. 449: M.E. Stickel (Ed.), 10th International Conference on Automated Deduction. Proceedings, 1990. XVI, 688 pages. 1990. (Subseries LNAI).

Vol. 450: T. Asano, T. Ibaraki, H. Imai, T. Nishizeki (Eds.), Algorithms. Proceedings, 1990. VIII, 479 pages. 1990.

Vol. 451: V. Marík, O. Stepánková, Z. Zdráhal (Eds.), Artificial Intelligence in Higher Education. Proceedings, 1989. IX, 247 pages. 1990. (Subseries LNAI).

Vol. 452: B. Rovan (Ed.), Mathematical Foundations of Computer Science 1990. Proceedings, 1990. VIII, 544 pages. 1990.

Vol. 453: J. Seberry, J. Pieprzyk (Eds.), Advances in Cryptology – AUSCRYPT '90 Proceedings, 1990. IX. 462 pages. 1990.

Vol. 454: V. Diekert, Combinatorics on Traces. XII, 165 pages. 1990.

Vol. 455: C.A. Floudas, P.M. Pardalos, A Collection of Test Problems for Constrained Global Optimization Algorithms. XIV, 180 pages. 1990.

Vol. 456: P. Deransart, J. Maluszyn'ski (Eds.), Programming Language Implementation and Logic Programming. Proceedings, 1990. VIII, 401 pages. 1990.

Vol. 457: H. Burkhart (Ed.), CONPAR '90 – VAPP IV. Proceedings, 1990. XIV, 900 pages. 1990.

Vol. 458: J.C.M. Baeten, J.W. Klop (Eds.), CONCUR '90. Proceedings, 1990. VII, 537 pages. 1990.

Vol. 459: R. Studer (Ed.), Natural Language and Logic. Proceedings, 1989. VII, 252 pages. 1990. (Subseries LNAI).

Vol. 460: J. Uhl, H.A. Schmid, A Systematic Catalogue of Reusable Abstract Data Types. XII, 344 pages. 1990.

Vol. 461: P. Deransart, M. Jourdan (Eds.), Attribute Grammars and their Applications. Proceedings, 1990. VIII, 358 pages. 1990.

Vol. 462: G. Gottlob, W. Nejdl (Eds.), Expert Systems in Engineering. Proceedings, 1990. IX, 260 pages. 1990. (Subseries LNAI).

Vol. 463: H. Kirchner, W. Wechler (Eds.), Algebraic and Logic Programming. Proceedings, 1990. VII, 386 pages. 1990.

Vol. 464: J. Dassow, J. Kelemen (Eds.), Aspects and Prospects of Theoretical Computer Science. Proceedings, 1990. VI, 298 pages. 1990.

Vol. 465: A. Fuhrmann, M. Morreau (Eds.), The Logic of Theory Change. Proceedings, 1989. X, 334 pages. 1991. (Subseries LNAI).

Vol. 466: A. Blaser (Ed.), Database Systems of the 90s. Proceedings, 1990. VIII, 334 pages. 1990.

Vol. 467: F. Long (Ed.), Software Engineering Environments. Proceedings, 1969. VI, 313 pages. 1990.

Vol. 468: S.G. Akl, F. Fiala, W.W. Koczkodaj (Eds.), Advances in Computing and Information – ICCI '90. Proceedings, 1990. VII, 529 pages. 1990.

Vol. 469: I. Guessarian (Ed.), Semantics of Systeme of Concurrent Processes. Proceedings, 1990. V, 456 pages. 1990.

Vol. 470: S. Abiteboul, P.C. Kanellakis (Eds.), ICDT '90. Proceedings, 1990. VII, 528 pages. 1990.

Vol. 471: B.C. Ooi, Efficient Query Processing in Geographic Information Systems. VIII, 208 pages. 1990.

Vol. 472: K.V. Nori, C.E. Veni Madhavan (Eds.), Foundations of Software Technology and Theoretical Computer Science. Proceedings, 1990. X, 420 pages. 1990.

Vol. 473: I.B. Damgård (Ed.), Advances in Cryptology – EUROCRYPT '90. Proceedings, 1990. VIII, 500 pages. 1991.

Vol. 474: D. Karagiannis (Ed.), Information Syetems and Artificial Intelligence: Integration Aspects. Proceedings, 1990. X, 293 pages. 1991. (Subseries LNAI).

Vol. 475: P. Schroeder-Heister (Ed.), Extensions of Logic Programming. Proceedings, 1989. VIII, 364 pages. 1991. (Subseries LNAI).

Vol. 476: M. Filgueiras, L. Damas, N. Moreira, A.P. Tomás (Eds.), Natural Language Processing. Proceedings, 1990. VII, 253 pages. 1991. (Subseries LNAI).

Vol. 477: D. Hammer (Ed.), Compiler Compilers. Proceedings, 1990. VI, 227 pages. 1991.

Vol. 478: J. van Eijck (Ed.), Logics in AI. Proceedings, 1990. IX, 562 pages. 1991. (Subseries in LNAI).

Vol. 480: C. Choffrut, M. Jantzen (Eds.), STACS 91. Proceedings, 1991. X, 549 pages. 1991.

Vol. 481: E. Lang, K.-U. Carstensen, G. Simmons, Modelling Spatial Knowledge on a Linguistic Basis. IX, 138 pages. 1991. (Subseries LNAI).

Vol. 482: Y. Kodratoff (Ed.), Machine Learning – EWSL-91. Proceedings, 1991. XI, 537 pages. 1991. (Subseries LNAI).

Vol. 483: G. Rozenberg (Ed.), Advances In Petri Nets 1990. VI, 515 pages. 1991.

Vol. 484: R. H. Möhring (Ed.), Graph-Theoretic Concepts In Computer Science. Proceedings, 1990. IX, 360 pages. 1991.

Vol. 485: K. Furukawa, H. Tanaka, T. Fullsaki (Eds.), Logic Programming '89. Proceedings, 1989. IX, 183 pages. 1991. (Subseries LNAI).

Vol. 486: J. van Leeuwen, N. Santoro (Eds.), Distributed Algorithms. Proceedings, 1990. VI, 433 pages. 1991.

Vol. 487: A. Bode (Ed.), Distributed Memory Computing. Proceedings, 1991. XI, 506 pages. 1991.

Vol. 488: R. V. Book (Ed.), Rewriting Techniques and Applications. Proceedings, 1991. VII, 458 pages. 1991.

Vol. 489: J. W. de Bakker, W. P. de Roever, G. Rozenberg (Eds.), Foundations of Object-Oriented Languages. Proceedings, 1990. VIII, 442 pages. 1991.

Vol. 490: J. A. Bergstra, L. M. G. Feljs (Eds.), Algebraic Methods II: Theory, Tools and Applicatlons. VI, 434 pages. 1991.

Vol. 491: A. Yonezawa, T. Ito (Eds.), Concurrency: Theory, Language, and Architecture. Proceedings, 1989. VIII, 339 pages. 1991.

Vol. 492: D. Sriram, R. Logcher, S. Fukuda (Eds.), Computer-Aided Cooperative Product Development. Proceedings, 1989 VII, 630 pages. 1991.

Vol. 493: S. Abramsky, T. S. E. Maibaum (Eds.), TAPSOFT '91. Volume 1. Proceedings, 1991. VIII, 455 pages. 1991.

Vol. 494: S. Abramsky, T. S. E. Maibaum (Eds.), TAPSOFT '91. Volume 2. Proceedings, 1991. VIII, 482 pages. 1991.

Vol. 495: 9. Thalheim, J. Demetrovics, H.-D. Gerhardt (Eds.), MFDBS '91. Proceedings, 1991. VI, 395 pages. 1991.

Vol. 496: H.-P. Schwefel, R. Männer (Eds.), Parallel Problem Solving from Nature. Proceedings, 1991. XI, 485 pages. 1991.

Vol. 497: F. Dehne, F. Fiala. W.W. Koczkodaj (Eds.), Advances in Computing and Intormation - ICCI '91 Proceedings, 1991. VIII, 745 pages. 1991.

Vol. 498: R. Andersen, J. A. Bubenko jr., A. Sølvberg (Eds.), Advanced Information Systems Engineering. Proceedings, 1991. VI, 579 pages. 1991.

Vol. 499: D. Christodoulakis (Ed.), Ada: The Choice for '92. Proceedings, 1991. VI, 411 pages. 1991.

Vol. 500: M. Held, On the Computational Geometry of Pocket Machining. XII, 179 pages. 1991.

Vol. 501: M. Bidoit, H.-J. Kreowski, P. Lescanne, F. Orejas, D. Sannella (Eds.), Algebraic System Specification and Development. VIII, 98 pages. 1991.

Vol. 502: J. Bārzdiņš, D. Bjørner (Eds.), Baltic Computer Science. X, 619 pages. 1991.